Linux+™
Certification Study Guide

Linux+™
Certification Study Guide

Drew Bird and Mike Harwood

McGraw-Hill Osborne

New York Chicago San Francisco Lisbon London Madrid
Mexico City Milan New Delhi San Juan Seoul Singapore Sydney Toronto

McGraw-Hill/Osborne
2600 Tenth Street
Berkeley, California 94710
U.S.A.

To arrange bulk purchase discounts for sales promotions, premiums, or fund-raisers, please contact McGraw-Hill/Osborne at the above address. For information on translations or book distributors outside the U.S.A., please see the International Contact Information page immediately following the index of this book.

Linux+™ Certification Study Guide

1234567890 DOC DOC 01987654321

Book p/n 0-07-213493-3 and CD p/n 0-07-213494-1
parts of
ISBN 0-07-213492-5

Publisher Brandon A. Nordin	**Project Editor** Jennifer Malnick	**Copy Editor** Bill McManus
Vice President & Associate Publisher Scott Rogers	**Acquisitions Coordinator** Jessica Wilson	**Production** Apollo Publishing Services
Editorial Director Gareth Hancock	**VP, Worldwide Business Development Global Knowledge** Richard Kristof	**Series Design** Roberta Steele
Acquisitions Editor Nancy Maragioglio	**Technical Editor** Zonker Brockmeier	**Cover Design** Greg Scotts

This book was published with Corel VENTURA™ Publisher.

This book is dedicated to the summer we never knew

From Global Knowledge

At Global Knowledge we strive to support the multiplicity of learning styles required by our students to achieve success as technical professionals. In this series of books, it is our intention to offer the reader a valuable tool for successful completion of the Linux+ Certification Exam.

As the world's largest IT training company, Global Knowledge is uniquely positioned to offer these books. The expertise gained each year from providing instructor-led training to hundreds of thousands of students worldwide has been captured in book form to enhance your learning experience. We hope that the quality of these books demonstrates our commitment to your lifelong learning success. Whether you choose to learn through the written word, computer-based training, Web delivery, or instructor-led training, Global Knowledge is committed to providing you the very best in each of those categories. For those of you who know Global Knowledge, or those of you who have just found us for the first time, our goal is to be your lifelong competency partner.

Thank you for the opportunity to serve you. We look forward to serving your needs again in the future.

Warmest regards,

Duncan Anderson
President and Chief Executive Officer, Global Knowledge

The Global Knowledge Advantage

Global Knowledge has a global delivery system for its products and services. The company has 28 subsidiaries, and offers its programs through a total of 60+ locations. No other vendor can provide consistent services across a geographic area this large. Global Knowledge is the largest independent information technology education provider, offering programs on a variety of platforms. This enables our multi-platform and multi-national customers to obtain all of their programs from a single vendor. The company has developed the unique Competus™ Framework software tool and methodology which can quickly reconfigure courseware to the proficiency level of a student on an interactive basis. Combined with self-paced and on-line programs, this technology can reduce the time required for training by prescribing content in only the deficient skills areas. The company has fully automated every aspect of the education process, from registration and follow-up, to "just-in-time" production of courseware. Global Knowledge Network through its Enterprise Services Consultancy, can customize programs and products to suit the needs of an individual customer.

Global Knowledge Classroom Education Programs

The backbone of our delivery options is classroom-based education. Our modern, well-equipped facilities staffed with the finest instructors offer programs in a wide variety of information technology topics, many of which lead to professional certifications.

Custom Learning Solutions

This delivery option has been created for companies and governments that value customized learning solutions. For them, our consultancy-based approach of developing targeted education solutions is most effective at helping them meet specific objectives.

Self-Paced and Multimedia Products

This delivery option offers self-paced program titles in interactive CD-ROM, videotape and audio tape programs. In addition, we offer custom development of interactive multimedia courseware to customers and partners. Call us at 1-888-427-4228.

Electronic Delivery of Training

Our network-based training service delivers efficient competency-based, interactive training via the World Wide Web and organizational intranets. This leading-edge delivery option provides a custom learning path and "just-in-time" training for maximum convenience to students.

ARG

American Research Group (ARG), a wholly-owned subsidiary of Global Knowledge, one of the largest worldwide training partners of Cisco Systems, offers a wide range of internetworking, LAN/WAN, Bay Networks, FORE Systems, IBM, and UNIX courses. ARG offers hands on network training in both instructor-led classes and self-paced PC-based training.

Global Knowledge Courses Available

Network Fundamentals

- Understanding Computer Networks
- Telecommunications Fundamentals I
- Telecommunications Fundamentals II
- Understanding Networking Fundamentals
- Implementing Computer Telephony Integration
- Introduction to Voice Over IP
- Introduction to Wide Area Networking
- Cabling Voice and Data Networks
- Introduction to LAN/WAN protocols
- Virtual Private Networks
- ATM Essentials

Network Security & Management

- Troubleshooting TCP/IP Networks
- Network Management
- Network Troubleshooting
- IP Address Management
- Network Security Administration
- Web Security
- Implementing UNIX Security
- Managing Cisco Network Security
- Windows NT 4.0 Security

IT Professional Skills

- Project Management for IT Professionals
- Advanced Project Management for IT Professionals
- Survival Skills for the New IT Manager
- Making IT Teams Work

LAN/WAN Internetworking

- Frame Relay Internetworking
- Implementing T1/T3 Services
- Understanding Digital Subscriber Line (xDSL)
- Internetworking with Routers and Switches
- Advanced Routing and Switching
- Multi-Layer Switching and Wire-Speed Routing
- Internetworking with TCP/IP
- ATM Internetworking
- OSPF Design and Configuration
- Border Gateway Protocol (BGP) Configuration

Authorized Vendor Training

Cisco Systems

- Introduction to Cisco Router Configuration
- Advanced Cisco Router Configuration
- Installation and Maintenance of Cisco Routers
- Cisco Internetwork Troubleshooting
- Cisco Internetwork Design
- Cisco Routers and LAN Switches
- Catalyst 5000 Series Configuration
- Cisco LAN Switch Configuration
- Managing Cisco Switched Internetworks
- Configuring, Monitoring, and Troubleshooting Dial-Up Services
- Cisco AS5200 Installation and Configuration
- Cisco Campus ATM Solutions

Bay Networks

- Bay Networks Accelerated Router Configuration
- Bay Networks Advanced IP Routing
- Bay Networks Hub Connectivity
- Bay Networks Accelar 1xxx Installation and Basic Configuration
- Bay Networks Centillion Switching

FORE Systems

- FORE ATM Enterprise Core Products
- FORE ATM Enterprise Edge Products
- FORE ATM Theory
- FORE LAN Certification

Operating Systems & Programming

Microsoft

- Introduction to Windows NT
- Microsoft Networking Essentials
- Windows NT 4.0 Workstation
- Windows NT 4.0 Server
- Advanced Windows NT 4.0 Server
- Windows NT Networking with TCP/IP
- Introduction to Microsoft Web Tools
- Windows NT Troubleshooting
- Windows Registry Configuration

UNIX

- UNIX Level I
- UNIX Level II
- Essentials of UNIX and NT Integration

Programming

- Introduction to JavaScript
- Java Programming
- PERL Programming
- Advanced PERL with CGI for the Web

Web Site Management & Development

- Building a Web Site
- Web Site Management and Performance
- Web Development Fundamentals

High Speed Networking

- Essentials of Wide Area Networking
- Integrating ISDN
- Fiber Optic Network Design
- Fiber Optic Network Installation
- Migrating to High Performance Ethernet

DIGITAL UNIX

- UNIX Utilities and Commands
- DIGITAL UNIX v4.0 System Administration
- DIGITAL UNIX v4.0 (TCP/IP) Network Management
- AdvFS, LSM, and RAID Configuration and Management
- DIGITAL UNIX TruCluster Software Configuration and Management
- UNIX Shell Programming Featuring Kornshell
- DIGITAL UNIX v4.0 Security Management
- DIGITAL UNIX v4.0 Performance Management
- DIGITAL UNIX v4.0 Intervals Overview

DIGITAL OpenVMS

- OpenVMS Skills for Users
- OpenVMS System and Network Node Management I
- OpenVMS System and Network Node Management II
- OpenVMS System and Network Node Management III
- OpenVMS System and Network Node Operations
- OpenVMS for Programmers
- OpenVMS System Troubleshooting for Systems Managers
- Configuring and Managing Complex VMScluster Systems
- Utilizing OpenVMS Features from C
- OpenVMS Performance Management
- Managing DEC TCP/IP Services for OpenVMS
- Programming in C

Hardware Courses

- AlphaServer 1000/1000A Installation, Configuration and Maintenance
- AlphaServer 2100 Server Maintenance
- AlphaServer 4100, Troubleshooting Techniques and Problem Solving

ABOUT THE AUTHORS

Drew Bird

Drew Bird, Linux+, Server+, CNI, MCT, has been working in the IT industry since 1988, and during that time has spent six years as a technical trainer. In addition to writing technical books, he is a contributor to a number of Web- and paper-based magazines. Drew lives with his wife, Zoe, in Kelowna, B.C., Canada.

Mike Harwood

Mike Harwood, Linux+, Server+, A+, MCSE, MCT, is Network Manager for a multisite network. In addition to writing technical books, he is involved in courseware and curriculum design for a variety of certification programs. Mike lives in Kelowna, B.C., Canada, with his wife, Cindy, and their two children, Paige and Breanna.

ACKNOWLEDGMENTS

It takes a great deal more than the efforts of two authors to produce a book such as this. There are many people who have contributed to this project, and without them the book you hold in your hands would not have been possible.

Of these people, we have been privileged to know only a few. To the others we don't know, our thanks have no less meaning.

Of all the people involved in this project, two have had more affect than any other. These are Nancy Maragioglio, our flamboyant and always cheerful editor, and our diligent and enduring technical reviewer, Joe "Zonker" Brockmeier. Special thanks also go to Jessica Wilson and Jennifer Malnick for their guidance, and to Bill McManus for the correction of our misteaks.

Finally, a big thank you to our friends and families, who offered support and encouragement. It makes all the difference.

CONTENTS AT A GLANCE

CONTENTS

XV

PREFACE

This book's primary objective is to help you prepare for and pass the Linux+ exam so you can begin to reap the career benefits of certification. We believe that the only way to do this is to help you increase your knowledge and build your skills. After completing this book, you should feel confident that you have thoroughly reviewed all of the objectives that CompTIA has established for the exam.

In This Book

This book is organized around the actual structure of the Linux+ exam administered at Sylvan Prometric and VUE Testing Centers. CompTIA has let us know all the topics we need to cover for the exam. We've followed their list carefully, so you can be assured you're not missing anything.

In Every Chapter

We've created a set of chapter components that call your attention to important items, reinforce important points, and provide helpful exam-taking hints. Take a look at what you'll find in the chapters:

- Each chapter begins with the **Certification Objectives**—what you need to know in order to pass the section on the exam dealing with the chapter topic. The Certification Objective headings identify the objectives within the chapter, so you'll always know an objective when you see it! These certification objectives are provided to allow you to cross-reference the material within the book with the CompTIA objectives. They are directly related to the CompTIA objectives, but are in a more logical and sequential order than those provided by CompTIA. To help you relate the book certification objectives to those supplied by CompTIA, we have created a matrix in the following table.

Chapter Number	CompTIA Objectives Covered
Chapter 1	None
Chapter 2	7.8
Chapter 3	7.1, 7.2, 7.3, 7.4, 7.5, 7.6, 7.13
Chapter 4	7.7, 7.9, 7.10, 7.11, 7.12
Chapter 5	1.1, 1.3, 1.5, 1.6, 1.7, 1.8, 1.9, 1.10, 1.11
Chapter 6	1.2, 1.3, 1.4, 2.1, 2.6, 2.7
Chapter 7	2.2, 2.3, 2.4, 2.5, 2.8, 2.9, 2.10, 2.11, 2.12, 2.13, 2.14, 2.15, 2.16, 2.17, 2.18, 2.19
Chapter 8	3.1, 3.2, 3.3, 3.4, 3.5, 3.6, 3.7, 3.8, 3.9, 3.10, 3.11, 3.12, 3.13, 3.14, 3.15
Chapter 9	4.1, 4.2, 4.3, 4.4, 4.5, 4.6, 4.7, 4.8
Chapter 10	4.9, 4.10, 4.11, 4.12, 4.13, 4.14, 4.15. 4.16, 4.17, 4.18
Chapter 11	5.1, 5.2, 5.3, 5.4, 5.5, 5.6, 5.7, 5.8, 5.9, 5.10, 5.11, 5.12, 5.13
Chapter 12	6.1, 6.2, 6.3, 6.4, 6.5, 6.6, 6.7, 6.8, 6.9, 6.10, 6.11, 6.12, 6.13, 6.14, 6.15, 6.16

EXERCISE

■ Certification Exercises are interspersed throughout the chapters. These are step-by-step exercises that help you master skills likely to be an area of focus on the exam. Don't just read through the exercises; they are hands-on procedures that you should be comfortable completing. Learning by doing is an effective way to increase your competency with the language and concepts presented.

■ **From the Classroom** sidebars describe the issues that come up most often in the training classroom setting. These sidebars give you a valuable perspective into certification- and product-related topics. They point out common mistakes and address questions that have arisen from classroom discussions.

■ **Scenario & Solution** sections lay out specific scenario questions and solutions in a quick and easy-to-read format.

SCENARIO & SOLUTION

You want to quit vi without saving changes to the file.	Use the :q! command.
You want go to line number 135 by the quickest way possible.	Use the :135 command.
You want to quit vi and save your changes.	Use the :wq command.

- ■ The **Certification Summary** is a succinct review of the chapter and a restatement of salient points regarding the exam.

 ■ The **Two-Minute Drill** at the end of every chapter is a checklist of the main points of the chapter. It can be used for last-minute review.

Q&A ■ The **Self Test** offers questions similar to those found on the certification exam. The answers to these questions, as well as explanations of the answers, can be found in Appendix A. By taking the Self Test after completing each chapter, you'll reinforce what you've learned from that chapter, while becoming familiar with the structure of the exam questions.

Some Pointers

Once you've finished reading this book, set aside some time to do a thorough review. You might want to return to the book several times and make use of all the methods it offers for reviewing the material:

1. **Re-read all the Two-Minute Drills**, or have someone quiz you. You also can use the drills as a way to do a quick cram before the exam.

2. **Review all the S & S scenarios** for quick problem solving.

3. **Re-take the Self Tests**. Taking the tests right after you've read the chapter is a good idea, because it helps reinforce what you've just learned. However, it's an even better idea to go back later and do all the questions in the book in one sitting. Pretend you're taking the exam. (For this reason, you should mark your answers on a separate piece of paper when you go through the questions the first time.)

4. **Complete the exercises**. Did you do the exercises when you read through each chapter? If not, do them! These exercises are designed to cover exam topics, and there's no better way to get to know this material than by practicing.

5. **Check out the Web site**. Global Knowledge invites you to become an active member of the Access Global Web site. This site is an online mall and an information repository that you'll find invaluable. You can access many types of products to assist you in your preparation for the exams, and you'll be able to participate in forums, on-line discussions, and threaded discussions. No other book brings you unlimited access to such a resource. You'll find more information about this site in Appendix C.

Linux+ Certification

Although you've obviously picked up this book to study for a specific exam, we'd like to spend some time covering what you need in order to attain Linux+ certification status. Because this information can be found on the CompTIA Web site, http://www.comptia.org/index.asp?ContentPage=certification/certification.htm, we've repeated only some of the more important information in the Introduction of this book, "How to Take an Linux+ Certification Exam." Read ahead to the introduction.

The CD-ROM Resource

This book comes with a CD-ROM that includes test preparation software and provides you with another method for studying. You will find more information on the testing software in Appendix B.

How to Take an Linux Certification Exam

This Introduction covers the importance of your Linux+ certification as well as prepares you for taking the actual examinations. It gives you a few pointers on methods of preparing for the exam, including how to study, register, what to expect, and what to do on exam day.

Importance of Linux+ Certification

The Computing Technology Industry Association (CompTIA) created the Linux+ certification to provide individuals with an industry recognized and valued credential. Due to its acceptance as an industry-wide credential, it offers individuals an edge in a highly competitive computer job market. Additionally, it lets others know your achievement level and that you have the ability to do the job right. Prospective employers may use the Linux+ certification as a condition of employment or as a means of a bonus or job promotion.

Earning Linux+ certification means that you have the knowledge and the technical skills necessary to work with Linux systems in a variety of roles. Computer experts in the industry establish the standards of certification. Although the test covers a broad range of computer software and hardware, it is not vendor-specific. In fact, many organizations, directly and indirectly linked to the Linux industry contributed and budgeted the resources to develop the Linux+ certification.

To become Linux+ certified you must pass one exam. The exam measures essential competencies for a specifying, installing, administering and troubleshooting Linux systems and their associated hardware. The exam also covers basic networking topics. The exam is designed to validate the skills of someone with six months of Linux experience.

Computerized Testing

As with Microsoft, Novell, Lotus, and various other companies, the most practical way to administer tests on a global level is through Sylvan Prometric or VUE testing centers, who provide proctored testing services for Microsoft, Oracle, Novell, Lotus, and the Linux+ certification. In addition to administering the tests, Sylvan Prometric and VUE also score the exam and provide statistical feedback on each section of the exam to the companies and organizations that use their services.

Typically, several hundred questions are developed for a new exam. The questions are reviewed for technical accuracy by subject matter experts and are then presented in the form of a beta test. The beta test consists of many more questions than the actual test and provides for statistical feedback to CompTIA to check the performance of each question.

Based on the performance of the beta examination, questions are discarded based on how good or bad the examinees performed on them. If a question is answered correctly by most of the test takers, it is discarded as too easy. The same goes for questions that are too difficult. After analyzing the data from the beta test, CompTIA has a good idea of which questions to include in the question pool to be used on the actual exam.

Test Structure

Currently, the Linux+ exam consists of a *form* test (also called *linear* or *conventional*). This type of test draws from a question pool of some set value and randomly selects questions to generate the exam you will take. We will discuss the various question types in greater detail later.

Some certifications are using *adaptive* tests. This interactive test weights all of the questions based on their level of difficulty. For example, the questions in the form might be divided into levels one through five, with level-one questions being the easiest and level-five being the hardest. Every time you answer a question correctly you are asked a question of a higher level of difficulty, and vice versa when you answer incorrectly. After answering about 15–20 questions in this manner, the scoring algorithm is able to determine whether you would pass or fail the exam if all the questions were answered. The scoring method is pass or fail.

The exam questions for the Linux+ exams are all equally weighted. This means that they all count the same when the test is scored. An interesting and useful characteristic of the form test is that questions may be marked and returned to later.

This helps you manage your time while taking the test so that you don't spend too much time on any one question. Remember, unanswered questions are counted against you. Assuming you have time left when you finish the questions, you can return to the marked questions for further evaluation.

The form test also marks the questions that are incomplete with a letter *I* once you've finished all the questions. You'll see the whole list of questions after you finish the last question. The screen allows you to go back and finish incomplete items, finish unmarked items, and go to particular question numbers you may want to look at again.

Question Types

The computerized test questions you will see on the examination can be presented in a number of ways. The Linux+ exams are comprised entirely of one-answer multiple-choice questions.

True/False

We are all familiar with True/False questions, but due to the inherent 50 percent chance of guessing the right answer, you will not see any of these on the Linux+ exam. Sample questions on CompTIA's Web site and on the beta exam did not include any True/False type questions.

Multiple Choice

There are currently no multiple-choice questions on the Linux+ exam, though CompTIA can change this at any time.

Graphical Questions

Some questions incorporate a graphical element to the question in the form of an exhibit either to aid the examinee in a visual representation of the problem or to present the question itself. These questions are easy to identify because they refer to the exhibit in the question and there is also an Exhibit button on the bottom of the question window. An example of a graphical question might be to identify a component on a drawing of a motherboard.

Test questions known as "hotspots" actually incorporate graphics as part of the answer. These types of questions ask the examinee to click on a location or graphical element to answer the question. As a variation of the above exhibit example, instead of selecting A, B, C, or D as your answer, you would simply click on the portion of the motherboard drawing where the component exists.

Free Response Questions

Another type of question that can be presented on the form test requires a *free response* or type-in answer. This is basically a fill-in-the-blank–type question where no list of possible choices is given. You will not see this type of question on the Linux+ exam.

Study Strategies

There are appropriate ways to study for the different types of questions you will see on a Linux+ certification exam. The amount of study time needed to pass the exam will vary with the candidate's level of experience working with Linux. Someone with several years experience might only need a quick review of materials and terms when preparing for the exam.

For others, several hours may be needed to identify weaknesses in knowledge and skill level and working on those areas to bring them up to par. If you know that you are weak in an area, work on it until you feel comfortable talking about it. You don't want to be surprised with a question knowing it was your weak area.

Knowledge-Based Questions

Knowledge-based questions require that you memorize facts. The questions may not cover knowledge material that you use on a daily basis, but they do cover material that CompTIA thinks a computer technician should be able to answer. Here are some keys to memorizing facts:

- **Repetition** The more times you expose your brain to a fact, the more it "sinks in" and increases your ability to remember it.

- **Association** Connecting facts within a logical framework makes them easier to remember.

- **Motor Association** It is easier to remember something if you write it down or perform another physical act, like clicking on the practice test answer.

Performance-Based Questions

Although the majority of the questions on the Linux+ exam are knowledge-based, some questions are performance-based scenario questions. In other words, the performance-based questions on the exam actually measure the candidate's ability to apply one's knowledge in a given scenario.

The first step in preparing for these scenario type questions is to absorb as many facts relating to the exam content areas as you can. Of course, actual hands-on experience will greatly help you in this area. For example, knowing how to add and remove user accounts is greatly enhanced by actually performing the procedure. Some of the questions will place you in a scenario and ask for the best solution to the problem at hand. It is in these scenarios that having a good knowledge level and some experience will help you.

The second step is to familiarize yourself with the format of the questions you are likely to see on the exam. The questions in this study guide are a good step in that direction. The more you're familiar with the types of questions that can be asked, the better prepared you will be on the day of the test.

The Exam Makeup

To receive the Linux+ certification, you must pass the Linux+ Exam. For up-to-date information about the number of questions in the exam and the passing scores, check the CompTIA site at www.comptia.org, or call the CompTIA Certification Area: (630) 269-1818 extension 359.

The Structure of the Linux+ Exam

The Linux+ exam is comprised of seven domains (categories). CompTIA lists the percentages associated with each domain as the following:

Planning the Implementation	4%
Installation	12%
Configuration	15%
Administration	18%
System Maintenance	14%
Troubleshooting	18%
Identify, Maintain and Install System Hardware	19%

Refer back to the section "In Every Chapter" to determine which chapters of the book contain information on which domains and objectives.

Signing Up

After all the hard work preparing for the exam, signing up is a very easy process. Sylvan operators in each country can schedule tests at any authorized Sylvan Prometric Test center. To talk to a Sylvan registrar, call 1-800-77 MICRO (1-800-776-4276). There are a few things to keep in mind when you call:

1. If you call Sylvan during a busy period, you might be in for a bit of a wait. Their busiest days tend to be Mondays, so avoid scheduling a test on Monday if at all possible.

2. Make sure that you have your social security number handy. Sylvan needs this number as a unique identifier for their records.

Payment can be made by credit card, which is usually the easiest payment method. If your employer is a member of CompTIA you may be able to get a discount, or even obtain a voucher from your employer that will pay for the exam. Check with your employer before you dish out the money. The fee for the exam is $140 for members and $190 for non-members.

Taking the Test

The best method of preparing for the exam is to create a study schedule and stick to it. Although teachers have told you time and time again not to cram for tests, there just may be some information that just doesn't quite stick in your memory. It's this type of information that you want to look at right before you take the exam so that it remains fresh in your mind. Most testing centers provide you with a writing utensil and some scratch paper that you can utilize after the exam starts. You can brush up on good study techniques from any quality study book from the library, but some things to keep in mind when preparing and taking the test are:

1. Get a good night's sleep. Don't stay up all night cramming for this one. If you don't know the material by the time you go to sleep, your head won't be clear enough to remember it in the morning.

2. The test center needs two forms of identification, one of which must have your picture on it (i.e. driver's license). Social security cards and credit cards are also acceptable forms of identification.

3. Arrive at the test center a few minutes early. There's no reason to feel rushed right before taking an exam.

4. Don't spend too much time on one question. If you think you are, just mark it and go back to it later if you have time. Unanswered questions are counted wrong whether you knew the answer to them or not.

5. If you don't know the answer to a question, think about it logically. Look at the answers and eliminate the ones that you know can't possibly be the answer. This may leave with you with only two possible answers. Give it your best guess if you have to, but most of the answers to the questions can be resolved by process of elimination.

6. Books, calculators, laptop computers, or any other reference materials are not allowed inside the testing center. The tests are computer-based and do not require pens, pencils, or paper, although some test centers provide scratch paper to aid you while taking the exam.

After the Test

As soon as you complete the test, your results will show up in the form of a bar graph on the screen. As long as your score is greater than the required score, you pass! A hard copy of the report is also printed and embossed by the testing center to indicate that it's an official report. Don't lose this copy; it's the only hard copy of the report that is made. The results are sent electronically to CompTIA.

The printed report will also indicate how well you did in each section. You will be able to see the percentage of questions you got right in each section, but you will not be able to tell which questions you got wrong.

After you pass the exam, a Linux+ certificate will be mailed to you within a few weeks. You'll also receive a lapel pin and a credit card–sized credential that shows your new status: Linux+ Certified Technician. You're also authorized to use the Linux+ logo on your business cards as long as you stay within the guidelines specified by CompTIA. If you don't pass the exam, don't fret. Take a look at the areas where you didn't do so well and work on those areas for the next time.

Once you pass the exam and earn the title of Linux+ Certified Professional, your value and status in the IT industry increases. Linux+ certification carries along an important proof of skills and knowledge level that is valued by customers, employers, and professionals in the computer industry.

COMPUTING TECHNOLOGY INDUSTRY ASSOCIATION

I

Introduction to Linux

I t has been said that in order to understand where we are going, we have to know where we have been. With regard to Linux, this statement is particularly true. The decisions made early on in Linux development, whether through design or coincidence, have had a huge impact on operating system (OS) technology and, in fact, the entire computer industry as it exists today.

The origins of the Linux OS can be traced back to 1991 when Linus Torvalds, then a student at the University of Helsinki in Finland, developed his own version of a "Unix-like" OS. Whatever motivates someone in their early twenties to spend weekends and evenings developing an OS, particularly on a university campus, is somewhat beyond these authors' understanding. Fortunately for us, though, Mr. Torvalds did, and from that original work and with the help of eager developers, Linux has grown exponentially in both popularity and functionality.

Today, Linux is a major feature of the OS landscape. Already popular as a server network operating system (NOS), Linux has recently started to make inroads into the desktop market, where the stranglehold that Microsoft has with its Windows products is the strongest. While it might be unfair to suggest that Linux will become a common sight on desktop systems over the next few years, there is certainly a growing movement of users who are looking at Linux as a possible future alternative to the current offerings.

It is as a network server, though, that Linux is gaining ground most rapidly. As understanding and acceptance of the Linux OS has grown, and as pay-for OSs have demanded more investment in terms of both hardware and software, Linux has been noisily building a strong following and a growing market share.

Another indication, if it were needed, of Linux's increasing impact is the creation of certification programs like the Linux+ certification program. Certification programs are designed as a mechanism to give individuals the skills and knowledge needed to support systems, and are offered in technology areas where too few skilled people are available. The existence of other certification programs and the advent of Linux+ serves to reinforce two things: Linux is a growing technology area, and there are not enough people with appropriate skills to fulfill current needs—and that's where you come in. By buying and reading this book, you are taking the steps toward becoming Linux+ certified, but you'll need more than just a comprehension of command line and a love of LILO to put this exam in the bag.

e x a m
ⓦa t c h *It's hard to put an exact figure on it, but a good portion of the Linux+ objectives and exam are related to PC hardware and networking. Not only that, but the hardware and networking aspects of the exam are very broad in their coverage. Taking the exam without fully understanding these subject areas could prove to be a costly exercise!*

The focus of Linux+ is not just the Linux OS but the things that make the magic happen. By this we mean the hardware and networking components that are used in PC servers and networks.

e x a m
ⓦa t c h *Linux is available for more hardware platforms than just the PC, but the Linux+ exam focuses on the PC hardware platform and related peripherals. The Linux skills included in the certification are, however, transferable between hardware platforms.*

To take and pass the Linux+ test, you'll need to demonstrate not just an understanding of Linux, but also a thorough knowledge of computer hardware and networking terms and technologies. For that reason, this book is structured to provide the foundation material first, before moving on to the Linux-specific information. If your networking and PC hardware knowledge is already strong, you might be tempted to skip through Chapters 2, 3, and 4 and move straight to the Linux material. You may well be able to do this, but beware, because CompTIA is relatively specific in what it expects you to know for the exam, a review of the material in these first few chapters is strongly recommended.

Insofar as the Linux material is concerned, CompTIA makes much mention of the fact that you are expected to demonstrate basic understanding of Linux, though of course the term "basic" can be open to interpretation. In reality, the knowledge of Linux required by the exam *is* at a fundamental level, though there is a breadth to the overall certification that still serves to make it challenging.

Before we jump right into the technical stuff, we thought this would be a good opportunity to introduce Linux and see why it is what it is today. We'll start by looking at the largest single factor in the success of Linux since its introduction: the people who use, develop, and support it.

The Linux Community

One of the first things you are likely to notice as you work with Linux is that it is very unique from other OSs, not only in terms of operation but also in terms of support, development, and application. Within the Linux world there is a certain camaraderie. Developers and users work together to create a solid end product, promoting more of a decentralized development design. This peer-based approach is particularly evident with regard to Linux support. Whereas other more mainstream OSs rely on formalized and sometimes costly support methods, Linux support often comes from peers in an online discussion forum or other less formal venues. Perhaps the strength of Linux lies in the relationship Linux has with its users—it is, without question, a community.

on the
ꭩ o b

As an individual working with Linux, you will need to become part of this community. You don't have to buy a subscription or wear a badge, but you do need to participate in Internet newsgroups and other help-based forums. In the early stages, you will find that you are taking more from than you are giving to these sources. Consider it an I.O.U. Over time, as your skills increase, the scale will tip the other way, and you will be helping the next generation of Linux users with their problems.

Unless you experience it, the culture of Linux is difficult to explain, but it is important to understand this culture because it permeates every aspect of working with and supporting Linux. Amongst many users, Linux represents more than an alternative OS: it is the tool to bring down the Microsoft giant, in a sort of David and Goliath mentality. For some, this is the goal that motivates and inspires the development of Linux. For those of us who work with Linux and integrate it with other OSs, the freedom fighter approach does not work well; it is, after all, business, and the end result is more important than the means.

on the
ꭩ o b

In many environments, Linux is used as a complement to other OSs. There are, of course, environments that have nothing else but Linux installed, but these are still relatively hard to find. Those familiarizing themselves with Linux would do well to remember that there is more chance of working in a mixed operating system environment than one in which all servers run Linux.

So what is the glue that binds the Linux community together and causes some of the brightest stars in technology today to give their time, free of charge, to the development of something that belongs to no one? Therein lies the answer. People give their time and effort to the development of Linux because it is a product for the people, of the people. There is no one collecting license fees here, and all enhancements are for the common good. When was the last time someone offered you something for nothing? If you are looking for a catch, you are wasting your time.

Anyone for a Free Operating System?

Imagine reading an advert in a computer magazine that went something like this:

> Free to a good home: Advanced network operating system with comprehensive hardware support and configurable kernel. Includes full file and print sharing capabilities, robust application server software, and too many other features to list. Serious inquiries only please.

Sounds too good to be true? Well for once, it isn't. One of the decisions made by Torvalds early on was certainly one of the most important, and is undeniably one of the major reasons that Linux is still around today. In a move rarely seen in the IT world, Torvalds decided to distribute Linux and its source code freely to anyone who wanted to access, modify, or improve it. Linux is distributed and protected under the GNU General Public License (GNU GPL), which permits users to access and modify the software source code as they see fit. The significance of the open source code model cannot be overstated. This approach takes the responsibility of software development out of the hands of a few and puts it into the hands of whoever has the skill and inclination to do so.

Giving anyone the ability to contribute to the development and direction of Linux is a tempting proposition for people. How many times when working with another OS have you thought of things you would do differently? Open source gives you the ability to roll up your developer sleeves and get your hands dirty making those changes. The open source access to Linux has created an OS that is very dynamic, with enhancements and fixes occurring at a staggering pace. With a worldwide pool of countless eager developers and programmers, it will be very interesting to see where Linux is headed in the future.

While all this is great, some people still doubt the open source model will survive. The only problem with the position of these detractors is that they have been predicting Linux's demise for years.

Open Source: Fact and Fiction

In today's often-distrustful world, anything given away for free is greeted with a bit of skepticism mixed with a hint of doubt. Open source licensing for all its good points does have a few people in the business and private worlds wondering if they can rely on a free product. Open source distribution often brings with it unknown factors; commercial products have a comfort to them in that they are familiar and, as far as we know, dependable. Businesses rely on their software, and they want and need the reassurance their systems are backed and supported by a major company.

Traditionally, programs like Linux that have been distributed under a free or open source license have struggled to gain the respect and credibility needed to be a threat to commercial programs. It is likely that commercial product vendors themselves have amplified and promoted the potential hazards of using open source programs. In an attempt to set the record straight, the following sections dispel a few of the myths that surround Linux as an open source product.

Linux Is a Toy for Techies

For a while, Linux has had a certain exclusivity to it. Many feel that it belongs in the exclusive domain of superusers who tinker with it incessantly for reasons unknown. In truth, Linux really is a great toy for the techie—it gives a little of the hands-on feeling back to software that closed source commercial programs have taken away. However, if you do not hunger for the experience of hardcore computing, recompiling kernels, or analyzing source code, and simply want to print a document, you have nothing to worry about. Linux, while appealing to the superuser, is not just a techies' tinkering tool; it is a solid server and desktop solution. Much of this accessibility has been brought about by the vastly improved installation routines and the increasing functionality of GUIs.

There Is No Support for Linux

One of the image problems that Linux has been struggling with for some time is that it doesn't have adequate support for those who use it. At one time this may have been true, but it is certainly no longer the case. Linux has very strong support, but it's a little different than the traditional support methods offered by the more commercial and conventional software vendors. While many Linux distributions offer formalized support on their Web pages, Linux's main support often comes from mailing lists, message boards, newsgroups, and chat forums such as IRC. Those who respond to support queries are typically people who have gone through the same things you are going through and have found a solution. Such an arrangement provides very solid support.

In addition, many commercial companies, Linux distributors, hardware vendors, and independent consultants now offer paid-for Linux support that is every bit as good as paid support for other software platforms.

Linux Is Not User-Friendly

In its infancy, Linux followed Unix, and the command-line interface was the name of the game. As you might expect, the command line is a little intimidating for many users, so Linux was left to those who had the patience and inclination to learn to use it effectively. While the command line is still the core of a Linux system, several strong and easy-to-use front-end graphical user interfaces (GUIs) now are available. For those of us who like the comfort of a mouse click, this is what we have been waiting for. Today's Linux can be as user-friendly as any commercially available product, just different.

on the job *While the GUI for Linux has come a long way, many Linux users feel it has no place on a Linux server. They see the GUI as a means to move Linux to the desktop, not as a tool to be used on servers.*

There Are Limited Software Applications for Linux

Here again is a complaint that is simply no longer true. Naturally, when Linux was first introduced, applications were scarce, but as Linux evolved, so too did the applications that were written for it. Today, Linux has a huge library of applications and utilities available for it. Many of these applications are also free, and given that their commercial equivalents cost hundreds to thousands of dollars, it is understandable that many would question the reliability and strength of these applications. As the saying goes, the proof is in the pudding, and many of today's Linux applications— free or otherwise—can stand up to most commercial applications available today. For an example of a free software package, try StarOffice from Sun Microsystems. This full-featured office productivity suite is designed to be as easy to use and as functional as, ahem, some other more commercial office (with a small *o*) software suites. Perhaps the best example of pay-for software is Oracle database software that is used by not just some but all of the Fortune 100 companies. They may not all be using Oracle on a Linux system, but the availability is there. That is not to say that there is not still room for improvement in this area, but things are certainly much better than they were, even as recently as a few years ago.

So, with all of this going for it and being free to boot, why isn't a Linux box under every desk and a penguin on every T-shirt? Much of it has to do with perception, some of it choice, and some of it ignorance. Increasingly, though, the number of Linux users is increasing, and its not just those looking to save a few dollars.

Who Uses Linux and Why?

Historically, Linux has been the domain of hardened computer users, those who consider a GUI a crutch and open-toed sandals the peak of fashion. Today, much to the chagrin of the more passionate Linux users, Linux has made significant steps in improving its GUI. In doing so, it has opened the floodgates to a new and eager audience, happy to sacrifice a degree of performance in exchange for being able to use a mouse.

Linux has moved away from a tool used strictly by the command-line superuser and now finds a strong market base in all areas of IT, including, to some extent, as a desktop OS. Linux has evolved from its humble beginnings to become the darling of NOSs. However, it takes more than a dedicated community and a price tag full of zeros to assure the success of an OS. Linux is a success story because it is a full-featured, robust OS. We'll look at those features next.

on the job

Not only does Linux have the open source approach going for it, it also has the coolest mascot, a rather happy-looking penguin. Apparently, Linus Torvalds likes penguins, making them a natural symbol for Linux. We are not quite sure of the connection, but we figure that anyone who has the skills and tenacity to create an operating system should at least get to choose the logo!

The reasons for the huge success of Linux are as diverse as the people who have developed it. Linux means different things to different people, but for the most part, those who are the most passionate about Linux are so because of the features it provides. The following are a few reasons why Linux's popularity continues to grow.

Speed

Linux is able to manage its resources—such as disk space, CPU utilization, and memory—in a highly efficient manner, making it extremely fast even on older computer systems on which other modern commercial OSs can no longer be run. Many reasons are given for Linux's high performance, some myth, some reality. One of the real reasons is that Linux has a configurable kernel, which allows administrators to compile and recompile the kernel to include only the functionality they need, and omit what they don't need. As well as improving performance, this approach has security benefits, because a kernel that doesn't offer unneeded services poses fewer security risks.

Additionally, Linux, like Unix, is command-line driven and not bogged down with the heavy graphical considerations found in other commercial OSs. While we are on the subject of GUIs, it's worth emphasizing the distinction between Linux with a GUI and another OS such as Windows 2000. Linux is a command-line-based OS that can run a GUI application. Windows 2000 is a GUI-based OS that can run some command-line utilities. It's very important to understand this distinction, because it accounts for many things, including the less-demanding hardware requirements of Linux.

Another distinction that should be made at this point is that more than one GUI is available. The most popular GUIs are the K Desktop Environment (KDE) and the GNU Network Object Model Environment (GNOME). The actual appearance of these GUIs depends on another piece of software called a window manager, but more about that later. For the Linux+ exam, it may be worth the time to familiarize yourself with the GUIs that are available and choose the one that you prefer. Of course, nothing says that you can't just stick to the command line, but where is the fun in that?

Stability

Even if you give an OS away for free, it still has to work, and work reliably. Without question, Linux does not suffer from a lack of stability; in fact, quite the opposite is true. A well-designed Linux system has the ability to run consecutively for months or even years without crashing, freezing, or even needing to be rebooted. Those who are not familiar with Linux may find these claims hard to believe, but in many business environments, Linux servers are relied upon to provide this level of stability and continuation of service. Keep in mind that claims of servers that run for years are not unique to Linux. Every major vendor will have supporters who claim to have had servers up and running for just as long and even longer. The longest-running server we've heard about was a NetWare server that was reported to have been up since 1942. We'll let you be the judge of that one.

Security

Within the IT industry, there is some debate as to which offers better security, the open source model or a closed source model such as Microsoft's. From a Linux standpoint, many feel that there is a huge advantage of having countless developers on the lookout for security holes, which, when found, can be quickly resolved. Of course, who is to say that security holes will be found only by honest developers? Open source gives access to everyone, including those who are looking not to fix the hole, but to take advantage of it. In a way, open source security is similar to taking a leisurely stroll on a nude beach; there is nowhere to hide, and all flaws are viewable to anyone interested enough to take a peek. The closed source approach tends to use a "security through obscurity" method, taking special precautions to hide every flaw. This model depends, and is hoping, that security holes go undetected or are at least harder to find as a result of the restricted access to source code.

Which model is more secure is open to discussion. A visit to the Microsoft support site reveals countless security patches and upgrades to a number of high-end programs, including Internet Explorer and Windows itself. In fairness, Linux Web sites offer numerous security fixes as well, so neither can claim that it hasn't has issues that needed to be addressed.

All OSs, whether closed or open source, are susceptible to security breaches. Linux, with its open source approach, might appear to be more cooperative in helping you address these problems, but that doesn't mean that it doesn't have security issues to deal with. At the end of the day, those of us who manage Linux servers, or any other for that matter, are responsible to monitor the vendor's Web site carefully for security patches or report ones if they are detected.

So, how secure is Linux? When configured correctly, Linux is a very secure OS that offers a significant level of resistance to accidental or malicious attacks. Poorly configured Linux systems are as easy to get into as a Barry Manilow concert, and the result is equally undesirable.

By now, hopefully, you are chomping at the bit, eager to get your hands on a little Linux action, but before we get to that, let's take a brief look at what makes a Linux system.

The Structure of Linux

A Linux system is much more than a single piece of software. It is a grouping of elements, each providing a certain facet or function to the overall system. Many of the parts described in this section can be obtained separately from each other, but in general they are all supplied together in what is called a distribution. (More about that soon.)

The basic parts of a Linux system are these:

- **The Kernel**   This is the core operating system, which among other things acts as the interface between software and the underlying hardware for the system. This is one of the reasons why kernels are platform dependant or, in other words, why a certain kernel only works on one type of hardware. When a system is booted, the kernel is loaded into the memory of the system and can then subsequently provide services to applications.

- **Init**   Init, or, to put it more accurately, the init process, is the right-hand man of the kernel. Once the kernel has loaded, the init process takes care of establishing how the system is to be configured, what services should (and should not) be loaded, and so on. Because the init process calls all other services and applications, it is said to be the "parent" of all other processes.

- **Daemons**   These are applications that run in the background on a Linux system and provide services. Daemons can be for any purpose. For example, the Advanced Power Management (APM) daemon provides facilities for managing the power on a system. Another example is the http daemon (httpd), which provides Web server services. Daemons can be loaded at startup, loaded manually, or can be triggered by another process, and they derive their configuration from text files. They are often called applications, but they should not be confused with an application such as a word processor or database. Daemons run behind the scenes, providing core system services.

- **Shells**   These provide an operating environment for users and programs, allowing them to execute preset commands. The shell in use dictates the appearance of the screen and what commands are available. The shell program is launched after a user logs in to the system. There are many different shells available, but by far the most popular is the Bourne Again Shell (BASH).

- **GUIs** As we have mentioned a couple of times already, there are a number of GUIs that can be used on a Linux system. The X Window system provides the GUI functionality, and there are numerous window managers that can further be used to customize the appearance of the GUI.

- **Applications** In the same way as on other OSs, there are applications, such as a word processor or a graphics application, that can run on a Linux system. Many of the applications are free, but there are also an increasing number of paid-for applications available as well. Many applications now take advantage of the GUI, but some others remain firmly attached to the command line.

At this point, don't worry too much about these components and how they work; we'll be talking more about each of them as we go through the book. For now, that you know they exist is sufficient.

Introducing Linux Distributions

Have you ever wondered why there appear to be so many different types of Linux available? The reality is that there aren't. There are, however, many different *distributions* all based around a common Linux kernel.

Linux in its purest definition is not an OS, it is an OS *kernel.* As mentioned earlier, the kernel forms the foundation of the OS. This Linux kernel is available for use by anyone, to do whatever they please with, and many companies have chosen to package it in a specific way. These packages are called distributions. You may have heard of some of these—they are produced by companies such as Red Hat, SuSE, and Debian.

Today, there are a number of Linux distributions to choose from, each built on the Linux kernel and each offering a range of systems tools, utilities, and bundled applications. As you might expect, each distribution has its own advantages and disadvantages, so before choosing one, it is necessary to understand the features available in each.

exam
ⓦatch

Linux+ certification is a distribution-independent certification. As much as possible, it focuses on the characteristics, commands, procedures, and tools that are common across all distributions. Where it does cover information confined to only certain Linux distributions, we'll make sure to point it out in this book.

Before choosing a specific Linux distribution, you need to consider many different factors. For the purposes of studying for the Linux+ exam, it may be wise to choose one of the more commercial and recognizable Linux distributions. When choosing a distribution(s) to use to prepare for the exam, consider the following criteria:

- **Availability**   Perhaps the easiest way to get any of the Linux distributions is a direct download from the Internet. Web sites such as http://delaware.linux.tucows.com/distribution.html and www.linuxiso.org provide links to the various Linux sites for download. If you prefer, many of the more commercial Linux distributions provide their offerings on CD-ROM, which are available for purchase from the manufactures' Web sites or from a local software reseller. Additionally, many Linux books include Linux software with the book, but be careful, because some of these may not be the most current distribution.

- **Package management**   Each Linux distribution requires some method of packaging and distributing files. Many of today's distributions use the Red Hat Package Manager (RPM) or the Debian DEB format, while others use the TAR (tarball) package format.

- **Support**   Some Linux distributions offer better, or at least more formalized, support than others. When first using Linux, it may be worthwhile to stick to some of the more mainstream distributions just for the support. Of course, like most everything Linux-related, the choice is yours.

- **Graphical interface**   Not to arouse the anger of the Linux purists, but the Linux GUI is a good way to get into the Linux world. Rest assured, there will still be plenty of command-line work to do, but a familiar interface can certainly reduce the learning curve. When it comes to Linux distributions, some simply include better interfaces than others, and choosing a mainstream distribution is the best way to ensure that you will be using one of the best of the available interfaces.

To sum up—and we are not trying to influence your decision here (okay, we are really!)—stick with one of the mainstream distributions, for now at least, and you are more likely to find help, information, and advice more readily.

Distribution Overview

There are simply too many Linux distributions to list and explain them all in any detail. Thus, this section describes some of the more popular distributions being used today and outlines some of the major features of each. To prepare for the Linux+ exam, you need to use one of these distributions. This will almost certainly be of value for the real world as well.

Red Hat Linux

Red Hat is arguably the most popular and commercial of all the Linux distributions. The current version of Red Hat, 7.1, is available for download from the Red Hat Web site, www.redhat.com. The installation of Red Hat is fairly straightforward and supports a wide range of hardware. Red Hat offers both the GNOME and KDE.

The Linux Red Hat Web site offers plenty for those new to Linux, including reference documents, a searchable knowledge base, application downloads, and access to support discussion groups. When first configuring your system with Linux, such resources will prove invaluable.

Caldera

Caldera offers some very strong graphical administration tools and an easy-to-follow installation. Like Red Hat, the Caldera Web site provides support for those who are trying to troubleshoot problems along the way. Caldera uses RPM packaging for application distribution, which is the same packaging system used with Red Hat Linux. For more information on Caldera, refer to its Web site at www.caldera.com.

Debian

Debian differs from other Linux distributors in that it is an organization and not a corporation. Debian is not directly promoted as an introductory Linux distribution, relying much more on the command line than Caldera and Red Hat. Having said that, Debian offers perhaps the easiest upgrade and package management mechanism and offers over 3,950 packages available for download, which are accessible from its Web site at www.debian.org.

Mandrake

With its recent release, Linux-Mandrake 8, Mandrake continues to provide an easy-to-use and friendly Linux system. Mandrake uses a preconfigured graphical version of Linux, and uses both the KDE and GNOME graphical interfaces, with KDE version 2.1.1 being the default desktop. Mandrake uses RPM packages and provides strong and well-polished graphical administrative tools. Like other Linux distributions, Mandrake relies on and encourages developers to contribute to the development and evolution of Linux-Mandrake. Its Web site, www.linux-mandrake.com, offers access to support pages, as well as various discussions groups that offer peer support and troubleshooting suggestions.

SuSE Linux

Both the SuSE Linux professional and SuSE personal distributions are very strong Linux distributions offering solid utilities and graphical tools, making it an ideal option for new users and those interested in using Linux on the desktop PC. SuSE has a very clean installation procedure, but if you do encounter trouble along the way, the SuSE Web site, www.suse.de/en, offers installation troubleshooting help. Like many of the other Linux distributions, SuSE uses RPM packaging for its downloadable applications and utilities.

Slackware Linux

Slackware Linux may be the grandfather of the Linux distributions. It is not for the faint of heart and is recommended for users who already have a certain level of knowledge and skills using Linux. For those who want to put their Linux knowledge to the test, a visit to www.slackware.com should get you started. The latest version, Slackware 8.0, which was released in July 2001, offers the latest versions of X-Window and KDE and a range of other updated utilities.

Don't get too worried about these different Linux distributions; although there are many of them, at the end of the day, they all, for the most part, are managed and behave in the same way. If you are proficient in one distribution, you will have little difficulty using the others. The thing to keep in mind is that some distributions are easier to use out of the box, and for the purposes of the Linux+ exam, the more friendly distributions are the best way to go. In that light, those new to Linux may find the best success with the Red Hat, Caldera, or Mandrake versions of Linux. These distributions are good choices, because they offer familiar GUIs, strong Web page support, and easy installation.

But You Said It Was Free!

So if Linux is free, and the development of new software is performed through the GNU GPL system, what do companies like Red Hat and Corel stand to gain by offering free products for a charge? Well, it's all in the packaging.

While the core Linux kernel is free, companies like Red Hat, SuSE, Caldera, and Mandrake provide Linux boxed packages that incorporate applications, utilities, and documentation in a single shrink-wrapped package. In some cases, you also get access to technical support resources. When you buy one of these boxed packages, you are not paying for the Linux kernel—you are paying for the extras that are supplied with it. Should you wish to do so, many Linux distributions are available free of charge by download, but many people choose to pay the comparatively small amount of money simply for the conveneince of a one-box solution.

Linux Today

While Linux has been slow to reach the desktop arena, the same can certainly not be said about Linux use in the network world and in servers. Inherent in each Linux distribution is the networking strength of Unix, making Linux the choice for such network devices as routers, firewalls, proxy servers, and virtually any other network component. In today's large networks, Linux machines are used as print servers, application servers, file servers, and Web servers. In fact, Apache, a Web server

FROM THE CLASSROOM

Why Pay?

If you're a Linux professional, or hope to be, buying a Linux distribution is a small consideration that promotes further development of Linux as a platform. Companies and organizations that offer distributions contribute greatly to the Linux movement, particularly in its aim to become a viable alternative to paid-for software. It's kind of like supporting public television. Sure, you don't have to, but if enough people have that attitude, it will wither away.

—Drew Bird, Linux+ Certified

application run on many Linux servers, is the most widely used Web server in the world.

Increasingly, Linux is being used as a means to reclaim "antiquated" hardware. Companies and organizations with limited IT budgets are beginning to take advantage of the lower hardware requirements of Linux, and in doing so, are realizing the advantages of free or low-cost software. As with most things in life, it is momentum that moves things forward, and the growing Linux user base and the need for alternatives to current OS offerings is propelling Linux forward at an increasingly rapid pace.

In fact, it is becoming less of an issue of whether the software can do the job, and more a case of whether there are enough people capable of supporting it. As more organizations use Linux in their network environment, a new problem has arisen, that of a lack of qualified personnel to support the growing number of Linux systems. Due to the lack of formalized licensing, it is difficult to pinpoint the number of Linux systems in use, but it most certainly exceeds the number of skilled individuals needed to support them. And the situation is likely to get worse before it gets better. As Linux continues to threaten the status quo in the server room and on the desktop, the shortage will become even more pronounced. CompTIA, the Linux+ certification, and this book(!) are steps toward addressing this need.

Linux Future

So now you know where Linux came from and have a good idea of where it is today, but what about the future? Much to the dismay of commercial OS vendors, the future of Linux looks very bright indeed. The open source approach and the ever-growing community of developers are creating a momentum that shows no indication of slowing down. Stronger applications continue to be developed, and improvements on the utilities and GUIs are making Linux more accepted both inside and outside of the server room. One of the important factors in the ongoing success of Linux will be people like you who have made the effort to become Linux support professionals. Linux may have been around for almost ten years, but in commercial terms, it has only just started getting going.

Summary

From its humble beginnings, Linux has grown to become a major contender in the battle for OS supremacy. As discussed, Linux offers a variety of benefits, including high levels of performance and a secure and reliable OS. Although Linux is truly free, a number of companies work to make your Linux experience more complete by offering shrink-wrapped distributions. These distributions serve to increase the exposure of Linux as an OS and, in doing so, bring it to a wider market.

One of the factors that may limit Linux's progress as a mainstream OS is the lack of enough skilled individuals to install and support it, but that's where certification programs like Linux+ come in. And for those who consider the penguin to be a poor mascot for Linux, consider the following quote from Linus Torvalds himself, "Some people have told me they don't think a fat penguin really embodies the grace of Linux, which just tells me they have never seen an angry penguin charging at them in excess of 100 mph. They'd be a lot more careful about what they say if they had."

2

Networking Basics

While the primary focus of Linux+ is the Linux operating system, an understanding of basic computer networking is essential for the test, not to mention the real world. Although Linux is quite content to work in a stand-alone configuration, its strength as a network operating system (NOS) is one of the main reasons it has become so popular. In almost all cases, those working with Linux systems will be working in a networked environment, so knowledge of networking media, protocols and systems will most certainly be an asset.

In this chapter, we will look at some of the networking technologies that you will need to understand when you take the Linux+ exam. Although there is only a single Linux+ exam objective covered, the breadth of networking as a topic makes it necessary to provide this level of coverage. That said, this chapter is not intended to be a complete tutorial on networking—we could use the entire book for that and still not cover everything. Instead, this chapter is intended to provide you with information on the most commonly used network technologies.

In simple terms, a network is a group of devices connected by some means for the purpose of sharing data or resources such as printers. If we could leave the definition at that, the test and the job certainly would be easier, but unfortunately we can't. We need to delve just a little deeper.

A number of elements are required to create a network. We must have the physical structure of the network, which is provided by cables and network devices. We also need mechanisms for managing access to the network media so that all connected devices are able to communicate. In addition, we also need mechanisms for transporting data once we are on the network, which is a function provided by network protocols. Protocols are essentially languages that provide a means for computers to communicate with each other in a reliable fashion. Finally, we need software that makes the functionality of the network usable. In our case, this software is Linux, which we will be discussing throughout the rest of the book.

We'll start our discussion by looking at the physical layout of the network, known as the topology.

Identify Basic Network Concepts, Including How a Network Works

Networks have *topologies* that dictate how they are laid out. There are three basic topologies—bus, star, and ring. There is also another topology called hybrid, or mesh, but a hybrid topology is a sort of "anything goes" setup that uses elements of the three basic models. It is more associated with wide area networks (WANs) than local area networks (LANs), so we won't discuss it separately. Let's start by looking at the most common topology in use today, the physical star.

Star Topology

In a star topology, devices on the network are connected to a centralized device called a hub or switch. The upside of this configuration is that devices can be plugged and unplugged from the network at will, and a faulty cable or computer will likely have no effect on the network. The downside is that the hub or switch becomes a single point of failure, so if it does fail, all the devices connected to it will not be able to access the network. Fortunately, hubs and switches are relatively simple devices with few moving parts (normally just a cooling fan), so they don't fail too regularly. Figure 2-1 shows the basic makeup of this topology. The star topology is most commonly associated with Ethernet networks that use unshielded twisted pair (UTP) cable, but it can be used with other cable types as well.

Bus Topology

Less common now than it was in the past is the bus topology. In a bus topology, all devices on the network are connected directly to a length of cable. The cable, in this context, is likely to be thin coaxial, though the same principle applies to bus networks created with thick coaxial cable, as well. We'll look at thick and thin coaxial cable later in this chapter. Figure 2-2 shows the basic layout of a bus network.

FIGURE 2-1

Star topology

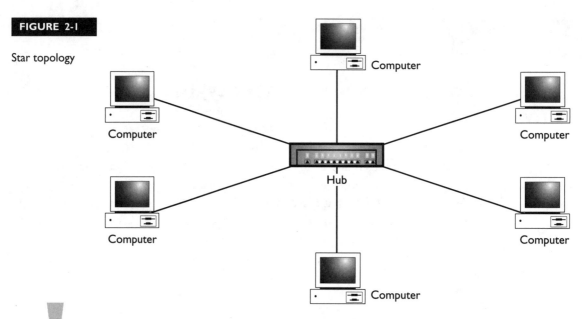

To confuse the issue, you might hear people talk of physical topologies and logical topologies. The physical topology is, as you might expect, the physical makeup of the network. The logical topology is the way the network is viewed by devices on it. The best example of this is Ethernet networks created using UTP cable. In this example, Ethernet operates a logical bus topology on a physical star topology. Don't worry too much about this aspect, but it's useful to know.

FIGURE 2-2

Bus network

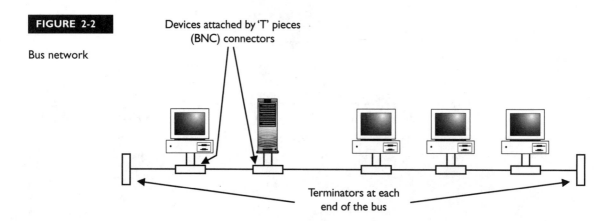

Ring Topology

In a ring topology, all devices are connected to a cable segment that has no start or end, as depicted in Figure 2-3. The advantage to this layout is that data can run on the cable in both directions. The downside is that the ring must be complete to function, a requirement that makes it necessary to use specialized networking equipment. If a problem were to occur at some point on the ring, the system can automatically move data around the ring in the opposite direction to avoid the problem area, although this capability depends on the networking system being used.

The Bigger Picture

While these basic layouts are all valid on their own, you should remember that only the smallest implementation will have a single network. More commonly, a group of networks will be created, the whole being divided in network areas called segments. A *segment* is an area of the network that is separated from the rest of the network by a router or other device. It's this device that defines where the network segment ends and facilitates the connectivity between the network segment and the rest of the network. We'll talk more about routers later on, but for now, have a look at Figure 2-4 to see how the router fits into the picture and makes connectivity between the segments possible.

FIGURE 2-3

Ring topology

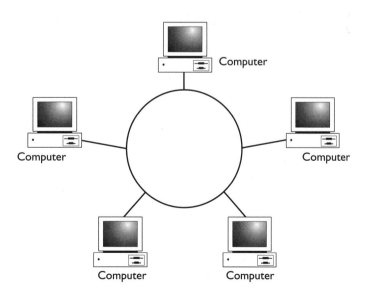

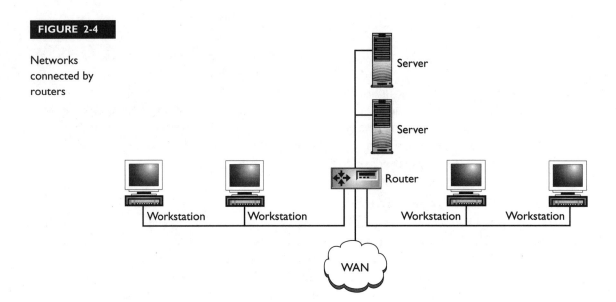

FIGURE 2-4

Networks
connected by
routers

Of the designs discussed here, by far the most common is the physical star layout, which is used by Ethernet networks made up of UTP network cabling. We'll talk more about Ethernet and UTP in the sections that follow.

Topologies might dictate how the network is laid out, but we need a means of constructing the topology, which is where network cabling and network devices come in.

Network Cabling

Network cables are the "ties that bind." The network cables used today commonly fall into three categories: coaxial, twisted pair, and fiber optic. Each has different characteristics, such as the maximum distance over which they can be used, resistance to interference, and the maximum supported speeds. Let's look at each technology and see what they can and can't do.

Coaxial Cabling

Coaxial cabling has been around for many years, and is slowly falling out of favor to faster and more flexible cable types such as UTP. Coaxial cable has a solid copper core, which is surrounded by a plastic sheath, which in turn is surrounded by a copper braid, which in turn is protected by an outer plastic sheath. Figure 2-5 shows an example of coaxial cable.

Two types of coaxial cable are commonly used for data transmission. Thin coaxial cable, which is sometimes referred to as "thinnet cable," has a maximum speed of 10Mbps and supports a maximum bus length of 185 meters. Devices connect to the network cable by using T pieces, which normally plug directly into the back of the network card. The proper name for the T pieces is British Naval Connectors, or *BNC* connectors. Figure 2-6 shows a BNC connector and the corresponding network card port.

To prevent signals from being reflected back down the length of the cable, each end of the cable segment must be terminated using a terminator. Figure 2-7 shows the basic layout of a coaxial network segment.

Note: Ethernet bus networks use a 50-ohm terminator at each end.

One of the big disadvantages of coaxial cable is that if a break occurs in the cable, none of the devices on the network will be able to communicate with each other. This not only makes adding devices and removing devices from the network awkward, it is also a nightmare to troubleshoot, because if the network stops working, you must divide the cable into sections to isolate the problem. Devices can be plugged in and out of the network without causing any problems, although all network connections should be treated carefully, because moving them too much can create problems with the cables.

Note: Thin coaxial and thick coaxial cable are sometimes referred to as thin Ethernet and thick Ethernet cable, respectively. Although the reference is not entirely accurate, it is used because, by far, the most common applications for these cables are on Ethernet networks.

FIGURE 2-5

Coaxial cable

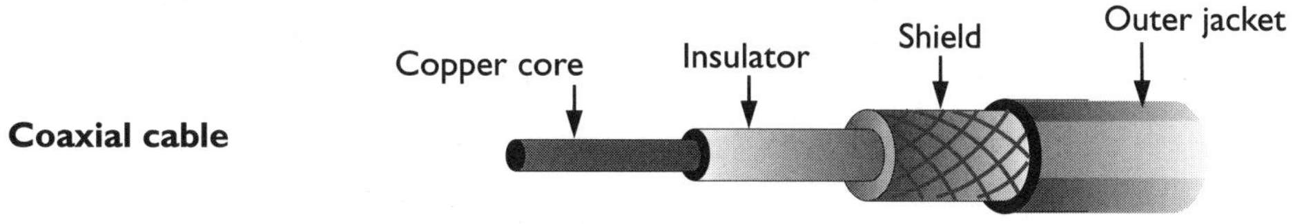

Coaxial cable

Copper core   Insulator   Shield   Outer jacket

A version of coaxial cable that is encountered much less frequently is thick coax, which has the same basic makeup as thin coax but is twice as thick at 3/8-inch diameter. The thickness of the cable and the relative inflexibility that this brings makes thick coax difficult to work with, and expensive. Thick coax really only gained a foothold in environments that have significant distances to cover—it's good up to 500 meters, but this is an area in which fiber optics have all but taken over. Thick coax was never

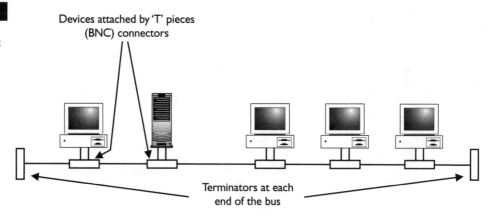

Devices attached by 'T' pieces
(BNC) connectors

Terminators at each
end of the bus

really popular for connecting workstations to the network, partly because special fittings, called vampire taps, are needed to attach devices to the cable. Again, these were relatively expensive and so did nothing to help thick coax's cause. If you are lucky/unlucky enough to work with thick coax, you can consider yourself fortunate/ unfortunate, depending on your point of view. The small number of installations that use thick coax are not likely to do so for long.

Twisted Pair Cabling

Twisted pair cabling has firmly cemented its position as *the* most popular cabling system in use today. Twisted pair is easy to work with, cheap to buy, and can cover reasonable distances. The only drawback, if you can call it that, is that twisted pair–based networks require networking devices called hubs or switches to create the physical star topology needed. In the early days of twisted pair, these devices had to be specially ordered and were quite costly. Now, you can practically buy them at the local gas station. There is more information on these devices in the "Networking Devices" section later in this chapter.

Twisted pair cabling is called such because it is made up of pairs of wire that are twisted together. These wires are protected by a protective plastic outer sheath. You can see the basic structure of twisted pair cable in Figure 2-8.

An alternative to UTP, shielded twisted pair (STP) cable, incorporates a protective shield around the pairs of cable to prevent outside sources interfering with the signal on the cable. You would use STP cable in environments where you think that interference may cause problems.

There are seven categories of twisted pair cabling, which are defined in Table 2-1. Of the seven, by far the most commonly implemented is Category 5 UTP.

FIGURE 2-8

Twisted pair cabling

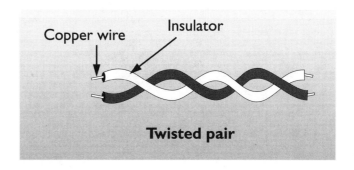

Tip: Although the likelihood of working with a category of cable other than Category 5 UTP is fairly low, technical personnel still use the tag when referring to the cable. If you here the phrase "cat 5," the reference almost certainly is to Category 5 UTP, or a variation of Category 5 cable.

Note: A new twist, if you'll excuse the pun, on twisted pair cabling is that of Cat 5e (the *e* stands for enhanced). The new cable provides better support for higher-bandwidth applications such as Fast Ethernet (discussed later) and Asynchronous Transfer Mode (ATM).

Fiber Optic

When the distance you need to cover is greater than that supported by the other cable types mentioned, and you need superior performance, there is only one way to go: fiber optic. Although still relatively expensive (in comparison to other cabling types), fiber-optic cable has become increasingly popular over recent years as understanding and support for the media has increased.

Fiber-optic cable consists of a central core that is protected by a cladding, which in turn is protected by a plastic outer sheath. The core carries the data, which travels in the form of light. Figure 2-9 shows the components of fiber-optic cable. Because, unlike the other cable types mentioned here, fiber optic uses light instead of electrical

TABLE 2-1 Categories of Twisted Pair Cabling (Reproduced with permission from *Computer Desktop Encyclopedia* © 1981–2001 The Computer Language Co., Inc., www.computerlanguage.com)

Category	Cable Type	Application
1	UTP	Analog voice
2	UTP	Digital voice, 1Mbps data
3	UTP, STP	16Mbps data
4	UTP, STP	20Mbps data
5	UTP, STP	100Mbps data
Level 6	UTP, STP	155Mbps data
Level 7	UTP, STP	1,000Mbps data

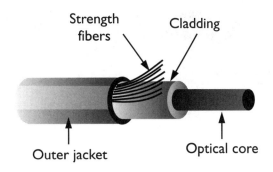

FIGURE 2-9

Fiber-optic
cabling

Strength
fibers

Cladding

Outer jacket

Optical core

Fiber-optic cable

signals, it is very resistant to outside interference. On the downside, it requires special consideration for its use and implementation.

exam
ⓦatch

Of all the cable types listed, fiber optic is the most resistant to outside interference.

Premade fiber-optic cables are available, but if custom lengths are required, special skills and tools are necessary in order to make cables of your own. Also, fiber-optic cable must be handled with care, and although it is quite flexible, there are limits to how much it can be bent. In addition, fiber-optic cable is comparatively easier to damage than the other cable types discussed. Run the castor of your office chair over a piece of UTP cable and it is unlikely that you will do any damage. Do the same thing to a length of fiber-optic cable and chances are that you will do damage. Don't ask us how we know that; we just do!

Notwithstanding these considerations, fiber-optic cable has so many advantages that it is likely to become even more popular over time. Presently, it is seen as a media mainly for connecting equipment over long distances, but it is increasingly being used as a means to connect servers to network switches and as a backbone connection between network segments.

So there you have it, a brief rundown of the various cable types in use today. To summarize this section, the relevant information is presented in Table 2-2.

TABLE 2-1	Cable Type	Maximum Speed	Maximum Distance
Common Cable Types and Characteristics	Thin coax	10Mbps	85 meters
	Thick coax	10Mbps	500 meters
	Category 5 UTP	100Mbps	100 meters
	Fiber optic	1,000Mbps (1 gigabit)	2,000 meters

Signal Enemies

Having established what the common cable types are in use today, let's look at what the potential threats are to the signals that travel across the cable, and why certain cable types are able to be used across greater distances and are better in certain applications, locations, and situations.

Electromagnetic Interference

The term *electromagnetic interference*, or EMI, is used to refer to the disruptive electrical fields created by electronic devices or mechanical equipment as they operate. EMI can interfere with the data signals as they travel along the cable. In some cases, the interference can be so bad that the signal is degraded to the point at which it becomes unusable. In less-extreme cases, the signal may remain usable but degrades much faster as it travels over distance because it has been weakened. Common causes of EMI are such things as data cables run next to power cables, fluorescent light fittings, or heavy machinery such as elevator equipment. You should be aware of EMI because it may help you determine the cause of a sporadic or mysterious network problem. You should also consider it when you are locating networking equipment or running data and power cables.

exam
ⓦatch

For the Linux+ exam, you will be expected to identify and diagnose problems caused by signal interference, including their causes and effects.

Crosstalk

In a similar fashion to EMI, signals on the cable can also be affected by the signals on other data cables that are running close to them. Crosstalk applies to not just two separate cables that run close to each other, but also to individual wires, or pairs of wires, like the ones you find in twisted pair cabling. In fact, the purpose of the twists in twisted pair cabling is to reduce the interference from other wires in the same cable.

on the job *Pop quiz: In what decade was the patent registered for twisted pair cabling? Answer: 1880s. Alexander Graham Bell, the inventor of the telephone, registered the patent for twisted pair cabling in 1881. There's nothing like being ahead of your time!*

Some cables are more susceptible to crosstalk than others. Of the cable types discussed in the preceding section, UTP is the worst in this respect and, once again, fiber optic is the best. In fact, as with EMI, fiber-optic cable has no susceptibility to crosstalk whatsoever.

Attenuation

As the signal travels along the cable, it gets weaker and weaker, a condition known as *attenuation*. Various methods are available to reduce attenuation. One is to simply use a thicker cable; the bigger the cable, the better able it is to hold on to the signal. The best example of this is the difference between thick and thin coaxial cable. Thick coax, which has the same basic construction as thin coax, just with more of everything, has a far greater maximum supported distance—500 meters, as opposed to 185 meters. Another method is to use shielding, such as that used in STP cable.

All cables suffer from attenuation, though some are better than others in this respect. Once again, the winner is fiber optic, which of the cable types discussed suffers the least from loss of signal strength over distance.

Networking Devices

When you are building a network, cables are only half the story. In almost all cases, you are likely to need networking devices, the only exception probably being a single segment thin coaxial network, which does not need anything but the cable, connectors, and terminators to operate. Such networks are becoming rare, and most networks are likely to have at least one or more of the devices discussed in this section.

SCENARIO & SOLUTION

You need to run a cable in the elevator shaft of your building, but you know the passing elevators creates EMI. What cable should you use?	Fiber optic
Copper-based network cables running next to electrical cables are suffering from signal degradation. Why?	EMI
What kind of network is it if it is described as 100BaseT?	It is a 100Mbps network using twisted pair cabling

exam

ⓌatcH

For the Linux+ exam, you are not expected to have a detailed knowledge of each of the devices discussed here, but you are expected to understand how networks operate and are constructed.

Repeaters

Repeaters are rarely seen nowadays, but they warrant a brief discussion, just in case you happen across one in your travels. Repeaters are devices that regenerate the signal transmitted along the cable so that the distances covered can be increased. There are two kinds of repeaters: an amplifying repeater simply regenerates the signal, complete with any noise, whereas a more thorough approach is taken by a signal repeater, which takes the data off the wire, repackages it, and places it back on the wire again. As mentioned, repeaters are uncommon, particularly in LANs, where the signal-repeating function is now commonly built into devices such as hubs and switches.

Hubs and Switches

In networks that use UTP cabling, hubs and switches are used to connect devices to the network. Multiple hubs and switches can be connected together to allow for larger numbers of devices to be connected.

exam

ⓌatcH

Networks that use coaxial cabling do not need hubs or switches, because devices connect directly to the cable.

Hubs and switches come in a variety of configurations. Some have only a small number of ports, such as four, while others, sometimes referred to as high-density, have as many as 48 ports. Each port on the hub or switch is capable of having a single device plugged into it, either a system or another hub or switch. More details about that are given later.

The Difference Between a Hub and a Switch

At first glance, a hub and a switch appear identical. The ports are the same, and most have the same selection of flashing lights, but that is where the similarity ends. Switches operate very differently from hubs and, in doing so, offer a number of performance improvements that can turn a sluggish network into a speedy one.

At the most basic level, a hub is a simple device that allows communication between connected devices. The hub does not manage the data in any way. For example, when a device plugged into port one of the hub wants to send data to a system on port eight, the data is forwarded to all of the ports on the hub, irrespective of the fact that, if it were an eight-port hub, six of the ports wouldn't need the data. In other words, all the hub does is provide an electrical pathway between the devices plugged into it.

A switch, by contrast, has a much more complex modus operandi, a fact that is reflected in the higher price of these units. A switch functions by, as the name implies, switching data between the ports on the switch as needed. Using the same example as before, if a device plugged into port one of the switch wants to send data to a device connected to port eight, the data is received by the switch on port one and forwarded to port eight. No other port gets the data because they don't need it.

This approach has two distinct benefits. The first is that, because systems don't hear data they don't need to, they are able to communicate with the switch more effectively. Second, it allows two devices connected to the switch to talk without the interruption of other devices. This reduces the number of *collisions*. Collisions occur on a network when more than one device attempts to talk on the network at a time. We'll talk more about collision in the section "Media Access Methods" later in this chapter. Because switches are able to provide a dedicated path between two nodes, for the period of the communication, the two will appear to each other as if they are the only devices on the network. This strategy is known as *microsegmentation*.

Another big benefit of the switched approach is that the device connected to the switch can drop the conventional-based media access method in favor of a much more selfish approach. It is the switch that deals with the media access management, and the device and the switch are able to communicate on an assumption that there will be no collisions. No collisions means there is no need to detect them. The upshot of all of this is that the switch and device can communicate in a mode called full-duplex. A full-duplex connection between a device and a switch doubles the maximum data rate that could be obtained with a standard connection. Full-duplex gets its name from the fact that communications can occur in both directions (for example, switch to server, server to switch) at the same time. This is in contrast to a standard connection, which operates in half-duplex mode. In a half-duplex configuration, communication can go one way or the other at a given time.

exam

✪atch

In a full-duplex communication, the data transfer rates are double the standard rate. So, a 100Mbps connection will operate at 200Mbps, and a 10Mbps connection will operate at 20Mbps. Half-duplex connections simply operate at the standard rate; in other words, a 100Mbps connection will work at 100Mbps, and a 10Mbps connection will work at 10Mbps. The term is half-duplex, but the speed is not halved; it remains the same.

Connecting Hubs and Switches to Create Larger Networks   Regardless of the technical differences that hubs and switches have, they do have one thing in common; the methods by which they can be connected to create larger networks. In a lot of cases, a single hub or switch does not offer enough capacity for all the devices that are to be attached. There are a number of strategies to get around the problem. One is to create multiple networks. Another, more popular, method is to simply connect multiple hubs and switches together. The process is not a difficult one, but it does require an understanding of how the ports on a hub or switch are configured and the cables that are used to connect them.

There are two types of cables commonly associated with hubs and switches: a straight-through cable, which is shown in Figure 2-10, and a crossover cable, shown in Figure 2-11.

As you can see, the difference between the two is that in the crossover cable, wires 1 and 3, and 2 and 6 are crossed with each other. The purpose of the crossover is simple. It makes the data from the transmit line of one device appear on the receive line of the other. In light of the fact that this is the most common application for the wire, switches and hubs are manufactured with the crossover made in the wiring of the port, negating the need for it to happen on the cable. These ports are known as Medium Dependant Interface-Crossed (MDI-X) ports. So, if you are conecting a

FIGURE 2-10

A straight-through
UTP cable

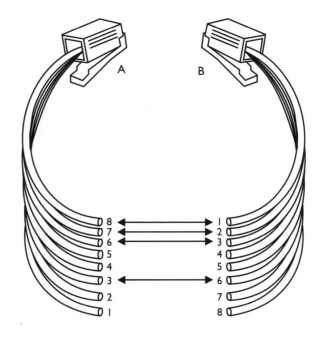

FIGURE 2-11

A crossover UTP
cable

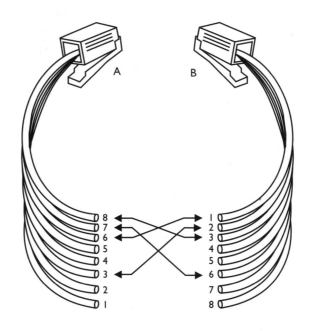

device such as a server directly to a wall outlet or directly to a hub or switch, you would use a straight-through cable, leaving the crossing part to the hub.

At the start of this discussion, the focus was on connecting hubs or switches together, and that's where crossover cables come in. When connecting two hubs or switches together, the connection actually needs to be straight-through, so that the hubs or switches appear to each other as if they were actually a single device. Mindful of this, hubs and switches will typically come with an uplink port, technically called a Medium Dependant Interface (MDI) port. This port is configured in such a way that the wiring inside the switch is not crossed internally. This allows two switches or hubs to be connected together using a straight-through UTP cable. If, in the unlikely situation, your switch or hub does not have an MDI port, you'll need to use a crossover cable to connect two devices together. This is achieved by plugging the crossover cable into a standard MDI-X port on each device. The crossover cable actually serves to cancel out the internal crossover of the ports, turning it into a straight-through connection.

In some cases, the hub or switch may have the ability for a port to be used in either an MDI or an MDI-X configuration. If this is the case, you normally switch between the two by using a toggle button. If you don't need the MDI port for connecting into another hub or switch, you can set it to MDI-X and use it for connecting to a server or workstation.

exam
ⓦatch

For the Linux+ exam, you will be expected to demonstrate a detailed knowledge of the connections for Ethernet switches and hubs. You will need to understand cable types and which cable to use in a given situation. Review the information presented in this section carefully.

Multistation Access Unit

While similar in appearance (depending on the cable type) to a switch, devices on a Token Ring network connect to a special kind of hub called Multistation Access Unit (MSAU). MSAUs are quite a bit more expensive than Ethernet switches due to the complexity of the devices and the relatively few that are manufactured. An MSAU that uses UTP cabling looks very similar to an Ethernet switch, while MSAUs that use other types of cable, such as IBM Type 1 cable, look distinctly different. In a similar fashion to Ethernet switches that have an MDI or uplink port, MSAUs have a Ring In (RI) and Ring Out (RO) port on them. The big difference is that because

Token Ring uses a ring topology, the RO port of the last MSAU must be plugged into the RI port on the first MSAU to create the full circle.

Bridges

At one point, bridges were popular networking devices because they provide a mechanism for segmenting the network, thereby reducing the number of collisions and the overall network traffic on each segment. Bridges are not very sophisticated in the task they perform, but they do the job well.

A bridge sits between physical network segments and manages the flow of traffic between the segments. By keeping traffic off of network segments that don't need to see it, a bridge reduces the overall traffic levels and so improves performance. Bridges work by determining which systems are connected to which segment, and then each time a packet of data arrives, the bridges decides whether to let it pass or to block it. To do this, it looks at the media access control (MAC) address of the devices on each side of the bridge. The bridge can learn dynamically about which devices are attached to which networks, or it can be manually configured with the information. Modern bridges tend to fall into the first category and so are sometimes referred to as *learning bridges*.

Now, if you are familiar with how a router operates, you might think to yourself "Well isn't that what a router does?" The answer is yes, it is what a router does, but the router makes its decisions based on the software-configured network address, as opposed to the hardware-derived MAC address. In some cases, bridges are faster than routers, although today's high-speed routers would take some beating.

on the
Job

You may hear someone mention that NetBEUI is bridgeable, but not routable. This is true, but the fact that bridges use the MAC address and not the software address means that any protocol is bridgeable. The MAC address is completely independent of the protocol.

One of the big reasons that bridges have fallen out of favor is that network switches basically perform the same function as bridges, in that they manage data based on the MAC address of the device on a port. In other words, a switch is a bit like a multiport bridge. Another reason for bridges' fall in popularity is the increased availability and support for routers. They offer more features than a bridge for a similar level of investment.

Routers

As the name implies, routers are used to route information around networks. In doing this, they are able to decide what is supposed to go where. Routers are used to create physical divisions within the network and then manage the flow of data between these networks. Routers make their decisions based on the software-configured network address of the device, such as a TCP/IP or an IPX address. Being able to determine the forwarding decisions in this way adds a level of flexibility (and complexity!) to router configuration. Access lists can be created to allow or deny access by certain hosts or to certain hosts. Tables can also be configured that forward data on the network in a certain way or to a certain host. Another feature is the ability to convert between one network protocol and another. Strictly speaking, this is a function of another network device called a gateway, but is also a function that a router can perform.

Routing capability can be provided through a server, such as a Linux server, or through a hardware-specific device. Each approach has its advantages and disadvantages. If you use a dedicated hardware-based router, the performance will be better, and reliability will likely be higher as well, because there are simply less things to go wrong. If you use a Linux server as a router, it is likely that you will have less performance, but also less investment dedicated to a single task. You can also add or remove functionality on the router more easily (and cheaply) if you are using a Linux server–based router.

Media Access Methods

Now that we have discussed topologies, cable types, and networking devices, the next piece of the networking puzzle is the media access method, which dictates how the network media is controlled and accessed. For example, Ethernet networks use a contention access method called Carrier Sense Multiple Access/Collision Detection (CSMA/CD). Token Ring networks, on the other hand, use a token-passing method. Because the media access method is defined by the networking system in use, it also governs, to an extent, what cable types can be used.

Contention (CSMA/CD)

On Ethernet networks, all devices operate on a system known as CSMA/CD, a contention-based media access method that allows devices to "talk" on the network. When a device wants to transmit, it first checks to see whether the cable is being used by another device. If it's not, it transmits data on the network. Simple. The complications come when more than one device decides to transmit at the same time. It is possible that more than one system will determine that the coast is clear and so begin to transmit simultaneously. The result of this faux pas is a collision, which causes fragments of the data to appear on the network. The sending nodes detect this collision (the CD part of the acronym) and wait a random amount of time, called the backoff, before retransmitting. Because the two systems use a random number to calculate the backoff, the chance of another collision is relatively low, but it can happen. If it does, the systems go through the whole routine again until they can either get the data to its destination or *timeout* and report an error.

This process may sound a little complex, but it really isn't. One of the problems, though, is that it does make for a busy network. In a small network environment, the number of collisions should be relatively low, but as the number of users starts to grow, the number of collisions grows exponentially. The end result of this is that CSMA/CD does not scale well to a large number of users on each network segment. There are two strategies to get around this problem. The first involves dividing the network into multiple segments by using devices such as routers or bridges. Because the collisions are confined to the segment of the devices, each network segment becomes its own collision domain. The other strategy is to use network switches, which, as discussed earlier, create multiple collision domains through microsegmentation.

The fact that CSMA/CD is the media access method used on Ethernet networks makes it by far the most popular system in use today. By managing the collisions with switches, Ethernet has dealt with the scalability issues and so looks to remain with us for the foreseeable future.

Token Passing

Token passing differs from CSMA/CD in that it does not permit multiple devices to transmit at the same time. Instead, a special packet called a token is passed around the network, which any system can grab and add data to. The token then travels to the destination system, where the data is extracted and the empty token is placed back on the network. The upside of this is that everyone gets a fair chance to transmit data. The downside is that the generation of a token, the maintenance of the token, and the passing of the token utilize valuable system resources. In a large network, this is less of an issue because the performance advantages of a token-based system outweigh the problems caused by collisions. On smaller networks, the overhead of the token-passing process is more noticeable, and so less suitable. Token passing is the media access method used in Token Ring networks.

Polling

The last, and least used, of the available contention methods is that of polling. In a polled contention system, a centralized device is responsible for granting permission to "speak" for network devices. Polling's centralized management approach means there are no collisions and that each device can talk at the maximum speed possible. It also means that if the device granting permission fails, the network will be unavailable. Polled systems are more likely to be seen in the world of WANs than in LANs, and so are a little outside the scope of Linux+, whose focus is on the far more common contention-based systems (Ethernet) and token-passing (Token Ring) systems.

Networking Standards

Networking standards define how data is placed on the cable and in what formats. From these standards, companies can create networking products that are compatible with the standards, and subsequently each other. Currently, there are only two networking standards that are commonly used on LANs, Ethernet and Token Ring. Of the two, Ethernet, is considerably more popular, with some industry sources suggesting that Token Ring accounts for one in 100 networks. Even so, an awareness of Token Ring is important, because you never know when you might be working on that one!

Ethernet

If someone says they have a network, you can almost assume that it is an Ethernet network. Ethernet can be implemented using thin coax, which coined the term "thin Ethernet," thick coax, which coined the term "thick Ethernet," twisted pair cabling, or fiber optic. As discussed earlier, Ethernet uses the CSMA/CD contention-based media access method.

on the job

Ethernet is defined by the IEEE 802.3 standard.

Ethernet supports various speeds, including 10Mbps, which is simply labeled Ethernet, 100Mbps, known as Fast Ethernet, and 1000Mbps, which is called Gigabit Ethernet. In general, networks that have been in place for some time will run a mix of 10 and 100Mbps, whereas newer networks are more likely to be 100Mbps, even if not all the devices on the network run at that speed. That's one of the good things about Ethernet. If the network devices support 10 or 100Mbps, devices that can use 100Mbps use it while other devices can operate at 10Mbps. Gigabit Ethernet is still relatively uncommon, but it is becoming increasingly popular as a server-to-switch connection method and when there is a great deal of traffic that needs to travel across a single segment.

Token Ring

On the surface, Token Ring seems a little complex in comparison to Ethernet, but because all of the details are taken care of by the electronics, those using it need only a basic knowledge of the system.

FROM THE CLASSROOM

Ten Base Who?

You may be used to seeing numbers like 10BaseT, 100BaseFX, and so on to describe networking standards. The numbers are useful because you can use them to determine the specifications of the standards being discussed. The numbers can be split up into three sections. The first part (10, 100, and so on) defines the speed of the standard. The second part (Base or Broad) determines whether the standard works on a baseband or a broadband media. The third part (T, FX, 2, and so on) defines the cable type. For example, 10BaseT is a 10Mbps standard that uses a baseband transmission media and twisted pair cabling.

—*Mike Harwood, Linux+ Certified*

Token Ring networks use the token-passing method of media access described earlier in the section on access methods. When the first system is started on a Token Ring network, a special data packet called a token is generated. The token is passed around the network and used by whichever system wants to talk. Because the system can't talk unless it has the token, the collisions experienced in Ethernet systems do not occur, and performance of the network does not degrade as much as Ethernet under heavy load conditions. That said, the use of a token-based system does create an overhead, which makes it slower in very small networks than Ethernet.

Token Ring can run at either 4Mbps or 16Mbps. Most Token Ring hardware components can support either speed, but the rule is that all devices on the ring must operate at one or the other speed. You can't use mixed speeds. New implementations of Token Ring are being developed, including a high-speed version that supports speeds similar to those of Ethernet. Whether or not these standards will ever become widely deployed remains unseen, but with the market dominance of Ethernet, you would have to be a very speculative gambler to put much money on Token Ring. And while we are on the subject of money, we should mention one other thing. Almost anything to do with a Token Ring network is more expensive than the Ethernet equivalent.

Network Protocols

Now that we have our network cables, network devices, and a mechanism to access the network, we need a mechanism to use this functionality to communicate data between systems. This is the job of the network protocol. Network protocols dictate how network devices, including servers, workstations, routers, printers, and the like, communicate with each other. For two devices to talk to each other, they must first have the means to communicate, and then they must know what language to talk in. On a typical network, there may be many different protocols in use, but each of these falls under the banner of one of the more common network protocols.

Development of a network protocol is an onerous task, and as a result, only a handful of protocol suites have been adopted over the years. By far the most popular is the Transmission Control Protocol/Internet Protocol (TCP/IP), but others such as Internetwork Packet Exchange/Sequenced Packet Exchange (IPX/SPX) and NetBIOS Extended User Interface (NetBEUI) can still be found on many a network.

For the purposes of Linux+, a discussion of each is warranted, but our main focus will be on TCP/IP because you are far more likely to be working with it than any of the other protocols discussed.

on the **job**

Even though we need network protocols, these still rely on the hardware-based MAC address that is programmed into each network interface, be it a network card or port on a router. Each of the protocols here has a mechanism for resolving the network address to the MAC address to facilitate communication. The assignment of MAC addresses is controlled to ensure that no two devices have the same address. MAC addresses are an important principle for any networking scenario.

TCP/IP

If there were a gold watch for long service to the IT industry, TCP/IP would have earned one some time ago. TCP/IP was developed in the 1970s when the Department of Defense needed a protocol to use on its WAN. The key requirements were that the protocol be routable and that delivery of data could be guaranteed if necessary. Much effort was expended on the development of both the WAN, which became the foundation for the Internet, and the protocol, which is basically the same TCP/IP protocol that we know and love today. Apart from lava lamps, how many other things from the '70s are still with us and in fashion?

There are a number of reasons why TCP/IP has endured the ravages of time so well. For a start, it is not a proprietary technology, its development being performed through a process called Request For Comment (RFC), to which anyone can contribute. The RFC process may seem more cumbersome than it could be, but it really is a good way of cooperatively developing protocols and standards that can be used in real-world applications.

on the **job**

In a sense, TCP/IP is to network protocols what Linux is to operating system software, in that it is developed through a cooperative process in which anyone can be involved. The only real difference is that there is a centralized control function, through the Internet Engineering Task Force (IETF), which is a subgroup of the Internet society (ISOC).

The TCP/IP protocol suite is continually under development, but some developments are more significant than others. One of the hottest topics in recent years has been the development and introduction of the next version of TCP/IP, version 6. No one appears entirely sure when the new version will be deployed on a wide scale, but many products are now IPv6-capable.

TCP/IP: More than Just a Protocol

More than just a single protocol, the term TCP/IP is used to refer to the TCP/IP protocol suite. There are protocols within the suite that deal with the routing of data through the network (IP), protocols that ensure the delivery of data to its destination (TCP), and a range of other protocols. Rather than go through every one of the protocols in the TCP/IP protocol suite, we have elected to explain just the most-used ones, which you can see in Table 2-3.

TCP/IP Addressing

Of all the aspects of TCP/IP, it is the addressing that requires the most attention. At first, the numbers that comprise a TCP/IP address might seem like they have been made up, but there is a method to the madness. When discussing TCP/IP addressing, the terms "TCP/IP address" and "IP address" are used interchangeably. Of the two, however, "IP address" is more accurate, because the addressing of a device is the function of the IP protocol, not the TCP protocol. For our purposes, we'll use the term "IP address."

How IP Addressing Works

To be scalable to multiple networks, TCP/IP must have an addressing scheme that allows devices to be placed on different physical network segments and still be able to communicate with each other. It must also do this while at the same time allowing for a very large number of segments, or networks, and a correspondingly large number of hosts.

exam
ⓦatch

For the Linux+ exam, even if you are not quizzed directly about your knowledge of TCP/IP addressing, you are likely to get questions that will require an understanding of the subject to answer correctly. Either way, make sure you are familiar with, and understand, the information presented here before you take your test.

IP addressing works by assigning a number to each segment, which is then referred to as the *network number*. Then, each device on that network is assigned a number, which is called the *node number*. This allows a kind of street and house number

TABLE 2-3   Commonly Used Protocols in the TCP/IP Protocol Suite

Protocol Name	Acronym	Purpose
File Transfer Protocol	FTP	A mechanism for transferring files between systems. FTP requires a server and a client program in order to function.
Simple Network Management Protocol	SNMP	Allows devices to communicate with, and be configured by, a network management system.
Internet Control Message Protocol	ICMP	Used for the testing and detection of network layout and configuration. The most popular use of ICMP is the PING command, which issues a special kind of ICMP packet called an echo.
Routing Information Protocol	RIP	One of a variety of protocols used for communicating network configuration information between routers.
Transmission Control Protocol	TCP	A transport protocol that provides connection-oriented delivery of data. This connection-oriented approach offers guaranteed data delivery. Because TCP requires that communications be monitored at two ends, it has a higher overhead than connectionless protocols such as UDP.
User Datagram Protocol	UDP	A transport protocol that has a lower overhead than TCP, but offers a best-effort delivery method for data.
Internet Protocol	IP	Transport protocol that coordinates network communications and routes data through the network.
Address Resolution Protocol	ARP	Used for determining the hardware (MAC) address of a network device.
Network Time Protocol	NTP	Used for the communication of time information between NTP-enabled devices.
Post Office Protocol 3	POP3	Protocol for e-mail retrieval that allows data to be stored on a server and downloaded when necessary.

format to be created, as in two devices can be on the same street, but they must have different house numbers. When one system wants to "visit" a system on the same street, it can just walk up the street to do it. Talking to a system on another street takes a bit more information, but by knowing the way to get out of the street, by accessing the *default gateway*, the system is able to send data to nodes on other streets, or networks.

The default gateway is a router, which can be either a server system acting as a router or a hardware device designed for the purpose. As discussed earlier, Linux, like other popular network operating systems, can act as a router. All that is needed, in hardware terms at least, is an additional network card in the server. Depending on the configuration of the router, the amount of software configuration necessary will vary. Figure 2-12 shows an example of how this addressing might work on a sample network.

Although the network in Figure 2-12 is relatively simple, imagine a network many, many times the size of this one and you will have some idea how large internetworks, like the Internet, are built. Okay, there is a little more to it than that, but at a very basic level, that's all the Internet is—one huge collection of connected networks.

Having established the reason for having IP addresses, we must now turn our attention to looking at how these network and node numbers are derived.

An IP address is comprised of four sets of 8 bits, known as octets. Within each octet, the 8 bits can be set to a 1 or 0, the result being a numerical value between 0

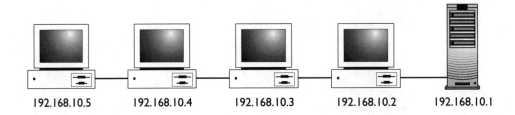

FIGURE 2-12

IP addressing on a sample network

Network Address = 192.168.10.0
Subnet Mask = 255.255.255.0

Useable Address Range for this network =
192.168.10.1 - 192.168.10.254.

192.168.10.5   192.168.10.4   192.168.10.3   192.168.10.2   192.168.10.1

and 255. For example, an octet of (10011101) is equal to 157. You can see how this number is derived by looking at the binary conversion chart in Figure 2-13.

The four octets are combined to create a 32-bit address, which is expressed in a dotted-numerical format, such as 192.168.12.46, which gives us the IP address, but the address alone is not enough for a system to communicate.

Subnet Masks   The IP address actually tells us two things: what the IP number is of the network it is attached to and what the address of the node is on that network. But how does it know which numbers refer to what? Along with the IP address, we also need a subnet mask, which, like the IP address, is a four-octet number expressed in a dotted-numerical format. With the subnet mask, each bit in the address that forms part of the network address is assigned a 1, and each bit that represents part of the node address is assigned a 0. Then, through a process called ANDing, the system is able to determine the necessary information.

To simplify things, let's use an example. Imagine you have an IP address of 167.54.122.12, and a subnet mask of 255.255.0.0. This would mean that the system would look at the first two octets to determine the network number and the last two octets to determine the node number. In this case, the device would be on network 167.54 and have a node address of 122.12. Add a third octet's worth of bits to the subnet mask to make it 255.255.255.0, and the network address would become 167.54.122, and the node address would become 12. You can see how this scheme might work in an example network with three segments in Figure 2-14.

Default Gateway   So far, we have established that we need a TCP/IP address and a subnet mask to communicate on the network, but there is one more piece of information we are likely to need. As discussed earlier, for a system to be able to communicate with another system on a different network, it must be able to find a way off of the current network and on to the other one. This is the function of a

FIGURE 2-13

Binary conversion chart

128	64	32	16	8	4	2	1	=	255
1	0	0	1	1	1	0	1	=	157

FIGURE 2-14

IP addressing
scheme

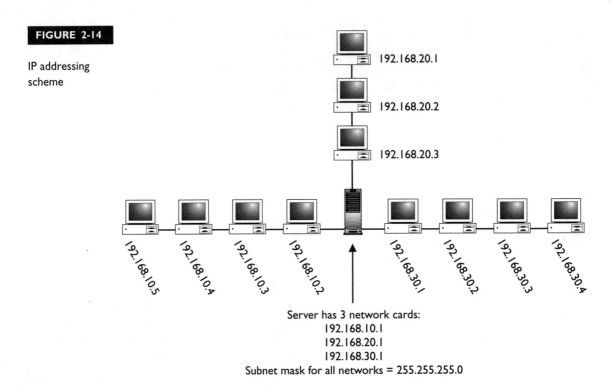

192.168.20.1

192.168.20.2

192.168.20.3

192.168.10.5
192.168.10.4
192.168.10.3
192.168.10.2
192.168.30.1
192.168.30.2
192.168.30.3
192.168.30.4

Server has 3 network cards:
192.168.10.1
192.168.20.1
192.168.30.1
Subnet mask for all networks = 255.255.255.0

default gateway, which is a router that provides access to other networks. It does not guarantee to know how to get to other networks (that is a function of routing tables and routing protocols), but it is the place to start the journey. For a workstation to send information to the default gateway, it must have its IP address, and the address must be on the same network as it is. A common problem with IP addressing is that a router on a different network is specified as the default gateway. When the system attempts to communicate with the gateway, it cannot be found, and so communication is limited to the segment.

To bring all of this together, we have incorporated IP addressing, subnet masks, and default gateway configurations into our sample network, which you can see in Figure 2-15.

IP Address Classes   Now that we have discussed TCP/IP addressing, we'll just throw another principle into the pot—that of TCP/IP address classes.

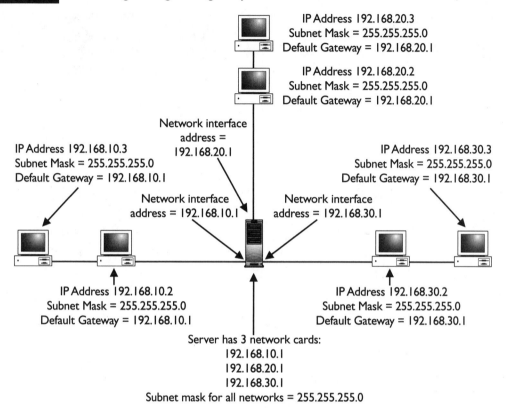

FIGURE 2-15 IP addressing showing default gateway addresses

There are five classes of address, each with its own range of numbers and available networks. These are shown in Table 2-4. For classes A, B, and C, Table 2-4 also includes the default subnet mask that you would use for each class. The standard subnet mask is the subject of much debate, because some say there is no such thing as a "standard" subnet mask, but in reality, if you get a Cass B address assigned to you, you are also guaranteed to be given the subnet mask of 255.255.0.0. What you do with that subnet mask is up to you.

By looking at Table 2-4, you can determine that certain classes of address have more network numbers and fewer node numbers available than others. For example, in the Class A range, there are only 126 networks available, but each can have a huge number (over 16 million) node addresses. On the other end of the scale, there are

TABLE 2-4 TCP/IP Address Classes

Address Class	Address Range	Standard subnet mask	Purpose
Class A	1–126	255.0.0.0	Addressing
Class B	128–191	255.255.0.0	Addressing
Class C	192–223	255.255.225.0	Addressing
Class D	224	NA	Multicast addressing
Class E	225–255	NA	Future development

many Class C networks available, but each can only have 254 nodes. This brings up numerous issues, some of which you may not need to worry about.

Class D addresses are used for multicasting. Multicasting is a type of network communication that lets groups of devices, such as routers, share addresses and receive information that is sent to that address. Class E addresses are reserved for future development.

Network and Broadcast Addresses

Two important TCP/IP-related addressing principles that must be understood for the Linux+ exam are that of how we refer to *this network*, and the addresses used for transmitting broadcasts.

This network   Addresses that are used to refer to this network are represented as all 0's. In other words, if you have a network of 124.15.6.231 and a subnet mask of 255.0.0.0, the address you would use to refer to this network would be 124.0.0.0.

Broadcast Addresses   Broadcast addresses use the entire octect, 255, to indicate that transmissions sent to this address should actually be sent to all addresses on that network. Using the same example as the one just used, the broadcast address for the network would be 124.255.255.255.

To give another example of each of these, with an address 203.16.12.171 and a subnet mask of 255.255.255.0, the number used to refer to this network would be 203.16.12.0 and the broadcast address for would be 203.16.12.255.

on the
(!)ob

In this chapter, subnet masks have been discussed only as they pertain to using full octets. In a working environment, you might find you are working with subnet masks that use only parts of an octet. For example, the PC being used to write this text has a subnet mask of 255.255.252.0. This means that the entire first and second octet, and the first six bits of the third octet, are being used as the network number, and the last two bits of the third octet and the entire fourth octet are being used to represent the node address. Understanding this "partial octet" subnet masking is outside the scope of the Linux+ exam, but it is a skill you may need to master for the real world.

Assigning IP Addresses

Assigning IP addresses has certain rules that must be observed. If you are connecting a server or other device to the Internet, you must obtain a registered IP address for that device. If you think about it, this is reasonable. Each device on the Internet must have a unique address; otherwise, it would not be able to send and receive data. To ensure that each node on the Internet fulfills this requirement, the assignment of IP addresses is closely controlled.

Around the world, three organizations shoulder the responsibility for assigning IP addresses. In the Americas and parts of the Caribbean, the responsibility falls to the American Registry for Internet Numbers (ARIN). In the Asia Pacific, it is the Asia Pacific Network Information Centre (APNIC). In Europe, the Middle East, and parts of Africa, it is Réseaux IP Européens Network Coordination Centre (RIPE NCC). In addition to applying to the appropriate organization to obtain a registered IP address, you can also get one from an ISP, which, given that you are most likely going to be connecting to one anyway, is probably the easiest choice.

Although you need to have a registered IP address for all devices that will be connected to the Internet, more flexibility is available for internal IP addressing. In all but the most exceptional circumstances, companies will employ a firewall system to protect a network that is connected to the Internet from outside influences.

on the
(!)ob

The use of the term firewall implies that there is a single device, but in many cases, this is not true. Firewalls, or to put it more accurately, Firewall systems, are often a group of devices, servers, and routers that work together to protect the network. Another thing to consider is that while we normally consider firewalls a measure to protect a network from Internet-based hackers, some organizations use them internally to protect areas of the network, such as the R&D department or accounts and payroll.

One of the functions that these firewalls often offer is that of Network Address Translation (NAT). NAT allows multiple devices to use a single (or a small number of) registered IP address for external communications. It does this by watching the communications coming in and remembering what data is supposed to go to which devices. You can see an example of NAT in Figure 2-16.

NAT effectively gives you two things. It allows you to use only a single (or small number) registered IP address, which is good because there are not that many to go round. It also gives you complete flexibility in IP addressing on our internal network.

Because, when using NAT, you no longer have to abide by the rules of assigned IP addresses, the addressing scheme can be whatever you want it to be, within the basic restrictions of IP addressing. For example, if you had an internal network with four segments, you might decide to call them 20.20.1.0, 20.20.2.0, 20.20.3.0, and 20.20.4.0. Using a subnet mask of 255.255.255.0, this would give you a huge number of possible networks with a maximum of 254 nodes on each network.

FIGURE 2-16

NAT in action

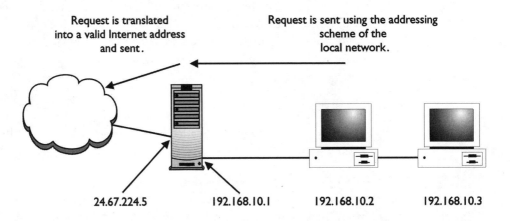

on the **job**

There are special ranges of IP addresses, called private ranges, which anyone can use on their internal network. Two of the most commonly used private ranges are 10.X.X.X and 192.168.X.X. They are special because routers on the Internet are programmed not to forward data that shows these addresses as the source or destination address. This allows you to create an internal network and not worry about using assigned IP addresses. The only drawback to this method is that systems using this IP address will not be able to access the Internet directly. You must use a proxy server or another type of server that provides NAT services if you are going to use this method and want to access resources on the Internet.

Whether you use a private range, NAT, or an assigned IP address range, you must observe the basic rules of IP addressing, which are that each node must have a unique address, and that nodes on the same network must share the same network address. Network addresses must be unique within that network, and if you want to reach another network, you must have a mechanism to do so.

TCP/IP Ports

TCP/IP offers so many different services that it needs to differentiate between incoming requests so that the data can be routed to the correct place. Take, for example, a server that provides e-mail and Web hosting services. When data is sent to the machine, it needs to know whether the information pertains to e-mail or a request for a Web page. The mechanism used to do this are *ports*, which are predefined identifiers assigned to requests so that they can be routed correctly.

TCP/IP has 65,535 ports available, though they are broken down into three designations. "Well Known" ports run from 0 to 1023; "Registered" ports from 1024 to 49151; and "Dynamic" or "Private" ports from 49152 to 65535. For our purposes here, we are concerned primarily with some of the services that use the Well Known port range.

on the **job**

When you want to specify the service on a specific server, you can combine the IP address and the port number. For example, if you were referring to the Web server application on a server with the IP address 211.16.24.215, you could use 211.16.24.215:80. That's the IP address, followed by a colon and the port number.

TABLE 2-5	Protocol Name	Port Number
Common TCP/IP Ports	FTP	21
	HTTP	80
	NNTP	119
	NTP	123
	POP3	110
	SMTP	25
	SNMP	161
	SSH	22
	Telnet	23

Table 2-5 shows some of the more commonly used TCP/IP ports.

An understanding of ports is important for those working with any system that offers TCP/IP-based services to clients, because quite often the ports must be opened up on a firewall to allow access. Imagine that you have a firewall server that protects a Web server and an e-mail server on a network. For users on the Internet to access either of these servers, the firewall needs to be configured to allow data through on those ports. At the same time, the firewall should be configured to block any ports that are not needed, and any servers that should not be accessed by outside sources.

IPX/SPX

If you are looking for a routable network protocol that requires minimal addressing configuration, then the Internetwork Packet Exchange/Sequenced Packet Exchange (IPX/SPX) protocol may offer a solution. Originally developed by Novell for use on NetWare networks, IPX/SPX's popularity was linked to the popularity of NetWare, though Novell licensed IPX/SPX functionality to other manufacturers, including Microsoft, who wanted to create IPX/SPX-compatible protocols.

Even Novell now acknowledges that the future of IPX/SPX looks bleak, and in the latest versions of Novell NetWare, TCP/IP is used as the default protocol. IPX is still supported, but Novell is gently nudging existing users to TCP/IP by introducing more and more TCP/IP services with each release.

exam

⚠ **atch**

If you are installing Linux into an environment that uses IPX/SPX, such as those with older NetWare servers, you need to know that Linux can be configured to use IPX/SPX if needed.

Like TCP/IP, IPX/SPX uses single address string that represents both the network number and the node number in the same string, but the portions of the address are fixed so a subnet mask or similar device is not needed to determine which part is the node and which part is the network address. An example of IPX/SPX addressing is DA25:CB8F:0074:DDE3:2A2A, where the portion {DA25:CB8F} is the network address, and the portion {0074:DDE3:2A2A} is the node address. Fortunately, most of the addressing in an IPX network is taken care of by defaults.

The number of installed IPX networks is expected to decline drastically over the next few years, and while anyone studying network protocols should be aware of IPX's existence, effort should be directed toward an understanding of TCP/IP rather than IPX.

NetBEUI

No discussion of networking protocols would be complete without the inclusion of NetBEUI, but you won't find NetBEUI and Linux working together. Although there have been attempts to incorporate NetBEUI into Linux, the attempts failed, and given that NetBEUI offers little advantage over the other supported protocols, motivation for its inclusion is low.

NetBEUI was developed by Microsoft and IBM as a simple-to-configure protocol for use on small LANs, but its designed use ultimately became its downfall. It is not a routable protocol, and as people moved from single-segment networks to larger ones, the lack of routing capability became the limiting factor in NetBEUI's popularity.

CERTIFICATION SUMMARY

Although Linux can operate in a stand-alone configuration, its use is far more likely to be as a network server, or at least connected to a network. As such, anyone working with Linux must have a good understanding of common networking methods, protocols, and cabling systems. This includes different cable types and the relative characteristics of each, their shortcomings, and their advantages. Modern networks also use various hardware and software devices such as hubs, switches, and routers to facilitate connection to, and operation of, the network. While a detailed understanding of the operation of these devices is not necessary, an appreciation for the functions that these devices perform and their physical configuration within the network, is also needed.

Those taking the Linux+ exam should also be aware of media access methods and how they apply to popular networking methods such as Ethernet and Token Ring. Network protocols, and in particular TCP/IP, play an important part in the networking picture, and an understanding of how these protocols work and are configured is essential.

All of these skills are important for taking and passing the Linux+ exam and will also be invaluable in real-world applications.

TWO-MINUTE DRILL

Here are some of the key points from this chapter.

Identify Basic Network Concepts, Including How a Network Works

❑ Toplogies dictate how a network is structured. The most common topology in use today is the physical star.

❑ Various cable types can be used in networks, including coaxial, fiber optic, and twisted pair. By far the most popular is twisted pair.

❑ Hubs and switches are used in to build networks.

❑ To ensure that equal access is granted to devices on the network, access methods are employed. The most common access method CSMA\CD.

❑ The most popular networking system in use today is Ethernet.

❑ Network protocols provide a range of functions including allowing devices to communicate with each other.

❑ TCP/IP is by far the most popular network protocol in use today.

SELF TEST

The following questions will help you measure your understanding of the material presented in this chapter. Read all of the choices carefully because there might be more than one correct answer. Choose all correct answers for each question.

Identify Basic Network Concepts, Including How a Network Works

1. You need to connect a PC to an Ethernet switch. What type of port on the switch would you connect it to?

    A. MDX

    B. MDI-X

    C. MDI

    D. MDX-I

2. Which of the following TCP/IP address classes is used for multicast addresses?

    A. Class B

    B. Class C

    C. Class D

    D. Class E

3. The condition through which a data signal degrades as it travels over a distance is called what?

    A. Crosstalk

    B. Loss

    C. Degradation

    D. Attenuation

4. You are implementing an Ethernet network using UTP cabling. What physical layout will your network take?

    A. Mesh

    B. Star

    C. Bus

    D. Ring

5. Ethernet switches forward information to a given port based on what information?

    A. The MAC address of the system connected to that port

    B. The IPX address of the system connected to that port

    C. The TCP/IP address of the system connected to that port

    D. The NetBEUI address of the system connected to that port

6. Which of the following network protocols are routable?

    A. IPX

    B. NetBEUI

    C. CSMA/CD

    D. TCP/IP

7. Which of the following IP addresses represents a class B address?

    A. 127.12.56.212

    B. 28.14.87.233

    C. 171.63.264.12

    D. 188.188.188.188

8. Which of the following cable types has the greatest resistance to EMI?

    A. Fiber optic

    B. Thick coax

    C. Shielded twisted pair

    D. Unshielded twisted pair

9. Which of the following is the correct broadcast address for the network 136.12.203.217 with a subnet mask of 255.255.255.0?

    A. 136.12.255.255

    B. 136.255.255.255.0

    C. 136.12.203.255

    D. 136.12.203.0

10. Which of the following network protocols does Linux support?

    A. NetBEUI

    B. IPX

    C. TCP/IP

    D. 10BaseT

11. What would be the maximum data rate of a fully duplexed 100BaseT network connection?

    A. 50Mbps

    B. 100Mbps

    C. 200Mbps

    D. 200Mbps

12. You need to connect two Ethernet switches together, but neither has an MDI port. Which of the following cable types should you use?

    A. Crossover

    B. Straight-over

    C. Straight-through

    D. Cross-through

13. The condition by which a signal receives interference from a signal on another cable lying near to it is called what?

    A. Crosstalk

    B. Crossover

    C. Attenuation

    D. Blocking

14. Fast Ethernet is an Ethernet standard that supports data transmission at what speed?

    A. 100Mbps

    B. 100Mbps

    C. 10Mbps

    D. 1,000Mbps

15. What type of media access method is CSMA/CD?

    A. Carrier detection

    B. Token passing

    C. Multiple access

    D. Contention

16. You examine the TCP/IP configuration for your Linux server and determine that the IP address is 192.168.5.203 and the subnet mask is 255.255.255.0. What is the node number of the server you are working on?

    A. 5.203

    B. 192.168.5

    C. 203

    D. 168.5.203

17. Consider the IP address 194.17.63.221. Which of the following subnet masks would you use for this address?

    A. 255.255.255.0

    B. 0.0.255.255

    C. 255.255.0.0

    D. 194.17.63.0

18. In a crossover UTP cable, which lines are crossed?

    A. 1 and 3

    B. 2 and 4

    C. 2 and 6

    D. 3 and 5

19. Which of the following types of address does a router use to make its routing decisions?

    A. IP address

    B. MAC address

    C. CSMA/CD address

    D. Routing address

20. How many meters can a device be from a switch on a UTP network cable segment?

   A. 25 meters

   B. 185 meters

   C. 500 meters

   D. 100 meters

LAB QUESTION

You have been tasked with designing a network addressing scheme for your company. You Have been assigned the Internet address of 25.67.233.17 as the external interface for your firewall/Proxy server, which is used for Internet access. The subnet mask for the connection is 255.255.254.0 and the default gateway is 25.67.233.1.

For the internal networks, of which there are two, you will be using the network address range 192.168.X.X. Using this information, label the systems in Figure 2-17 with the appropriate IP addresses, subnet masks and default gateway.

FIGURE 2-17

Template for
Lab Question

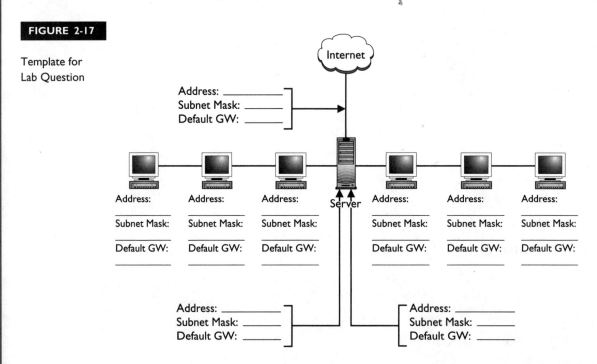

SELF TEST ANSWERS

Identify Basic Network Concepts, Including How a Network Works

1.   ☑   **B.** On a network switch or hub, all of the ports you use for connecting equipment are Medium Dependant Interface-Crossed (MDI-X) ports. The use of an MDI-X port allows you to use a standard straight-through cable. If the connection is not directly into the hub and is into a wall socket or floor box, a straight-through cable can also be used because these cables are wired directly to the patching units.

   ☒   **A.** The only two types of valid port on a hub or switch are Medium Dependant Interface (MDI) and MDI-X. MDX is not a valid port type. **C.** MDI ports are provided to allow multiple hubs or switches to be connected to create larger networks. The MDI ports of a hub or switch can be connected using a straight-through UTP cable. If no MDI ports are available on a hub or switch, they can be connected by using a crossover cable plugged into an MDI port. **D.** MDX-I is not a valid type of port.

2.   ☑   **C.** The IP address range that starts 224.X.X.X is used for multicast addressing. Multicast transmissions are those sent to a group of computers that all share the same multicast address. Multicasting is often used for communication between routers or other networking devices.

   ☒   **A.** Class B addresses (in the range 128.X.X.X to 191.X.X.X) are used for assigning addresses to clients, as are Class C addresses (192.X.X.X to 223.X.X.X), **B. D.** Class E addresses are reserved for future-development purposes.

3.   ☑   **D.** Attenuation. The degradation of a signal as it travels over distance is called attenuation. Different types of cables can cope with this attenuation better than others. Do not confuse attenuation with crosstalk or EMI.

   ☒   **A.** Crosstalk refers to interference from other data cables that run close to the cable. Crosstalk can weaken or even corrupt the signal, making it unusable. **B.** The term loss is sometimes used to refer to the degradation of a signal as it travels over a wire, but this is not a technical term. **C.** Degradation is the general term given to the reduction in quality of a signal. Degradation can be the result of crosstalk or electromagnetic interference (EMI), which is caused by electrical or mechanical machinery operating in close proximity to the cable.

4.   ☑   **B.** UTP cabling is configured in a physical star topology and requires the use of networking devices called switches or hubs. Each cable from the switch or hub is connected to a single device, creating the appearance of a star.

   ☒   **A.** The physical mesh layout is a term given to a network that has multiple paths between nodes. The mesh layout is most commonly associated with wide area networks (WANs) that may have redundant routers. **C.** The bus physical layout is associated with thin or thick Ethernet cable. **D.** Physical ring networks are associated with fiber optic.

5. ☑ **A.** Ethernet switches work by only forwarding packets that are intended for a given host on the cable connected to that host. It determines this information by looking at the Media Access Control (MAC) address of the device attached to that cable. Performance is improved because this approach reduces the number of collisions and provides dedicated bandwidth between two devices on the switch.

☒ **B.** IPX addresses are network addresses and so are configured through software. Ethernet switches use the MAC address to forward data. This applies to answers **C** and **D** as well.

6. ☑ **A, D.** Both IPX and TCP/IP are routable protocols. For a protocol to be routable, it must have an addressing scheme that allows the network and the node to be identified separately.

☒ **B.** NetBEUI is not a routable protocol. **C.** CSMA/CD is a media access method and not a networking protocol.

7. ☑ **D.** The address 188.188.188.188 falls into the Class B range for IP addresses. The Class B range runs from 128.X.X.X to 191.X.X.X. The fact that all numbers in the address are 188 has no bearing on the validity of the address.

☒ **A.** Addresses that start with 127 are reserved for loopback addresses. The loopback is a software element within the TCP/IP protocol stack that can be used to verify the correct operation of TCP/IP on a given device. **B** is an address from the Class A range, which runs from 1.X.X.X to 126.X.X.X. **C** appears, at first, to be a Class B address, but because the third octet is 264, the address is actually invalid. Each octet in an IP address can be a maximum of 255.

8. ☑ **A.** Electromagnetic interference (EMI) is caused by electrical or mechanical equipment. These harmful emissions can corrupt or weaken data signals as they travel along the cable. Fiber-optic cable is not affected by EMI because it uses light instead of electrical signals to transmit data.

☒ **B.** Thick coaxial cable is more resistant to EMI than thin coax or UTP cable, but it still does suffer from EMI. **C.** Shielded twisted pair is more resistant to EMI than UTP, thanks to a protective shield that covers each wire and the cable itself. **D.** Of all the cable types listed, UTP is the most susceptible to EMI

9. ☑ **C.** Broadcast addresses are used by systems when a message must be sent to all devices on a network. To denote the broadcast address for a given network, 255 is used to represent all nodes on that network. From the subnet mask, you can deduce that the first three octets

(136.12.203) represent the network address, so the broadcast address for this network would be 136.12.203.255.

☒ **A.** If the subnet mask were 255.255.0.0, then this answer would be correct. **B** is invalid. **D** would represent the correct designation if the question were referring to this network.

10. ☑ **B, C.** Linux supports TCP/IP natively and can support IPX, although reconfiguration of the Linux kernel is required to provide this support.

☒ **A.** At one time, developers worked on making a NetBEUI-compatible protocol to work with Linux, but the work was never completed because the benefits of using NetBEUI were outweighed by the work involved in implementing it. **D.** 10BaseT is an Ethernet standard that runs at 10Mbps over twisted pair cabling. It is not a network protocol.

11. ☑ **C.** In a fully duplexed network connection, the standard CSMA/CD approach is dropped in favor of a more efficient access method that allows the connection to be run at double the standard speed. Therefore, a 100BaseT network connection will run at maximum of 200Mbps.

☒ **A.** The opposite of a full-duplex connection is a half-duplex connection. However, although the term "half" is used, it does not reduce the speed of the network connection. Therefore, a half-duplex 100Mbps network connection will run at 100Mbps. **B.** 100Mbps is the correct number for a half-duplex network connection. **D.** 200Mbps may seem right at first, but notice that the figure has a capital **B**. This indicates megabytes per second, not megabits per second as it should be. Therefore, this answer is incorrect.

12. ☑ **A.** When two Ethernet hubs or switches are to be connected that do not have MDI ports, an MDI-X port can be used, provided you connect them using a crossover UTP cable. All "standard" ports on a switch or hub are MDI-X ports

☒ **B.** There is no such thing as a straight-over cable, or a cross-through cable (**D**). **C.** A straight-through cable is a common term used to describe a twisted pair cable that has all the pins connected the same at both ends.

13. ☑ **A.** Crosstalk occurs when a signal from one cable interferes with the signal on another cable that runs close to it. Crosstalk can occur between individual wires within a cable, as in the case of twisted pair, or it can occur between physically separate cables in a situation such as a wiring closet or in a cable run.

☒ **B.** The term crossover is used to refer to a twisted pair cable that is used to connect two network devices, such as switches or hubs that don't have purpose-designed uplink ports available on them. **C.** Attenuation is the term used to refer to the degradation of signal quality as it travels over distance. **D.** Blocking is not a valid term in this context.

14. ☑ **B.** Fast Ethernet supports data transmission at 100Mbps. This can be increased to 200Mbps if the connection between the device and the network switch can be configured as a full-duplex connection. Two other standards of Ethernet are available. Standard Ethernet operates at 10Mbps and Gigabit Ethernet operates at 1,000Mbps.
    ☒ **A.** This answer appears to be correct, but the number is followed by the megabytes per second designation (MBps), not the megabits per second designation (Mbps). **C.** 10Mbps is the speed of standard Ethernet. **D.** 1,000Mbps is the speed of Gigabit Ethernet.

15. ☑ **D.** Carrier Sense Multiple Access/Collision Detection (CSMA/CD) is a contention-based media access method. It is associated with Ethernet networks.
    ☒ **A.** Carrier detection is part of the mechanism by which CSMA/CD operates but it is not, in itself, a media access method. **B.** Token passing is a media access method that uses a special packet called a token. For a device to transmit data on the network, it must be in possession of the token. The most common implementation of the token-passing method is Token Ring. **C.** As with carrier detection, multiple access is part of the mechanism by which CSMA/CD operates, but it's not a media access method.

16. ☑ **C.** On a system that uses TCP/IP, both the IP address and the subnet mask are needed to determine the network and node number of the device. In this question, the subnet mask is 255.255.255.0, meaning that the first three octets are used to represent the network address, and the last octet is used to represent the node address. Therefore, the network number is 192.168.5 and the node number is 203.
    ☒ **A.** If the subnet mask had been 255.255.0.0, this answer would be correct. **B.** 192.168.5 correctly identifies the network number for this question, not the node number. **D.** If the subnet mask had been 255.0.0.0, then 168.5.203 would have been correct.

17. ☑ **A.** Assuming that you are using standard IP subnet masks, which you would do in the absence of any other information, you would select the subnet mask 255.255.255.0 for this address. The address is a Class C address, in the range 192.X.X.X to 223.X.X.X, so the first three octets would be used to represent the network number, and the last would be used to represent the node number.
    ☒ **B.** Network numbers are always assigned from the left side of the IP address, so this subnet mask is invalid. **C.** 255.255.0.0 would be correct if the address had been in the Class B range (128.X.X.X to 191.X.X.X). **D.** 194.17.63.0 is the number that would be used to refer to the network 194.17.63.

18. ☑ **A, C.** In a twisted pair crossover cable, wires 1 and 3, and 2 and 6 are crossed over. This is in contrast with a straight-through cable, in which all the wires run uncrossed.
    ☒ **B** and **D** are both incorrect.

19. ☑ **A.** Routers make forwarding decisions on the software-configured network address of a device. On local area networks, these addresses are commonly TCP/IP or IPX addresses.
    ☒ **B.** The MAC address is used by bridges and network switches to make forwarding decisions. These devices are not capable of routing information based on the network address. **C** is invalid because CSMA/CD is a media access method and not a network addressing system. **D** is not a valid term in this context.

20. ☑ **C.** UTP cable segments can be up to 100 meters in length.
    ☒ **A.** All commonly implemented cable types are capable of more than 25 meters. **B.** 185 meters refers to the maximum permitted length of thin coaxial cable. **C.** 500 meters is the maximum cable distance for thick coaxial cable.

LAB ANSWER

There are various ways in which the addressing can be supplied. The basic principles are that each system must have a unique host address, and each network segment must have a unique network address. The default gateway information for each machine should direct the system to the local interface for the system acting as a router, which in this case is Server1.

Any network address that uses the 192.168.X.X is acceptable. In this example we have used 192.168.100.X and 192.168.200.X, with a subnet mask of 255.255.255.0. The interfaces for the local network in this example are not provided a default gateway, though depending on the configuration of the server and the desired result may be necessary. See Figure 2-18 for a sample solution.

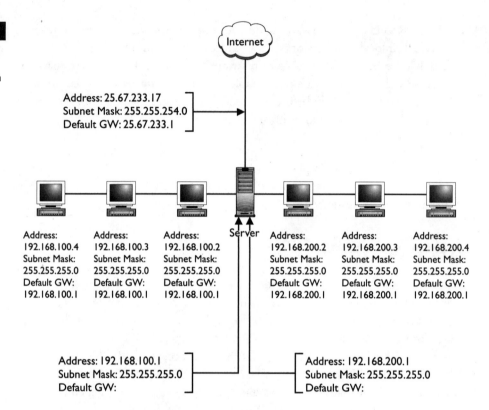

FIGURE 2-18

Sample solution
for Lab Question

Internet

Address: 25.67.233.17
Subnet Mask: 255.255.254.0
Default GW: 25.67.233.1

Address:
192.168.100.4
Subnet Mask:
255.255.255.0
Default GW:
192.168.100.1

Address:
192.168.100.3
Subnet Mask:
255.255.255.0
Default GW:
192.168.100.1

Address:
192.168.100.2
Subnet Mask:
255.255.255.0
Default GW:
192.168.100.1

Server

Address:
192.168.200.2
Subnet Mask:
255.255.255.0
Default GW:
192.168.200.1

Address:
192.168.200.3
Subnet Mask:
255.255.255.0
Default GW:
192.168.200.1

Address:
192.168.200.4
Subnet Mask:
255.255.255.0
Default GW:
192.168.200.1

Address: 192.168.100.1
Subnet Mask: 255.255.255.0
Default GW:

Address: 192.168.200.1
Subnet Mask: 255.255.255.0
Default GW:

3

Hardware Configuration

T he inclusion of a chapter on hardware in a book focusing on the Linux operating system may seem a little unusual, but it actually makes pretty good sense. Whereas most of the other vendors' Linux exams focus on the operating system only, the CompTIA certification goes right into hardware, including all major system components and what it takes to have them function correctly within the system. As we are preparing you to take the Linux+ exam, this book will do the same.

Linux, like any other operating system, will often require a little hardware tinkering to get things where they need to be. Knowing how to determine whether system components are functioning as they should and being able to make adjustments when they are not represents half the battle when it comes to computer management. The rest, of course, is up to the operating system.

The CompTIA Linux+ exam objectives cover a broad scope of personal computer hardware, including all the major system components you are likely to encounter when working with Linux, both new and past technologies. For some, much of this may be review, but for others it may be new. In either case, make no mistake—without a detailed knowledge of key system components, passing the Linux+ exam will prove difficult indeed.

With that understanding, this chapter will examine core system computer components, including their basic characteristics and installation considerations. Before any discussion of hardware, it is a good idea to first review some electrostatic discharge (ESD) practices.

Electrostatic Discharge

Have you ever scurried across a carpet and then touched something only to get a shock? This can be quite entertaining if you are bored and the object you are touching is not a computer component. Static discharge and computer equipment are like oil and water; they don't mix. Even with this knowledge, many people handling hardware do not observe the proper ESD practices, a very undesirable and potentially costly practice.

Perhaps what makes proper ESD handling so deceptive is the fact that ESD may not immediately damage a system component; rather, the static discharge can cause a gradual degradation of a component. After a few weeks or months, this degradation is hard to pin down as a result of ESD damage. Some components, such as system

FIGURE 3-1

Equipment used for ESD prevention (Copyright © 2001, Intel Corporation)

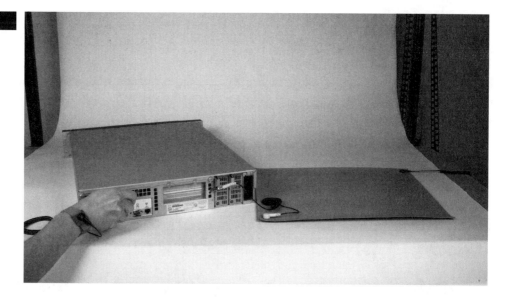

memory, are particularly susceptible to ESD, meaning your new 256MB memory module can die in your hands before it reaches the system board. Figure 3-1 shows equipment used for ESD prevention.

ESD Best Practices

Without question, ESD represents a major risk to system components, but with proper handling, the threat can be minimized. The following are a few precautions to take whenever handling computer components:

■ Leave components in the antistatic bag until you are ready to install them. All components when purchased and when transported should be in the antistatic bag.

■ As much as possible, work on computer components while standing on hard floors. Working on components while standing on a carpeted area is asking for trouble.

■ Never place the component on the outside of the antistatic bag. Antistatic bags are designed to pull static outward; placing components on the bag may in fact be worse than placing them on the counter.

- Handle devices such as memory and expansion cards by the edges, never touching the connectors or onboard circuitry. Wear an approved antistatic strap around your wrist or ankle.

- Use an antistatic mat to rest components on when placing them down.

- Never run components through your hair and then try to make them stick to a wall.

on the Job

When it comes time to storing components not currently in use, ensure that they are placed in an antistatic bag and stored in a cool, dry place.

CERTIFICATION OBJECTIVE 3.01

Identify Basic Terms, Concepts, and Functions of System Components

Before you sit down to install your Linux system, you'll likely need to know about the hardware in your system and what this hardware is designed to do. The following section outlines major system components and what you may need to know about them to install Linux successfully.

Memory

All computers need random access memory (RAM) to function because it provides temporary storage for information so that the information can be quickly accessed by the various components of the system. RAM is available in two basic types: dynamic (DRAM) and static (SRAM). SRAM is the more costly of the two and is used primarily for cache memory in systems. DRAM, being the more affordable, is plentiful in the modern PC.

The first implementations of DRAM required that individual dual inline package (DIP) chips be plugged directly into the board, but there have been significant changes since this was the case. Today, a more efficient approach of attaching memory chips directly to a printed circuit board is used with these boards plugging directly into memory slots onto the system board.

Today, the most commonly used types of these RAM boards are the dual inline memory modules (DIMMs), but you may still see single inline memory modules (SIMMs) in older, legacy systems. For laptops, small outline DIMMs (SO-DIMMs) are used.

Physical Design

It is possible to distinguish between the various memory types by looking at them, because they all have a slightly different form factor. What is sometimes confusing when talking about memory is that familiar terms such as SIMMs and DIMMs refer to the physical layout of the memory, not the specific type of memory. Memory still comes in different types, such as extended data output (EDO) and SDRAM. SIMMs and DIMMs simply refer to the physical layout of the plug-in board, which is known as the *packaging*.

Single Inline Memory Module   SIMMs were popular in 386, 486, and early Pentium-class computer systems. The early SIMMs came in a 30-pin variety, which could transfer data in or out of the module 8 bits at a time, and a 72-pin option, which had a 32-bit maximum transfer rate. SIMMs are most commonly associated with the older EDO memory, and it is unlikely that you will encounter SDRAM on a SIMM, because SDRAM is typically used with DIMMs. Figure 3-2 shows a 72-pin memory module.

on the
ᶤob

Although SIMMs are associated with older PCs, Linux's undemanding hardware requirements mean that often these older PCs are called into service as Linux systems. Therefore, an understanding and awareness of SIMMs is necessary.

FIGURE 3-2

72-pin
SIMM module
(Copyright
© 2001, Intel
Corporation)

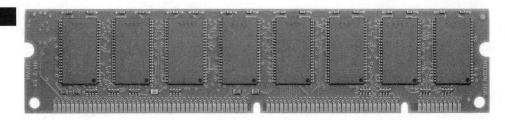

Dual Inline Memory Module   DIMMs are the most common type of memory used today. DIMMs use a 168-pin design. They are installed vertically and are secured by catches that engage the module at each end. DIMMs are most likely to contain SDRAM or maybe EDO RAM, because those were the prevalent technologies when DIMMs were introduced. Figure 3-3 shows a 168-pin DIMM.

EXERCISE 3-1

Identifying, Installing, and Removing Memory Modules

1. Power down your system and unplug it from the wall socket.

2. Remove the case from the system.

3. Observe appropriate ESD practices as discussed in the beginning of the chapter.

4. Locate the memory modules on the system board, remove the clamps from either side of the memory, and remove the module from the memory slot. Be careful to handle the memory by the edges only.

5. To reinstall the memory, clear a path to the memory module, removing cables that may be in the way. Align the module to the correct position for the socket. Both 72-pin and DIMMs have notches that must be aligned before installing.

6. Once aligned, fit the memory into the socket, push the module securely in place, and connect the latches to lock it there. SIMMs fit in the sockets on an angle, whereas DIMMs push straight in.

7. Return the system to normal, reboot the system, and confirm that memory is counted during POST.

8. If memory is not counted, ensure that it is properly seated in the memory slot on the system board.

Rambus Inline Memory Module   The Rambus inline memory module (RIMM) is designed specifically for use with systems that use Rambus memory. A RIMM resembles a DIMM but uses 184-pin connectors. However, because of their proprietary nature, RIMMs are found only in a few servers.

Small Outline DIMM   Notebooks and laptops need memory too, and that is where the small outline DIMMs (SO-DIMMs) come into play. SO-DIMMs are typically a 72- or 144-pin variety and may be a single module or require matched pairs. SO-DIMMs are typically installed under the keyboard or in a panel located on the back of the laptop.

Types of Memory

Not all memory is created equal, and there are many types of RAM, making it important to know the characteristics of each type before installing it into your system. For those who are installing or upgrading memory into an existing system, the trick is being able to match and buy the memory that is supported by the system. This section outlines the characteristics of the more common RAM implementations that you are likely to encounter when installing Linux:

- **Extended data output RAM**   Developed in 1994, EDO memory is all but extinct, but those installing Linux on older systems may encounter it. Once an impressive statistic, EDO RAM has a maximum bandwidth of 320MBps, but it is restricted to be used only on systems that have a processor and system board that support its use.

- **Synchronous dynamic RAM**   SDRAM was a significant improvement over EDO RAM, providing speeds almost double that of EDO. The performance capabilities of SDRAM have given it a firm foothold in high-performance computer systems and it is supported by major server and desktop manufacturers. SDRAM is available in a number of speeds, including PC66, PC100, and PC133 versions, which provide 528MBps, 800MBps, and 1.1 GBps of maximum bandwidth, respectively. Expect to see SDRAM somewhere along the way.

- **Double data rate (DDR) SDRAM**   As with most things computer-related, improvements are just around the corner. DDR-SDRAM is the newcomer on the block and provides considerable speed performance over regular SDRAM. DDR-SDRAM provides a maximum bandwidth of 1.6 GBps for PC100, and 2.1 GBps for PC133. Due to compatibility concerns, many computers continue to use SDRAM, but servers are increasingly turning to DDR-SDRAM to take advantage of its performance capabilities.

■ **Rambus DRAM** RDRAM is unlikely to be seen a great deal, but a discussion of memory would not be complete without it. RDRAM is the result of a joint effort from Intel and Rambus and provides high-performance RAM with up to 1.6 GBps maximum bandwidth transfer. Due to licensing considerations, RDRAM is more expensive than alternatives such as SDRAM, a fact that has meant RDRAM has been deployed in limited numbers.

on the

jo b

As far as Linux and RAM compatibility are concerned, Linux currently supports all the major memory types and configurations. There should be few compatibility issues with Linux itself; however, the system board still has to support the memory.

Error-Correcting Code and Parity RAM

When good-quality memory is purchased, it usually has little go wrong with it and works error-free within the system. Like everything computer-related, errors will eventually happen, but in the case of memory, there are methods in place to help handle them automatically.

Older computers had something called *parity* that was designed to detect errors in memory and report it. Parity was limited in that, although it could detect the error, it had no mechanism in place to correct errors. Today's systems require a higher level of error correction, which is where error correcting code (ECC) memory comes in.

Like parity memory, ECC can detect errors in memory, but ECC can take it one step further. By using a mathematical calculation called a *checksum,* ECC RAM has the ability to correct the errors it finds, and if it can't, it reports them. SDRAM of today often uses ECC, making it an efficient type of memory and the choice for high-end servers. ECC RAM costs more than non-ECC, but in most applications, the performance of the ECC modules justifies the cost.

Processors

Processors are the heart of the computer system and one of the major components in determining the performance capabilities of a system. There are two main CPU manufacturers competing in the processor market, AMD and Intel, each holding a certain amount of the market share, with Intel leading the way. These companies have produced a number of different processors over the years, many of which will be seen when installing Linux on new computers as well as older systems. Today, there is pretty much 100 percent Linux compatibility for these two processor manufactures. The only real compatibility issues are encountered in the world of CYRIX processors.

The Linux community is working with both AMD and Intel to support the latest in processor technology, the 64-bit processor.

The System Bus

Many people become acquainted with buses and expansion slots the first time they open the computer case and try to install a new expansion card. Essentially, a bus is a communication pipe that the CPU can use to communicate with other devices on the system board, and "bus speed" refers to the rate at which the information can travel from the CPU to these devices. Only a handful of expansion bus slots are used in modern PCs, each offering various speeds and having different form factors. The following section looks at the types of bus expansion slots commonly used in today's systems.

Many of these bus technologies are not used on modern computer systems and therefore are obsolete as far as commercial computer systems go. Linux, however, is less hardware-demanding, so the use of these bus types on older machines is still relevant.

Industry Standard Architecture

Introduced in the mid 1980s, the Industry Standard Architecture (ISA) bus was the first I/O bus. Originally, the bus was designed as an 8-bit bus. Later, in 1984, a 16-bit version of the ISA bus was developed. The 8-bit version of the bus is no longer seen today; the 16-bit version is another story. Though becoming increasingly less common, 16-bit ISA slots are still in many of today's computer systems, primarily because there are many legacy cards around, such as sound cards and modems, that use the ISA slot.

MicroChannel Architecture

A new bus to be used with IBM's PS/2 computer systems, the MicroChannel Architecture (MCA) bus, was introduced in 1987. The MCA bus offered two significant improvements over the standard ISA bus. It was the first to offer 32-bit capability, and it introduced *bus mastering*, which is a technique that allows a system's peripheral devices to transfer data to other peripheral devices without using either the CPU or system memory. This strategy significantly improved the system's overall performance.

Despite its significant speed enhancement over the ISA bus, it never really caught on. It failed partly because it was proprietary technology used exclusively by IBM PS/2 systems and partly because its design was incompatible with existing ISA expansion cards. MCA is gone now but deserves a footnote as being the first 32-bit system.

on the
j o b

MCA is not well supported by Linux, so refer to the specific distribution's hardware compatibility list to confirm.

Extended Industry Standard Architecture

As mentioned, MCA was designed as a proprietary technology used by IBM. However, it wasn't long before a group of other well-known IT companies developed its own 32-bit bus in response to MCA. What came out of their joint venture was the 32-bit Extended Industry Standard Architecture (EISA) bus. EISA was instantly popular for its 32-bit capabilities as well as its backward compatibility, with the capability to support both the 8- and 16-bit ISA devices. EISA became a relatively common sight in 386 and 486 computers, and because of its faster bus, it was used in many servers of the time. Today EISA is gone, having been replaced by the newer bus technologies such as PCI.

VESA Local Bus

The Video Electronics Standards Association (VESA) local bus (VL-bus) was used in 386 and 486 computers and offered 32-bit capability. VL-bus performed very well for devices such as graphic cards, and for a while, VL-bus was the AGP of its time. Despite its high-performance capabilities, VL-bus suffered from two major drawbacks. First, it did not use bus-mastering, meaning that the CPU had to be used for all data transfers from the VL-bus to the system, thereby creating a bottleneck and performance lag. Second, the bus did not accommodate software setup of the device and required jumpers to be set on the card. The world was going to Plug and Play, so this type of manual intervention was not welcome. VL-bus has given way to PCI and is not found in newer computer systems.

Peripheral Component Interconnect

All of this brings us to where we are today with the Peripheral Component Interconnect (PCI) bus. PCI was designed by Intel as a replacement to the VL-bus, and it wasn't long before PCI was the leader in bus technologies. PCI developers were able to take advantage of the strengths offered by the VL-bus and develop a significantly improved bus. PCI provided support for Plug and Play and could be configured by the software. Further, PCI allowed for bus mastering, which increased the performance capabilities over VL-bus. There was no competition for bus supremacy, and today PCI is the standard for attaching peripheral devices.

PCI-Extended Bus

The PCI bus has undergone some improvements, giving us the PCI-extended (PCI-X) bus. PCI-X is a 64-bit bus, increasing the speed of the PCI bus from 132MBps to 1 GBps, a rather significant improvement. The PCI-X bus is backward-compatible and can accommodate existing PCI expansion cards, a factor that could eventually lead to PCI-X being the only PCI bus included on modern system boards. Figure 3-4 shows a system board with both 32- and 64-bit PCI slots.

Accelerated Graphics Port

Perhaps the most performance-demanding expansion card of all is the video card. To accommodate the demands of video performance, Intel developed the Advanced

FIGURE 3-4

System board with 32- and 64-bit PCI slots (Copyright © 2001, Intel Corporation)

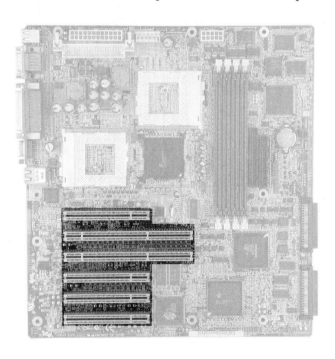

Graphic Port (AGP), which has the capability to produce video images up to eight times faster than PCI can. To accomplish these speeds, AGP has a direct connection between the video adapter and the system's memory. Most modern systems come with an AGP port, and in so doing, free up an existing PCI slot for another expansion card.

Figure 3-5 shows examples of the various expansion cards.

exam
ⓦatch

Be prepared to answer questions pertaining to card and expansion slot compatibility. Also ensure that you are familiar with the physical appearance of each bus type.

BIOS and the Boot Process

Somewhere located on every system board is a read-only memory (ROM) chip known as the basic input/output system (BIOS). The BIOS provides the basic

---

FIGURE 3-5

Examples of various expansion cards (Reproduced with permission from *Computer Desktop Encyclopedia* © 1981–2001 The Computer Language Co., Inc., [www.computerlanguage.com])

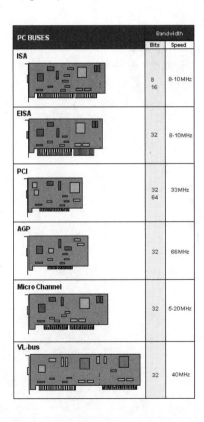

SCENARIO & SOLUTION

You are installing a 16-bit legacy sound card in a system. Which slot should you use?	The ISA slot is used for legacy 16-bit expansion cards.
Which slots support 32-bit data transfer?	MCA, EISA, VL-bus, PCI, AGP, and PCI-X all support 32-bit bus transfer.
You want a type of memory that can correct memory errors on the fly. What should you use?	ECC memory has the ability to correct memory errors as well as report them. Parity, an early version of memory, could only report errors.

set of instructions the computer needs to get up and running. These instructions let the CPU know what it needs to do when the system is booted; without these instructions, the computer has no idea what to do. Because the processor needs to use these BIOS instructions on every boot, it makes sense to have these instructions stored permanently on the system itself, which is why the BIOS is stored on read only memory (ROM). ROM provides permanent storage, often called nonvolatile memory because it retains settings even when the computer is off. Older ROM could only be written to once and that was it. Today, systems use something called electrically erasable programmable read-only memory (EEPROM), which allows the instructions on the BIOS to be overwritten.

exam
ⓦatch

Every now and then, the BIOS may need to be upgraded for new features or to accommodate new hardware. BIOS is upgraded in a process called flashing, but before you ever flash a BIOS, make absolutely sure it is necessary and that you follow the manufacturer's documentation. Improperly flashing a BIOS can cause irreparable damage.

BIOS Boot Process

Once the CPU finds the initial set of instructions on the BIOS, the system boot process begins. Part of this boot process is the Power On Self Test (POST). The POST routine is responsible for checking the status of components within the system. Any errors found during POST can be displayed on the screen or by a series of audible beeps, just letting you know something is amiss. Both the visual and audio error messages can vary from BIOS to BIOS, so it may be necessary to consult your system's documentation to find out exactly what the system is trying to tell you. Common visual error messages include the following:

- **Error 101**   System board interrupt failure
- **Error 201**   Memory test failure
- **Error 301**   Keyboard error
- **Error 501**   Color video test error

Beep error codes may be a little trickier to isolate. Table 3-1 shows the BIOS beep codes for the American Megatrends, Inc. (AMI) BIOS.

exam
ⓦatch

One very short beep usually indicates a successful POST process; anything else is undesirable.

After the BIOS has successfully completed the POST process, it does a quick system inventory, which brings us to the familiar memory test on the screen during startup. During this inventory procedure, the system will look for I/O devices, such

TABLE 3-1   AMI BIOS Beep Codes

Number of Beeps	Problem	Cause
1	Memory refresh errors	Incorrectly installed or bad RAM
2	Parity circuit error	Incompatible or faulty RAM
3	Base 64 memory failure	Possible faulty or poorly installed RAM
4	System timer failure	Likely main board failure
5	Processor failure	Faulty or poorly installed CPU
6	Keyboard controller error	Possible faulty keyboard controller
7	Virtual mode exception error	System board failure
8	Video card error	Incorrectly installed or faulty video card
9	ROM BIOS checksum error	Incorrect version of BIOS ROM
10	CMOS checksum error	Faulty system board
11	Cache memory error	Faulty or poorly inserted cache tips
1 long and 2 short	Video error	Poorly seated or bad video card

as keyboards and mice, and also will display onscreen messages of devices found, such as SCSI or IDE hard drives or tape devices. After the system has been inventoried, the BIOS looks for a bootable device and the master boot record. LILO, the Linux boot loader, is typically located in the MBR and so is loaded. The LILO is then responsible for loading the Linux kernel.

on the
Uob

When troubleshooting a system, it is a good idea to keep an eye on what is happening during the boot process. For instance, you may notice that not all of the memory is being counted during the memory count or that the system inventory does not include a hard drive.

CMOS

The complimentary metal-oxide semiconductor (CMOS) is closely associated with and often mistaken for the BIOS; however, they are very different. The CMOS provides the storage for the BIOS settings. The CMOS is volatile memory, meaning that when powered down, it will lose the BIOS settings. Having to reenter system configuration settings each time the system boots would be impractical, so instead, the CMOS retains these settings by having constant power supplied to it with the use of a battery that is on, or connected to, the system board.

The BIOS setup allows you to configure your system, but be warned that incorrect changes in the BIOS can have a negative effect on the system's performance. The settings that can be set in the BIOS include those for the disk drive, memory configuration, and floppy drives. These settings are then stored on the CMOS. To see what the settings are, the BIOS setup program must be accessed, which is normally done by pressing the DELETE or F1 key at the appropriate place in the startup process. The exact key combination will vary from manufacturer to manufacturer, so consult your documentation if you are unable to access your BIOS settings. Before experimenting too much with these settings, it would be a good idea to document the current ones.

on the
Uob

Like any other type of battery, the CMOS battery won't last forever. If you notice that hardware settings and the system clock information are not being saved, the battery likely is dead. In this case, you need to replace the battery or locate a really small set of booster cables!

SCENARIO & SOLUTION

Each time you boot your computer, you notice it does not retain your hard drive settings. What is wrong?	Most likely, your CMOS battery is dead or dying. Replacing the battery should fix the problem.
When you boot your system, you hear one short beep and the system continues to boot. What is the problem?	There isn't one. One short beep usually indicates everything has been checked and your system is ready to go
What is meant by nonvolatile memory?	Nonvolatile memory refers to ROM chips where the information is burned on the chip and stays there, even when the system is powered down. The system's BIOS is an example of nonvolatile memory.

Storage Devices

Continuing our discussion on hardware, we now turn our attention to arguably the most important set of components in any computer, the storage devices. Having your memory, system board, or network card fail is bad enough, but imagine losing the device that holds all of those spreadsheets, documents reports, and databases. The loss of this data can range from a mild inconvenience to a severe financial blow, crippling an entire business. With so much at stake, the management and maintenance of hard drives becomes a crucial consideration.

When it comes to working with storage devices, there are only two interfaces from which to choose, the Small Computer Systems Interface (SCSI) and the Advanced Technology Attachment (ATA) interface.

on the **job**

The type of interface used will affect the installation, maintenance, and recovery procedures, making it critical to know the differences and characteristics of each.

Identify Proper Procedures for Installing and Configuring ATA Devices

By far the most widely used hard drives today are the ATA standard disk drives. These ATA drives are most likely the ones you are using in your workstation, with SCSI being reserved primarily for servers and high-end workstations. The ATA interface is commonly referred to as IDE (short for Integrated Drive Electronics), and the terms are used interchangeably in this book.

In the early days of IDE hard disk development, there were no standards in place to regulate the advancement of the interface. As a result, there were numerous compatibility issues between different hard drive manufacturers. This is no longer the case, because several standards are in use to prevent these issues. The key ATA standards used today are the ATA-33, ATA-66, and the latest and greatest, ATA-100. Each of these introduced new features and speeds. ATA-33 was the first to use the ATAPI interface for IDE CD-ROMS. ATA-66 doubled the speed from 33MBps to 66MBps, and in doing so, required a new 80-conductor, 40-pin cable. Finally, ATA-100 brought us the fastest IDE transfer rates available at 100MBps. Before all of these were on the scene, there were the ATA-1 through ATA-3 standards, but they are no longer in use. A detailed knowledge of the ATA standards is not required for the Linux+ exam, but knowing that they exist is good to know.

exam
⚙atch
To view the IDE hard drives currently installed and a summary of their characteristics, type dmesg | grep hd *at the command prompt.*

IDE Identification Under Linux

Like SCSI hard disks, Linux references the devices as files, which are also kept in the /dev directory. IDE drives carry the *hd* designation for referencing. Table 3-2 shows the designation for IDE devices in Linux.

EXERCISE 3-2

Identifying IDE Hard Disks Under Linux

1. Boot the Linux computer and go to the command line or, alternatively, enter an X Window session and start a terminal session.

2. Type the following command: **dmesg I grep hd**.

3. The **dmesg** command will list all detected hardware, whereas the **grep** command filters through the list to take you directly to specific hd references.

4. Identify the IDE hard disks currently used in your system.

Master and Slave

The successful installation of an IDE device is usually a straightforward process offering only a fraction of the complexity found with SCSI installations. There are only a few considerations when installing IDE devices, making it far less intimidating than SCSI. Most system boards today have two IDE channels built onto them, with each channel capable of supporting up to two devices, allowing a total of four IDE devices within a standard system. This is considerably fewer than the SCSI interface, which is one of the reasons people opt for SCSI.

The onboard controllers are typically referred to as the primary controller and secondary controller. Unlike SCSI, which uses ID numbers to distinguish between devices on a bus, IDE devices are distinguished on the channel from each other by using a master/slave setting or, as discussed later, by the cable itself. If only a single drive is present, it must be connected to the primary controller. The primary controller

TABLE 3-2	IDE Device	Device Name
IDE Designations Under Linux	Primary master	/dev/hda
	Primary slave	/dev/hdb
	Secondary master	/dev/hdc
	Secondary slave	/dev/hdd

on the system board is often labeled Channel 0, with the secondary controller labeled Channel 1. Once a hard disk is connected to the primary channel as a master, additional hard disks can then be added as a slave on the primary channel or as a master or slave on the secondary channel. Figure 3-6 shows the IDE channels on a system board.

Devices are set to be a master or a slave by the use of jumpers, typically located on the back of the device. Setting the jumpers may be different between manufacturers, but they are all very similar. These jumpers have to be set correctly, or the devices may not be recognized by the system. If there are two masters or two slaves on an IDE bus, they will not work. Further, if a CD-ROM is set as master on the primary channel, the system will likely be unable to boot. To determine if IDE hard drives have the proper master and slave setting, check the system's BIOS settings to see if they are recognized; if they are present, you are ready to go. Figure 3-7 shows the master/slave selection jumpers on an IDE hard disk.

exam
ⓦatch

If a newly installed IDE device is not recognized by the system, the first thing to check is whether the jumpers have been set correctly.

FIGURE 3-6

IDE channels on
a system board

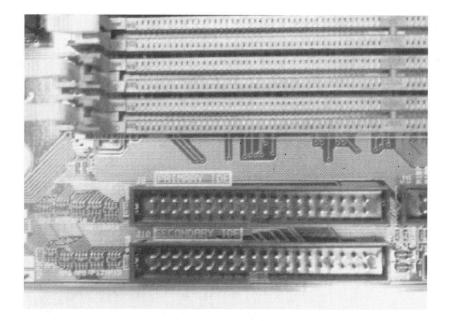

A standard IDE cable has three 40-pin connectors on a standard flat cable, and when connecting IDE devices in a jumper set master and slave configuration, it does not matter which cable connector is used to connect the devices, because the jumper settings determine the master or slave setting of the device. There is another option, however: the cable select jumper. By setting the jumpers on the hard drive to the cable select (CSEL) option, the location of the devices on the cable will determine which device is the master or slave. The cable select option makes things a little bit easier when installing devices, and changing devices between master or slave is as simple as changing the cable connectors between devices. Even so, configuring master/slave jumpering is not the most difficult task, so cable select has not really caught on.

on the
job

A common faux pas that can happen when installing IDE devices is to bend the pins when installing the device. Ensure that the cable and pins are correctly aligned before applying pressure.

FIGURE 3-7

Master/slave
selection
jumpers on an
IDE hard disk

CERTIFICATION OBJECTIVE 3.03

Identify Proper Procedures for Installing and Configuring SCSI Devices

Those who have worked with storage devices under another operating system are no doubt used to a letter-naming convention such as C, D, E, and so on. Linux does not use this type of convention to identify drives or partitions within the system. In the Linux naming convention, and UNIX for that matter, all peripherals and devices are referred to as files, and all devices are kept in the /dev directory. SCSI hard drives are referenced as *sd* devices and lettered in order of their place on the SCSI chain. Table 3-3 shows the SCSI drive device names.

SCSI

When it comes to hard drive performance and reliability, your choice will almost always be SCSI. SCSI has been around the computer industry for some time and has continued to evolve, providing a solid solution for today's most demanding computer systems. In terms of performance, SCSI has no equal but unfortunately when it comes to implementation difficulty, it again stands alone.

Part of the SCSI evolution has been the development of a number of different SCSI standards or implementations, each offering its own speeds, cabling, and compatibility issues. When working with SCSI, it will be necessary to understand the characteristics of each of these standards.

TABLE 3-3	SCSI Device	Device Name
SCSI Device Naming Convention	First SCSI hard disk	/dev/sda
	Second SCSI hard disk	/dev/sdb
	Third SCSI hard disk	/dev/sdc
	Eighth SCSI hard disk	/dev/sdh

e x a m
ⓦ a t c h

To view the SCSI hard drives currently installed and a summary of their characteristics, type dmesg | grep sd *at the shell prompt.*

SCSI Standards

Discussion of the various SCSI standards can become confusing very quickly, leading some to rename Small Computer Systems Interface to Simply Confusing Systems Interface. When working with Linux systems using the SCSI interface, it is important to understand the different standards and how they function in order to configure and maintain the systems correctly. Considering that Linux has had huge success on server systems and the SCSI interface is dominant in the server environment, it stands to reason that the paths of Linux and SCSI are linked.

The first SCSI standard introduced was the appropriately named SCSI-1 standard, also known as narrow SCSI. SCSI-1 introduced data transfer speeds of 5MBps and an 8-bit bus, and allowed up to eight devices attached to a single cable. SCSI-1 did not receive industry-wide support, but the obvious advantages of the system, especially the benefits of connecting numerous devices on a single bus, caught the imagination of many. SCSI-1 is not used today and is unlikely to be seen in a real work environment.

The SCSI-2 standard was introduced soon after SCSI-1 and was far more successful than its predecessor. Under the SCSI-2 standard, two separate implementations were defined: Fast SCSI and Fast Wide SCSI. Fast SCSI increased the clock speed and transfer rates from 5MBps to 10MBps, and Fast Wide SCSI doubled the transfer rate again to 20MBps. Another difference between these two standards lies in the number of devices they can support. By using a wide cable and a 16-bit bus, Fast Wide SCSI was able to support 16 devices on the bus, while narrow SCSI implementations support only 8 devices.

o n t h e
ⓙ o b

One device on both a narrow SCSI bus and a wide SCSI bus is reserved for the SCSI host adapter card, leaving only a total of 7 devices on a narrow bus and 15 devices available for a wide SCSI bus.

Things really started to get cooking with the introduction of the SCSI-3 standard. Numerous implementations fall under the SCSI-3 banner, and keeping them straight is certainly not an easy task, made more confusing with the often conflicting naming scheme found in many books and Web sites.

Ultra SCSI, also known as Fast-20, was the first of the new SCSI-3 standards offering a data transfer rate of 20MBps and support for up to eight devices. Next up was Wide Ultra SCSI, which as a wide implementation increased the data transfer rate to 40MBps and supported up to 16 devices. Along comes Ultra2 SCSI, supporting eight devices and a maximum transfer rate of 40MBps. As you might expect, a wide version followed. Wide Ultra2 SCSI provides support for 16 devices and an 80MBps transfer rate. Got all of that?

All of this brings us to where we are today, the Ultra 160 or Ultra3 SCSI, and the more recent Ultra 320 SCSI. Both Ultra160 and Ultra320 are only available in the wide bus. As their names suggest, Ultra 160 has a maximum transfer rate of 160MBps, and Ultra320 has a maximum transfer rate of 320MBps. Table 3-4 displays the SCSI standards and their respective characteristics.

SCSI Signaling

Now that you have a grasp of the SCSI standards that are used, you are ready to move on to the specific SCSI signaling methods used. Signaling methods are the means by which signals are electrically driven on the bus. There are three different methods that can be used on a SCSI bus: single-ended (SE), high-voltage differential (HVD), and low-voltage differential (LVD).

SE signaling is the most cost effective of the methods, and therefore is quite commonplace. Single-ended SCSI is highly susceptible to cable interference, so devices attached cannot exceed a total bus length of 6 meters, and sometimes less depending

TABLE 3-4   SCSI Standards

SCSI Standard	Bus Width	Devices Supported	Bus Speed (MBps)
SCSI-1	8	8	5
Fast SCSI	8	8	10
Fast Wide SCSI	16	16	20
Ultra SCSI	8	8	20
Wide Ultra SCSI	16	16	40
Ultra2 SCSI	8	8	40
Wide Ultra2 SCSI	16	16	80
Ultra3 SCSI (Ultra160)	16	16	160
Ultra320 SCSI	16	16	320

on the SCSI standard being used. SE SCSI is often associated with the older SCSI standards and is not defined for the newest SCSI standards, Ultra2 SCSI and higher. However, SE SCSI was widely implemented, so it is likely that more than a few of the Linux systems you manage will have SE SCSI devices in use.

HVD SCSI is far less susceptible to interference and has a bus length of up to 25 meters, making it ideal for connecting SCSI devices that are far away from each other. HVD devices cost more than SE ones, and HVD and SE are incompatible on the same bus. In today's SCSI environments, HVD is not that popular, having given way to LVD signaling.

If while working with SCSI you see the terms "multimode LVD" and "LVD/MSE (multimode single-ended)," understand that they are one in the same. The terms refer to an implementation of SCSI that has the ability to switch between the LVD and the SE mode. Remember when working with LVD and SE that if a SE device is connected to a multimode LVD/MSE bus, the entire bus switches to the SE mode. Otherwise LVD/MSE devices operate in the LVD mode.

| TABLE 3-5 | Cable SCSI Standards and Corresponding Bus Lengths |

SCSI Standard	SE (Meters)	HVD (Meters)	LVD (Meters)
SCSI-1	6	25	*
Fast SCSI	3	25	*
Fast Wide SCSI	3	25	*
Ultra SCSI	1.5	25	*
Wide Ultra SCSI	1.5	25	*
Ultra2 SCSI	**	25	12
Wide Ultra2 SCSI	**	25	12
Ultra3 SCSI	**	***	12
Ultra320 SCSI	**	***	12

*LVD was not defined for original SCSI standards.
** SE was not defined for speeds beyond Ultra SCSI.
*** HVD was not defined for speeds beyond Ultra2 SCSI.

LVD is the first choice for most SCSI implementations today because it offers a maximum bus length of 12 meters and backward compatibility with older SE devices. This compatibility, however, comes at a cost; when LVD and SE devices are used on the same bus, the bus is restricted to SE speeds and SE cable lengths. Table 3-5 shows the SCSI standards and the signaling characteristics of each.

SCSI Host Adapters

At the heart of the SCSI magic is a SCSI host adapter. The SCSI adapter may be a separate expansion card or it may be integrated into the system board. These SCSI host adapter cards are available for a variety of functions and speeds, with the more complex adapters housing their own processors and memory on board.

The SCSI host adapter requires an IRQ and I/O address similar to other expansion cards, but the devices attached to it do not. From the adapter, devices are connected to the SCSI bus in a chain configuration. Internal devices are connected to the cable using a single connector, whereas each external SCSI device on the chain requires two ports—one to receive the signal and the other to send the signal out. Once the chain is configured, all communication between the SCSI devices and the computer passes through the SCSI controller.

on the job *Because SCSI devices are connected with a cable in and a cable out, they are often referred to as being daisy-chained.*

The Linux kernel supports a large number of SCSI host adapters, although a trip to the distribution's Web site to confirm compatibility is always a good idea. Figure 3-8 shows a SCSI host adapter.

SCSI Termination

There are several rules that those working with SCSI must adhere to. One of the more crucial of these is to ensure that the SCSI bus has adequate termination. When a signal reaches the end of the bus, it can reflect back if it isn't stopped or terminated. If it is not stopped or terminated, the old signal mixes with the new and may corrupt the newly sent signal. Therefore, both ends of a SCSI bus must be terminated to prevent this signal reflection. Figure 3-9 shows an external LVD/SE terminator.

Two main types of termination strategies are used to prevent signal reflection on the SCSI bus: active and passive termination. Passive termination is the oldest form

A SCSI host
adapter
(Copyright
© 2001, Intel
Corporation)

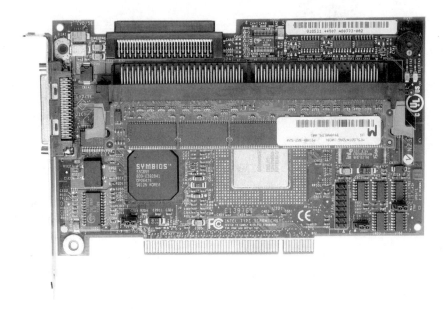

of termination and is associated with the earlier SCSI standards. Passive termination uses a series of resistors to absorb the signal as it reaches the end of the bus. Active termination is a more advanced form of termination and is used with the faster SCSI standards; in fact, some of the faster SCSI standards require active termination to work effectively. Unlike passive terminators, which use a collection of resistors to absorb the signal, active terminators use voltage regulators. Unless termination for SE SCSI is required, active termination is the preferred method. Figure 3-10 shows the proper termination for a SCSI bus.

on the **job**

When troubleshooting a SCSI bus, confirming proper termination is often the first step in the troubleshooting process. The first and last devices on the SCSI bus must have terminating resistors installed, and any devices in the middle of the bus must have termination disabled.

SCSI Cabling and Connectors

With so many different SCSI implementations, it stands to reason that there are numerous SCSI cables and connectors designed to support them. It is certainly not easy to keep track of all the different cables and which cable goes with which device, but it is necessary to know the differences when working with SCSI devices.

FIGURE 3-9

An external
LVD/SE
terminator
(Copyright
© 2001, Intel
Corporation)

FIGURE 3-10

An example of
SCSI bus
termination

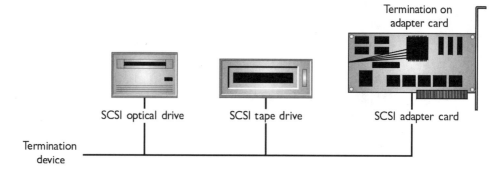

Termination on
adapter card

SCSI optical drive   SCSI tape drive   SCSI adapter card

Termination
device

Don't be surprised on the Linux+ exam if you are required to identify the various cables and connectors because it is an important part of implementing the SCSI interface.

Internal SCSI Cabling

Unlike the more familiar IDE interface, SCSI can have both internal and external devices connected to the bus, and therefore both internal and external cables. The construction of these cables is very different, as are their cable connector types. There are a few things to keep in mind when maintaining or troubleshooting internal cables on a SCSI system. If you are connecting an 8-bit, or narrow, internal SCSI device, you will likely need a 50-pin cable, referred to as an A-cable. A-cables resemble the internal cables used for IDE, but instead of 40 pins, the A-cables use 50. The 50-pin design is often associated today with legacy SCSI devices, but you can expect to see them in your travels, especially for connecting tape and CD-ROM devices. For internal wide SCSI devices, 16-bit implementations, a 68-pin cable also known as a P-cable is used. Figure 3-11 shows the 50- and 68-pin internal SCSI connectors.

In addition to the types of internal SCSI cable connectors used, there are also variations in the types of internal cabling used. Older and slower SCSI standards used a standard unshielded flat cable, similar to that of an IDE cable. Today, these

---

FIGURE 3-11

50- and 68-pin internal SCSI connectors

Standard 50-pin female

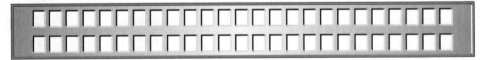

High-density 68-pin male

flat cables are most likely seen on SE SCSI, whose speeds do not exceed Ultra SCSI. Beyond this, a new cable is needed.

As SCSI reached the speeds of Ultra2, the standard flat cables became inadequate and increasingly susceptible to interference and potential data corruption. To manage the new SCSI speeds, a new cable was introduced, a twist-and-flat cable. As the name suggests, the cable actually twists between the connectors on the cable, which gives it greater resistance to interference. Figure 3-12 shows a standard and twist-and-flat internal SCSI cable.

The characteristics of internal SCSI cabling are outlined in Table 3-6.

on the
ⓙ o b *SCSI cables inside a system can get a little confusing, so take the time during the installation to label all cables and secure them inside the case in an orderly manner. This will certainly make your job easier when troubleshooting or adding new devices.*

External SCSI Cabling

External SCSI cabling started off with a 50-pin D-shell connector for the early SCSI-1 implementations. However, it was not widely used and rarely is used with SCSI today. The original D-shell connectors gave way to something called *Centronics* connectors, which are not unlike the parallel cables used with today's printers. Unlike

FIGURE 3-12

A standard and
twist-and-flat
SCSI cable

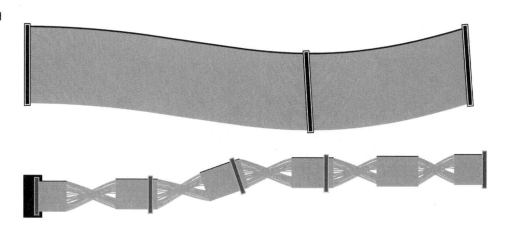

TABLE 3-6

Summary of
Internal SCSI
Cabling

Cable Type	Pinouts	Connector Type
Internal high-density A cable	50	High-density
Regular-density A cable	50	Regular-density
High-density P cable	68	High-density

the D-shell connectors, Centronics connectors do not use pins for contact; rather, they use two rows of flat contacts, and the cable is locked into place with the use of clamps on either side of the cable.

With the introduction of SCSI-2, D-shell connectors were once again used, but this time they were improved by reducing the number of pins. These high-density D-shell cables, known as P-cables, are in common use today and are available in a narrow, 8-bit, 50-pin version and a wide, 68-pin version. The newest external cable to be introduced after the high-density D-shell connector is the creatively named very high-density cable interconnect (VHDCI) connectors. VHDCI connectors are available in a 68-pin version and are often referred to as micro-Centronics connectors. Figure 3-13 displays the various external SCSI connectors. Table 3-7 outlines the characteristics of external SCSI cabling.

FIGURE 3-13

External SCSI
connectors

High-density 50-pin male

Very high-density Centronics 68-pin male

Centronics 50-pin male

TABLE 3-7	Cable Type	Pinouts	Connector Type
	High-density A cable	50	High-density D-shell
Summary of External SCSI Cabling	Centronics external A cable	50	External Centronics
	High-density P cable	68	High-density D-shell
	VHDCI P cable	68	VHDCI D-shell

SCSI IDs

A typical SCSI system consists of multiple devices on a single bus, where each of the devices needs some method of distinguishing itself from the others. This is done with the use of SCSI IDs. On any narrow, 8-bit SCSI implementations, SCSI IDs can range from 0 to 7, allowing it to support up to eight devices on a bus. One ID number, however, has to be reserved for the system's SCSI host adapter. On any wide SCSI bus, there can be a total of 16 devices, whose numbers can range from 0 to 15. SCSI IDs are typically set using a jumper, thumbwheel, or DIP switch; however, some of the newer devices use SCSI Configuration Automatically (SCAM), a utility that allows SCSI IDs to be automatically assigned (imagine that!). SCAM requires that the operating system, SCSI host adapter, and SCSI device support the feature.

When manually assigning SCSI IDs, it is important to remember that the lower SCSI IDs have the higher priority. For example, if two SCSI devices want access to the bus at the same time, the one with the lower ID will win. With this consideration, hard drives are typically given the lowest SCSI ID numbers, 0 or 1, and the highest ID number typically goes to the SCSI host adapter, which will be 7 for 8-bit SCSI and 15 for 16-bit SCSI.

on the
job

To muddy the ID waters a bit more, once a SCSI device has a unique ID, it can be divided into eight logical unit numbers (LUNs), allowing more than one physical device to be connected on each SCSI ID. LUN numbering ranges from 0 to 7. As if that were not enough, each LUN can have subdevices under them as well. Each LUN can have a sub logical-unit number (SLUN), allowing for yet more devices. But now we are getting into the ridiculous....

SCSI Installation Procedures

After reading all the various SCSI standards and related information, you may be wondering just how difficult a SCSI installation is. It is certainly not as easy as IDE devices, but with an understanding of SCSI standards, cable length, and device compatibility, you are halfway there. The following is a list of general SCSI installation procedures. These practices vary depending on whether you are installing a new SCSI bus or adding devices to an existing bus, but the general guidelines are the same.

- **Connect SCSI devices to the SCSI bus** Connecting devices to an existing SCSI chain is generally a fairly straightforward process if a few things are kept in mind. Be aware of the total number of devices the bus can support, recommended cable lengths, and the signaling method used. If all of these are matched, there should be little difficulty in adding devices.

- **Set the SCSI IDs** As previously mentioned, each device on the SCSI bus must have a unique ID. If problems arise after an installation, ensure that a duplicate ID isn't used on the bus.

- **Set the SCSI termination** Termination is one of the hotspots for SCSI troubleshooters. Two, and only two, terminators should be present on the bus. The terminators must be located at the physical ends of the bus, and if you're using one of the faster SCSI standards, ensure that active termination is used.

The previous section on SCSI was full of interesting and not so interesting facts; it would be a good idea to see how much stuck by considering the following scenarios.

SCENARIO & SOLUTION

After installing a new SCSI hard disk, other devices on the bus fail.	Improper termination or nonunique SCSI IDs are the first places to look for trouble after installing a new SCSI device.
Your SCSI bus has three hard disks and a SCSI controller. Where should termination be?	Regardless of the devices used, termination should be set at devices on both of the physical ends of the cable.
You need to install 12 SCSI devices on a single bus. Which SCSI standards could you use?	16-bit SCSI, or wide SCSI standards allow 16 devices attached to a bus, including Fast Wide SCSI, Wide Ultra SCSI, Wide Ultra2 SCSI, Ultra3, and Ultra320.

SCSI or IDE

Now that you have some understanding of the two interfaces, it's time to determine which one is better. A direct comparison between IDE and SCSI isn't necessarily easy, because they simply have different needs. When it comes to servers, SCSI is the name of the game. Performance and reliability are primary considerations for server machines, so IDE devices should only be used in a support role to SCSI. Desktop systems are another story. Single-device environments, like most desktops PCs, are well suited for IDE devices.

The following is an overview of how IDE and SCSI stack up against each other:

■ **Speed**   One of the most important of all hard drive characteristics is the speed at which the hard drive can transmit data. The fastest SCSI hard disk is far and away faster than the fastest IDE disk; however, many home and small business users simply do not need the high-end SCSI speeds. With that in mind, the newer ATA-100 drives are as fast as Ultra2 SCSI, making IDE hard disks sufficient for most nonserver computer systems.

■ **Number of connected devices**   SCSI is far superior with regard to the total number of supported devices on a single bus. IDE can only support a total of 4 devices, whereas a SCSI bus can support 8 to 16 devices, and many more by using LUNs. In environments where numerous devices or peripherals are required, SCSI is the choice.

■ **Implementation**   If you are looking for an easy installation, choose an IDE device. The various SCSI standards and related cabling offer a sea of confusion for those unfamiliar with the interface. Additionally, maintaining and troubleshooting a SCSI bus is far more difficult.

■ **Cost**   IDE is considerably less expensive, but SCSI supporters combat this claim by suggesting that SCSI devices typically last twice as long and, therefore, in the end are actually cheaper than IDE devices. However, by the time IDE devices are wearing out, they are usually out of date anyway. You can be the judge of this debate.

In the final analysis, SCSI is far and away the choice when performance and reliability are the primary considerations, making it well suited for high-end workstations and servers. Of course, everyone would like high performance and reliability, but despite SCSI's performance superiority, it is expensive and often difficult to implement, which all but excludes it from the cost-driven desktop market. Therein lies the distinction between the two interfaces: You are unlikely to see SCSI devices and hard disks on the average desktop system, and are equally unlikely to see ATA hard drives holding a server's critical data.

IEEE 1394

Perhaps one of the more poorly named of all interfaces is the IEEE 1394 interface, although to many, the interface is referred to as FireWire. FireWire, however, is a registered trademark of Apple Computer Corp., so for now at least, we are stuck with IEEE 1394. IEEE 1394 supports Plug and Play and, like USB, has the ability to hot-swap devices. IEEE 1394 can transmit data at 400MBps and supports 63 devices from a single port. IEEE 1394 requires a separate controller card that can be installed like any other expansion card, these cards support Plug and Play, making their installation that much easier. IEEE 1394 is widely used for high-speed devices such as digital video cameras. As far as Linux is concerned, great strides are being made, and the support for IEEE 1394 gets more and more solid with each kernel release.

on the **Ⓙob** *IEEE stands for Institute of Electrical and Electronics Engineers (www.ieee.org), an organization that sets standards for computers and communications.*

Universal Serial Bus

The universal serial bus (USB) has become very popular over the last few years. It is a physical port included on the back of all new computer systems that allows up to 127 devices to be attached to a single computer. USB currently supports speeds of up to 12MBps; however, a new version of USB soon will be introduced that offers speeds up to 480MBps. USB supports Plug and Play, making it easy to attach, and the system can allocate system resources such as IRQs and I/O addresses. The USB port will typically use IRQ 9 or 11. As of Kernel 2.4, there is large support for a wide variety of USB devices, such as scanners, modems, cameras, keyboards, mice, hard drives, and CD-ROMS, although with some of these devices, the performance may leave something to be desired. Figure 3-14 shows a picture of a USB cable.

Before purchasing a USB device, ensure that Linux supports the device.

One of the best features of USB is hot-swap technology. Any device attached to a USB connector can be plugged in or out while the system is up and running.

FIGURE 3-14

A USB cable

CERTIFICATION OBJECTIVE 3.04

Identify Proper Procedures for Installing and Configuring Peripheral Devices

Peripherals devices are typically those that are attached to the computer as an input or output device, the noncritical add-on components. Included in this category are such devices as printers, scanners, mice, joysticks, modems, digital cameras, and microphones. The following section will review some of the more common peripheral devices and how they are installed on computer systems.

Modems

Like other peripheral devices, modems require an IRQ and I/O address in order to function, and in the days before Plug and Play, the configuration of modems was often a bit of a nightmare. External modems can be connected to one of the computer's serial ports, typically COM2. The modem will then use COM2 resources, I/O 2F8–2FF, and IRQ 3. Alternatively, an external USB modem can also use the external USB port and its associated resources.

If the modem is connected internally, it will still require one of the computer's serial ports, even though it is not physically connected to the port. Modems can be set as to which COM port to take, but when this is configured, it is important that two devices are not competing for the same COM port and the same resources. Legacy modems were all designed for ISA slots, but new modems are designed to fit with the PCI slots. In either case, they are installed like a regular expansion card.

Testing the Modem

Modems can be a bit tricky to get working and can sometimes cause conflicts within the system. After installing a modem in Linux, it is a good idea to give it a test to make sure everything is running as it should. Testing modem operation is quite easy in Linux, because most Linux distributions include a utility called minicom or xminicom. Running the minicom program will provide a method to establish your modem's communication parameters. Table 3-8 shows a list of commands you can use from within the minicom utility to test your modem.

TABLE 3-8	Common Modem Commands	Description
Modem Commands	AT	Tests whether your modem is working with Linux.
	ATA	ATA answers an incoming call.
	ATD	Once all is confirmed you are now ready to dial to an outside number. ATDT is followed by the number you wish to dial, ATDT 555-4444.
	ATZ	Resets the modem.
	ATH	Hangs up the modem.
	ATI3	Displays the name of the modem.

TABLE 3-9	Standard Printer Port	Linux Printer Port
Parallel Port Naming Under Linux	LPT1	/dev/lp0
	LPT2	/dev/lp1
	LPT3	/dev/lp2

exam

ⓦatch   *Incorrectly installed modems will often conflict with a serial mouse.*

Parallel Printers

Parallel ports are used to connect a variety of devices to the computer, including external hard drives, scanners, and printers. A computer can support up to three parallel devices—LPT1, LPT2, and LPT3—although it is rare to see more than LPT1 used on the system. Printers connected to a parallel port typically use IRQ 7 and I/O address 378h. As with the serial ports, the parallel ports also have a unique naming convention under Linux. Table 3-9 shows the equivalent names within Linux.

Parallel ports used to be unidirectional, meaning that communication between the port and the system itself only occurred in one way; this is no longer the case. The parallel ports we have come to know and love offer bidirectional communication, improving the capabilities of the port. Choosing whether a parallel port is to provide unidirectional or bidirectional data transfer is done in the BIOS setup screen. When configuring the parallel port in the BIOS, you have three choices: use the unidirectional mode, use an enhanced parallel port (EPP) mode, or use an enhanced capability port (ECP) mode. EPP ports allow for bidirectional data transfer. ECP ports are also bidirectional but use a DMA channel, making them significantly faster than EPP. Figure 3-15 shows the various connectors available on a standard computer system.

exam
ⓦatch

Be prepared to know what the available options are for parallel ports and where they are set.

Connecting USB Peripherals

Numerous peripherals are available that are designed to work with the USB ports. These peripherals range from Web cams, scanners, and digital cameras to external hard drives and printers, to name a few. The devices designed to work with the USB port all take advantage of the hot-swap capability of USB, meaning that the devices can be plugged into the system while it is running and be automatically recognized and configured—a very neat feature indeed. USB has the ability to provide the power to most devices, so extra power cables are not needed. USB supports 127 devices on the chain, with the maximum cable length between devices being 5 meters.

Cabling, Connectors, and Peripheral Ports

All of those devices that sit outside of the computer case have to have a way to connect to the system. The mouse, printer, scanner, and removable hard drive need a physical

FIGURE 3-15

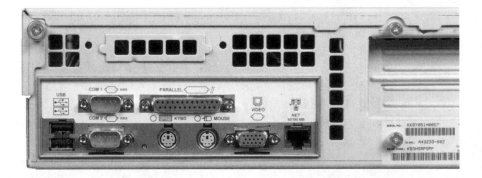

port so that they can transfer their data to the computer. Some of the more common ports include the parallel port, USB, IEEE 1394, and the standard serial port. The following section looks at the connectors and cables used with various ports and introduces the communication method used by each.

Parallel and Serial Communication

Parallel and serial are often associated with the actual port, but they also describe the method of communication used by the port. Serial devices transmit data one bit at a time in series, and the transfer can either be *synchronous,* a steady stream of data, or *asynchronous,* data sent in intermittent bursts. Synchronous serial communications require data to be continually sent, even when no data needs or is ready to be sent. Devices that do not need this steady stream and only send data intermittently, such as a serial mouse or modems, use asynchronous serial communication. The Recommended Standard-232 (RS-232) defines serial communications, which is why serial ports are sometimes referred to as RS-232 ports.

Parallel communication can transmit data more than one bit at a time, meaning larger packets of data can be transmitted, and faster. Many external devices, including printers, scanners, and external hard drives, use parallel communication that allows them to send large amounts of data simultaneously.

DB Connectors

There are several DB connectors that are used on computer system to connect external device DB connectors come in a 9-, 15-, 25-, 37-, and 50-pin variety. Each of these connectors has a different function, with some using parallel communication and some using serial. Of these, the most commonly used are DB-9, typically used with COM1 and connected to a serial mouse, DB-25, often used with printers, and DB-15, which is commonly used with the VGA port on the back of the computer. Figure 3-16 shows the various DB connectors and their uses.

PS/2 and Mini-DIN

A DIN is a port used to connect mice, keyboards, and other devices to the system. On modern systems, a 6-pin DIN is used, whereas older systems used a larger, 5-pin DIN connector. IBM was first to use the 6-pin DIN on its PS/2 computers, but

FIGURE 3-16

DB connectors and their associated usage (Reproduced with permission from *Computer Desktop Encyclopedia* © 1981–2001 The Computer Language Co. Inc., [www.computerlanguage.com])

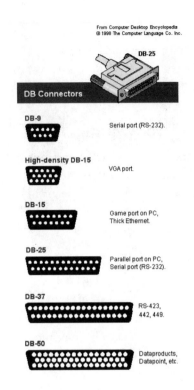

since then, it has been adopted to be used in most modern systems. The 6-pin DIN is often simply referred to as a PS/2 port now.

CERTIFICATION OBJECTIVE 3.05

Identify Available IRQs, DMAs, I/O Addresses, and Procedures for Device Installation

Physically installing hardware is just the first step in getting hardware working in a computer system; it also has to be allocated system resources to make it work. These resources include input/output (I/O) addresses and interrupt request lines (IRQs).

The management and allocation of these devices in today's systems is often managed through Plug and Play, but not always, and even when it is, it doesn't always work successfully. Each kernel release brings Linux closer to true Plug and Play compatibility, but even some of the more seasoned Linux administrators prefer to disable Plug and Play rather than tangle with it. Chapter 4 has more information on Linux and Plug and Play.

When working with a Linux system, at some point it will be necessary to view the resource allocation within your system. The utilities and methods to view system resources are covered in Chapter 4.

exam
ⓦatch

Be prepared to answer questions regarding the allocation of system resources and which hardware devices are associated with specific resources.

IRQs

In the early days of computer development, PCs were restricted to eight IRQs, but as more devices were developed for computers, each of which devices requires a unique IRQ, eight IRQs simply couldn't cut it. To accommodate new devices, the original number of 8 IRQs was doubled to 16, ranging from 0 to 15.

Before the days of Plug and Play, fighting with IRQs was a daily occurrence for computer support technicians, a battle not easily won. Many IRQs are reserved for use with specific devices. Table 3-10 shows the standard IRQ assignments.

exam
ⓦatch

The exam will require an understanding of the various IRQs and their corresponding devices.

EXERCISE 3-3

Identifying IRQ Ports in Linux

1. Boot the Linux computer and go to the command line or, alternatively, enter X Window and start a terminal session.

2. Type the following command: **cat /proc/interrupts**.

3. Identify the IRQs being used in your system.

TABLE 3-10	IRQ	Device
Standard IRQ Assignments	0	System timer
	1	Keyboard
	2	Redirect to IRQ 9
	3	Serial ports, COM2, and COM4
	4	Serial ports, COM1, and COM3
	5	Parallel port(LPT2)
	6	Floppy drive controller
	7	Parallel port (LPT1)
	8	Real-time clock
	9	Redirected from IRQ 2 (often used by USB)
	10	Available
	11	Available
	12	PS/2 mouse
	13	Math coprocessor
	14	Hard disk controller
	15	Secondary hard disk controller

I/O Addresses

I/O addresses provide a mechanism for the operating system and the devices to communicate. Like IRQs, all I/O devices within the computer must have a unique I/O address. The devices may use assigned I/O addresses or may be dynamically assigned. Table 3-11 shows the standard assignment of I/O addresses.

As a point of clarification, ports are still referred to as COM1 though COM4, but within Linux, they have an alternative naming convention. Table 3-12 shows the naming convention for serial ports in Linux.

DMA

Those who have hooked up an older ISA sound card will no doubt remember Direct Memory Access (DMA), because those sound cards often required the use of a DMA channel to work, although very few people new why or what it did. DMA is used exclusively with older ISA devices and refers to the ability of peripherals to talk

TABLE 3-11	I/O Device	I/O Address
Standard IRQ Address Assignments	COM1	3F8h
	COM2	2F8h
	COM3	3E8h
	COM4	2E8h
	LPT1	378h
	LPT2	278h

TABLE 3-12	Serial Communication Port	Serial Communication Port Under Linux
Naming Conventions for Serial Ports Under Linux	COM1	/dev/ttyS0
	COM2	/dev/ttyS1
	COM3	/dev/ttyS2
	COM4	/dev/ttyS3

directly to the system's memory without using CPU resources. Within Linux, DMA is managed by the kernel; however, any device that needs DMA needs to be set up properly. Modern Linux, through the use of loadable kernel modules (LKMs), can make most of this semiautomatic. To view any DMA usage on your system, type **cat /proc/dma** at the command line.

CERTIFICATION OBJECTIVE 3.06

Identify Basic Procedures for Adding and Removing Field-Replaceable Units

A field-replaceable unit (FRU) refers to any system component that can be replaced in the field rather than fixed. For example, if you were called to repair a faulty monitor, you are more likely to replace the monitor than to clear a space on the person's desk and start taking it apart. Two reasons for this are that, in general, monitors cannot be repaired without specialized tools and that the electrical charges contained in a monitor can be fatal.

Considering the hourly cost of a technician and the low cost of hardware components, most system components today are replaced instead of repaired. The replacement of components in the field is generally a straightforward process. However, there a few things to keep in mind during the process:

- **Replace the correct part** As obvious as it sounds, the correct component needs to be replaced. Some problems can be deceptive, like whether the video problem is a card, cable, or monitor issue. Part of the purpose of FRUs is to have everything up and running as soon as possible, and replacing wrong parts is at odds with this goal.

- **Use similar components** In the interests of compatibility, it is a good idea to replace the failed component with one of the same. This way, you know it is compatible with the system and that the correct drivers are already installed. Of course, this is not always possible or practical, but with components such as memory and expansion cards, it can be a huge time saver.

- **Test new configuration** New components do not always work, and sometimes they take extra configurations and settings to make them work. After replacing an FRU, take the time to ensure that the component is functioning within the system. Doing so can prevent being called back again for the same problem.

- **Return the system to its normal state** Often, when replacing parts, the case is taken off the computer and stuff on the desk is disrupted. As a courtesy, after replacing the system component, put everything back to normal.

CERTIFICATION OBJECTIVE 3.07

Identify and Maintain Mobile System Hardware

Dealing with portable systems—notebooks or laptops—presents its own unique challenges. With desktop computers, it is fairy easy to pop off the case and take a look inside. With such easy access, it is possible to swap components in and out to help troubleshoot the problem. You do not have this luxury with portable systems. Not only are the parts of a portable system difficult to access, but they are often integrated components and proprietary. If, for instance, a video card fails in a

FIGURE 3-17

A PCMCIA card

desktop, you can remove the card and replace it in a short time. This is simply not possible with a laptop system. Troubleshooting such components as memory, monitors, mice, and hard drives becomes very difficult. These integrated components can also create compatibility issues for Linux.

Not all components in portable systems are integrated. Some of the expansion cards will be PCMCIA cards, which are designed exclusively for use with portable systems. PCMCIA cards come in three types: Type I and Type II, which are 16-bit cards, and Type III, which are 32-bit cards. They are all the same form factor and can fit and work in any PCMCIA slot. Like any other expansion card, these sometimes fail, and when they do, they need to be replaced. Linux supports a wide range of these PCMCIA cards, but as always, check with the hardware compatibility list just to make sure your device is supported. Figure 3-17 shows a PCMCIA expansion card.

on the
Job
Keep an eye out for systems that use Winmodems. These modems are not supported by Linux and are most certainly going to cause you trouble.

Advanced Power Management

Advanced Power Management (APM) is an application programming interface (API) developed by Microsoft and Intel that enables power management for separate devices on a system. Through APM, devices such as hard disks and monitors can be configured to "power-save" after periods of inactivity. Although an increasing awareness has meant that almost all systems are now APM-enabled, it is most commonly associated with laptop and other mobile systems, where it serves to extend battery run times. On a Linux system, APM functionality is provided through the APM daemon.

CERTIFICATION SUMMARY

As with any operating system used, correctly functioning hardware is an important piece of the puzzle. This chapter focused on the details and characteristics of core system components, as well as peripheral devices and the resources they use. It provided a discussion on the relationship between the BIOS and the CMOS, identified memory packaging and the specific memory types, and examined the devices within the computer and the resources they need in order to function correctly.

A working knowledge of this material is needed when repairing or upgrading a computer system. Hardware knowledge and resource management will also prove invaluable when installing Linux on a system. Perhaps most importantly, in the short term at least, CompTIA has put a strong emphasis on hardware knowledge in the Linux+ exam, so passing the test without an understanding of the concepts provided in this chapter may be very difficult.

TWO-MINUTE DRILL

Here are some of the key points presented in this chapter.

Identify Concepts and Functions of Key System Components

❑ Storage devices are the most important components in a system, because they hold data. Above all else, data must be protected.

❑ Memory comes in many types and is typically packaged as a SIMM or a DIMM design, except for in portable systems, in which it is packaged as a SO-DIMM design.

❑ Common types of memory include EDO, DRAM, SDRAM, DDR-SDRAM, and RDRAM.

❑ ECC memory can detect and correct a memory error.

❑ Common system buses include ISA, PCI, PCI-X, and AGP.

❑ The BIOS is provided on a ROM chip and provides the instructions the computer needs when it first boots. BIOS settings are stored on the CMOS.

Identify Proper Procedures for Installing and Configuring SCSI and IEEE 1394 Devices

❑ Each SCSI device requires a unique SCSI ID number to distinguish it from other devices on the bus.

❑ A SCSI bus requires terminators at each end of the bus to absorb signals to prevent signal reflection.

❑ A SCSI bus uses one of three types of signaling: LVD, SE, or HVD. These signaling methods determine the length of the SCSI bus.

❑ A wide SCSI bus can support up to 16 devices, while a narrow SCSI bus can support 8 devices.

❑ Several SCSI standards have been developed, each offering its own unique characteristics.

❑ The SCSI host adapter requires an IRQ and I/O address, but the devices attached to it do not.

❑ IEEE 1394 supports Plug and Play and, like USB, has the ability to hot-swap devices.

❑ IEEE 1394 requires a separate controller card, which can be installed like any other expansion card.

Identify Proper Procedures for Installing and Configuring Peripheral Devices

❑ External peripherals are connected to the system using ports. Common ports are the DB connectors, USB, IEEE 1394, and SCSI external connectors.

❑ Peripheral devices must be assigned system resources to function.

❑ IEEE 1394 and USB support hot-swap technology and can be installed while the system is up and running.

❑ The Linux kernel continues to advance and provide increased support for both USB and IEEE 1394 devices.

Identify Available IRQs, DMAs, I/O Addresses, and Procedures for Device Installation and Configuration

❑ Devices attached to a computer require system resources to function. IRQ and I/O addresses must be unique to the device.

❑ Two devices sharing the same resources will not function and may cause the system to hang.

❑ To view used resources under Linux, use the *proc* file system.

Identify Basic Procedures for Adding and Removing Field-Replaceable Units

❑ Due to time and budget considerations, systems components are often replaced instead of repaired.

❑ FRUs are generally used to remove or add a component on site quickly.

❑ Monitors, keyboards, mice, and power supplies are examples of FRUs.

Identify and Maintain Mobile System Hardware

❏ Portable systems use integrated and proprietary components, which makes solving compatibility issues difficult.

❏ Access to the hardware is restrictive on portable systems and finding replacement parts often is hard.

❏ Portable systems use PCMCIA expansion cards and are available in 16-bit and 32-bit varieties.

SELF TEST

The following questions will help determine your level of understanding of the material presented in this chapter. Some of the questions may have more than one correct answer, so be sure to review all answers carefully before choosing all that apply.

Identify Concepts and Functions of Key System Components

1. Which port is associated with ttyS0?

    A. COM1

    B. COM2

    C. LPT1

    D. LPT2

2. What is the process of upgrading the BIOS referred to?

    A. Flooring

    B. Charging

    C. Flashing

    D. Toasting

3. Which of the following memory types uses 168-pin connectors?

    A. SIMMs

    B. SO-DIMMs

    C. DIMMs

    D. RIMMs

4. Which of the following best describes the CMOS?

    A. The CMOS is nonvolatile memory.

    B. The CMOS is volatile memory.

    C. The CMOS is upgraded using a process called flashing.

    D. "CMOS" and "BIOS" refer to the same thing.

5. Which of the following mechanisms do modern memory modules use to report or correct errors within memory?

    A. Parity

    B. EDO

    C. ECC

    D. ECP

Identify Proper Procedures for Installing and Configuring ATA Devices

6. Due to a shortage of disk space, James has added an additional IDE hard drive into his computer. After the drive is installed, neither drive is recognized in the BIOS. What is the likely cause of the problem?

    A. The new hard drive is damaged.

    B. The jumpers are set incorrectly.

    C. The drives are incorrectly terminated.

    D. The cable is damaged.

7. You have decided to upgrade your system to use a larger hard disk. You would like to use the new disk as the boot device but keep the old drive in the system to use to keep backup files. The system also has a single CD-ROM attached. What is the best configuration for this scenario?

    A. Set the new drive to master on the primary controller and the old drive to master on the secondary controller.

    B. Set the new drive to master on the secondary controller and the old drive to slave on the secondary controller.

    C. Set the new drive to slave on the primary controller and the old drive to master on the secondary controller.

    D. No jumper changes are required to accommodate this configuration.

Identify Proper Procedures for Installing and Configuring SCSI Devices

8. You are installing a non-Plug and Play SCSI host adapter card in your system. Which of the following best describes the steps you need to take?

    A. Install the card in the middle of the SCSI chain, terminate both ends of the new card, and assign the card an IRQ address and a unique SCSI ID.

    B. Install the host adapter card, terminate it only if it is at the end of the bus, and assign the card an IRQ address and a unique SCSI ID.

    C. Install the card in the middle of the SCSI chain, terminate both ends of the new card, and assign the card an IRQ address and a unique SCSI LUN.

    D. Install the host adapter card, terminate it only if it is at the end of the bus, and assign the card a unique SCSI ID.

9. Which termination method uses resistors to absorb signal reflection?

    A. Passive termination

    B. Active termination

    C. High-density termination

    D. Standard SCSI termination

10. Martin is using SE devices on his SCSI bus, he wants to add a new LVD device for the increased speeds. What is the result of this configuration?

    A. The LVD device will operate at SE speeds.

    B. LVD and SE are incompatible on the same bus.

    C. All devices will operate at LVD speeds.

    D. Only the new device will operate at LVD speeds.

11. Karen has ordered components to install a new SCSI system in her computer. When the order is delivered, she receives the following: Ultra2 SCSI controller, two SE SCSI hard disks, two active terminators, and a 40-pin internal cable. Which of these devices will have to be returned?

    A. SCSI controller

    B. SE SCSI hard disks

    C. Active terminators

    D. 40-pin internal cable

12. What is the maximum transfer rate of Ultra SCSI?

    A. 10MBps

    B. 20MBps

    C. 30MBps

    D. 40MBps

Identify Proper Procedures for Installing and Configuring Peripheral Devices

13. Which of the following ports is considered hot-pluggable?

    A. Serial ports

    B. COM ports

    C. USB ports

    D. PS/2 mouse port

14. Which of the following devices would likely use the DB-15 connector on the back of the computer system?

    A. Serial mouse

    B. Printer

    C. PS/2 mouse

    D. Monitor

15. Which of the following ports is associated with LPT2?

    A. /dev/lp1

    B. /dev/lp0

    C. /dev/sda

    D. /dev/sdb

Identify Available IRQs, DMAs, and I/O Addresses and Procedures for Device Installation

16. Which I/O port and IRQ are associated with the LPT1 port?

    A. I/O 378h and IRQ 7

    B. I/O 278h and IRQ 5

    C. I/O 3F8h and IRQ 4

    D. I/O 2F8h and IRQ 3

17. Which IRQ and I/O are typically used by an external modem?

    A. I/O 2F8–2FF and IRQ 3

    B. I/O 378h and IRQ 2

    C. I/O 2F8–2FF and IRQ 4

    D. I/O 278h and IRQ 2

18. Which of the following devices uses IRQ 6?

    A. Hard drive controller

    B. Parallel port

    C. Real-time clock

    D. Floppy disk controller

Identify Basic Procedures for Adding and Removing Field-Replaceable Units

19. Which of the following are advantages of using similar components when replacing FRUs?

    A. Compatibility

    B. Saves time

    C. Driver support

    D. Cost

Identify and Maintain Mobile System Hardware

20. You are installing a Linux on a laptop computer. You are attempting to configure the internal modem but are unable to get Linux to recognize it. Which of the following could explain your difficulties?

    A. Linux does not support modems on older laptop computers.

    B. The modem built into the portable computer is a Winmodem.

    C. Linux does not support integrated modems.

    D. The modem is not powered on.

LAB QUESTION

Complete the following table to test your knowledge of SCSI standards and characteristics.

SCSI Standard	Bus Width	Devices Supported	Bus Speed (MBps)

SELF TEST ANSWERS

Identify Basic Terms, Concepts, and Functions of System Components

1. ☑ **A.** Within Linux, the COM1 port is referenced by the system as ttyS0.
   ☒ **B.** COM2 is associated with ttyS1. **C.** LPT1 is associated with lp0. **D.** LPT2 is referenced as lp1.

2. ☑ **C.** Modern BIOS chips can be flashed, or upgraded, to accommodate new hardware that is introduced. For instance, if a new 80GB hard drive is installed, the BIOS may need to be upgraded to accommodate the drive's capacity. Flashing of the BIOS requires the download of a program from the manufacturer's Web site.
   ☒ **A, B, D.** These are fictitious terms with regard to the BIOS.

3. ☑ **C.** DIMM memory modules use 168-pin connectors. DIMM modules use notches on the bottom of the module to ensure that they are placed in the correct way and are secured in place using latches.
   ☒ **A.** SIMMs have been replaced with the newer DIMMs. SIMM memory was packaged in a 30-pin variety, and the more modern SIMMs used a 72-pin design. **B.** SO-DIMMs are typically a 72- or 144-pin design and are used with portable computer systems. **D.** A RIMM uses 184-pin connectors and was designed specifically for use with systems that use Rambus memory.

4. ☑ **B.** The CMOS stores the BIOS settings and is volatile memory, meaning that every time the system is shut down, the CMOS could lose its information. It does not lose its information, however, because it is powered by a battery located on the system board.
   ☒ **A.** The term "nonvolatile" refers to the chips like the BIOS, that does not lose its information when the system is shut down. Without the battery, CMOS would lose its data and is therefore not nonvolatile memory. **C.** CMOS is not upgraded; it simply stores the BIOS settings. The BIOS is upgraded using a process called flashing. **D.** "CMOS" and "BIOS," while often used interchangeably, are two different things. The BIOS is a set of instructions stored on a ROM chip, whereas the CMOS holds BIOS settings.

5. ☑ **C.** ECC RAM check the integrity of the information held in memory by using a mathematical calculation called a *checksum*. ECC RAM has the ability to correct the errors it finds, and if it can't, it reports them to the system.
   ☒ **A.** Parity was designed to detect errors in memory and report them to the system. Although parity was able to detect a memory error, it had no mechanism in place to correct it. **B.** EDO is

a specific type of memory developed in 1994 and is no longer used in modern systems. **D.** ECP, or enhanced capability port, is a bidirectional port that uses a DMA channel to enhance performance.

Identify Proper Procedures for Installing and Configuring ATA Devices

6. ☑ **B.** When installing new IDE devices, if the jumpers are not set correctly, the hard disks may not be recognized in the system's BIOS. Often this will be the case if two devices are set as master and they are competing with each other. The first place to look when troubleshooting IDE problems after an installation is the jumper settings.
☒ **A.** The question asks which is the most likely cause of the problem. Although it is possible to have a damaged hard disk that will cause problems, it is more likely that the problem is a result of an improper installation. **C.** IDE devices do not have to be terminated; termination is for SCSI devices. **D.** Although the cable could be damaged, it is more likely that the issue is a result of incorrect jumper settings.

7. ☑ **A.** During an upgrade of IDE hard disks, the old hard disk is often kept in the system to add hard disk space. To do this, you could set the new drive to master on the primary controller and the old drive to master on the secondary controller. It is also possible to set the new drive to master on the primary controller and the old drive to slave on the primary controller.
☒ **B.** You would need to set the new drive as master on the primary drive; setting it as a master on the secondary controller would not accomplish want you need to do. **C.** The new drive would have to be set as master and not as slave. **D.** Jumper settings are required to properly configure a IDE device.

Identify Proper Procedures for Installing and Configuring SCSI Devices

8. ☑ **B.** When installing a new device into an existing SCSI chain, the device is terminated only if it's the end of the bus; further, each device on the SCSI bus requires a unique ID and an assigned IRQ address.
☒ **A.** Additional devices can be either installed anywhere in an existing SCSI chain; however, only if they are on the ends of the bus do they require termination. SCSI host adapter cards have an additional consideration if they have termination built into them and it is often set as "on" by default. If a SCSI host adapter in not at the end of a SCSI bus, termination has to be turned off on the card. **C.** Both ends of the card should not be terminated. Further, SCSI devices do not require a unique LUN assigned to them. LUNs, or logical unit numbers, can be assigned to individual SCSI devices after they have been assigned a unique SCSI ID. **D.** A SCSI card requires an IRQ assigned to the device.

9. ☑ **A.** Termination is used to absorb the data signal as it reaches the end of the SCSI bus. If this is not done, the signal will reflect and cause data corruption and errors on the SCSI bus. Passive terminators are associated with older SCSI standards and SE signaling. Passive terminators use resistors to absorb signal reflection.

   ☒ **B.** Active termination uses voltage regulators to dampen signal reflection. Active termination is used for the faster SCSI standards and offers better performance than passive termination. **C, D.** No such termination methods exist.

10. ☑ **A.** The newer LVD SCSI signaling method is compatible with SE devices on the same bus but will be restricted to using the characteristics of SE, including bus speeds and cable length.

    ☒ **B.** LVD and SE are compatible on the same bus; it is HVD that is incompatible with SE on the same bus. **C.** If there is a single SE device on the bus, LVD will use SE characteristics. **D.** This is fictitious.

11. ☑ **D.** All the devices listed except for the 40-pin cable are required to set up a SCSI bus. Older internal SCSI devices are connected using a 50-pin cable, and newer SCSI devices will use a 68-pin connector; 40-pin connectors are used to connect internal IDE devices.

    ☒ **A.** Every SCSI bus requires a SCSI controller on the bus. The controller may be a separate expansion card or may be built into the system board. **B.** The SE hard drives can be used with the controller on the SCSI bus. **C.** A SCSI bus requires termination at both ends of the bus; the two active terminators would be needed to accomplish this.

12. ☑ **B.** Ultra SCSI has a maximum transfer rate of 20MBps.

    ☒ **A.** Fast SCSI has a transfer rate of 10MBps. **C.** No SCSI standards list a maximum transfer rate of 30MBps. **D.** Wide Ultra SCSI and Ultra2 SCSI have a maximum transfer rate of 40MBps.

Identify Proper Procedures for Installing and Configuring Peripheral Devices

13. ☑ **C.** One of the advantages of USB ports is that they allow devices to be attached to the system without powering down the computer. Once plugged in, the system will automatically recognize and configure the device.

    ☒ **A, B, D.** Each of these ports does not allow devices to be attached on the fly. The system will not automatically detect the presence of devices plugged into these ports while the computer is turned on.

14. ☑ **D.** The DB-15 connector on the back of a computer system is used to connect a monitor to the computer's video adapter. It is commonly known as the VGA port.

    ☒ **A.** The serial mouse uses a DB-9 connector, which is a serial port, often referred to as

RS-232. **B**. The printer typically uses the system's parallel port, which is a DB-25 connector. **C**. PS/2 devices, whether a keyboard or a mouse, use a 9-pin DIN connector.

15. ☑ **A**. Unlike other operating systems, Linux references devices as files, which may take you some time to get used to. The LPT2 port is referenced under Linux as /dev/lp1.
    ☒ **B**. /dev/lp0 is the Linux reference for LPT1. This Linux naming scheme has a pattern; /dev/lp2 is LPT3. **C**. The Linux reference /dev/sda refers to the first device on a SCSI bus. **D**. /dev/sdb refers to the second device on a SCSI bus, and /dev/sdc refers to the third. Easy, huh?

Identify Available IRQs, DMAs, I/O Addresses, and Procedures for Device Installation

16. ☑ **A**. I/O address 378h and IRQ 7 are most commonly associated with the LPT1 port, which is often used by printers.
    ☒ **B**. I/O 278h and IRQ 5 are associated with the LPT2 port. **C**. I/O 3F8h and IRQ 4 are used with COM 1 and 3. **D**. I/O 2F8h and IRQ 3 are used with COM 2 and 4.

17. ☑ **A**. When installing a modem, it will typically use COM2. COM2 resources are I/O 2F8–2FF and IRQ 3. If any other devices, including a serial mouse, are using these resources, there will be conflicts and the devices will not work as they should, possibly causing the system to hang.
    ☒ **B**. I/O address 378H and IRQ 7 are typically used with LPT1 for a parallel device such as a printer. **C**. I/O address 3F8H and IRQ 4 are usually associated with COM1. **D**. I/O address 278h and IRQ 5 are commonly used with a secondary parallel port, LPT2.

18. ☑ **D**. Devices used within a computer system have to be assigned unique IRQ addresses, and IRQ 6 is reserved for the floppy drive controller.
    ☒ **A**. The primary hard drive controller uses IRQ 14, while the secondary hard disk controller uses IRQ 15. **B**. The LPT1 parallel port is typically used with IRQ 7, and the LPT2 port usually uses a free IRQ such as 10 or 11. **C**. The real-time clock in the system uses IRQ 8.

Identify Basic Procedures for Adding and Removing Field-Replaceable Units

19. ☑ **A, B, C**. If you are replacing a failed component with a new one, using a component from the same manufacturer will ensure compatibility because it is already proven to work in the system. Using a similar component can also save time, because it is not necessary to install new drivers and many system settings will not need to be changed. Using the same type of component will also ensure that the drivers for the hardware function with the system.
    ☒ **C**. It is unlikely that using a similar component would affect the cost of replacement.

Identify and Maintain Mobile System Hardware

20. ☑ **B.** Winmodems are designed to be used with Windows operating systems and, as such, are a nightmare to try to configure under Linux. If you are installing Linux on a laptop and plan to use the modem, first check the documentation to see if the internal built-in modem is a Winmodem. If it is, then you'll likely have to find an alternative.

☒ **A.** Linux has support for many hardware devices, for new devices, as well as older components. Linux does have trouble with a few components, including using Winmodems. **C.** Linux has support for add-on modems, as well as integrated modems. To ensure compatibility, it is often better to choose your modem than have one built into the system board. **D.** Internal modems are powered by the system and so are not powered on separately.

LAB ANSWER

SCSI Standard	Bus Width	Devices Supported	Bus Speed MBps
SCSI-1	8	8	5
Fast SCSI	8	8	10
Fast Wide SCSI	16	16	20
Ultra SCSI	8	8	20
Wide Ultra SCSI	16	16	40
Ultra2 SCSI	8	8	40
Wide Ultra2 SCSI	16	16	80
Ultra3 SCSI (Ultra160)	16	16	160
Ultra320 SCSI	16	16	320

4

Hardware Troubleshooting

Despite our best efforts, computers simply do not always behave the way in which we would like. In the computer world, hardware troubleshooting is just part of life, and while monitoring and proactive maintenance can reduce the amount of troubleshooting needed, it can never eliminate it. This is not to suggest that you toss out your maintenance procedures; far from it, but the reality is that at some point, you will need to crack open the case and repair, replace, or upgrade components. This chapter deals with some of the general hardware troubleshooting procedures used in the repair of systems. As much as possible, it stays clear of specific software and operating system troubleshooting by introducing only some of the utilities used in Linux to identify correct installation of components. Software troubleshooting is covered in more detail in Chapter 12.

As with Chapter 3, some of the information provided in this chapter may be review, but as far as the test is concerned, you will be expected to identify troubleshooting strategies for both core system components and peripheral devices.

CERTIFICATION OBJECTIVE 4.01

Identifying, Troubleshooting, and Isolating Common System Problems

Before ripping apart a computer system and replacing components, it is a good idea to follow a few basic troubleshooting guidelines that can help to isolate the exact cause of the problem. The procedures used to help isolate a computer problem vary, depending on who you ask. However, there are a few common troubleshooting steps that will reduce the time it takes to track down a problem and ensure that it is fixed.

Troubleshooting your own computer is bad enough, but when it comes to troubleshooting systems you are unfamiliar with, it can be a bit more involved. In such a case, identifying the problem is the first step. To do this, you need to get information from two key sources: the person who uses the system, and the computer itself. Both of these sources can offer valuable information, and having information from only one source will most likely make the troubleshooting process more difficult than it needs to be. That said, in certain instances, getting information from users can often be tricky, especially if they do not have technical experience to convey the problem accurately. Regardless, they often hold the key to the problem, and a little active listening and reading between the lines can get you your answer. The rule of thumb here is to listen first before starting any troubleshooting.

If the problem is less serious and your system is still running, system logs provide a great source for information, though at times they can be very cryptic and seemingly not that helpful. However, armed with these cryptic codes, you can search the distribution's knowledge base, Internet newsgroups, or other help sources to track down the error. If you are still unsuccessful, phone support is available who usually can identify and get to the bottom of the problem.

More information on support sources can be found in Appendix C.

Common System Errors and Resolutions

If you have spent any time trying to troubleshoot errors, then you may already know that it is often a difficult endeavor. Table 4-1 lists a few of the more common hardware errors you may encounter while managing your system, as well as the possible solutions. Keep in mind, however, that often several possible reasons exist for a problem.

TABLE 4-1   Common Hardware Problems and Solutions

Problem	Possible Solution
Floppy light stays on.	Floppy cable is connected backward.
Floppy drive not accessible.	Damaged disk in drive; damaged floppy drive.
System does not detect the IDE hard drive.	Verify that the hard drive is recognized in the BIOS and that the hard drive cabling is correctly attached to the drive. The red line on the cable should be attached to pin 1. Confirm the drive is jumpered correctly with the correct master/slave settings. The IDE cable may be damaged; confirm by replacing with a known working cable. The drive may be faulty; replace with a known working drive to test it. Finally, you may need to verify that automatic detection of IDE devices is enabled in the BIOS.
System does not maintain time and/or hard drive settings.	The most common fix for this problem is to replace the CMOS battery.
System reports that no operating1 system is present.	Once the BIOS finishes POST, it looks in the master boot record (MBR) for a bootable device. If not found, you will receive an error message. Ensure that a disk isn't in the floppy drive. The OS may be damaged and need to be reinstalled. The MBR may be damaged and need to be repaired, using the fdisk /mbr command.

TABLE 4-1   Common Hardware Problems and Solutions *(continued)*

No display on the monitor during bootup.	Cable is not connected from the monitor to the video card. The monitor or video card may be damaged. Replace the monitor or video card with a known working one to test it.
Flickering monitor.	Flickering can be a result of a faulty monitor, the refresh rate setting for the monitor, or if the monitor is located near a strong electric current, such as another monitor.
System does not recognize the entire size of the hard drive.	Confirm the settings in the BIOS to ensure that the entire size of the disk is recognized. If it is not, the hard drive settings may have to be manually set, or the BIOS may need to be upgraded to a newer version.
Modem is not recognized by the system.	If the modem is an expansion card, ensure that it is properly seated in the bus slot. If it is, ensure that a resource conflict doesn't exist with another device. If you are using a portable system, verify that it is not a Winmodem.
USB or IEEE 1394 device is not recognized by the system.	Verify the Linux kernel version used and that the devices are supported with that version.
Computer sporadically reboots itself.	May be a result of inconsistent or insufficient power to the system. Damaged or incompatible memory or a problem with a processor could be the problem.
Failed SCSI devices.	Confirm that the SCSI device is terminated correctly. Confirm that the SCSI cable length does not exceed the recommended length. Verify that no SCSI ID conflicts exist.
Failed network connectivity.	Confirm the physical cable connection and that the link light is active on the network card.
Parity error or errors in applications.	Likely a problem with memory; insert known working memory.
Keyboard/mouse not working.	Confirm physical connections; if the device is not plugged in, power down the system and reconnect the device.

Once again, it is necessary to point out that a hardware problem can be caused by many things. Table 4-1 by no means is a comprehensive list, but it will steer you in the right direction.

Getting a Hardware Overview

It is hard to identify and isolate a problem if you do not know what hardware the system is or is not recognizing. During the initial Power On Self Test (POST) process, the hardware within your system is identified. You need to check carefully during the POST phase, because if your system is experiencing hardware problems, an indication of the problem likely will be displayed during this time.

If you believe that the system is recognizing your hardware correctly, but you are still experiencing problems within Linux, you will need to use some of the Linux tools to determine what is being detected.

Things happen fast when the computer system first boots, and if you look away for an instant, you might miss the hardware summary provided by Linux. Fortunately, you can use the dmesg command to see all of this hardware information after the system is booted. This command can be used from a terminal session in an X Windows session or from the console. The hardware information provided by the dmesg command can help isolate the cause of hardware-related problems and help you to understand better what is going on within your Linux system. The following is a sample from a printout using the dmesg command. As you can see, it is quite detailed. When reviewing it, try to identify the hardware installed on the system, such as the processor, SCSI devices, IDE devices, and peripherals.

on the **!** **job** *Information such as that provided by* dmesg *should be included in system documentation that you create.*

```
Detected PS/2 Mouse Port.
Serial driver version 4.27 with MANY_PORTS MULTIPORT SHARE_IRQ enabled
ttyS00 at 0x03f8 (irq = 4) is a 16550A
ttyS01 at 0x02f8 (irq = 3) is a 16550A
pty: 256 Unix98 ptys configured
apm: BIOS version 1.2 Flags 0x03 (Driver version 1.13)
apm: disabled - APM is not SMP safe.
Real Time Clock Driver v1.09
RAM disk driver initialized:  16 RAM disks of 4096K size
PIIX3: IDE controller on PCI bus 00 dev 39
PIIX3: not 100% native mode: will probe irqs later
    ide0: BM-DMA at 0xffa0-0xffa7, BIOS settings: hda:pio, hdb:pio
    ide1: BM-DMA at 0xffa8-0xffaf, BIOS settings: hdc:pio, hdd:pio
hda: ST32132A, ATA DISK drive
hdc: FX120T, ATAPI CDROM drive
ide0 at 0x1f0-0x1f7,0x3f6 on irq 14
ide1 at 0x170-0x177,0x376 on irq 15
hda: ST32132A, 2015MB w/120kB Cache, CHS=1023/64/63
Floppy drive(s): fd0 is 1.44M
FDC 0 is a post-1991 82077
md driver 0.90.0 MAX_MD_DEVS=256, MAX_REAL=12
```

```
raid5: measuring checksumming speed
   8regs      :   334.518 MB/sec
   32regs     :   196.596 MB/sec
using fastest function: 8regs (334.518 MB/sec)
scsi : 0 hosts.
scsi : detected total.
md.c: sizeof(mdp_super_t) = 4096
Partition check:
 hda: hda1 hda2 < hda5 >
RAMDISK: Compressed image found at block 0
autodetecting RAID arrays
autorun ...
... autorun DONE.
VFS: Mounted root (ext2 filesystem).
(scsi0)  found at PCI 1/4/0
(scsi0) Wide Channel A, SCSI ID=7, 16/255 SCBs
(scsi0) Cables present (Int-50 NO, Int-68 NO, Ext-68 NO)
(scsi0) Downloading sequencer code... 422 instructions downloaded
(scsi1)  found at PCI 1/5/0
(scsi1) Wide Channel B, SCSI ID=7, 16/255 SCBs
(scsi1) Cables present (Int-50 NO, Int-68 NO, Ext-68 NO)
(scsi1) Downloading sequencer code... 422 instructions downloaded
scsi0 : Adaptec AHA274x/284x/294x (EISA/VLB/PCI-Fast SCSI) 5.1.31/3.2.4

scsi1 : Adaptec AHA274x/284x/294x (EISA/VLB/PCI-Fast SCSI) 5.1.31/3.2.4

scsi : 2 hosts.
autodetecting RAID arrays
autorun ...
... autorun DONE.
VFS: Mounted root (ext2 filesystem) readonly.
change_root: old root has d_count=1
Trying to unmount old root ... okay
Freeing unused kernel memory: 76k freed
Adding Swap: 411224k swap-space (priority -1)
3c59x.c:v0.99H 01Aug00 Donald Becker
http://cesdis.gsfc.nasa.gov/linux/drivers/vortex.html
eth0: 3Com 3c905 Boomerang 100baseTx at 0xef00,  00:60:08:17:63:bf, IRQ 16
  8K word-wide RAM 3:5 Rx:Tx split, autoselect/MII interface.
  MII transceiver found at address 24, status 786d.
  Enabling bus-master transmits and whole-frame receives.
hdc: ATAPI 12X CD-ROM drive, 256kB Cache
Uniform CD-ROM driver Revision: 3.10
```

Once you have an overview of the hardware installed and recognized by your system, you can begin to look at specific hardware components.

EXERCISE 4-1

Using the dmesg Utility

1. From the command line, or from within a terminal session in an X Window session, type dmesg | more.

2. To view information about the hard disks in your system, you can use the grep command with the **hd** parameter—**dmesg | grep hd**.

3. To create a text file with the **dmesg** information in it, type **dmesg >** *filename*.

4. You can then use a text editor such as vi (explained in Chapter 9) to view the information.

Using the proc File System

To get information on specific hardware components, the /proc file system is often used. The /proc file system is a unique directory included in all Linux distributions that is used to provide information about a variety of devices found within the system. The first place to go when looking for what is really going on in the system may be /proc.

The /proc directory is unlike other file systems because it is a virtual file system, meaning that it isn't actually permanently stored on the hard disk; rather, it is kept in memory. The /proc directory puts system information at your fingertips and is an invaluable tool for troubleshooting the system. Table 4-2 shows some of the common options found within the /proc directory.

Numerous other virtual files worth looking at are in the /proc directory. Some of the information provided is a bit cryptic, but other information is fairly straightforward and easy to understand. In either case, don't be afraid to snoop around, but be careful not to make any changes to the files.

A common way to view the information provided by /proc is with the **cat** command. For example, to view information on the CPU(s) in your system, you should type the following:

```
$cat /proc/cpuinfo
```

TABLE 4-2	Proc Usage	Information Provided
	/proc/cpuinfo	CPU speed, stepping number, vendor, cache size
proc Options	/proc/interrupts	IRQs in use by the system and any duplicate used that is causing hardware conflicts
	/proc/meminfo	Physical and swap memory in use and total system memory
	/proc/net	Network configuration information
	/proc/pci	PCI devices on the system, including video and network adapters
	/proc/ioports	I/O ports in use and the devices attached to them
	/proc/dma	DMA channels in use
	/proc/filesystems	File systems installed on the system
	/proc/scsi/scsi	Information on installed SCSI devices
	/proc/ide	Information on installed IDE devices

Alternatively, you can view the information in an editor such as vi.

Confirming System Resources

You can expect from time to time to have some system resource conflicts, and troubleshooting these in a Linux environment is very different from other OSs. Common throughout Linux distributions are the utilities that make viewing the system's resource allocations, such as IRQs and I/O addresses, quite easy.

Your first indication of a resource conflict is that a device, typically an expansion card, is not working. Most devices cannot share resources, and those forced to share often will not work at all. Resource conflict is most apparent after a new device has been installed into the computer, which makes the isolation of the problem a little easier. Some resource conflicts will appear on the screen by identifying the location of the conflict, while others just leave you guessing.

on the **job**

In some cases, installing a device that conflicts with another will often render both devices unusable. If this is the case, it actually makes the problem easy to troubleshoot, because, by looking at documentation, you should be able to determine the resources that were being used by the device that has now stopped working.

The allocation of system resources in most modern systems is managed by Plug and Play, which prevents many of the potential resource conflicts. Many Linux users, however, choose to disable the Plug and Play feature in the BIOS due to potential problems within Linux. Plug and Play support is improving with each release of the Linux kernel, but there are still issues.

Viewing Resources in Linux

Viewing resource configuration and use in Linux is a straightforward process and again the proc file system is perhaps the best way to do it. When manually setting an expansion card to use a specific IRQ, type the following Linux command to determine whether the IRQ is already in use or is free:

```
#cat /proc/interrupts
```

The results of this command are shown in Figure 4-1.

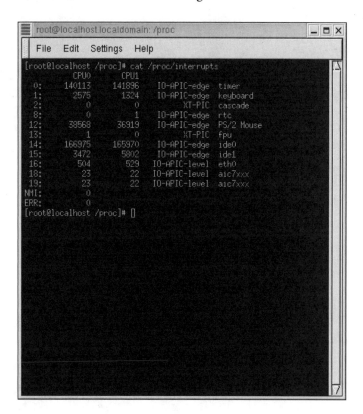

FIGURE 4-1

The output from a **cat /proc/interrupts** command

In a similar vein, to view the I/O ports that are in use, type the following Linux command:

```
#cat /proc/ioports.
```

The printout from the command should look something like that in Figure 4-2.
To view the DMAs the system is currently using, if any, type the following command:

```
#cat /proc/dma.
```

Linux Kernel

When troubleshooting hardware-related problems on your Linux computer, it is a good idea to know what kernel version you are using and whether some of your problems may in fact be caused by the version you are using. As already discussed, the Linux kernel is the root of the OS itself and is constantly under development,

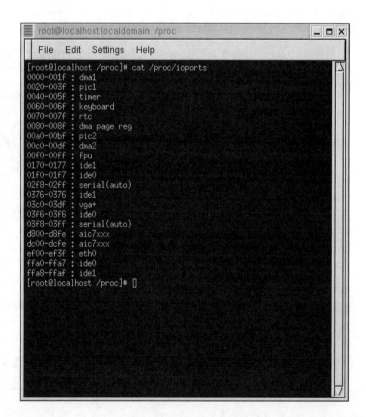

```
root@localhost.localdomain: /proc
File   Edit   Settings   Help

[root@localhost /proc]# cat /proc/ioports
0000-001f : dma1
0020-003f : pic1
0040-005f : timer
0060-006f : keyboard
0070-007f : rtc
0080-008f : dma page reg
00a0-00bf : pic2
00c0-00df : dma2
00f0-00ff : fpu
0170-0177 : ide1
01f0-01f7 : ide0
02f8-02ff : serial(auto)
0376-0376 : ide1
03c0-03df : vga+
03f6-03f6 : ide0
03f8-03ff : serial(auto)
d800-d8fe : aic7xxx
dc00-dcfe : aic7xxx
ef00-ef3f : eth0
ffa0-ffa7 : ide0
ffa8-ffaf : ide1
[root@localhost /proc]# []
```

with newer versions being introduced at a staggering pace. There are several reasons why a kernel upgrade is a good idea; the following are just a few:

- A newer kernel will have more support for the newest devices. If you want the latest and greatest, you will need a kernel that can support it.

- Nothing is perfect, and this includes the Linux kernel. Each new kernel offers fixes to bugs found in earlier versions. When it comes to troubleshooting, this is very important to know.

- Each new Linux kernel introduced seems to offer better resource management, enabling it to handle hardware more effectively.

- Each new Linux kernel release seems to provide increased stability; just ask those who have used earlier Linux versions and compared them to the newer ones. Some of the hardware instability issues you may face can be resolved by simply updating the kernel.

EXERCISE 4-2

Verifying Kernel Version

1. Start your Linux system and go to the command line. If in an X Window session, open a terminal session.

2. At the command line, type the command #cat /proc/version.

on the **Job**   *The kernel version can also be verified by using the command* uname -a.

From the screen display, identify the kernel version being used. The printout from the command should look something like that in Figure 4-3. Refer to the distributor's Web site to ascertain what hardware devices are supported by this version.

Verifying Hardware Compatibility

You can save yourself a lot of time and energy by verifying hardware compatibility before installing it into your system. To verify hardware compatibility, most of the Linux distributions offer a hardware compatibility list on their Web sites. Generally speaking, if your hardware is on the list, you are good to go. As an additional

The output from
a cat
/proc/version
command

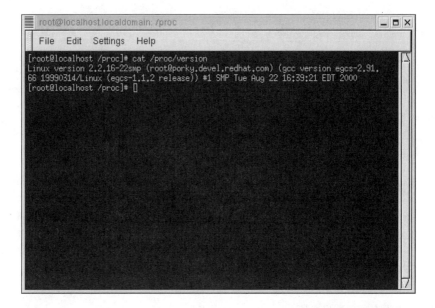

measure, some people use the USENET groups to confirm compatibility or to look for suggestions on installation procedures. Perhaps more than any other operating system, it pays to do a little hardware homework before installing something in your Linux system.

exam
ⓦatch

Verifying hardware compatibility before installing a hardware device is a mandatory requirement.

FROM THE CLASSROOM

Bring on the Subs

One of the easiest and most effective troubleshooting methods is that of substituting a suspect component for another. For example, if you suspect a problem with a network card and you have a known working card of the same type available, swapping them over will prove whether the problem is with the network card or something else. The key to making this strategy work is to ensure that the component you are swapping works. If it does not, you may find yourself going in a very wrong direction when troubleshooting.

—Mike Harwood, Linux+ Certified

EXERCISE 4-3

Verifying Hardware Compatibility

1. Log on to the Internet and go to the Internet home page for the distribution you are using.

2. By following links or using the search feature, locate the hardware compatibility list.

3. Verify that the hardware installed in your system is included in the list.

4. Create a bookmark for the page so that it can be accessed for future reference.

CERTIFICATION OBJECTIVE 4.02

Identifying Proper Procedures for Diagnosing and Troubleshooting IDE Devices

Installing, maintaining, and troubleshooting IDE devices is a required skill when working with computer systems. IDE devices have very few failure points, but even so, there are some troubleshooting areas to be aware of. In case of a problem with an IDE device, consider the following:

- The primary hard drive needs to be connected as the master on the primary controller. Other IDE devices can be connected as a slave on the primary channel or on the secondary channel as either the secondary master or slave. Having two devices configured the same on the same channel will prevent both devices from working.

- If an IDE drive is not recognized by the system after installation, check the master and slave settings to make sure they are set correctly. The hard disk will usually have the correct settings labeled right on it. If not, the hard drive manufacturer's Web site will have the correct settings listed.

- If the entire size of the hard drive is not recognized in the BIOS, the BIOS may need to be upgraded to accommodate. Consult the system board manufacturer's Web site for details.

- If the system is booted and no drives are recognized, ensure that the system is configured to automatically recognize IDE devices.

- Two infrequent—but possible—related IDE problems include a damaged IDE cable, which may prevent the device from working altogether or create intermittent problems, and a bent pin, which is often a result of an impatient installation. Trust us on that one!

- While not so much of an issue nowadays, some older kernels may have problems seeing ATA 66/100 controllers. This is just an issue to be wary of when you are working with an older kernel version.

If while starting the system you receive the error message, "Drive not bootable, insert system disk," you may have a corrupt master boot record.

CERTIFICATION OBJECTIVE 4.03

Identifying Proper Procedures for Diagnosing and Troubleshooting SCSI Devices

Working with SCSI can be a very frustrating experience when things start to go wrong, simply because there are so many places where the problem can lie. The diverse range of problems that can arise on a SCSI bus makes finding the exact cause difficult, often requiring a great deal of patience and systematic elimination. The following section describes some basic and very general steps to take when troubleshooting SCSI devices.

When troubleshooting SCSI devices, or anything else for that matter, be sure to make only one change at a time. Making multiple changes can make things confusing really fast and may make it difficult to determine what the exact cause of the problem was.

Confirm SCSI IDs

As mentioned in Chapter 3, all devices on a SCSI bus require a unique ID to make them distinguishable from each other on the bus. You will have problems if two devices on the bus are set to share IDs. SCSI IDs are usually assigned by priority; the lower the SCSI ID, the higher the priority. SCSI hard drives are typically assigned the lower IDs, 0 or 1, and the highest IDs, 7 through 15, are reserved for the SCSI host adapter.

Confirm All Cabling

The myriad SCSI cabling and connectors can bring with it a host of problems, most of which are not difficult to fix—finding the problem is the difficult part. Perhaps the first thing to check with SCSI cables is that all the cables are securely connected. A poorly attached cable can cause intermittent problems or prevent devices from working altogether.

Another consideration when troubleshooting SCSI cabling is the recommended length of the SCSI cable. If the recommendation is exceeded, a variety of problems can arise on the SCSI bus. SCSI cable lengths are determined by the signaling method used. To review recommended cable lengths, refer to Chapter 3.

The quality of cable may also be a factor that can lead to cable-related problems. Wherever possible, purchase good-quality SCSI cable from an established vendor. Saving a few dollars on poor-quality cable can come back to haunt you.

Termination

It is not uncommon after the installation of a new SCSI device to have termination issues. It is very important to get termination right, but termination is often overlooked. The SCSI bus must have two, and only two, points of termination. Any more or less will cause a problem. Terminators have to be located at the physical ends of the bus, and if any device between the terminators, such as a SCSI host adapter, has built-in termination, it must be turned off.

The type of termination used might come into play as well. Passive terminators are associated with the older SE SCSI standards and are not recommended for the higher-speed SCSI implementations. If you are using the faster SCSI standard, be sure to use active termination.

SCENARIO & SOLUTION

You need a list of the PCI devices on the system, including video and network adapters. What command should you use?	/proc/pci
What command could be used to view the SCSI drives currently installed?	/proc/scsi
You want a printout of the hardware currently installed on your Linux system. What utility could you use?	dmesg

If you power on your system first and then power on external SCSI devices, you may not see all the devices. Therefore, it is recommended to power on external SCSI devices first to ensure they are recognized by the system.

CERTIFICATION OBJECTIVE 4.04

Identifying Proper Procedures for Diagnosing and Troubleshooting Peripheral Devices

Given that "peripheral device" refers to anything that is connected to a computer system, it is difficult to provide coverage for all eventualities. Therefore, this section provides information on some of the more commonly troublesome devices and those focused on by CompTIA in its exam.

Network Cards

Networks cards provide the means to get to the outside world. Without one, networking your computer could prove a very difficult task. Usually after installing a new network card, it works fine, but from time to time, it doesn't. Keep in mind that these are hardware-specific resolution strategies. Chapter 12 on operating system troubleshooting isolates software-related causes. When troubleshooting network cards, consider the following areas:

- Check whether the network card is firmly inserted into the system board. It may be necessary to remove the card and install it into a different expansion slot.

- Confirm the IRQ and I/O settings to ensure that there are no conflicts with another device. These settings can be determined by using the **proc** commands.

- Replace the card with a known-working one. Hardware, even new hardware, can be faulty. By installing a known-working network card, you can determine whether the original is faulty.

- If the card seems to be working in the system but won't access the network, confirm that the link lights on the back of the card are lit and that the network cabling is securely attached.

exam

ⓦatch

Observation techniques play a large part in troubleshooting.

Sound Cards

Depending on the sound card you are using, getting it to work within Linux can be a bit of a challenge. The physical installation is straightforward: simply put it into an available expansion slot, but that is just the beginning. Older ISA sound cards can be particularly troublesome, often causing resource conflicts and, depending on the sound card, you may need to configure the Linux kernel to use sound. Sound complicated? It certainly can be, but it often boils down to just how badly you want MP3s playing on your Linux system.

The exact procedures used to install sound cards fall outside of the Linux+ objectives. However, you should know where to look to resolve resource conflicts. The following commands are a good place to start. Type **dmesg | grep sound**. Alternatively, you can type **cat /dev/sndstat** at the command line.

on the

ⓙob

Sound card compatibility often comes down to whether or not the sound card is Sound Blaster compatible. It is best to stick to the mainstream for sound cards.

Floppy Drive Failures

Like any other device in the computer, floppy drives will periodically fail. However, the floppy disk is more likely to be at fault than the drive itself. The first thing to do when a failed floppy drive is suspected is to try another disk in the drive, maybe even a few, just to make sure. If none of the disks works, you are likely looking at a failed floppy drive.

Perhaps one of the more common floppy drive–related problems occurs when a new floppy drive is installed and the floppy cable is plugged in backward. If this happens, the floppy drive light will always stay on. Make sure that the red edge of the floppy drive cable is plugged into pin 1, as marked on the floppy drive cable connection.

Troubleshooting Modems

Dealing with modems that do not work can be a very frustrating experience. Many different things can cause the modem not to respond. As with all troubleshooting procedures, you should start with the most basic solutions and work out from there.

The first thing to check when the modem is not working is whether the cable is correctly installed into the wall socket and the modem itself. Many modems have two slots on them: one for a connection to the telephone line and one for the modem connection. Confirm that the right one is used. After you have confirmed the cabling, the next step is to verify that there is no resource conflict with another device. Again, using the proc file system may be the easiest way to do this.

on the job

External modems are generally less hassle to configure and easier to troubleshoot than internal modems. What they do add, however, is considerations for cabling between the PC and the modem and an external power cable.

Peripheral Ports

The ports on the back of computer systems, including the serial, parallel, USB, and perhaps IEEE 1394 ports, provide the path for the data from peripheral devices to get to the computer. When it comes to troubleshooting peripheral devices, verifying that the ports are functioning as they should is a good place to start.

Perhaps the first thing to do when troubleshooting a port is to ensure that it is communicating with the system. To do this under Linux, the **proc** commands discussed earlier provide the best way of gathering information and verifying the port is configured correctly and is using the correct IRQ and I/O address.

If problems with a port persist after confirming the resources, check that the cabling is connected properly and is functioning. Over time, cables have a way of sometimes squirming loose. Often, fixing a problem is as easy as reattaching a cable. Sometimes the cables themselves are faulty. If this is suspected, all that can be done is to replace the cable with a known working one and see if the problem is corrected.

Troubleshooting problems with other peripheral devices such as those connected to IEEE 1394 and USB ports may be a bit more involved. Each new kernel release brings Linux closer to supporting all the devices that can be connected to these interfaces, but there is still a ways to go. If you are having trouble with devices connected to the ports, it is often a good idea to check the distributor's Web site to see if you have the latest kernel and, therefore, the best support for such devices.

When troubleshooting peripheral devices, confirm that the kernel supports the device.

Dealing with Plug and Play

Enabling Plug and Play (PnP) in Linux can create a number of unwanted configuration issues. In today's systems, PnP has become the name of the game, and we have become somewhat dependent on it, but when working with Linux, you may not be able to rely on PnP technology, especially for ISA devices.

ISA cards that support PnP present a challenge for Linux and those who are trying to install such devices. For ISA PnP devices, Linux has a built-in set of applications, *isapnptools,* for just that purpose. These tools allow you to manually configure the resource configuration of the ISA cards. Using these tools is not easy, but there is another option: disable Plug and Play.

Many computers today offer an option to disable PnP in the BIOS, and setting your BIOS to enable PnP for Linux may not yield positive results. Linux continues to improve its PnP capability with each kernel release, but it is far from perfect. For the purposes of an easy installation, it may be a good idea to disable PnP in the BIOS.

Remember that PnP is often disabled in the BIOS when using Linux.

Hardware or Virus?

Often, knowing what to troubleshoot is as difficult as fixing the problem itself. Determining whether a problem is hardware or software related is often complicated enough, but throwing in virus considerations and identifying the cause of a problem makes it much more difficult. The following are some signs that your troubles may be a result of virus activity:

■ **New files or directories**   Though often hard to spot, your system may include new files or directories. It can be hard to know whether these files should or should not be there, and erasing important system files is never a good practice. If you find any files that make you wonder what they are, log on to a Linux USENET group and post a question. Doing so can get you to the root of the problem in short order.

■ **Increased system errors**   Some viruses may cause an increase in system errors, such as memory or swap file errors. If you have not added new software or made system changes and such errors appear, you have cause to be suspicious.

■ **Disappearing files**   If the document you have just spent four hours working on suddenly vanishes or becomes corrupt, you could have virus activity.

SCENARIO & SOLUTION

You have been called to help troubleshoot a problem where a user complains that several of her documents will no longer open.	Check the computer with a recent virus checker. Missing or damaged files can be an indication of virus activity on the system.
You want to manually configure the resources used by your ISA cards.	Linux provides isapnptools to manually configure ISA devices.
You are installing Linux on a laptop and discover it is using a Winmodem.	Linux does not support Winmodems, and the device should be disabled.

Identifying Proper Procedures for Diagnosing and Troubleshooting Core System Hardware

The procedures for troubleshooting core system hardware components are much the same for all systems, regardless of the operating system used. At the end of the day, hardware is hardware, and knowing how to maintain and troubleshoot it will be part of your responsibilities. The following section looks at some of the core system components and what it takes to troubleshoot them.

BIOS

As mentioned in Chapter 3, the BIOS holds the initial set of instructions the system needs to boot, and during the boot process, the BIOS reports any errors it detects. When new hardware components are added, you may need to go into the BIOS settings and confirm that they are recognized by the system. Here comes the tricky part: The BIOS on older computer systems, and even on some of the newer systems, may not support the latest and greatest components. For instance, the new 1 GHz processor or the 80GB hard drive may not have BIOS support, and when this happens, you have to upgrade the BIOS. Because of the lower hardware requirements for Linux as compared to more-commercial operating systems, it is likely that, at some point, you will be using Linux on a system with an older BIOS. The troubleshooting process for Linux on these older system often requires identifying the current BIOS version and possibly upgrading it.

The BIOS chips on the system board are upgraded by using a program from the BIOS manufacturer. These programs can be downloaded and are typically installed by rebooting the computer and running the BIOS upgrade program from a floppy disk. The process of updating the BIOS is called *flashing*, but beware—flashing the wrong program on your BIOS chip or disrupting the flashing process can irreparably destroy your BIOS, and there is no easy way to recover from this.

Memory

Work around computers long enough, and you will at some point find yourself troubleshooting memory-related errors. Like many other system components, diagnosing the cause of, and correcting, a memory error is a systematic process, starting with the most obvious cause and working from there. Perhaps the most difficult aspect of dealing with memory errors is that they are often misleading, giving no obvious clue that they are at the root of the problem. However, with a little direction and a methodical approach, it is possible get to the bottom of a memory-related error.

When you do have a memory error, the cause can usually be isolated to one of three things: incompatible memory or configuration, poorly installed memory, or a damaged memory module.

Incompatible or Misconfigured Memory

Before purchasing any memory for a system, you must verify that it works with the current configuration, including both the operating system and the hardware. To verify memory with the hardware, it may be necessary to visit the system board manufacturer's Web site, where the vendors will list any memory-related compatibility issues. Further, some system boards require that memory be installed in a certain configuration. For instance, some require matching of equal capacity modules or may require that all memory sockets be filled.

Using incompatible memory in your system may prevent the system from running altogether or may cause more subtle errors, which can be far more difficult to isolate. The trick to avoiding compatibility and configuration errors is to do your homework before purchasing new memory; it could save you a lot of headaches at the end of the day.

Before doing a major upgrade to system memory, it is a good idea to check to see if a BIOS upgrade is needed. BIOS upgrade information can be obtained from the system board manufacturer's Web site.

Memory Installation

If you are going to have a memory-related problem, it is most likely going to occur after the installation of new memory modules. Memory errors after an installation will usually be caught during the POST process, but not always. There are two indicators that the new memory module is not installed correctly. The first is if POST only counts part of the memory, which may mean the new memory installed may not be seated properly or is not being recognized by the system. After the installation of new memory, keep an eye on the POST memory count, just to make sure everything is as it should be. Second, the system may halt during the POST memory count, notifying you with an audible warning that something is wrong. This too can indicate improperly installed memory.

If memory isn't working after an installation, take the time to reinsert the memory module, perhaps even in a different socket, ensuring that the RAM is secured in place with the appropriate clamping mechanisms. If the memory does appear to be seated properly, it may be necessary to place the new memory into a different slot or clean the socket and pins with compressed air.

Damaged Memory Module

Isolating a damaged memory module can require a little trial and error and may involve swapping memory in and out to find the specific memory module that is defective. Swapping different memory modules and testing memory in different sockets can help determine whether the memory itself is at fault or if the memory slot is at fault. Always remember when installing memory modules to use ESD best practices; you can save yourself some potentially frustrating errors by doing so. Just one note from experience: faulty memory sockets are very rare.

**on the
() o b**

Most vendors will be willing to replace memory if it is damaged, but some are far more reluctant and prefer to install the memory themselves. It may be a good idea to confirm the return policies from the vendor before purchasing.

Memory Errors, Signs, and Symptoms

Every computer-related problem has a way to let you know if things are not working. Memory is no exception. A large part of memory troubleshooting involves translating system messages and being able to determine which of these messages are related to memory problems and which are not. The following are a few signs and symptoms that may be a result of memory-related issues.

Computer Does Not Boot   Although a computer that does not boot seems more dramatic, it is often easier to troubleshoot than one that does boot but has periodic problems. As mentioned in Chapter 3, when the system first starts, as part of the boot process, the BIOS performs an inventory check of the system components, including the memory. A computer that does not boot because of a memory error will often beep to let you know of the problem. The exact sequence of beeps will depend on the BIOS manufacturer. The remedy in this case is to confirm that all memory modules are properly seated and also to verify the memory module configuration. It may be that the module is defective and may need to be replaced.

All Memory Is Not Counted During the Boot Process   An astute person may notice that sometimes after a memory upgrade, all the memory is not counted during the boot process. Of course, it is nice to have the new memory working in the system. There are a few things that can cause a system not to recognize all or some of newly installed memory. First among these would be improperly seated memory; if it isn't fastened down and installed correctly, the BIOS in its boot process may not see the memory. Memory configuration and compatibility may also cause the problem. It may be necessary to confirm with the system board manufacturer to verify the memory configurations that are acceptable.

A less likely explanation, especially with newer computer systems, is that the system's current configuration does not actually support the amount of RAM installed. There is a maximum amount of RAM that a system can support, and if this is exceeded, all of the RAM will not show up. Often, this can be corrected by upgrading the BIOS; however, before installing large amounts of memory in a machine, confirm that it is supported.

Computer Freezes, Periodically Reboots, or Crashes   Erratic system functioning within Linux, such as freezing, crashing, and periodic reboots, can be a result of defective memory. Pinpointing any of these errors to the system's RAM is a difficult task because many other factors, including the system board and even applications, can cause the problem. ESD damage during the installation may cause these types of problems, but how can anyone prove it? If you are trying to isolate the cause of periodic freezing or reboots, you can try swapping out the memory to see if the situation resolves itself.

on the job   *If you receive a "segmentation fault" after installing new RAM, the new RAM likely is faulty. Segmentation faults are, for the most part, the Linux equivalent to the Windows Illegal Operation error. A segmentation fault may close down a program and log error information to the Linux /var/log directory.*

To view and confirm that all memory is properly configured and accounted for within Linux, there are a few utilities that can be used, each of which shows much the same information. One of the more commonly used is proc, described earlier. By using the proc directory, it is possible to determine all resources used by the system, including memory. To view memory configurations with proc, use the following command: $cat /proc/meminfo.

An example of the information provided by this command can be seen in Figure 4-4. Alternatively, the free command also displays memory-related information.

EXERCISE 4-4

Viewing Memory Information on a Linux System

1. If in an X Window session, open a terminal session. If not, use the command line.

2. At the command line, type the following command: cat /proc/meminfo.

3. From the screen display, identify the memory configuration used in your system, including overall memory and the swap space used

The results of the command should display the relevant memory information.

FIGURE 4-4

Output from the
cat
/proc/meminfo
command

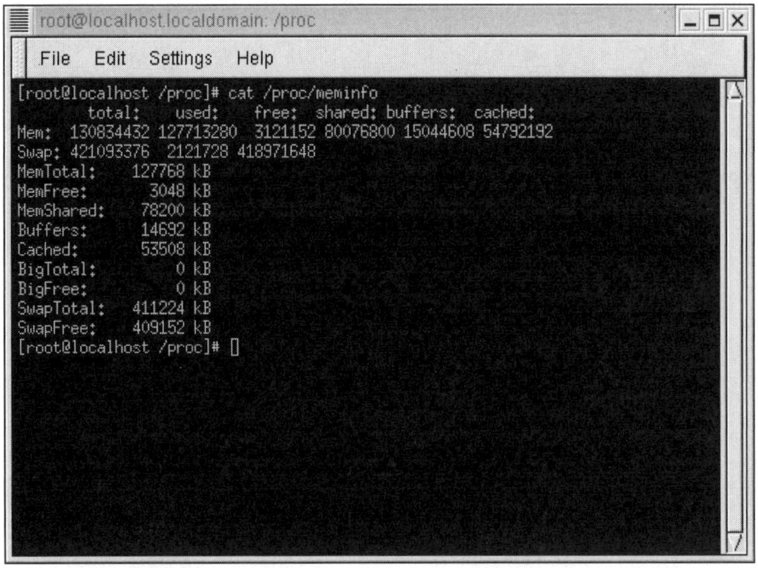

If Linux does not recognize all the memory you are using in the system, you may need to upgrade your kernel or add a command to the appropriate entry in the boot loader file.

Processors

Unfortunately, the first indication that there is a problem with the processor is usually that the system will not start, or worse still, the smell of burning in your office. Processor failures are very rare and are generally due to overheating, which is an effect of an inadequate or broken CPU fan. Not much can be done with a processor that has overheated and burnt out, other than replacing it. Fortunately, there are a few safeguards in place to help prevent this from happening. Newer computer systems support a temperature sensor connected to the CPU. When a threshold is surpassed, the CPU will power down. This feature is set in the system BIOS and is commonly set to be on by default. The second, less technical, indicator is a loud noise coming from the computer case itself. When a CPU fan is failing, it will typically make a lot of noise on its way out. If you do hear this, you have a little time to buy a new fan and replace it.

If you have a system that is inexplicably locking up, the CPU might be overheating. In this situation, check that both the power supply fan and the CPU fan are operating correctly, and ensure that the system is adequately ventilated.

EXERCISE 4-5

Viewing CPU Information on a Linux System

1. From the command line, in an X Window terminal session, type the following command: $cat /proc/cpuinfo.

2. From the screen display, identify the CPU used in your system.

Video Cards

Many of today's systems use integrated video cards, meaning they are built onto the system board. If this is the case, compatibility can be a nightmare if the integrated

FROM THE CLASSROOM

Take Your Time

One of the most common mistakes when troubleshooting is that of attempting to fix the wrong thing. In many cases the cause of the problem may be obvious, such as when a power supply fails. In other instances, the cause of the problem may be harder to determine. The key thing to remember is that a minute spent determining the problem is a minute spent more wisely than 20 minutes wasted trying to fix a problem that doesn't exist. Troubleshooting is a systematic process. When it comes to troubleshooting, there really is no substitute for practical experience. Try and get hands-on experience when you can, and your troubleshooting skills will benefit as a result.

—Drew Bird Linux+ Certified

card is not supported. It is possible to disable the onboard video adapter and install a new one, but this sometimes creates more problems than it solves. In other systems, video cards are not built onto the system board; rather, they are expansion cards. They will typically use an AGP bus slot or sometimes a PCI slot. Like other expansion cards, video cards require a unique IRQ and I/O address. Generally speaking, video cards either work or they do not, and they do not have many configurable settings. You do need to pay special attention to video cards if you are using XFree86 and the X Window System.

CERTIFICATION SUMMARY

Maintaining and supporting computer systems will at times require troubleshooting hardware components. Having knowledge of how these components function in normal operations can increase your success in troubleshooting a system error and reduce the time it takes to isolate the problem. A good practice when troubleshooting hardware problems is to start with the easiest solution and work to the more difficult.

Not all hardware problems are easy to diagnose, but they can all be resolved, whether this involves replacing a CMOS battery or the entire system board. Questioning the user about the errors, as well as reviewing system-generated errors, can help isolate problems within a computer system. The correct functioning of the operating system will depend on the configuration of the hardware and whether this hardware is doing what it is designed to do.

TWO-MINUTE DRILL

Here are some of the key points presented in this chapter.

Identifying, Troubleshooting, and Isolating Common System Problems

❑ To help isolate the cause of a problem, use the appropriate questioning techniques and monitor system-generated log files.

❑ During the system boot process, the BIOS startup procedure will identify and report hardware problems it encounters.

❑ When isolating a potential hardware problem, start with the most accessible solution and work to the more difficult.

Identifying the Proper Procedures for Identifying and Troubleshooting IDE Devices

❑ Ensure that the jumpers are set correctly on the IDE device.

❑ Ensure that the IDE cable is securely connected to both the system board and the device itself.

❑ To boot from a specific hard disk, ensure that it is connected to the primary channel on the system board.

Identifying the Proper Procedures for Identifying and Troubleshooting SCSI Devices

❑ If you have intermittent problems on a SCSI bus, ensure that it is properly terminated on both ends.

❑ Ensure that the SCSI bus does not exceed the number of devices it can support.

❑ When adding devices to a SCSI bus or troubleshooting it, ensure that each device has a unique ID.

Identifying the Proper Procedures for Identifying and Troubleshooting Peripheral Devices

❑ Confirm that the peripheral device is on the distribution's hardware compatibility list.

❑ Ensure that the kernel version you are using accommodates the peripheral device.

❑ When troubleshooting a peripheral device, ensure that the cables are securely attached to the system.

❑ Confirm that there is not a resource conflict between devices. Each peripheral will require a unique IRQ and I/O address.

Identifying the Proper Procedures for Identifying and Troubleshooting Core System Hardware

❑ Linux excels in its ability to be used in older hardware systems due to its more efficient use of resources. However, there may be some compatibility issues with this older hardware that can cause problems.

❑ When installing new core system components, ensure that they are on the distribution's hardware compatibility list.

❑ Using the proc file system, it is possible to monitor what is going on in your system, including resource conflicts and which devices are recognized by the system.

SELF TEST

The following questions will help determine your level of understanding of the material presented in this chapter. Some of the questions may have more than one correct answer, so be sure to review all answers carefully before choosing all that apply.

Identifying, Troubleshooting, and Isolating Common System Problems

1. You need to purchase a new video card for your Linux system. Before purchasing the new card, where should you verify the card's compatibility?

   A. Xfree86 Web site.

   B. System board manufacturer's Web site.

   C. Linux distribution Web site.

   D. Linux supports video adapters from all the major manufacturers; confirming compatibility before a card is purchased is not necessary.

2. Which of the following is a valid reason to update your Linux kernel?

   A. Increased hardware support

   B. The ability to dual-boot the Linux system

   C. Need to use IDE devices

   D. Need to use SCSI devices

3. After installing a new USB device, it does not work with your Linux system. You suspect that you may need to upgrade your Linux kernel. Which of the following commands could you use to verify your current kernel version?

   A. cat /proc/version

   B. cat /proc/kernel

   C. cat /proc/lkernel

   D. cat /proc/vkernel

4. You walk into a server room and hear a loud buzzing noise coming from the server. Which of the following is most likely the cause of the noise?

   A. Faulty hard disk

   B. Faulty CD-ROM

   C. Faulty monitor

   D. Faulty CPU fan

5. After installing a floppy disk into your system, you notice that the light on the drive always stays on. What, if anything, is wrong with the floppy drive?

A. The cable is inserted backward.

B. There is likely a disk in the drive.

C. The power cable is faulty.

D. The floppy drive is incompatible.

6. You suspect that some of the devices installed on your system are using the same IRQs. Which of the following Linux commands could you use to view the IRQs used in your system?

A. cat /proc/irqinfo

B. cat /proc/interrupts

C. cat /proc/pci

D. cat /proc/ioports

7. Recently, every time you have reboot your computer system, you receive an error message and have to reenter your hard drive settings upon each boot. Which of the following best describes the problem?

A. Faulty hard drive

B. Corrupt boot record

C. Faulty memory

D. Failed CMOS battery

8. You have been asked to install a second network card into you company's main server. After checking the cards compatibility on the manufacturer's Web site, you install the card. After it is installed, neither of the network cards are recognized by the system. Which of the following is most likely the cause of the problem?

A. Incorrect network settings.

B. The network cards are incompatible with each other.

C. This is a known bug in Linux and was corrected in the 2.2 Linux kernel and later.

D. The two network cards are trying to use the same resources.

Identifying Proper Procedures for Diagnosing and Troubleshooting IDE Devices

9. Which of the following commands would give you a list of the IDE hard disks installed on your system?

   A. dmesg | grep hd

   B. dmesg | hd grep

   C. dmesg | sd grep

   D. dmesg | grep sd

10. After installing a new IDE device on your computer system, you receive an error that says, "Non-system disk or Disk error." What is the most likely cause of the problem?

   A. The ID assignments are incorrect.

   B. The operating system is not installed.

   C. You have the IDE disk set as master on the primary controller.

   D. You have a multiboot configuration set on the system.

Identifying Proper Procedures for Diagnosing and Troubleshooting SCSI Devices

11. Which of the following need to be checked when troubleshooting a SCSI bus? Choose three.

   A. Termination

   B. Number of devices on the bus

   C. SCSI IDs

   D. Master/slave setting

12. You are troubleshooting the SCSI devices on your company's application server. As the first part of your troubleshooting procedure, you decide to review the SCSI devices in your system. Which of the following Linux commands do you use?

   A. cat /proc/scsi/scsi

   B. cat /proc/sda

   C. cat /proc/sdb

   D. cat /proc/sd

13. At the request of your supervisor, you have installed an external scanner on an existing SCSI bus. After the scanner was installed, nothing seems to work properly. Which of the following is the next logical step in the troubleshooting process?

    A. Verify the scanner's compatibility with Linux.

    B. Consult the scanner manufacturer's Web site.

    C. Verify SCSI termination.

    D. Verify that the Linux kernel supports the scanner.

Identifying the Proper Procedures for Identifying and Troubleshooting Peripheral Devices

14. You are having difficulty configuring an ISA expansion card under Linux and would like to disable Plug and Play on your system. What is the method to accomplish this?

    A. Use the Linux isapnptools.

    B. Disable Plug and Play in the CMOS.

    C. Disable Plug and Play in the BIOS.

    D. Modify the Linux kernel.

15. Which of the following can be used to configure ISA Plug and Play devices?

    A. isapnptools

    B. cat /proc/ioports

    C. cat /proc/interrupts

    D. cat /proc/isa/devices

16. You are inspecting a system and suspect that it may have a virus on it. Which of the following may indicate the presence of a virus?

    A. Unfamiliar files or folders

    B. Increased error messages on the screen

    C. Incompatible memory

    D. A corrupt document

17. You have just installed a new USB device into your Linux computer. Which of the following commands could you use to verify USB devices on your system?

    A. cat /proc/usb

    B. cat /proc/bus/usb/devices

    C. cat /proc/version

    D. cat /proc/sysinfo

18. You want to buy a new network card for your Linux server. What is the first thing to do before purchasing the new network card?

    A. Shop for the best price on the card.

    B. Observer appropriate ESD practices.

    C. Determine the network protocols that you will be using.

    D. Verify hardware compatibility.

Identifying the Proper Procedures for Identifying and Troubleshooting Core System Hardware

19. You have just installed a new 800 MHz processor in your Linux server. After the processor is installed, it is not recognized by the system. Which of the following could fix the problem?

    A. Upgrade the BIOS.

    B. Upgrade the CMOS.

    C. Replace the BIOS chip.

    D. Replace the CMOS chip.

20. After installing a new memory module, not all of the memory is recognized by the system. Which of the following are possible explanations for this?

    A. Maximum memory capacity exceeded.

    B. You are mixing SIMMs and SO-DIMMs in the same system.

    C. Memory is not installed correctly.

    D. ESD-damaged memory module.

LAB QUESTION

A user calls you to help him troubleshoot a problem with his computer. After purchasing and installing a new monitor for the system, there is no video display. The system seemed to be working fine previously. Describe the steps, in the proper order, you might take to isolate the cause of the problem.

SELF TEST ANSWERS

Identifying, Troubleshooting, and Isolating Common System Problems

1. ☑ **A, C.** The XFree86 Project is an organization that produces XFree86, an open-source implementation of the X Window System. XFree86 provides the magic for such graphical interfaces as KDE, GNOME, Enlightenment, and Blackbox. The site maintains a list of hardware that is supported by XFree86, and if your video card appears here, you should be okay. To further verify video compatibility, refer to the distributor's Web site, because most of them have a well-documented hardware compatibility list. If your card isn't on the list, it doesn't mean it won't work; it just might be quite a job to get it to work.

   ☒ **B.** Unless the video card is integrated on the system board, visiting the system board manufacturer's Web site will not provide the information you are looking for. **D.** Verifying hardware compatibility is the first step and needs to be done before purchasing hardware, whether the hardware is from a major manufacturer or not.

2. ☑ **A.** There are several reasons to upgrade your Linux system with a new kernel version, including increased hardware support. The Linux kernel is dynamic and constantly under development. With each new kernel release, Linux provides increased hardware support. To view what the new kernel offers, visit your Linux distribution's Web site and review the documentation on the kernel release.

   ☒ **B.** All the Linux systems have the ability to multiboot your system, and upgrading the kernel is not needed to accomplish this. **C.** Linux supports IDE devices, and it is not necessary to upgrade the kernel to achieve IDE support. However, if it is a new IDE device and not supported with the kernel, then an upgrade is needed. **D.** The Linux kernel already supports SCSI devices, and upgrading the kernel is not needed.

3. ☑ **A.** At Some point in your Linux administration, it will be necessary to confirm the kernel version you are using. Of the commands listed, the easiest way to do this is to use **cat /proc/version**. You could also use the uname –a command.

   ☒ **B, C, D.** These are not valid Linux commands.

4. ☑ **D.** When the CPU fan becomes worn out, it often makes a noise, letting you know that it will need to be replaced. If you suspect a damaged or broken processor fan, it is a good idea to open the case to confirm. A broken fan can cause the processor to overheat, in which case either your processor will burn out or the system will shut down as the processor temperature reaches a predefined threshold.

☒ **A, B, C.** Each of these components can make a noise when it is failing; however, it is more likely that a loud noise is caused by the system fan, and that is the first place to look.

5. ☑ **A.** A common problem encountered after the installation of a floppy drive is that the power light to the drive is always on and the drive will not work. The cause of this problem is simply that the cable connecting the floppy drive to the system board is connected backward. To fix the problem, turn off the system, use ESD practices, and replace the cable the correct way.
☒ **B.** A disk in the floppy drive would not cause the error. If the disk in the drive is nonbootable and is in the drive when the system is booted, it may give a non-system disk error. **C.** If the light on the floppy is on, then there is sufficient power to the drive and the power cable is not faulty. **D.** Floppy drives are standard, and it is very unlikely that there would be compatibility issues.

6. ☑ **B.** Devices installed in a computer require a unique IRQ address to be recognized by the system. If two devices are trying to use the same IRQ, there is a resource conflict and the devices will not work properly. To view the IRQ resources being used in your Linux system, use the command cat /proc/interrupts.
☒ **A.** The command is fictitious. **C.** The command cat /proc/pci is used to view the characteristics of PCI devices currently used in the system. **D.** The command cat /proc/ioports is used to view the I/O addresses and the devices that are currently using them.

7. ☑ **D.** CMOS is volatile memory, which means that if the computer is turned off, the settings will be lost. To prevent this from happening, the CMOS uses a battery to maintain power after the system is powered down. If you have to reenter setting, such as hard drive settings on each boot, it is a strong indicator that the CMOS battery has failed and needs to be replaced.
☒ **A.** If the hard drive were faulty it would not require reentering settings on each boot. More likely the hard drive would not be recognized, and no settings would be visible.
B. A corrupt boot record would not cause a failure of the hard drive settings to be kept in the CMOS settings. **C.** Faulty memory would not force hard drive settings to reentered each time the computer is booted.

8. ☑ **D.** If after installing a new expansion card, like a network card, you discover that it or other existing components no longer work then there is likely a resource conflict. In this instance, it would be necessary to confirm which resources each of the network cards are using.
☒ **A.** Network settings may prevent the cards from accessing the network but would not prevent the system from recognizing the cards. **B.** There are no real compatibility issues between the network cards themselves only with Linux and the respective card. **C.** From its early days, Linux was designed to support multiple network cards in a single PC, there is no bug that would prevent this.

Identifying Proper Procedures, for Diagnosing, and Troubleshooting IDE Devices

9. ☑ **A.** During the boot process, your Linux computer will list the hardware that has been detected by the system. After the boot process, it is possible to view this information using the dmesg command. The hardware list can be quite extensive and take some time to read through. To go directly to the devices you want to see, you can use the **grep** switch with the dmesg command. To view the IDE drives installed, the correct syntax of the command is dmesg I grep hd.

   ☒ **B.** The syntax of the command is invalid. The **grep** switch needs to be used before listing the devices you are searching for. **C.** The command is invalid. **D.** The command dmesg I grep sd is used to scroll through the **dmesg** hardware list to find the SCSI drives currently installed.

10. ☑ **B.** After the POST process during the boot phase, the BIOS looks for instructions in the MBR and a device to boot from. This could be a floppy, CD-ROM, and the hard drive. If a bootable device is not found, you may receive the non-system disk error. You may receive this error, even when the operating system is installed on your system, which may mean your MBR or system files are corrupt. It may, however, be something as simple as a having a nonbootable floppy disk in the drive during bootup.

    ☒ **A.** IDE devices do not use ID assignments; SCSI devices use ID numbers. **C.** To boot the system, you would need to set a hard drive as a master on the primary controller. If the hard drive is not the master on the primary controller, you may get the non-system disk error. **D.** The Linux systems can successfully multiboot with a number of different operating systems. Unless the multiboot configuration is corrupt, it would not cause the problem.

Identifying Proper Procedures, for Diagnosing, and Troubleshooting SCSI Devices

11. ☑ **A, B, C.** Troubleshooting a SCSI bus requires attention to a number of details. Each SCSI bus requires a terminator at each end to prevent signal prevention. If there are problems on the SCSI bus, ensure that the termination is properly set. A SCSI device can typically support 8 devices for narrow SCSI devices and 16 for wide SCSI. If the number of devices exceeds the recommended number, the SCSI bus could fail. To differentiate between SCSI devices on the bus, each has to have a unique SCSI ID. If there are duplicate IDs, the devices could fail to work properly.

    ☒ **D.** IDE devices are distinguished from each other on an IDE bus using a master and slave setting. SCSI devices do not use the master/slave jumper configuration.

12. ☑ **A.** To view the SCSI devices and their associated characteristics, the cat /proc/scsi/scsi command can be used.

☒ **B.** cat /proc/sda is not a valid command; sda is associated with the first SCSI hard drive installed in the system and can be used in the command dmesg I grep sda. **C.** You would not see the listed SCSI devices by using the command cat /proc/sdb; sdb is the Linux reference for the second SCSI hard disk in the system. **D.** cat /proc/sd is not a valid Linux command.

13. ☑ **C.** If a SCSI device is not working after the installation, the first place to look is at the SCSI termination. The SCSI bus should only be terminated at each of the physical ends of the bus.

☒ **A.** As part of best practice, the devices must be confirmed that they are supported by Linux before they are installed, not after. **B.** While it may be necessary to contact the vendors Web site, the first step in troubleshooting requires to verify the most likely problems first. In this case it is the SCSI termination. **D.** Hardware compatibility should be verified before the device is installed.

Identifying the Proper Procedures for Identifying and Troubleshooting Peripheral Devices

14. ☑ **C.** Many Linux users recommend disabling Plug and Play on Linux systems to avoid potential conflicts. Disabling PnP is done in the system's BIOS and is usually on by default. If you are installing legacy ISA cards, it is often a good idea to disable Plug and Play.

☒ **A.** The isapnptools set is used to configure ISA cards and the resources they use; it cannot be used to disable Plug and Play. **B.** The CMOS provides the storage for the BIOS settings, so the changes to the PnP configuration are changed in the BIOS and saved to the CMOS. **D.** It is not necessary to modify the kernel to disable Plug and Play.

15. ☑ **A.** The isapnptools set is a utility in Linux that allows you to manually configure the resources used by ISA Plug and Play devices. If you wish, you can also use the pnpdump command, which displays all the resource configurations that the devices on your system support.

☒ **B.** cat /proc/ioports is used to view the I/O ports currently used in the system, but is not used to configure the ISA cards in the system. **C.** cat /proc/interrupts shows the IRQs that are being used and the devices using them. **D.** cat /proc/isa/devices is not a valid command.

16. ☑ **A, B, D.** While each of these problems can be explained by other means, they can be a result of virus activity as well. That may sound vague, but that is often the nature of chasing a virus. Over time, it gets easier to distinguish between hardware, software, and virus problems.

☒ **C.** A virus would not cause incompatible memory in the system.

17. ☑   **B.** To verify USB devices on your system, you can use the cat /proc/bus/usb/devices command, which will show the USB devices currently installed.
    ☒   **A.** cat /proc/usb is not a valid command. **C.** cat /proc/version is used to verify the kernel version you are currently using in your system and provides no information on USB devices. **D.** cat /proc/sysinfo is not a valid Linux command.

18. ☑   **D.** Linux supports numerous types of network cards from a variety of manufacturers. However, there are some that are not supported and some that do not work as well as others. Before buying any device, including network cards, it is important to visit your Linux distribution and verify that the card you are using is on the hardware compatibility list. Some users go one step further and post a question on a USENET group to see if any other people have had difficulty with the hardware in question. The important thing is that the new hardware is verified compatible with you system configuration.
    ☒   **A.** Although the cost of a network card may be a consideration for some companies, especially if buying many of them, it is far more important to verify that the hardware is on the distribution's hardware compatibility list and tested to work with your configuration. **B.** While installing a new network card, it is necessary to observe appropriate ESD practices. ESD practices are not a consideration when buying the card. **C.** Network cards support all protocols and are not a consideration when purchasing the card.

Identifying the Proper Procedures for Identifying and Troubleshooting Core System Hardware

19. ☑   **A.** To accommodate newly developed hardware, the BIOS on older systems may have to be upgraded. To do this, a program needs to be downloaded from the manufacturer's Web site. When run, it will update the information held on the BIOS chip. Care should be taken to follow the manufacturers procedures when updating the BIOS. If done incorrectly, the BIOS chip can be irreparably damaged.
    ☒   **B.** The CMOS holds the settings for the BIOS and does not need to be upgraded to accommodate new hardware. The BIOS and CMOS are often considered to be the same thing, but they are not and it is important to understand the difference between the two. **C.** To accommodate new hardware, it is not usually necessary to replace the entire BIOS chip. Flashing the BIOS chip is the preferred method. **D.** As mentioned, the CMOS holds the BIOS settings; therefore, replacing the CMOS chip would not help.

20. ☑ **A, C, D.** When newly installed memory is not recognized by the system, it could be result improperly seated memory, a damaged memory module and if the system does not support all of the memory installed. To correct the problem, start with the easiest answer first, check that the RAM is properly seated, replace the module with a known working one, and refer to the system board's documentation to determine the amount of memory the system can support.
☒ **B.** SIMMs are 72-pin modules used primarily on 486 and Pentium-class computer systems. SO-DIMMs are used in portable computer systems and therefore are not used in the same systems as SIMMs.

LAB ANSWER

1. On arrival at the site, question the user to gather more information about the error. Ask why the new monitor was the old one faulty.

2. Identify whether the users obtained any system errors before the problem and the steps, if any, they used to try to fix the problem on their own.

3. Check that the monitor has power going to it and that it turns on. If there is power, the light on the front of the monitor should turn on, and you will hear the monitor starting. If it does not have power, ensure that the electrical cord is plugged in both to the wall and the computer. If the cord is plugged in and there is no power, then the electrical cable may be faulty.

4. Once power has been confirmed, ensure that the monitor cable is connected to the computer at the back of the system. If it is connected and there is no picture, confirm that none of the pins were bent when the cable was installed.

5. If the monitor cable is attached securely, no pins are bent, and there is still no picture, you may need to try the monitor on a known working system. If the monitor works with the system, the problem most likely lies with the video card on the failed system and not the monitor. If the monitor does not work on the working system, then the monitor is likely faulty.

5

Planning the Implementation

I nstalling Linux is a bit like painting a house. The key is in the preparation. OK, it's nothing like painting a house, but we had to work in the "preparation is the key" line somehow! All joking aside, the implementation of a Linux server requires a range of information to be in place and a number of decisions to be made. Many of them have more to do with analysis of needs, determination of requirements based on those needs, and fulfilling those needs than specific technical information. However the importance of these steps should not be underestimated. The recognition of requirements, issues, and needs is just as important as knowing how to fulfill those needs on a technical level.

In today's corporate IT environment, it is not enough for individuals to have excellent technical skills. Just as important is an understanding of how technology enables the business process and how, in many cases, the availability of the server and the data it holds are inextricably linked to the fortunes of the company. Part of this understanding involves knowing why a certain solution is right for an application or, in other words, what solution to use in a certain scenario. Much of this chapter is devoted to that subject; it is about deciding why and for what purposes Linux should be used. After establishing what Linux can do, we look at what software needs to be installed to satisfy the customers' needs, and we also look at some of the more common uses for a Linux server. Next, we look at some of the choices you might consider when selecting software for your server, such as which distribution to choose and how the various methods of licensing might affect your choices.

We also look at how you can make sure you are using the appropriate version of the Linux kernel and where you can get software and other resources you may need for your installation. We conclude our discussion by looking at some of the broader topics that must be considered when installing a new server, such as technical support requirements and training.

Generally speaking, the coverage in this chapter is primarily focused on the objectives defined in Domain 1 of the Linux+ exam outline, though there are some exceptions that should be noted. Objective 1.2 deals with hardware compatibility verification, a topic that we have chosen to include in Chapter 6, which addresses preinstallation activities. The same goes for Objective 1.3, which covers the selection of services prior to installation, and Objective 1.4, which discusses actual disk partitioning considerations.

We'll begin our discussion of planning the implementation by looking at some of the common roles in which a Linux system can be employed.

CERTIFICATION OBJECTIVE 5.01

Identifying the Purpose of the Linux System Based on Predetermined Requirements

The first question that must be asked and answered when planning the Linux implementation is what the purpose of the server will be. The versatility of Linux means that it can be used in a variety of roles, including as a desktop system, mail server, database server, Web server, and so on. Of these roles, some are more popular than others. In general, customers are likely to have some knowledge of what they want from a server, but in many cases, those not familiar with Linux will be unaware of its capabilities. For example, we visited a customer recently who wanted to install a Linux system to act as a proxy server. They already had a Microsoft Windows NT system, which they used as a file and print server, but they were opting not to upgrade this server. When it was pointed out to the customer that the Linux system could offer all of the required functions (file server, print server, and proxy server), they were surprised. In this case, the perception was that the Linux server is only able to do "Internet-type stuff." In the end, the customer still opted for a separate Linux system as the proxy server, but is looking to upgrade the file and print server to a Linux system.

An understanding of what functions a Linux server can perform, and what is needed to fulfill that role, is essential. In this section, we'll discuss some of the more common Linux system roles and what some of their specific requirements are. Remember, as previously described, there is a good chance that a single physical server may offer a number of these services rather than just one.

File and Print Server

While perhaps not the foremost role that springs to mind, Linux makes an excellent file and print server platform in certain environments. Two of the more popular mechanisms available for these services are Network File System (NFS) and Samba.

Many companies choose to use an operating system such as Novell NetWare or Windows NT/2000 as a file and print server platform, and in some respects, these platforms are more suited to the task, with advanced file security capabilities and more powerful user management tools. That said, from a pure performance perspective, Linux is able to rival these platforms in even the most demanding environments.

File and print servers are likely to be relatively powerful servers. However, as with the other server types discussed here, the actual amount of power will depend on how many people are using the server's resources and for what tasks. Because file and print serving normally satisfies a core business requirement, it is highly likely that a file and print server will accommodate fault-tolerant strategies such as a redundant array of independent disks (RAID).

Mail Server

Whereas ten years ago, business communication relied on the phone and fax, today's e-world is firmly dependant on electronic mail. The basic way in which e-mail is handled by a server makes it a reasonably simple process, but the volume and increasing size of e-mail can make for a stiff workload on even the most powerful servers. Numerous mail software systems are available, the most popular being Sendmail, which is included with a number of the popular Linux distributions.

So important is e-mail as a function that some companies, such as SuSE, sell Linux-based solutions targeted directly at the e-mail server market. Even if your Linux server is not a dedicated server such as this, the chance that it will be running a mail program such as Sendmail is relatively high.

As with file and print servers, e-mail is normally a business-critical function, so servers providing e-mail services will often employ fault-tolerant measures. For a true indication of how important e-mail is to people, try turning the e-mail server off at 9:00 A.M. on a Monday morning. Just make sure to stand well back!

Database Server

Today's database systems are more than just a means of storing copious amounts of information; they are also the means by which that data can be managed, extracted, and secured. Almost every organization can justify using a database, whether it is a small system for storing business contacts or a worldwide booking system for an airline.

Linux's ability to host database applications has prompted some of the largest database software manufacturers in the world to release Linux-compatible versions of their products. The fact that companies like Oracle and IBM have backed Linux has had a twofold effect. First, people see the backing of big-name companies as validation of Linux as a platform, and second, the availability of actual products causes people to consider a Linux-based solution in cases where they may not have done so before.

Servers acting as database servers will typically have large hard disks and lots of memory, because a plentiful supply of both is needed to move around the large amounts of data required. In many cases, hardware or software fault-tolerance measures are used to increase reliability. In many cases, such as a hotel booking system or an e-commerce outfit, the availability of a database may be the core business requirement. In these instances, higher levels of fault tolerance are often considered, such as clustered servers or failover configurations, that can cope with a complete system failure.

DNS Server

Have you used a DNS server today? If you have been on the Internet, it is almost certain that you have. The Domain Name System (DNS) performs a very important role in that it translates host names, such as www.kernel.org, into IP addresses, such as 209.10.41.242. This process is necessary because of the human limitation of remembering lots of numbers, such as IP addresses (we have problems remembering our own postcodes). Imagine seeing an ad for a new Internet site that was giving away free Ferraris. All you need to do is log on to 24.77.144.17. It just doesn't have the same impact as www.afreecarforyou.com. And no, before you put this book down and head to the nearest Web browser, we made that site up.

DNS servers don't just resolve host names for Internet Web sites; they also resolve host names for other types of servers, including e-mail servers such as smtp.mail200.com. They can also translate IP addresses into host names through a process called *reverse lookup*.

on the **Job**

If you can ping a system by its IP address but not by its host name, there is most likely a problem with the DNS configuration, either at the server's end or on your workstation.

The DNS namespace is arranged in a hierarchy that prevents the need for a single server to hold information for all the hosts on the Internet. DNS servers are assigned to hold records for each host on a specific zone and are configured so that if they don't hold the information needed, they can ask another DNS server for the information. Figure 5-1 shows an example of the name resolution process and the DNS namespace structure.

FIGURE 5-1

DNS namespace
and host name
resolution

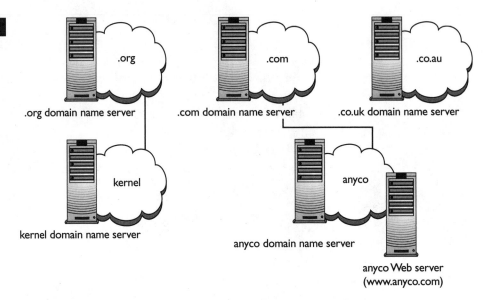

Whether a company needs a DNS server will depend on a number of factors, such as whether there are sufficient servers internally to warrant a DNS server and the relationship you have with your Internet service provider. In a lot of cases, organizations prefer to use the DNS, or name server, facilities of the ISP rather than use a machine of their own.

Desktop System

As we have discussed already in this book, Linux's emergence as a desktop operating system has gained pace over recent years to the point where some organizations are looking to Linux as a replacement for existing desktop operating systems. That said, software availability is still the thorn in the side of Linux as a desktop operating system, though products such as StarOffice from Sun Microsystems and WordPerfect from Corel are going a long way toward addressing this issue. In addition, there are many specialized applications, particularly academic and scientific applications, designed to run on Linux.

The developments and enhancements in installation programs and graphical tools have also helped Linux as a desktop OS. Recognizing the potential market for this, many Linux distributors offer "workstation" or "desktop" versions of their products.

Many of the popular Linux distributions have a Workstation installation option that includes the functionality needed for the system to operate as a desktop, and omits some of the more server-based options and utilities.

One of the attractions of using Linux as a desktop system is the relatively modest hardware requirements in comparison to other workstation operating systems. Also, licensing costs can be significantly reduced, a big factor in organizations that have hundreds or even thousands of systems.

Web Server

One of the most popular uses for a Linux server is as a Web server; that is, a server that provides Web pages to clients. The process of a Web server is a relatively simple one. Clients request Web pages using a specific protocol, most likely the Hypertext Transfer Protocol (HTTP). The server responds to the request by supplying files that contain the text, related graphics, and any programs that are embedded within the page. The files supplied by the Web server are stored in directories on the server or, if necessary, can be pulled from another server. Figure 5-2 shows the basic function of a Web server system.

While the basic process of Web serving is straightforward, the increasing complexity of Web pages and the high-resolution graphics, animation, and other

Basic function of
a Web server

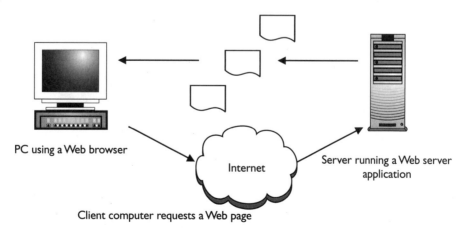

Server returns Web page and associated
graphics to client

PC using a Web browser

Internet

Server running a Web server
application

Client computer requests a Web page

SCENARIO & SOLUTION	
You want users to access your internal Web server by its host name rather than its IP address.	Install a DNS server.
Users want to send and receive e-mail.	Install a Linux server and configure mail services.
A user wants Linux as a desktop operating system.	Install a Linux distribution in a workstation configuration, or use a distribution specifically geared toward this use.

Web page additions mean that the Web serving process often places high demands on the underlying system hardware. In addition, the need to have Web sites available on a constant basis, particularly for outfits such as commercial organizations, means that Linux servers acting as Web servers are often configured with fault-tolerant hardware or software solutions. Linux is particularly suited for this, because it includes a variety of programming and scripting tools that are well suited for Web application development.

CERTIFICATION OBJECTIVE 5.02

Comparing and Contrasting How Major Licensing Schemes Work

Now that we have looked at some of the things that Linux is capable of, we will soon look at how you actually obtain the applications that make these services possible. But before we do, a discussion of some of the more common licensing schemes is in order.

As discussed in Chapter 1, Linux is free. The software that you may be using on it may not be, however. To work effectively with Linux, an understanding of how different licensing methods work and what you are, and are not, allowed to do with them is needed.

GNU/GPL

The GNU licensing system is the most generous concept possible, because the software and/or source code for a product can be obtained, manipulated, improved, or changed as you wish. No permission is required to do any of these things, but you must maintain the free principle. A fee may be charged for the distribution of the software, but the software itself and the source code must be available for no charge. A further condition of the GNU licensing is that any modifications or improvements to the software cannot change the conditions of the license. In other words, if you change a piece of software that was created and licensed under a GNU license agreement, you can't place any new restrictions on the software.

on the **Job** *If the feeling grabs you, check out the full GNU/GPL license at http://www.gnu.org/copyleft/gpl.html.*

Shareware

Software distributed under a shareware agreement can be used free of charge for a preset time period, which is normally 30 or 60 days, although there are no standards as to what the duration might be. After the trial period, users are asked either to register the software and pay the registration fee or discontinue use and remove the software from their computer. Because the honor system doesn't work too well, many developers and companies have elected to use *timeouts*, wherein if the product isn't registered after a certain period, it simply stops working.

Shareware is a popular approach because it gives users the opportunity to try before they buy. If the developer has enough confidence in the product, this approach works well because people are generally happy to pay the fee. If you do use shareware that doesn't have a timeout, register it and pay the fee when the time comes. If too many people don't pay the fees, the encouragement for the developer to continue releasing new software is removed, so new software is not released. Ultimately, this will mean that there will be less choice of different software applications.

Given the fact that much of the Linux software available is distributed free of charge, shareware is not as popular as it may be on other platforms.

Freeware

Software that is distributed without charge, and that can be used indefinitely without payment, is labeled *freeware*. Software that is truly freeware can be further distributed, but cannot normally be changed in any way, and no monies can be collected from the distribution. A company or developer may sometimes distribute freeware because they want to whet your appetite for the product before encouraging you to upgrade to a more feature-rich version for which you have to pay. Other developers take a slightly more aggressive approach in that they might make a version of one product available as freeware, but make subsequent versions of the product paid software. This is an effective way to build a following for a product, particularly if the newer version offers considerable enhancements over the older version. The key difference between freeware and open source software is that freeware does not usually make source code available.

Open Source

As its name suggests, the principle behind open source licensing is that anyone can have access to the software source code, and anyone can contribute to the development and improvement of the software. This is in contrast to freeware, in which the compiled software is available free of charge, but the source code isn't made available to developers.

Open source software development has many proponents, who cite the open approach as a means to create better software. Certainly, some of the most popular software products, particularly for the Linux platform, are the products of open source licensing. An excellent example is the Apache Web server, discussed later, which is the most popular Web server product in use today.

Open source software not only enables developers to understand better the workings of the software, it also allows them to implement special features and functions that may be needed.

Closed Source

The opposite of open source, *closed source* refers to code that is not available for developers to improve or enhance. Any commercial software application for which the source code is not available can be termed closed source. Closed source software may sometimes be referred to as *proprietary* software.

Artistic License

One of the less frequently used licensing methods is the artistic license. Software distributed under an artistic license allows individuals to modify or alter the software, but restrictions are placed on the use of the software, and the inclusion of the software within other packages. In an artistic license situation, the original copyright holder continues to own the license irrespective of what changes are made by developers. This allows the copyright holder to maintain a level of control over the software itself and the subsequent distribution of the software. Developers who subscribe to the artistic license are normally able to charge a realistic fee to cover duplication and distribution costs, but must not charge a fee for the software itself.

CERTIFICATION OBJECTIVE 5.03

Identifying the Function of Different Linux Services

On its own, a Linux server is an interesting thing, but after you have bored of the games and configured your X Window System to within an inch of its life, you might want to install a few services and, as the saying goes, see what this baby can do.

The truth is that this baby can do quite a lot. In fact, more than we can explain here, and certainly more than you need to know for your Linux+ exam. So, for the purposes of brevity, and so that we don't pollute your mind with nonessential facts, we'll take a look through some of the more popular Linux services that you may choose to run on your server. You may find yourself installing just one of these services, or you might install them all. Hey, it's a free country!

Apache

Given that the popularity of Linux has much to do with the explosive growth of the Internet, it comes as little surprise that one of the most popular uses for a Linux server is as a Web server. Of the available Web server products, Apache HTTP Server is by far the most popular Web server product, and is included with all major Linux distributions.

Research performed in July 2001 shows that Apache is streets ahead of its competitors in terms of market share. Over 58 percent of all Web server installations use Apache. Its nearest competitor, Microsoft Internet Information Server (IIS), is a relative straggler, with "only" 25 percent of the market share.

As described earlier in this chapter, the functions that a Web server performs are relatively simple, in that they make files available to users who request them using a protocol such as HTTP. However, behind this simple function, a number of other functions can be used, including detailed reporting and error logging, authentication so that password-protected Web pages can be configured, and virtual hosting, which allows a single Web server implementation to service a number of different Web sites. Apache does all of this and more.

Like many other Linux applications, configuration of Apache is performed through a series of text-based configuration files. Also, as with many other Linux services and applications, the range of possible configuration parameters is quite astounding, though to set up a basic configuration, only a fraction of the options is needed.

The popularity of Apache means that support, both free and pay for, is plentiful, as are support resources, documentation, and books. So popular is Apache that, as one seasoned system administrator puts it, "You would have to pay me to use anything else."

You can download the latest version of apache from http://www.apache.org.

ipchains and iptables

Another very popular use for Linux systems is that of firewalling. A firewall system helps protect computers on a network from attack from outside sources. A number of software applications are available for firewall purposes, but many Linux administrators choose to use ipchains or iptables because the functionality is built into the Linux kernel.

If your Linux kernel does not support ipchains or iptables, it will need to be recompiled to provide this support. ipchains has been available in all kernel versions since 2.1.

Both ipchains and iptables are packet-filtering systems, which manage the network traffic that passes through them. Depending on the configuration of the packet filter, data is read as it comes into the system and can then be blocked or forwarded. Figure 5-3 shows the basic function of a Linux firewall system and how it might fit into complete firewall solution.

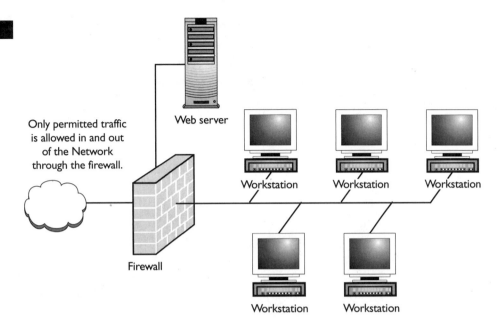

FIGURE 5-3

An example
Linux firewall
installation

Although the functions of ipchains and iptables are basically the same, there is one significant difference. ipchains is used with versions 2.1 and 2.2 of the Linux kernel, whereas iptables is used with some later revisions of 2.3, and 2.4.

As you would expect from a newer product, iptables has more functionality than ipchains, though both provide the basic features needed from a firewall system. These features include packet filtering (as previously mentioned) and address masquerading, which is also referred to as Network Address Translation (NAT). For an explanation of NAT, refer to Chapter 2.

Configuration of ipchains and iptables requires a good understanding of both the tools themselves and TCP/IP addressing. Many of the configuration files require address ranges to be entered, and entering the wrong range can have the complete opposite of the desired effect.

Samba

Unless you have spent the last 15 years on a desert island, you'll know that Microsoft Windows is by far the most popular operating system in use today. As well as versions designed for the desktop market, such as Windows 98, ME, and XP, Microsoft has also had considerable success with its server operating systems, Windows NT and Windows 2000. In many organizations, desktop PCs running Windows software connect to servers running Windows software.

Rather than trying to beat Microsoft, in 1992 Andrew Tridgell created Samba, a software package that allows Windows-based clients to connect to a Linux system and then use the resources of that Linux system as if it were a Windows server. From the user's perspective, once they have logged in to the server, they would have a hard time telling the difference between saving a file on a Windows NT Server, for example, or a Linux server.

Specifically, Samba offers the ability to map drives to a Linux server using the same mechanisms that would be used to store files on a Windows server. Printers that are set up on the Linux server running Samba are also available to Windows users. Linux servers running the Samba application can also participate in *browsing*, the mechanism by which Windows servers and workstations locate each other on the network.

Samba runs as two small programs on the server, and there is also a client program that needs to be loaded on client computers if needed. The client software is not needed on Windows systems, because they already have a client that can access resources on Samba servers.

Samba features highly on people's needs from a Linux system, so it is included with most distributions. If your distribution does not come with it, or you want to download and install the latest version, you can get it from http://samba.org. This site acts as a central portal for accessing the dozens of Samba mirror sites around the world.

BIND

As discussed earlier, a popular role for a Linux server is that of a DNS server. For a Linux server to perform name resolution, it must have an application loaded. By far the most popular of these DNS server applications is the BIND server. BIND stands for the Berkeley Internet Name Domain. The BIND application is an open source implementation that provides DNS server capabilities on a range of server platforms, not just Linux.

exam
ⓌatchWatch

If you can ping a server using the IP address but not the host name, you will need to check the configuration of the BIND server.

The BIND server runs as a daemon on the Linux server and includes tools that allow the functionality of the server to be tested. You can find out more information about BIND and download the latest version of BIND from http://www.isc.org/products/BIND.

Squid

The rather oddly named Squid proxy-caching product answers the needs of users who want to increase Internet performance and decrease the bandwidth used on Internet connections. It also allows Internet access to be controlled from a central location.

Squid is a proxy server system, which means that it sits on the network and processes requests for network users who want to access Internet sites. The Squid service takes the request and goes to the Internet to retrieve the Web page. When it brings back the data, the information is forwarded to the user and a copy is placed in the *cache*. Storing the data in the cache means that if anyone else wants the same information, it is retrieved from the cache rather than from the Internet. This is how Squid is able to improve performance, by serving requests locally, and reduce bandwidth use, by not having to go onto the Internet each time a request is placed.

To the clients, the entire process is transparent. They have no indication that they are retrieving information through a proxy server. It is worth mentioning, however, that Squid is not as powerful as some of the more commercial proxy server applications, and does not support certain services that users might need. The following are the Internet services supported by Squid:

- **Hypertext Transport Protocol (HTTP)**   Used to retrieve Web pages and associated files
- **File Transfer Protocol (FTP)**   Used to send and retrieve files to/from servers that support FTP
- **Secure Sockets Layer (SSL)**   Used for secure transactions
- **Gopher**   Used to search for Internet-based files and resources
- **Wide Area Information Server (WAIS)**   Used to search for documents on Internet-based indexes

Saving money and increasing performance are only half the story, however. Squid also accommodates the filtering of Web sites by allowing or denying access to sites based on the configuration. This is a useful feature if you don't want people to look at certain sites or groups of sites.

Squid uses the Internet Caching Protocol (ICP), which allows groups of Squid servers to be configured in an *array*. Servers within the array can ask each other for pages, rather than going to the Internet. In larger organizations, this further reduces the need to pull information from the Internet.

How much of a benefit a Squid server will be depends on the volume of Web browsing being performed and the likelihood that more than one person will want to see the same information as someone else. In certain environments, such as academic ones, the benefits may be huge, because an entire classroom will be able to retrieve a graphics-heavy Web page from cache after the teacher has accessed it once. In a smaller environment where just a few users access disparate Web pages, the performance benefits will be harder to realize, though the ability to filter sites may still be useful. You can find out more information on Squid and download the latest version from http://www.squid-cache.org.

DHCP

If you recall from Chapter 2, the task of IP addressing can be a complex one, particularly on networks that have multiple segments and lots of systems. A solution to this often time-consuming task is to use the Dynamic Host Configuration Protocol (DHCP) service, one that Linux happily hosts.

A system that hosts DHCP services can automatically issue IP addresses and other pieces of TCP/IP-related addressing information to clients from a predefined pool of addresses known as a *scope*. Scopes can be defined for more than one network, and a single DHCP server can issue addresses to clients that are on a different network from it, thanks to a special function that routers perform when they see a DHCP packet on the network. DHCP addresses are given to clients, normally for a limited amount of time called a *lease*, though this lease can be renewed at various points during the lease period if both the server and client agree to it.

The basic process of a client obtaining an IP address is broken down into four phases. When a system that is DHCP-enabled boots up, it broadcasts a message to discover what DHCP servers are available on the network. On hearing the message, the DHCP server sends out an offer, which includes the IP address, the lease information, and any other configuration information included in the offer. If more than one DHCP server responds to the request, the client selects which offer to choose and sends a request back to the DHCP server, notifying them of the selection. If the server is

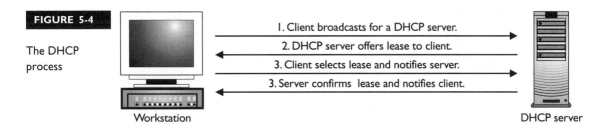

FIGURE 5-4

The DHCP
process

1. Client broadcasts for a DHCP server.
2. DHCP server offers lease to client.
3. Client selects lease and notifies server.
3. Server confirms lease and notifies client.

Workstation   DHCP server

still okay with the arrangement, an acknowledgment is sent back to the client and it begins to use that IP address. You can see how this process works in Figure 5-4.

This automatic assignment process means two things. First, after a system is configured to use DHCP, no further configuration of the system is needed. If the entire IP addressing scheme is changed, only the server needs to be reconfigured, not the DHCP clients. The other benefit, as mentioned earlier, is that duplicate DHCP addresses are a thing of the past, as the human factor is removed from IP address configuration.

DHCP is a popular service in almost any environment where TCP/IP is used, but is particularly useful in situations where a large number of IP addresses are being used, such as in a large corporation, and by ISPs who may need to grant addresses to clients as they dial into the ISP but who can then reuse that address for another client when the original connection is disconnected. DHCP, particularly in smaller environments, is a relatively low-overhead process, so it is unlikely that a server would be dedicated purely to this task, though it is possible in a situation such as an ISP.

DHCP services on Linux are provided by a single daemon called DHCPD. Configuration of the addresses and the other information that will be supplied by DHCPD is a simple process of editing a text file.

SCENARIO & SOLUTION

You need to provide security and network address translation capabilities.	Configure Linux to use ipchains or iptables, depending on the kernel version being used.
Windows clients want to store files on the Linux server and use its printing capabilities.	Install and configure Samba on the Linux server.
You need to improve Internet access times and restrict access to certain sites.	Install a proxy server application, such as Squid, and configure an exclusion list.

CERTIFICATION OBJECTIVE 5.04

Identifying Strengths and Weaknesses of Different Distributions and Their Packaging Solutions

As we discussed in Chapter 1, when we talk about Linux itself, we are referring to the Linux kernel. The kernel can be downloaded from a number of sites, many of which can be accessed through the Linux Kernel Archives site at http://www.kernel.org. This site can also tell you what the latest stable version of the kernel is.

However, as we also mentioned in Chapter 1, the kernel alone is just a component of a Linux system and does not provide many of the services and functions that are likely to be needed, which is why we have Linux distributions. Just to recap, Linux distributions are basically groups of Linux components (kernel, utilities, programs, code, tools, and so forth) combined into a convenient format. Distribution vendors also create their own utilities and, in some cases, packaging formats to simplify the addition and removal of applications.

Generally speaking, no one distribution can be said to be better than another, although some are more complete than others and some are easier to use than others. Also, some companies offer better levels of support for their distribution than others offer. Particularly, you may want to consider the following before deciding on a specific distribution:

- **Support**   When you pay for a Linux distribution, you are generally entitled to a certain level of free support. This may take the form of e-mail or telephone support or a more informal method, such as a dedicated newsgroup. There are also numerous companies who are willing to provide support for Linux on a paid basis. However, the more mainstream distributions are likely to be better catered for than some of the more niche distributions. Remember, no matter what distribution you choose, there is an abundance of free support sources for you to use, and in the future contribute to.

- **Packaging format**   One of the big factors that can influence the choice of distribution is the packaging method, which has an effect on how simple it is to add or remove packages. Packaging schemes allow files to be downloaded in a specific format so that they can be installed easily. Choosing a distribution that supports one of the more popular formats, such as the Red Hat Package

Manager (RPM) or the DEB package format, will make it easier to download and install new applications to your server. Although RPM and DEB were developed by Red Hat and Debian, respectively, many of the other distributions accommodate these formats, or formats of their own, so that applications can be added to their distributions easily, as well. Outside of the packaging formats already discussed, Linux distributions support archive files created with the Tape Archive Utility (tar), which are known as tarballs, so even if your choice of distribution doesn't support a particular package format, getting your software will not be a problem.

■ **Utilities**   Some distributions include certain utilities that others do not. An easy example of this is the partitioning utility Disk Druid, which is included with Red Hat but not with other distributions such as Mandrake or Debian, which have their own utilities.

■ **Documentation**   Buying a packaged product will almost certainly mean that you will get some documentation. How useful this documentation is depends on the distribution and your understanding of Linux. Given the availability of high-quality Linux books (like this one!), the inclusion of documentation may not be the biggest factor, but it may be a consideration.

■ **Designed application**   Some Linux distributions are aimed at a specific market or application. In some cases, using one of these purpose-designed distributions may be wise. Good examples of this strategy are SuSE Email Server, and the Linux Mandrake single-purpose firewall solution.

■ **Included applications**   Even though applications are not hard to find, the applications included with the distribution may be a factor in the choice of a distribution, particularly as some distributors choose to include specialized applications such as database or groupware products.

Based on these criteria, and any other you need to consider, you can download your chosen Linux distribution and install it. Then you can start to think about what additional applications you want to install.

Popular Linux Distributions

If you really want to evoke emotion in a Linux expert, simply start poking holes in his or her favorite Linux distribution, but stand well back when you do it, and let us

FROM THE CLASSROOM

Choosing a Distribution

A common question is "Which is the best operating system?" The question of "Which Linux distribution is best?" comes up just as often. Again, there is no simple answer to either question. Many factors affect the suitability of a distribution for a given situation. For example, using a Linux distribution that has no GUI included with it may prove very challenging to a new user. On the other hand, it could be seen as a way of speeding up the user's education of the command-line configuration capabilities. If that is the goal, then such a version may be appropriate. More likely, the availability, applications, support, and package format will be the major considerations. We have a favorite, but we are not telling!

—*Drew Bird, Linux+ Certified*

know because we want to watch. Seriously though, discussions of which Linux distribution is best can tend to get heated, as people have their favorites, and still others have opinions about why certain distributions are not as good as another.

In your capacity as a vendor-independent Linux professional, you would do well to steer clear of these discussions and instead form your own opinions as to how good, or bad, a specific distribution is. But what's the best way to do this? Well, there are no strict guidelines, but in many cases, it goes something like this. To start, you pick a mainstream distribution such as Red Hat or Caldera. These easy-to-install one-box solutions offer the most convenient way to get started in Linux, and so make a natural starting point. Support is plentiful and resources abound.

on the
job

It is common for people to refer to Linux distributions as "distros." For example, "Red Hat is one of the more popular distros." We'll stick with "distribution" in this book, but don't be surprised if you hear the phrase or see it in documentation or support material.

After you have developed an understanding of Linux and its capabilities, you start to try out a few of the less well-known distributions, like Kondara or Gentoo. Because you are now better able to determine what is, and isn't, a problem, you will be better able to judge what are the upsides and downsides of a specific distribution. What happens next, whether you go back to one of the more popular distributions or keep trying other versions, is, of course, up to you.

In many cases, a Linux server is installed for a specific task or purpose. In other cases, a single Linux system is expected to satisfy a range of requirements. Whether a single system can satisfy the needs placed upon it will depend on the hardware of the system and the products that are installed on it. It may be necessary to install more than one system, and nothing says that you have to run the same Linux distribution across all of your servers, though it does have administrative advantages in terms of maintenance and support.

In Chapter 1, we took a very brief look at some of the more popular distributions, but we must now look slightly deeper into each offering, and examine why you might, or might not, use it.

on the
ⓙob

Your preference for a given distribution really cannot be determined by reading about it. The best way to make a choice is to download some of the available distributions and give them a test drive. You'll be surprised by how quickly you will develop an opinion.

Red Hat

Although there are no concrete statistics, it is accepted by many that Red Hat Linux is the most widely used of the Linux distributions. As well as producing a completely open source operating system, as a company, Red Hat has made some significant contributions to the world of open source software and Linux. Most notable is the Red Hat Package Manager (RPM), which is now the most popular package management system across Linux distributions.

Another reason that Red Hat has been able to garner its large market share is that the structure and approach of its service, support, and training options are in line with those that you would expect from a leading network operating system supplier. This "big picture" approach serves to reassure customers, particularly those new to Linux, that there is tangibility to Red Hat and its offerings, which some of the other, smaller offerings lack.

Of all the distributions discussed here, support for Red Hat Linux—in both a formal and informal capacity—is the easiest to come by. The snowball effect is certainly in play here, and Red Hat now has a momentum that will make it difficult to catch, in terms of installed numbers at least, by the other distributors.

Red Hat Linux can be downloaded from the Red Hat Web site. In addition, you can purchase Red Hat Linux from Internet-based and traditional retailers.

Caldera OpenLinux

Viewed by some as the Linux distribution for beginners, to label it as such is unfair, particularly as it is just as capable and complete as any of the other Linux distributions discussed here. Caldera earned the "for novices" tag because of its simplified installation routing, called LIZARD, and its intuitive and easy-to-use admin utility, COAS. One feature of LIZARD that is particularly useful is a demonstration mode that allows you to step through a Linux installation without actually making any changes to the system or installing any products. Also included is an enhanced version of Webmin, the browser-based administration tool.

Caldera currently provides two versions of OpenLinux. The workstation version is targeted at those developing Linux-based applications, whereas the server version is targeted at the more traditional server market, and can be installed in a number of predetermined configurations including File and Print server, Web server, and Network server.

Like many of the other mainstream distributions discussed here, OpenLinux has a complete training and support structure in place that can significantly ease the transition to Linux.

SuSE

Like Red Hat, SuSE have one of the more polished corporate images of the Linux distributors and has built many relationships with large software vendors, resulting in a distribution that includes a large number of applications and services. The basic Linux product is available for Intel, PowerPC, and Sparc platforms and comes in a Personal or Professional version. The former is targeted at desktop users, and the latter is aimed at servers.

As well as providing the basic Linux distribution, SuSE has bundled together some leading applications to create more specific applications, such as a mail server, groupware server, and a database server, using products from companies such as Lotus and IBM.

SuSE Linux products are available from the SuSE Web site and from online and traditional software retailers.

Debian

Unlike the other distributions mentioned here, Debian is not a commercial organization, and is maintained and improved upon by a group of people who are committed to furthering Debian as a distribution. Development and maintenance of Debian is governed by a social contract.

Over time, Debian has attracted the tag of being difficult to install, causing other distributions, based on Debian, to be created but that address this issue. After installation, however, Debian comes into its own, its ace-in-the-hole being an up-to-date application installation format.

One of the most significant aspects of note for Debian is the packaging retrieval method, the latest implementation of which, apt-get, allows you to add or remove applications from the server with relative ease. The Debian packaging system (DEB) is widely regarded as the simplest to use, and when combined with the apt-get retrieval process, it makes for a very simple and effective package system.

Debian is available by download or can be purchased through a number of Debian-appointed CD distributors.

Slackware

One of the more popular Linux distributions and one of the oldest, Slackware has made a name for itself as a stable and functional Linux distribution. The aim of Slackware is to be "the most 'Unix-Like' Linux out there."

Unlike other distributions that have various different server and workstation variants, Slackware has one offering, though there are two special versions, ZipSlack and BigSlack, available. The first is a cut-down version of Slackware that only requires 100MB of disk space to install. The name is derived from it ability to be placed on a single 100MB Zip cartridge, thus enabling a complete Linux system to be carried around. ZipSlack uses a FAT file system to enable it to be used on systems without repartitioning the disk. BigSlack is similar in this respect but includes a much more comprehensive Linux system including preconfigured versions of the X Window System and GNOME.

Slackware has its own application packaging system and includes a menu-based utility called pkgtool. Application packages use the standard tar format, described later in this chapter, but are tracked and monitored by the system.

Slackware is available by download from www.slackware.com or can be purchased from retailers.

on the **job** *Slackware now comes with RPM, though the native Slack packages are tarballs.*

Mandrake

Mandrake is actually a Red Hat variant that has proved particularly popular in environments where the simplified installation program and comprehensive help capabilities are most appreciated.

The Linux Mandrake product range includes basic products that provide the basic Linux operating system, applications and add-ons, as well as solutions targeted directly at specific uses such as a corporate server and a firewall solution.

Mandrake comes replete with a range of applications and other software that makes setting up a server and configuring it simple, including a range of tutorials and demos. Use of the Red Hat Package format also makes downloading and installing new applications simple.

For more information on Linux Mandrake, visit http://www.mandrake.com.

Packaging Formats

Although the downloading of applications, as previously described, is not complex, it can get complicated, particularly if things do not go as planned. For this reason, and in an effort to bring Linux to the masses, package formats have been created to simplify the installation of an application.

on the **job** *A utility called alien allows packages to be converted from one format to another. Some distributions include the alien utility.*

Applications that are created in a packaging format can be used with an automated package manager that allows the application to be installed or removed with just a few commands. In some cases, the package manager will attempt to ensure that any additional applications needed to run the application being installed are available, although how effective this detection process is varies. This reliance by an application on another module is a condition known as a *dependency*. Of the packaging formats available today, by far the most popular is the Red Hat Package Manager (RPM). RPM comes in both command-line and graphical-based versions and is used with other popular distributions, including Caldera and SuSE. Another popular format is the DEB package format that is used with the Debian distribution of Linux and its derivatives. In most cases, the type of package can be identified by the file extension used for the package. The commonly used extensions are listed in Table 5-1.

Each packaging format has its supporters and detractors, but the general feeling is that the DEB format is simpler to use because it removes the need to make decisions

TABLE 5-1	Package Format	File Extension
Package Manager File Extensions	Red Hat Package Manager	.rpm
	Debian	.deb
	Slackware	.tgz
	Stampede	.slp

about the installation process. The DEB utility, apt-get, will even locate the appropriate package for you and take care of the downloading. While the packaging format does not necessarily make or break a distribution, in some cases, it can be a deciding factor with regard to which Linux distribution to choose.

CERTIFICATION OBJECTIVE 5.05

Describing the Functions, Features, and Benefits of a Linux System

In the objectives, CompTIA asks us to be able to "Describe the functions, features, and benefits of a Linux solution as compared with other operating systems." Now, given that this is a Linux+ book, it might seem odd that we would give any air time to other operating systems, but to draw comparisons, it is necessary.

on the *Job*

The verve with which some Linux techies protect "their" OS can be frightening. While we are all in favor of a bit of partisanship, proclaiming that Linux is the best operating system for every situation would be a hard-to-justify claim indeed. As a technical professional, your role is to make the best recommendation possible for the customer, whether or not that solution is a Linux system. Convincing a customer to use Linux when another OS would be more suited to the task might seem like a strike at the heart of the paid software industry, but the customer will become disillusioned with Linux (not to mention you) if they face a continual battle of trying to shoehorn a Linux system to fit where another OS could have done the job better. No matter what your technical preference is, the customer's needs and requirements come first. Remember: this is the mark of a true technical professional.

The Operating System Market Today

For the past few years, Linux has seen its market share increase to the point where it can now be considered one of the major players in the operating system market. Some of its strengths, or weakness, depending on your point of view, come from the distributed nature in which Linux is developed, supported, and sold (in both the actual and metaphorical sense). To clarify what is meant by this, consider one of the other mainstream operating systems, such as Windows 2000/XP. One company sells it, and while that company (a small concern based in Washington State) (oh no, here come the lawyers!) produces updated versions of the product, it is still within the control of a single entity and so moved forward by that entity. There is a single focus for marketing drive, product development, and support. In the eyes of many corporate users, this single focus adds up to accountability and stability, which are two of the reasons that people buy things. It could be said that the Linux community offers the same single-entity format, but the community is not formalized (nor does it want to be), and while there are many entities within the Linux community, it is still a more-devolved structure than any other of the mainstream operating systems. That's not to say that the single entity model is better, or worse, just that organizations and individuals have become comfortable with purchasing software from these single entities. The reasons? Well that's different things to different people.

People buy products from Microsoft for reasons which range from "they are good" to "well everyone else is using it" to "I know I can get support." Another factor contributing to the success of Microsoft products is that many manufacturers ship systems with Microsoft products already installed. Whatever the reasons, the fact that Microsoft sells so many products annoys many in the Linux community, who see Microsoft products, particularly the Windows range of products, as inferior.

Irrespective of how you perceive OSs from vendors like Microsoft and Novell, there are certain instances where they are more suited to an application than Linux. We challenge anyone to claim that it is as easy to administer 20,000 user accounts with the built-in tools available on Linux as with the tools included with Novell NetWare. Likewise, some of the features of Windows 2000 make the same task on Linux seem like reversing a large truck into a small-car space. You can do it, but would you want to? Of course, some people will, and that, ultimately, is the point. The suitability of a network operating system for a given task has a lot to do with personal opinion, sometimes in denial of the actual facts. This is not a good state to be in.

There are also environments that, while they might benefit from a Linux system, simply don't have the knowledge base or capabilities to support it. Unless considerations are included for training, implementation support, and maintenance, such environments may not actually benefit from using Linux at all.

exam
ⓦatch
The Linux+ test does not require that you have a knowledge of other popular operating systems, but you must be able to determine Linux's suitability for a given task.

Before we take a look at Linux's competitors, it is perhaps worth mentioning that the likelihood that you will be working in an environment that has more than one of these operating systems is high, and likely to increase over time. As companies discover that their needs can be served better by using the most appropriate OS for the task, the use of multiple OSs will become commonplace. Even if you choose to stick completely with Linux, an appreciation of what other OSs are available and what their respective capabilities are is important.

A Brief Operating System Comparison

To draw this brief "which operating system should be used" discussion to a logical conclusion, a comparison of the mainstream OSs is perhaps in order. We'll start with Linux!

FROM THE CLASSROOM

What's the Best NOS?

Many people ask "What is the best operating system?" There really is no simple answer. A better question would be "What is the best operating system for a certain task," but even then, the answer is not an easy one. As OS manufacturers include more and more features, functionality, and applications in their offerings, the capabilities of each OS become very similar. Perhaps the best example of this is Novell NetWare. Generally accepted as the best file and print server platform, Novell has, for the past few versions, included Web server functionality and a range of other features. Does that now make it the ultimate platform for those wanting file, print, and Web services? Perhaps, but all the other mainstream OSs also offer file, print, and Web server services. There are so many other factors involved, as well. If operating system A has a better Web server platform than B, but A needs a much higher level of technical knowledge, which is the best for a customer that has little technical skill in house? Like we said, there really is no simple answer.

—Drew Bird, Linux+ Certified

Linux Linux has carved itself a place in the corporate server room through its ability to provide numerous services at a fraction of the cost associated with other commercially available OSs. Although Linux is capable of performing almost every common server role, it is as a server that supplies Internet- and network-related services that it has found its niche. Many large ISPs use Linux servers as Web servers, proxy servers, and firewall servers. The increasingly simple installation and management utilities have meant that it is also being used by an ever-growing number of small businesses whose limited budgets limit the use of more expensive and hardware-demanding application software. That said, big businesses and larger organizations have been equally, if not more so, keen to adopt Linux. In these environments, where technical skills may be more varied and available, and the numbers of servers far greater, the savings and capabilities of Linux provide huge benefits.

Much of Linux's performance strength is placed on its ability to be configured to provide only those services that are needed. If the server does not need to offer a specific service, the service can be stopped so that it does not occupy valuable system resources. In some cases, the kernel can be recompiled so that the overall size, and so the associated system resources, can be reduced. This advantage is making Linux the OS of choice in everything from gas pumps to PDAs to pizza boxes. Think we are joking? Check out this link at http://www.kyzo.com.

The ability of Linux to be pared down to the bare minimum does not mean it is lacking in any features, however. Linux servers are often called into play as database servers using any one of the powerful commercial database products or as a platform for operating e-commerce applications. It is equally adept at being a firewall server, DHCP server, proxy server, or a Web server. Thanks to the configurable kernel, Linux is able to perform the chosen task without being held back or bogged down by features and functions that are not required.

Administration of Linux is performed through a wide variety of command-line, menu-based, and GUI utilities. Some critics of Linux claim that it is difficult to configure, but in truth, Linux is no more difficult to administer than any other NOS, if you know how to do it. Even so, the relatively recent acceptance of Linux as a mainstream OS has meant that more people are familiar with OSs such as Windows NT, Windows 2000, and Novell NetWare. This level of familiarity has, to some extent, hampered the progress of Linux.

Linux is a portable OS, meaning that it can be run on a wide range of different hardware platforms, including PC, PowerPC, Sparc, and a variety of platforms based on the Motorola 68000 range of processors, such as Amiga's processors and Atari.

A strong indicator of the increasing popularity of Linux is that many of the larger hardware manufacturers, such as IBM and Dell, will now supply systems with Linux preloaded.

Unix   Although Linux is a "Unix-like" operating system, we thought we would give Unix its own heading because it is an OS in its own right. As you might expect, much of the information is the same for Linux and Unix, so we have elected to provide only the briefest of overviews here, especially since an understanding of Unix is not required for the Linux+ test.

To a great extent, Unix is the domain of big business, government departments, and academic institutions. Much of this is historic. Unix has been with us since 1969, a time when the need for a powerful OS to run on a variety of hardware was present, but few options were available.

Unix is a fully featured multiuser OS that has been ported to various platforms and is available in both free and paid-for versions. Unlike Linux, most versions of Unix are not distributed under an open source agreement.

Novell NetWare   Traditionally seen as the file and print server king, Novell NetWare has made significant advances into other services, such as a Web and FTP server. The NetWare of today is no longer seen as purely a file and print platform, but as a full-service Internet platform as well.

NetWare features strongly in larger companies and governmental installation, though it has lost a great deal of ground in recent years to other OSs such as Windows NT/2000 and Linux. Even so, NetWare is still a prominent feature of the corporate IT landscape.

One of NetWare's greatest strengths is Novell Directory Services (NDS), or to give it its up-to-date name, eDirectory. eDirectory is a standards-based directory service system that provides user and network resource management capabilities. Information stored in the directory can be distributed across multiple servers and can also be duplicated to foster availability and fault tolerance. Although Novell initially designed NDS for use with NetWare servers, it is now marketed as a separate product, and versions are available for Linux, certain versions of Unix, and Windows NT/2000 as well. Understandably, Novell is very keen to push eDirectory as *the* cross-platform management tool, and while adoption is still at relatively low levels, Novell is making inroads into larger organizations.

Although recent versions of NetWare (perhaps reluctantly) have provided a GUI-based interface for server administration (which is a Java-based implementation of the X Window System), much of the server administration is performed from the command line or through menu-based utilities at a connected workstation.

NetWare includes many of the functions that are provided by mainstream Linux distributions, including file and print services, Web server and FTP applications, and DHCP and DNS functionality. Other facilities, such as proxy server and firewall capability, are available through add-on products. Unlike Linux, the OS kernel includes all the system capabilities and cannot be recompiled. NetWare has higher minimum hardware requirements than Linux but tends to need less in practical applications than Windows 2000.

From a networking perspective, NetWare supports TCP/IP and IPX. Novell actually invented IPX, and for many years set it as the default protocol for NetWare servers. Using TCP/IP required additional configuration and often additional products to be installed. Since version 5.*x*, Novell has configured TCP/IP as the default protocol.

Windows 2000/XP   Microsoft's NOS offerings are currently the best selling of those listed here. There are many reasons for this, and they are not just due to the Microsoft marketing machine.

By using the same interface as its desktop OS offerings, Microsoft has made a systems administrator of everyone, from the guy in accounts who has his MCSE to the seasoned tech who has been supporting it since the days of LAN Manager. The familiarity of the interface makes Windows server products simple to use and administer, and Microsoft includes almost every conceivable system management and monitoring tool in the server software, although many of the applications offer only the basic levels of functionality. Windows 2000 offers a complete set of network services, including DHCP and DNS services, various network management capabilities, and a thin client server product called Terminal Services.

But while Windows 2000/XP has its admirers, it also has its detractors. Some people point to the fact that the graphics-heavy OSs place too many demands on the underlying hardware, and the closed source software approach causes people to speculate as to just how many bugs are present and how secure Windows really is.

In Windows 2000, the introduction of a standards-based directory system called Active Directory presented welcome additions to the user management capabilities of Windows 2000. Like eDirectory, Active Directory is designed to be a standards-based directory services system that allows the management of users and other network objects. Unlike eDirectory, Active Directory is currently available only for Windows server platforms.

FROM THE CLASSROOM

Directory Services

Its difficult to have a discussion of modern OSs without the subject of directory services coming up, and reasonably so. Directory services systems are designed to allow the storage and management of network objects within a single database. The database can be stored on a single system or can be distributed across multiple systems as needed. The latter is the drive behind directory services systems generally, and here's why. Imagine you have four servers and one user that needs access to all four. In a server-centric user account system, the user account would have to be created four times, once on each server. In a directory services environment, the user account is created just once in the directory services database, and the database is made available to all four servers. It might be that all four servers actually get a copy of the database, or that they simply know how to access it. Either way, the timesaving in resource management can be incredible. Imagine if there were 100 users and 50 servers and the accounts had to be created individually! Although user accounts are an easy example, directory services systems can be used to store a range of information, such as printers, groups, server configurations, and so on. As well as reducing the administration overhead, directory services can also provide fault-tolerance advantages, by creating duplicate copies of the database so that one is available if another should become corrupt or unavailable.

—*Mike Harwood, Linux+ Certified*

CERTIFICATION OBJECTIVE 5.06

Identifying How the Linux Kernel Version Numbering Works

The first full release version of Linux, 1.0, was released in 1994. Since then, many updates have been made, and various new versions released. In addition, as releases have been made, bugs (errors in operations) have been corrected using software updates called *patches*. To help you determine what version of the kernel you are using, the kernel numbering is formatted so that you can tell what the major and minor version of the kernel is, and what level of bug fixing or patching has occurred.

The Linux version numbering works in an *a.b.c* format. At the time of writing, the latest version of Linux is 2.4.7. The 2 represents the major kernel version, the 4 represents the minor version number, and the 7 represents the level of patching in place. The minor version number is further used to indicate whether the kernel version is stable, represented by an even number, or in development, represented by an odd number. Some of the warnings about not using the development version in a live environment make it sound like any system using it will come crashing down around your ears, which may not be the case. The development tag is more an indication that the version has not been developed completely or tested under all circumstances. When a new version is being developed, the existing version is placed into a feature freeze, and enhancement work is targeted at the new version. Once work on the new version is complete, it is assigned the next even identifier, and the whole process starts again.

exam
Watch

An understanding of the Linux version numbering is essential for the exam. You may not be asked direct questions about the suitability for a specific version, but you may be asked to identify why a version would not be used, such as a development version.

So, the bottom line is that for a production server, you should only use a Linux kernel version that has an even second number, such as 2.2.2 or 2.4.1. Nothing is stopping you from downloading and installing a development version (one with an odd number as a second digit), but you need to be aware of the fact that it may not operate quite as expected. You should certainly never consider using a development version of the kernel in a live environment.

on the
Job

Some of the larger distribution vendors have a version-numbering game going, but remember that between distributions, a higher version number does not mean a more up-to-date product. Version 2.1 from one vendor may be newer than 6.0 from another. There are no rules and regulations about distribution numbering, and the distribution version numbering is unrelated to the Linux kernel version numbering.

One other important point about version numbering is that companies like Red Hat release products that have a more conventional numbering system, such as 7.0 or 7.1. These numbers are reflective of the version of the distribution that is in place, not of the Linux kernel version that is included with the package.

EXERCISE 5.1

Downloading the Latest Linux Kernel

1. Using a Web browser, go to www.kernel.org.
2. Click the link next to the 'Protocol HTTP field'.
3. Click the link next to the Linux Repository, including kernel source field.
4. On the following screens, click Kernel, then v2.4/, then linux-2.4.6.tar.gz, or the latest stable version number.
5. In the dialog box that appears, click to save the file to your local hard disk.

SCENARIO & SOLUTION

You need to find the latest stable version of the Linux kernel.	Visit one of the Linux kernel FTP mirror sites and download the latest version of the kernel that has an even number of the minor revision.
You want to get and install a Linux distribution.	Download one of the distributions available on the Internet, buy a distribution by mail order, or buy a boxed product from your local computer store.
You are not sure that certain services you need are included in your chosen Linux distribution.	Visit the Web site of the distributor and check what is, and is not, included. Post a message to Internet newsgroups for advice.

CERTIFICATION OBJECTIVE 5.07

Identifying Where to Obtain Software and Resources

With many of your planning choices now made, the next step is to obtain the software you need for the installation. Depending on what your requirements are, this may be a simple one-step process or it may require a little digging.

If the Linux distribution you choose does not have an application you need, or if you want to download the latest version of an application, you will need to get hold of it. If you are familiar with downloading software for other platforms, such as Windows, the process of downloading might take a little adjustment.

Applications for Linux systems are made available in a number of formats. Whereas for a Windows system you simply run an executable and away you go, some Linux applications are distributed as source code, others are distributed as precompiled binaries, and still others are packaged together to make downloading and installing easier. For the Linux+ exam, you'll need to understand what the various types of download formats are. You will also be expected to know the basic instructions for downloading and installing applications, but we leave that to the appropriate chapter later in the book.

Source Code

Of all the options available, downloading the source code for an application is probably the most complicated approach. Source code is the raw program data that must be compiled before it can be used, a process that can bring with it issues that, unless you are familiar with the compilation process, may be hard to get past. Unless the software you want is only available in source code, you should try to use one of the other methods. Getting help with compilation problems is often easy. Understanding what to do with the help is often not easy.

exam
ⓦatch

To simplify the process of compiling source code, a makefile script is often included with the download. The makefile is an executable script that simplifies the process of compiling the source code.

Binaries

A binary is an already-compiled version of the program. Binaries are easier to use than source files because they are designed to be used with certain versions of Linux and in certain configurations. Therein lies perhaps the biggest disadvantages of binaries. Because they are designed to work on a given platform, trying to install them on another platform will almost certainly bring with it problems. If a binary of an application is not available for your chosen platform, you may need to download the source and go through the compilation process.

tar

Files that you download, be they binaries or source code, are often grouped into one file called a tar archive. tar, which is short for Tape Archive Utility, allows multiple files to be combined into a single file, making it easier to download. tar is able to combine files in such a way that, when it is expanded again, the original directory structure is preserved. This is useful for situations where one file expects to see another file, such as a configuration file, in the same location each time it runs.

On its own, tar does not perform any compression, the result of which is that when a group of files are "tar'd," a file that's the combined size of all the files within it is produced. If you want to reduce the size of the file produced by tar, you can use the -z switch with the command, which results in a compressed archive being produced. Files that have been packed using the tar utility have a .tar extension; for example, utility_1.1.tar. If the file has been compressed, it will normally carry the .tar.gz or the .tgz extension; for example *utility_1.1.tar.gz.*

on the *Other compression utilities are available, such as pkzip and bzip2, but gzip is* **job** *still the most popular.*

As we mentioned briefly earlier, tar files are often referred to as *tarballs.* To create a tarball, you first create the tar file using the tar utility and then compress them using the gzip utility. By naming the resulting file as a .tar.gz or a .tgz file, you will have created a tarball.

Because tar is available across all Linux systems and is not a distribution-dependant packaging method such as RPM or DEB, discussed next, some utilities or applications are available only as tar archives, and an understanding of tar and its use is essential. Specific information on tar is included in Chapter 9.

Finding Applications

In many cases, you will be able to determine the location of an application simply by searching for it on the Internet, though some ways exist to shortcut this process, such as visiting a site that provides links to application libraries.

Many of the Linux distribution organizations maintain databases and archives of applications, and a variety of other sites also provide downloads for Linux.

on the
job

When downloading and installing applications, be careful where you get them from. Where possible, only download software from a trusted source, such as your chosen Linux distribution Web site.

CERTIFICATION OBJECTIVE 5.08

Determining Customer Resources for a Solution

One of the less technical but important considerations is that of evaluating a customer's resources to see if the Linux implementation can be supported. "Support" in this context refers to things such as whether enough technically capable staff are available to support the newly installed Linux system and whether those staff need to be trained to support the solution. In almost all cases, this training will have costs associated with it that will add to the cost of the implementation.

These considerations are important, particularly because they can negate any costs savings that might be gained by using free software. Installing the first Linux system into an environment that has no other Linux systems installed will have implications that may not be fully understood by the customer. For example, the customer may not be aware that Linux has different support requirements than other OSs that they may be using. There may also be issues with applications that are currently in use or pieces of specific hardware, though the latter is likely to be less of an issue nowadays than in the past.

Whatever the issues, the key thing is communicating them to the customer and ensuring they understand the issues that they may face as they start to use Linux.

CERTIFICATION SUMMARY

Before installing Linux, or any other OS for that matter, certain factors must be considered, such as what the purpose of the server is to be, and what, if any, special hardware or software considerations must be made for this. These considerations will include what software components must be loaded to fulfill these requirements.

When installing these software packages and selecting which services to load, the principles of licensing must be fully understood, as must the function and purpose of each service. In particular, a basic understanding of the major different Linux services is necessary.

Even though all Linux distributions are based around the same kernel, they differ in terms of what is included with them, what utilities are available, and what level of support is included. A particular consideration should be that of packing methods, which play an important role in the ease with which applications can be added to or removed from the system.

Once a distribution has been selected, the suitability of the distribution must be determined, including the Linux kernel version included. To do this, an understanding of Linux kernel numbering is necessary. Any knowledge of where distributions can be obtained is useful, as is an understanding of what resources are available for that distribution.

TWO-MINUTE DRILL

Here are some key points from this chapter.

Identifying the Purpose of a Linux Machine Based on Predetermined Customer Requirements

Linux is a versatile operating system that can fulfill many roles. Some of the more popular roles are the following:

❏ **Database server**   A server that is used to store and manage large amounts of data.

❏ **Mail server**   A server that provides e-mail facilities to users.

❏ **Web server**   A system that provides Web page content to users over the Internet or an intranet

❏ **Desktop system**   Installed when Linux is to be used as a workstation

❏ **Appliance**   Used when a system is designed to fulfill a specific singular purpose

Comparing and Contrasting How Major Linux Licensing Schemes Work

❏ Software distributed under the GNU/GPL license can be modified and distributed freely. Source code for the software must be made available so that others can further develop the software.

❏ Shareware can typically be used for a trial period before a royalty fee must be paid.

❏ The phrases "open source" and "closed source" refer to whether or not the source code for a given piece of software is available to the public.

❏ Freeware is software that can be used free of charge for an indefinite period.

Identifying the Functions of Different Linux Services

Some of the more popular Linux applications include the following:

❏ **Apache**   This Web server product allows a Linux server to act as a host for Web pages.

❑ **Squid**   A caching proxy server that improves performance by making local copies of frequently accessed Web pages. Squid can also be used to restrict access to Web pages.

❑ **Samba**   Allows Windows clients to use a Linux server to store files and perform printing tasks. Samba also allows the Linux server to participate in browsing activities.

❑ **ipchains**   A service that allows a Linux server to be configured as a basic firewall system and to perform Network Address Translation duties. ipchains has been replaced by iptables in kernel versions 2.4 and above.

❑ **Sendmail**   A service that allows a Linux server to act as a Message Transfer Agent and route SMTP-based messages. Sendmail provides the basic functionality required to use e-mail services.

❑ **BIND**   The Berkley Internet Naming Daemon is an implementation of the Domain Name System service. Servers that provide BIND services are able to resolve host names to IP addresses.

❑ **DHCP**   A service that allows IP addresses to be assigned to clients automatically. DHCP reduces the overhead of individually configuring systems and can eliminate problems of duplicate IP addresses.

Identifying the Strengths and Weaknesses of Different Distributions and Their Packaging Solutions

❑ A distribution is a set of software that includes the Linux kernel, applications, and utilities.

❑ Numerous distributions are available, each of which has its respective pros and cons.

❑ Linux distributions use *packages* to aid in the installation, management, and removal of application software.

❑ Of the packaging formats available, the Red Hat Package Manager (RPM) is the most widely adopted.

❑ Software that is not distributed in a package is distributed in source code, or a compiled binary. In each case, the tape archiving utility tar is commonly used to create archives.

Describing Functions, Features, and Benefits of a Linux System

❑ Linux is a free software operating system that supports a range of hardware platforms and is distributed under an open source licensing agreement.

❑ Linux and its associated applications are typically less resource intensive than other operating systems offering similar levels of services.

❑ An increasingly wide range of software is available for the Linux platform, and customized distributions are available to fulfill specific needs.

Identifying How the Linux Kernel Version Numbering Works

❑ Linux kernel numbering is comprised of a major version number, a minor version number, and a patch-level designator, all of which are separated by periods. An example of this is 2.4.2.

❑ Kernel versions that have an even number as the second number indicate stable versions, whereas odd numbers indicate versions still under development.

Identifying Where to Obtain Software and Resources

❑ The latest Linux kernel can be downloaded from www.kernel.org.

❑ Many suppliers of Linux offer downloadable versions of their distributions. Also, some suppliers provide shrink-wrapped versions that can be purchased from online or conventional stores.

❑ A huge range of Linux applications are available, either from Linux distributors' Web sites or from other Internet-based resources.

Determining Customer Resources for a Solution

❑ When implementing a Linux solution, the customer's ability to support and manage the system must be considered.

❑ If necessary, technical staff may need to be trained in the support of the Linux system, and budget should be made available to do this.

SELF TEST

The following questions will help determine your level of understanding of the material presented in this chapter. Some of the questions may have more than one correct answer, so be sure to review all answers carefully before choosing all that apply.

Identifying the Purpose of the Linux System Based on Predetermined Requirements

1. Your client has asked you to install a server that will allow host names to be translated into IP addresses. Which of the following server types would you implement?

    A. BOND

    B. BIND

    C. Proxy

    D. ipchains

2. Which of the following Linux services can protect the internal network from attacks by external sources?

    A. Samba

    B. Squid

    C. ipchains

    D. BIND

Comparing and Contrasting How Major Licensing Schemes Work

3. Which of the following statements best describe the GNU/GPL licensing method?

    A. You can change the software but you cannot add or remove functionality.

    B. You can change the software and then sell it, as long as it has significant differences from the original version.

    C. You can change the software and redistribute it, but you must include the source code in the redistribution.

    D. Once it is changed, the copyright of the software belongs to you.

4. Which of the following statements is true regarding software licensed as shareware?

    A. You can use the software indefinitely without paying a fee.

B. You can use the software for a trial period, but if you continue to use it after that period, you must pay a royalty.

C. You can amend and freely distribute the software, but the copyright remains with the original owner.

D. You can provide the software to others but must not charge for it.

Identifying the Functions of Different Linux Services

5. Which of the following services makes it possible for Windows clients to store files and print through a Linux server?

A. DHCP

B. Samba

C. ipchains

D. BIND

6. The process by which a DNS server resolves IP addresses to host names is called what?

A. Name resolution

B. Proxy resolution

C. Iterative lookup

D. Reverse lookup

7. The period of time for which a DHCP address is assigned to a client is known as a what?

A. Scope

B. Lease

C. Let

D. Rent

8. Which of the following Linux services can reduce IP addressing tasks?

A. Samba

B. Squid

C. ipchains

D. DHCP

Identifying Strengths and Weaknesses of Different Distributions and Their Packaging Solutions

9. Files that have the .tar suffix indicate that the file is what?

   A. An application package

   B. Compressed

   C. Created with tar

   D. Created using the -x switch.

10. You want to download and install a package for your Caldera Linux system. Which of the following files are you most likely to download?

    A. package.rpm

    B. package.cal

    C. package.deb

    D. package.slp

11. The requirement of an installed application to have another piece of software in order to run is known as a what?

    A. Reliance

    B. Link

    C. Dependency

    D. Relationship

12. Which two of the following Linux distributions use the Red Hat Package Manager as their default package management format?

    A. Debian

    B. Red Hat

    C. Caldera

    D. Slackware

13. Files that have the .tar.gz suffix indicate what?

    A. They were created using tar.

    B. They contain a software package.

    C. They are compressed.

    D. They are uncompressed.

Describing the Functions, Features, and Benefits of a Linux System

14. A customer wants to install a database server that can use one of the large commercial database products. Which three of the following platforms would you recommend?

- A. Linux
- B. Windows 2000
- C. Novell NetWare
- D. Windows ME

15. Which two of the following factors would influence your choice of a certain Linux distribution?

- A. Availability
- B. Support
- C. Higher version numbering
- D. Packaging format

Identifying How the Linux Kernel Version Numbering Works

16. You are considering using a 2.3.5 version of the Linux kernel for your new file and print server. Why would you not do this?

- A. This is not a valid kernel version.
- B. Because this release is not for public use.
- C. Because this is a development version.
- D. Because this version does not provide printing support.

17. Consider the kernel version 2.2.7. What does the 7 represent?

- A. The minor version
- B. The major version
- C. The stepping number
- D. The patch level

Identifying Where to Obtain Software and Resources

18. Your client wants to use a Linux server as a DHCP server, but you find that the DHCP daemon is not available on the server. Which of the following might you do to install DHCP functionality on the server?

    A. Recompile the kernel.

    B. Download and install the dhcpsrvr utility.

    C. Update the kernel to 2.3.1.

    D. Use the **ADD MODULE** command.

19. Which of the following locations could you use to get a copy of the latest Linux kernel?

    A. http://www.kernel.org

    B. http://www.kernel.com

    C. Linux newsgroup

    D. http://www.microsoft.com/kernel

Determining Customer Resources for a Solution

20. Which of the following should you consider when implementing a Linux system for a customer?

    A. Support capabilities of existing staff

    B. Application compatibility

    C. Hardware compatibility

    D. Training expenses

LAB EXERCISE

You have been tasked with specifying a Linux distribution for your company's new Web server. You have very little in-house skills with Linux, so using a distribution that is easy to use, manage, and update should be a top priority. The ease with which new applications can be installed is also a consideration. You want to be able to purchase a support contract from the distribution supplier directly, rather than through a third-party consultancy.

You have already narrowed your search to the following distributions: Red Hat, Caldera, Debian, Mandrake, and SuSE.

Research each distribution and make the most appropriate recommendation.

SELF TEST ANSWERS

Identifying the Purpose of the Linux System Based on Predetermined Requirements

1. ☑ **B.** Servers that host the Berkeley Internet Naming Daemon (BIND) service translate IP addresses into host names on TCP/IP-based networks.

   ☒ **A.** This answer is fictitious. **C.** Proxy is a function performed by products such as Squid. Servers providing a proxy service are able to intercept requests from clients for Internet Web pages and then store the retrieved results in cache to improve performance. **D.** ipchains is a function that provides firewall services on a Linux server.

2. ☑ **C.** ipchains is a firewall mechanism that can protect internal systems from attack by external sources. In versions of the Linux kernel after 2.2, this functionality is also provided by an enhanced utility called iptables.

   ☒ **A.** Samba is a system that allows Windows clients to store files on a Linux server, and to access the printing functionality of a Linux server. **B.** Squid is a proxy product that improves Internet access response times by caching frequently accessed pages to disk. **C.** BIND servers are responsible for translating host names into IP addresses.

Comparing and Contrasting How Major Licensing Schemes Work

3. ☑ **C.** GNU/GPL licensing dictates that software can be changed but that the copyright ownership of the software does not change. It also dictates that only a fee to cover duplication and distribution can be charged. The actual software and the source code must be supplied free of charge.

   ☒ **A.** Changes to GNU/GPL-licensed software are not subject to any restrictions. Functionality can be added or removed at the discretion of the developer. **B.** Even if the software is changed substantially, the terms of the GNU/GPL license remain the same. **D.** Developers are permitted to change software developed under the GNU/GPL license, but the license of the changed software remains the same as before the software was amended.

4. ☑ **B.** Shareware is designed as a "try before you buy" format, so if the software continues to be used after a trial period, a royalty must be paid to the copyright holder of the software.

   ☒ **A.** Software that can be used indefinitely without paying a fee is referred to as freeware. **C.** This statement is generally representative of software that is created under the artistic license format. **D.** This statement is often true of software produced under the shareware banner, but does not in itself describe shareware.

Identifying the Functions of Different Linux Services

5. ☑ **B**. The Samba service provides a number of features that allow Windows clients to store files and use the printing capabilities of Linux servers.
☒ **A**. DHCP servers automatically assign IP addresses to clients. **C**. ipchains is a firewall function that prevents outside sources from accessing systems on an internal network. **D**. BIND servers translate host names into IP addresses.

6. ☑ **D**. DNS servers can resolve an IP address to a host name through a process called reverse lookup. It is called *reverse* because it is the reverse of the normal DNS function, which is to resolve host names to IP addresses.
☒ **A**. Host name resolution is the term given to the resolution of host names to IP addresses. **B**. There is no such term as proxy resolution. **C**. Iterative lookup is a term given to the process by which a DNS server consults another DNS server for information on a host name that is outside its managed namespaces.

7. ☑ **B**. The length of time a DHCP-assigned address is allocated to a client is known as the lease.
☒ **A**. Scope refers to the range of addresses that are available for assigning to clients. **C, D**. Let is not a term associated with DHCP, nor is rent.

8. ☑ **D**. DHCP servers allow clients to obtain IP address and configuration automatically. This eliminates the need for IP configuration to be performed on individual systems and reduces the overhead that altering the IP addressing scheme may bring.
☒ **A**. Samba is a network service that allows Windows clients to store files on, and use the printing facilities of, a Linux server. **B**. Squid is a proxy product that can improve the performance of Internet browsing and can be used to restrict access to Internet sites. **C**. ipchains is a feature of the Linux kernel that allows basic firewall functionality to be implemented on the Linux server.

Identifying Strengths and Weaknesses of Different Distributions and Their Packaging Solutions

9. ☑ **C**. Files that have been created with the tar utility are normally named with the .tar extension.
☒ **A**. The file may, or may not, be an application package. The tar utility is simply used to place a number of files into a single easy-to-use format; it does not indicate what the possible contents of the file are. **B**. Tar files that are compressed are conventionally named as .tar.gz or .tgz files to indicate their status. **D**. The **-x** switch is actually used when unarchiving a tar file.

10. ☑ **A.** Caldera supports the Red Hat Package Manager (RPM) format. Therefore, of the files listed, you are most likely to download the package.rpm file.
☒ **B.** There is no package format that uses the .cal extension. **C.** DEB files are associated with the Debian package format. **D.** Files with the .slp extension are associated with the Stampede package format.

11. ☑ **C.** When an application is installed, it often requires that other software components be available on the system. This condition is known as a dependency.
☒ **A, B, D.** Reliance, link, and relationship are not terms associated with application installation.

12. ☑ **B, C.** Of the distributions listed, both Red Hat and Caldera use the Red Hat Package Manger format for installing, managing, and removing applications.
☒**A.** Debian-based distributions use the DEB packaging format. **D.** Slackware Linux uses tar packages.

13. ☑ **A, C.** Files that have the .tar.gz extension indicate that they have been created with the tar utility and are compressed. Such files are referred to as tarballs.
☒ **B.** The fact that a file has been archived using the tar utility and compressed does not indicate what kind of files are included in the file. **D.** The fact that the file has a tar.gz extension indicates that it is compressed.

Describing the Functions, Features, and Benefits of a Linux System

14. ☑ **A, B, C.** Of the products listed, Linux, Novell NetWare, and Windows 2000 are all capable of being a server for a large commercial database product. The client's needs would have to be fully analyzed to determine which of the three platforms is the most appropriate for its needs.
☒ **D.** Windows ME is a desktop operating system and thus is unsuitable for use as a commercial database server.

15. ☑ **B, D.** Of the factors listed, only the availability of support and the packaging format are likely to play a major part in your selection criteria.
☒ **A.** Most, if not all, Linux distributions are available for download from the Internet, and a great many are available on CD-ROM in a consumer package. The availability of a specific distribution should not be an issue. **C.** Companies that produce Linux distributions can assign their own version numbers to the release. One company using a higher release number than another does not necessarily indicate a more up-to-date product.

Identifying How the Linux Kernel Version Numbering Works

16. ☑ **C.** The second part of a Linux kernel version number indicates whether it is a release or a development version. An odd number indicates that it is still under development and thus not a stable release. Only stable releases, those with an even second identifier, should be used in production environments.

☒ **A.** This is a valid kernel version number. The first identifier designates the major version, the second the minor version, and the third the patch level. The issue is that this version is a development release. **B.** Kernel versions are not restricted by how they can be used in this way. **D.** All Linux kernel versions provide printing support.

17. ☑ **D.** Linux kernels are numbered in a dotted format that indicates the major version, the minor version, and the patch level. So, in this case, the 7 refers to the patch level installed in this version of the kernel.

☒ **A.** The minor revision is indicated by the second number. In this case the minor version number is 2. **B.** The major version is indicated by the first number, which in this case is 2. **C.** Stepping numbers are associated with processors rather than Linux kernel versions.

Identifying Where to Obtain Software and Resources

18. ☑ **A.** If you find that the Linux kernel on your system does not support DHCP, you will need to recompile the kernel to provide the functionality.

☒ **B.** This is not a valid answer. The dhcpsrvr utility is not a valid Linux application. **C.** The second number of this Linux kernel version indicates that it is a development version, so it should not be used in a production environment. **D.** The **ADD MODULE** command is not a valid Linux command.

19. ☑ **A.** The Linux kernel can be downloaded from http://www.kernel.org or any of the mirror sites around the world.

☒ **B.** This site is a commercial site and not a mirror site for the Linux kernel. **C.** Linux newsgroups are a useful source of information for anyone installing Linux, but they are not a source for the Linux kernel. **D.** The Microsoft support site is, understandably, not a source for obtaining the Linux kernel.

Determining Customer Resources for a Solution

20. ☑ **A, B, C, D.** When considering a customer's needs and capabilities, the support capabilities of existing staff, application and hardware compatibility issues, and any additional expenses that may arise from training support staff must be considered.

☒ None. All answers are correct.

LAB ANSWER

This exercise doesn't actually have a "right" answer, but certain things need to be considered in each example. For instance, not all of the distributions mentioned offer direct support. On another criteria, Debian has arguably the easiest to use packaging method, though this is still subjective.

The point of the exercise is that this kind of scenario mirrors real life. Often, you will be asked to evaluate and make recommendations based on a number of criteria. Whether there is a right or a wrong recommendation depends on what the criteria are and how specific they are.

COMPUTING TECHNOLOGY INDUSTRY ASSOCIATION

6

Pre-Installation Procedures

General Pre-Installation Considerations

When it comes to installing operating systems, most of us choose to install first and ask questions later. This approach, while perhaps the most widely implemented, is not the best way to go, especially for a Linux installation. While it is true that Linux installations are much easier than they used to be, there are still many unwanted surprises that can arise. Perhaps more than any other operating system, it is important to do a little legwork before jumping in and resist the temptation to head right into an installation. This chapter focuses on the things you need to be aware of before installing Linux, including background information on file systems, hard-disk partitioning strategies, choosing the appropriate installation method, and the Linux directory structure. Such considerations are fair game for the Linux+ exam. Before we get started on the real detail, let's take a look at some of the topics covered in this chapter.

Determining the Server Role

Before you install Linux, it will be good to know what exactly its intended use will be. This factor will greatly influence the installation strategy and hardware design of your system. Will you install Linux as a desktop solution, or will you choose to install Linux in a server configuration? If it is a server, will it be an Apache server, firewall server, or perhaps a file and print server? Either way, the hardware requirements for these systems vary, and you need to be aware exactly how to ensure that your hardware is up to the task.

During the installation procedure, some distributions will ask whether you want to install Linux as a desktop system or as a server system, with a preset list of applications. Other distributions offer a more free-form approach, requiring you to specify packages individually. In either case, for the purposes of the Linux+ exam, it would be a good idea to install Linux using the different options to get a feel for how they are the same and how they are different. Make special note of the differences in hardware requirements, such as which installations need more hard disk space, and which ones need more memory.

Distribution

Part of the pre-installation process will include familiarizing yourself with the strengths and weaknesses of the various distributions. Chapter 5 covers this topic, but to make a really informed decision, it would be a good idea to visit the distribution-specific Web sites. Once there, look for the ones that offer easy-to-use support, FAQs, and discussion groups. When the real installations begin, you might need these resources.

Many of the procedures and commands used during the installation are the same throughout all distributions, but there are some subtle differences. For the most part, however, if you can use one, you can use them all. When it does come time to install Linux, it would be a good idea to install several of the distributions to see which one you prefer to use, not just for the Linux+ exam but for ongoing use. Keep in mind, however, there are some distributions that are more accommodating for beginners than others, not to suggest that they are any less powerful, but they are easier to work with than other distributions

Installed with Another Operating System

Many people, especially when learning Linux, choose to install Linux on a system that already has an operating system installed. This is not a bad strategy and has some definite advantages, but if you are planning on installing Linux on a computer that already has an operating system installed, there will be extra considerations and steps.

Because Linux supports native Microsoft file systems, some distributions allow you to install Linux into a Windows partition. This is not the recommended way to go, as the performance of Linux is somewhat compromised, but it makes for an interesting setup and might be worth a try. Mandrake 7.2, for instance, makes this type of arrangement really easy.

 on the **job**

Linux does not support the NTFS file system used by some Windows versions, including Windows NT and Windows 2000.

The other option is to partition your hard disk and keep the operating systems on separate partitions. Linux has built-in utilities you can use to accomplish this. Be warned, however, that you have to concentrate when partitioning you disks; one wrong move, and you can wipe your other operating system and lose your data. This is said from experience.

Method of Installation

Before installing Linux, you should probably know *how* you are going to install it. Linux supports many different types of installation methods, each of which are discussed further in this chapter. Before installing Linux, choose the installation method you intend to use and gather the materials you need to perform the installation. For instance, if you are installing from CD, then you will need either to order the CD from one of the distributors Web sites or download Linux and burn it to CD. Some of the other installation methods, such as network installations, require even more preparation. To familiarize yourself with the various Linux installation methods, it would be a good idea to try several to see the differences between each.

exam
watch

For the Linux+ exam, be prepared to know the different options available for installing Linux.

Packages Installed

There are many programs and packages that you can download and install for Linux. These can be added during or after the installation, but if you intend to use them, you should examine their requirements and see if you need to upgrade your system. For instance if you are going to install StarOffice or other programs, ensure that the hard drive and memory are capable of supporting it. Depending on the distribution you use, the packages need to be in the format that the distribution supports. Packaging formats were covered in Chapter 5.

on the
job

Unfortunately, finding package information is not always easy. One approach to find out what you might need in terms of hardware is to post a message to a newsgroup and find out from other administrators what the real-world requirements for a package are.

Hardware Support

While Linux does support a wide variety of hardware, it is a good idea to confirm that the hardware you are using in your system is on the manufacturer's hardware compatibility list. This is particularly important when installing on laptop systems or older computers where the hardware configuration might be unusual and proprietary.

Networked or Stand-Alone

You will have to determine if your system is going to be on a network or if it's going to be a stand-alone system. Considering that Linux has strong networking capabilities, most installations will certainly be on networked systems. There are a few additional considerations when connecting the system to a network. First off, before the installation, be sure you have the network settings you will need during the installation. These settings might include the IP address, the subnet mask, gateway, or the domain name. If you are using a DHCP server, these settings will be assigned automatically. Additionally, you might need to track down drivers for the network card. Remember that the Internet is, in fact, a network. If you intend your Linux system to use the Internet, be ready with ISP settings.

on the
ⓞo b   *The methods and procedures used in the installation of Linux are often matters of contention among accomplished Linux installers. We focus our content based on CompTIA exam objectives, but feel free to experiment and try things your own way. That is how Linux has gotten as far as it has.*

CERTIFICATION OBJECTIVE 6.01

Identifying Required System Hardware and Validating That It's Supported by Linux

Confirming hardware compatibility is covered briefly in Chapter 4, but because it is such an important consideration, it warrants another, more thorough, discussion. The natural temptation when you first get the operating system is to just pop in the CD and begin the installation. While this method is perhaps the most widely implemented, there is a more cautious approach that is recommended by both the authors and CompTIA.

Before installing Linux on a computer, take the time to acquaint yourself with the hardware configuration first. To be honest, considering the automated installation of today's Linux distributions, getting hardware specifics of your machine before the installation begins is not as important as it was on earlier versions. The reason for this is that although Linux can detect a wide range of hardware, it can't detect it all. During the installation you might be required to set undetected hardware information manually before the installation can continue. If you do not have the information, the installation might not be able to continue, and you will be left wishing you paid more attention to this chapter.

Hardware Documentation

If you are lucky enough to be setting up a new computer system, you likely have the hardware documentation that came with the system. Admittedly, most of us never use this documentation, and recycle it before ever opening its packaging. When installing Linux on your system, however, it is a good idea not to recycle it too quickly. Take a look through the documentation and information on the specific hardware used in your system. If the computer comes with documentation on the system board, for instance, you might want to know if the components on the board are integrated, and if they are, whether these integrated components are Linux compatible or there are any issues related to them.

on the
Job *In an ideal world, you will be able to check Linux compatibility before you buy your hardware, but you might be installing Linux on hardware you already have, so this isn't always possible.*

An astute system administrator will take the time to review the components in the system and compare the hardware with the specific Linux distributions Web site. The hypercautious might even chat on a few discussion groups to confirm any hardware they are concerned about. If you find that the hardware you want to use is not supported, you might need to install an updated kernel.

on the
Job *Keep the documentation somewhere it can be easily accessed. Having to check manually what hardware is installed is not a good use of time.*

Using Windows

Having both Linux and Windows installed on the same computer system is becoming a popular choice for many. Such a configuration can be especially useful when you are learning Linux. If you are installing Linux on a machine that is also using Windows, gathering hardware information is easy. From within Windows, right-click on the My Computer icon located on the desktop and select Properties. The Windows System Properties dialog box opens. By selecting the Device Manager tab from the top menu, you can view the hardware currently installed on your system. Once you have the hardware information, you can then verify its compatibility for Linux and get the necessary drivers. Figure 6-1 shows the Windows System Properties dialog box.

Using Linux

Once Linux is installed on your system, you can use the Linux utilities to determine the hardware in the system. Hardened Linux users might disagree, but for the most part, the Linux tools used to verify hardware are not as polished as more commercial operating systems. That said, they do the job just as well.

The first place to go when looking at the hardware in your system is the dmesg command. This command provides a summary on all the detected hardware in the Linux system. More information on the dmesg command can be found in Chapter 4. The proc file system is another place to look for hardware configuration information. As with dmesg, proc is covered in detail in Chapter 4.

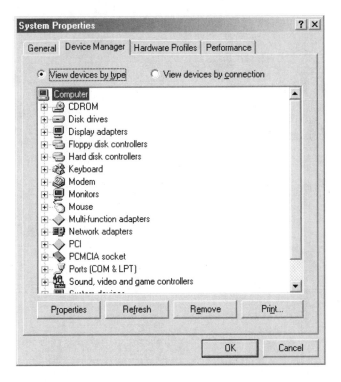

FIGURE 6-1

Windows System Properties dialog box

Other tools that can be used under Linux include the scanpci command, which as you might expect, includes PCI information; the isapnp command, used to configure plug and play for ISA devices; and the SuperProbe utility, which lets you identify characteristics of the video card. Before using the SuperProbe utility, read the related manual pages. It can lock up your system. There are also several graphical tools that can also be used to gather hardware information in the system. Figure 6-2 shows a hardware information screen from KDE, and Figure 6-3 shows a hardware information screen from GNOME.

FIGURE 6-2

KDE Control Center

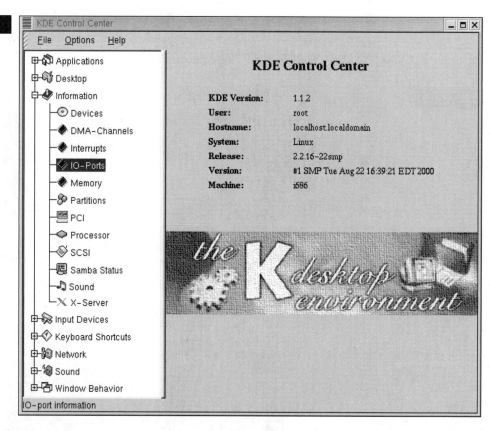

FIGURE 6-3

GNOME System
Information
screen

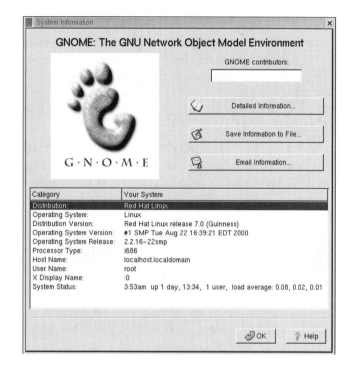

EXERCISE 6-1

Access Hardware Information from the Desktop

1. Start an X Window session. This exercise is using a GNOME desktop.

2. From the main menu, choose Programs | System | System Info.

   If using KDE, select KDE menus | KDE control center.

3. If using GNOME, the GNOME system information screen will be displayed.

   If using KDE, the KDE control center will be displayed.

4. From these screens, you will be able to determine hardware-specific information about your system.

on the **Job**

Linux commands are case sensitive. Take care to remember to use the right case. For instance, typing superprobe *at the command line will returne a "command not found" error. The correct command is SuperProbe. If a command you use does not work right away, confirm that you have typed it correctly.*

Gauging Your System Requirements

Linux has long been promoted as the operating system that can run on hardware that would make some other operating systems choke. While it is true that Linux can be far less hardware-demanding than its commercial counterparts, the stories of just how low Linux can go have become almost urban legends. To hear it from some Linux users, you get the impression that, if installed correctly, you could run Linux on an Etch-A-Sketch. The fact is that Linux can be installed on a system with very minimal hardware but, and here is the catch, you can't do much with it after it is installed, and you certainly won't be using a GUI. With that in mind, the minimum recommended hardware configuration for Linux is something like a 386-based PC with 8MB of memory. Some Linux users might get Linux up and running on less, though given the time it would take to find slower hardware, the motivation behind this is somewhat of a mystery.

When we talk about minimum hardware requirements, we are referring to the minimum hardware your system needs to perform a useful service. This does not necessarily mean using the X Window system, as this is just an interface, but the system needs to be able to function as a useful machine. With this consideration in mind, we know of companies still using 486 and low-end Pentium Linux systems in their operation. These systems might be acting as firewalls, gateways, or routers, but they are performing a function and, on machines that commercial operating systems simply cannot touch.

The minimum requirements might vary, depending on the distribution you decide to install and the services you wish to use with it. Keep in mind that the minimum recommended requirements listed on the specific distributions Web site are often just enough to get it going. Adding new services and programs might require additional resources to keep them functioning properly and at acceptable performance levels. The next section lists general recommended installation requirements. These are not set in stone and might vary, depending on the services installed. Table 6-1 shows the general requirements for both a Linux server and a Linux workstation installation.

TABLE 6-1   Linux Real World Installation Requirements

System Resources	Linux Server	Linux Workstation
Memory	128MB	32–64MB
Processor	Pentium II class or AMD K6	Pentium-speed CPU
Video	VGA/SVGA	SVGA
Hard disk	20GB and up typically SCSI	4GB and higher usually IDE

CERTIFICATION OBJECTIVE 6.02

Determining Which Software and Services Should Be Installed

It is difficult to make sweeping statements about what you will need from hardware for your Linux system. Quite simply, hardware and system requirements ultimately depend on the purpose of the system and on the software and services required to support these roles. With this in mind, the first step in determining the hardware requirements for a Linux system is to identify the role the system will have. Once you determine if the system will function as a server or desktop system, you can then identify the services and software needed to support these systems. Desktop systems, for instance, will use a graphical interface and productivity tools such as StarOffice. Installing graphical tools will increase the hardware requirements over straight command-line interface, and installing graphical applications will require significant hard-disk space and possibly more RAM.

Software and Services for a Linux Server

Deciding to set up your system as a server is often just the first step. The next thing you have to decide is what services you will need. Listed next are some of the more common server services that can be configured during the installation. Exactly which ones you need will depend on the role of the server you are installing.

- Proxy server

- Firewall server
- File and print server
- News server
- NFS server
- SMB (SAMBA) server
- FTP server
- Web server
- DNS name server

Your server system can be configured to perform any one of these server roles individually or to function in all these roles as a single-box server solution. Each type of server service you choose to install has an impact on the resources the system needs to fulfill the function. During the installation, you might be prompted to choose between the server and workstation setup and will have the option to choose the server components you wish to install. The hard-disk space required to install components will usually be reported when you choose each package, but be prepared. A typical server installation ranges from 1 to 2GB, depending on the packages selected.

Software and Services for a Linux Workstation

If your new system is to be used exclusively as a desktop system, then the server packages and programs are not needed. Desktop systems have a different range of needs, and during the installation, you can select various packages to customize to your requirements. Common desktop systems will typically include some common software and components. As an example, Table 6-2 shows the workstation options when installing Mandrake Linux 7.2 and their approximate sizes.

exam
ⓌAtch

You will not be expected to know disk space requirements for applications for the Linux+ test. This is included to give you an idea of hardware requirements.

As you can see, the software and components that you can install add up very quickly. Keep in mind that these do not include other programs, such as StarOffice, which you are likely to install at a later date. Be prepared to reserve 1.5 to 2GB of hard disk space for the installation. When you get more used to Linux, you can

TABLE 6-2	Mandrake Workstation Installation Options and Requirements

Software	Hard Disk Space
KDE	140MB
Gnome	110MB
Other graphical desktops: Icewm, Window Maker, Enlightenment, FVWM, etc.	100MB
Internet tools: tools to read and send e-mail and news, pine, mutt, tin, etc.	90MB
Communication tools: IRC, Xchat, licq, gaim, etc.	70MB
Office tools: Kword, Kspread, PDF viewers, etc.	260MB
Multimedia support	40MB
System documentation, how tos	30MB
Graphical utilities: Gimp, etc	70MB
C, C++ Library, and development tools	180MB
Other development tools: perl, Python, etc.	150MB
Console tools: shells, file tools, editors, etc.	160MB

streamline the installation to include only those tools you will be using. For now, however, install everything, so you can to get some idea which utilities and programs are available and which you prefer to use.

General Considerations When Choosing Components

Whether you choose to install the server or desktop options, there are some general considerations and best practices to observe when installing Linux. When setting up your Linux system, consider the following.

- **Plan for growth**   If the services and packages installed during the initial setup are already encroaching on system capacity, there is no room to install future services or packages. It is best to leave yourself some room, in terms of both memory and in hard drive capacity. A good example of this is the /home directory, which holds user account information. A general rule of thumb is to allow between 10 and 100MB per account (that's a big thumb). If your network currently has 10 users, but you expect the number of users to increase to 100, then you need to plan for this growth *now*.

- **Prepare for future hardware** Install the services and components needed to support the hardware you currently have, but also install those needed to support hardware you intend to include on your system. For example, if you intend to install an ISDN adapter, install the utilities you will need to manage the device. This helps to determine if your current hardware configuration can support this future growth.

- **Partition ahead** Choose your partitions well. A strong partition strategy can help with system availability and increase scalability. Partitions must allow for current software and components, but must also leave room for future growth.

- **Include network support** Linux is a network operating system. Even if you are installing Linux as a stand-alone computer, it is likely that, at some point, it will be used on a network. When installing Linux, therefore, have a network card in the system, and install the necessary components and services needed to support network services. They can be added later, but this way, your system is ready to go.

- **Include language libraries** For developers, or those wanting to try their hands at programming, be sure to include the compilers and libraries you will need. For instance, you will need to install gcc if you plan to be doing C programming.

- **Consider dependencies** Packages often need other pieces of software in order to run. This is known as a *dependency*, and it can significantly increase the amount of space required by an application. Most distributions determine dependencies and calculate the total amount of required space, but be aware that the total disk space required may be more than is specified in documentation.

- **Consider security** Do not install any services you will not need, as they might represent a security risk.

Depending on your available hard-drive space, you might want to install every option. Given the size of today's hard disks, this certainly can easily be done. For the purposes of the Linux+, it would be good to have everything installed just to try it out.

Determining How Storage Space Will Be Allocated to File Systems

Understanding the Linux directory tree is very useful when performing installations and making informed decisions when partitioning your hard disk. At first glance, the Linux file system is very confusing, and to be honest, it is not much better after the second. The file system is divided into many parts, and those used to working with Windows are going to have to think outside of the box a bit on this one.

Root File System

During the installation of Linux, you must create a root (/) directory. This root partition is designated as /, so when we refer to the /usr directory, it represents two distinct directories—the / directory and the usr directory. In Windows terms, the same directory structure would be represented as c:\usr. The / directory is synonymous with c:, and the usr directory would be a file folder within the c: directory.

The root file system is typically kept small, as it will usually contain only key system files. To look at what is in the root directory, type **ls** at the command line, and you will see the other subdirectories in the root system, but probably not individual files. The following is a sample of a printout from using the ls command:

```
#ls
bin     dev     home    mnt     proc    sbin    usr
boot    etc     lib     opt     root    tmp     var
```

The root directory is the primary directory, with the other subdirectories being standardized Linux directories, meaning you can expect to see them throughout all Linux distributions. Listed as follows is a brief introduction to each of these subdirectories:

- **/bin**   Holds the commands needed for bootup and contains common Linux user commands including grep, chown, ls, sort, chmod.
- **/boot**   Holds the boot loader and the kernel images.

- **/etc**   Holds administrative configuration files and computer-specific system configuration.

- **/home**   Used to store the user's data. Because this data can be large, it is often kept on its own partition. Also, by separating it, it will not be lost if the / partiton becomes corrupt.

- **/lib**   Holds the shared libraries and kernel modules.

- **/mnt**   Mount point for removable media.

- **/proc**   Provides information on the kernel status routines. The file system interface to the Linux kernel.

- **/root**   Home directory for the root user.

- **/sbin**   Contains administrative commands.

- **/tmp**   Holds temporary files for applications.

- **/usr**   Holds system software such as compilers and other user tools. The /usr directory is most certainly going to grow as more software is added, which is why many prudent installers put it in its own directory.

- **/var**   A dynamic directory holding those files that change, such as log files. The log files in the /var directory have been known to grow out of control, and it is advised to keep it on its own partition to prevent files from falling into other partitions.

- **/dev**   Within Linux, all devices are referenced as files. The /dev directory holds these referenced names. If you go into the /dev directory and view these files, it seems pretty confusing, and for those not used to Linux, it is. For the Linux+ exam, it will not be necessary to know all the entries in the /dev directory, but you might need to know what the /dev directory holds. Chapter 9 covers these directories in greater detail.

Understanding the Linux directory and being able to navigate it will be required for the Linux+ exam.

The newer hard drives we now install in our systems are very large and are often divided into sections for both performance and organizational reasons. When a hard drive is partitioned, we have both physical and logical drives to deal with. The physical drive refers to the actual drive. The logical drives, on the other hand, are conceptual.

The physical drive is divided up in a process called *partitioning*, and these partitions are known as *logical drives*.

Primary and Extended Partitions

Whether you want to segment your hard drive into sections or keep it as a single large disk, each hard drive must have a partition. For the operation system to be able to use the hard disk, it must be able to recognize a partition on the disk, even if it is just a single large one.

The concept of partitioning drives can at first seem confusing, but once you get your head around it, it is straightforward. Partitioning is an important concept, as it will most certainly be a consideration during the Linux installation. Also, if things are not partitioned as they need to be, the installation might be unsuccessful, or you might find yourself reinstalling in pretty short order. In a worst-case scenario, you might even lose data on other partitions on the disk. Disk partitioning should be performed only when you are sure of the goals.

A hard disk can contain up to four primary partitions. This is not a restriction of Linux but rather of PC architecture. To be more specific, the restriction is a limitation of the computer's master boot record. There is no getting around the four primary-partition limit. If we were using an 80GB hard drive, we could partition the drive to four 20GB primary partitions, but even these might be too large for some applications. That's where extended partitions come into play.

Extended partitions provide the means to slash the partition sizes to whatever we want them to be. To create an extended partition, you can exchange a primary partition for an extended partition, using a program such as FDISK, leaving three primary partitions on the disk and one extended. Extended partitions act as if they were actually an independent drive and are able to have different operating systems or even different file systems installed on them. Extended partitions are divided further into logical drives, giving you the ability to reduce your 80GB hard drive into very small sections.

Before installing Linux, it is important to determine the partitioning strategy you will be using. Some people choose to install Linux alone on the system, meaning that the entire hard disk can be used for Linux. This is not a bad strategy to take; however, for those who will want to keep their current operating system, things get a bit more involved. In this situation, Windows should be installed in its own partition and then Linux installed in a separate partition.

It is possible to install Linux in the same partition your Windows files are kept in, but Linux takes a performance hit in doing so. This is not a recommended strategy.

If you do plan on configuring a dual-boot system, you will have to leave enough hard drive space outside your Windows partition to install Linux. If you are just setting up Windows, then you can use the FDISK utility. If Windows is already installed, however, and it is using the entire hard disk as a single partition, FDISK can't help.

During the Linux installation, you will be required to select a partition on which to install the operating system. If the entire disk is already occupied by another partition, space will need to be made for Linux. There are two approaches to this. The first is to wipe the hard disk completely and repartition as needed. The other is to repartition the drive dynamically.

There are a few utilities that allow you to repartition the drive dynamically, both third-party and Linux-native. Red Hat and other distributions provide a utility called the First Nondestructive Interactive Partition Splitting (FIPS) utility. To review the documentation on FIPS, consult the distribution documentation. Some of the other third-party partitioning tools include Partition Commander (http://www.v-com.com), Partition It (http://www.quarterdeck.com), and Partition Magic (http://www.powerquest.com).

Figure 6-4 shows the partitions and the how they are referenced in Windows and Linux.

Some of the utilities for partitioning disks are easier to use than others. Trying different distributions will allow you to determine which partitioning utility you prefer.

Creating Partitions for Linux

Once we have the partition ready for the Linux installation, we can now look at how we're going to set up the Linux partitions. Linux typically requires at least three partitions: one for the root file system, which is where the Linux kernel itself is kept, the / partition, and a swap file partition, but Linux is not restricted to using just these partitions. In fact, many users decide to make multiple partitions for Linux, sometimes one for each of the key directories. There is a distinct advantage to making these multiple partitions, namely, the protection of data and system files.

FIGURE 6-4

Partitioning
design

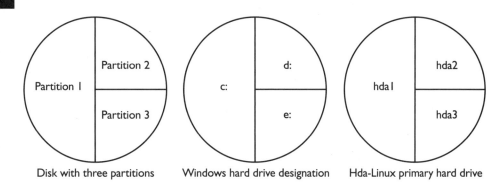

Disk with three partitions   Windows hard drive designation   Hda-Linux primary hard drive

It works like this: during the installation, you have to make a partition for the root
(/) directory. If this directory were ever to fail, and Linux needed to be installed,
everything within that directory would be lost as well. If during the installation,
however, you made the root directory a partition and the /home directory a partition,
if the root directory failed, the /home directory would be safe on another partition.

FROM THE CLASSROOM

A Word of Warning

We would be neglectful at this point if we did
not wave a few red flags in the air. Partitioning
your drive is a risky process and should never
be done without doing a backup of anything
you want to keep. When partitioning your
disk, it is best to assume the worst-case
scenario and prepare for it. In other words,
never attempt to repartition a drive without
first taking a full backup (or two) and verifying
that the backups are valid. The utilities are
generally reliable, but you just never know.

—*Drew Bird, Linux+ Certified*

The ability to create multiple partitions to store the various Linux directories opens up a lot of possibilities. On a Linux server we maintain, for instance, because the root directory holds few files, it sits by itself in a small partition, while the /var directory, which holds user programs, has a large partition, as does the /home directory. To help clarify Linux partitioning, let's look at a few examples.

```
Mount Point    Type    Size
/ (root)    ext2    1GB
Swap    Swap    100MB
```

This represents a conservative approach to Linux partitioning, where there are only two partitions, one for the root and one for the swap. In this example, all files will be saved on the root directory. The size of the root file is OK, but would not leave much room for the addition of a lot of extras. You will notice that when you start to do your installation, the space gets used up pretty fast. The purpose of swap file space is discussed in the section "A Little on Swap," later in the chapter, but when it comes to sizing a swap file partition, there is no hard and fast answer, as it depends on what the machine is to be used for and what kind of loads it will be experiencing. Some say that in many cases, making the swap file larger than the amount of physical RAM invokes the law of diminishing returns, while others insist you can't have enough of a good thing. A common approach is to make the swap space the same size as the physical RAM.

on the **Job**

It used to be that the limit for the swap file was 128MB. This is no longer the case. Linux swap files can now be as large as 2GB!

```
Mount Point    Type    Size
/ (root)    ext2    2GB
/var    ext2    500MB
Swap    Swap    100MB
```

In this example, the root directory might be too big for what is needed. Remember that the root directory contains the key system files, and nothing else really needs to be stored there; therefore, it is unlikely that it would need this much space. The /var directory can grow large fast, as it contains programs that can often be in excess of hundreds of megabytes. Depending on the use of the computer, this directory can get big; 500MB might be too small.

on the
job *For those who have experience in DOS, notice that the forward slash, not the backslash, is used in reference to directories in Linux.*

```
Mount Point     Type      Size
/ (root)     ext2      500MB
/var     ext2      2GB
/home     ext2      1GB
Swap     Swap      150MB
```

This example shows a well-rounded approach to Linux partitioning. The /var and /home directories should have sufficient room to account for growth, and the root partition is not taking up more room than it needs. Of course, if required, additional partitions can be made for other key Linux directories, such as the /tmp or /dev directories.

exam
Watch *It is a good practice to put the /var and /home directories on separate partitions because they fluctuate, and if they fill up the partition, they will not effect the rest of the system.*

A Little on Swap

So what is the swap partition? Swap is a special partition used to store data on the hard drive in the same way as if it were physical RAM. The swap partition provides virtual memory to the system and augments the physical memory. Even though swap file speeds are not that of the physical memory, using swap files allows you to run more applications than you have the physical RAM for.

During the installation of Linux, you are given the option to choose the size of the swap file partition, and as we mentioned earlier, this is a point of some debate. Some determine swap space by calculating the systems total memory needs, assuming all programs are running. Once the total memory requirement is determined, they subtract the physical memory from the total memory needed the remainder is how much swap space required. This is a dangerous strategy, as swap space isn't as fast as physical memory. Further, the relatively low cost of RAM makes this approach unnecessary. Assuming you have enough physical memory to cover your software needs, a common approach is to match your swap space and physical RAM.

on the
job *For those who want to see the available memory, you can use the free command, which is helpful when estimating swap file needs.*

Partition Quick Reference

It is not possible to make hard and fast rules that dictate the exact sizes of the Linux partitions. The best that can be done is to say that it all depends on the intended use of your Linux system, and with experience you are sure to develop your own opinion on Linux partition sizes. With that in mind, Table 6-3 provides a list of general recommendations for common Linux partitions. The estimates are based on a Server Linux system and will not necessarily hold true for a desktop system.

CERTIFICATION OBJECTIVE 6.04

Identifying the Best Method of Installation

There are many different ways that Linux can be installed onto a system. Some of these are easy, and some of these are a little trickier. It is important, however, to consider these different installation methods to prepare the required materials, depending on the one that you choose to use. This section explores some of the common Linux installation methods and what will be needed to complete and installation in each case. As far as the Linux+ exam, as well as real-world application, is concerned it might be worthwhile to try a few of them.

TABLE 6-3 Linux Partition Sizes

Linux Partition	Recommended Sizes	Reason
/var	200MB to 10GB and higher	Overall size may expand and contract. Holds spool and log files which can grow large.
/usr	500MB to 5GB and higher	Holds Linux related data and program files.
/home	100MB to 10GB and higher	Contains users and must accommodate all user activity
/boot	10MB to 50MB	Holds only essential boot files and therefore does not need to be large.
/tmp	10MB to 10GB and higher	Holds temporary files of which there are many.

CD-ROM

By far the most popular means of installing Linux is using the CD-ROM. In fact, you could spend the rest of your Linux days never having to use a different installation method. If you have Linux available on CD, and your system allows you to boot from it, then this truly is the way to go. If you want to do a CD installation, you can purchase the CD from one of the vendor Web sites or from a local computer retailer. Alternatively, you can download and burn Linux from the Internet. This step poses a few additional considerations, and download times might be a problem if you are working with a slow Internet connection. For the first installation, it might be worth your while buying your first copy of Linux. It is still far cheaper than commercial systems, plus you get the documentation. Of course, the choice is yours.

on the job

If your system does support booting from CD, you may need to reconfigure the boot order in the BIOS to make the CD the first bootable device.

Installing Linux from CD can be as simple as putting the CD in the drive and rebooting your system. This works only if your computer supports booting from a CD. New computers support this feature, but if you are installing Linux on an older PC, you might not have this luxury. In this case, you will need to make a boot disk, and that is another story altogether. Making Linux boot disks is covered at the end of this section.

Network Access Installations

Suppose for minute that you do not have a CD or perhaps you are looking for an alternative way to install Linux. Then you have the option of performing some network-based installations. You have several choices when conducting a remote installation, including FTP, HTTP, SMB, and NFS.

If you have network access, then an FTP or HTTP installation might be what you are looking for. FTP and HTTP installations are network based. The system connects and downloads the installation files from an FTP or HTTP server. This server can be on the local network or on the Internet. If you are doing an installation over the Internet, make sure you have a fast connection, or you could have a long wait. With network access, you can also perform an NFS (network file system) installation of Linux. During an NFS installation, the Linux installation files are transferred from an NFS-mountable drive on another system on the network.

To perform a network installation, you will need to make a network installation boot disk. Creating installation boot disks is covered in the next section, but as a summary, you can make a network boot disk in DOS using the rawrite command, or you can make a boot disk from Linux using the following command:

```
dd if=network.img of=/dev/fd0
```

Once the boot disk is made, when you restart your system, you will be guided through a menu and given the choice to install through FTP, NFS, or HTTP. Be prepared to have network configuration on hand to complete the installation.

The final network installation strategy involves using Samba. Samba is software that allows Windows clients to connect to a Linux server, and it will appear as a Windows server. You can install Linux using an SMB shared directory. More on a Samba server can be found in Chapter 5. For the purposes of installation, all you need to know is that it can be used to install Linux.

Making Linux Boot Disks

Most recent PCs can boot from the CD, but rest assured, at some point you will be installing Linux on a system that doesn't. That's where the Linux installation boot disk comes in. The following section explains how to create a boot disk both from a DOS prompt and inside Linux. For the purposes of the Linux+ exam and your own practice, it is worth your time to try both methods.

Making a Boot Disk from DOS

Part of the pre-installation process is gathering the tools you will need to complete the Linux installation. If you are just installing Linux on a computer system and do not currently have access to Linux files, you might find yourself needing to make a boot disk from DOS so that you can install Linux. For those of you anxious to get going, this might seem like a step back, but it might make your life a lot easier one day.

To make a boot disk from DOS, you need to go directly to a DOS prompt and use the Linux rawrite command. This command is in the dosutils folder on the CD, and is available for most of the major distributions, including Red Hat, Mandrake, turboLinux, and SuSE. Once the command is located, execute it by typing **rawrite**, and you will be prompted for an image file to use.

The image file it is looking for is located on the CD in the appropriately named images directory. When prompted, enter the path to the image file, and rawrite will copy the boot.img file to the disk. You now have a Linux installation boot disk.

on the
()ob

The rawrite **command might not be included with all Linux distributions but is available on the many of the popular ones**.

EXERCISE 6-2

Creating an Installation Boot Disk from DOS

1. Insert the Linux CD and follow these commands.

2. Change to CD-ROM drive by typing the following command:

   ```
   C:\> d:
   ```

3. Change directories to the dosutils directory: **D:\> cd \dosutils**. It is assumed your CD-ROM drive is designated as D:. Replace with correct letter designation if it is not.

4. Run the rawrite program located in this directory: **D:\dosutils> rawrite**.

5. When requested by the program, enter the appropriate disk image name and target diskette drive. In this case, it's the boot.img. Enter the disk image source file name: **D:\images\boot.img**.

6. When prompted, enter target diskette drive: **a:**.

7. Insert a formatted diskette into drive A: and press ENTER.

Creating Boot Disks from Linux

If you have access to a Linux system, you can use it to create installation disks for another system. Making boot disks from within Linux is a straightforward process. During the creation of the boot disk, you might have to *mount* the CD. The topic of mounting devices is covered later in Chapter 9, but is essentially the process of making a device visible to the rest of the system. The command to mount the CD is # mount -t iso9660 /dev/cdrom /mnt/cdrom. This mount point is true for many, but not all, Linux distributions.

Once the CD is visible to your system you can enter the images directory on the CD. You might notice other .img files in the directory. Feel free to use these in place of the boot.img file. The .img files represent the disk creation for the different installation methods. Once you have located the appropriate .img file, type the following Linux command:

```
# dd if=boot.img of=/dev/fd0
```

Once this is entered, Linux copies the appropriate files to your disk. Notice the reference in the command fd0, which as we now know, is the first floppy drive. After the files are copied, you can unmount your CD by typing **umount /mnt/cdrom**. Pay close attention to the command; it is *umount*, not *unmount*—who knows why! Reboot your system, and the floppy will start the installation process.

EXERCISE 6-3

Making an Installation Boot Disk in Linux

1. Log in as root.

2. If necessary, insert the CD in the drive and mount the CD.

   ```
   mount /mnt/cdrom
   ```

3. Using the cd command, change to the directory containing the image files.

   ```
   cd /mnt/cdrom/images
   ```

   Note that this directory is not the same for all Linux distributions.

4. Run the following command:

   ```
   dd if=boot.img of=/dev/fd0
   ```

5. Unmount the CD using the umount /mnt/cdrom command and reboot your system with the disk in the drive.

SCENARIO & SOLUTION

You need to install Linux an older 486 system that does not have a CD. The computer is on a local network.	Many older systems might not have CDs to install from. If the computer is on the network, you can use an FTP, HTTP, NFS, or SMB installation.
You want to create a Linux installation boot disk but do not have access to a Linux system.	It is possible to create Linux installation boot disks from a DOS prompt using the rawrite command.
You are working with your Linux system and are trying several new commands, however, some of them appear not to work. What could explain this?	Many Linux commands are case sensitive; while using them if they do not work, confirm their correct usage.

CERTIFICATION OBJECTIVE 6.05

Partitioning According to Your Pre-Installation Plan with FDISK

There will be a point when you will have to put away the graphical utilities and partition your disk with perhaps the oldest and one of the most awkward of the partitioning tools, FDISK. If you are just setting up your system to be used with Linux, you might be using the FDISK utility to partition. To get you more familiar with FDISK we will walk through the process of setting up Linux partitions on the hard disk.

Using FDISK can lead to a loss of data if used incorrectly. Make sure all data is backed up before using FDISK.

To start the FDISK process, we need to access the hard drive we want to partition. For this exercise, we will be using a 2GB disk. To start, type **fdisk** and the drive you want to partition. like so:

```
#fdisk /dev/hda
```

This command will begin the process of partitioning the first IDE hard disk, hda. Once the command is run, you will be prompted to type **m** to see a list of the options available for FDISK. For our purposes, we need only a few of these listed options to create the Linux partitions. To begin with, we need to use the p switch to view the current partition table. Using the p option should look something like in Figure 6-5 but will depend on your current partitions and hard disk used. Figure 6-5 shows the menus options for fdisk and disk partition information.

Once the disk is identified, your next move is to delete the current partitions. Be very sure that you have information backed up and you can afford to lose the partition if it gets erased. Once you press D, you will be prompted to enter a partition you want deleted. Once all partitions are deleted, you can confirm that no partitions are present by using the p command.

Once you confirm that no partitions are present, you can now begin to partition your disk for a Linux installation. The first thing to do is to use the *n* command to add a new partition. You will be prompted to set up an extended or primary partition, we will need to set up primary partitions first. Press P to select primary partition, then select the starting partition number, 1, to create the partition. Figure 6-6 shows the steps taken to partition the drive.

Once we have the primary partition set, we can create a swap partition. To do this, follow the previous steps for creating a partition. When it comes to creating our swap partition, there is one extra step we need to take. By default, FDISK creates ext2

FIGURE 6-5

Menu options for FDISK and disk partition information

```
root@localhost.localdomain: /root                                    _ □ X

File   Edit   Settings   Help

[root@localhost /root]# fdisk /dev/hda

Command (m for help): m
Command action
   a   toggle a bootable flag
   b   edit bsd disklabel
   c   toggle the dos compatibility flag
   d   delete a partition
   l   list known partition types
   m   print this menu
   n   add a new partition
   o   create a new empty DOS partition table
   p   print the partition table
   q   quit without saving changes
   s   create a new empty Sun disklabel
   t   change a partition's system id
   u   change display/entry units
   v   verify the partition table
   w   write table to disk and exit
   x   extra functionality (experts only)

Command (m for help): p

Disk /dev/hda: 64 heads, 63 sectors, 1023 cylinders
Units = cylinders of 4032 * 512 bytes

   Device Boot    Start       End    Blocks   Id  System
/dev/hda1   *         1       762   1536160+   83  Linux
/dev/hda2           763      1023    526176    5  Extended
/dev/hda5           763       966    411232+   82  Linux swap

Command (m for help):
```

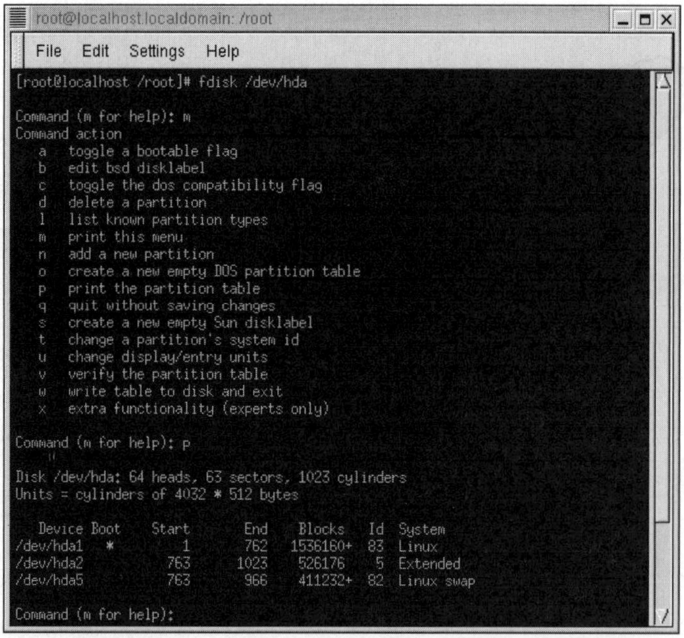

FIGURE 6-6

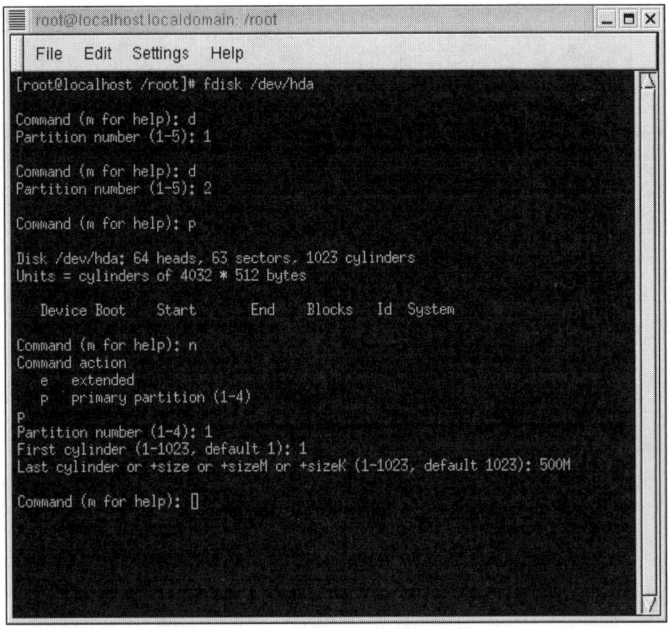

Creating a
primary partition

```
root@localhost.localdomain: /root                          _ □ ×

  File   Edit   Settings   Help

[root@localhost /root]# fdisk /dev/hda

Command (m for help): d
Partition number (1-5): 1

Command (m for help): d
Partition number (1-5): 2

Command (m for help): p

Disk /dev/hda: 64 heads, 63 sectors, 1023 cylinders
Units = cylinders of 4032 * 512 bytes

   Device Boot    Start      End    Blocks   Id  System

Command (m for help): n
Command action
   e   extended
   p   primary partition (1-4)
p
Partition number (1-4): 1
First cylinder (1-1023, default 1): 1
Last cylinder or +size or +sizeM or +sizeK (1-1023, default 1023): 500M

Command (m for help): []
```

Linux partitions, therefore, we need to change this to a swap partition. Using the
t command, we can change a partitions system's ID, in this case, from ext2 to swap.
To add additional partitions for Linux subdirectories, such as /usr, /var, or /home
for instance, create additional partitions using the n command to allow for them.

That is how to use FDISK to create Linux partitions, however, it is one thing to
read about it, it is another to do it. Understanding fdisk and partitioning is a Linux+
objective, so get in there and give it a try, and if you mess things up on your system,
refer to Chapter 11 on troubleshooting.

CERTIFICATION OBJECTIVE 6.06

Understanding and Configuring File Systems

The basic role of a file system is to provide a mechanism to organize the hard disk
and establish the way files are stored, secured, and accessed on the hard disk. It is
important to have an understanding of the file system Linux supports, as you will

SCENARIO & SOLUTION

You want to manage the partitions on your hard drive using FDISK.	When using FDISK under Linux, you need to identify the hard disk you want to partition. If you want to manage partitions on the primary hard drive, the usage is **fdisk /dev/had**. If it is on the second hard drive in the system, it is **fdisk /dev/hdb**.
You are working with a 20GB hard drive and want to partition space for both Windows and Linux.	If working with a disk that does not have an operating system installed, then the FDISK utility can be used to partition. For the 20GB drive, half the partition could go for each operating system.
You decide to partition your hard disk using only primary partitions. How many partitions can you use?	A computer system will allow no more than four primary partitions. To get around this limitation, extended partitions can be used.

have to choose the one you will use during the installation process. Each of the supported file systems offers its own unique characteristics, and although there are many, only a few are used in typical operation. Table 6-4 outlines the file systems supported by Linux.

In some cases, it might be necessary to recompile the kernel to use certain file systems.

Linux Favorites

Although Linux supports a large number of file systems, the average user will use only a few of these. The ext2 file system is likely to be the one you will use and is perhaps the most widely used file system throughout the Linux community. Over time, the ext2 file system has proved to be a stable system and offers excellent performance. Now, despite being initially developed for use with Linux, ext2 is being ported to other operating systems.

On the heels of the ext2 file system comes the ext3 file system, which includes the same features as ext2 but brings an extra feature to the table: journaling. Journaling is just a means the system uses to keep a record of what goes where, and in the event of failure, the system can use this information to repair things quickly. After a file system failure, journaling results in reduced time spent recovering a file system after a crash. Because of this, when it becomes more readily implemented, you are likely

| TABLE 6-4 | File Systems Supported by Linux |

File System	Description
ext	Known as the Linux extended files system, this was the file system of choice before ext2. Today, ext has been replaced by ext2.
ext2	Replacing ext, ext2 is by far the most common Linux file system used today. Enhancements include the ability to use big disks without needing to create many partitions and a maximum filename size of 255 characters.
ext3	Still under development, ext3 has the characteristics of the ext2 file system but uses journaling, a fault-tolerant measure.
ReiserFS	As is ext3, ReiserFS is another journaling file system.
iso9660	The iso9660 is the standard file system used by CDs.
mini Unix	Mini Unix is history now, but was the first file system used by Linux, and according to some, the most reliable.
msdos	As you might have guessed, this is the Microsoft DOS file system. Compatibility with MS-DOS allows you to access floppy disks that come from the Microsoft operating system.
usmdos	The usmdos file system enhances the features of regular MS-DOS, including support for long filenames. With umsdos, you can install Linux within a DOS partition.
nfs	The network file system allows the sharing of files between networked computers regardless of the file system used on the remote computer.
vfat	This is the file system used by Windows 95/98 that provides enhanced features of the regular fat file system.
swap	The Linux file system used for the swap space.
ffs	Here is one that will never appear on any test, but could be a trivia question at some point. ffs is the Amiga file system. Who knew?

to see ext3 in environments where high system availability is important, such as on Linux servers.

A fairly recent addition to the file system arena is the ReiserFS. This new file system promotes itself as being much faster than ext2, and as does ext3, offers journaling capabilities. The latest version of ReiserFS, version 4, is scheduled for release in 2002. The current version of ReiserFS is being shipped with a few of the major Linux distributions.

CERTIFICATION SUMMARY

Planning the Linux installation is an important step and helps to ensure that the installation is successful. Planning involves gathering the information you will need to complete the installation, deciding what the Linux system is intended to do, and developing a disk partitioning strategy.

Understanding the role of the Linux system, whether server or desktop, is an important consideration. There are different services and components that need to be installed for a server or workstation, and these components invariably have a huge impact on the system's hardware requirements.

Before installing Linux, it is important to understand the methods and purpose of partitioning. To install Linux on a system that already has an operating system present, room must be made on the partition to install Linux. Several utilities are available that will help you to repartition an existing drive, including third-party utilities and the FIPS Linux utility. If you're setting up Linux on a new partition, you might be using the Linux FDISK utility, and although it's not graphical and perhaps not that user friendly, it does the job.

TWO-MINUTE DRILL

Here are some of the key points presented in this chapter.

Identifying Required System Hardware and Validating That It's Supported by Linux

❏ Always confirm that the hardware you intend to use in your system is on the manufacturer's hardware compatibility list

❏ If you intend to use a graphical interface, verify video card compatibly before the installation

Determining Which Software and Services Should Be Installed

❏ The software and components installed during installation will depend on the intended use of the system.

❏ Desktops and server Linux installations require the installation of different software and components.

❏ The hardware requirements for the Linux installation will vary, depending on the software and services installed.

Determining How Storage Space Will Be Allocated to File Systems

❏ Numerous partitioning choices are available for Linux installations. The exact choice depends on the intended use of the system.

❏ A system can have four primary partitions. To increase the number of partitions available, a primary partition can be switched to extended, and the extended divided.

❏ The size of a partition and the number of partitions will depend on the type of system you are installing.

Identifying the Best Method of Installation

❏ Numerous methods are available to install Linux, including CD, NFS, FTP, HTTP, and SMB.

❏ Choosing an installation method depends on the resources you have available. The most common method is installing Linux from a bootable CD-ROM drive.

❏ Setting your computer to boot from CD is done in the BIOS. If not supported, a boot disk is required.

Partitioning According to Your Pre-Installation Plan with FDISK

❏ Many Linux users prefer to put key Linux subdirectories on a unique partition, creating a little fault tolerance if the root directory should fail.

❏ The number of Linux partitions used will depend on the purpose of the system. A common strategy is to create a partition for the /home, /usr, and /var directories.

Understanding and Configuring File Systems

❏ Linux supports a number of different file systems.

❏ The most widely used Linux file system is ext2.

❏ Linux supports the ext3 and Reiser file systems, both of which support journaling.

❏ Linux can support DOS and FAT partitions.

SELF TEST

The following questions will help you measure your understanding of the material presented in this chapter. Read all of the choices carefully because there might be more than one correct answer. Choose all correct answers for each question.

Identifying Required System Hardware and Validate That It's Supported by Linux

1. Which of the following utilities can you use to detect your video card and monitor?

    A. SuperProbe

    B. Superprobe

    C. vidprobe

    D. superprobe

2. You have located an older computer system that has a 500MB hard drive, 64MB of memory, an SVGA video card, a Sound Blaster–compatible sound card, and a nonbootable CD-ROM drive. You want to install Linux as a desktop solution, including both GNOME and KDE, an office package, multimedia tools, and Internet tools such as Xchat and a browser. You are not connecting to a network, so you are forced to install locally. Which of the following hardware components do you need to upgrade to get your system functioning?

    A. Hard drive

    B. Sound card

    C. CD-ROM drive

    D. Memory

Determining Which Software and Services Should Be Installed

3. Which of the following are you least likely to include in a Linux server installation?

    A. Web server

    B. Graphics manipulation software

    C. FTP server

    D. KDE

4. What term is given to the relationship between a software application and a separate code library or application?

   A. Relativity

   B. Dependency

   C. Proxy

   D. Reliance

Determining How Storage Space Will Be Allocated to File Systems

5. Consider the following Linux partitioning strategy:

   ```
   Mount Point    Type    Sizea
   / (root)     ext2    3GB
   /usr    ext2    500MB
   Swap    Swap    100MB
   ```

   Which two of the following might you suggest to improve the partition strategy?

   A. Increase the size of the root partition.

   B. Decrease the size of the root partition.

   C. Increase the size of the /usr partition.

   D. Decrease the size of the /usr partition.

6. Which of the following is not an advantage of creating separate partitions for Linux directories?

   A. Disaster recovery

   B. Organization

   C. The ability to use journaling

   D. Future growth

7. What is the function of a Linux swap partition?

   A. Provide fault tolerance for the system

   B. Help to organize disk space

   C. Provide the system with virtual memory

   D. Increase hard disk space

8. You want to design a partition strategy in which a separate partition holds the user's data on a separate partition. Which of the following partition strategies would you use?

    A. /, /swap, and /var

    B. /, /swap, and /home

    C. /, /swap, and /proc

    D. /, /swap

9. You are installing Linux on a system and want to make a system with the least amount of partitions. Which of the following partition strategies are you likely to use?

    A. /, /swap

    B. /, /home

    C. /, /usr

    D. /, /

10. You are the network administrator and are tasked with installing a new Linux server. When the system is set up, you want to ensure that the /home directory is secured, even if the root directory becomes corrupt. What step during the installation can you take to accomplish this?

    A. Backup the /home directory

    B. Put only the /home directory on a ext3 partition

    C. Make two /home directories

    D. Create a single separate partition for the /home directory

Identifying the Best Method of Installation

11. You are installing Linux on a system that has a blank hard drive and a CD-ROM drive, and you are sure it can boot from CD. When you boot the system with the CD in the drive, you receive an error message stating that a boot disk cannot be found. What can you do to remedy the error and install Linux?

    A. Format the hard disk using the format c: /s command.

    B. Change the BIOS settings to boot from CD.

    C. Change the BIOS settings to boot from hard disk.

    D. Confirm that the hard drive is connected and cabled correctly.

12. You are installing Linux on a computer system that has no CD-ROM drive attached but does have network access. Which of the following installation methods could you use to install Linux? (Choose three.)

    A. FTP

    B. NFS

    C. Boot disk

    D. SMB

13. You want to remotely install Linux on several computers in your office. You decide to install using NFS. Which of the following is the correct command for making a network installation boot disk?

    A. dd if=network.img of=/dev/fd0

    B. dd if=network.img of=/fd0

    C. dd if=boot.img of=/dev/fd0

    D. dd if=network.img if=/dev/hda1

14. Which of the following commands is used to make a boot disk from within Linux?

    A. rawrite

    B. format /boot.img/fd0

    C. dd if=boot.img of=/dev/fd0

    D. dd if=boot.img of=/dev/hda

15. Which of the following commands is used to make a Linux boot disk under DOS?

    A. rawrite

    B. format c: /s

    C. rawrite c: /s

    D. cd \dosutils

Partitioning According to Your Pre-Installation Plan Using FDISK

16. You are installing Linux on a computer system that already has a version of Windows installed on it. Windows is currently using the entire hard disk on a single partition. To install Linux in a separate partition and keep your Windows installed, what must you do?

    A. Use FDISK to repartition the drive to make room for Linux.

    B. Use the Linux rawrite command to free space on the hard disk to install Linux.

C. Save all Windows files to an alternative location and format the hard disk.

D. Use third-party partitioning software to free space on the disk.

17. Which of the following commands can you use to determine the amount of swap space that is being used on your system after an installation?

A. /proc/free

B. free

C. ms

D. /proc/memuse

Understanding and Configuring File Systems

18. Which of the following file systems is most used by Linux in current installations?

A. ext

B. ext2

C. ffs

D. Minix

19. You are installing Linux on a server that is going to act as the company's main server, reliability and availability are of key concern. You decide to use a file system that supports journaling. Which of the following could you use? (Choose two)

A. ext3

B. ext2

C. swap

D. ReiserFS

20. Part of your role as system administrator is to monitor system logs. Which of the following directories are you likely to be looking in for the logs?

A. /usr/logs

B. /tmp/logs

C. /var/logs

D. /logs

LAB EXERCISE

By now the installation CD is likely burning a hole in your pocket, and you are confident you have everything you need to begin the installation. Just to make sure, an installation checklist follows. Fill it out to test your knowledge of your system.

Component	Manufacturer	Model	Component Specifics
Motherboard			
Processor			
Video adapter			
Monitor			Refresh rate
SCSI adapter			
Network card			IRQ I/O
Sound card			IRQ DMA I/O
Mouse			
Hard drives			
Keyboard			

Network settings	
IP address	
Subnet mask	
Domain name	
Gateway address	
DNS server	

SELF TEST ANSWERS

Identifying Required System Hardware and Validate That It's Supported by Linux

1. ☑ **A.** The SuperProbe can be used to detect video cards and monitors.

☒ **B.** Linux commands are case sensitive. The correct command is SuperProbe. **C.** There is no such utility as vidprobe. **D.** Linux commands are case sensitive. The correct command is SuperProbe

2. ☑ **A.** Given the packages that need to be installed, the 500MB hard drive is not big enough to accommodate them. The KDE and GNOME windows managers are more than 100MB each, and an office package can be even larger. If you did manage to fit all the required components into 500MB, there would be no room for anything else.

☒ **B.** A Sound Blaster–compatible sound card should be sufficient to work in the system and should be detected and configured properly on the installation. **C.** Even if you are unable to boot from the CD, you can make a installation boot disk and from there install from the CD. There would be no advantage to upgrading the CD. **D.** Given the required components and the fact that it is a desktop system, 64MB of memory should be sufficient. Remember that there will be a swap partition in use that will augment this 64MB of memory.

Determining Which Software and Services Should Be Installed

3. ☑ **B.** Of the applications listed, graphics manipulation software is the least likely to be installed on a server system.

☒ **A, C.** Linux servers are particularly well suited to Web hosting and FTP serving, and so are quite likely to have these applications installed on them. **D.** Although not essential, many administrators choose to install the X Window system and a GUI for the graphical administration tools.

4. ☑ **B.** Many applications require code libraries or other applications to run. This is known as a dependency.

☒ **A.** Apart from Einstein's theory, which applies to all things, the term relativity has no relevance to Linux. **C.** Proxy means to act on behalf of another and is not the term used to describe package dependencies in Linux. **D.** Reliance is not the term used to describe package dependencies in Linux.

Determining How Storage Space Will Be Allocated to File Systems

5. ☑ **B.** The root directory can usually be kept small, as it contains only key system files. If other, larger subdirectories are located on their own partitions, such as /usr, then the size of that the root partition needs to be decreased. **C.** The /usr directory holds application data and can grow significantly, depending on the software installed. It is always a good idea to give yourself some breathing room for such directories.

☒ **A.** Unless all the Linux subdirectories are in the root partition, the root partition does not need to be that big. During the initial setup, the preferred method is to partition many of the subdirectories, leaving the root directory by itself. **D.** Depending on the role of the computer, the /usr directory can get large; 500MB does not leave much room for growth. Decreasing it further is probably not a good idea.

6. ☑ **C.** The ability to use journaling is not a function of partitions; it is a function of file systems. Both ext2 and Reiser support journaling, a feature that allows the system to recover from file system errors much faster.

☒ **A.** By partitioning key subdirectories, it is easier to recover after a root directory failure. If the root directory fails, the data stored on a separately partitioned subdirectory is intact and will stay that way, even if you have to reinstall Linux. **B.** Things can get very confusing inside Linux directories very fast. By partitioning your Linux system, it can be easier to navigate and can certainly help to organize things within the system. **D.** Having key Linux subdirectories can help for future growth. It allows for expansion of individual partitions, not the entire operating system.

7. ☑ **C.** The Linux swap partition is used as virtual memory for the system. The swap partition is one of two partitions you will need to create during the installation of Linux. There does not seem to be any consensus about the size of the swap partition, however, many users keep around the size of physical memory and a throw in a few more MBs for kicks.

☒ **A.** The swap partition does not provide fault tolerance for the system. Fault tolerance is providing mechanisms for increasing system availability in case of failure. The swap partition does not do this. **B.** The function of the swap file is not to organize the hard disk, but to provide virtual memory. **D.** The swap partition does not increase hard disk space.

8. ☑ **B.** The user's data is kept in the /home directory, therefore, if you wanted to create a partition that housed user data, you would create a separate /home partition. The / represents the root partition, and the /swap is, of course, the swap partition.

☒ **A.** The /var directory does not contain the user's data and, therefore, putting it on its own partition would not help. Among other things, the /var directory holds logging information. **C.** The /proc directory holds kernel status routines and not any user data. **D.** The scenario was asking for a separate partition to house the user data, this configuration would house the /home directory on the same partition as the / directory.

9. ☑ **A.** To set up Linux with a minimum of partitions, you can choose to use a single / directory and a swap partition. In a real-world application, it is recommended to make more partitions for other key Linux subdirectories.
    ☒ **B.** The minimum required partition strategy is to partition the / and swap directories. Depending on the use of your Linux system, however, it might be wise to create a separate /home partition. **C.** Depending on the use of your Linux system, it's a good idea to partition of /usr directory, however, not necessary. **D.** You would not set up two / directories on a system.

10. ☑ **D.** If the /home directory is managed on its own partition, should the root directory fail, the user's information is secured in the /home directory in another partition. If the root partition needs to be reinstalled, it can be without loss to the data in /home.
    ☒ **A.** While backing up the data in the /home directory is a good idea, it does not secure the data should the root directory become corrupt. It would, however, provide a means to restore the data should a reinstall be necessary. **B.** Putting the /home directory on an ext3 partition would help fix file system errors on that partition should they arise, but is not good for securing the data within the /home directory in case the / directory fails. **C.** Making two /home directories is not needed and could be very confusing. The easier solution is to just put /home on its own partition.

Identifying the Best Method of Installation

11. ☑ **B.** To be able to install from the CD, the BIOS has to be set to boot from CD. To do this, enter the BIOS screen when the system starts, locate the boot order, and change it to CD. If your system does not have this option, it might not support booting from CD, in which case it will be necessary to make an installation boot disk. Most new computer systems support CD booting.
    ☒ **A.** The command format c: /s is a DOS command used to format and copy system files to the hard disk. Remember, Linux does not use letters to reference physical disks or devices. **C.** It is likely that the BIOS is already set to boot from the hard disk, which explains the error message. The BIOS has to be changed to boot from the CD. **D.** If the hard drive has an operating system and the error is received, it is possible that a cable is at fault. This error is caused because the system cannot find the MBR to boot from.

12. ☑ **A, B,** and **D.** When installing Linux, you have the option to install locally or remotely using the network. Three of the common methods for remote installation include FTP, NFS,

and SMB installations. Remote installation requires a network installation boot disk.

☒ **C.** By itself, a boot disk is not an installation method, but rather a tool needed to start the installation process for a network installation or a local installation on a system that does not have a CD-ROM drive.

13. ☑ **A.** To install Linux over the network, you will need to make a Linux network installation boot disk. To do this, you will use the network.img file located on the distributions CD in the images file folder. The correct syntax for making the command is dd if=network.img of=/dev/fd0.

☒ **B,C,** and **D.** None of these options represent valid Linux commands.

14. ☑ **C.** If you find yourself trying to install Linux on a machine that does not support booting from the CD, you will need to make a Linux installation disk. To make an installation disk from within Linux, you need to specify the location of the boot.img that needs to be transferred to the floppy disk. Once you have the boot.img file, the correct command to create the disk is dd if=boot.img of=/dev/fd0.

☒ **A.** The rawrite is a utility that is used to create a Linux boot disk from within DOS. The rawrite utility is typically found in the dosutils file folder on the distributions CD. **B.** It is not a valid Linux command. **D.** The command is directing the image file to an IDE hard disk and not the floppy drive. The first floppy drive under Linux is designated as fd0.

15. ☑ **A.** The rawrite command, located in the dosutils file folder on the Linux CD, is a utility that can be used under DOS to make a Linux boot disk. To use the rawrite command correctly, you will need to identify a boot.img file to transfer to the floppy disk. The boot images are usually kept in the image file folder on the respective distributions CD, or they can be downloaded from their Web sites.

☒ **B.** The format c: /s command is used under DOS to make a bootable DOS system disk, not a Linux boot disk. **C.** This is not a valid command. **D.** It is a command to change to the \dosutils directory, not make an installation disk.

Partitioning According to Your Pre-Installation Plan with FDISK

16. ☑ **D.** If you find yourself wanting to install Linux on a system on which the current operating system is occupying the entire partition, you can use third-party software to dynamically resize the partition and free disk space to install Linux. There are other utilities that also accomplish this, such as the FIPS utility found on the Red Hat and other distribution CDs.

☒ **A.** If you are setting up a system from scratch, the FDISK utility can be used to segment your hard disk into partitions, leaving enough room to install both operating systems. If, however, there is already an operating system installed that is occupying the entire hard disk,

FDISK cannot create partitions to install Linux, as all disk space is being used. **B.** The rawrite command is used to make a Linux installation disk from within DOS and is not used as a partitioning tool. **C.** Although it is possible to save all necessary files and repartition your hard disk from scratch, you will have to reinstall both operating systems.

17. ☑ **B.** Of the commands listed, free is the only valid Linux command and hence the only one that can provide information on the swap space usage after an installation.

☒ **A, C,** and **D.** They do not represent valid Linux commands.

Understanding and Configuring File Systems

18. ☑ **B.** Current Linux installations are most likely to be using the ext2 file system. The file system has proven to be reliable while offering strong performance. Though ext3 has been developed and offers additional features to ext2, ext2 remains popular.

☒ **A** is incorrect; ext was once the favorite of Linux, but it has been all but eliminated by ext2. **C.** We imagine that finding someone using ffs might be difficult. It is the file system used for the Amiga computer systems, and they are few and far between. **D.** Minix was the first file system used by Linux, and while it still has supporters out there, it is no longer the first choice.

19. ☑ **A** and **D.** Both ext3 and the recent ReiserFS support journaling. Journaling is a method the system uses to log and keep track of what is what with the file system. In the unlikely event of a corrupt or failed file system, this information can be used to rebuild the file system and get things running.

☒ **B.** ext2 does not support the journaling feature. **C.** The swap partition is used to augment the system physical memory by providing virtual memory.

20. ☑ **C.** The /var directory holds such things as the spool directory and log files. If left unchecked, log files can grow out of control and grow beyond their allocated space. If this is the case, these files can start falling into unwanted parts of the system. To prevent this, the /var directory is often kept on its own partition.

A, B, and **D.** They are not standard Linux log file locations or names.

LAB ANSWER

The table filled out will be different for every system it is done for. The purpose of the exercise is to identify hardware and network information that you might need during the installation process. The task might seem a little cumbersome, but it is a good habit to get into, and the table can be used after the installation for upgrade purposes, or if you need to troubleshoot your system.

7

Linux Installation

CERTIFICATION OBJECTIVES

By this point of the book, you have gained an understanding of the various Linux distributions, identified the hardware within your system, and reviewed common Linux partitioning strategies, file systems, and the various installation methods. Perhaps the only thing left to do is actually install Linux. That is what this chapter is all about.

All the various Linux distributions share some common installation procedures. This chapter identifies these and provides a step-by-step installation of two popular Linux distributions. Before getting to the actual installations, we will outline the general steps and procedures common throughout all the major Linux distributions.

CERTIFICATION OBJECTIVE 7.01

Describing the Different Types of Linux Installation Interaction and Describing Which One to Use for a Given Situation

Not too long ago, the installation of Linux was, well, esthetically unpleasing, using large text boxes and keyboard-driven screens that could sometimes be awkward. For many of the major Linux distributions, things have changed, and the slick graphical installation screens and menus are as clean and visually appealing as anything else offered. GUI installation has become what users have come to expect, and Linux has delivered. The graphical installation method is commonly used, but in case there is a problem, or you have a hankering for a large text box, the other methods are still available.

on the job

As with any system, there are instances in which the GUIs might fail, so be prepared to work with the text box if necessary.

To give the graphics some so desperately crave, Linux attempts to start the installation process using a scaled-down X Window system. The problem is, if Linux cannot detect the video card, which does occasionally happen, it cannot start the graphical installation screens. If this is the case, then you are stuck with the old text installation screens, and while not as pretty, they still do the job as good as the graphical. Some people who have grown accustomed to text installation screens even choose this method over the graphical. We are not that nostalgic.

Installing in a text mode might be as simple as typing **text** at the boot: prompt when starting the installation. If this is not an option, review your distributions documentation to find the procedures for a nongraphical installation. The steps are the same as the graphical installation, however, navigating the screens is a bit different. The text mode installation is a keyboard-based installation and uses the ARROW keys to move the cursor, TAB and ALT-TAB to jump between options on the screen, and SPACEBAR to select options on the screen. Refer to the section on installing SuSE Linux at the end of this chapter to see an example of text installation screens.

exam
Watch

The text installation option is often used when Linux does not detect the video card and cannot start a graphical installation.

In addition to the straight text and GUI installation modes, some distributions offer a variety of other installation modes, including the following:

- **Low-resolution mode** Sometimes the graphic card cannot support the resolution mode used for the installation, and you have the option at the boot: prompt to specify using a lower resolution mode. If you've tried the regular mode and have had no success, you might try low-resolution mode.

- **Expert mode** For advanced features and more control over the installation, you can choose the expert mode. To install in expert mode, type **expert** at the boot: prompt. Although it says expert, do not be afraid to use this feature. It is not all that dissimilar from a regular installation. It simply provides more options and control over the installation.

- **Rescue mode** Knowing that the rescue mode option is available might save you a lot of grief one day. The rescue mode lets you try to repair a damaged Linux system.. After you have successfully installed Linux, try reinstalling with the rescue feature to see what you are able to do and the extra options you have to choose from. Rescue mode is often accessed by typing **rescue** at the boot: prompt or making a rescue floppy.

CERTIFICATION OBJECTIVE 7.02

Selecting Appropriate Parameters for a Linux Installation

The first few screens of the Linux installation require you to set some general parameters so the installation can continue. Take the time to get these initial settings correct, as this can make the rest of the installation a lot easier, and if you do not, you might find yourself reinstalling.

Language

The first installation screen you are likely to encounter requires you to set the appropriate language, and when you think about it, it only makes sense. The number of languages you can choose from is quite amazing, but we recommend, just to make the installation easier, choosing a language you can read and write; well, at least read. For those wanting an extra challenge during the installation, feel free to install in a different language. Bonne chance!

Configuring the Mouse

Installing a mouse with the newer Linux distributions is generally a straightforward process, and it is likely that your mouse will be auto-detected and very few problems should arise. When on the mouse configuration screen, you will notice a menu of numerous types of mice, both serial and PS/2. If your mouse is not auto-detected, you will be able to configure the mouse settings manually, including the port to use if connecting a serial mouse, /dev/ttsy0, /dev/ttsy1, /dev/ttsy2, or /dev/ttsy3.

If your mouse is not detected, you can navigate the screen by using TAB to move between the different menu options and SPACEBAR to select them. Be sure to test your mouse settings after you have selected you mouse configuration. If the mouse is not working, ensure that the cables are properly connected and that the correct mouse settings are chosen.

on the job

As a word of caution, never connect or disconnect PS2 devices while the computer is running. They are not designed for this purpose, and there is a chance for damage to the system.

If you have only a two-button mouse, you might be able to select an option to emulate a three-button mouse. This is recommended because some features in the X Window system require a three-button mouse. When the emulate option is used, clicking both mouse buttons will function as the third mouse button.

Configuring the Keyboard

The options on the keyboard selection screen are self-explanatory. You have the option to select your keyboard from a list of available keyboard options, with the default being the standard 104-key PC keyboard, perhaps the most widely used keyboard style.

Time Zone

All Linux installations will require you to set the time zone you are in. Many people do not take the time to select the correct time zone. Setting the time zone is important because the system uses time stamps. If you fail to set the time zone correctly, your e-mail, applications, and anything that uses the time or date will be incorrect. Take the extra few seconds and set the correct time zone.

CERTIFICATION OBJECTIVE 7.03

Selecting Packages Based on the Machine's Role

After all the general installation parameters are set, the real fun begins. In every Linux installation, you will have to decide the role that the computer will have, either a server or workstation or something in between. Most installations provide the option to choose one or the other and might have an additional custom option, which allows you to hand-pick the software packages and services you would like installed.

Be careful when choosing the role of your system, as the default options might have some surprises. For instance, during the Red Hat installation, you are given the choice for a workstation, server, or custom installation.

The workstation installation is preconfigured and will install standard workstation programs, including desktop environments such as KDE and GNOME, and other desktop utilities. The workstation installation will completely remove current Linux partitions on the system, so make sure that all important data is backed up. Fortunately, the workstation installation will ignore any non-Linux partitions.

A server installation, however, will wipe out your entire hard drive whether there is a non-Linux partition or not—quite the surprise if you are unaware of the risk.

Finally, you have the custom option, which gives you control over the packages you do and do not want installed. The custom option is recommended only for expert users, however, when learning Linux, it is good to use the custom option just to see what is available and what packages are being installed to your system.

Most of the major distributions offer an installation guide of some sort on their respective Web sites that will describe the various installation procedures, including the installation of servers and workstations. It is worth the effort to track down these guides as a reference during the installation.

During the pre-installation procedures, you likely identified the role of your computer and the packages it would take to support this role. Workstations, for instance, will typically use a window manager, office tools, and desktop utilities. A server installation is less likely to use any of these packages and more likely to use programs such as Apache, Samba, or Squid. Choosing the packages to install is an important consideration and must be matched with the purpose of your system. Refer to Chapter 6 for more information on choosing packages to install.

CERTIFICATION OBJECTIVE 7.04

Selecting Appropriate Options for Partitions Based on Pre-Installation Choices

No matter what distribution you are using, at some point during the installation, you will need to partition your disk. As discussed in Chapter 6, there are many different methods to do this, and the method used will depend on whether you are installing Linux on a system that already has an operating system installed or if it is on a system all by itself. Listed below is a review of a few of the tools that can be used when preparing you Linux partitions.

- **fdisk**   fdisk is the grandfather of partitioning tools and might, in fact, be the one you will find yourself using during the installation. fdisk can take some time to get used to but is a powerful partitioning tool. Each Linux distribution includes fdisk as an option for partitioning.

- **cfdisk**   cfdisk is an easier-to-use fdisk-type utility. Although it is more user friendly, it is perhaps not as versatile as the fdisk utility and not as commonly used.

- **Distribution-specific tools**   For some reason, each distribution seems to have its own partitioning tools. Red Hat has Disk Druid, Mandrake has DiskDrake, and so on. Fortunately they all do the same thing. Some do have a few additional features, but if you are familiar with using one, then the others should not be too difficult to work with.

- **fips**   When it comes to resizing a partition to make room for Linux, a common utility to use is fips. Although the process of resizing a partition is complex, fips makes the process simple and is not a complicated utility.

- **Third-party partition tools**   Many companies create partitioning software utilities that are very easy to use and efficient for partitioning the disk. These third-party tools come with documentation, making them the tools of choice if you have the money to afford them.

After you have chosen the tools you will be using to partition your disk, the next installation procedure is to identify a specific Linux partitioning strategy to be used. Linux requires at least two partitions during the installation, one for the swap partition and one for the root, which is typically formatted with the ext2 file format. Once the Linux-specific partitions are set, you can make additional partitions for the other Linux key subdirectories such as /home, /var, or the /usr directories. Chapter 6 outlined the Linux partitioning strategies that can be used.

CERTIFICATION OBJECTIVE 7.05

Selecting Appropriate Networking Configuration and Protocols

If your machine will be part if a network, you will need to set network settings during the installation. Setting the network settings is straightforward—that is, of course, providing that you have access to all the network information you need. Listed next are the possible network settings you will be required to input. Depending on your type of network and distribution used, you might be asked to input one or all these criteria.

IP Address

TCP/IP is the protocol of choice for Linux and during the installation, if your system is going to be connected to a network, you will need to enter an IP address. There are two ways in which your system can get the IP address: through a DHCP or BOOTP server, which automatically assign the IP addressing information, or by manually setting the number yourself. The method you choose will depend on the network configuration used.

If your new Linux system is not connected to a local area network but will be connected to the Internet, you will also need an IP address. Part of the pre-installation process is to identify these numbers from your Internet Service Provider (ISP) so they are ready for the installation. Most, but not all, ISPs use DHCP to assign addresses automatically. IP addresses are covered in greater detail in Chapter 2.

If your system has more than one network card, each network card will require its own address. Network cards are referred to as eth0, eth1, eth2, and so on.

Subnet Mask

The function on the subnet mask was covered in Chapter 2. It is essentially a means to identify which part of the IP address represents the host and which part of the address represents the network. The subnet mask can be automatically assigned by a DHCP server, but on many networks, this number is manually assigned. You will need the correct subnet mask to join an existing network or to log on to the Internet successfully.

Default Gateway

The default gateway identifies the device on the network that allows your system to access networks outside your local network. A router or server often act as the gateway device on a network. Not all local area networks will require your system to have a default gateway, however, if you want to connect to the Internet or another network, you will need one.

Hostname

There has to be a way to identify computers on a network, and this is the function that the hostname provides. If, for instance, your computer was named comp1 and you were in the linux.com domain, then your full system hostname would likely be comp1.linux.com. When searching for your system on the network and you have DNS installed, it is possible to ping the hostname to find it on the network. If your computer is not part of a network and you choose not to give it a hostname, then you will be given the default hostname of localhost.

Primary DNS

A DNS server is responsible for translating computer names to IP address. During the installation, you will be required to enter the address of the system that is providing DNS function. If connecting to the Internet, you will likely have a secondary DNS server and sometimes even a third for fault tolerance purposes.

on the **Job**

Many Linux distributions will allow you to input only a single DNS number during the installation. To add the additional numbers, you will need to edit the /etc/resolv.conf file manually.

If for some reason you do not have access to the network information, or if it changes at some point, it can be easily changed after the installation. Each distribution has its own GUI tools to accomplish this, such as the netconfig utility for Red Hat. In addition, the ifconfig command can be used to set certain information.

Connecting to the Internet

Many of the Linux systems you install will be connected to the Internet. To accommodate this, Linux installations often include the configuration of devices needed to access the World Wide Web. Mandrake 7.2, for instance, allows you to configure such devices as ISDN, DSL, cable, and modems during the installation, making connecting to the Internet that much easier.

Of course to configure these devices, you will need hardware and configuration information. When installing a modem, for instance, you will need to identify the type of modem you are using, the serial port it will use, the DNS server, phone number, and login ID. If you do not have this information, you can set up the modem after the installation, but the pre-installation planning makes sure it is all ready to go.

Other devices such as the ISDN, DSL, and cable are all configured in much the same way in that you will require ISP information as well as hardware-specific information. For the most part, as long as the pre-installation information is gathered and accessible, the installation of such devices is a smooth process.

CERTIFICATION OBJECTIVE 7.06

Selecting Appropriate Security Settings

Regardless of the operating system used, system security is a major consideration. Part of a secure Linux system is to create strong passwords; easily deciphered passwords are often the cause of a compromised system. For any user, including the root user, to log on, Linux requires an entry in the /etc/passwd. The /etc/passwd file holds passwords for each user, however, the passwords kept in this file are easy to read, causing a security issue. To remedy this potential security risk, during the installation you will have the opportunity to use shadow passwords. Shadows passwords are encrypted and kept in the /etc/shadow file. The shadow passwords are readable only by the root user, adding an extra level of security to the equation.

In the constant struggle for a secure system, a technique called MD5 has been developed. The details of MD5 surpass the Linux+ objectives, so for our purpose, just an awareness of MD5 is needed. Interestingly, MD5 allows you to have passwords that are up to 256 characters in length. Passwords of that length would be like typing an essay to log onto the system. During the installation for increased security, enable MD5 passwords.

FROM THE CLASSROOM

Shadow Passwords

The subject of why we use shadow passwords can be a confusing one, but there is interesting background behind it. Originally, passwords were stored in an encrypted format in the /etc/password file. The encryption used was sufficiently strong in that it was not practical for it to be cracked. Nowadays, the processing power available could crack the passwords relatively easily. So, rather than storing the passwords in the /etc/password file that is viewable to everyone, the passwords are stored in the /etc/shadow file, which is visible only to the root user. The /etc/password file is still needed, as the information provided in it is used by the system at various levels.

—*Mike Harwood, Linux+ Certified*

Often times the only way to know if a password has failed is when someone has accessed your system. In a more proactive approach, you can download Linux crack utilities that test the strength of your passwords. Remember, such utilities are to be used only for good!

CERTIFICATION OBJECTIVE 7.07

Creating Usernames and Passwords During Installation

During the installation, you will be required to input at least one password for the root account, and more if you are setting up other user accounts at the same time. When setting up passwords during the installation, there are some general guidelines to help ensure that the passwords you choose are secure. Listed next are some of these considerations to keep in mind when setting passwords.

- Passwords should use at least eight characters, but the more, the better.

- Refrain from using simple, easy-to-guess passwords, such as your name or birthday. Oddly, many passwords are chosen for their ease of remembering rather than their difficulty in deciphering.

- Linux is case sensitive, so don't be afraid to mix up the letters a bit. Strong passwords will take advantage of case SeNsitiVity.

- Passwords are a lot harder to guess if symbols and numbers are mixed in with letters. Unfortunately, they might also be harder to remember.

Armed with these general guidelines, we can now make some very secure passwords for the accounts we need to set up during the installation. For example, for the root account, a strong password would be something like $MXd56eR*. The problem is, of course, that the password bobscomp is a lot easier to remember than *Y3ie7&4, so you will have to find the middle ground. One easy method is to combine numbers into words and mix the case. For example, the root password on our server is Expl0reR. We tell you this because we trust you!

on the **!**
() o b

During the installation, you will be required to enter a password before the installation can continue. For the purposes of the course, security might not be a concern, but it is best to get into the habit of establishing strong security procedures now.

umask

Every file, when created, has to have a default file permission set to it. Of course, we can change the file permission after files are created, but they have to start somewhere. The default mode to set file permissions is done with the umask command. There are a several file modes that can be set using umask. Table 7-1 shows the range of values available.

On most systems you will find that the default value is set to 022 or 077, though there is no set rule on this. For 022, new directories will have a mode of read and write for the owner, and read for everyone else. New files will have the mode of read, write, and execute for the owner, and read for everyone else. To display the current umask setting on your system, type **umask** from the command line. The printout will list the file mode you are currently using.

TABLE 7-1	umask Values	

umask	File Permission	Directory Permission
000	rw-rw-rw-	rwxrwxrwx
022	rw-r—r—	rwxr-xr-x
027	rw-r-----	rwxr-x---
077	rwx------	rw-------
777	--------	--------

on the job

The umask and file mode values are derived from subtracting the umask value from the 777 value of complete rights. For instance to understand the umask value of 022, you have to subtract the values of the file permissions, which are 4 for read, 2 for write, and 1 for execute, from the full value of 777. For more information on file permissions, refer to Chapter 9.

EXERCISE 7-1

Modifying umask File Mode Settings

1. At the command line, type the following command:

   ```
   umask
   ```

2. Identify the current **umask** setting, which, for example, might be the 022 or 077 settings. Create a new text file using the following command:

   ```
   dmesg | grep hda > test
   ```

3. The command will create a text file. To view the file permissions, type the following command:

   ```
   ls -l.
   ```

   Make special note of the file permissions of the file you created.

4. Modify the file mode using the umask command to a different umask setting:

   ```
   umask 077 (022)
   ```

5. Create another text file using the following command:

   ```
   dmesg | grep hda > test2
   ```

6. Using the ls -l command review the file permissions for the new test file.

Creating Users and Passwords During Installation

Although it is not mandatory, it is recommended to make a few users during the installation simply because the root account should be used only when administrative tasks need to be performed. You will likely have the opportunity to create user accounts after the root account has been established. Setting up a user account during the installation is as simple as typing in the name for the user and typing in a password twice. As soon as the installation is completed, the account will be active.

Many administrators do not give the addition of user accounts much thought, but they do require special consideration, as each account poses a potential threat to the security of your system. Before creating user accounts, it is important to verify that shadow passwords and, potentially, MD5 passwords, are enabled. Not using shadow passwords leaves your passwords insecure.

on the **job** *Linux uses the Pluggable Authentication Mode (PAM) that is intended to prevent the creation of easy-to-pick or inappropriate passwords. It would not be a good idea to depend on PAM for password security. Implement a strong password policy just to make sure.*

EXERCISE 7-2

Testing Shadow Passwords

1. Log on to the system as a regular, non-root user.

2. At the command line, type the following command:

   ```
   $cat /etc/shadow
   ```

3. If shadow passwords are enabled you should receive the following message:

```
$cat: /etc/shadow: permission denied
```

4. Issue the command:

```
$cat /etc/passwd
```

The password field (the second field in each entry) should be set to *x*. This indicates that shadow passwords are being used.

---

exam **Watch**

A simple way to see if shadow passwords are being used is to check whether the second field in the user's entry of the /etc/password file is set to x. If it is, then you are using shadow passwords.

on the **Job**

Users can be added after the installation using the useradd command. Refer to Chapter 9 for more information on the useradd command.

CERTIFICATION OBJECTIVE 7.08

Installing and Configuring Xfree86 Server

A graphical interface is not much use if the keyboard, mouse, and other such devices can't interact with it. To allow hardware to be used with the graphical interface, an X server must be installed. That's where XFree86 comes in. XFree86 provides the means for the hardware and graphical interface to be used together.

exam **Watch**

To see what version of XFree86 you are using, type X -showconfig at the command prompt.

Installing XFree86

XFree86 comes with every major Linux distribution and is most often installed by default. This means that it is generally not necessary to install XFree86 as a separate package; however, there might become a time when you need to upgrade or perhaps reinstall, in which case you will need to download and install it.

Before even downloading XFree86, you should verify that it works with your current hardware configuration. The XFree86 Web site offers a comprehensive list of supported video cards and, to be honest, you will need to have a fairly unusual piece of hardware for it not to be supported by XFree86, but it does happen.

The first step in downloading the X server is deciding on the exact server you will need. There are many server types available for download, and choosing the right one is essential. Some of the servers available include the following:

- **X8514.tgz**   Used for 8514-based boards
- **XAGX.tgz**   Server for AGX-based boards
- **XI128.tgz**   Server for the Number Nine Imagine 128
- **XMach32.tgz**   Server for Mach32-based boards
- **XMach64.tgz**   Server for Mach64-based boards
- **XS3.tgz**   Server for S3-based boards
- **XS3V.tgz**   Server for the S3 ViRGE system boards
- **XVGA16.tgz**   Used for VGA 16
- **XSVGA.tgz**   Server for Super VGA-based boards

If you have any questions about which of these servers to use, refer to your documentation to confirm your hardware. If you are still unsure, you can play it safe and install the XVGA16.tgz server. It will be enough to get you going.

Once you have downloaded the correct package, you can then start the installation process. XFree86 needs to be installed in the /usr/X11R6 directory, and if this directory does not exist, you will be required to create it. Once the files have been unpackaged to the directory, you are ready for the next step, configuring XFree86 server.

Running the preinst.sh script file will test your system, looking for anything that might cause a problem, such as hardware or missing files.

Configuring XFree86

With the necessary files unpacked in the /usr/X11R6 directory, you are ready to configure your X server. During the installation, you will be prompted for some information on your system, so be prepared. Specifically, you will need to know your monitor and video card capabilities. The utilities used to reconfigure XFree86 after the installation are covered in greater detail in Chapter 8.

CERTIFICATION OBJECTIVE 7.09

Selecting Video Card Support

During the installation of Linux, it will try to automatically detect the video card you are using in your system. If you use a mainstream card and it's not too new, Linux is likely to pick it up. If it doesn't, you can enter the settings manually. Once the correct card is identified, you will need to set the amount of video RAM used by the card, which you will know as part of the pre-installation. Finally, you will be required to set the video resolution you will be using.

Once again, it is important to know what your hardware is capable of supporting to choose the correct resolutions for your video card. You will have the option of choosing from several different resolution modes. Don't forget to test the resolution mode before continuing. To do otherwise could prove frustrating when it doesn't work.

on the
Job

Using unsupported video modes can damage hardware.

During the X configuration part of the installation, you will also have to choose the color depth you will use. As a quick reference, remember that 8-bit color uses 256 colors, 16-bit color uses about 65,000 colors, and 24- and 32-bit use almost 17 million colors. Your window manager looks a little bland with 8-bit colors, so use a higher depth and test the configuration to see if it works with your system.

Once these settings have all been successfully entered, you are ready to use the graphics capabilities of your system.

CERTIFICATION OBJECTIVE 7.10

Selecting Appropriate Monitor Manufacturers and Settings

When it comes to choosing your monitor, you will be thankful that you took the time to review and document your hardware before the installation. You will need to choose your monitor from a list of preset monitors. There are many monitors to choose from, some distributions boast more than 1,700! It is your job during this part of the installation to choose your monitor from this extensive list. If you do not know which monitor you are using, you might have to refer to the manufacturer's documentation.

If you are unable to find your monitor in the list, you might have to input your monitor settings manually. To custom-install your monitor, you will need to input your horizontal sync range and vertical sync range. The horizontal sync is measured in kilohertz, with the typical range for a monitor being between 30 and 64 kHz. The vertical sync, or vertical refresh rate, is measured in hertz, and is typically set between 50 and 90 Hz. It is important not to set the monitor range beyond what it can support, as it is possible to damage your monitor.

CERTIFICATION OBJECTIVE 7.11

Selecting Appropriate Window Managers or Desktop Environments

The window managers and desktop environments give us something other than a command prompt to look at. Unlike many other operating systems, Linux gives us a choice as to which one we will use on our systems. Although the decision of which to use often boils down to personal preference rather than any feature or functionality, it is nice to have the choice.

Linux Window Managers

There are many window managers that you can choose to use on your Linux system. Each of these window managers provides a basic level of functions, including moving, hiding, resizing, and closing windows. Others offer far more advanced features. To give you some idea of what is available, here is a list of some of the window managers you might use.

- **BlackBox (http://blackbox.alug.org)**   BlackBox prides itself on being a fast window manager. To accomplish this, it puts little emphasis on looks and a lot on performance. BlackBox does provide the tools and methods to function, but doesn't put them in a pretty box. Perhaps not for the beginner, but for future use, BlackBox might be the one.

- **Sawfish (http://www.sawfish.org)**   The Sawfish window manager is a configurable window manager that allows you to customize the look of your system. To get some idea of what Sawfish allows you to do, refer to the Sawfish theme page at http://www.sawmill.org. Sawfish is designed to use minimal resources and to be easy to configure. If you get stuck using Sawfish, the site offers support links.

- **WindowMaker (http://www.windowmaker.org)**   If you are looking for a window manager to download and use for the first time, WindowMaker might be it. Visit the site at http://wm.themes.org/ to get a better idea of what you can do with WindowMaker.

- **Enlightenment (http://www.enlightenment.org)**   Enlightenment is a popular window manager, and a good one to use for an initiation. Enlightenment offers many features, and at the Enlightenment Web site, you can view screen shots and download various themes.

- **IceWM (http://www.icewm.org)**   The Ice window manager is built from the ground up and offers many of the features found throughout other popular window managers. As do the other window manager Web sites, the one for Ice offers a variety of themes to customize the look and feel of Linux.

This is by no means a comprehensive list of window managers available for Linux, but it is enough to get started. For a list of available window managers, check out the Web site at http://www.plig.org/xwinman/.

Desktop Environments

Desktop environments take the window manager one step further to include many new features and a veritable cornucopia of applications. Desktop managers are very user friendly, and offer all the graphical tools you could want. When it comes to desktop environments, there are two that are the key players, KDE and GNOME.

GNOME itself is not a window manager and, in fact, needs to be used with one. You will need to have a GNOME-compliant window manager in order for it to work. GNOME comes with most of the major Linux distributions and can be installed as the default, standard desktop environment. GNOME is built using free-open source software and is, therefore, distributed under this agreement. Figure 7-1 shows the desktop screen of GNOME.

Like GNOME, KDE offers numerous graphical utilities and features. Unlike GNOME, however, KDE comes with its own built-in window manager called KWM, although you can use a different window manager if you choose. Figure 7-2 shows the KDE desktop screen.

FIGURE 7-1

GNOME desktop screen

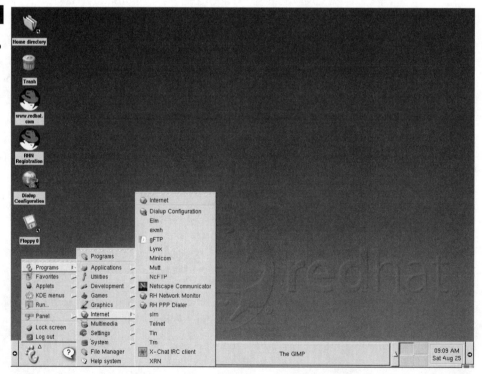

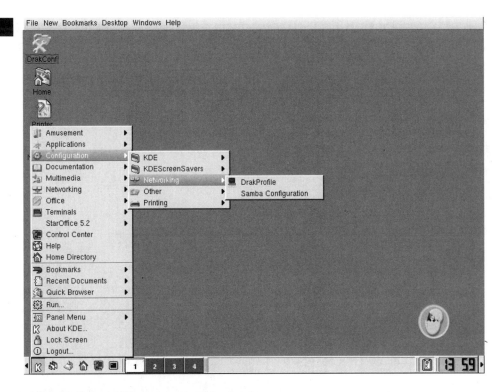

FIGURE 7-2

KDE Desktop
screen

Explaining When and Why the Kernel Needs to Be Recompiled

Deciding to recompile the kernel might seem like a fairly momentous decision, but in reality, the automated tools that are available make it less of an issue. It is still, however, a task that should be approached with a degree of caution and a measure of preparation.

There are a variety of reasons why you might recompile the kernel, but it basically involves adding or removing components and, subsequently, functionality. Here are some of the main reasons why you would recompile a kernel.

- **Add or remove modules** Although it is possible to add or remove modules on the fly (see Chapter 8 for more information on this), such actions are really meant only for situations when you require a module on an occasional basis. If you are going to use the module on a regular basis, it is far more efficient to compile that module into the kernel so that it is always run. Likewise, if there are modules within the kernel that you don't use, it is more efficient to remove that feature than leave it in. Doing so reduces the size of the kernel and, subsequently, memory usage. Reducing the size of the kernel can also improve performance, though you have to remove a number of modules to get a noticeable improvement (Linux is fast anyway!).

- **Add or change hardware support** Kernels are designed to accommodate a wide range of hardware but, even so, you might find yourself in a situation in which the kernel needs to be recompiled to add or change support for hardware. It is also possible to recompile the kernel optimized for a certain type of processor.

- **Fix bugs or problems** In some cases it might be necessary to recompile the kernel to fix a bug or problem. Sometimes, rather than recompiling the kernel, a patch can simply be applied to. In other instances, a recompile is necessary.

Because distributions come with a standard kernel, it is common practice to recompile the kernel straight after installation to customize it as required. This allows you to start from a solid base. One word of warning, however: for the uninitiated, compiling the kernel is a process that has many steps and associated downfalls. While process itself is not complex and is well documented, it is worth a few practice tries before you try it on a production system.

CERTIFICATION OBJECTIVE 7.13

Installing a Boot Loader

A boot loader is a program that is installed on the hard disk that allows you to choose the operating system you would like to boot into. The boot loader is one of the initial programs that run when the computer starts, and it's responsible for transferring control to the operating system, which can then continue with the boot process. There are many different types of boot loader programs available, but the Linux Loader (LILO) is the one you are far more likely to encounter and use during your Linux installation.

on the **Job**

Keep in mind that LILO, while the most popular boot loader, is not the only option available. Mandrake Linux, for instance, uses the Grand Unified Boot Loader (GRUB) as a default option and is preferred over LILO by many.

LILO is used to start Linux on your system or, if you're using multiple operating systems, it allows you the option of booting into any one of them. With many distributions, during the installation of Linux, you will be prompted to install LILO and determine exactly where it should be installed. For this, you have two choices, install LILO on the primary hard drive's master boot record (MBR) or on the first sector of the partition where you installed Linux. Other distributions will automatically install LILO to the MBR.

LILO will most often be installed on the MBR, which is read directly by the system's BIOS. LILO will usually be installed on only the first sector of your root partition when another boot loader is being used on the system such as the Windows NT or 2000 NTLDR boot loader. During the installation, when you are prompted for the location to install LILO, just install it on the MBR, unless you are using an alternative boot loader. If during the installation you choose not to install LILO, you might not be able to boot into Linux directly, and will need another method, such as a boot disk, to get your system running.

exam **Watch**

During the LILO installation step, remember that it is ordinarily installed on the MBR unless your system is using an alternative boot loader program.

Another alternative you have when choosing a boot loader is the Loadlin program. Loadlin uses the DOS MBR to boot into your Linux system. To use Loadlin, you will need the loadlin.exe program, which is included with many Linux distribution CDs. Additionally you will need a copy of your kernel image on your DOS partition. All this will allow you to dual-boot your system.

CERTIFICATION OBJECTIVE 7.14

Installing and Uninstalling Applications After Installing the Operating System

As you might imagine, at some point, you will need to add an application to your system, such as a word processor or some other type of utility. As you are looking for these packages to download, understanding package formats becomes an important consideration. When you start to look for packages to download, you will come across a number of different ones, and you will need to know which packages go with which distributions.

RPM

The most common of all Linux package formats is the Red Hat Package Manager (RPM). Although it is referred to as the Red Hat Package Manager, it is used by far more than the Red Hat distribution. Mandrake, SuSE, and Caldera use the RPM package format.

Installing RPM

RPM packages can be installed using the specific X tools within the graphical interface or from the command line. This section refers to the installation of the packages from the latter.

When installing an RPM package, there are three key switches that are used.

- **rpm -I** can be used to install a new RPM package.
- **rpm -F** is used only to upgrade a package and will not install the package if it is not already installed.
- **rpm -U** is used to upgrade an RPM package and will install the package if it is not already installed.

In addition to these major switches, there are two minor switches often used with the rpm command. The **-v** switch is used to see verbose messages, and the **-h** switch is used to see the hash marks (#) during the installation as progress markers. The most common use of these switches when installing an RPM looks like this:

```
#rpm -Uvh package_name.rpm
```

Using this command upgrades or install an RPM package, using hash marks for progress and verbose messages.

As you might imagine, if you have the option to install an RPM package, you also have the option to uninstall an RPM. Uninstalling a package is a simple process. Simply use the *-e* switch as follows:

```
#rpm -e package_name
```

Note that when removing a package, the .rpm extension is not required, only the package name.

Installing and uninstalling are just two of the features you can do with the rpm command. You can also use the command to identify the RPM packages you have installed. By using the **-q** switch, you are able to determine if there is a specific RPM package installed. For instance, the following command can be used to determine if the Apache Web server is installed:

```
#rpm -q apache
```

To see a list of all the RPM packages currently installed on your system, you can use the **-qa** switch as follows:

```
#rpm -qa | more
```

There are plenty of other switches that can be used with the **rpm** command. We have just identified some of the more commonly used. To see a comprehensive list of the available options for the rpm command, type **rpm — | help | more** at the command line.

Installing from tar

You might find an application, download it looking for the familiar .rpm extension, only to be greeted with a .tar, .tar.gz, or tgz extension. Now what? Files using such formats are referred to as tar files and offer a clear advantage in that they are package-manager independent. Also, because it sometimes takes a while for packages distributed in tar format to be made into RPMs or the like, you might find that tar files offer more current software.

tar files are not as slick as the RPMs and require an extra step during the installation. These files have to be both untarred and unzipped to be installed. To do this, use the following command:

```
#tar xzvf filename
```

The **x** switch in the command is used to extract the files from the archive, the **z** switch is needed if the tar file is zipped (which is common), and the **v** is used to display verbose messages. The **f** refers to the name of the archive file. As you can see, the switches can be used next to each other, but the **f** must be followed by the filename. Refer to Chapter 10 to see a list of the switches and their usages for the tar command.

Table 7-2 shows some of the common distribution formats you can expect to see when you are looking for packages to install.

on the

Job *The Martian and Alien programs allow conversions between package formats such as .deb, .rpm, and tar.gz. Using these utilities makes packages accessible to all Linux distributions.*

TABLE 7-2	Common Package Formats

Format	Description
.rpm	Red Hat Package Manager. The main file archive format used not only for Red Hat but a number of other distributions.
.deb	File archive format used with the Debian Linux distribution. Can be converted for other distributions using the *Martian* or *Alien* programs. Both the dpkg and the apt-get utilities are used to install, extract, and query packages.
.tar	The .tar extension signifies that the package was made using the tar command; tar command switches can be seen by typing **tar --help** at a command interface.
.gz or .z	The archive was compressed using the gzip utility. The file can be unzipped using the gzip or gunzip commands.
.tar.gz or .tgz	A tar archive that has been compressed with the gzip utility. Such files will need to be both untarred and gunzipped.
.bz2	File was compressed with the bzip utility.

SCENARIO & SOLUTION

You need to install a new RPM package. Which switch are you likely to use with the rpm command?	**rpm -i** can be used to install a new package.
You want to upgrade an RPM package with verbose messaging. Which RPM switch would you use?	**rpm -Uv** will upgrade a package and provide verbose messages.
You want to get a list of all the RPM packages currently installed on your system.	Using the rpm -qa command will provide a list of the RPMs on your system.

CERTIFICATION OBJECTIVE 7.15

Reading Log Files Created During Installation to Verify the Success of the Installation

For the most part, you will know if the installation has worked simply by whether it boots up or not; however, sometimes there are those subtle things that did not install correctly. In either case, it is good practice to review a few logs after the installation to make sure everything is running as it should. Listed here are a few of the log files you might wish to view.

■ **boot.log (/var/log)** The boot.log provides a comprehensive look at the services that were loaded during the boot process. Using this log, you will be able to determine if the service started correctly, and it might help you isolate a problem if they did not.

■ **install.log (/tmp)** The install.log gives you a good look at what was loaded during the installation and what did and did not install properly. The log file is quite long and might take some time to read through, but it is worth it to make sure everything was installed correctly.

■ **dmesg (/var/log/)** dmesg allows you to see the hardware that the kernel has detected the correct hardware during the installation. If you are having trouble accessing hardware after the installation, you can peruse the dmesg output to confirm that the system recognizes it.

There are numerous other log files that you can review, far too many to list here. If you would like to view these other log files, you can use the find command to locate the files and the **vi** command to view them. A great number of these log files are kept in the /var/log directory. This is a good place to start when exploring log files.

CERTIFICATION OBJECTIVE 7.16

Testing an Installed Application's Performance in Both a Test and a Production Environment

Once the installation is complete and before the system is released to end users, it's worth testing the installation of the applications to make sure that they are operating properly. What form this testing takes depends on what the application is and who will be using it. Let's say, for example, that you have elected to install Samba on the system to provide file and print sharing capabilities to Windows clients. You can make sure the Samba daemons are running, but that alone does not prove that clients will be able to access the system.

The only way to test such a system effectively is to use it just as a client would. In other words, you go to a client workstation, map a drive to the Linux server, print to the printer on the Linux server, and so on. If all that works as you expect, then you can release the system, or at least that application, to users.

Now, because at this point you might not know how the server will react under load, it might be worth releasing the application to only a small group of users and have them to use the system on the understanding that they are acting as testers. If you pick the right audience for this kind of limited trial, it is possible that any shortcomings can be detected and addressed with ease.

Once any bugs have been worked out, you can release the product to all the users, however, the testing and checking should not stop there. As more people start using the service, the ability for the server to support the demands placed on it should be monitored.

Outside of testing systems in a practical situation, you can also use the rpm command with the -V switch to confirm the package was installed correctly. If while testing a package, the command finds something wrong with the package, it will print it to screen. As an example, you might want to test and verify the Apache package. To do this the command is **rpm -V apache**. If anything is wrong in the Apache package, it will be detected and reported. Of course, this must be used in conjunction with a real-world practical test.

Red Hat Installation

So far in this chapter, we have outlined the general procedures you will encounter as you install your Linux system. To get a better idea of an actual Linux installation, we will walk you through the specific steps of a real Red Hat installation. The exact steps might vary depending on the exact version of Red Hat you are installing. This installation example will use Red Hat 7.0.

The first screen requires you to choose the language you will use for the installation process. Even without too much pre-installation preparation, this should be straightforward.

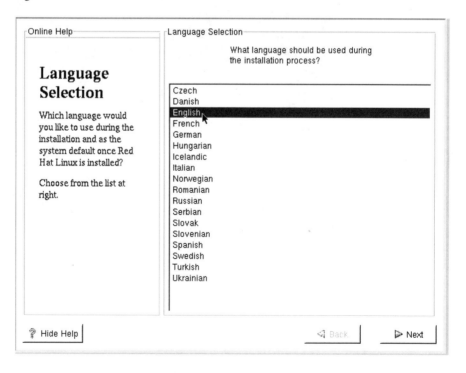

This screen allows you to choose the model and layout of your system and whether dead keys will be enabled. Dead keys allow the use of accent letters, for instance, à, ō, and ü. The default setting will typically work with most keyboards.

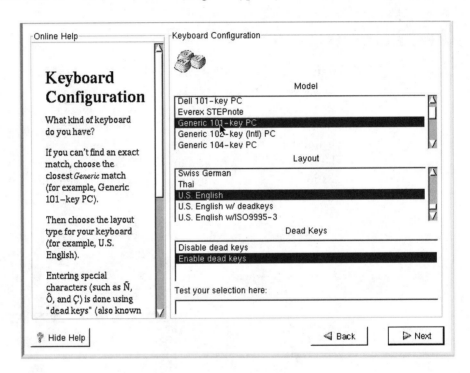

The third installation screen allows you to configure the mouse. If it is a serial mouse, you will need to configure the com ports. If not, choose your mouse from the list. You may use the Emulate 3 Buttons option, which in a Windows Manager, lets you press both mouse buttons simultaneously to emulate a three-button mouse. Some features require three mouse buttons.

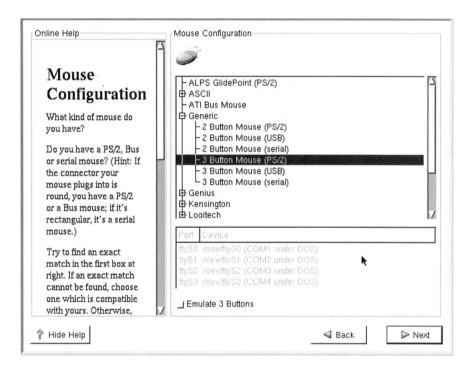

After the general parameters are set, the Linux installer introduction screen is displayed. The screen encourages you to read the installation documentation, which is a very good idea.

At this point in the installation, you will be required to choose the role of your Linux system. Your options for Red Hat are Server, Workstation, or Custom. You also have the option to choose the Upgrade option. Only this option will allow you to preserve any existing data. The others will require repartitioning and will destroy existing data.

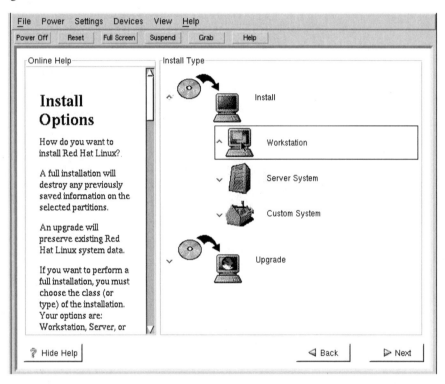

After choosing the system's role, you will need to partition your disk. You have the option to partition your drive automatically, partition using the Red Hat Disk Druid utility, or use fdisk. For most installations, the Disk Druid is the choice, but the familiar fdisk utility is there if you prefer.

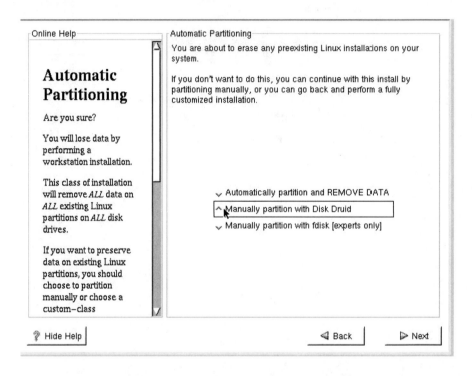

Partitioning with the Disk Druid straightforward, but if you are installing Linux on a disk with another operating system, be careful not to erase it.

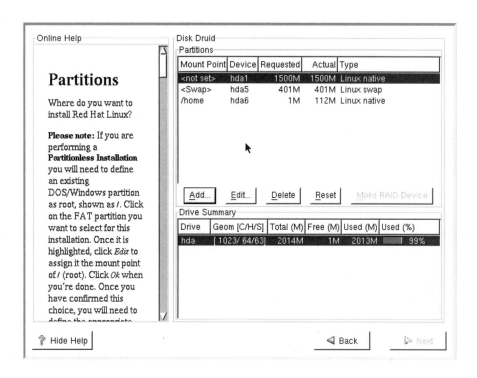

Once the partitions have been chosen, you will be taken to a screen to format the Linux partitions. You will have the option to check for bad blocks during the formatting. It is worth your time to do so, as any bad blocks will be marked and not written to.

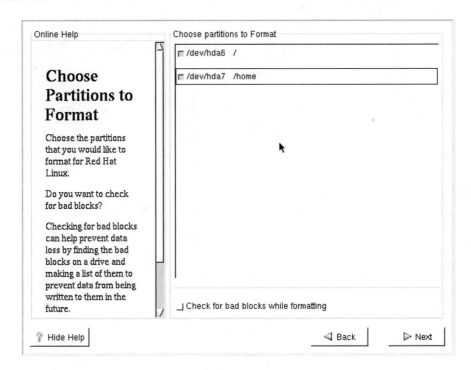

There is not much to setting the time zone, just choosing your location. It is important to set the correct time, as it is used by the system.

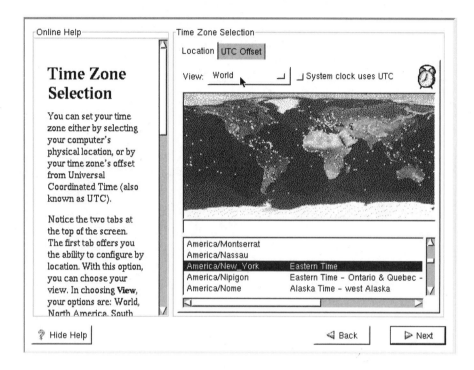

The following illustration shows the screen to set the root account password and any additional user account passwords. It is recommended to make at least one additional user account in addition to the root account.

During this part of the installation, you can choose the packages you want to install. More options are available if you are using the custom option during installation.

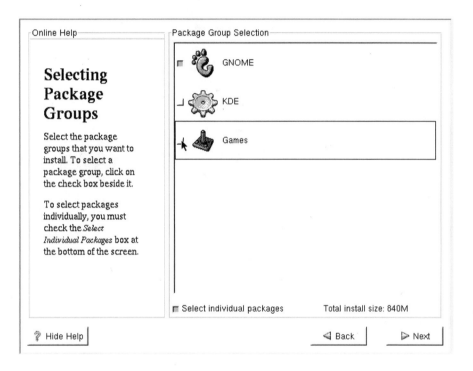

Part of the X configuration requires choosing the monitor settings. The following illustration shows the Red Hat screen for configuring the monitor. You have many preset choices to choose from, or you can custom set your monitor settings. The settings for your monitor will be included with your monitor's documentation.

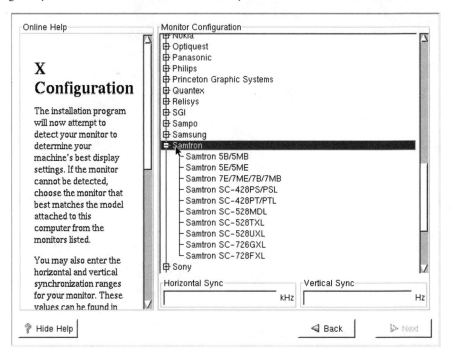

After the monitor is selected, you can choose your video card. Linux will try its best to detect you video card and settings. If it is incorrect, you can input your own settings. You will need to know you video memory, manufacturer, and possibly video chipset.

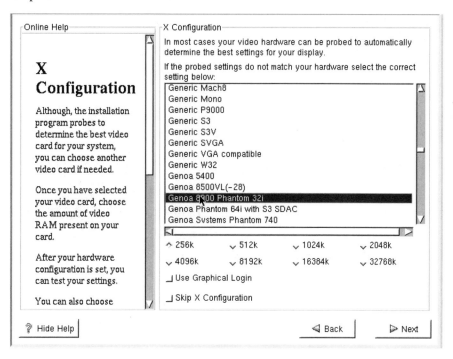

After you have configured all the previous screens, you have one last chance to back out and go back to change anything. If you are sure you have correctly installed everything, click the Next button, and Red Hat Linux will be installed.

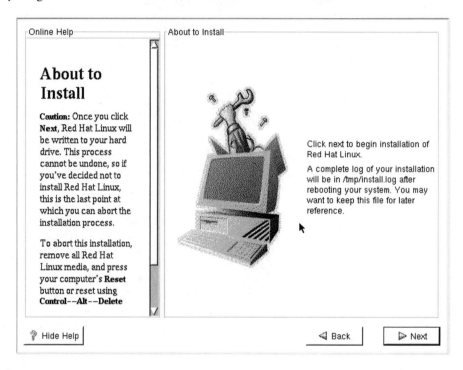

SuSE Text-Based Installation

Now that you have seen what a graphical installation, you can see what you can expect from a text-based installation. For a text installation, we have chosen to use SuSE. SuSE can be installed in both a graphical and text mode, and whenever possible, a graphical installation should be used. For now, however, let's take a look at a text installation.

As with any installation, the first screen you can expect to see is the language selection screen. Right from the start, you will notice how unpolished the text-based screens are. Still, choosing a language is choosing a language, no matter how you package it.

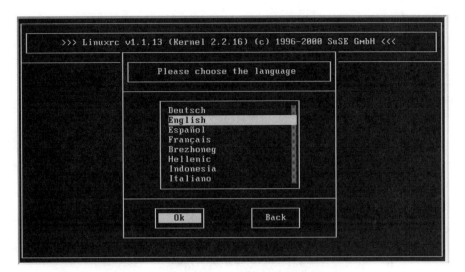

Graphical installations are unlikely to have this type of screen, but you can choose from a color or monochrome display. We would recommend going with color unless you are troubleshooting or are curious about what a monochrome display looks like.

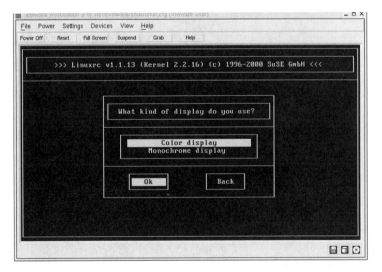

The keyboard selection screen is familiar, and despite the absence of graphics, should offer little difficulty.

Once the keyboard map has been chosen, you will be greeted with the SuSE installation main menu screen. You can explore the various options available on this screen, but when you are ready to carry on with the installation, select the Start Installation / System option.

This dialog box offers a few important options, including performing a regular and rescue boot. For the purposes of the installation, however, we need to select the Start Installation / Update option. Once selected, we can choose the installation method we will use.

By this point in the installation, you might have had your fill of keyboard-driven text menus. Here is your chance to bail out. You can select to use a graphical installation from here, but if you have problems, you might have to return to the text installation. For this example, we will continue with the text installation.

This screen allows you to install a fresh copy of Linux, upgrade an existing installation, or install using Expert mode. All these modes are very helpful options, but for now, we are installing a new copy of Linux.

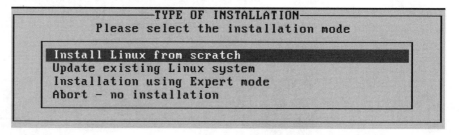

Graphical or text-based installation, there is no escaping the fact that you will have to partition your disks. This screen gives you the opportunity to use your entire hard disk for Linux or partition some off, just in case you have something else on the drive.

It isn't pretty, but it works. The partitioning tool used is a very basic utility, but provides the same function as one with all the pretty packaging.

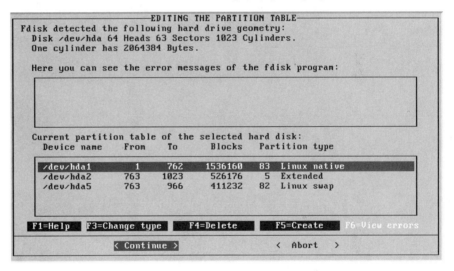

After the hard disks have been partitioned, you can now choose the file systems used for the respective partitions. The following illustration shows ext2 being used for hda1, but you will have other options, including swap.

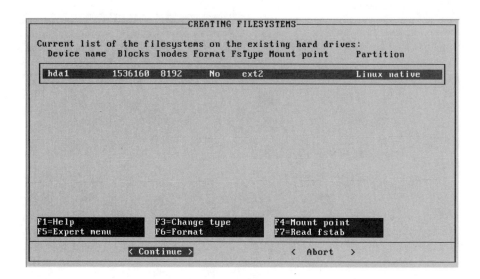

Once you have set the hard disk with partitions and file systems, you are now ready to install SuSE Linux. Select the Install Packages option to choose the packages you want to install; then select the Start Installation option, and you are on your way to installing SuSE on your system.

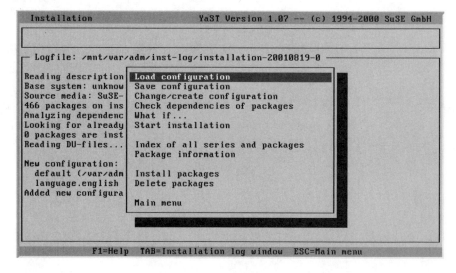

CERTIFICATION SUMMARY

Despite the large number of Linux distributions, they all share some common installation procedures. Many of the major Linux distributions allow you to use a graphical installation or a text-based installation. Text-based installations are commonly used when there is a problem with hardware. Once you know the installation method you will use, you will be guided through general installation procedures, including mouse settings, keyboard settings, and the language to be used for the installation.

In addition to all the general installation procedures, you will be required to do some more advanced installation steps, including partitioning your disk, configuring the X Server, choosing the packages to install, and choosing a security strategy for your system.

During the installation, you will need to set a password for the root account and maybe some for some of the user accounts. For these accounts, strong passwords should be created that use uppercase letters, numbers, and symbols.

After the installation, you can review the boot.log and the install.log to verify that the installation was successful. All applications should also be tested individually to verify that they work in a practical environment and a production environment.

TWO-MINUTE DRILL

Here are some of the key points presented in this chapter.

Selecting the Appropriate Linux Installation Interactions

❑ Most of the major Linux distributions will auto-detect the video card and will use graphical installation screens.

❑ If a graphical installation isn't working, you can use other installation interaction methods, including a text mode and an expert mode.

Selecting Appropriate Parameters for a Linux Installation

❑ During the Linux installation, you will be required to identify several general installation parameters, including time zone, language, and keyboard and mouse settings.

❑ These settings can be readily changed after the installation using tools readily available throughout all Linux distributions.

Selecting Packages Based on the Machine's Role

❑ During the installation, you will be required to choose the software and packages to be installed. The packages installed will depend on whether the system is intended to be a server or a workstation.

❑ Packages can be installed after the installation if the intended role of the system changes.

Selecting Appropriate Options for Partitions Based on Pre-Installation Choices

❑ There are many Linux native tools available for creating partitions including fips and fdisk

❑ In addition to the Linux native partitioning tools, several third-party utilities are available.

Selecting Appropriate Networking Configuration and Protocols

❑ During the installation, you will have the chance to set your system's network settings, including IP address, subnet mask, default gateway, DNS server, and hostname.

❑ If you are connecting to the Internet or to an existing LAN, you will need the settings for the respective network.

Selecting Appropriate Security Settings

❑ During the installation, you will have the option of using shadow passwords, adding an extra level of security to the system.

❑ Passwords should follow a certain criteria, making them harder to crack. This involves using both upper- and lowercase letters, symbols, and numbers to make up a password.

❑ The default file permissions of a system can be changed using the umask command.

❑ During the installation, you will be required to set the root password for the system.

Creating Usernames and Passwords During Installation

❑ During the installation, you will be prompted to make regular user accounts in addition to the root account. It is recommended to make at least one regular account during the installation and use the root account only for administrative purposes.

❑ When creating user passwords, they should follow general policies for creating strong passwords.

Installing and Configuring Xfree86 Server

❑ XFree86 server comes with most of the Linux distributions available. If needed, it can be downloaded and installed as a separate package.

❑ To configure XFree86 server successfully, you will need to input settings for both the monitor and the video card.

Selecting Video Card Support

❏ To install your video settings manually, you will need to input your video memory, resolution supported, and manufacturer or chipset.

❏ Video settings can be changed after the installation using the Xf86setup utility.

Selecting Appropriate Monitor Manufacturers and Settings

❏ When manually configuring your monitor, you will need to input the vertical and horizontal sync ranges.

❏ Monitor settings can be altered after the installation using the Xfree86 setup utility.

Selecting Appropriate Window Managers or Desktop Environments

❏ Numerous window managers are available for Linux. All provide a similar, basic functionality.

❏ Both GNOME and KDE make a solid desktop environment choice. Both KDE and GNOME require a window manager to function. Many of the popular window managers are GNOME-compliant. KDE has a built-in manager

Explaining When and Why the Kernel Needs to Be Recompiled

❏ The kernel is often recompiled to remove features you don't want, or to add features you do.

❏ The kernel can be reconfigured to customize the kernel for your specific hardware. configuration.

Installing a Boot Loader

❏ Linux supports a variety of boot loaders, including LILO and GRUB, which allow the system to multi-boot operating systems.

❏ If a system already has a boot loader installed, such as the NTLDR, then the Linux boot loader should not be installed on the MBR.

Installing and Uninstalling Applications After Installing the Operating System

❑ Files with the .tar, .tgz, and tar.gz extensions must be unzipped and unpacked before installing.

❑ The most common Linux application package is RPM. Numerous options are available when using the rpm command.

Reading Log Files Created During Installation to Verify the Success of the Installation

❑ Part of the installation process involves reviewing log files to ensure that all has been installed correctly and is functioning.

❑ Common log files to review after the installation include the boot.log, install.log, and running the dmesg command.

Testing an Installed Application's Performance in Both a Test and a Production Environment

❑ After the installation, test the system and applications as if you were the user to ensure it has complete functionality.

❑ The **rpm -V** *package_name* can verify the RPM package installation.

SELF TEST

The following questions will help you measure your understanding of the material presented in this chapter. Read all of the choices carefully because there might be more than one correct answer. Choose all correct answers for each question.

Describing the Different Types of Linux Installation Interaction and Describing Which One to Use for a Given Situation

1. After trying several times, you cannot get your Linux system to install using a graphical screen. At the boot prompt, what interaction method should you choose?

    A. Rescue mode

    B. Text mode

    C. Safe mode

    D. Recovery mode

Selecting Appropriate Parameters for a Linux Installation

2. After installing Linux, you find out that the mouse does not work the way you would like. Which of the following are you most likely to do to reconfigure the mouse?

    A. Reinstall Linux and change the mouse settings.

    B. Modify the /etc/mouse directory.

    C. Edit the /var/mouse.conf file.

    D. Use the mouseconfig command.

Selecting Packages Based on the Machine's Role

3. You are installing Linux on a computer with limited hard disk space. You will be using the system as a Linux file and print server. Which of the following are you least likely to install?

    A. KDE

    B. Resource monitoring utilities

    C. Network monitoring utilities

    D. RPM packages

Select Appropriate Options for Partitions Based on Pre-Installation Choices

4. Which of the following partitioning utilities is included with all Linux distributions?

    A. Partition-it

    B. Diskdruid

    C. fdisk

    D. Partition Magic

Selecting Appropriate Networking Configuration and Protocols

5. You are installing Linux on a server that is going to be your company's new file and print server. Which of the following pieces of information will you need to complete the network configuration part of the installation?

    A. IP address

    B. Hostname

    C. DNS

    D. Kernel version

Selecting Appropriate Security Settings

6. Which of the following commands would you use to change the default file mode values?

    A. chmod

    B. Umask

    C. umask

    D. modfile

Creating Usernames and Passwords During Installation

7. You are required to input a password during the Linux installation. Which of the following passwords are the most secure?

    A. bob1

    B. Bob101

    C. R1o1b1B1

    D. Robert4

Installing and Configuring XFree86 Server

8. What Linux directory holds the XFree86 files?

  A. /usr/bin/X11R6

  B. /usr/X11

  C. /usr/bin/X11

  D. /usr/X11R6

Selecting Video Card Support

9. What is the last step when configuring a video card?

  A. Locate and input the video chipset information.

  B. Identify the video memory.

  C. Test the video settings.

  D. Document the video card settings.

Selecting Appropriate Monitor Manufacturers and Settings

10. When manually configuring a monitor, which of the following settings do you need to set?

  A. Vertical sync range

  B. Video memory

  C. Horizontal sync range

  D. Color resolution

Selecting Appropriate Window Managers or Desktop Environments

11. Which of the following is the built-in window manager used by KDE?

  A. KVM

  B. KWM

  C. KMV

  D. KMW

Explaining When and Why the Kernel Needs to Be Recompiled

12. Which of the following is least likely to be a reason to recompile the kernel?

  A. Adding or removing modules

  B. Correcting application errors

C. Supporting new hardware

D. Modifying user accounts

Installing a Boot Loader

13. You are installing Linux on a computer system that already has Windows 2000 installed on it. Where are you likely to install LILO?

A. On the MBR.

B. On the first sector of the root directory.

C. You would install GRUB, not LILO.

D. /mnt/winnt directory.

14. Which of the following programs can be used to make a dual-boot system?

A. GRUB

B. /root

C. LILO

D. TDboot

Installing and Uninstalling Applications After Installing the Operating System

15. After downloading and installing a specific RPM package, your system seems to be performing more slowly. You decide to remove the package. Which of the following commands would you use?

A. rpm -e *package_name*

B. rpm -e

C. rpm -E *package_name*

D. pm -E

16. You are downloading a new Linux application that has a .tgz extension. What does this extension mean?

A. The file was created using the tar command.

B. The file was compressed using the gzip utility.

C. The file was designed for Slackware Linux.

D. The file was designed for Debian Linux.

17. You need to determine if Apache is installed on a new Linux system. Which of the following commands could you use to determine whether apache is installed?

A. rpm -q apache

B. rpm -e apache

C. rpm -Uvh apache

D. rpm -v apache

Reading Log Files Created During Installation to Verify the Success of the Installation

18. After installing Linux, you want to review a log file that reviews the services that were loaded during the boot process. Which of the following log files might you review?

A. install.log

B. dmesg

C. /var/log

D. boot.log

Testing an Installed Application's Performance in Both a Test and a Production Environment

19. After installing Linux, you decide to upgrade an application on the system. The extension on the file is .rpm. Which of the following commands could you use?

A. rpm -U

B. rpm -i

C. rpm -F

D. rpm -C

20. After installing an RPM Apache package, you suspect something might have gone wrong during the installation. What command might you use to test your suspicions?

A. rpm -v apache

B. rpm -V apache

C. rpm -E apache

D. rpm -e apache

LAB QUESTION

It must come as no surprise that the lab question on a chapter focusing on Linux installations will be a Linux installation. Follow the procedures outlined in this chapter to install any distribution of Linux you are interested in. If this is your first time installing Linux, it might be a good idea to stick to one that offers an easy and perhaps graphical installation.

SELF TEST ANSWERS

Describing the Different Types of Linux Installation Interaction and Describing Which One to Use for a Given Situation

1. ☑ **B.** If you are installing Linux and are having difficulty with the graphical installation, you can install Linux using text mode by typing **text** at the installation's **boot:**.

   ☒ **A.** Rescue mode is an option but is used to try and repair an existing Linux installation, not to correct graphical installation problems. **C.** Safe mode is a recovery option for the Windows operating system. **D.** Recovery mode is not a valid Linux option.

Selecting Appropriate Parameters for a Linux Installation

2. ☑ **D.** If after installing Linux you need to change or modify your mouse settings, you can use the mouseconfig command. The mouseconfig command can be used from within a Window Manager or from the console. Both options provide the same functionality.

   ☒ **A.** It is possible to reinstall Linux to change the mouse settings, but that just a bit extreme. **B.** There is no such directory as the /etc/mouse directory. **C.** There is not a /var/mouse.conf file.

Selecting Packages Based on the Machine's Role

3. ☑ **A.** KDE is a graphical interface and is not required of a Linux server; in fact, many seasoned Linux administrators will not install a graphical interface, whether there is hard disk space or not.

   ☒ **B.** Regardless of the intended use of the server, it is necessary to install resource-monitoring tools. If a GUI is not installed, these can be used from the command line. **C.** As with resource monitoring tools, it is best to have network monitoring utilities available. **D.** RPM is package format.

Select Appropriate Options for Partitions Based on Pre-Installation Choices

4. ☑ **C.** fdisk is a powerful utility included with all Linux distributions. It may not be as user friendly as some of the more commercial tools, but it is the most widely used.

   ☒ **A.** Partition-it is not a valid Linux utility. **B.** Diskdruid is not included with all Linux distributions, it is supplied with Red Hat Linux. **C.** Partition Magic is a third-party utility and not included with all distributions.

Selecting Appropriate Networking Configuration and Protocols

5. ☑ **A, B,** and **C.** If your new Linux server will be on a TCP\IP network, your system will need a unique IP address. The IP address can be assigned by DHCP if another server on the network is providing DHCP service, or it can be manually set during the installation. To set the IP address manually, you will need to know the correct IP address to use. A hostname is used to identify your computer on the network. The hostname can be changed after the installation using the hostname command. During the installation, you will have the option to enter the DNS server you will be using. The DNS server is responsible for converting hostname addresses to IP address.

☒ **D.** When setting up the network information during the installation, you will not need to input the Linux kernel version.

Selecting Appropriate Security Settings

6. ☑ **C.** The umask command is used to set default file mode values.

☒ **A.** The chmod command is used to change file permissions on a file after it has been created. **B.** Linux commands are case-sensitive and so the correct command is umask, not Umask. **D.** There is no such command as modfile.

Creating Usernames and Passwords During Installation

7. ☑ **C.** When making Linux passwords, it is recommended that the passwords be at least 8 characters in length using both upper- and lower case letters and using numbers or symbols. Only answer C meets these criteria.

☒ **A.** Bob1 is not a secure password, it is less than 8 characters and is in lower case. **B.** Although Bob101 is more secure than answer A, it is not a recommended character length. **C.** Robert4 is not secure and would not be difficult to guess. Names are usually not recommended.

Installing and Configuring XFree86 Server

8. ☑ **D.** The XFree86 files are kept in the /usr/X11R6 directory, if you are installing XFree86 and the directory does not exist, you will need to create it.

☒ **A, B,** and **C** are not valid Linux directories.

Selecting Video Card Support

9. ☑ **C.** Once all the settings for the monitor and video card are input, they need to be tested to see if they work OK.

☒ **A.** Locating and inputting video information is one of the first tasks that are to be performed. **B.** Identification of the video memory is performed during the configuration. **D.** The documentation of the video card settings is a pre-installation task.

Selecting Appropriate Monitor Manufacturers and Settings

10. ☒ **A and C.** The vertical sync and horizontal sync range specifications are needed if the monitor configuration is to be entered manually.

☒ **B.** The video memory setting is part of the video card specification. **D.** Color resolution is also specified as part of the video card specification.

Selecting Appropriate Window Managers or Desktop Environments

11. ☑ **B.** Neither GNOME nor KDE are themselves window managers and require a window manager to function. KDE has a built-in window manager known as kwm.

☒ **A, C, and D.** None of these are valid Linux options.

Explaining When and Why the Kernel Needs to Be Recompiled

12. ☑ **A, B, and D.** The kernel may need to be recompiled to add or remove modules, correct application errors, or add new hardware functionality.

☒ **C.** The Linux kernel will not need to be recompiled to modify user accounts.

Installing a Boot Loader

13. ☑ **B.** Windows 2000 and Windows NT have a boot loader, NTLDR, installed, therefore, LILO should not be installed on the MBR, as it would prevent Windows from booting. In this case LILO should be installed on the first sector of the / directory. If you accidentally install LILO on the MBR, it is possible to correct the situation by modifying the lilo.conf file.

☒ **A.** Installing LILO on the MBR would overwrite the Windows boot loader, NTLDR, and prevent Windows from booting. **C.** GRUB is an alternative boot loader, but it, too, would need to be installed on the first sector of the / partition. **D.** LILO would never be installed in such a directory.

14. ☑ **A** and **C**. Both GRUB and LILO are boot loaders, which is software that makes it possible to configure dual booting on a system.
☒ **B**. /root is not a program. **D**. FIPS is a partitioning utility. While it can be used to create multiple partitions for different operating systems, it is not a boot loader system like GRUB or LILO. **D** is not a valid Linux option.

Installing and Uninstalling Applications After Installing the Operating System

15. ☑ **A**. To remove an existing RPM package from your system, you can run the rpm command using the -e switch along with the package name.
☒ **B, C,** and **D**. To remove the program, the package name has to be specified, and Linux commands are case-sensitive, meaning only -e will work to erase the package.

16. ☑ **A** and **B**. The extension .tgz indicates that the file was created with tar and that during the creation of the tar file, gzip was used to compress the tar.
☒ **C** and **D**. A .tgz file can be used for Slackware Linux or Debian, but the file extension of .tgz does not indicate use for any specific platform.

17. ☑ **D**. The command rpm -q will show information about currently installed RPMs.
☒ **A**. The rpm -v command is not valid. **B**. The rpm -e command is used to erase an RPM. **C**. The rpm -Uvh command is used to unpack RPMs.

Reading Log Files Created During Installation to Verify the Success of the Installation

18. ☑ **C**. The install.log file contains information on the Linux installation.
☒ **A**. /var/log is a directory that contains log files from the system. **B**. dmesg is a utility that provides information in the configuration of the system. **D**. There is no such file as boot.log.

Testing an Installed Application's Performance in Both a Test and a Production Environment

19. ☑ **A**, the rpm -U command allows an existing application to be upgraded.
☒ **B**. The rpm -i command allows a new application to be installed. **C**. The rpm -q command will show information about an RPM. **D**. the rpm -e command uninstalls packages from the system.

20. ☑ **B**. to verify the installation of an RPM package the -V switch can be used with the rpm command. To test the apache installation, the command rpm -V apache is correct.

☒ **A**. Linux commands are case sensitive and the verify command requires a capital *V*. **C** is not a valid Linux command. **D**. **-e** used with RPM is meant to erase existing packages, not exactly what was intended.

LAB ANSWER

The completion of the lab should see the successful installation of Linux on your system. If you have run into trouble during the installation, you can refer to Chapters 4 and 12 on troubleshooting. Additionally, some common installation problems can also be found by doing a newsgroup and Google search.

8

Configuration

CERTIFICATION OBJECTIVES

After the installation, and before the system is made available to users, it's often necessary to perform a number of configuration tasks. These tasks include reconfiguring the X Window system; setting up, configuring, and managing access to server services; reconfiguring the boot loader, and setting up printing. There is no set order in which the tasks must be performed, which is just as well, as the CompTIA objectives move quickly between tasks in an apparently random order.

For many of the tasks discussed in this chapter, there is more than one way to perform the task. For example, reconfiguration of the X Window system, which is the first topic we cover, has a variety of utilities that achieve the same goals. In the real world, it's likely that you'll develop a preference for doing things a certain way with a particular tool. For the Linux+ exam, however, you'll need to show an understanding of all the utilities discussed. In addition, it is also worth mentioning that in some cases, only the basic information is provided on a certain topic. Configuration of network servers, for example, is a subject on which it is possible to write an entire chapter for each of the services discussed; however the Linux+ exam does not require that you understand these services to that level of detail. If, as is likely, you find yourself using these services in the real world, consider the information presented in this chapter as a starting point for further reading, rather than a complete tutorial.

CERTIFICATION OBJECTIVE 8.01

Reconfiguring the X Window System with Automated Utilities

The configuration of the X Window system is stored in the XF86Config file, which is normally found in the /etc/X11 directory. While the file can be edited manually, the layout is sufficiently complex that you will want to avoid doing so unless it is absolutely necessary. There are numerous tools available for automated configuration of the file, and it is common practice to use one of these to perform the majority of the configuration, making only minor changes through the manual method. The utilities in question are Xconfigurator, XF86Setup, and xf86config. In the following sections, we'll look at each of these tools and run though the X server configuration process with each.

Xconfigurator

Xconfigurator is a Red Hat utility that allows the X Window system to be configured through a series of menus. It can be run from a command prompt or from within the X Window system. Because of its origins, Xconfigurator is found only in Red Hat–based distributions. Unlike XF86Setup and xf86config, Xconfigurator assumes that the mouse is already working.

on the **job** *When the Xconfigurator process is complete, a new XF86Config file is written, overwriting the existing one. If you want to keep the existing file for any reason, make a copy of it before you start Xconfigurator.*

Using Xconfigurator

The Xconfigurator is started by using the following command. Note the capital *X*:

```
#Xconfigurator
```

The screens are displayed as follows:

- **Welcome**   Provides information about the Xconfigurator process.
- **PCI Probe**   If you have PCI devices, the PCI probe screen attempts to discover your video card.
- **Monitor Setup**   Displays a list of monitors that can be selected. Choices include a range of generic monitor options and a "Custom" option that lets you specify the vertical and horizontal sync settings for your monitor. If you select the Custom option, you are taken through a Custom Monitor Setup Process. You can pick from preconfigured lists of settings or specify them manually.
- **Video Memory**   If you select a preconfigured monitor from the list, you are taken directly to the Video Memory page. From the options listed, pick the one that matches the amount of memory on your video card.
- **Clockchip Configuration**   This screen allows you to select a clockchip setting. In all but the most exceptional circumstances, use the "No Clockchip Setting (recommended)" option.
- **Select Video Modes**   Because the X Window system can support various resolutions and color depths, it's necessary to specify which modes you want to configure the system for. Choose as many as you want.

Once you have clicked OK on the Select Video Modes screen, the X Window configuration you have chosen is tested. The message, "Can You See this Message?" appears on the screen. You have 10 seconds to click OK. Doing so tells Xconfigurator that the settings work. Not clicking OK returns you to a screen that lets you reenter the program and reconfigure as necessary.

xf86config

Of the tools discussed here, the most basic, in terms of appearance at least, is the xf86config utility. This text-based, menu-driven system allows the complete configuration of all the X server components. As with the other utilities mentioned, the result of using Xf86Setup is the production of an XF86Config file with the settings chosen.

Start the utility by using the following command:

```
#xf86config
```

After the initial screen explaining the purpose and function of the utility, available options are listed and you use numbers to select them. The screens are as follows:

- **Mouse Selection**   A variety of mouse types is displayed covering all but the most unusual devices. Depending on your choice, you might be asked a question about third-button compatibility.

- **Mouse Device**   You are asked to enter the device name that the mouse is connected to, for example, /dev/tty0. The default, if nothing is entered, is /dev/mouse.

- **Keyboard Device**   Next you have to choose the keyboard type you are using. If in doubt, choose the Generic 102 Key PC option.

- **Keyboard Layout**   Select the layout that corresponds to your keyboard.

The next phase of the utility is the monitor configuration. Again, it is important to know the correct information for your monitor so you don't damage it.

- **Select Horizontal Sync Range**   You can choose from 10 predefined monitor types or select to enter your own horizontal sync range.

- **Vertical Sync Range**   Choose from four predefined vertical sync ranges or choose to enter your own.

- **Identification/Description Strings**   Enter a free-form description of your monitor.

- **Video Card Specific Settings**   Next you are informed about the process of choosing the correct video card type. If you choose to see the list of video cards, you can select from more than 700. Alternatively, select "no," and you will be taken straight to the video memory selection screen.

- **Video Memory Selection**   Enter the amount of video memory your card has. If it is more that 4MB, choose option 6 to enter the number yourself in kilobytes.

- **Identification/Description Strings**   As before, you can add free-form text as descriptors for your video card entry. Just hitting enter uses the defaults.

- **Color Depth**   The next screen lets you choose the desired color depth. Options range from monochrome to 16 million colors.

- **File Creation Confirmation**   The utility informs you that it is about to create a new XF86Config file and reminds you that it will overwrite the existing one. Answering "no" to the prompted question allows you to specify the filename and location for the new file. CTRL-C will exit the utility completely.

XF86Setup

The XF86Setup utility launches a basic graphical interface that allows you to configure the X Window system further. The basic options that can be configured are Mouse, Keyboard, Video Card, Monitor, Mode Selection, and Other. Clicking on each option takes you through a series of self-explanatory screens to configure your X Window system. As with the other utilities, when you are finished, a new XF86Config file is written.

Whichever of the utilities you elect to use, the basic procedures and results are all the same, so moving between one utility and another should not present too much of a challenge.

CERTIFICATION OBJECTIVE 8.02

Configuring the Client's Workstation for Remote Access

Whether a Linux system is connected to a LAN or not, there is often a need to connect to other systems or networks such as the Internet. By far the most popular way of doing this is by modem, the configuration of which is covered in Chapter 3. Other methods of connection include ISDN, xDSL, and cable. Some of these services are available only in certain locations, whereas modem access is universal.

The physical means of access is only half the story. You also need a software mechanism of connecting to another machine, the most popular method being the Point-to-Point Protocol, or PPP.

Configuring PPP

PPP is the most poplar method of establishing a remote connection over a dial-up link. That link might be to a corporate network, in which case the information needed for configuration will come from within. More likely, the connection will be to an Internet service provider (ISP), which will provide the necessary information, which will most likely include the following:

- ■ **Phone number**   Your ISP will supply you with a phone number of its dial-in system. It's likely that, although there will be only one number, there will be many incoming channels.

- ■ **Username and password**   The ISP will supply a username and password for you to use when you access the system. If you get the opportunity to set your own password, which is normal, you should use a different password than the one you use to access your Linux system.

exam
ⓦatch   *Entering the wrong username and password combination will result in a "PPP Authentication Failure" message.*

- **IP address** Most ISPs nowadays use dynamically assigned network addresses, but in some cases you might be required to add your addressing information manually, in which case you'll need to get the address information from the ISP.

- **Domain name server information** It's common for ISPs to give two DNS server addresses for fault tolerant reasons. This information needs to be added to the /etc/resolv.conf file.

- **Mail and news server Information** If you want to send and receive e-mail, you'll need the address of the respective servers. ISPs supply this in host name format, such as smtp.attcanada.net, or news.myservice.ca. This information will need to be provided to applications that you will use to read mail or connect to news services.

Before you actually start configuring PPP, you need to make sure that the kernel being used has PPP support, which you can do with the following command:

```
#dmesg | grep PPP
```

The output from the command will vary depending on the distribution of Linux you are using, but if any output at all is produced, this indicates that PPP is loaded. After you have verified that PPP functionality is available, it needs to be configured. As with other things Linux, the configuration of PPP is performed through a series of text files, and editing the files directly requires a solid understanding of the syntax, commands, and options.

Starting PPP

The PPP daemon, pppd, provides the PPP functionality on the server. A number of configuration files are used by pppd , including ppp-on, which brings up the connection, and ppp-off, which, as you might expect, takes down the connection. The exact location and the existence of the files will depend on the distribution of Linux you are using, the version of PPP installed, and how much prior configuration has taken place.

Because the configuration of the PPP files can be confusing, there is a variety of tools that can be used to configure the connection. Of those available, the most popular are kppp, a graphical utility that ships with KDE; rp3-config, a Red-Hat, GNOME-based utility; and wvdial, a text-based utility that uses a configuration file.

For actually initiating a connection, a script called a "chat script" is used to talk to the modem. The chat script contains commands that will initialize the modem and can pass phone numbers and other information.

Configuring ISDN

Because modems are limited to 56K, it is no surprise that people often look for a faster way to connect to the Internet and remote sites. While cable Internet access and technologies such as xDSL have become popular in recent years, ISDN is often used as well. Although installing an ISDN terminal adapter, which is the equivalent of a modem, requires drivers and, subsequently, configuration, PPP treats an ISDN connection in the same way it does a dial-up link through a modem. Also, because ISDN terminal adapters use a serial port assignment, configuration is made even easier. The upshot of this is that the configuration of an ISDN connection, as far as PPP is concerned, should be very similar to that of a modem.

There are various utilities for configuring ISDN, the most popular probably being isdn-config utility found in GNOME.

Configuring Cable/DSL

Configuration of remote access using cable and DSL can be simple, tricky, or in some cases, impossible. Both cable and DSL connections require the use of a special modem that can be either internal or external. With external modems, the setup is the same as that for a standard network connection in that a network card is installed in the PC, and then a cable connects the system to the modem. Internal modems can be trickier, as they must be installed in the system and configured through the operating system software. Some of these internal modems are not designed to work with Linux, so be sure to check before signing up. Once you have configured the modem correctly, IP addresses and associated information are generally supplied automatically. PPP is not required because there is not a dial-up element to the connection.

CERTIFICATION OBJECTIVE 8.03

Setting Environment Variables

When you log in to the system and start a shell session, a range of values, known as environment variables, are set by the system to customize the appearance and behavior of the session. In addition, environment variables can be used to store values, which can then be used when processing commands or to influence the behavior of the shell itself. A good example of an environment variable is the PATH statement, which is used to list all the directories that the shell should look in when a command is issued. A typical path statement for the user ROOT might look something like this:

```
/usr/local/sbin:/usr/sbin:/sbin:/usr/local/sbin:/usr/local/bin:/sbin:/bin
```

As you can see, directory paths are listed, each separated by a colon. When a command is executed, the shell looks through the path command, in order, and executes the first occurrence of the program that it finds. The path command can be added to, reordered, or taken away from as necessary.

While some environment variables can be changed, others, such as the UID variable, are provided a value by the system; thus they are labeled as read-only.

Viewing Environment Variables

You can view the currently assigned environment variables in a number of ways. To see a single variable, type **printenv** followed by the variable you want to view. So to view the PATH variable, the command is as follows:

```
#printenv PATH
```

Note that the name of the variable must be exactly as it appears in the environment variables, which can be upper or lower case. To see a complete list of the environment variables, you can use the printenv command on its own or type **set**. You might want to redirect the output to the **more** or **less** utilities (| **more**) as

FIGURE 8-1

Print of
environment
variables

```
root@localhost.localdomain: /root

 File   Edit   Settings   Help

[root@localhost /root]# lsmod
Module                Size  Used by
ide-cd               23632  0  (autoclean)
lockd                31656  1  (autoclean)
sunrpc               54116  1  (autoclean) [lockd]
3c59x                20136  1  (autoclean)
aic7xxx             137528  0
[root@localhost /root]#
```

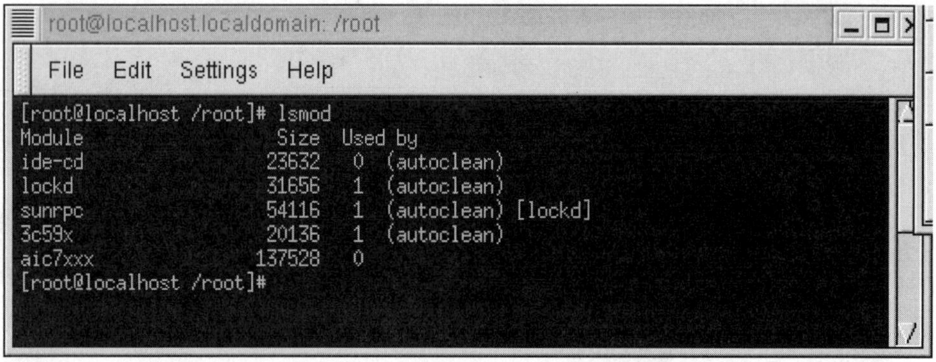

it is common for the listing to be more than a single page. Figure 8-1 shows and
example of both commands used to view environment variables on a test system
that has undergone no other configuration.

By default, the shell configures values for the variables that it needs to function, and
leaves out others. Table 8-1 shows some of the more commonly used environment
variables and their meanings.

Setting Environment Variables

To set an environment variable, you can type the name of the variable followed by
the equal sign, as:

#HISTSIZE=500

TABLE 8-1

Commonly Used
Environment
Variables and
Their Purposes

Variable	Purpose
PATH	Defines the directories through which the shell will search to find a program
DISPLAY	Defines where the X Window output will be displayed
TERM	The type of the terminal currently in use
HISTSIZE	Defines the size of the command buffer history (in commands)
PRINTER	Used to define the default printer
MAIL	Path to the user's mailbox

A variable set like this, however, remains in effect only for the duration of the session. Logging out from the system or closing the shell session loses the new setting for the environment variable. To make the environment variable permanent, the appropriate shell configuration file, which can be found in the user's home directory, must be edited. The file will already have environment variables in it, so it's not difficult to set a new variable; in any case it is the same syntax as setting it at the command line.

Exporting Environment Variables

Once you have set an environment variable, it is available to you within the shell but not to other programs, such as shell scripts that might run. To make the variable available to other programs after it has been set, it must be exported, which you can do with the following command:

```
#export variable_name
```

If you had an environment variable called DEFLOG, the command would look like this:

```
#export DEFLOG
```

Unsetting Environment Variables

On occasion, you might find it necessary to unset an environment variable, which can be easily achieved by using the following command:

```
#unset VARIABLE_NAME
```

Variables are great because if you don't want to change any of them, you can leave them at the system default, and chances are you won't even really notice them. On the other hand, they are easy to set, add, and change.

CERTIFICATION OBJECTIVE 8.04

Configuring Basic Network Services and Settings

As you might recall from Chapter 2, for a system to participate on the network, there are a number of settings that must be configured. These settings include TCP/IP address information, DNS information, and the like. In general, the settings chosen during installation are rarely changed, though you might find yourself needing to do it at some point.

For the most part, network configuration information is stored in a couple of files, the exact names and locations of which will depend on the Linux distribution you are using.

on the
Job

DHCP client functionality is provided through the dhcpcd daemon. If the system is configured to use DHCP, the daemon starts at boot and retrieves the TCP/IP addressing configuration from the DHCP server. For more information on DHCP, refer to Chapter 2.

If you want, you can edit the files manually, though once again, you need to be careful of command usage and syntax. If you prefer, you can configure the network settings through a variety of utilities including netcfg, netconfig, and Linuxconf. There are other utilities available as well, but these are some of the most common. Again, the exact tools available will depend on what distribution you are using. What follows is a very brief explanation of some of the available tools. We highly recommend that you take a look at each one, but be careful when changing settings, as making the wrong change will render a machine unable to connect to the network.

netconfig

netconfig is a Red Hat–created, menu-based utility that allows the network settings to be configured through a series of screens. The utility is self-explanatory in its use and some of the fields will autofill by using TAB. The main Configure TCP/IP screen is shown in Figure 8-2.

Once you have entered the necessary information, the results are saved into the appropriate configuration files.

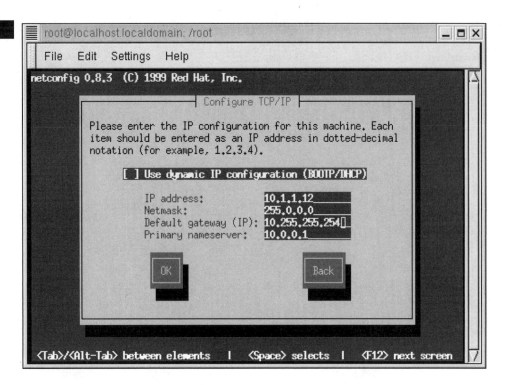

Linuxconf

If a GUI is more your thing, the Linuxconf utility lets you configure network settings
as well. Once again, the information that is required is the same; only the method of
entering is different. When changes have been made in Linuxconf, you are prompted
to activate the changes. Choosing "yes" in this dialog causes the changes to take effect
immediately. Figure 8-3 shows a sample screen from the network card configuration
dialog of Linuxconf.

netcfg

The graphical utility netcfg provides a simple interface for configuring network
settings. The Interfaces screen of netcfg is shown in Figure 8-4.

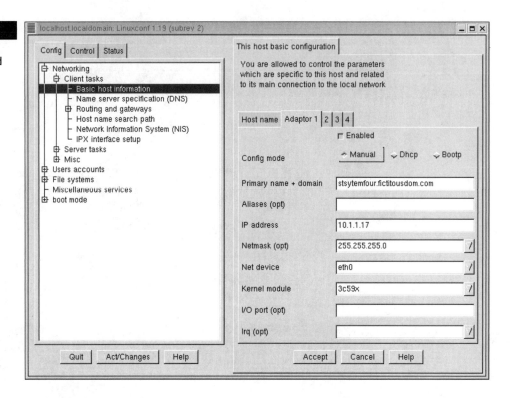

FIGURE 8-3

Network Card
Configuration
dialog from
Linuxconf

Configuring DHCP Server Functionality

While the complete configuration of a DHCP server is somewhat outside the scope of Linux+, it is useful to know some of the details about configuring Linux as a DHCP server. The actual process is well documented, so you should have no problem finding out more information if you want to go this way.

The DHCP server functionality is provided by the DHCP daemon, called dhcpd. Configuration information for dhcpd is supplied through the text file /etc/dhcpd.conf. Once the file has been configured as appropriate, you can have the DHCP service start automatically on boot or use the following command from the directory that contains the script file, such as /etc/rc.d/init.d:

```
#./dhcp start
```

To stop the DHCP server, use the same command and substitute *stop* for *start*.

FIGURE 8-4

The Interfaces
screen in netcfg

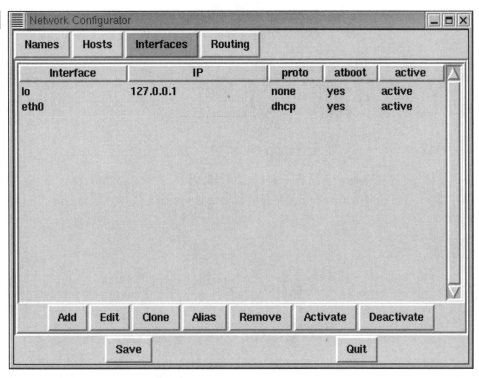

Configuring DNS Server Functionality

The mechanism for configuring a server to provide DNS services is very similar to that of DHCP, in that there is a DNS daemon called "named" and a configuration file called /etc/named.conf. After configuring the file, the DNS server functionality

SCENARIO & SOLUTION

After the installation, you want to reconfigure networking on your system.	Use a utility such as Linuxconf or netconfig.
You want to configure your system as a DHCP server.	Edit the dhcpd.conf file and start the Dhcp daemon.
You want to configure your system as a DNS server.	Edit the named.conf file and start the named daemon.

can be started and stopped using the same command format as DHCP, though of course you must substitute named for dhcpd.

Configuring Basic Server Services

There are such a wide range of services that a Linux server can provide that a single server can often provide all the services needed by an organization. This section looks at some of the services you might find yourself configuring on your server.

NIS

The network information service (NIS) allows a centralized server to act as a host for specified files and then allows those files to be accessed by other hosts transparently. This process has many benefits including the ability to allow information, such as usernames and passwords, from one system to be used across other systems. Whether you use NIS in your network will depend on how big your network is and exactly what your needs are. Many organizations find that they can do without NIS completely, while for others it forms an important part of the network infrastructure. One thing that you should know about NIS, however, is that it's not very secure.

How NIS works

In the most basic NIS configuration, a single server is nominated as the master server, and other systems are configured as clients. Once the hierarchy is set, when a certain file is accessed, it is accessed from the central host rather than the local system to which the user is connected. This allows a single set of information to be maintained across the network.

As with DNS, NIS uses domains to create logical groups of systems, though it is common practice to name NIS domains differently than DNS domains (or any other domains such as Windows NT domains) to prevent confusion.

on the **job**

NIS commands are prefixed with yp, which stands for Yellow Pages. The original implementation of NIS was called that, but a trademark infringement in the UK caused yp to be renamed NIS. They didn't, however, change the commands that are used, hence the yp prefix.

The yp Commands   As we just mentioned, many of the commands associated with the NIS service start with the prefix yp. The actual commands and their respective uses are defined in Table 8-2.

Configuring the NIS Client

The client-side configuration of NIS is performed through the /etc/yp.conf file. There are two methods in which the NIS client can access the server. The first, broadcast, requires the NIS server to be contacted to be on the same subnet as the client, which is not always practical. The second, known as the server hostname method, requires that the target NIS server be specified. In either case, the yp.conf file must be edited.

For the broadcast method, all that is required is to specify the domain name and the fact that it is to be the broadcast method. In the following example, the domain name is headoffice.

```
domain headoffice broadcast
```

The server hostname requires that you specify the domain name and the hostname, which in this example is hqserver, as follows:

```
domain headoffice server hqserver
```

It is also possible to just specify a hostname, as follows:

```
ypserver hqserver
```

In certain respects, NIS performs some of the same functions as Directory Services platforms such as Novell eDirectory, though the latter offer far greater functionality.

TABLE 8-2	Command	Purpose
Common Commands Used with NIS	ypserv	Starts the NIS daemon
	ypinit	Creates the NIS databases
	ypwhich	Shows which NIS server is being used by the client
	yppasswd	Used to set the password on an NIS server

NFS

The Network File System (NFS) is a mechanism to mount and access file systems from other servers across the network. The beauty of NFS is that once the remote file system is mounted, it can be accessed as if it were a local, enabling you to move between the two transparently. Figure 8-5 shows how NFS might work in a practical implementation.

There are two configuration elements to NFS, a client and a server. Whether your system will need to be configured for both roles (and there is no reason why it shouldn't) will depend on your needs.

Configuring NFS Client Functionality

Because NFS is so well integrated, the process of accessing a remote file system is much the same as accessing a local one, in that it uses the /etc/fstab file. This file defines what file systems are to be mounted by the system on bootup, and all that is needed to access an NFS share across the network is for the appropriate entry to be added to the fstab file. For more information on the structure and layout of the /etc/fstab file, refer to the section on configuration files later in this chapter.

A sample fstab file with the entry (last line) to mount a remote NFS share looks something like this:

```
LABEL=/                 /                  ext2     defaults          1 1
/dev/cdrom              /mnt/cdrom         iso9660  noauto,owner,ro   0 0
/dev/fd0                /mnt/floppy        auto     noauto,owner      0 0
none                    /proc              proc     defaults          0 0
none                    /dev/pts           devpts   gid=5,mode=620    0 0
/dev/hda5               swap               swap     defaults          0 0
server2:/data/docs      /data/s2data       nfs
```

The NFS entry, which, as you have probably guessed, is the last line, is formatted as follows. The first column defines the name and directory, separated by a colon, of the remote server that is to be accessed. The second column defines the mount point within the file system on your local host, and the third defines the type of file system that is being mounted. If connection to the remote NFS share is successful, you can change into the /data/s2data directory and access data from the remote system as easily as you could access other directories on your local system, though obviously performance might not be quite so sprightly.

This example, which is the most basic usage, does not optimize the communication in anyway and uses defaults where appropriate. It is likely that in a live environment, you will explore some of the mount options to fine-tune the NFS access.

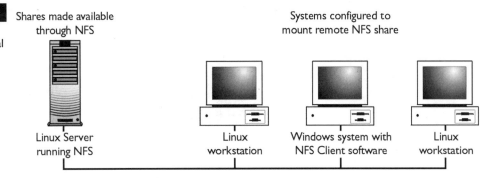

Shares made available through NFS

Systems configured to mount remote NFS share

Linux Server running NFS

Linux workstation

Windows system with NFS Client software

Linux workstation

FIGURE 8-5

NFS in a practical implementation

Configuring to Provide NFS Server Capabilities

As with the client side of NFS, serving tasks are configured through a text file, though it is the /etc/exports file instead of fstab. The layout of the exports file is basic, in that there are only a small number of required parameters though, as usual, there is a gamut of other options that can be used if necessary. The following is an example of an entry in an exports file:

```
/data/docs    john(rw)    sue(ro)
```

This entry makes the directory /data/docs mountable by John, who has read-and-write access, and Sue, who has read-only access. It is also possible to grant access rights based on host, domain, and group name.

Once changes have been made to the exports file, the NFS services will need to be stopped and started or restarted for the changes to take effect. This can be performed with the following commands:

```
#./nfs stop
```

and

```
#./nfs start
```

NFS is a popular service on Linux, but while it does allow Linux and Unix systems to access each other, it doesn't let Windows clients use the shares unless special software is installed which is why, in addition to NFS, you are just as likely to be using SMB on your network as well, which brings us nicely on to that subject.

SMB

Given the proliferation of Microsoft Windows, the likelihood that a server will be providing SMB based services is relatively high. As we have discussed previously, SMB services allow Windows clients to attach to and use the file system of a Linux server. It also allows Linux printers to be accessed. There are two daemons that provide SMB services. The smbd daemon provides file and print services while the nmbd daemon offers name resolution services. Figure 8-6 shows how a server running SMB services might fit into the network.

Configuring SMB

The settings for SMB are defined in the text file smb.conf, which is normally found in the /etc or /etc/samba directories. The file can be in other locations as well, so make sure you are editing the right file for your system. The file is broken down into a number of sections. One section deals with the global settings for the configuration, such as the workgroup name that should be used; another lists the information for sharing directories to user and another details the printing configuration. The following is an example of a very basic smb.conf file.

```
#Global Settings

[global]
     workgroup = ourdom
     server string = Linux Server

#Shares
[datadir]
     comment = The data directory
     path = /data
     valid users = mary john steve chris
     public = no
     writable = yes
[publications]
     comment = The publications directory
     path = /data/public
     public = yes
     writable = no
```

In this example, the workgroup field defines the name of the domain or workgroup to which this server will be a member, and the server string defines the description

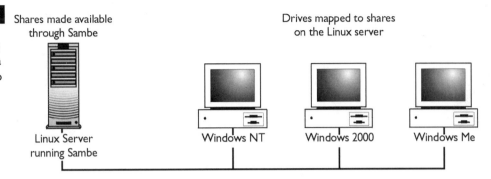

FIGURE 8-6

A server running SMB services in a practical scenario

Shares made available through Sambe

Drives mapped to shares on the Linux server

Linux Server running Sambe

Windows NT

Windows 2000

Windows Me

that will be used in browsing for this system. In the following share sections, each share is named, surrounded by square brackets ([ ]), and then specific configuration options are applied to each one.

In the first share, datadir, a list of users, is defined that can access the share. Each person's name is added to the list and separated by a space. The public setting is "no," which means that all other users will be unable to use the share. The writeable parameter is set to "yes," thereby allowing the named users to write to the directory.

In the second share, publications, everyone has access to the files in the /data/public directory, but the use of the "writable = no" setting means that users will not have write permissions.

on the

job

The permissions for shares in Samba do not override the Linux assigned permissions, and they are subjected to them. If a user is given write access to a share but they have only read access in Linux, they will have only read access. In reverse, if the Linux permission is read and write but the share permission is read only, the permission will be read only. In either case, the most restrictive permission applies.

Testparm

As it is quite possible to make mistakes in the smb.conf file, the testparm utility is available to test the file and look for any errors or typos. The command is run as follows:

```
#testparm configfilename
```

The utility reports any errors that are found or reports that all is OK. It then offers to show the summary of the settings from within the file. Once the changes to the smb.conf have been tested, the SMB daemons must be restarted for the changes to take effect. This can be achieved with the following commands:

```
#./smb stop
#./smb start
```

Once the SMB daemons have been restarted, you need to create user accounts for users that will be accessing the system through SMB. They should be able to connect to the machine from a Windows system and access the shares that you have created, or you can use the smbclient program.

Creating SMB Users

There are two command utilities that you should be aware of when working with SMB, namely smbadduser and smbpasswd. As you can probably guess from their names, the commands add users and set passwords for accounts that will connect to the system using smb. The user IDs and passwords for connection to Samba are different from those used by the Linux system. They are also stored in different files, namely /etc/samba/smbusers and /etc/samba/smbpasswd. Any user that will connect to the Linux system through SMB must have a Linux user ID and an SMB user ID. Trying to add a user that does not exist on the Linux system using the smbadduser command will result in an error.

The basic usage of the smbadduser command is as follows:

```
#smbadduser linuxuserid:windowsuserid
```

So, for example, if you want to create an SMB account for a user who has a Linux ID of sarah and a Windows ID of sarahw, the command looks like this:

```
#smbadduser sarah:sarahw
```

Passwords can be set at the time the user account is created or subsequently changed using the smbpasswd command as follows. Note that the Linux user ID is specified, not the SMB username.

```
#smbpasswd sarah
```

You will be prompted to enter and retype the new password for the user, at which point the /etc/samba/smbpasswd file is updated.

FROM THE CLASSROOM

The Simplicity of Samba

Understanding how simple Samba is to set up and use causes many people to start thinking about replacing their existing Windows servers with Linux systems. Such an approach might be valid, but there are so many more aspects to a server's role than just file sharing and print sharing. Applications installed on an existing server might not run on Linux, or certain specialized hardware devices might not be supported. Also, the ability to support and manage a Linux system requires specialist skills that might not be present in house. The ease with which products such as Samba can be configured can lead server administrators into a false sense of security. That is not to say that the substitution of Windows server with a Linux system is not a practical measure—it is—just that there are often more things to consider than just file sharing and print sharing.

—*Mike Harwood, Linux+ Certified*

If you prefer to use a GUI for the administration of Samba, there are a number of graphical utilities available including the Samba Web Administration Tool (SWAT), which is shipped with the Samba software. Like other GUI administration tools, however, all SWAT does is take your selections and write a new smb.conf file. Thus, an understanding of the file itself is still important.

SCENARIO & SOLUTION

You want to create an SMB share that is accessible by selected users for write access.	Create a share and use the valid users entry to define which users are able to access the share.
You have made changes to the smb.conf file and want to validate the changes are correct	Use the testparm utility to make sure there are no errors in the file.
You have made changes to the smb.conf file, but the changes do not seem to have taken effect.	Stop and restart the SMB services.

CERTIFICATION OBJECTIVE 8.06

Configuring Basic Internet Services

The fact that Linux has made its name partly on the back of its abilities as a network server should make it no surprise that it is able to offer a complete set of network services, including Web server (HTTP), e-mail server (POP, SMTP), FTP server, and a range of other network services.

Configuring Mail Services

So commonplace has our use of e-mail become that it makes you wonder how we managed without it. Every network operating system platform available has the ability to provide e-mail server services, but few offer the function so integrally as Linux. The mail function of Linux is rooted in many of the processes, and it is assumed that users on the system have a mail account.

E-mail services on a Linux server are typically provided through two protocols, the Simple Message Transfer Protocol (SMTP) and the Post Office Protocol (POP), though many organizations are now using Internet Messaging Access Protocol (IMAP) because of its increased functionality. SMTP is used for sending and routing e-mails. POP, most commonly POP3, is used for retrieving e-mails from a server, as is IMAP, though the latter also has the ability to read e-mail and still leave it on the server.

While SMTP might be the protocol for sending and retrieving e-mail, a mail application, most commonly Sendmail, is used to perform the message management functions of the server. Sendmail is configured through a text file called sendmail.cf. Although sendmail.cf is a standard text file, editing it is the stuff of legend and has been compared with everything from a black art to just plain impossible. In view of this, there are numerous tools, including configuration macros and graphical utilities that allow you to configure the file. For the Linux+ exam, you will not need to understand or use these tools, but you should know that they work with the sendmail.cf file.

SMTP uses TCP/IP port 25 for communication, while POP3 uses 110.

The Sendmail functionality is provided by the sendmail daemon. Depending on what Linux distribution you are using, you can start the sendmail daemon with the following command.

```
#./sendmail start
```

The daemon can also be used with the stop and restart commands as needed. If configuration changes are made to the Sendmail configuration, the daemon must be restarted for the changes to take effect. It might also be necessary to restart the daemon if the there is a problem with processing of mail.

You can check the status of the mail queue by using the *sendmail –bp* **command.**

The complexity of Sendmail has caused people to look to other packages, such as qmail, as an alternative, though Sendmail still remains the package of choice for many implementations.

The available options for a daemon (stop, start, restart, and so on) can be obtained by using *./daemonname* **but no other information. For example, to find the options available for the smb daemon, simply type** *./smb* **and press RETURN. A list of the options will then be displayed.**

Sendmail Aliasing

One of the e-mail features that's often used is that of aliasing. By using the alias feature, a user or group of users can receive e-mail that is sent to a user that does not have a user account, such as info@company.com or help@company.com. A text file, /etc/aliases, is used to configure this feature. Entries that are placed in the file look something like this:

```
help:      dthomas
```

Any time a mail is sent to the user ID "help," the mail is actually forwarded to user dthomas on the local system instead. This is useful if you have a rotation system for people who answer queries from users. You can also have mail sent to a group of users by using the following syntax:

```
help:dthomas, jgreen, spenot
```

You can also configure the aliases file to forward mail to an external address as well as an internal one. For example, if you want mail addressed to the help e-mail address to be sent to one internal account and one external account, use an entry like this:

```
help:      dthomas, dthomas@hisdom.net
```

When changes have been made to the aliases file, the command newaliases must be run for the new entries to be recognized.

In addition to the /etc/aliases file, users can set up personal e-mail forwarding by creating or editing a file called .forward in their home directory. The file is consulted after the /etc/aliases, but before the mail is actually delivered to the user.

The syntax for the .forward file is different than that for the /etc/aliases file, in that only the e-mail address(es) to which the mail is to be sent is (are) listed. For example, if a user called Mary wants e-mail to go to her local mailbox *and* her mailbox at her home, the entry in the .forward file looks something like this:

```
\mary, mary@marysdom.com
```

The backslash before the user's name indicates that the mail is to be sent to a local mail account. The comma is then used to specify a different, in this case external, user account.

FROM THE CLASSROOM

SMTP and POP

The relationship between SMTP and POP can sometimes seem confusing, but it really isn't. SMTP is a mechanism for transmitting e-mail messages, which are basically text files. The gist behind SMTP is that the receiver will always be able to receive the mail, and will always read it on that system. Of course the reality might be different. While SMTP is able to deliver the mail to the mailbox, it might be that the user is not on the system and will want to retrieve mail and read it on another system. That's where POP comes in. POP allows e-mail messages to be listed, retrieved, and deleted from a central system remotely. After logging in, POP manages user requests and executes them against the user's mailbox. This allows users to download mail from a central system and store it on another machine. If you have ever used Microsoft Outlook Express with an ISP, chances are you were using POP. You dial in, and provide a username and password, and then your mail is downloaded to the local system. That way, your central mailbox does not fill up. If you want to send an e-mail, however, that is done via SMTP.

—Drew Bird, Linux+ Certified

POP and IMAP

Although SMTP allows you to send e-mail and route it, to download e-mail from a central location you'll need POP or IMAP functionality. This functionality is provided separately from the main SMTP function of applications such as Sendmail or Qmail and instead implemented through a separate daemon. The daemon might include just POP or IMAP capability but will most likely include both.

To find out if there is a POP daemon configured in your system, you can use the grep command to examine the /etc/inetd.conf file as follows:

```
#cat /etc/inetd.conf | grep pop
```

If a POP daemon is configured, the output from the command should look something like this:

```
pop-3   stream tcp    nowait  root    /usr/sbin/tcpd    ipop3d
```

In this example, the name of the daemon is ipop3d, a POP daemon that is supplied with Red Hat and Mandrake. Other popular daemons include qpopper and cyrus.

Configuring HTTP

The http daemon provides Web server service, which allows the Linux system to host Web sites. As we have already discussed, the most common Web server in use is Apache, but that doesn't affect the configuration of the http daemon, which is still performed using the httpd.conf file. The exact location of this file differs between distributions, so if you can't track it down, use the following command to locate it:

```
#find / -name httpd.conf
```

The file is lengthy and has many options to allow for sophisticated configuration of the Web server. Two entries that are worthy of particular mention are the ServerRoot parameter, which dictates the location of the server configuration and log files, and DocumentRoot, which specifies the directory from which your Web site files will be served. Earlier versions of Apache actually used three files, but the function of the three files is condensed into a single file in later versions.

For the Linux+ exam, understand the filenames that are associated with the configuration of FTP, HTTP, and so on, rather than concentrating on the formats. Some of these configuration files contain so many parameters and options that even some veterans do not know what they all do. Remember that the Linux+ exam is about demonstrating a "basic" understanding. This means knowing what files and daemons do what and why you would use them.

The httpd services can be stopped and started using the following commands:

```
#./httpd start
```

and

```
#./httpd start
```

You can also use the reload and restart commands if preferred.

For more information on configuring the Apache Web server, visit the Apache Web site at http://www.apache.org.

Configuring FTP

Outside of e-mail and Web-server services, FTP is one of the most popular functions for an Internet server. FTP, which is a mature standard, allows files to be retrieved from a central host using a range of simple commands. Many Linux distributors provide FTP download abilities for their software, and almost every other software supplier provides FTP capability. Whether you will need an FTP server boils down to one simple thing: do you want people to download files, via FTP, from your server? For many organizations, such a service is not necessary, and it is less likely that you will configure an FTP server than, say, a Web or mail server. Even so, understanding the basic process of configuration is handy if you decide you do want it.

Although, as with everything else in the Linux world, there are exceptions, the most common FTP server in use is Washington University FTP, or WU-FTP. The configuration file used by the FTP server is /etc/ftpaccess. The file governs how the server behaves and how clients can use the server.

As are the other daemons discussed here, FTP is started and stopped using the following commands:

```
#./ftpd start
```

```
#./ftpd stop
```

You can also use the reload and restart commands if necessary.

Configuring SNMP

The Simple Network Management Protocol, SNMP, allows devices on the network, including servers, to communicate with a central system to inform it of problems with the network or any other condition for which it is configured.

SNMP operates by having participating systems in one of two modes. In manager mode, it can receive the messages from systems that are configured to report to it. In agent mode, it is able to send messages to a manager about a condition on the system.

Configuration of SNMP on a system is performed though the etc/snmp/snmpd.conf text file. The layout of the file is relatively complex, though there are a large number of comments that attempt to make the purpose of the file clearer.

The SNMP daemon, snmpd, can be started and stopped in the same way as the other daemons mentioned in this section, by using the stop and start commands. Here is an example of the command to start the SNMP daemon:

```
#./snmpd start
```

CERTIFICATION OBJECTIVE 8.07

Identifying When Swap Space Needs to Be Increased

When it comes to demands placed on system hardware, Linux treads very lightly. That's why it can run on levels of hardware that designers of other operating systems can only dream about. Part of this undemanding approach translates into the swap file usage. As you might recall from the chapters on installation, swap space is configured so that if the physical RAM becomes used up, a portion of the hard disk can be used as if it were physical RAM as well. That way, the system can use the space instead of physical RAM. Unlike other operating systems, however, Linux tends to use the swap space only when it's experiencing particularly high usage or in systems that have very little physical RAM in the first place. High usage of the swap file indicates two things: first, your system probably does not have enough RAM, and second, the workload on your system is probably quite high.

Using the free Command to See Swap Usage

The free command, which shows physical memory usage, also shows the swap space in use. Figure 8-7 shows the free command from a system that has very low usage.

As you can see from Figure 8-7, we used the **-m** switch with the free command. This serves the simple purpose of showing the figure in megabytes rather than bytes, making it easier to read. As you can also see from the figure, none of the swap space on this system is being used either. This is because the system has 128MB RAM, and is offering only a basic set of services.

If users are complaining that the system is slow, or even worse, if they are being disconnected, the swap space usage should be checked, though not to the exclusion of other system components. If you find that the used figure reported by the free command represents a sizable chunk of the swap file, you should consider increasing the available swap space on your system, but you should also consider adding RAM as well. Given that RAM is relatively inexpensive nowadays, there should be few instances, particularly in production environments, where it is necessary to run a system with too little RAM.

If you do find it necessary to increase the amount of swap space on your system, it is a task that can be achieved with the mkswap command. There are a number of parameters for the mkswap command, some of which can be dangerous, so be sure to know what you are trying to achieve before jumping in. For full details on mkswap, refer to the appropriate manual or information page.

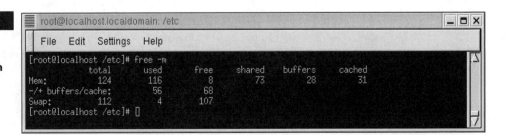

FIGURE 8-7

The output from a **free -m** command on a system with 128MB RAM

```
[root@localhost /etc]# free -m
             total       used       free     shared    buffers     cached
Mem:           124        116          8         73         28         31
-/+ buffers/cache:          56         68
Swap:          112          4        107
[root@localhost /etc]# []
```

CERTIFICATION OBJECTIVE 8.08

Adding and Configuring Printers

In many cases, one of the functions that a Linux server will provide is that of a print server. Printing is a core task for many network servers, and the likelihood that you will need to configure printing at some point is high.

on the
job

If you come across CUPS, or the Common Unix Printing System, you might find yourself asking what the future holds for Linux printing. CUPS is a relatively new product that provides more functionality than lpd and promises to make printing on Linux as simple as on any other platform. Some distributors, such as Mandrake and Caldera, have already started including CUPS as their primary printing system while other distributors support it but opt for lpd as the default. For more information on CUPS, visit http://www.cups.org.

The printing functionality is provided through the line printer daemon (lpd), which deals with the processing of print jobs. Print jobs are sent to lpd in the form of a file, which is first stored in the specified spool directory. Generally speaking, this directory is /var/spool/lpd/*printername*, but you can change this location if you are concerned about print jobs filling the disk. Once the complete file has arrived in the spool directory, lpd looks in the /etc/printcap file for printer specific configuration information. If the print configuration is specified to use a filter, the file is processed according to the filter (analogous to a driver on other platforms) and subsequently sent to the printer. Lpd is able to route jobs to printers on other servers almost as easily as it is able to print to a device that is connected locally. Only minor configurations in the printcap file are required. Given that the printcap file provides the configuration information needed by lpd, it's necessary to understand how it is structured.

The /etc/printcap File

On a system that does not have any printers installed, you might find that the /etc/printcap file does not exist, making it necessary for you to create one. Within the file, each printer is defined, along with configuration parameters that dictate how the printer should be treated by lpd. The following is a typical example of a printer configuration from an /etc/printcap file.

```
# The laserjet in the main office
    HPLaserjet | laser | lp
    :sd=/var/spool/lpd/laser
    :lp=/dev/lp0:
    :if=/var/spool/lpd/lp0/filter:
```

Table 8-3 lists the definitions for each field in the /etc/printcap file. The printcap file can hold information for more than one printer. Each new printer configuration starts with the name of the printer and is followed by the printer configuration. In other words, each new printer definition follows the format of the first.

If you change the configuration of an existing printer or add a new printer to the printdef file, lpd must be restarted for the changes to take effect. If you have not created the spool directory manually, lpd will create the directory and set the appropriate permissions for you.

In the preceding example, we define that the printer is connected to the first parallel port (lp0) on the local system, but as you can see from Table 8-3, it's also possible to redirect the printer output to a network printer by using the **rm** and **rp** parameters. When you do this, it is still necessary to specify the configuration information for the remote printer. If we were to use the same configuration as in the previous sample printcap file but instead of sending it to lp0, we sent it to

TABLE 8-3	Parameter	Purpose
Parameters Used in the printcap File	lp	Specifies the print device that should be used for this printer.
	sd	The spool directory that should be used for this printer.
	rm	If the printer is not local, this parameter provides the remote host name.
	rp	Used with the rm parameter, this defines the remote printer name.
	if	Specifies the location of the text file that reformats the job ready for printing.
	mx	Defines the maximum size of the print job. A setting of 0 or no setting means there is no limit.
	lf	Specifies that name and location of an error log for this printer.

a remote host called adminserv and a printer called secondfloor, the printcap entry would look like this:

```
# The laserjet on the second floor
    HPLaserjet | laser | lp
    :sd=/var/spool/lpd/laser
    :rm=adminserv
    :rp=secondfloor
```

When using utilities such as lpr and lpq, the first entry in the printcap file is used as the default if no other printer is specified. So the printer you most frequently use should appear first in the file.

Testing Your Configuration

With your printing now configured, you can test the configuration by using the line printer (lpr) command, which lets you send print jobs from the command line to the printer. You can, of course, send a print job from within a GUI, but a basic knowledge of the lpr command is useful, just in case the GUI is not available.

lpr   The basic usage of lpr is as follows:

```
#lpr filename
```

This takes the file specified and sends it to the first printer specified in the printcap file, provided this is not overridden by the PRINTER environment variable, and processes it using the information provided. Chances are that if the printer is properly configured and the correct filter is being applied, the output will be exactly as you expect. It is also possible to add switches to the lpr command that affect how it processes the request. Some of the more commonly used switches are described in Table 8-4, along with sample usage.

If you prefer, a number of GUI tools are available to help you with the configuration of your printers, but all they do, in effect, is edit and update the /etc/printcap file

TABLE 8-4	Switch	Purpose	Sample Usage
Commonly Used Switches with the lpr Command	-p	Specfies the printer to use	lpr -p laser myfile
	-K	Specified the number of copies to print	lpr -K,20 myfile
	-m	Sends e-mail to the specified user when the job is complete	lpr -m john myfile

configurations. So by having an understanding of the manual process of adding and configuring printers, you can better interpret what the GUI tools are doing in the background. Also, in some cases, such as if you are using an unlisted printer, you will need to configure printers manually.

There is more information on managing and controlling of printers in Chapter 10.

CERTIFICATION OBJECTIVE 8.09

Reconfiguring Boot Loader

Although there are various boot loaders available, LILO is by far the most popular. As a result, you need to understand the layout and format of the LILO configuration file, lilo.conf, to be able to make any necessary changes.

exam
ⓦatch

Understand the function and purpose of the lilo.conf file, including the basic layout and why you would edit it.

The lilo.conf file is found, like many of the other Linux configuration files, in the /etc directory. Before editing it, you should make a copy of the file so that you can recover it if necessary. A sample lilo.conf file might look something like this:

```
boot=dev/hda
map=/boot/map
install=/boot/boot.b
default=linux
lba32
prompt
timeout=50
message=/boot/message

image=/boot/vmlinuz-2.2.5.15
      label=linux
      root=/dev/hda2
      read-only
other=/dev/hda1
      label=windows
      table=/dev/hda
```

As you can see, the basic structure of the file is that there is three sections. The section at the top of the file specifies general settings. This is known as the global section. Under this, there are sections that begin with the fields "image" or "other," each of which specifies a different way of starting the operating system or a different operating system altogether. There can be numerous images specified for a single installation of Linux because it can be booted into various modes.

on the **Job**

The lilo.conf file can contain entries for up to 16 different boot options.

Table 8-5 explains the components of the global section. In the images section, there are fewer fields. Table 8-6 explains the most commonly used.

The heading of "other" is used if there is an operating system other than Linux installed on your system, in which case the only information needed is the label field and the table field, which specifies where the other operating system can be found.

	Field	Explanation
TABLE 8-5 Fields Used in the Global Section of the lilo.conf File	boot	Specifies the location of the bootable partition
	map	Specifies the location of the map file, which provides the location of bootable kernel images
	install	Specifies that file named should be used as the new boot sector
	default	Specifies the image that is to be used by default if no other image is selected from the boot loader menu
	timeout	Specifies, in tenths of a second, how long to wait for user input before using the default image
	message	Specifies a file that contains text that can be displayed as a message

	Field	Explanation
TABLE 8-6 Fields Used in the Image Section of the lilo.conf File	Image	Specifies the Linux kernel image to be used.
	djustrightLabel	Specifies the text that will be displayed in the boot loader menu
	Root	Specifies the location of the root file system for this image
	read-only	Specifies that the file system should be mounted initially as read-only, though it will most likely become read-write when the boot is completed and file system checks have been performed.
	password	It is possible to provide a password that must be supplied when selecting an image, thereby preventing unauthorized users from booting into it. It should be noted that if you are using this option, the permissions on the lilo.conf file should be changed to prevent any user other than root from viewing it.

Editing and Saving lilo.conf

There are likely to be relatively few instances when it will be necessary to edit the lilo.conf file, but some reasons might include adding a new image, changing the label values for existing images or changing fields such as the timeout. Once you have made the changes to your file, you need to rewrite the system boot sector, which is done with the following command:

```
#/sbin/lilo
```

A message will be displayed listing any images that have been changed. Now, when you restart the system, your new changes will be in effect.

on the **ⓙob**

When changing the configuration of the boot loader, be sure to have a boot floppy on hand in case the system does not start as you expected it to.

EXERCISE 8-1

Editing the lilo.conf File

1. Use the cp command to create a copy of your lilo.conf file.

   ```
   #cp /etc/lilo.conf /etc/lilo.bak
   ```

2. Using a text editor such as vi, open the /etc/lilo.conf file for editing.

3. In the label section of your default image entry, change the description of the image.

4. Change the default field in the global section of the file to match the new description.

5. Change the timeout value to 150.

6. Save your changes and then rewrite the boot sector with the #/sbin/lilo command.

7. Restart the system by using the #shutdown -r now command.

8. When the system restarts, you should see the new label you created. How long does the system wait before using the default selection?

CERTIFICATION OBJECTIVE 8.10

Identifying the Purposes and Characteristics of Configuration Files

The fact that Linux uses configuration files makes it necessary for system administrators to be able identify what the purpose of each file is, and to understand how editing of the files should be performed. Specifically, for the Linux+ exam, we will focus first on the files that customize the Bash shell, then we will look in detail at the fstab and inittab files. Finally, we'll take an overall look at the /etc directory, which is home to a great many of the Linux-related configuration files.

Bash Files

The Bourne Again Shell (Bash) is the most widely used shell, so there is a good chance you will be working on a system that uses a Bash shell. As such, understanding the configuration files used by Bash is essential. Bash has a number of configuration files, which are located in each user's home directory. Table 8-7 details the files and their respective purposes.

By default, these files are copied to the user's home directory when the user account is created. The files themselves are stored in the /etc/skel directory, so if you want to change the "defaults" for the files, simply edit those files, and each time a new user is created, the newly modified files will be copied to the user's home directory. Unfortunately, for existing users, you will have to copy the files manually if you want them to have the new settings.

TABLE 8-7	File	Purpose
Bash Configuration Files and Their Purposes	.bash_profile	Specifies environment variables.
	.bashrc	Used to specify commands to be run each time a new instance of the shell is opened. By default this file points to the /etc/.bashrc file.
	.bash_logout	Lists commands that should be executed when the user logs out.

inittab and fstab

Although there are many configuration files in the etc directory, two that are worthy of special mention are inittab and fstab.

inittab

The inittab file is used by the system to denote what actions the *init* command is to do at a certain run level or under certain conditions. In addition, the file specifies the default runlevel and the settings for the creation of virtual terminals, which are described in Chapter 10. Following is a sample of an innitab file. To save space, we have taken out some of the lines where the information is purely commentary.

```
#This line sets the default run lelvel
id:3:initdefault:

# System initialization.
si::sysinit:/etc/rc.d/rc.sysinit

l0:0:wait:/etc/rc.d/rc 0
l1:1:wait:/etc/rc.d/rc 1
l2:2:wait:/etc/rc.d/rc 2
l3:3:wait:/etc/rc.d/rc 3
l4:4:wait:/etc/rc.d/rc 4
l5:5:wait:/etc/rc.d/rc 5
l6:6:wait:/etc/rc.d/rc 6

# Things to run in every runlevel.
ud::once:/sbin/update

# Trap CTRL-ALT-DELETE
ca::ctrlaltdel:/sbin/shutdown -t3 -r now

# When our UPS tells us power has failed, assume we have a few minutes
# of power left. Schedule a shutdown for 2 minutes from now.
pf::powerfail:/sbin/shutdown -f -h +2 "Power Failure; System Shutting Down"

# If power was restored before the shutdown kicked in, cancel it.
pr:12345:powerokwait:/sbin/shutdown -c "Power Restored; Shutdown Cancelled"

# Run gettys in standard runlevels
1:2345:respawn:/sbin/mingetty tty1
2:2345:respawn:/sbin/mingetty tty2
```

```
3:2345:respawn:/sbin/mingetty tty3
4:2345:respawn:/sbin/mingetty tty4
5:2345:respawn:/sbin/mingetty tty5
6:2345:respawn:/sbin/mingetty tty6

# Run xdm in runlevel 5
# xdm is now a separate service
x:5:respawn:/etc/X11/prefdm -nodaemon
```

As you can see, there are comments throughout the file that do a good job of explaining the various options. The most likely change you will make to the inittab file is to the default runlevel, a procedure described in Chapter 10.

fstab

The fstab file is used during the boot process to determine which devices should be mounted. The file format is relatively simple and has six possible fields. The definitions for each of these fields can be seen in Table 8-8.

The following sample file is a printout of a /etc/fstab file from a system in which the CD-ROM is automatically mounted. So that you can correlate the information from the table with the information in the file, we have added numbers (in bold) to

	Column Number	Field	Purpose
TABLE 8-8 Fields in the /etc/fstab File	1	/dev/device	Specifies the device and partition that is to be mounted.
	2	/dir	Specifies the directory within the file system to which this device is to be mounted.
	3	fstype	Specifies the file system of this partition, for example, ext2, swap.
	4	mount options	Specifies the options that the file system should be mounted with. For example, **noauto** means that the file system will should not be automatically mounted..
	5	fs_freq	Specifies the frequency with which the dump utility shroruld create a backup of the partition
	6	fs_passno	Specifies the place in the file system check (fsck) order for this partition.

the top of the file to indicate the column numbers.

1	2	3		4	5	6
LABEL=/ /				ext2	defaults	1 1
/dev/cdrom		/mnt/cdrom	·	iso9660	noauto,owner,ro	0 0
/dev/fd0		/mnt/floppy		auto	noauto,owner	0 0
none		/proc		proc	defaults	0 0
none		/dev/pts		devpts	gid=5,mode=620	0 0
/dev/hda5		swap		swap	defaults	0 0

Other Important Files and Directories in the Etc Directory

While the fstab and inittab files might have been singled out for special attention in the Linux+ objectives, they are by no means the only files and directories of importance in the /etc directory. The names and purpose of some of the other configuration files that can be found in the /etc are given in Table 8-9.

Table 8-10 provides a brief rundown of some of the directories that you'll find in the /etc directory.

The files and directories are by no means comprehensive, and it's a good idea to take some time to examine the structure and contents of the etc directory structure.

TABLE 8-9	File Name	Purpose
Some Configuration Files Found in the /etc/ Directory	hosts	Can be used for static hostname resolution. The IP address of the host that is to be resolved is added to the left of the file. The host names and aliases are then separated by tabs.
	resolv.conf	Provides information on the DNS server availability. The first line is the search domain. Subsequent lines consist of the name of the DNS server, a tab, and then the IP address of that server. It is common practice to list at least two DNS servers for fault tolerance.
	hosts.allow	Specifies the hosts that are allowed to use the network services provided by this system.
	hosts.deny	Specifies the hosts that are not allowed to use the network services provided by this system.
	crontab	Provides configuration information to the cron daemon.
	group	Used to store information on groups created on the system.
	passwd	Used to hold user account information for the system.
	shadow	Used to hold shadow passwords for user accounts.
	gshadow	Used to hold shadow passwords for groups.
	services	Defines services, ports, and aliases for this system. Used by inetd for service designations.

TABLE 8-10	Directory	Function
Selected Directories from the /etc Directory	/skel	Contains files that will be copied to user's home directory on user creation
	/X11	Contains configuration information for the X server, including the XF86Config file
	/ppp	Contains scripts and other PPP related information
	/cron.*	A number of directories used by the cron daemon for running scheduled jobs

CERTIFICATION OBJECTIVE 8.11

Editing Basic Configuration Files

Having looked at what the key configuration files are and where they are located, we now look at what you need to edit those files.

Making Copies of Your Files

Many of the text editors available on Linux do not make backup copies of the files being edited, and many also do not prompt you when you overwrite an existing file. For this reason, its good practice to make a backup copy of any file that you are going to edit. The easiest way to do this is with the cp command. For example, if you were going to edit the /etc/fstab file, you could do the following:

```
#cp fstab fstab.bak
```

SCENARIO & SOLUTION

You want to configure name resolution for your system.	Edit the /etc/resolv.conf file and enter the appropriate information.
You want to change the default run level for your system.	Edit the /etc/inittab file and change the default runlevel entry.
You want to configure the storage devices that are mounted at boot.	Edit the /etc/fstab file and make the appropriate changes.

Chapter 8: Configuration

This would copy the fstab file to another called fstab.bak. Then, if any of the changes you made didn't work, or simply if you wanted to revert back to the original file, you could use the command in reverse to copy the backup file over the original. The preceding example assumes that you are in the correct directory to perform the command.

Using a Text Editor

There are dozens of text editors available for Linux, some of which are easier to use than others. Whether you are a command-line junkie or GUI fan, getting to know at least two editors is worthwhile, and you should make sure that one of those is a generic utility such as vi, which is described in Chapter 10. In fact, if you prefer, you can choose to just use vi.

General Considerations for Editing

Apart from making copies, there are some other general guidelines you should observe when editing files.

■ **Be sure of changes when you make them**   Many of the files we have discussed are essential for the operation of the system. Making an incorrect change might have you reaching for a recovery disk in short order. Be careful of what you change and how you change it. If in doubt, retreat to the documentation or another support source and return later.

■ **Understand the syntax for the changes you make**   Making a change to a certain file might enable or disable a service, mount a file system, or restrict access. Also be sure that you are editing the correct file. Many Linux services use more than one file for configuration.

■ **Place comments in the file**   If others are editing them, they know what you have changed. Comments can be placed in files using the # character. Any text that appears after the character is ignored by the system. The # character can also be useful if you no longer want the system to use a certain line, but you don't want to delete it.

■ **Be aware of configuration filenames**   Many utilities will overwrite a file without prompting. This might mean you mistakenly save a file over an old one.

■ **Familiarize yourself with recovery procedures**   If you are working with a file such as inittab or fstab, understand the process of recovering your system should you subsequently be unable to boot. Understanding the process before you need to do it is a lot easier (and less stressful) than poring through documentation once the problem has occurred.

■ **Know how to exit without saving changes**   Even on a good day, fingers don't always work they way they are supposed to. If you think you have mistakenly deleted something or overwritten something else, exit the editor without saving and start again.

When you first start working with Linux, you might think that the proliferation of text files makes for complex administration, but as time goes on, you'll realize that it really is a very efficient way to do things.

CERTIFICATION OBJECTIVE 8.12

Loading, Removing, and Editing List Modules

We have mentioned at several points that Linux is a modular system that allows the administrator to manage closely what services and modules are loaded by the system. For example, if a certain device is not needed by the system, such as a parallel port, the administrator can choose not to include the functionality in the kernel, which makes the kernel smaller and more efficient. Then, if the parallel port is needed temporarily at some point, the relevant modules can be loaded manually, providing that functionality.

Loading Modules at Boot

When a Linux system boots, modules that have been configured as part of the kernel are automatically loaded, as are any modules that are listed in the /etc/modules.conf or /etc/conf.modules files, depending on your distribution. Don't be surprised if, when viewing this file, there are very few entries. Most Linux installations will have the required functionality compiled as part of the kernel, rather than having the files loaded in this way.

Viewing a List of Loadable Modules

Modules are kernel specific, that is, a module will work only with the kernel for which it is designed. For this reason, the available modules are placed into a directory in the /lib/modules directory that corresponds to the kernel version number for which they are designed. Figure 8-8 shows the directory listing of this directory from a sample server. As you can see, there are a variety of subdirectories that are used to break down the available modules by type.

Because modules often depend on other modules, a file called the dependency tree is created on the system that defines which modules have which dependencies. The dependency tree file can be found in the same directory as the module subdirectories. If you add new modules to the system, you can build a new dependency tree by using the depmod -a command.

insmod

If you want to load a module that is not currently loaded, you can use the insmod command to do it. The basic usage of the *insmod* command is as follows:

```
#insmod modulename
```

FIGURE 8-8

Sample listing
of modules
from a server

```
root@localhost.localdomain: /lib/modules/2.2.16-22                    _ □ ×

  File   Edit   Settings   Help

[root@localhost 2.2.16-22]# pwd
/lib/modules/2.2.16-22
[root@localhost 2.2.16-22]# ls -l
total 84
drwxr-xr-x    2 root     root         4096 Aug 26 01:36 block
lrwxrwxrwx    1 root     root           21 Aug 26 01:36 build -> /usr/src/linux-2.2.16
drwxr-xr-x    2 root     root         4096 Aug 26 01:36 cdrom
drwxr-xr-x    2 root     root         4096 Aug 26 01:36 fs
drwxr-xr-x    2 root     root         4096 Aug 26 01:36 ipv4
drwxr-xr-x    2 root     root         8192 Aug 26 01:36 misc
-rw-r--r--    1 root     root        36501 Aug 26 01:47 modules.dep
-rw-r--r--    1 root     root           99 Aug 26 01:47 modules.pcimap
drwxr-xr-x    2 root     root         4096 Aug 26 01:36 net
drwxr-xr-x    2 root     root         4096 Aug 26 01:36 pcmcia
drwxr-xr-x    2 root     root         4096 Aug 26 01:36 scsi
drwxr-xr-x    2 root     root         4096 Aug 26 01:36 usb
drwxr-xr-x    2 root     root         4096 Aug 26 01:36 video
[root@localhost 2.2.16-22]#
```

If the module is able to load successfully, a message such as the following will be displayed:

```
Using /lib/modules/2.2.16-22/net/modulename.o
```

In some cases, the modules you are trying to load might require that another module be loaded before it. If this is the case, you might see a message such as that shown in Figure 8-9.

As in this case, there is generally some indication of the module that is required, so you can load the dependency module and then the module you want, which should now load successfully. You can then use the *lsmod* command to see the list of loaded modules, including the one you have just loaded. There are a number of switches for the *insmod* command, which can be viewed on the man page (*man insmod*). One of the more commonly used switches is -k, which allows the kernel to remove a module if it not used after a certain amount of time. This process is called autocleaning.

exam
ⓦatch

Understand the purpose and function of the module commands such as insmod and rmmod.

rmmod

The Remove Modules command, rmmod, allows you to unload modules from the system that are no longer needed. The basic usage of the rmmod command is as follows:

```
#rmmod modulename
```

FIGURE 8-9	
A failed module load	

```
root@localhost.localdomain: /lib/modules/2.2.16-22/net                    _ □ ×

 File   Edit   Settings   Help

[root@localhost net]# insmod ppp
Using /lib/modules/2.2.16-22smp/net/ppp.o
/lib/modules/2.2.16-22smp/net/ppp.o: unresolved symbol slhc_remember_Rsmp07972313
/lib/modules/2.2.16-22smp/net/ppp.o: unresolved symbol slhc_toss_Rsmpa152cec0
/lib/modules/2.2.16-22smp/net/ppp.o: unresolved symbol slhc_free_Rsmpb99033d9
/lib/modules/2.2.16-22smp/net/ppp.o: unresolved symbol slhc_init_Rsmp1ca65fca
/lib/modules/2.2.16-22smp/net/ppp.o: unresolved symbol slhc_uncompress_Rsmp3bb36b01
/lib/modules/2.2.16-22smp/net/ppp.o: unresolved symbol slhc_compress_Rsmpcfd3a418
[root@localhost net]# insmod slhc
Using /lib/modules/2.2.16-22smp/net/slhc.o
[root@localhost net]# insmod ppp
Using /lib/modules/2.2.16-22smp/net/ppp.o
[root@localhost net]#
```

In addition, it's possible to list more than one module on the command line, in which case the modules are removed in the order they are specified. There are also two useful switches for the command. The **-r** switch will try to unload all modules in a stack. In simple terms, this means that if unloading one module frees up another, it is also unloaded, and so on. The **-a** switch can be used to unload all the currently loaded modules that are not in use.

lsmod

The lsmod command, which has no switches, displays a list of the currently loaded modules. You can see an example printout from an lsmod command in Figure 8-10.

The information displayed by the lsmod command can be broken down as follows. The first column lists the name of the module, the second this size, the third the number programs that are using that module. The fact that some of the modules have a [driver] next to them indicates that the driver is used by another driver in the list. The same information provided by lsmod can be also be viewed with the proc command as follows:

```
#cat /proc/modules
```

modprobe

As does **insmod, modprobe** allows kernel modules to be loaded and unloaded as needed. The difference between the two is that the single command can be used for both the loading and unloading.

FIGURE 8-10

The printout from an **lsmod** command

```
root@localhost.localdomain: /root

 File   Edit   Settings   Help

[root@localhost /root]# lsmod
Module              Size  Used by
ide-cd             23632   0  (autoclean)
lockd              31656   1  (autoclean)
sunrpc             54116   1  (autoclean) [lockd]
3c59x              20136   1  (autoclean)
aic7xxx           137528   0
[root@localhost /root]#
```

SCENARIO & SOLUTION

You want to view a list of the currently loaded modules.	Use the lsmod command.
You want to remove any unused modules.	Use the rmmod command with the -a switch.
You want to have a modules automatically load at boot.	Add the module to the modules.conf file or recompile the kernel to include the functionality.

While loading and unloading modules manually or though the modules.conf file is all well and good, if the functionality is required on an ongoing basis the kernel should be recompiled to include that module. Doing so makes for a "tighter" configuration and improves performance.

CERTIFICATION OBJECTIVE 8.13

Documenting the Installation of the Operating System, Including Configuration

Documentation is the task the most system administrators love to hate, but there is really no need for this to be the case, and in times of trouble, a solid set of documentation can also be your best friend. Here are some tips on how you can best prepare your documentation.

■ **Include as much as you need, but don't include information you don't** For documentation to be effective, it has to be relevant and up to date. Including information of little relevance makes the documentation less efficient and increases the workload associated with updating it. If information is included that is not updated, it might as well not be included in the first place.

■ **Dedicate time to maintaining the documentation** Set aside a certain amount of time each week for the maintenance of the documentation. What tends to happen is that documentation gets relegated far enough down the task list that it never gets done. This results in documentation that is of little use when you come to use it. Take care of the documentation and, when the time comes that you need it, the documentation will take care of you.

■ **Remember the purpose** Documentation is not meant as a means to convince someone else that you are doing your job properly. It is a tool designed to help you manage, administer, and, if necessary, recover your server more efficiently. Remember this when deciding what to include in documentation set. Fancy network maps are well and good, but not at the expense of other, more important information.

■ **Make copies** Make more that one copy of the documentation, and ensure that a hard copy is available at all times. The one time you might need the documentation more than ever is when the system is down—the exact time you won't be able to access information on the server. Also, if support is performed on remote locations, such as at home, ensure that you have a copy of the documentation available there as well.

Now that we have looked at the guidelines for creating, maintaining, and storing your documentation, let's go over what kind of information should, and should not, be included in your documentation set.

What to Include in the Documentation

There really is no simple answer to this question, but it can be answered by another question. Ask yourself what information would be needed for someone with a reasonable knowledge of Linux, who might not be you, to be able to re-create the existing system configuration. Whatever you come up with is probably what should be included in the system documentation. It is also worth mentioning that a server system is likely to need far more detailed documentation than a system that is used as a workstation.

on the job

When creating documentation, remember that the person using the documentation in the future might not be you or might not even work for your company. For this reason, be very careful about the assumptions you make.

Here are some suggestions for inclusion in the system documentation:

- **Basic system information** This includes things such as software versions, the purpose of the system, the location and contact information for anyone connected with the system.

- **Hardware configuration information** In some cases, the need to rebuild or reconfigure a system might come from the fact that you have experienced a hardware failure. Having accurate information about what devices are already installed in the system, or how the system was configured previously, will be extremely useful. Hardware configuration information of most use is things like resource usage, device driver information and so on.

- **Configuration files** Because Linux configuration is based on text files, making copies and printouts of the files is really easy, and doing so can significantly decrease the amount of time it takes to rebuild a system. System and application specific files should be included.

- **Information on patches and updates** Information on the versions of patches and updates that have been applied to should provided, along with dates of when the patches were applied. This information is critical if you are to be able to reload the system to its running state.

- **Network information** Although much of the actual network configuration information will be included in the files previously mentioned, extra information such as the configuration of the network on which the system resides and any dependencies that the server might service should be detailed. For example, if the server provides DNS lookup services, you might include information on how to ensure that DNS services can continue in the event of a system failure.

- **Information on password recovery procedures** Although, for security reasons, passwords themselves should not be included in system documentation, procedures for the recovery of passwords including the root account should.

- **Change log** A way that updating documentation can be made easier is to use a change log. Each time a change is made that affects the documentation, the change is noted in the change log. Then, at an appropriate time, the documentation itself is updated with the change. If the documentation is called into service between the change being made and the log being updated, the change log can be consulted to see recent changes.

■ **Contact information** Contact information for anyone associated with the system should be included and, if appropriate, escalation procedures in case of a failure should also be noted.

During this section, we have talked about documentation as if it is used only for re-creating or rebuilding the system, which perhaps paints a lopsided picture of documentations function. It is just as useful, and will more likely be used more frequently, in the day-to-day administration of the system, so you should make sure it contains information that facilitates both situations.

CERTIFICATION OBJECTIVE 8.14

Configuring Access Rights

While Linux is able to provide a wide range of services to clients, it's reasonable that only authorized users be able to use them. For access to system services to be controlled, it's necessary to understand how access rights to the various services are managed.

inetd

Inetd is a most useful creature that saves valuable system resources while still enabling the system to perform a range of functions. inetd intercepts incoming requests for network services an then sends those requests to the appropriate service. There are many analogies for inetd, but the most useful is that of a switchboard operator. As calls (requests) come in for certain numbers (services, specified by TCP/IP port numbers), the calls are routed to that service and then acted upon. The great thing about inetd is that rather than have all the services running on the system and using valuable resources, inetd can wake services on demand. So, if the server provides FTP services, but they are used on a very occasional basis, the FTP daemon can load at the request of inetd, when an ftp request comes in, rather than being loaded all the time.

on the **Job** *Some distributions use xinetd and /etc/xinetd.conf in place of inetd.*

Generally speaking, there are more services configured on a system than are actually needed, which can lead to security problems. One of the first steps toward securing your Linux server is to remove services that are not needed from the /etc/inetd.conf file, which is what inetd uses to determine what services are available on the system. If inetd does not find a requested service in the inetd.conf file, it stops the remote host from trying to access it.

A typical inetd file from a freshly installed server system will most likely contain dozens of unnecessary services. To disable them as far as inetd is concerned, simply step through the file, commenting out (using #s) the services you don't want to offer. Don't delete the lines, as you never know when you might want to start offering the services. In the following excerpt from an /etc/inetd.conf file, the ftp and telnet services are enabled, but the other services listed are disabled, as the lines that describe the services are commented out with #.

```
#time stream    tcp    nowait   root     internal
#time dgram udp    wait    root     internal
#
# These are standard services.
#
ftp           stream  tcp      nowait  root    /usr/sbin/tcpd   in.ftpd -l -a
telnet        stream  tcp      nowait  root    /usr/sbin/tcpd   in.telnetd
#
# Shell, login, exec, comsat and talk are BSD protocols.
#
#shell        stream     tcp   nowait     root   /usr/sbin/tcpd   in.rshd
#login        stream     tcp   nowait     root   /usr/sbin/tcpd   in.rlogind
#exec         stream     tcp   nowait     root   /usr/sbin/tcpd   in.rexecd
```

As mentioned earlier, inetd relies on TCP/IP ports to determine which service the remote host is requesting. To do this, it uses another file, /etc/services, for information on which TCP/IP ports relate to which service. Although it doesn't represent a serious security measure, changing the ports associated with a service might be warranted. The change is made by editing the /etc/services file and specifying another port number for a service. Here are some example lines from an etc/services file:

```
ftp-data       20/tcp
ftp            21/tcp
fsp            21/udp          fspd
ssh            22/tcp                          # SSH Remote Login Protocol
ssh            22/udp                          # SSH Remote Login Protocol
telnet         23/tcp
#              24 - private
smtp           25/tcp          mail
#              26 - unassigned
time           37/tcp          timserver
```

The first column specifies the name of the service, and the second the port number to be used and the protocol type.

If the remote host is requesting a service that is supported by inetd, the request is passed on to that service, but the quest for access is not over yet. There are still the access control files, called hosts.allow and hosts.deny, which if configured, must be passed.

hosts.allow and hosts.deny

Among the key files in managing access to the network services are the hosts.allow and hosts.deny files, both of which can be found in the /etc directory. There are different ways to configure the entries in the files, but before we get on to that, let's look at how the system used the two files.

When a remote host requests a network service, let's say HTTP for argument's sake, the hosts.allow file is examined. If an entry in the file matches the client trying to access the system, access is granted. If not, the system attempts to match the host with an entry in the hosts.deny file. If a match is found, then access is blocked; if not, access is granted. What this adds up to is this: if the hosts.allow and hosts.deny files are blank or do not exist, any host will be able to access the service.

So, to prevent access by unauthorized hosts, you add all the hosts you do want to access the system to the hosts.allow file and list all hosts (including the ones you do want to have access) in the hosts.deny file. Because the system looks at the hosts.allow file before is gets to the hosts.deny file, the users you do want to provide access to will be allowed on the system before the access control system gets to the hosts.deny file. Simple!

hosts.allow and hosts.deny File Entries

The format for entries in the hosts.allow and hosts.deny files are the same for each. The basic usage is as follows:

```
service: who_is_allowed_or_denied
```

So, for example, an entry in the hosts.allow file that lets everyone access the HTTP service looks like this:

```
http: ALL
```

You can also create entries based on criteria such as an IP address range:

```
http:  10.10.10.
```

This statement allows access from all systems that have an IP address in the range of 10.10.10.1–10.10.10.255.

It is common practice on a secure system to have an entry of ALL:ALL in the hosts.deny file and then add the appropriate access in the hosts.allow file. This catch-all makes it easy to manage your security of services. As well as the ALL wildcard, you can also use a range of other options including LOCAL, which provides access only to systems on a local network, and UNKNOWN, which applies to a system with a name or address that cannot be resolved correctly.

Make sure you understand the purpose of the hosts.allow and hosts.deny files and the order in which they are processed. Also, make sure you understand the basic syntax for adding entries to the file.

In addition to the system-wide restrictions applied by inetd and the hosts files, many services also have the ability to restrict access specifically. For more information on controlling access for specific services, refer to the man pages or HOWTOs. Links to these resources are provided in Appendix C.

Linux security is an incredibly complex subject, and as such warrants further research and reading. If you find yourself managing a Linux server that provides services to outside clients, be sure to understand the issues involved and find out about any potential security issues—before someone else does it for you!

CERTIFICATION SUMMARY

We covered a wide range of topics in this chapter, from configuring the X server to setting up and installing printing. We also looked at how you set and configure services and the access rights for those services. We also looked at the process of updating server configuration files and what some of those files are.

As the Linux+ exam requires that you have a "basic" knowledge of many of these topics, we have covered those topics in only the most basic terms. For the real world, you'll most certainly benefit from some further reading and experimentation.

TWO-MINUTE DRILL

Here are some of the key points from this chapter.

Reconfiguring the X Window System with Automated Utilities

❏ A variety of tools are available to automate the X server configuration process.

❏ Xconfigurator is a menu-based system, XF86Setup uses a minimal GUI, and xf86config uses a text-based system.

❏ All the utilities serve the same function: to create an XF86Config file for the X server.

Configuring the Client's Workstation for Remote Access

❏ PPP provides a mechanism for establishing dial-up links with remote hosts such as an ISP.

❏ PPP functionality can be compiled in the kernel or loaded through a module.

❏ PPP can be used for standard modem or ISDN connections.

Setting Environment Fariables

❏ Environment variables allow the workspace to be customized by using standard values.

❏ Variables can viewed by using the set or printenv command.

Configuring Basic Network Services and Settings

❏ In some cases, it might be necessary to reconfigure network settings such as IP address, subnet mask, and DNS information.

❏ Network information is stored in configuration files.

❏ A number of utilities, including Linuxconf, netconfig, and netcfg, are available to automate the configuration of network settings.

Configuring Basic Server Services

❑ Samba allows a Linux server to make resources such as directories and printers available to SMB clients such as Windows workstations.

❑ NFS allows remote file systems to be mounted into the local file system and accessed as if they were part of the system.

❑ NIS allows files to be accessed from a central system so that information is kept consistent across the network.

Configuring Basic Internet Services

❑ Linux is capable of offering a range of network services including Web server, e-mail, and FTP services.

❑ Configuration of services is performed through text files. Each service has its own files, or sets of files, for configuration.

❑ Daemons provide the functionality for each service and can be started, stopped, and restarted as needed.

Identifying When Swap Space Needs to Be Increased

❑ Swap space is used when the system does not have enough physical RAM to satisfy user requests.

❑ The amount of free swap space, and other memory related information, can be viewed with the free command.

❑ If you need to add more swap space, you can use the mkdir command.

Adding and Configuring Printers

❑ Information on printer configuration is stored in the /etc/printcap file.

❑ Filters can be used to format print jobs into the correct form for the printer.

❑ Printer configurations can be defined for local or remote printers.

Reconfiguring Boot Loader

❑ Boot loaders dictate how the system boots.

❑ The file is divided into two parts. The global section dictates what parameters should be used at all boots. The images section specifies the particulars for each of the bootable configurations.

❑ Once changes have been made, the boot sector must be rewritten for the changes to take effect.

Identifying the Purpose and Characteristics of Configuration Files

❑ Text-based configuration files are used for the configuration of almost all Linux services.

❑ Certain files, such as inittab and fstab, are key to the operation of the system.

❑ Many of the configuration files are stored in the /etc directory, or subdirectories of it.

Editing Basic Configuration Files

❑ Editing of configuration files is an essential skill for Linux administrators.

❑ Copies of key files should be made before editing so that they can be rolled back if necessary.

❑ Any changes to files should be commented so that others are aware of the changes.

Loading, Removing, and Editing List Modules

❑ Modules can be loaded and unloaded by the administrator.

❑ Modules are kernel-version dependant.

❑ The lsmod command can be used to see the loaded modules. The insmod and rmmod commands can be used to load and unload modules respectively.

Documenting the Installation of the Operating System, Including Configuration

❑ Documentation is important for the maintenance, administration, and recovery of the system.

❑ Multiple copies of the documentation should be kept, including at remote sites from which administration is performed.

❑ The documentation set for a server should include copies of configuration files, network configuration information, disk layout information, and any application-specific information.

Configuring Access Rights

❑ Services that are not needed should be disabled through inetd.conf.

❑ The hosts.deny and hosts.allow files provide a mechanism for managing access to the system.

❑ Respective services also have files that can further restrict access.

SELF TEST

The following questions will help determine your level of understanding of the material presented in this chapter. Some of the questions may have more than one correct answer, so be sure to review all answers carefully before choosing all that apply.

Reconfiguring the X Window System with Automated Utilities

1. Which of the following is a text-based configuration utility for X?

    A. Xconfigurator

    B. xf86config

    C. XF86Config

    D. XF86Setup

Configuring the Client's Workstation for Remote Access

2. Which of the following pieces of information do you *not* need when setting up a PPP connection with an ISP?

    A. PPP dial-in server hostname

    B. PPP dial-in server phone number

    C. Username

    D. Password

Setting Environment Variables

3. Which of these files do you edit to make a permanent change to an environment variable for the root user?

    A. /etc/inittab

    B. /root/.bash.profile

    C. /root/.bash_profile

    D. /root/.bash.env

Configuring Basic Network Services and Settings

4. Which two of the following utilities can you use to reconfigure the network settings on a Linux system?

   A. netcfg

   B. netconfig

   C. ipconfig

   D. inetcfg

Configuring Basic Server Services

5. Which of the following commands do you use to see which NIS server is responding to your requests?

   A. ypmatch

   B. ypwhich

   C. ypwich

   D. ypinit

6. Which of these files contains the information that Samba uses for configuration?

   A. samba.conf

   B. samba.dat

   C. smb.conf

   D. testparm.conf

Configuring Basic Internet Services

7. Which of the following commands successfully restarts the Apache Web server?

   A. ./http start

   B. ./httpd start

   C. ./httpd restart

   D. ./http restart

Identifying When Swap Space Needs to Be Increased

8. Which of the following commands do you use to view the amount of swap space in use on a system?

A. free

B. freeswap

C. swap

D. mkswap -m

Adding and Configuring Printers

9. In the /etc/printcap file, what does the :lp field dictate?

A. The name of the printer

B. The local device that the printer is connected to

C. The spool directory

D. The filter to be applied

10. What does the command lpr -m root report cause to happen?

A. The file "report" is formatted by lpr and then e-mailed to root.

B. All print jobs called "report" and all print jobs owned by root are removed from the default print queue.

C. The file report is printed with a masthead of "root."

D. The file report is printed to the default printer, and root receives an e-mail notification when the job was completed.

11. Which of the following lines from a printcap file correctly defines a new printer called HPLaser with an alias of HPLJ?

A. HPLaser:HPLJ

B. HPLaser | HPLJ

C. #HPLaser | HPLJ

D. #HPLaser:HPLJ

Reconfiguring Boot Loader

12. Which of the following two fields in the lilo.conf file do you edit to change the name of the default operating system image that is loaded?

    A. image

    B. default

    C. defimg

    D. label

13. Which of the following commands do you use to rewrite the boot sector after changes have been made to the lilo.conf file?

    A. /bin/lilo

    B. /usr/lilo

    C. /sbin/lilo.conf

    D. /sbin/lilo

Identifying the Purposes and Characteristics of Configuration Files

14. What function does the /etc/skel directory provide?

    A. It contains configuration file templates.

    B. It holds files that will be copies to user's home directory.

    C. It holds information for the skel daemon.

    D. It holds the skel daemon.

15. Which of the following lines do you add to the /etc/fstab file in order to mount a NFS share of /data/docs from server 7 to a mount point of /data/s7data?

    A. `server7:/data/docs    /mnt/data/s7data     nfs`

    B. `/data/docs    /data/s7data    nfs`

    C. `server7:/data/docs    /data/s7data     nfs`

    D. `server7:/data/docs    /data/s7data`

Editing Basic Configuration Files

16. While editing a text file, you want to place a comment in the file detailing what changes you have made. Which of the following characters do you use to do this?

    A. ""

    B. &

    C. #

    D. "

Loading, Removing, and Editing List Modules

17. Which of the following commands do you use to remove all the loaded modules that are not currently in use?

    A. lsmod -r

    B. rmmod -r

    C. rmmod -a

    D. rmmod -removeall

Documenting the Installation of the Operating System, Including Configuration

18. Which of the following are you *least* likely to include in the system documentation?

    A. Contact information for hardware suppliers

    B. Configuration files

    C. Root account passwords

    D. Network settings

Configuring Access Rights

19. Which of the following files would you edit if you wanted to prevent FTP services from being accessed on your system?

    A. inetd.conf

    B. ftpaccess

    C. hosts.allow

    D. hosts.deny

20. Which of the following entries would you add to the hosts.allow file to give access to the Web server from a network of 10.10.10.0?

    A. http: 10.10.10.

    B. smtp: 10.10.10.

    C. http: 10.10.10.1

    D. http – 10.10.10.

LAB QUESTION

Configure basic printing by manually creating an /etc/printcap file. After opening the file in an editor, create an entry for a printer called laser, with aliases of hplaserjet3 and lp. Use the default spool location and use lp0 as the output device.

After creating and saving your printcap file, start or restart the lpd daemon to recognize the new printer, and then use the lpr command to print to the printer using the printer name and one of the aliases. If you don't have a printer connected to your parallel port, use the lpq command to verify that the print jobs are in the print queue.

SELF TEST ANSWERS

Reconfiguring the X Window System with Automated Utilities

I. ☑ **B.** xf86config is a text-based utility for configuring the X server.
☒ **A.** Xconfigurator is a menu-based system for configuring the X server.
C. This is not a valid utility. **D.** XF86Setup uses a basic GUI as its interface.

Configuring the Client's Workstation for Remote Access

2. ☑ **A.** To establish a PPP connection, you do not need the hostname of the PPP dial-in server.
☒ **B, C, D.** To establish a dial-in connection to an ISP, you will at least need the phone number, username, and password. If TCP/IP information is not supplied automatically, you might also need TCP/IP addressing information as well.

Setting Environment Variables

3. ☑ **C.** Environment variables are stored in the bash_profile file, which is stored in the user's home directory. In the case of root, this is /root.
☒ **A.** The /etc/inittab file stores configuration information that is used by the system on boot. **B.** The correct filename is .bash_profile, not .bash.profile. **D.** There is no such file as .bash.env.

Configuring Basic Network Services and Settings

4. ☑ **A. B.** Both of these are valid networking configuration utilities on a Linux system.
☒ **C.** ipconfig is used on Windows platforms, not Linux. **D.** inetcfg is a Novell NetWare utility, not a Linux utility.

Configuring Basic Server Services

5. ☑ **B.** The ypwhich command will show which NIS server is currently servicing your requests.
☒ **A.** The ypmatch command allows specific entreis from files to be pulled from the server.
C. The correct command is ypwhich, not ypwich. **D.** The ypinit command is used to initialize the NIS server.

6. ☑ C. The smb.conf file is used by Samba to determine settings and share information.

☒ A. B. These filenames are not valid. D, testparm is a utility that allows smb.conf files to be checked for errors and incompatibilities.

Configuring Basic Internet Services

7. ☑ C. The http daemon is called httpd, and the restart command will stop and restart the daemon.

☒ A. The daemon is httpd, not http, and the correct command is restart, not start.
B. The correct command is restart, not start. **D.** The daemon is httpd, not http.

Identifying When Swap Space Needs to Be Increased

8. ☑ A. The free command can be used to see how much swap space is being used. The -m switch can be applied to allow information to be presented in megabytes rather than bytes.

☒ B, C. The freeswap and swap commands are not valid. **D,** the mkswap command is used to create swap space. It does not have a -m switch

Adding and Configuring Printers

9. ☑ B. The :lp field of the /etc/printcap file determines what local device the printer is connected to.

☒ A. The name of the printer appears on its own line with no characters before it.
C. The spool directory is defined by the :sd field. **D.** The filter to be applied to the print job is defined by the filter parameter.

10. ☑ D. The **-m** switch of the lpr command causes an e-mail to be sent to the user specified when the job has finished printing

☒ A. Root is only sent an e-mail indicating that the print job has completed, not of the job itself. **B.** The lpr command is not used to remove jobs from the print queue. The lprm command can be used to do this. **C.** There is no option that prompts a masthead to be printed.

11. ☑ B. The entry in a printcap file that defines a printer configuration should start with the printer name with any aliases separated by a | .

☒ A. The printername and any alias should be separate by a |, not by a :. **C. D.** The line that defines the printer name does not start with any special characters.

Reconfiguring Boot Loader

12. ☑ **B. D.** The label field of the image needs to be changed, and so does the default entry in the global sections, as it is the label that is used by the default entry for reference.
☒ **A.** The image field is used to specify the Linux kernel image that is to be used. **C.** This is not a valid field in the lilo.conf file.

13. ☑ **D.** The command /sbin/lilo writes a new boot sector allowing changes in the lilo.conf file to be recognized.
☒ **A. B.** The lilo command is run from the sbin directory. **C.** The lilo.conf file is located in the /etc directory and is used as a configuration file for the rewriting of the boot sector, not the program.

Identifying the Purposes and Characteristics of Configuration Files

14. ☑ **B.** Files that exist in the /etc/skel directory are copied to a user's home directory when the user account is created.
☒ **A.** The only files that are generally in the /etc/skel directory are Bash configuration files. **C. D.** There is no such thing as the skel daemon.

15. ☑ **C.** Entries in the fstab file to mount a remote NFS share must define the server name and share separated by a colon, then a tab and the local mount point, then a tab and the file system type NFS.
☒ **A.** In this command, the first and last portions are correct, but the mount point is specified as /mnt/data/s7data which is incorrect. **B.** The name of the remote server, in this case server7 must be specified in the first column. **D.** The remote server information and mount point are both correct, but the type of file system, in this case NFS must also be specified.

Editing Basic Configuration Files

16. ☑ **C.** The # character can be used to place comments in configuration files. Anything that appears after the # will be ignored by the system.
☒ **A. B. D.** None of these characters allow comments to be placed into files.

Loading, Removing, and Editing List Modules

17. ☑ **C.** The rmmod -a command will unload any modules that are not currently in use.
☒ **A.** The lsmod command is used to list the modules that are loaded on the system, not to remove them. **B.** The -r switch, when used with the rmmod command is used to recursively unload modules. When using the -r switch, the module are the top of the stack must be specified. **D.** The -removeall switch is not a valid rmmod switch.

Documenting the Installation of the Operating System, Including Configuration

18. ☑ **C.** Passwords should not be included in system documentation, though procedures for the recovery of passwords should be included.
☒ **A. B. D.** All these pieces of information should be included in the system documentation.

Configuring Access Rights

19. ☑ **A.** The inetd.conf file defines what network services are provided by the server. If the ftp entry is commented out of the inetd.conf file, the inet daemon will not respond to any requests for ftp access.
☒ **B.** The ftpaccess file is used to configure the ftp server characteristics. While it can be used to reatrict access, if no access is requires at all, it is more effective to edit the service from inetd.conf. **C.** The hosts.allow file defines which hosts are allowed to access the system. **D.** The hosts.deny system defines what hosts cannot access the services of the system. In each case, it is possible to control access through these files, but it is more effective to disable the service by editing the inetd.conf.

20. ☑ **A.** The syntax for entries in the hosts.allow is servicename : allow_restrict.

☒ **B.** The Web server service is provided by the HTTP protocol, not SMTP which is used for the sending and receiving of e-mail. **C.** This entry would grant access to only one host, not the entire network range. **D.** The syntax is service:, not service -.

LAB ANSWER

1. Use the following command to open the /etc/printcap file:

   ```
   #vi /etc/printcap
   ```

2. Press I to enter the vi insert mode (for more information on using vi, refer to Chapter 10).

3. Enter the following information into the file, exactly as it appears:

   ```
   # The laserjet in the main office
           laser | hplaserjet3 | lp
           :sd=/var/spool/lpd/laser
           :lp=/dev/lp0:
   ```

   Press ESC; THEN TYPE **:wq** and press ENTER.

4. Stop and restart the lpd by using the following command:

   ```
   #/etc/rc.d/init.d/./lpd restart
   ```

   The lpd deamon will stop and restart. You should receive a warning message about the changing of ownership of the new spool directory, but no other errors.

5. Use the following lpr command to print files.

   ```
   #lpr /etc/hosts
   ```

6. Now use the same command, but this time specify an alias of the printer by using the -p switch with the lpr command.

7. If you have a printer attached, the files should have printed. If not, you can use the lpq command to see the print jobs held in the queue.

COMPUTING TECHNOLOGY INDUSTRY ASSOCIATION

9

Linux Administration: Part One

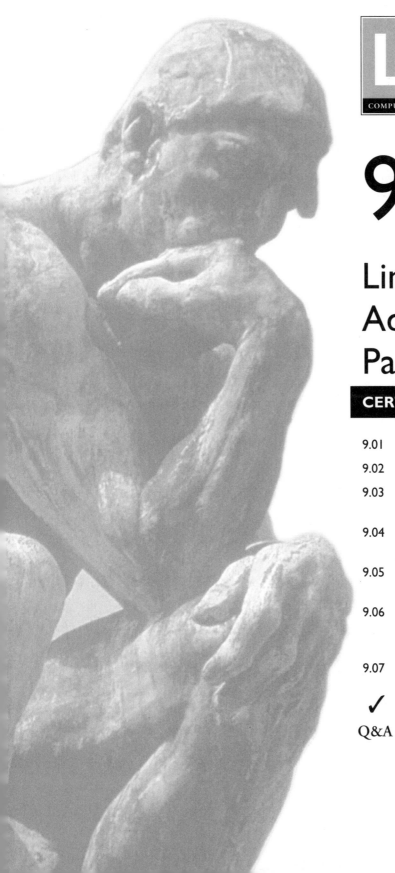

Whereas installing and configuring a system is performed on an occasional basis, the administration of a system is performed daily. Many of the tasks are relatively simple, but there is enough variety to make them interesting. The disciplines and skills needed to administer your system form the cornerstone of your Linux skills and will help you in a variety of situations and circumstances.

The Administration domain of Linux+ has a large number of objectives, which is why we have chosen to split the objectives up into two chapters. In fact, Administration is one of the largest of the Linux+ domains at 18 percent.

Among other things, this chapter takes you through common administration tasks such as managing user and group accounts, managing file permissions, managing devices and file systems, and a variety of other administration-related tasks. Some topics are not strictly administration tasks but are included because they provide the base skills necessary to administer the system.

exam
⚙atch

You are very likely to be asked questions in the Linux+ exam that relate to the use of the commands described in this section, so be sure you are familiar with the use and options of these commands before you take your exam.

CERTIFICATION OBJECTIVE 9.01

Creating and Deleting Users

One of the most often-performed administration tasks is that of creating and deleting user accounts. How often this actually needs to be done will depend on what kind of services the systems you manage provide. A server providing file and print services will most likely need more user accounts than one acting as, for example, a proxy server. Also, some software applications such as database systems may offer internal authentication processes, negating the need to create user accounts on the Linux system. Creating and deleting user accounts is a relatively simple process, though an understanding of what is happening in the background is useful as well, because if a problem occurs with the creation process, you will be able to determine what the likely cause is.

on the **job**

You must be logged in to the system as root to create user accounts.

User accounts are a vital part of any networked system because they provide accountability. In other words, a mechanism is required to ensure that each user is accountable for their actions, which a user ID provides for. Making users use a specific ID also allows file permissions to be set that restrict or allow access. We'll deal with application of permissions later; for now, we'll just concentrate on creating and managing user accounts.

on the **job**

Help for most commands found in this chapter can be obtained by typing - - help after the command. For example, ls - -help will provide help for the ls command. There are also man or info pages that can be used to obtain information on the various commands.

Creating a new user account is a simple process, though a number of different commands and utilities can be used to do it. The simplest way to add a new user is to use the adduser, or the newer useradd, command. For the purposes of our discussion, we will use the useradd command, which is now generally accepted as the standard. The basic syntax for the command is as follows:

```
#useradd username
```

So, if we were to create a user account for a user called Juan, we would use the command like this:

```
#useradd juan
```

You won't receive a message indicating that the user has been added correctly, but the lack of an error message lets you know that the user account was added without problem. As with other Linux commands, the basic command is only the beginning, and useradd has a range of options that can be added to the command line to customize the user account creation. Table 9-1 shows some of the more commonly used options and their sample usage.

Note: An additional option for the useradd command, -p, allows a password to be entered. The only problem is that it stores the password specified as clear text in the shadow password file, which is not a great idea. Plus, of course, the password won't work, because only encrypted values of the password can be stored in that file.

| TABLE 9-1 | Commonly Used Flags for the useradd Command |

Flag	Purpose	Sample Usage
-u	Specifies the user ID number to use	useradd -u 621 juan
-g	Specifies the user's initial login group	useradd -g students juan
-G	Specifies other groups the user should be added to	useradd -G softball,interns juan
-d	Specifies the home directory location for the user	useradd -d /data/users juan
-s	Specifies the location of the shell for the user	useradd -s /bin/csh juan
-c	Allows a comment to be included in the user's info	useradd -c summer student juan
-e	Specifies an expiration date for the account	useradd -e 2002-08-23 juan

on the job

In most Linux distributions, if no group is specified for the user, a group of the same name as the user is created, and the user is added to it.

When the options are used with the useradd command, they are placed between the command and the new user's name as follows (note that the quotation marks around the comment section are only necessary if the text has spaces in it; not doing so causes the command to misinterpret the information):

```
#useradd -c "Temporary user" -d /data/users/home Juan
```

exam watch

The useradd command is located in the /usr/sbin directory and is included in every Linux distribution.

Once the user account is created, it is imperative that the user account have a password set on it; otherwise, the user will not be able to log in. So, to create a password for the new user account, you can use the passwd utility. Again, assuming the user's name is Juan, the command would look like this:

```
#passwd juan
```

As we have discussed previously, Linux has rules about what is, and isn't, an acceptable password, so don't be surprised if users unfamiliar with Linux have problems setting a password. Be prepared to help them out, and make sure you remind them of the case-sensitivity issue. We will talk more about the passwd utility later in this chapter; creating strong passwords was covered in Chapter 7.

Using the passwd command without specifying a username will mean that you are changing the password for the account you are currently logged in as. If you are creating user accounts, you will be using the root account, so if you don't specify a username, you will be changing the root account password. Be careful!

Users' Home Directories

When you create user accounts, you also create users' home directories, which are intended as a storage point for the users' personal files and configurations. Both the adduser and useradd commands will create the directories and set the permissions on them automatically. Another automatically occurring process is that the contents of the /etc/skel directory are automatically copied to the users' home directory. In the default configuration, a number of configuration files are copied, including shell configuration files. This is useful if you want users to have a standard set of files, such as configuration files.

If you use the useradd command with the -D option, the options specified as the defaults will be set. You can do this if the system defaults, which are specified in the /etc/default/useradd file, do not suit your needs.

Several other mechanisms for creating user accounts are available, including GUI-based tools, such as Linuxconf and YaST. However, knowing how to create user accounts with command-line utilities is an essential skill for any Linux system administrator.

Rather that creating user accounts individually, you can use mechanisms such as the command newusers to create multiple user accounts in a batch format by using a text file as the source for information.

EXERCISE 9-1

Creating User Accounts

1. Log in to the system as root.

2. From the command line, type the following command:

   ```
   #useradd -c "A new user I created" james
   ```

3. Set a password for the new user by typing the following command:

`#passwd james`

4. When prompted, enter and reenter a password for the user.

5. Log out of the system.

6. At the login prompt, type **james** as the username, press the ENTER key, and then enter the password. You should log in to the system successfully.

How User Account Information Is Stored

An important part of the user account creation process is that of understanding how user accounts are stored. As with many other things in the Linux world, user account information is stored in a text file called passwd, which can be found in the /etc directory. The file contains a single line for each user account that has been created.

on the

job

If you view the /etc/passwd file on a system, you will notice that more user accounts appear than just those that you have created. Many of the services that the system runs have user accounts for various purposes.

Each line might seem a little complex, but the format is actually quite simple; fields of information are all separated by colons. Figure 9-1 shows what each field means.

You may have noticed that the password field in all of these examples is set to x. This isn't the password; the x simply indicates that the system is using shadow

SCENARIO & SOLUTION

You try to create a user account with spaces in the comment but receive an error.	Use quotation marks around the comment if it has spaces in it.
You want to specify an expiration date for a user account.	Use the -e option with the useradd command.
You try to create a user account but are unable to.	Check to make sure that you are logged in to the system as the root account.

Layout of the fields in an /etc/passwd file user entry

passwords. You may recall from our earlier discussions that shadow passwords are used to protect passwords on the system better.

exam
Watch

An understanding of the structure of a /etc/passwd file entries is important for the Linux+ exam.

User IDs

Each user account that is created on a system is assigned a unique user ID (UID). As you can see from Figure 9-1, the UIDs for users on this system start from 500, which could be changed if needed, with each subsequent account being assigned the next ID (501, 502, 503, and so on). UIDs are necessary because many of the internal system functions are performed using these IDs rather than the username.

on the
Job

Only the root account should have a UID of 0. If any other account has a UID of 0, you should consider it a security problem. Accounts with a UID of 0 have the same privileges as root.

In a single-server system, letting the system allocate UIDs using the default numbering system should be fine, but when you have multiple servers, some tasks are made easier by having user accounts across different servers use the same UID. For this reason, it's possible to override the system-created UID with one of your own choosing. As you may recall from Table 9-1, the option to use to do this is -u. So, for example, if you want to create a UID and specify the UID number instead of having it automatically assigned, you would use the following command:

```
#useradd -u 600 james
```

This would create a new user james with a UID of 600.

Anyway, enough of this creativity; let's turn our attention to deleting user accounts, another task you'll find yourself performing on a regular basis.

Deleting and Disabling User Accounts

As you might expect, deleting user accounts is somewhat more straightforward than creating them, though there are still considerations that need to be taken into account (no pun intended!). The first consideration is whether the user account is to be disabled so that it can be used again in the future or deleted. If your target is the former, then a little editing of the /etc/passwd or the /etc/shadow file is in order.

You will recall from our earlier discussion of creating user accounts that the second field in the user account entry in the /etc/passwd file is usually set to x, indicating that the password is shadowed. Changing this field to an asterisk (*) will render the account disabled, because the system no longer looks to the shadow password file for the password. You can also replace the password value (the second field) for the user in the /etc/shadow file with an asterisk to create the same effect. The following is an example of a disabled user account in the /etc/passwd file for mike:

```
postgres:x:26:26:PostgreSQL Server:/var/lib/pgsql:/bin/bash
mailnull:x:47:47::/var/spool/mqueue:/dev/null
trevor:x:500:500::/home/trevor:/bin/bash
mike:*:501:501::/home/mike:/bin/bash
```

You can also disable a user account by using the passwd command, discussed in the next section, or by changing the user's shell entry in the /etc/passwd file to read /bin/false. Here is an example:

```
mike:*:501:501::/home/mike:/bin/false
```

exam
watch

An asterisk (*) in the password field of a user entry in the /etc/passwd or /etc/shadow file indicates that the user account is disabled. An x in the password field of a user entry in /etc/passwd indicates that the system is using shadow passwords.

If your focus is more to do with deleting the user account completely, your command-line companion in this respect is the userdel command. In comparison to other Linux commands, which often have a large number of options, userdel has only one, and even that is optional. The basic usage is as follows:

```
#userdel juan
```

This command will successfully delete the user account, but the user's home directory will remain unless the -r option is added to the command line, as follows:

```
#userdel -r juan
```

In this instance, the user account entry is deleted from the /etc/passwd file and the user's home directory is deleted. For this reason, the -r option should be used only after you have verified that no files in the user's directory are needed. If you prefer not to delete user accounts from the command line, you can use one of the various GUI tools that are available, such as Linuxconf.

EXERCISE 9-2

Deleting a User Account

1. Log in as root.

2. Type **userdel -r james** and press ENTER.

3. Log out from the session and try to log in as the user James. What happens?

CERTIFICATION OBJECTIVE 9.02

Modifying Existing Users

Having looked at both the creation and deletion of user accounts, we now need to look at the process of modifying existing user accounts. The maintenance of existing user accounts should not take too much of your time, but this depends, of course, on how many users you are maintaining. For the purposes of the Linux+ exam, modification of existing user accounts is broken down into three parts, namely changing passwords, modifying group memberships, and updating personal information. Each is addressed in turn in the sections that follow.

Changing Passwords

Users are able to change their own passwords by using the passwd command, but on occasion, you will need to change a user's password for them. In both cases, the passwd command is used, though more options are available if you are using the utility as the root user. Some of the more commonly used options, available to the root user, for the passwd command are detailed in Table 9-2.

In addition to the passwd command, the chpasswd command allows password files in a batch process.

Managing Password Aging (chage)

In a networked system such as Linux, it is good practice to enforce periodic password changes on users so that they don't use the same password indefinitely. The chage command is available to set such things as the minimum and maximum password durations. It can also be used to expire a user account, thereby disabling it. Some of the more commonly used options for the chage command and their sample usage are shown in Table 9-3.

TABLE 9-2	Commonly Used Options for the passwd Command

Option	Result	Example Usage
username	Specifies the user account to have a new password	passwd mary
-l	Locks the user account	passwd -l mary
-u	Unlocks the user account	passwd -u mary
-d	Sets the password to blank, thereby disabling it	passwd -d mary
-S	Shows status information about the user's password	passwd -S mary

TABLE 9-3	Commonly Used Options for the chage Command	

Option	Result	Sample Usage
-m	Specifies the minimum number of days a user must retain the same password	chage -m 0 user
-M	Specifies the maximum number of days a user can use the same password	chage -M 30 user
-E	Sets expiration date for the user's password	chage -E 2002-08-23 user
-W	Specifies the number of days before password expiration the user receives warnings	chage -W 7

on the job   *A user can check to see when their password will expire and view other associated information, by using the command chage -l username. The root user can use the command to see the information on any user account.*

Changing Personal Information

A useful addition to any user account entry is personal information about the user, such as their full name or a contact phone number. This kind of information is stored in the comment field of the user's entry in the /etc/passwd file. You can either edit the file manually, using a text editor, or use the usermod command. In fact, usermod allows you to do that and much more.

usermod

The usermod command works in much the same way as the useradd command, except it doesn't create user accounts, it only modifies existing ones. The options that can be used with usermod are the same as with useradd, with the exception of -l, an option for usermod that allows you to rename a user. Renaming a user is not a big deal to a Linux system because, as you may recall from earlier, the system performs its tasks using the UID rather than the username. However, if you are renaming a user or setting a new UID for the user, you should ensure that they are logged out before you make the change. Otherwise, the system gets very confused.

As mentioned, the options for the usermod command are the same as for useradd, so refer to Table 9-1 if you need to use them. Here is an example of the usermod command in which we change the personal information for a user:

```
#usermod -c "Pager Number 555-7653" chris
```

and in this example, we rename a user from Chris to Christian:

```
#usermod -l christian chris
```

As you can see, any options and information that are to be used with the usermod command are passed before the username is specified. One point of note here is that if you rename a user, the user's home directory is not automatically renamed as a result. The user will still be able to use the home directory, but you might want to rename the user's directory and change the path to the user's entry for consistency reasons.

Changing Group Settings

Nestled in the options for the usermod command are, as with the useradd command, options that allow the group memberships for a user to be manipulated. The two options in question are the -g option, which allows you to modify the user's initial login group, and the -G option, which allows the user membership of other groups to be updated.

Changing the user's initial group is a fairly straightforward process, which can be achieved using the following command:

```
#usermod -g students Christian
```

This command switches the initial membership from whatever it is set to currently to the group students. The only stipulation for the -g option is that the group must already exist. If it doesn't, the usermod command will not create it.

on the **job**   ***Users must have a primary group specified.***

The -G option is a little more involved, in that it requires you to specify all of the groups that the user is to be a member of. Not specifying a group in the listing will cause the user to be removed from that group. The implications of this can be far reaching. For example, if a user is a member of 20 groups, and you were to issue a command that listed only one group outside of that 20, the user would be automatically removed from the 20 that they were currently a member of. So, if a user needs to be added to the students group, but is already a member of a group called research and another group called marketing, the usermod command must be used as follows:

```
#usermod -G research,marketing,students christian
```

Not naming the research and marketing groups would cause the person to be removed from them, so use the command with care!

on the **job** *Users can temporarily switch to a new primary group by using the newgrp groupname command. The primary group stays in effect until the user ends the session.*

That concludes our coverage of user accounts and account management. Now we'll look at another vital part of user administration on a Linux system, that of groups.

CERTIFICATION OBJECTIVE 9.03

Creating, Modifying, and Deleting Groups

On a system such as Linux, where many users may be using and sharing the resources, groups provide a mechanism for assigning rights and permissions to entire sets of users, rather than doing it on a per-user basis. Being able to do this significantly reduces the administration overhead of managing large numbers of users. If the

SCENARIO & SOLUTION	
A user is going on extended leave, and you want to disable their user account.	Use the passwd -l command to lock the account.
You want to set a user's configuration so that the password must be changed every four weeks.	Use the chage command to set a password expiration term.
You want to add a user to a new group.	Use the usermod command with the -G option but specify all of the groups that the user will be a member of.

system you are configuring will not have many users, you may be able to avoid creating groups completely, but an understanding of the procedures and processes involved is important because a number of system-created groups exist, a few of which you may find yourself using.

on the
Job
Do not delete the system-created groups unless you have a very good reason to do so. If you delete a system-created group, some of the services that are configured on your server might stop working completely.

As with creating users, there are numerous tools, graphic and otherwise, that can be used to create groups. For the purposes of our discussion, we will once again focus on the command-line utilities that are present on every Linux system.

on the
Job
You must be logged in as root to create group accounts.

Like user accounts, group information is stored in a text file. It can be found in the same /etc directory as the passwd file, but it's called group instead. Also like user accounts, the file is comprised of one-line entries that hold information about the group. The format is the same as the passwd file, though there are less fields. Here are some sample lines from a group file:

```
sales:x:600:paul,mike,holly,cindy,tracy
research:x:601:paul,tyler,james,christian,david
marketing:x:634:trevor,sally,steve,james
```

As you can see, each field is separated by a colon. An explanation of each field is provided in Figure 9-2.

FIGURE 9-2

Layout of the
fields in an
/etc/group entry

Password field. The x indicates
the password is shadowed.

List of users that belong
to this group

↓   ↓

marketing:x:879:juan,peter,sadi,christine,tyler

↑   ↑

Group name   Group ID
              (GID)

Adding Groups

The command to add groups to the system is groupadd. A number of options can be used with the groupadd command, but the only required one is the group name. The following is an example of the command to add a group called students:

```
#groupadd students
```

The command adds an entry to the groups file, with the default information, such as the group ID. To add users to the group, you can edit the groups file and add each username, separated by a comma, or use the usermod command as discussed earlier.

on the **Job**

Be careful not to add unnecessary spaces in the username listings of the groups file or when using the usermod command. When Linux encounters a space, it assumes that it has reached the end of the username listing and stops reading. All entries after the space will be ignored.

Armed with the information from Figure 9-2, you might have noticed that in the previous example entries from the beginning of this section, the password field on all groups is set to x. If you want to, you can set a password for each group that must be entered when a user wants to join a group. If the group does not have a password set and you want to put set one, you can use the gpasswd command. The gpasswd command can also be used to update a group's membership.

If you want to get a list of groups that you are a member of, you can simply type **groups** at the command line. For a listing of which groups a user belongs to, simply add the username to the groups command. Examples of both of these commands can be seen in Figure 9-3.

FIGURE 9-3

Output from the groups command

```
root@localhost.localdomain: /                                    _ □ ×
  File   Edit   Settings   Help
[root@localhost /]# groups
root bin daemon sys adm disk wheel
[root@localhost /]# groups juan
juan : juan research marketing sales students
[root@localhost /]#
```

Modifying a Group

In certain circumstances, you may find it necessary to modify the group ID or rename the group completely. Both of these tasks can be performed using the groupmod command.

The usage of the groupmod command is much the same as the use of the other commands mentioned in this section. The options are passed and then the group name is supplied. Here is an example of a command to rename a group from students to summerworkers:

```
#groupmod -n summerworkers students
```

Deleting a Group

Deleting a group is a simple task that can be achieved using the groupdel command, as follows:

```
#groupdel groupname
```

This command has no options. If you would rather, you can delete a group by directly editing the /etc/group file and deleting the corresponding line in the file. Just be careful to make sure that you are deleting the correct group!

EXERCISE 9-3

Creating, Editing, and Deleting Groups

1. At the command prompt, type the following command to create a group called newgroup:

```
#groupadd newgroup
```

2. Type the following command to see the new entry from the /etc/group file:

```
#grep newgroup /etc/group
```

3. Rename the group by using the following command:

```
#groupmod -n evennewergroup newgroup
```

4. To verify that the renaming was successful, use the same command as in Step 2, but substitute newgroup with **evennewergroup**. Notice that the group ID is the same as newgroup.

5. Delete the group by using the following command:

```
#groupdel evennewergroup
```

CERTIFICATION OBJECTIVE 9.04

Identifying and Changing File Permissions, Modes, and Types

On multiuser systems such as Linux, there is a need to ensure that users are only able to see, edit, and execute the files that they are supposed to. As we discussed earlier, this is one of the reasons we have user accounts, which give us the ability to grant permissions to individual users.

Whereas the root account is able to access all of the files on the system, it is very likely that other users will not need such a high level of access, and in fact, must be prevented from accessing certain files. Such protection is achieved through file permissions.

Each file or directory on a Linux system has a set of permissions that allows the system administrator to control who can access what, and it is through these permissions that user access is limited.

The Rights

Three basic rights can be assigned to a file:

- **Read**   Allows the user to see the file, open it, and view its contents
- **Write**   Allows the file to be edited and saved with the new changes
- **Execute**   Allows the file to be run

Working with these three basic rights, each file can then accommodate the rights in certain configurations. The rights can be set on a file for the owner, the group, or for everyone, which in this context is anyone who is authenticated on the system.

With us so far? Good. Okay, next comes the process of actually assigning the rights to the files. Each file has nine associated values that are used to hold the permissions. The first three values refer to the owner's permissions, the second three are the group permissions, and the third three are for the "everyone" permissions. Of the three that pertain to each, the field can be set to the values r, w, and x. So, if there were a file that could be read, written, and executed by everyone on the system, the permissions listing for it would look like this:

```
-rwxrwxrwx
```

If the file were only supposed to be read and written by the owner, the permissions listing would look like this:

```
-rw-------
```

Alternatively, if the file were to be read, written, and executable by the owner but read by everyone, the permissions listing would be this:

```
-rwx---r-
```

Now, the r, w, and x format works well for us humans who need easy ways to remember things, but in the background, Linux actually uses a numerical format for the assignment of permissions, which it does by giving a numerical value to each of them. You can see the numerical values in Table 9-4.

on the **job**

Because the values of a single permission can be a number between 0 and 7, eight numbers are available. As a result, these permissions are sometimes referred to as the octal values.

TABLE 9-4	Letter Value	Permission	Numerical Value
Alphabetical and Numerical Permission Values	r	Read	4
	w	Write	2
	x	Execute	1

By using these numerical values, Linux is able to short-form the permissions into just three numbers. It does this by simply calculating the sum of the three permissions to create a single number. A read and write combination results in 6, a write and execute combination (which is unusual) results in 3. By then assigning these numerical values to each of the three entities, Linux is able to use just three numbers to represent the entire file permission listing. A permission listing of 755, for instance, allows the owner read, write, and execute permissions (4+2+1), the group read and execute permissions (4+1), and everyone else read and execute permissions (4+1). When you come to assign permissions, which is done with the Change Mode command (chmod, discussed in a minute), you can opt to use either the alphabetical or the numerical format. First, though, take a look at some of the more common permission combinations and what their values would be, outlined in Table 9-5.

By now, you might have noticed that in each of the listings we have used, there has been a leading dash (-). This is a special field that, while unrelated directly to the permission values, is an important part of the permission listing because it can be used to define what the file is. There are three potential settings for this field, which are explained in Table 9-6.

So, if you see a permission listing that looks like this

```
drwxr-xr-x   11   root   root   3343 Aug 11 07:32 mydir
```

TABLE 9-5   Some Commonly Used File Permission Combinations

Alphabetical Permission	Description	Numerical Permission
-rwxrwxrwx	All users have complete access to the file. This is a potentially dangerous situation, because users can delete the file.	777
-rw-r-r--	The owner has read and write permissions; all other users have read permission.	644
-r-xr-xr-x	All users have read and execute permissions. This might be assigned to a utility executable. It is unlikely that anyone should be editing the file.	555
-rwxrwx---	The owner and the group have full rights, but no one else can use the file. This is a common setting for documents or other files that are used within a defined set of people.	770
-rw-rw-rw-	Everyone has read and write permissions. As with 777, this is a potentially dangerous situation as anyone can delete a file with this permission.	666

TABLE 9-6	Setting	Purpose
	-	Represents that the target is a file
Field Settings for First Permission Slot	d	Represents that the target is a directory
	l	Represents that the target is a symbolic link

you'll know that it is a directory to which the owner has full rights and everyone else has read and execute rights. See, it's easy when you know how!

Viewing The Current Permissions

The current permissions for a file can be viewed by using the ls command, which we will discuss in more detail later:

```
#ls -la filename
```

The filename can be omitted for a listing of all entries in the current directory, or you can use wildcards to limit the results. Figure 9-4 shows the results of the command from the / directory on a Red Hat Linux server.

Change Mode (chmod)

Now that we have established what the file permissions are, it's time to take a look at how they are set, which is by using the Change Mode, or chmod, command. The basic usage of the command is as follows; however, there is quite a bit more to it than just this:

```
#chmod permissions filename
```

To demonstrate the usage of chmod more effectively, imagine that we have a file called myfile, and that we want to set the permissions as rwx for the owner, and r for all other users. The command to do this would be

```
#chmod 744 myfile
```

To set the same permissions for all files in the directory, we could use the wildcard symbol, as in

```
#chmod 744 *
```

FIGURE 9-4

Results from an
ls -la listing of
the / directory

FIGURE 9-4

Results from an
ls -la listing of
the / directory

```
[root@localhost /]# ls -la
total 184
drwxr-xr-x   18 root     root      4096 Aug  8 12:55 .
drwxr-xr-x   18 root     root      4096 Aug  8 12:55 ..
-rw-------    1 root     root        41 Aug  2 13:43 .bash_history
drwxr-xr-x    2 root     root      4096 Jul 29 01:24 bin
drwxr-xr-x    2 root     root      4096 Aug  2 14:19 boot
drwxr-xr-x   11 root     root     98304 Aug  2 14:20 dev
drwxr-xr-x   40 root     root      4096 Aug  8 15:05 etc
-rw-r--r--    1 root     root         0 Aug  4 09:16 file1
drwxr-xr-x   20 root     root      4096 Aug  8 13:07 home
drwxr-xr-x    3 root     root      4096 Aug  8 15:15 images
drwxr-xr-x    4 root     root      4096 Jul 29 01:00 lib
drwxr-xr-x    2 root     root     16384 Jul 29 00:55 lost+found
drwxr-xr-x    4 root     root      4096 Jul 29 00:56 mnt
-rwxr--r--    1 root     root        13 Aug  4 08:19 myfile
drwxr-xr-x    2 root     root      4096 Aug 23  1999 opt
dr-xr-xr-x   72 root     root         0 Aug  2 07:19 proc
drwxr-x---   15 root     root      4096 Aug  8 15:02 root
drwxr-xr-x    2 root     root      4096 Jul 29 01:27 sbin
drwxrwxrwt    9 root     root      4096 Aug  8 15:01 tmp
drwxr-xr-x   16 root     root      4096 Jul 29 01:11 usr
drwxr-xr-x   21 root     root      4096 Jul 29 08:46 var
[root@localhost /]#
```

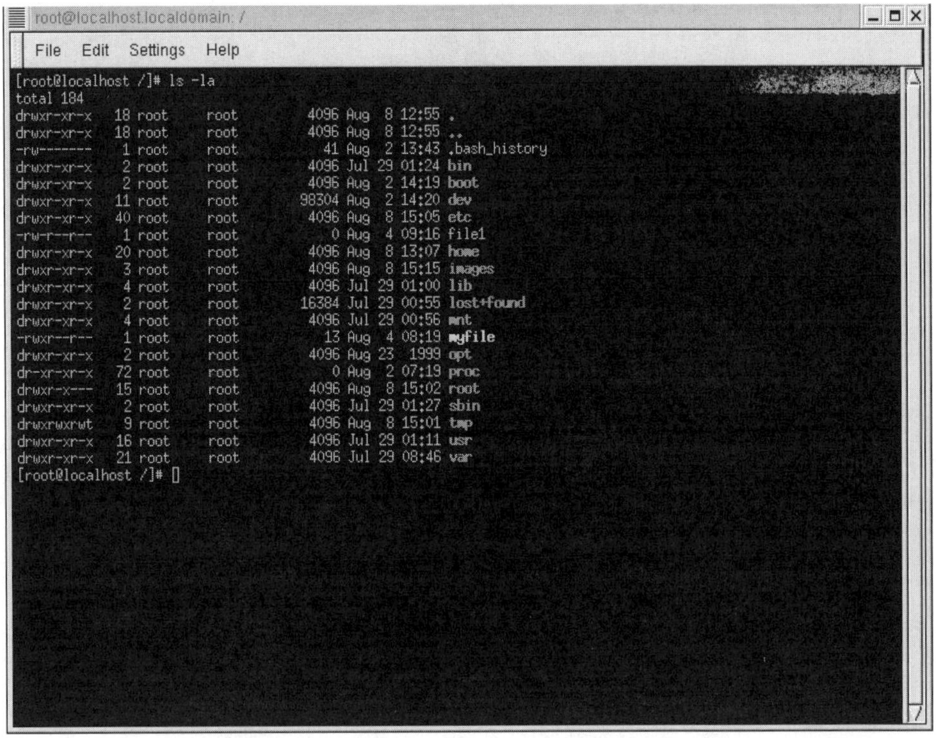

If you prefer, the rights can be assigned using the letters rwx and specifying the entity to which the rights should be assigned. Again, here is are a few examples of this format

```
#chmod u+rw,g-rw,o-rwx textfile
```

This command will add the read and write permissions to the owner (**u**), take away the read and write permission from the group (**g**), and give everyone else (**o**) all rights. In this way, the rights are added or taken away from the permission set, but it is also possible to assign them absolutely, as shown in the following command:

```
#chmod u=rw,g=r,o=r textfile
```

This gives the user read and write, the group read, and everyone else read. For our last example, we'll use an easy one:

```
#chmod a+rwx
```

In this example, the *a* refers to "all," as in all entities. Using the *a* is just another way to do the same thing as using "rwx." As you can see, the jumble of *r*'s, *w*'s, and *x*'s can be quite confusing, which is why many system administrators prefer to familiarize themselves with the numerical format and stick with that.

One last note on chmod is that it can be used to change a file from a "normal" file to one that can be executed. By setting the execute permission on the file, the file becomes executable by all users on the system. This is important in certain instances, such as shell scripts, which we will be discussing later in Cchapter 10.

EXERCISE 9-4

Viewing and Setting File Permissions

1. Use the following command to create a text file called myfile:

```
#vi myfile
```

2. When the vi screen opens, press I and then type in a few characters. What you type is not important. To save the file, press ESC, type **:wq**, and press ENTER.

   The file should save, close, and return you to the command prompt.

3. To see the permissions for the file you just created, use the following command:

```
#ls -la myfile
```

What are the permissions currently set to?

4. Change the permissions of the file to allow you full access and all other users read and execute access by entering the following command:

```
#chmod 755 myfile
```

5. Check the new permissions again using the command from Step 3.

FROM THE CLASSROOM

File Permissions

To anyone who has been working with other network operating systems, such as Windows NT/2000/XP and Novell NetWare, the permission structure of Linux may seem very rudimentary. However, while it does not offer some of the functionality provided by other NOSs, the entire Linux system benefits from its simplicity, which not only makes the assignment and calculation of rights simple, but also minimizes the amount of information that needs to be stored for each file in the file tables. Ultimately, this results in higher levels of performance and reduced memory usage.

—Mike Harwood, Linux+ Certified

Change Ownership (chown)

Given that the ownership of a file plays an important part in the permission assignments, the owner of the file on a Linux system is, perhaps, more important than it is on other NOSs. The upshot of this is that the Change Ownership command, chown, is provided so that the user or group ownership of a file can be easily changed. The basic usage of the chown command is as follows:

```
#chown [username|groupname] filename
```

So, if you wanted to assign ownership of a file called schedule, in the current directory, to a user called Zoe, you would use the following command:

```
#chown zoe schedule
```

Alternatively, the command to change the group ownership of a file would be as follows:

```
#chown sales schedule
```

There are a number of options that can be used with the chown command, but the only one you should be really concerned with is the -r option, which stands for "recursive." Using this option when changing the ownership of a directory applies the new owner to the directory, to all files and directories in that directory, and so on. Be sure that you want to do this, because putting all of the rights back after doing this by mistake can be a time-consuming process. If you want, you can use the –v (verbose) option with chown to display a listing of the files having their ownership changed.

exam
Watch

The chown **command can be used to change the user and/or group ownership of a file, whereas the** chgrp **command can only be used to change the group ownership.**

Change Group (chgrp)

The last of the permission-related commands we will look at in this section is the Change Group, or chgrp, command, which is used when you want to change the group settings of a file. In the same way that the owner of a file plays an important role in the Linux file permissions system, so does the group assignment, which counts for the second of the file permission assignations. In much the same way as you use chown, chgrp is used by naming the group that you want to assign to the file. So, if you want to assign group ownership of a file called newsletter to a group called faculty, you would use the following command:

```
#chgrp faculty newsletter
```

As with the chown command, chgrp can be used to change the ownership characteristics of directories as well as files, and can be used with the -r option to have the settings applied through a directory tree.

on the
job

Rights applied to all files and directories in a tree are said to have been assigned the rights recursively.

If you want to view the current owner and group assignments for a file, simply use the ls -la command as described at the beginning of this section.

Managing and Navigating the Linux Hierarchy and File System

So far in this book, we have mentioned several times the directory structure that Linux uses. In the chapters on installation, we discussed how you might want to separate certain directories onto separate disks or partition your file system in a certain way. In this section, we are going to look at the Linux file system and what the directories that are created on each system by default are used for. See Table 9-7 for an overview.

If you are used to working on a Windows system, you may be used to referring to directories that are separated by backslashes (\). In Linux, forward slashes are used (/), but they both perform the same function insofar as they serve to separate directories. Typing **cd ** at the command prompt of a Windows system takes you to the root of

| TABLE 9-7 | Standard Linux Directories and Their Purposes |

Directory Name	Purpose
bin	Contains binaries (programs) that can be used by anyone
boot	Contains binaries that will only be used by the superuser (root)
dev	Holds the boot loader files and the Linux kernel files
etc	Holds configuration files such as the /etc/passwd user information file
home	Default location for the users' home directories
lib	Holds code libraries used by other programs
lost+found	Used by the File System Check utility (fsck) to store bits of files found during the check
mnt	The default mount point for removable media such as CD-ROMs
proc	Mount point for the proc virtual file system
root	The root user's home directory
sbin	Programs that are used by the superuser (root)
tmp	Default directory for temporary file storage
usr	Used for nonessential programs

the file system. Typing **cd /** on a Linux system does the same thing. Now, we don't want to steal the thunder from the cd command, discussed in an upcoming section, but you can move around in much the same way on a Linux system as a Windows command session because the cd command allows you to move up and down through the tree.

For those not used to moving around a command-line–based environment, using commands for basic file system tasks may seem antiquated, but you just might be surprised. Once you are familiar with the commands and their use, moving around and managing the file system using the command line may come naturally.

Having looked at the file system structure, we will look at some of the commands that you will use to manage and navigate it. The commands we will be covering, and their functions are detailed in Table 9-8. We will only be providing basic coverage of the usage of each command, because providing complete usage information would most likely encompass an entire book.

We'll work through the table in order, so we'll begin our discussion of file system management commands with the **ls** command, but first we need to look quickly at wildcards, which play an important role in file and directory management tasks.

exam
ⓦatch

Wildcards are a subset of regular expressions. Chapter 10 discusses regular expressions in more detail.

TABLE 9-8 Common File System Management Commands and Their Functions

Command	Function
cd	Used to change between directories
ls	Used to list the files in a directory
mkdir	Used to create directories
rmdir	Used to remove (delete) directories
cp	Used to copy files from one location to another
mv	Used to move files from one location to another
rm	Use to remove (delete) files

Wildcards

Some of the commands we will discuss in this section allow the use of wildcards to make choices. For example the rm command, which is used to remove, or delete, files, can be used with wildcards to allow multiple files to be deleted at the same time. The wildcard characters (? and *) can be used in place of other characters of the filename. A question mark (?)is used to denote a single character, and an asterisk (*) is used as a substitute for a group of characters.. So, the phrase *sheet would be any files that end with "sheet," the phrase **sheet*** would include any files that start with "sheet," and the phrase *sheet* would include any files that have the word "sheet" in the name.

Although we haven't covered the commands just yet, we'll borrow the command rm from our upcoming discussion for the purposes of an example. The rm command deletes files and directories. By using wildcards with the rm command, we can delete groups of files based on their names. If, for argument's sake, we wanted to delete all the files that started with "invoice," we would use the following command:

```
$rm invoice*
```

All the invoice files would be deleted, without the need for each to be identified individually. Wildcards can be used in any place along the filename, including filling in for a specific character. Using a command line such as **rm ?n?o?c*** may look a little complex, and is of limited use, but it would still delete the invoice files as described in the preceding example.

You should try out commands with wildcards to get used to them, but remember, using wildcards with commands such as rm can have catastrophic results. Until you are completely comfortable with these wildcards, you should confine your tests to a set of sample files and directories. With wildcards taken care of, let's start our discussion of the commands.

Change Directory (cd)

The **cd** command, which is used to move between directories, is simplicity itself in that it has a limited number of options. The basic usage of the cd command is as follows:

```
$cd directory_name
```

This example works if the directory you want to navigate to is a subdirectory of your current position. If you want to reach a directory that is many levels below the one that you are at, you can use the full path to that directory, rather than stepping down each level individually. For example:

```
$cd /home/susan/data/docs/January
```

on the **job**   *Some Linux shells have a built-in feature that will allow them to guess the directory name that you want to use with a command. This is particularly useful if the directory you are using has a long name. For example, to change into a directory, all that is needed is to type* cd *followed by the first few letters of the directory. Press* **TAB,** *and the system will try to guess the directory name for you.*

When using the cd command, a single period (.) is used to refer to the current directory, while two periods (..) are used to refer to the parent directory. For example, you simply type **cd**, if you want to move to the directory above the one you are in.

The double period can be combined with a directory path as needed. For example, to change to a directory called data that is another subdirectory of the parent of the current directory (got that?), you would type **cd ../data**.

For each level you need to go up, you can simply type **../**. If the data directory were a subdirectory of a directory two levels above yours, you could type **cd ../../data**.

In a directory structure that has only a few levels, messing around with slashes and dots may seem a little unnecessary, but if you are working with a complex directory structure, going up through the directory structure and back down again in a single command is a whole lot faster than forever going up to the root and back down again.

on the **job**   *Using the command cd ~ will automatically take you back to your home directory from wherever you are in the file system, as will the cd command without any options. Alternatively, as the root user, you can go directly to a user's home directory by appending their username, as in cd ~john. Another useful trick is cd -, which will take you back to the previous directory.*

While we are on the subject of directories and moving around in them, it's a good time to introduce another command: present working directory, or pwd. This command will provide the entire path to your current location. pwd is just about the easiest way to figure out where you are.

List (ls)

You'll need to list the contents of the directory, which is achieved by using the ls command, almost as frequently as you'll need to change between directories. The most simple usage of ls is to type it at the command line. The result is a listing of all the files, and directories, in your current directory. As you might expect, though, ls has more than just a few tricks up its sleeve. Some of the more useful options for the ls command are provided in Table 9-9.

As you can see from the sample usage, the options can be combined where appropriate to customize the output further. For example, to get a listing of all the file and directory entries in the current directory that begin with "pro" sorted in reverse order by size, you would use the following command:

```
$ls pro* -l -S -r
```

If you prefer, the options for commands like ls can be combined in a single option, such as ls pro* -lSr.

As an alternative to **ls**, you can use the **dir** command, which fulfills the same function.

| TABLE 9-9 | Commonly Used Options for the ls Command |

Option	Result	Sample Usage
-a	Shows all entries, including files starting with a period	ls -a
-l	Lists files and directories including information such as permissions	ls m* -l
-h	Displays sizes in a readable format	ls g* -h -l
-r	Reverses the order of the display	ls g* -h -l -r
-R	Lists subdirectory contents as well as the for the current directory.	ls g* -l -R
-S	Sorts files by size	ls g* -l -S
-s	Lists file by size	ls g* -l -s
-X	Sorts alphabetically by extension	ls -lax

Make Directory (mkdir)

The Make Directory command, mkdir, is one of the simpler Linux commands in that it has only one option. The basic usage of the command is to name the directory you want to create, as in

```
$mkdir newdir
```

You can also add an option (-p) that will automatically create the structure specified in the command. So, if you wanted to create a complete directory structure from a single command, this can be accomplished as follows:

```
$mkdir -p dir1/dir/2/dir3/dir4/dir5/dir6
```

Using the -p option in this way can make it simple to create large numbers of directories with ease.

Remove Directory (rmdir)

The rmdir command deletes a specified directory, provided the directory does not have any files in it. The basic usage, assuming we are deleting a directory called olddocs, is as follows

```
$rmdir olddocs
```

As with mkdir, an option, -p, can be used with the rmdir command that will delete any directories above the one you are removing that become empty as a result of the command. When using the -p option, you must insert it before the name of the directory being removed, as in

```
$rmdir -p olddocs
```

Copy (cp)

The cp command is used to copy files from one location to another. The original file is left intact in its location. The cp command is one of the most commonly used and has a number of options that allow you to customize its behavior. The basic usage of the cp command is as follows:

```
$cp filename destination
```

Wildcards can be used to copy multiple files at a time, so if you wanted to copy all the files that started with the letter *g* from your current directory to a directory called /home/steve/data/docs, you would use the following command:

```
$cp g* /home/steve/data/docs
```

There are a number of options that can be used with the copy command, as detailed in Table 9-10.

Move (mv)

The mv command is used to move files or directories between locations and can be used to rename files. The mv command differs from the cp command because whereas cp makes a copy of the file in the new location while leaving the original in place, mv will actually remove the original file after it has arrived in its new home.

The basic usage of the mv command is as follows:

```
$mv testfile /home/johnny
```

In this example, the file testfile is moved from the current directory to the directory /home/johnny. Relatively few options are associated with the mv command. The most used are listed in Table 9-11 along with their sample usages.

TABLE 9-10 Commonly Used Options for the cp Command

Option	Result	Sample Usage
-R	Copies directories recursively	cp -R g* /home/data/docs
-f	Forces overwrite if file or directory exists in destination	cp -f g* /home/data/docs
-v	Switches into verbose mode	cp -v g* /home/data/docs
-u	Copies file only if the file does not exist in destination or is older	cp -u g* /home/data/docs

TABLE 9-11	Options for the mv Command with Sample Usages	
Option	**Result**	**Sample Usage**
-I	Interactive mode; prompts for input at each move	mv -i test* /home/Johnny
-f	Forces existing files to be overwritten without prompting user	mv -f test* /home/Johnny
-v	Switches the command into verbose mode, which causes each filename to be displayed as it is moved	mv -v -f test* /home/johnny

As you can see from Table 9-11, wildcards can be used to include files that match a certain pattern. By using the mv command with wildcards, it's possible to move large numbers of files to a new location with ease.

on the **Job** *When using wildcards and file management commands, make sure you understand what you are doing. Moving files from one location to another may render your system unusable.*

Remove (rm)

The rm command can delete both files and directories, and is a powerful command that should be used with care. The rm command not only can delete a file or directory in the current directory, it can also delete all files and directories below the current point. The basic usage of the rm command is as follows:

```
$rm testfile
```

This command deletes the file called testfile but prompts you to confirm the deletion, which can make deleting large numbers of files when using wildcards tiresome. A number of options can be used with the rm command. The major ones are detailed in Table 9-12 along with examples of usage.

You may have realized that the last of these sample usage commands is a pretty dangerous creature. The command deletes all directories, files, and subdirectories from the current position downward, ignoring all error messages and not prompting for any user input. If you were to execute this command from the / directory while

TABLE 9-12   Options and Sample Usages for the rm Command

Option	Result	Sample Usage
-r	Deletes all files and directories below the current location	rm -r -d dirname
-d	Indicates that the object being deleted is a directory, not a file	rm -d dirname
-I	Switches the command into interactive mode	rm -i -d dirname
-f	Specifies to ignore all errors or warnings	rm -r -d -f dirname

logged in as root, you would wipe the entire disk without warning. Again, this is a powerful command and should be used with care.

CERTIFICATION OBJECTIVE 9.06

Performing Administrative Tasks while Logged in as Root or by Using the su Command

On a day-to-day basis, even if you are the sole administrator for the system, you should be logged in as a normal user account. By normal, we mean one that has sufficient file permissions to perform your tasks, but not one that provides too many administrative possibilities. Logging in as the root account, which is what many systems administrators choose to do, is dangerous because it allows complete control over the system. Not

SCENARIO & SOLUTION

You want to see the permissions for all the files in the current directory	Use the ls -l command.
You want to create a directory structure from a single command	Use the mkdir command with the -p option.
You want to delete a group of files but don't want to be prompted for each one	Use the rm command with the -f option.

only that, but when logged in as the root account, you are not subject to standard file permissions, meaning that any file on the system can be moved or deleted. One moment's lapse of concentration, or even just a simple slip of the finger, and an entire system can be rendered useless and valuable data lost. Whenever possible, you should not log in as the root.

on the job

When you are logged in as the root account, the command prompt will generally start with a #. When you are logged in as a normal user, it will start with a $ symbol. This behavior can be set by editing the shell prompt and varies between distributions.

That said, it is likely at some point during the day that you will need to perform a task as the root user, such as creating new users' accounts, or you may need to log in to the system as another user to troubleshoot a problem or the like. So that you can do this, the Switch User (su) command is provided to allow you to switch between identities.

on the job

The Linux command sudo allows commands to be executed as the su user, which makes it unnecessary to keep logging in as root.

When you use the su command, if you don't specify the UID you want to switch to, the system assumes you want the root account. So if you use the su command while logged in as another user, you will be prompted for the root account password. If you want to access another user's account, simply append the username to the su command, such as this:

```
#su Johnny
```

You will then be prompted for the password for that user account, unless you are logged in as the root account, in which case you are taken straight in.

To switch back to the original UID, simply type **exit** at the command line. Nothing is stopping you from issuing the su command again from within another session, and all that is required to return to the original login ID is to type **exit** for as many sessions as you have open.

For more information on the options available for the su command, refer to the su infopages.

EXERCISE 9-5

Using the su Command

1. Create two new users on the system by following the steps from Exercise 9-1. Remember to set passwords for the new accounts.

2. Log in as one of the new users and then enter the following command to switch UIDs to the other new user you created:

   ```
   $su (other user id)
   ```

   What happens?

3. Use the exit command to close the session and return to your original login ID.

4. Log out from the original ID and log back in using the root account.

5. Repeat the su command from Step 2. What is different this time?

6. Exit and log out from the system.

CERTIFICATION OBJECTIVE 9.07

Mounting and Managing File Systems and Devices

As we have already established, the Linux file system differs from that file system on other operating systems because it views the entire file system as a single entity, whether the elements of the file system exist on other drives, removable media, or even other systems.

While this makes for a very flexible approach to file systems, it also requires that devices such as CD-ROMs, floppy drives, and other removable media be formally added or removed from the file system. The process to achieve this is called *mounting*. By default, a number of devices are set to mount automatically at boot. The instructions for which devices are mounted at boot are listed in the /etc/fstab file. Outside of these devices, it will be necessary to mount any devices you need manually.

When the mount command is used, the /etc/fstab file is searched for certain pieces of information. If a piece of information is not supplied on the command line, such as the file system type, and the entry for the device is defined in the fstab file, the information for the entry is used.

Viewing Mounted Devices

Seeing what devices are currently mounted is simply a case of using the mount command. You can see the output from a mount command as follows:

```
/dev/hda1 on / type ext2 (rw)
none on /proc type proc (rw)
none on /dev/pts type devpts (rw,gid=5,mode=620)
```

As you can see from the list of mounted devices, the floppy drive for this system is not available. Any attempt to access the floppy drive in this system would result in an error. So, the floppy drive must be mounted.

Mounting a Device

The mounting of a device, in this case a floppy disk, is a straightforward process, achieved by using the mount command. To mount a floppy drive, type the following:

```
#mount -t ext2 /dev/fd0 /mnt/floppy
```

The -t option defines the file system type, /dev/fd0 indicates what device is to be mounted, and /mnt/floppy defines the mount point for the device within the file system.

Using the mount command again, you can see that the floppy drive is now listed as a device:

```
/dev/hda1 on / type ext2 (rw)
none on /proc type proc (rw)
none on /dev/pts type devpts (rw,gid=5,mode=620)
/dev/fd0 on /mnt/floppy type ext2 (rw,nosuid,nodev)
```

As the mount point is /mnt/floppy, by changing to the /mnt/floppy directory, you can now access the contents of the floppy disk. Whether it is a floppy disk,

CD-ROM, or other removable media, there must be media in the drive for it to mount successfully. Also, the directory into which the device is to be mounted must exist for the mount process to complete.

Although the /mnt directory is the default for mounts, any directory can be specified as the mount point. However, mounting in a location other than the default can sometimes confuse the system, not to mention the users.

Mounting a CD-ROM is much the same process as mounting a floppy drive, although obviously the device name is different. Here is the command for mounting a CD-ROM drive. The default mount point for a CD-ROM is /mnt/cdrom.

```
#mount -t iso9660 /dev/cdrom /mnt/cdrom
```

Linux can accommodate almost any removable media. If you have a less-mainstream device, chances are that Linux will be able to work with it. Consult the device manufacturer or the Linux distributor for more information.

Unmounting a Device

Unlike some other operating systems, where you can remove and replace floppy disks and CD-ROMs at random, Linux requires that you unmount devices before removing the media. In some cases, such as CD-ROMs, Linux will physically prevent you from removing the CD. In other cases, such as the floppy drive, Linux won't prevent you from removing the floppy; however, you may find yourself with problems later on when you try to insert another disk.

Unmounting a device is a similar process to that of mounting it, except you use the umount command instead of mount. Notice that there is no n in the umount command. To dismount the same floppy device that we mounted earlier, the command would be as follows:

```
#umount /dev/fd0
```

The device should unmount, but if any files on the device are being accessed, you will get a "device is busy" message and be prevented from unmounting the device. To get around the problem, make sure that no files on the device are in use, and ensure that you are not in the directory structure of the device.

Checking Disk Space Usage

An important aspect of managing a file system is that of keeping track of how much disk space is being used, and how much space is free for the storage of files. Different systems will have varying disk space usage characteristics. A server that provides purely firewall services is unlikely to have large fluctuation in disk space usage, though over time the disk may fill up with log files and the like. In contrast, disk space usage in a file and print server may fluctuate considerably (though the trend will generally be up). In either case, a periodic check of disk space use is in order, a process easily achieved by using the Disk Usage (du) or Disk Free Space (df) command. We'll look first at the du command.

Disk Usage (du)

Executed on its own, the du command will list the size of all the files in the directory and subdirectories, which may not be the most useful way to view the information. A more practical way would be to use the -s and -h options, which simply provide a summary (the -s) and display the information in a "human-readable" format (the -h), meaning numbers that are understandable by us, such as 536M (536 megabytes). Commonly used options for the du command are provided in Table 9-13 along with sample usage.

One thing to note about using the -s option is that the du command still processes all the files, but it does it without displaying each file individually. This means that the screen will appear to "hang" while the command is processed. Be patient, it will come back.

TABLE 9-13   du Command Options, Results, and Sample Usage

Options	Result	Sample Usage
-c	Displays a total of all files scanned	du -c -h
-m	Displays totals in megabytes for each volume	du -m
-s	Provides only a summary	du -s -h
-h	Displays information in a human-readable format	du -h

Disk Free Space Command (df)

If you are more interested in the amount of disk space used, and the amount still available for storing files, using the df command is simpler and more concise than using the du command. Here is a printout from a df command. As with the du command, the -h option is used to provide a more human-friendly format to the numbers.

```
Filesystem          Size  Used  Avail Use% Mounted on
/dev/hda1           1.4G  826M  575M  59% /
/dev/fd0            1.4M  1.2M  198k  86% /mnt/floppy
```

As you can see, the information provided by the df command is more useful than that produced by the du command, which is one reason why many system administrators prefer df.

CERTIFICATION SUMMARY

Whereas other tasks are performed on an as-needed basis, administrative tasks are likely to be performed on a daily basis. Administrative tasks include such things as creating, modifying, and deleting user accounts and groups. Part of this user administration will involve managing and assigning file permissions. File permissions are necessary to ensure that users are only able to see the files and directories that they are supposed to see. To manage file systems from the command line, you need to know the structure of the Linux file system and understand how to navigate it.

Because many of the commands associated with the administration of a Linux system require that you be logged in as an account with special powers, you need to understand the risks associated with these accounts and understand what can be accomplished while logged in as these users.

In Linux, the file system is regarded as a single entity, and an understanding of the structure of the file system is essential, as is being able to mount and unmount removable devices such as CD-ROMs and floppy disk drives. Another important administration task is monitoring disk space usage and tracking free disk space, a task for which a number of commands are available.

TWO-MINUTE DRILL

Here are some key points from this chapter:

Creating and Deleting Users

❑ Users can be created by using the useradd command or through graphical utilities.

❑ When using the useradd command, options must be placed before the user's name

❑ User accounts can be deleted by using the userdel command, or they can be disabled by placing a * in the password field of the user's passwd file entry.

Modifying Existing Users

❑ A user's password can be changed by using the passwd command.

❑ The -l and -u options allow a user account to be locked and unlocked, respectively.

❑ Each entry for the user in the /etc/passwd file contains an area for comments. This can be used to enter personal information about the user.

Creating, Modifying, and Deleting Groups

❑ Groups can be added to the system by using the groupadd command.

❑ Information about the groups on the system is stored in the /etc/groups file.

❑ Groups can be deleted from the system by using the groupdel command.

Identifying and Changing File Permissions, Modes, and Types

❑ The chmod command is used to change file permissions.

❑ File permissions are assigned in three sets. The first set reflects the right of the owner of the file, the second the group, and the third everyone.

❑ The chown command is used to change file or directory ownership.

❑ The chgrp command is used to group associations with a file or directory.

Managing and Navigating the Linux Hierarchy and File System

❑ Linux uses a number of standard directories for storing files.

❑ The basic structure of the file system is a root directory called / and subdirectories of that which are denoted using a /.

❑ Wildcards can be used to manipulate multiple files at a time.

❑ The ls command allows files to be listed using a large number of criteria.

❑ The cp command and the mv command can be used to copy and move files, respectively.

❑ The mkdir and rmdir commands can be used to make and remove directories, respectively.

❑ The rm command can be used to delete files and directories.

Performing Administrative Tasks while Logged in as root, or by Using the su Command

❑ When logged in as the root user, you have complete control over the system.

❑ You should not log in as the root account unless you are performing system-related tasks.

❑ The su command can be used to log in as another user without logging out of your current session.

Mounting and Managing File Systems and Devices

❑ The /dev directory contains the device files for the system. Devices can be mounted at any point in the file system, but are typically mounted in the /mnt directory.

❑ Devices can be mounted and unmounted with the commands mount and umount, respectively.

❑ The amount of disk space being used on the system can be viewed with the df or du command.

SELF TEST

The following questions will help determine your level of understanding of the material presented in this chapter. Some of the questions may have more than one correct answer, so be sure to review all answers carefully before choosing all that apply.

Creating and Deleting Users

1. Which of the following commands disables the user account for a user called bhavesh, but allows him to keep his current password so that he can use it again in the future?

   A. passwd -d bhavesh

   B. passwd -r bhavesh

   C. passwd -u bhavesh

   D. passwd -l bhavesh

2. Which of the following commands successfully deletes a user account Sarah and removes the user's home directory?

   A. deluser -r sarah

   B. userdel sarah

   C. userdel -r sarah

   D. userdel -rh sarah

3. Which of the following commands correctly creates a user account for a new user called James with a comment of Student and an expiration date of 5 September, 2002?

   A. useradd -c Student -e 2002/09/05 james

   B. useradd james -c Student -e 2002/09/05

   C. Useradd -c Student -e 2002/09/05 james

   D. useradd -comm Student -exp 2002/09/05 james

4. Which of the following commands creates a new account for a user called George with a comment of Manager R&D?

   A. useradd -c Manager R&D george

   B. Useradd -c "Manager R&D" george

   C. useradd -c "Manager R&D" george

   D. useradd -p Manager R&D george

Modifying Existing Users

5. David is a member of the research and marketing groups. Which of the following commands add him to the group sales as well?

A. usermod -g research,marketing,sales david

B. usermod -G research,marketing,sales david

C. usermod -g sales

D. usermod -G sales

6. In the /etc/passwd file, what is the significance of an *X* in the password field?

A. It indicates that the password is set to X.

B. It indicates that the password is shadowed.

C. It indicates that the account is disabled.

D. It indicates that the password has yet to be set on this account.

Creating, Modifying, and Deleting Groups

7. Which of the following commands will create a group called research?

A. groupadd research

B. newgrp research

C. groupadd -n research

D. crgrp research

8. What is the purpose of adding a password to a group?

A. It prevents people from logging into the system as a group.

B. It prevents people from adding themselves to a group.

C. It requires that people provide a password to join a group.

D. It requires that the password be given before any changes are made to the group.

Identifying and Changing File Permissions, Modes, and Types

9. Which command is used to change the group ownership of a file or directory?

A. groupmod

B. groupperms

C. chgrp

D. chown

10. If a file has a permission listing of 644, which of the following statements is true about the file?

    A. It can be read and executed by all users.

    B. It can be read and written by the owner; all other users can only read it.

    C. It can be read and executed by the owner; all other users can only read it.

    D. It can be read and written by the owner; all other users can read and execute it.

11. What is the function of the chrgrp command?

    A. It allows a user to change their initial group for the duration of the login session.

    B. It allows the administrator to change a user's initial group setting.

    C. It allows the administrator to change the group ownership of a file.

    D. It allows the renaming of a group.

Managing and Navigating the Linux Hierarchy

12. Which of the following commands moves all of the files in the current directory that start with "doc" to the /userdata/wpdoc directory and automatically overwrites files if they exist already?

    A. mv -f doc* /userdata/wpdoc

    B. cp -f doc* /userdata/wpdoc

    C. mv -i doc* /userdata/wpdoc

    D. mv /f doc* /userdata/wpdoc

13. What does the pwd command do?

    A. Allows you to change your password

    B. Displays the full path to the directory in which you are currently residing

    C. Allows you to change a passwd in an FTP session

    D. Moves you straight to the directory specified in the present working directory variable

14. Which of the following commands lists detailed information on all the files in the current directory in reverse order sorted by size?

    A. ls -l -r -S

    B. ls -l -R -S

    C. ls -r -S

    D. ls -r -s

Managing and Navigating the Standard Linux File System

15. What kind of files are found in the /usr directory?

A. Users' home directories

B. User templates

C. User account information

D. Programs that are not essential to system operation

Performing Administrative Tasks while Logged in as root or by Using the su Command

16. When using the **su** command to switch from your current user to the superuser account, what information do you need to provide?

A. Username

B. Password

C. Type of shell to open

D. User ID

Mounting and Managing File Systems and Devices

17. What is the default mount point for the first floppy disk in a system?

A. /dev/fd0

B. /dev/fd1

C. /mnt/fd0

D. /mnt/floppy

18. Which of the following commands show the amount of free space on a drive?

A. freespace

B. %free

C. df

D. du

19. Assuming you have created a directory of /discs/cdrom, which of the following commands successfully mounts a CD-ROM to that mount point?

   A. mount -t iso9660 /dev/fd0 /discs/cdrom

   B. mount -t iso9660 /dev/cdrom /discs/cdrom

   C. mount -t iso9660 /dev/cdrom -mtp /discs/cdrom

   D. umount -t iso9660 /dev/cdrom /discs/cdrom

20. Which text file specifies what devices are to be mounted at system startup?

   A. /etc/fstab

   B. /etc/mount

   C. /etc/firstmount

   D. /mnt/fstab

LAB QUESTION

As a junior Linux network administrator, you have been tasked with several administration tasks that must be completed as soon as possible.

Create the following user accounts and be sure to include their full name in the comment field:

- Mary Smith
- Andrew Wiseman
- Peter Parker
- Steve Panta

Create the following groups and assign Mary and Andrew to the sales group and Peter and Steve to the marketing group. Also, all of the users must be assigned to the commercial group. Only Mary needs to be assigned to the publications group.

- Sales
- Marketing
- Commercial
- Publications

Log in as each user and verify group membership is correct. Finally, disable the user account for Mary and test to make sure that the restriction works.

SELF TEST ANSWERS

Creating and Deleting Users

1. ☑ **D.** This command locks the user account for the user ID bhavesh.

☒ **A.** When used with the -d option, the passwd command deletes the password for the user ID. This will disable the account, as required, but it will also delete the user's password, meaning that they will not be able to log back in with that password. **B.** There is no -r option used with the passwd command. **C.** The -u option actually unlocks the user account.

2. ☑ **C.** The correct command to delete a user and at the same time remove the user's home directory is userdel -r *username*.

☒ **A.** The correct command to remove a user account is userdel, not deluser. **B.** The omission of the -r option means that while this command removes the user account, it does not remove the user's home directory. **D.** The correct option for removing the user's home directory is -r, not -rh.

3. ☑ **A.** This command adds a user account called james with a comment of student and an expiration date of 5 September, 2002.

☒ **B.** The username parameter of the useradd command comes after all the options have been passed, not before. **C.** Linux commands are case-sensitive. The useradd command does not start with a capital *U*. **D.** The options that should be used are -c for the comment and -e for the expiration date.

4. ☑ **C.** This command creates a user account called George with the correct comment.
A. Because there are spaces in it, the comment must be surrounded by quotation marks.
B. Linux commands are case-sensitive. The correct command here is useradd, not Useradd.
D. The -p option is used to create nonshadowed passwords on a user account, not to add a comment.

Modifying Existing Users

5. ☑ **B.** To add a user to a group, the -G option must be used, and all groups to which the user belongs must be listed.

☒ **A, C.** Using the -g option with the usermod command will cause the user's initial group to be changed. **D.** The use of the -G command is correct, but all groups to which the user belongs must be added or the user will be removed from any groups that are not listed.

6. ☑ **B.** The existence of an *X* in the password field of a user's entry in the /etc/passwd file means the user's password is shadowed.

   ☒ **A.** This answer is not correct. **C.** Disabled accounts are often denoted by the use of * in the password field. **D.** This answer is not correct.

Creating, Modifying, and Deleting Groups

7. ☑ **A.** The groupadd command is used to create a new group. The basic usage is the command followed by the name of the group that is to be created.

   ☒ **B.** Users can use the newgrp command to option between initial groups for the duration of a session. **C.** The -n option is not valid with the groupadd command. **D.** There is no such utility as crgrp.

8. ☑ **C.** Placing a password on a group means that the password must be supplied before users can add themselves to the group.

   ☒ **A.** This answer is not correct. **B.** It does not prevent people from adding themselves to a group, but it does require that they provide a password. **D.** The root account has full privileges to manipulate a group's settings, and no passwords are required.

Identifying and Changing File Permissions, Modes, and Types

9. ☑ **C.** The chgrp command is used to change the group ownership of a file or directory.

   ☒ **A, B.** The groupmod and groupperms commands do not exist. **D.** The chown command is used to change user ownership of a file or directory.

10. ☑ **B.** The read file permission is assigned a value of 4, the write permission 2, and the execute permission 1. The first number refers to the owner's rights, the second to the group rights, and the third to everyone else's rights. Therefore, a permission value of 644 means that the owner can read and write to the file and all other users could only read it.

    ☒ **A.** This combination would result in a permission value of 555. **C.** This combination would result in a value of 544. **D.** This combination would result in a value of 655.

11. ☑ **C.** The chgrp command is used to change the group ownership of a file or directory.

    ☒ **A.** Users can option to a new primary group for the current session by using the newgrp command. **B.** Changing the user's initial group setting is performed with the usermod command. **D.** Renaming a group is achieved using the groupmod command.

Managing and Navigating the Linux Hierarchy

12. ☑ **A.** This command uses the correct wildcard configuration and the -f option, which automatically overwrites existing files.
☒ **B.** The **cp** command is used to copy files, not to move them. **C.** The -i makes the mv command run in interactive mode, which will require manual input should there be a conflict of overwriting files. **D.** The /f option is not valid with the mv command. The correct option is -f.

13. ☑ **B.** The pwd command stands for Present Working Directory, and executing it will display the full path to the current directory.
☒ **A.** The passwd command is used to change a password. **C.** This answer is not valid.
D. This answer is not valid.

14. ☑ **A.** The -l option provides detailed information, the -r option reverses the order of the listing, and the -S option causes the files to be sorted by size.
☒ **B.** The -R option causes all of the subdirectories to be displayed as well. **C.** The -l option is needed if detailed information is to be displayed. **D.** The -s option shows the size of the files in the folder; it does not sort by them.

Managing and Navigating the Standard Linux File System

15. ☑ **D.** The /usr directory holds files that are not essential to the system operation.
☒ **A.** Users home directories are, by default, stored in the /home directory. **B.** While there are no user templates per se, files that contain default user information are stored in the /etc directory.
C. User account information is stored in the /etc/passwd file.

Performing Administrative Tasks while Logged in as root or by Using the su Command

16. ☑ **B.** When you use the **su** command, if no user ID is specified, then the system uses the root account automatically. Therefore, the only information you will need is the password for the root account.
☒ **A, C, D.** None of these pieces of information is needed to option to the root account using the **su** command.

Mounting and Managing File Systems and Devices

17. ☑ **D.** The default mount point for the first floppy drive in a system is /mnt/floppy.

☒ **A.** /dev/fd0 is the default location for the device file for the first floppy drive, not the mount point. **B.** The /dev/fd1 directory is the default location for the second floppy drive device file. **C.** The default mount point is called floppy by default, not fd0.

18. ☑ **C.** The df command will show the amount of data currently on a drive and the amount of free space.

☒ **A, B.** Neither the freespace command nor the %free command is valid on a Linux system. **D.** The **du** command shows the amount of disk space used, but does not show the amount of space left free.

19. ☑ **B.** This command successfully mounts the CD-ROM drive with a mount point of /discs/cdrom.

☒ **A.** This command uses the device name fd0, which is associated with floppy disk drives, not CD-ROMs. **C.** The -mtp option is not a valid option, and so is not required by the mount command. **D.** The command umount is used to dismount devices, not to mount them.

20. ☑ **A.** The file that is used to list the devices that should be mounted on startup is the /etc/fstab file.

☒ **B, C, D.** All of these answers are incorrect, and in fact are fictitious.

LAB ANSWER

To create a new user, the **useradd** command is used. This command also allows you to specify a comment, in this case the user's full name, during the account creation. Groups are created using the groupadd command. The users are assigned to the group accounts using the usermod command. Remember that all groups to which the user should belong must be specified. Group membership can be viewed using the groups command.

Finally, user accounts can be disabled through a variety of methods, but perhaps the most common is to place an * in the password field of the user's entry in the /etc/shadow file. Try logging in as the user to check whether the account is actually disabled.

10

Administration: Part Two

I n this, the second chapter covering the administration domain, we start to look at some of the more technical aspects of Linux server administration. These include things such as using the shell and taking advantage of the multiuser aspects of the Linux operating system. We also cover how you can connect to, and use the resources of, your Linux system remotely with utilities such as FTP and Telnet.

As working with text files is a major part of Linux administration, vi, a text editor, is examined, as is the process of creating shell scripts that can help you automate tasks on your system. We also discuss the tape archive utility, tar, which is used to combine files as well as a mechanism for taking backups of the system. This chapter also includes the management and administration of printing on a Linux system.

CERTIFICATION OBJECTIVE 10.01

Describing and Using the Features of the Multiuser Environment

Linux is a multiuser operating system, meaning that a single Linux server is able to accommodate a number of sessions. These sessions can be local to the system, in which the user actually sits at the system, or remote, in which a utility such as SSH is used. In either case, the system is able to provide services to more than one user at a time, which is what makes it a multiuser system.

Virtual Terminals

When you start up a Linux system, you will be in one of two states. Either you will be at the login prompt of a terminal session or at the login screen of a GUI. In either case, each of these is simply a session, that is, a program generated by the system to enable you to use it. Given this, there is no reason why the system cannot create multiple terminals so that different actions can be performed on each, which is exactly what it does.

The maximum number of terminals, known as virtual terminals, available on a system is 12, though most are configured to provide fewer than that; six appears to

FROM THE CLASSROOM

Multiuser Operating Systems

If you are familiar with other network operating systems such as Novell NetWare or Windows 2000/XP, the idea of a multi-user operating system can take some getting used to. In effect, the system is able to host a large number of sessions from users who can connect to it using a variety of means and methods. The roots of this multiuser system can be traced to days gone by when "dumb" terminals, that is, computing devices with no processing power of their own, could connect to a system and use the system's resources as if it were local to them. This centralized approach fell out of favor to other computing models, such as the distributed method used by Windows and NetWare. Now, people are again looking to thin client technology as a computing solution, which uses the processing power of a central system, and the device the user employs simply becomes a mechanism to accept keyboard input and receive screen updates. In a sense, such configurations are the completion of a full circle.

—Mike Harwood, Linux+ Certified

be the norm. In the unlikely event that you do need more than six virtual terminals, you can increase the available number by editing the /etc/inittab file. In this file you'll find an entry that looks something like the following, although in some distributions, getty or a similar variation is used instead of mingetty.

```
1:2345:respawn:/sbin/mingetty tty1
```

To add another virtual terminal session, copy and paste one of the existing lines from the file and renumber the first character and tty designation to the next number.

You can switch between the virtual terminals in a number of ways, including pressing ALT-F*n* (where *n* is the number of the function key), or by using the following command from the console:

```
#chvt n
```

Having virtual terminals allows you to log in to each session as a different user and to use each of the terminals to perform different tasks. For example, you could set a task running on one session while going to another to carry on working. Each session operates completely independently of the others, so your actions in one won't affect another directly, though obviously there is a finite amount of processing power, so running large and complex programs in a number of sessions will cause the entire machine to slow.

Some administrators use the virtual terminal functionality as a means to have one session logged in as root at all times and another as a standard user ID. This approach is OK, but the only difference between the screens is minimal, so the possibility of error between the sessions is high. In addition, for security reasons, it is a very bad practice to leave a virtual terminal logged in as root.

Running Programs in the Background

As well as having multiple virtual terminals, it's also possible to run commands in the background, without switching to another terminal session. The ability to run commands in the foreground and background is another feature of Linux's multitasking capabilities.

By default, all programs run in the foreground. They are visible on the screen, and you can't input any other information while they are running. In contrast, a program run in the background does not actually appear on the screen as it runs. Because some programs take a long time to run, such as creating a very large zip file, you might choose to run a program in the background so that the terminal is still free to perform other tasks.

To run a program in the background, simply append an ampersand (&) to the command line. Here is an example of this:

```
#find / &
```

If you start a program without the ampersand and then realize that you should have run it in the background, all is not lost. By pressing CTRL-Z, you can break into the process and suspend the operation. Now, using the background command (bg) and specifying the job number, the program can be sent to the background, allowing you to continue to work in the foreground. The command to send a process to the background is as follows:

```
#bg 2
```

The 2 reflects the job ID, which is given when the processing is suspended. To bring the program back to the foreground, you use the fg command with the job's ID. For example:

```
#fg 2
```

As you can imagine, the ability to run jobs in the background can be very handy, as it allows you to have the system process more than one task without tying up the machine. This is particularity true when running a session on a remote utility such as SSH, when it is simpler to place a job in the background than start another session.

CERTIFICATION OBJECTIVE 10.02

Using Common Shell Commands and Expressions

In Chapter 9, we looked at some of the commands you can use to work with the Linux file system such as cd and rm. In this section, we'll look at some of the other common shell commands you might find useful and how you can manage the information that is supplied by the commands.

Getting Help with Commands

With all but a few exceptions, commands executed on a Linux system have a corresponding help page, which can be accessed as follows:

```
#command --help
```

The information provided in the help screen is generally very basic, and displays only what the valid switches for a command are, rather than an explanation of what the switches do. For a more detailed explanation of both the utility and the switches, consult the manual page for the command, which can be accessed by typing

```
#man command
```

Included in the manual page are detailed descriptions of the purpose of the command, as well as meaning and sample usage of the associated switches.

As useful as man is, there is now a more flexible and up-to-date utility called info. Information pages are accessed in much the same way as manual pages. You issue the command and then the utility you want help on. For example, the command

```
#info chmod
```

provides the information page on the chmod utility.

Chances are, if you have viewed the information supplied by the help command, the manual page, and the information page, but you still don't have the solution to your query, the possibility of finding the answer from another source is slim.

on the job

For a brief description of a command, you can use the **whatis command***. Type* whatis **followed by the name of the command.**

Manipulating Command Output

In a lot of cases, the information provided by a command will occupy more than one screen, making it difficult to read or making it impossible to see the information on the first line of the file. Because Linux relies so heavily on text files and command-line utilities, methods are provided that allow you to manage the information supplied from a command so that you can either view the information more easily, or do something with it.

Piping

When a command displays information that uses more than a page, the pipe feature can be used to restrict the display to a single page at a time. The pipe feature can be invoked by using the | **more** switch on the command line. For example, if you wanted to view the help page for the ls command page by page, you could use the command

```
#ls -help | more
```

Each page of the printout would be displayed with a -More- designation at the bottom of the screen. To move forward a page, press SPACEBAR. To move forward a line at a time, press ENTER. A more versatile command that can be used in place of **more** is **less**. The **less** command allows you to move back and forth through the file.

There is actually more to this command than at first appears. The pipe actually sends the information from the first command to the command in the second part. In this example, the more *command is actually a utility in its own right.*

Redirecting Output

In some cases, you might want to redirect the output from a command to a file rather than have it displayed on the screen. Such tasks are useful when, for example, you are compiling documentation that needs printouts from a device listing or the like.

The redirection process is simple, but you must be very careful as there are very few safeguards built into the process and it is quite easy to overwrite an existing file with the output from a redirection.

The basic command for piping information to another file is to use the greater-than (>) symbol. For example, if you wanted to redirect the output from a dmesg printout to a file called systeminfo, you would use the following command:

```
#dmesg > systeminfo
```

Once the command is complete, you can show the contents of the file by using the cat command. Using two greater-than (>>) symbols will cause the result of the command to be appended to the specified file rather than overwriting it. Input, as well as output, can be redirected, which is useful when you want information read from a file to serve as input for a command. To input information to a command, use the less-than (<) symbol.

Combining Commands

So far, all the command examples that we have given have been of a single command executed on the command line, but Linux can also take multiple commands from a single command line and execute them in order.

To do this, simply type the commands as you would do normally, but separate each by a semicolon (;), as shown in this example:

```
#mkdir -p /home/jsmith/data;cp /home/js/data/*
/home/jsmith/data;chmod /home/jsmith/* 744
```

In addition to the semicolon, you can also use two ampersands (&&) to string two commands together.

This command will create a directory called /home/jsmith/data, then copy all the files from the /home/js/data directory to the /home/jsmith/data directory, and finally, change the file permissions on all the files.

Any set of commands can be combined, and it is even possible to customize the processing of the commands, such as making the second command execute only if the first returns an error, and so on. Such features are commonly used in the construction of shell scripts, a topic covered later in this chapter, in the section "Programming Basic Shell Scripts."

Creating Command Aliases

Because, in some cases, a command is used with great frequency or for some other reason, commands can be aliased. In effect, this means that a command can be executed by using an alias of it.

An often-used example of this is the aliasing of the clear command to cls. Because many other operating systems use the cls command to clear the screen, those new to Linux are tempted to type cls instead of clear.

on the job

Some administrators see the use of aliases as lazy, but in reality it is just another way to save time. Anyone looking to make a task more work than it could be is defeating the entire purpose of using computers in the first place.

To get around this, it is possible to create cls as an alias of clear. After the alias is created, both commands will work.

Creating an alias requires that the alias command be used and that both the alias and the command to be aliased are specified. To create an alias of clear, as we just described, the command is as follows:

```
# alias cls='clear'
```

Once the command is executed, either cls or clear will result in the screen being cleared.

The alias feature can also be used to capture commands with switches and assign them an alias, which can be a real time saver if there is a certain command you use a great deal. For example, if you use the vi command frequently to edit the /etc/passwd file, you can create an alias of pe to execute the command automatically as follows:

```
# alias pe='vi /etc/passwd'
```

Aliases that are created in this way are in force only for the current session, and logging out will lose them. If you want to make them permanent, they must be entered into the startup files for your shell.

Commands can be unaliased by removing them from the startup file or using the unalias command from the command line as follows:

```
# unalias aliasname
```

Command History

The shell is able to store each typed command in a command buffer, which can be accessed by pressing the UP ARROW and a variety of other more complicated methods. Each command is stored, as typed, until a maximum number of commands is stored (normally 1,000), at which point, the oldest command is removed from the buffer and the newest added.

on the job

By far the most common shell is the bash shell, which accommodates all the features discussed in this section. There are, however, other shells that can be used that might not offer some of these features.

The great thing about the command buffer is that it even remains usable if you log out and log back in again. It is, however, user dependant. If you execute commands as a user and then su into the system as another user, a new command buffer is started, and the commands previously typed as the other user are not available.

Tab Completion

This was touched on briefly in Chapter 9, but it is worth a separate mention here, as it is a big time saver when it comes to performing multiple commands on separate directories.

Tab completion works by trying to guess what file, directory, or command you want to access. All that is needed to access tab completion is to type the first few characters of the file, directory, or command you want to access and press TAB. Tab-complete will automatically attempt to complete the entry you are looking for. If there is more than one thing that corresponds with the letters typed, tab-complete does not activate on the first press of TAB, but a second press will bring up a list of things that match. If there is a very large number of matches, tab-complete will show a message asking if you want to see a list of them.

Interrupting and Stopping Jobs

When a job is running, it is sometimes necessary to stop the job or suspend it, as described earlier. To stop a job, press CTRL-C. You will most likely end up using this command a great deal, particularly as you explore your system and try different commands and utilities. As we mentioned earlier, you can also use CTRL-Z to suspend a job.

Once a job is suspended, you are free to perform any commands that you want to. You can also restart the suspended job at any time. Use the jobs command to see what jobs are currently running or suspended, and then choose to restart the job either in the foreground or background.

Common Shell Commands

In Chapter 9, we discussed some of the file-management commands, such as cd and rm, that you will find yourself using on a regular basis. As well as these tasks, you will almost certainly need to use other commands during your day-to-day work.

There are many commands that are used on Linux to perform various tasks. Listing them all would simply occupy too much space, and CompTIA certainly don't expect you to know every command for the Linux+ test. So, we have chosen a range of useful commands and included them in Table 10-1. Other commands are covered in the section later in this chapter in creating shell scripts.

CERTIFICATION OBJECTIVE 10.03

Using Network Commands to Connect to and Manage Remote Systems

As we discussed earlier, Linux is a true multiuser operating system. Part of this multiuser functionality requires that other users have the means to log in and access the system, a process that is achieved by using a number of tools.

The tools discussed in this section serve different purposes. For example, Telnet and SSH allow a user to connect to a Linux server and run shell sessions from that server. FTP, in contrast, can be used to transfer files to and from the server but does not allow command execution on the remote host. The X Window redirection, or

| TABLE 10-1 | Some Commonly Used Shell Commands |

Command	Result	Sample Usage
clear	Clears screen and returns blank prompt at top of the screen.	clear
cat	Can be used to display text files and combine them.	cat /etc/passwd
more	Used to view a text file one page at a time.	more /etc/passwd
less	Lets you view a text file and move back and forth through it.	less /etc/passwd
diff	Displays text files and denotes differences.	diff file1 file2
cmp	Lets you compare two files and notifies you if they are different.	cmp file1 file2
env	Used to display environment variables.	env
head	Used to display the start of a text file. In this sample usage, the *n* refers to the number of lines to be shown.	head -*n*50 textfile
tail	Used to display the end of a text file. In this sample usage, the *n* refers to the number of lines to be shown.	tail -*n*50 textfile
history	Displays the list of commands that have been entered.	history

X11 forwarding, discussed last, allows you to have X Window output appear on a terminal other than the server. We'll start our discussion by looking at Telnet.

Telnet

Telnet is a utility that allows a text shell session on another host. This session can then be used to administer the system or perform other tasks that you would sit at the server to perform. Telnet has been around for a long time, but has one big black mark against it in that it is not a secure platform. For that reason, Telnet is really suitable for use only in an environment where security is not a concern. Such environments are few and far between!

Using Telnet

Most platforms, including many of the Microsoft Windows variants include a Telnet client. Opening a Telnet session can be achieved by using the following command. We have omitted the prompt from this command, as it can be issued on a Linux or a Windows system.

```
telnet ipaddress | hostname
```

Alternatively, you can just type **telnet**, which will take you to a telnet> prompt, at which point you can type **open** and then enter the ip address or hostname of the server you want to connect to. To quit a Telnet session, type **exit**. For more information on using Telnet, consult the appropriate manual or information page.

SSH

The Secure Shell, SSH, is like Telnet in that it allows a session to be opened on a system remotely. The big difference between the two is that SSH employs very tough encryption and security measures, making it suitable for use in situations where Telnet would not be used. The most common implementation of SSH is OpenSSH.

Using SSH

Provided that SSH is installed and configured, the command to open an SSH session with a host is as follows:

```
#ssh ipadrress|hostname
```

The big difference between Telnet and SSH is that on initiating an SSH session, an exchange of authentication keys take place. This exchange of keys can sometimes cause issues, particularly if the configuration of SSH has not been completed properly on either of the systems involved.

on the
()o b

In some cases, you might need to just transfer a single file from one server to another. This can be achieved with the Remote Copy (rcp) command. The basic usage of this utility is rcp localfile remotefile. This translates into something like rcp server1:thisfile server2:thisfile. If the server in the first part of the command is the local server, you won't need to specify the server name.

FTP

One of the most common methods of transferring files between two systems is the file transfer protocol (FTP). FTP has been with us for so long that it has become a standard application, and it would be hard to find a Linux distribution that does not offer an FTP server and client of one form or another. There are numerous graphical FTP client applications, but there is also a command line–based system, which is the focus of our discussion here.

Opening an FTP Session

You can open an FTP session by typing the **ftp** command, followed by the IP address or host name of the host you want to connect to. You can use the host name only if host name resolution is configured. Assuming you were going to connect to an IP address of 24.67.203.4, the command would be as follows:

```
#ftp 24.67.203.4
```

The remote system will respond to your request by either asking for a username and password or refusing the connection.

FTP Commands

Once you are connected to the remote host, you can start transferring files to and from it, but beware, some of the commands used in FTP are different from those you use in a shell session. Table 10-2 shows some of the more commonly used ftp commands and their uses.

A complete list of ftp commands can be found by typing **help** at the ftp> prompt.

TABLE 10-2   Commonly Used Commands for FTP

Command	Result	Sample Usage
ls	Lists the files in the current directory	ls
cd	Changes working directory on remote host	cd /data
lcd	Changes working directory on local host	lcd /home/data
put	Uploads a single file to the remote host	put myfile
get	Downloads a single file from the remote host	get myfile
mput	Uploads multiple files to the remote host	mput *doc
mget	Downloads multiple files from the remote host	mget *doc
binary	Switches transfers into binary mode	binary
ascii	Switches transfers into ASCII mode (default)	ascii

Quitting an FTP Session

Once you are done with the FTP session, simply typing **quit** and pressing RETURN will take you back to the shell prompt.

*The netstat **command can be used to view a list of network connections, including those opened by Telnet and other programs. You can view the connection information by using the** netstat -a **command. More information on netstat can be found in Chapter 12.***

Redirecting X Window

Such is the flexibility of the multiuser capabilities of a Linux system, that it is possible to redirect an X Window session from one host to another. Whether such an arrangement will be useful to you depends on your needs, but imagine being able to have the GUIs from three or four server systems visible on a single desktop. If you are in an intensive administration position, such a configuration might simplify your life considerably. It's possible to "forward" an entire session to another host or just one or more client windows.

Starting an X Window session from another system requires that you perform two steps. The first is that the xhost command be used to add the name of the system that you want to allow X Window services to come from to a permissions file. The next is to start a utility such as Telnet or SSH and redirect the X Window display to your local system.

X-11 forwarding, to give it its proper name, can also be achieved by using SSH with the -X switch, if the system is configured appropriately.

For more information on the exact usage of the xhost command, consult the appropriate manual page.

Creating, Extracting, and Editing File and Tape Archives with tar

As we have discussed previously, the tape archive utility (tar) is used to create and manage archive files. tar allows us to group files together into a single file, making it easier to copy and download. In addition, a tar archive can be unarchived into its original directory structure, which makes it ideal for distributing applications or, in fact, any instance where the preservation of the directory structure is important. The basic usage of tar is as follows:

```
#tar command switches filetocreate filestoinclude
```

Table 10-3 shows the options for the tar command.

TABLE 10-3	Switches Used with the tar Command

Option	Command
-c	Create.
-x	Extract.
-t	Test.
-z	Signifies that the tar being created or extracted is compressed. Uses gzip to provide this functionality (-Z, which uses the compress utility, can also be used).
-v	Causes tar to operate in verbose mode. Each file is included in or extracted form. An archive is displayed.
-f filename	The name of the file being created, updated, or extracted from.
-k	Will not overwrite newer files if they already exist.
-A	Adds files to an existing archive.
-m	Used when the archive must span more than one media volume.
-r	Appends files to the archive.

tar is a simple utility to use. Here are some examples of tar usage:

To create a compressed tar file called test.tgz that contains all the files from the /usr/sbin directory, type following:

```
# tar czvf /tmp/test.tgz /usr/sbin
```

This example does not precede the options with a hyphen (-), though you can if you prefer, that is, -czvf.

Now to extract files from the archive, type

```
# tar xf /tmp/test.tgz
```

To view the contents of a tar archive without extracting the files, you use the **t** switch, as in

```
# tar tvf /tmp/test.tgz
```

Because the path of the tar file that is to be created can be specified, and thanks to the fact that Linux mounts devices directly into the file system, tar can be used to back up the files on a system by specifying the location of the tarfile to be on a tape backup device such as /dev/st0. By using tar in this way, and by using the switches provided in Table 10-3, it's possible to use tar to create daily backups of your system. There is a further discussion of backups in Chapter 11.

EXERCISE 10-1

Creating, Testing, and Extracting tar Archives

1. Change to the /usr/bin directory.

2. Create a tar archive of all files starting with *z* by using the following command:

   ```
   # tar czvf testtar.tgz z*
   ```

3. Check to see the file has been created by using the ls z* command.

4. Test the archive using the following command:

   ```
   tar tf testtar.tgz
   ```

   What happens? Why?

5. Test the archive again, this time using the following command:

    ```
    # tar tzf testtar.tgz
    ```

    What happens? Why did the command work this time when it failed before?

6. Extract the files from the archive by using the following command:

    ```
    # tar xzf testar.tgz
    ```

    What would have happened if you had used the following command?

    ```
    tar xvzf testtar.tgz
    ```

---

on the job

tar is not the only utility that can be used to compress files. Three other popular compression utilities are bzip2, zip, and gzip.

CERTIFICATION OBJECTIVE 10.05

Managing Runlevels with init and shutdown

As we have discussed elsewhere in this book, one of Linux's most endearing qualities is its ability to run only the services that are needed for the operation of the system. An important part of this configurability is that services that are not needed can be stopped and others that are, started. It is possible, by using shell scripts (which we will discuss later), to stop a number of services at a time, but it is likely that once a predetermined server configuration is reached, the system will run with a standard set of services and you would want the server to boot into that configuration in most cases. So, to achieve this, Linux provides runlevels, which dictate the subsets of services that are to be run in various configurations, and the init process, which allows us to switch between them.

Runlevels and init

Linux accommodates various modes, which are basically configurations that dictate what services are, and are not, started on the system. These modes are known as runlevels, and can be switched between by using the init command. The runlevel definitions can differ slightly between distributions, so for the purposes of example, the runlevels for a Red Hat Linux system are shown in Table 10-4.

As you can see from the table, on a Red Hat Linux system, runlevel 4 is not used, which means that you can use it for your own purposes by configuring a certain set of services to be stopped and started.

on the
job

Setting the default runlevel to 0 or 6 will cause the system to automatically halt or reboot each time it starts, causing a loop. Do not set the default runlevel to these settings.

As mentioned, the init command usage is relatively simple. If you were currently in runlevel 3 and you wanted to move to 6, you would type

```
#init 6
```

Instead of the init command, the telinit command is often used as it allows a time option (-t) to be passed. The time option indicates the delay between the execution of the command and the changing of the runlevel.

The default runlevel is set in the /etc/inittab file, which can be changed if necessary. The line that dictates the default runlevel will look something like this:

```
id:3:initdefualt:
```

| TABLE 10-4 | Run Levels Used on Red Hat Linux |

Runlevel	Description
0	System halt.
1	Single user mode. All networking functions disabled and only one user can work at the console. Some distributions also use a runlevel of *S* for single-user mode. Single-user mode lets the root account log in to perform maintenance tasks.
2	Like single-user mode, but multiple users can log in at the console.
3	Full multiuser mode. This is the "normal" mode for most systems.
4	Unused.
5	Boots automatically into a graphical interface.
6	Causes the system to reboot.

In this example, the *3* refers to the default runlevel of the system.

While the runlevel system might seem a little complicated, it is actually quite simple. Under the /etc/rc.d directory there are seven subdirectories, named rc0.d through rc6.d. In each directory, the services that should be run and stopped at the corresponding runlevel are specified. When each level is run, based on the information in these directories, any needed services are started, and any unneeded services are stopped. Figure 10-1 shows the listing from an rc3.d directory on a Red Hat Linux server.

As you can see from the listing, there are files titled S*xx* service and K*xx* service. The service names that start with *K* are those that will be stopped (if they are running) and the services with an *S* at the beginning are those that will be started. The *xx* represents a number that is the priority for the service. When a runlevel is entered, the services to be stopped are processed in priority order, and then those that are to be started are processed in priority order.

If you want to have a service run at a specific level, you can add it to the appropriate directory, however, it should be noted that some services depend on others, so you must make sure that the order in which the services are loaded doesn't cause a dependency conflict.

Directory listing from the rc3.d directory on a Red Hat Linux server

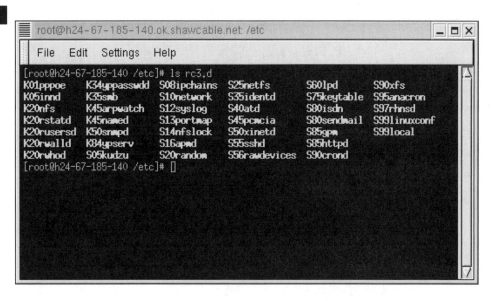

If you want a service to run at boot, irrespective of the default runlevel, you can add the information to the /etc/rc.d/local script file. Alternatively, you can add a script to the /etc/rc.d/init.d directory.

EXERCISE 10-2

Using the init Command and Determining Default Run Level

1. From the command line, while logged in as root, type **init 1**. What happens?

2. Type the following command:

   ```
   #init 0
   ```

   What happens?

3. Restart the system, if necessary by cycling the power. When the system comes back up, log back in as root.

4. From a terminal session, or through the console, determine the default runlevel of your system by opening the inittab file using the following command:

   ```
   #vi /etc/inittab
   ```

5. Once the file is open, locate the line that reads id:*n*:initdefualt: (where *n* is the default runlevel).

Shutdown

While init can be used to switch between runlevels and shut down the system, only the person at the console is aware of the fact that the system state is changing. As Linux is designed to be used in a networked environment, it is just as likely that when you shut down your system, users will need to be notified of the fact, a process that is achieved with the shutdown command.

The basic usage of the shutdown command is as follows:

```
#shutdown now
```

There are a number of switches that can be used with the command, but the only mandatory one is the **time** switch. The amount of time can be specified in minutes or can be now, which brings the system down without a delay. If you prefer you can use a -**t** switch, which allows you to specify seconds until shutdown. Some of the more commonly used switches that can be used with the shutdown command are given in Table 10-5, along with some sample usages.

In addition to the switches in Table 10-5, it is possible to include a warning message when issuing the shutdown command. For example, if you wanted to shut down the system with a reboot after 10 minutes and send a message of the fact to all users, you could use the following command:

```
#shutdown -r 10 The system will be unavailable for 20 minutes
for maintenance.
```

on the **Job**

Bringing down the system without first giving connected users a chance to save their files can result in corrupted data. Always warn users that the system will be taken down, and then, once the time to take the system down has arrived, give the users sufficient time to save their work before bringing the system down.

Shutdown Shortcuts

As well as the shutdown commands discussed, there are also some other commands and methods that you can use to shut down the system. These commands only

TABLE 10-5   Commonly Used Switches for the **shutdown** Command

Switch	Result	Sample Usage
-k	Sends the warning message that the system is going down, but does not actually initiate a shutdown.	shutdown -k
-r	Reboots the system after shutdown.	shutdown -r now
time	Specifies the amount of time (in minutes) to wait before going down. Instead, the command **now** can be used. Actual time can also be used, as in hh:mm.	shutdown -r 10
-c	Can be issued to cancel a shutdown in the time between the command being issued and the system going down. CTRL-C can also be used to cancel a shutdown.	shutdown -c

FROM THE CLASSROOM

The wall Command

Giving users a message when you are taking the system down is an important task, but there are many other times when you might want to send a message to users and not rely on the user reading their e-mail. The easiest way to do this is to use the wall command, as follows:

```
#wall The system will be taken down at 17:30 for routine maintenance. Please
call x245 for more information.
```

This command causes the message to appear on the screen of all connected users. Also displayed is the name of the user that generated the message, which can serve to reinforce the validity and importance of the message. It should be mentioned, however, that the message will not be displayed inside X Window sessions.

—Drew Bird, Linux+ Certified

trigger the same shutdown processes as the shutdown command and init, but they provide a different means to do it. The commands are detailed in Table 10-6.

on the job *Because CTRL-ALT-DEL restarts the system, users of other operating systems might issue the command by mistake. You can prevent this key combination from restarting the system by commenting the appropriate line out of the /etc/inittab file.*

TABLE 10-6 Alternative Commands for Shutting Down the System

Command	Result	Process
reboot	Reboots system	Same as shutdown -r or init 6
halt	Halts system	Same as shutdown -h or init 0
CTRL-ALT-DEL	Reboots system	Same as shutdown -r or init 6

EXERCISE 10-3

Shutting Down the System and Sending a Warning Message

1. From the command line, type the following command:

   ```
   #wall The system is being taken down. Please save all your
   work and logout!
   ```

2. Issue the following command:

   ```
   #shutdown -r 10
   ```

3. Cancel the shutdown by pressing CTRL-C.

CERTIFICATION OBJECTIVE 10.06

Stopping, Starting, and Restarting Services (Daemons) as Needed

As well as the batch stopping and starting of services (as with the init command), you will sometimes find it necessary to start and stop services on an individual basis. It is a process achieved with two simple commands, namely start and stop. In some cases, you'll want to stop a service simply because it is not needed. In other cases, stopping and starting is a way of "jumpstarting" a service that is having problems. To stop a service, use the following command:

```
#./servicename stop
```

To start one, use the following:

```
#./servicename start
```

Many services also have a restart, reload, or status option, which can be used and, in fact, is preferable if you want to restart a service. The reload option, if available, causes the service to reread its configuration files, which is handy if you have made a minor change and do not want to interrupt services.

exam
Watch

The files that are used in the launching and stopping of a service are usually held in the /etc/init.d or the /etc/rc.d/init.d directory. Alternatively, the daemons themselves are normally located in the /usr/sbin directory. Starting the daemon from this directory generally requires solid knowledge of the switches used with the daemon.

One thing to make sure of when starting and stopping services is that the correct service name is used. The files that start and stop them are usually labeled in a way that makes it clear which service the file corresponds to, such as dhcp, for the DHCP service, or smb, for the Samba service. In other cases, such as httpd, a *d*, for daemon, is appended to the service name.

on the
Job

When stopping and starting a service, leave a few seconds' gap between the commands to allow the service to stop completely before it is restarted.

Before stopping and starting services, you must consider what effect performing the action will have on users and the network. For example, if you were to stop the DHCP service, for the duration of the outage, no computers that connect to the network will be able to get an IP address. As you would expect, this could be a problem, though stopping and restarting a service should take only a few seconds. Always make sure you understand the implications of stopping and starting a service.

EXERCISE 10-4

Stopping and Starting a Service

1. Log in to the system as root.

2. Change to the /etc/init.d directory.

3. Type **ls -l** to see a list of the files in the directory.

4. Move the mouse to see the cursor move around the screen.

5. Type the following command to unload the gpm daemon:

```
#./gpm stop
```

You should receive a message informing you that the service has been stopped.

6. Move the mouse around again. You should not see a cursor.

7. To start the gpm service again, use the following command:

```
#./gpm start
```

You should receive a message that the service was started again OK. The mouse will now work again.

Note: Exercise 10-4 assumes that the console mouse services daemon (gpm) is loaded and that are you at the console and not in an X Window session.

CERTIFICATION OBJECTIVE 10.07

Managing Print Spools and Queues

In a great number of cases, a Linux server will not only store files but will provide printing services as well. In Chapter 8 we looked at how to set up and configure basic printing services. In this section we'll look at how to manage print spools and queues.

exam
ⓦatch
Managing printers with the lp commands is an important part of a Linux administrator's responsibilities. Make sure you understand the function of each command before you take the Linux+ exam.

Spooling

As we discussed in Chapter 8, print jobs that are sent to a Linux server are stored as files in a spool directory, which is typically /var/spool/lpd/*printername*. By and large, the spool directories are self-maintaining, lpd sees to that, but in some cases it might be necessary to manage the spooling process, a task that is achieved by using the lpc command.

If you find that the print queues are taking up too much space on the disk, it might be necessary to relocate the spool directory. To relocate the spool directory, edit the corresponding sd entry in the /etc/printcap file, create the directory if necessary, and, finally, restart the lpd service.

lpc

The line printer control program (lpc) allows printers to be controlled through tasks such as holding or killing jobs, or disabling printing to a printer completely. The lpc command can be found in the /usr/sbin directory.

Unlike the lpq and lprm commands that will be discussed in a moment, lpc can be used from the command line or as a stand-alone utility. Typing **lpc** at the command prompt takes you into the lpc utility, which while still using a command line, uses its own lpc prompt.

The lpc utility has many capabilities, and in fact there are too many to list here. Instead, we have chosen to list some of the more helpful commands in Table 10-7.

For a complete listing of the lpc commands, see the manual page for the utility by typing **man lpc**.

lpq

The line printer query command, lpq, allows you to view all the jobs that are currently in the queue for a printer. The only switch you need to use with the lpq command is the **-p** switch, which allows you to specify the name of the printer you want to view. If you don't name a printer, the printer named in the corresponding environment variable or the first entry in the /etc/printcap file is used. Figure 10-2 shows the output from an lpq command.8

TABLE 10-7   Commands Used with the **lpc** Command

Command	Function	Sample Usage
status	Shows the current daemon status, number of jobs in queue, and so on.	lpc status all
stop	Stops any more jobs, after the current one, from printing	lpc stop *printername*
start	Starts the queue printing after a stop or a daemon problem	lpc start *printername*

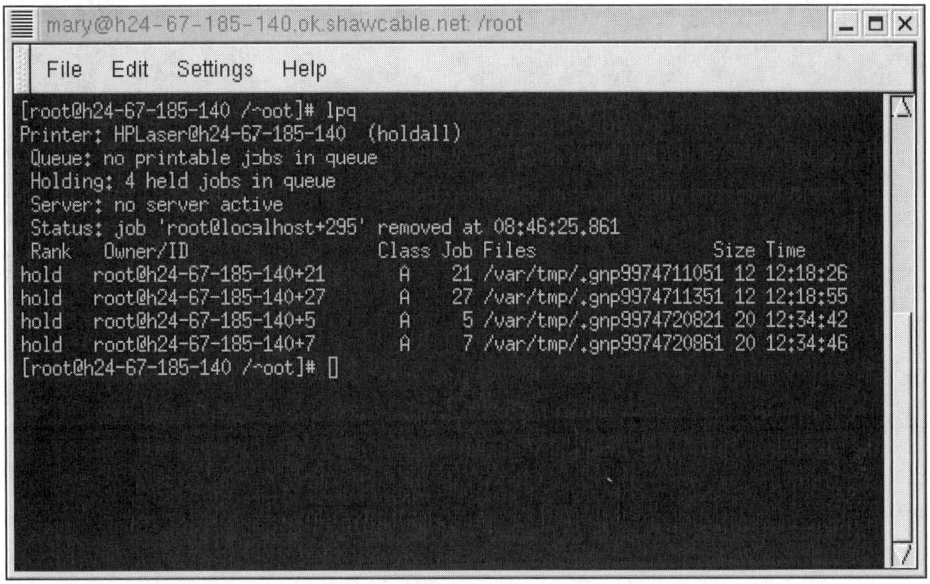

FIGURE 10-2

The output from
an lpq command

As you can see from the listing, information about the printer, as well as each job that is in the queue, is provided, including the job number, which is used to delete jobs from the queue.

lprm

Another useful command for managing printing is the lprm command, which allows you to remove print jobs from the queue, provided they haven't started printing. The basic usage of the lprm command is as follows:

```
# lprm -p printername jobnumber
```

As described above, the job number can be obtained by using the lpr command. As with the lpr command, if no printer name is specified, the printer defined in the environment variables or the first printer entry in the /etc/printcap file is assumed by lprm.

The output from an lprm command can be seen in Figure 10-3.

As the root user, you can delete any job from the print queue, but users can delete only jobs that they have submitted.

SCENARIO & SOLUTION

You want to see a list of the jobs in a print queue.	Use the lpr command and specify the printer name.
You want place a hold on printing from a queue.	Use the lpc command to hold all the jobs in the queue.
You want to remove a job from the printer queue.	Use the lpr command to find the job number and then use lprm to delete it.

CERTIFICATION OBJECTIVE 10.08

Creating, Editing, and Saving Files with vi

By this point, it should be obvious that many of the functions of a Linux system are based on text files. Often, you will need to work with these text files, which is why Linux distributions typically include a variety of utilities to edit them. Of all the various editors, however, vi, the granddaddy of the text editors, or a variation of it, is included with every Linux distribution.

FIGURE 10-3

The output from an lprm command

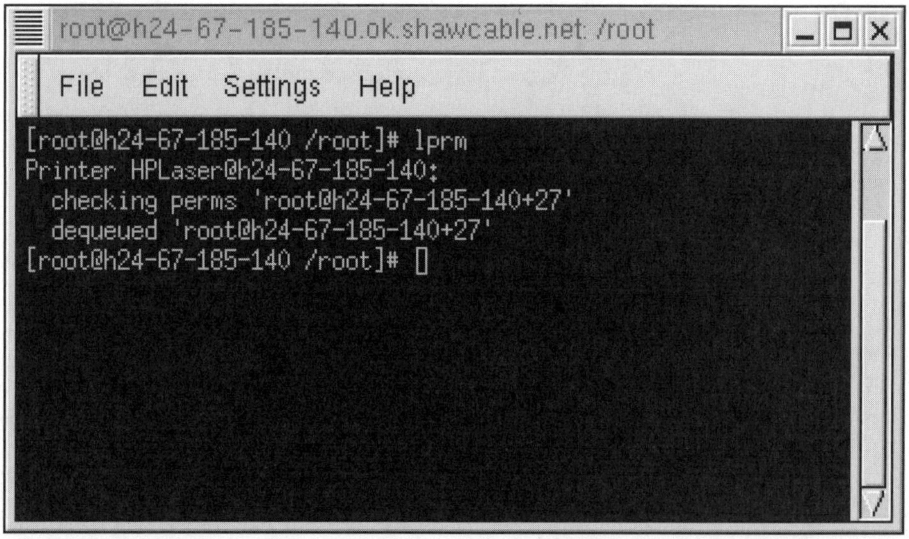

```
root@h24-67-185-140.ok.shawcable.net: /root

 File   Edit   Settings   Help

[root@h24-67-185-140 /root]# lprm
Printer HPLaser@h24-67-185-140:
  checking perms 'root@h24-67-185-140+27'
  dequeued 'root@h24-67-185-140+27'
[root@h24-67-185-140 /root]# []
```

on the **Job**

The version of vi included with Linux distributions is actually a clone of the original vi program.

If you have are used to editing text files in a graphical word processor, using vi for the first time can seem a little, well, bewildering. There are no menus and no pointers, but even without these accruements, vi is a powerful tool, and knowing how to use it is as close to mandatory as any utility can get.

exam **Watch**

You may choose to use a text editor other than vi, but you should still be aware of the basic usage. Any system you work on will have vi on it, there are no guarantees that other tools will be available.

You start vi by typing **vi** at the command prompt, though you can make it easier by adding the filename to the command line as follows:

```
#vi filename
```

You can also enter the path of the command if the file you want to access is not in the current directory. Just typing the vi command on its own will cause the editor to start, and using a filename of a file that does not exist will cause vi to assume that you are creating a new file of that name.

vi Basics

Once vi is started, you should see a screen very similar to that in Figure 10-4. In this example, we have actually opened a text file. As you can see from the figure, the name of the text file being edited appears at the bottom of the screen. This file is actually in the directory from which we started vi, but if were to edit a file from another directory by entering the complete path, the entire path would be shown in the screen.

vi operates in different modes, which dictate what you can and cannot do. When you first start vi, you are in what is called "visual mode." This mode allows you to move around the file, but does not allow you to edit it. Command (or colon) mode, which is entered by typing a colon (:), allows you to perform tasks such as saving files, moving around the file and quitting the program. A third mode, sometimes called "insert mode," allows you to make changes and edit the file. Insert mode is entered by pressing I, and exited by pressing ESC.

FIGURE 10-4

The basic vi screen

```
root@h24-67-185-140.ok.shawcable.net: /root        _ □ X

 File   Edit   Settings   Help

      Ide0: BM-DMA at 0xffa0-0xffa7, BIOS settings: hda:pio, hdb:pio
hda: ST32132A, ATA DISK drive
hda: ST32132A, 2015MB w/120kB Cache, CHS=1023/64/63
 hda: hda1 hda2 < hda5 >
~
~
~
~
~
~
~
~
~
~
~
~
~
~
"vitest" 4L, 174C
```

Moving Around in vi

Before we look at editing text in vi, we'll start by covering the basic commands you need to move around within the file. Although the ARROW keys can be used, there are vi-specific commands for each movement as well. Most of the commands are a single letter or a single key press. For example, pressing w moves you from word to word, which is a quick way to work your way through long lines of text. The commands listed in the following table work only in visual mode. Table 10-8 gives you some of the basic commands for moving around in vi.

When you are using a terminal emulator, the ARROW keys sometimes don't work properly. It is, therefore, useful to know the commands for moving up, down, and around a text file..

Searching for Text in vi

Given that some of the text files used in Linux configuration can be large and fairly complex, it should come as no surprise that one of the most used features in an editor is searching for a string of text. Table 10-9 shows the commands for searching for a string of text in vi. These commands can be entered directly from the visual mode.

TABLE 10-8	Basic Commands for Moving Around in vi

Command	Alternative	Result
CTRL-B	PGUP	Moves up one entire page
CTRL-F	PGDN	Moves down one entire page
J	DOWN ARROW	Moves down to the next line
K	UP ARROW	Moves up to the previous line
H	LEFT ARROW	Moves one character left
L	RIGHT ARROW	Moves one character right
W	N/A	Moves to the next word
B	N/A	Moves to previous word
n	N/A	Moves to the specified line number (where n is the number)
:n	N/A	Where n is the line number, entered from the command mode prompt, takes you directly to the specified line number

Basic Editing Commands in vi

vi has a language all its own when it comes to editing text, and knowing the difference between, for example, the **a** command and the **A** command is essential. The commands themselves offer almost every conceivable option for editing, including ones that you might wonder if you will ever use. Table 10-10 list some of the vi commands you might find yourself using when editing files.

TABLE 10-9	Commands for Searching for Text in vi

Command	Result
/*searchtext*	Searches forward through the document for the specified text
?*searchtext*	Searches backward through the document for the specified text
n	Moves to the next occurrence of the specified text

TABLE 10-10	Commonly Used vi Editing Commands

Command	Result
a	Inserts text after the cursor position
I	Inserts text before the cursor position
A	Inserts text at the end of the line
I	Inserts text at the beginning of the line
D	Deletes the text from the current cursor position to the end of the line
dd	Deletes the entire line
yy	Copies current line into buffer
P	Pastes line into position above the current location
p	Pastes line into position below the current location

on the **()ob**

If you are editing a large text file and know the line number that you want to edit, you can have vi go straight to that line number when it opens by adding the +linenumber switch into the command. For example, if you wanted to go straight to line 151 of a file called myconfig, you could type vi +151 myconfig.

Saving and Exiting

Once you are done editing or viewing the file, you will need to save your changes or just exit the program. This can be done from visual mode using special combinations of characters or from the command mode. Either way, if you have been editing the file, you must first press ESCAPE to exit the insert mode. The basic commands for saving and exiting in command mode are shown in Table 10-11.

In some cases, the commands can be combined, for example, the command :wq will write the file and quit vi. It should be noted, however, that the commands must be used in the correct order. Typing **:qw** will not work, as it is effectively telling vi to quit and then write.

on the **()ob**

From visual mode, you can use the zz command to save a file and quit or zq to quite a file without saving.

| TABLE 10-11 | Basic Commands for Saving and Exiting in vi |

Command	Result
:w	Writes (saves) file
:q	Quits vi and returns you to the command prompt
:w!	Forces a write on files that are protected
:q!	Quits without saving changes
:w *filename*	Saves the current file as a new file with the name supplied

As mentioned earlier, whether you choose to use vi or another editor, a basic understanding of vi will stand you in good stead for the real world, not to mention the Linux+ test.

CERTIFICATION OBJECTIVE 10.09

Managing and Navigating the Graphical User Interface

While the subject of GUIs might still be a matter of some debate in Linux circles, there is a very good chance that you will be using a GUI during your Linux administration tasks.

SCENARIO & SOLUTION

You want to quit vi without saving changes to the file.	Use the :q! command.
You want go to line number 135 by the quickest way possible.	Use the :135 command.
You want to quit vi and save your changes.	Use the :wq command.

Exactly what CompTIA means by manage and navigate the graphical user interface is unclear. The exam does not include any performance tasks, so you will not be expected actually to do anything with the GUI. Concentrate on the information provided here, and you should be OK.

Navigating the GUI

If you are used to using other operating systems with a GUI, such as Microsoft Windows, the X Window system will not yield too many surprises on the surface, though there are some subtle differences you will notice. For example, double-clicking on the button in the upper left of the dialog box on a Microsoft Windows system will close the box. Not so on certain X Window managers, where a right mouse-button click has the same effect. There are other differences as well, some subtle, others not so subtle.

The thing about window managers is that there are so many of them and no standards that dictate how they look or operate. How the GUI will appear and react really depends on what you are using. For a more detailed explanation of Window managers, refer to Chapter 7.

Layout of the GUI

There are numerous GUIs available, but we have to pick one for demonstration purposes, so we have chosen to show the GNOME desktop. The major features are identified in Figure 10-5.

We'll briefly run through each of the areas and their meaning.

- **Root window**   The root window is effectively the background for the screen. The root window can have icons placed on it, and is often referred to as the desktop.

- **Panel bar**   The panel bar has a number of components by default, but is completely customizable. It acts as the starting point for navigating the menu system. In GNOME, the button for the panel is a paw, but it differs for other systems. There are also shortcuts for opening terminal windows (xterm), and in this case, a shortcut for accessing utilities and Netscape Navigator. When an application is started, a button for that application appears on the panel, allowing you to switch between applications easily.

FIGURE 10-5

Major components of the GNOME desktop

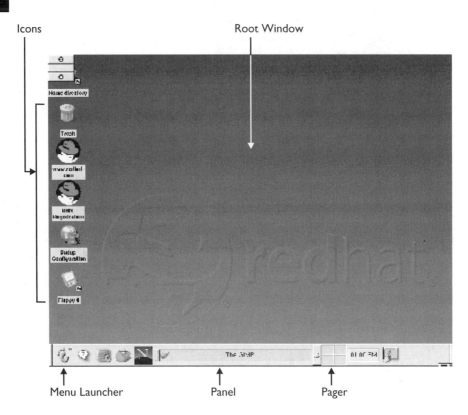

Icons

Root Window

Home directory)

Trash

www.redhat.com

HTTP Configuration

Dialup Configuration

Floppy disk

The GIMP

Menu Launcher

Panel

Pager

■ **Pager**   Referred to as the Desktop Guide in GNOME, the pager allows you to have multiple window sessions running and switch between them. This is particularly useful if you have a number of windows open but want to switch to a "blank page" to do other tasks. Another feature is the button with the caret (^) symbol on it. Clicking this brings up a list of tasks from all window sessions, allowing you to switch between them instantaneously.

Menus   The menus in X Window systems are all pretty much the same in that they contain shortcuts to applications, utilities, and files. Shortcuts can be added or removed from the menus as needed. Apart from the actual menu system that is accessed from the control panel, right-clicking or left-clicking at almost any place on the screen or on any element will bring up a menu. What the menu contains, and what actions can be performed, will depend on the element being selected. Also, you might recall from earlier chapters that Linux uses the capabilities of a three-button mouse, pressing the third button (or whichever combination emulates it) causes a another menu to be displayed. This menu often includes useful features such as cut and paste.

Terminal Emulators Terminal emulators are programs that allow a console prompt to be displayed in a window. One common program used for this is xterm. The terminal emulator functionality is provided because, whether pro-GUI or otherwise, the chances of needing to perform command-line operations during a session is fairly high. The terminal emulator window acts much the same as the normal command line, though whereas exiting from a terminal session will log out the user, doing the same in an terminal emulator window will simply return you to the X Window screen. If you wish to do so, the size and type of the fonts in an terminal emulator session can be changed for clarity. Figure 10-6 shows a GNOME desktop with a number of applications loaded and a terminal emulator session.

FIGURE 10-6

A GNOME desktop with applications and a terminal emulator session

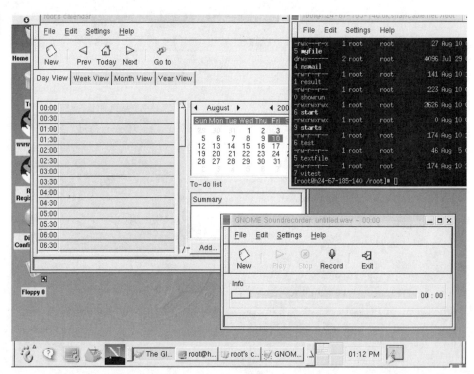

This has been only the briefest of overviews of using a GUI, and is no substitute for a little hands-on experience. Spend some time using the GUI and working out how to navigate around. Even if you don't have to demonstrate your skills on the Linux+ test, you can be sure that you will be using a GUI in the workplace.

CERTIFICATION OBJECTIVE 10.10

Programming Basic Shell Scripts with Common Shell Commands

In some instances, it will be necessary to perform certain tasks on a regular basis. Examples might include daily housekeeping tasks or routines that have to be performed on occasion. In fact, any task that will be performed regularly is a candidate for a shell script.

So that you don't have to keep typing the same commands in day after day, the commands can be written into a special text file called a shell script. Actually, the only thing special about a shell script is that it is an executable file. To create a shell script, we must have an understanding of some of the more common tasks, and the commands, that we might include.

Basic Shell Script Structure

When you are writing a shell script, you might elect to include comments that describe the function of a command, or you might choose to note the date a specific change occurred. To make a comment in your file, simply place a crosshatch (#) symbol at the beginning of the line. This tells the shell to ignore the line. If you want to, you can also choose to include spaces in your shell script to break up sections or simply to make it easier to read. Blank lines are ignored by the shell, so feel free to add as many as you like.

For an example, we'll do just a simple shell script and then go through what each component of the script means.

For the Linux+ exam, you are not expected to display a detailed knowledge of shell scripts, but you are expected to demonstrate an understanding of their purpose and function.

A Simple Shell Script

In our basic example, we will create a shell script that will find all the files that are owned by a particular user and write the information to a text file. It is called find4me. The script might take some time to run, as it starts its search from the root of the file system. Also, if it is run as a normal user, you'll get some "permission denied" errors, but as this is only for example purposes, don't worry too much.

```
#! /bin/sh

# This script will search for files that are owned by the
specified user.
echo Which user do you want to search on?
read name
echo Looking for files that belong to $name
find / -user $name -print > ownedby_$name
echo Thanks for using find4me!

exit 0
```

The Elements   The shell script comprises a number of elements, each of which is described here.

- **The shell designator**   The first line of a shell script is used to denote the shell that the script is to be used with. Even though the line is prefixed with a hatch symbol, the system still reads the line to determine this information. This line is a vital part of the shell script.

- **Blank lines**   Lines can be left blank anywhere through the script. Blank lines can be used to separate sections of the script or to make the script look less cluttered. In this example, they are not used, but in a complex script they can be very useful.

- **Comments**   Lines that start with a hatch mark denote a comment. Comments should be used so that anyone reading the shell script can determine its function. You might also want to include contact information for yourself in case someone wants to contact you about the file. You can also place comments on the same line as code, though it must be after the code itself.

- **Echo**   The echo command is used to display text on the screen. This is useful for prompting users or showing when a script has completed.

- **User input**   In the sixth line, the read command is issued with a tag of *name*. This produces a blank line for the user to type on, and whatever is typed is assigned the *$name* variable. This is used in numerous places throughout the script. Each time, the information the user entered replaces the $name field.

- **Commands**   Commands are placed in the file as if they were executed at the command prompt.

- **exit command**   In a script such as this, the exit command is not strictly necessary, though convention dictates that it is included.

As far as shell scripts go, this is about as simple as you can get. Although input from the user is collected, the commands completed with the input are relatively simple. More complex shell scripts can contains hundreds of lines and require a very strong understanding of the subject to work with. The script must be made executable before it can be used, but we'll get to that later.

Common Shell Commands Used in Scripts

Because shell scripts are basically just lists of commands formatted in a certain way, there is nothing stopping you using any of the commands that we have already discussed, or any other for that matter. The following sections discuss some of the commands you might find using on regular basis.

grep   The grep command is used to search for text within files or the results of a command. In Chapter 3, you might recall that we used the grep command to pull information on the IDE drive configuration from a dmesg output. The same basic format can be used for pulling information from a text file. Let's say we want to pull the information on a user called Mary from the /etc/passwd file. Executing the following grep command will display that line from the file.

```
#grep mary passwd
```

The result of the command might look something like this:

```
mary:x:600:600::/users/mary:/bin/bash
```

You can use other criteria as well, such as in this example, which shows all users that have an asterisk (*) in their field, which as you might recall, is used to disable a user's account. Because, however, the asterisk can be misinterpreted as a wildcard by the grep command, you must put the asterisk in quotation marks, like so:

```
#grep "*" /etc/passwd
```

As with the other commands listed in this section, a full explanation of grep usage can be obtained by typing

```
man grep
```

find   The find command is particularly useful, as it allows you to find files based on a variety of criteria, including the filename, modification date, and size.

It would take pages and pages to explain the entire usage of the find command, so instead we'll just give you some examples of the more commonly used options and point you toward the documentation for more information.

To search for files based on a name, use the following command:

```
$find / -name textfile -print
```

There are various elements to this command. The / specifies that the search is to start at the root. The -name switch is used to designate that the search criteria is the name of the file, and the -print tells the utility to print, on the screen, the full path of the files location. As with other commands, find can be used with wildcards to produce multiple matches. For example, to find all filenames on the system that start with *pas* and print the information to the screen, use the following command:

```
#find / -name 'pas*' -print
```

It is also possible to have find use criteria such as size. The following command searches the entire directory structure looking for files that are more than one megabyte in size.

```
#find / -size +1024 -print
```

There are a range of other capabilities of the find command. You can view the full listing by consulting the manual page for find, which can be viewed by typing **man find**.

cut   The cut command allows you to extract specific characters of text from a file by specifying the columns of text that should be included. This command can be useful if you need to extract information from a file and that information appears in the same place all the time. A typical us of the command would be

```
#cut -c 2,4,6,12-15 textfile
```

In this example, the **-c** switch specifies that it is the characters that are to be referenced. The *2,4,6* reference indicates that the text should be pulled from the second, fourth, and sixth columns, and the *12-15* reference is used to specify that the characters in that range should be extracted. If the file textfile were to look like this,

```
The quick brown fox jumped
over the lazy dog
```

the output from the above command executed against it would be

```
h urown
vrtzy d
```

If you don't specify the filename, the cut command interprets your command line inputs as specific until you CTRL-C out of it.

Conditional Statements   Conditional commands are those that react to information produced by other commands. Conditional commands include if, which allows a command to make a decision based on a result; then, which allows the script to determine what to do; and else, which allows the script to execute a command if the condition is not met. If you get into shell scripting in a serious way, you'll need to understand how the if, then, and else commands work. For the Linux+ exam, knowing that they exist should be sufficient.

Running a Shell Script

Once you have created your shell script, the file must be made executable, a task that is achieved with the chmod command. As you might recall from Chapter 9, the chmod command changes the permissions on a file. You might also recall that a value of 7 makes the file read, write, and execute for a certain entity. If you want everyone to be able to read, write, and execute the file, you can use the following chmod command:

```
#chmod 777 filename
```

You don't have to make it executable for everyone, you can just choose to have yourself use the file instead.

Once the permissions are set, you can execute the file by using the ./ prefix to the command, such as in this example:

```
#./myshell
```

If you are lucky, the script will run OK first time around. If it doesn't, use an editor to figure out what is amiss. Even if changes are necessary, you don't need to use the chmod command again. The permission will remain on the file no matter how many times it is changed.

CERTIFICATION SUMMARY

Linux is a multiuser operating system meaning that a single host can be accessed by a number of users simultaneously. As well as remote users being able to access the system with a variety of tools such as Telnet, the Secure Shell, and X Window redirection, the system also allows multiple virtual terminal sessions on a single system, thereby allowing multiple login sessions. When working on the system, there are a variety of common commands and expressions that are used to manage the information produced by commands.

Linux uses a system called runlevels to switch the system in and out of certain states of configuration. The init or telinit command is used to switch between the levels. Sometimes it can also be necessary to stop or start a service on an individual basis.

The Linux system provides the tape archiving utility, tar, to create a single file from multiple files. It also allows for these files to be compressed to reduce space usage.

Shell scripts can be used to combine commonly performed tasks into a file so that they can be performed in a single command, which reduces the time it takes to perform tasks and reduces the possibility for errors.

✓ TWO-MINUTE DRILL

Describing and Using the Features of the Multiuser Environment

❏ Linux is a multiuser system that allows people to log in through a variety of methods and use the resources of the server.

❏ One feature of a multiuser environment is that from the console, virtual terminal sessions can be used.

❏ You can move between the sessions, and each operates separately from the others.

Using Common Shell Commands and Expressions

❏ Information can be viewed a page at a time by redirecting the output into another utility such as **less** or **more** by using a pipe symbol (**| more**).

❏ Information can be redirected to a file using the > operator or appended to a file by using the >> operator.

❏ The shell command line has many features, including a command history and auto-complete, though the availability is shell dependant.

Using Network Commands to Connect to and Manage Remote Systems

❏ A number of utilities are available to connect to and manage remote systems.

❏ Telnet is a popular tool for remote access but is not secure. SSH is the preferred to tool, as it provides encryption capabilities.

❏ FTP can be used to transfer files between hosts and is the most popular format for doing so.

❏ X Window sessions can be forwarded to other hosts using X-11 forwarding.

Creating, Extracting, and Editing File and Tape Archives with tar

❏ The tar utility allows multiple files to be incorporated into a single file, called an archive.

❏ tar archives can be uncompressed, which means they have an extension of .tar, or can be compressed, in which case, they receive an extension of .tar.gz or .tgz. Files like this are sometimes referred to as "tarballs."

❏ The tar format is often used to distribute software, but it is also used for backup purposes.

Managing Runlevels with init and shutdown

❏ There are seven runlevels numbered 0 through 6.

❏ You can switch between runlevels by using the init command.

❏ The default runlevel is set in the /etc/inittab file.

❏ The shutdown command can be used to shut down the system with various options.

Stopping, Starting, and Restarting Services (Daemons) as Needed

❏ On occasion, it is necessary to stop or restart services.

❏ The ./servicename stop | start | restart | reload commands can be used to stop, start, and restart services. Some service offer all these options, while others might offer only stop and start.

❏ Make yourself aware of the correct service name for services that you have on your server.

Managing Print Spools and Queues

❏ Directories are used to hold print jobs while they wait to print. These are referred to as spool directories.

❏ The lpq command can be used to view the print jobs that are waiting to print.

❏ The lprm command allows print jobs to be removed from the print queue.

❏ The lpr command can be used to send print jobs to a printer.

❏ The lpc command allows you to control a printer.

Creating, Editing, and Saving Files with vi

❑ vi is a text editing utility that is available, in one form or another, on all Linux platforms.

❑ vi can be used in one of three modes. One mode allows you only to view the file, one to edit, and another to issue commands that let you manipulate and save the file.

Managing and Navigating the Graphical User Interface

❑ Linux is a command line–based operating system, but numerous GUIs are available.

❑ Use of a GUI is optional.

❑ The GUI operates much as the Microsoft Windows interface does.

Programming Basic Shell Scripts with Common Shell Commands

❑ Shell scripts are files that contain commands you would normally execute at the command line.

❑ Basic shell scripts can be created to automate commonly performed tasks or to perform tasks that require input from multiple commands.

❑ Some common commands used in shell scripts include grep, find, cut, and if.

SELF TEST

The following questions will help you measure your understanding of the material presented in this chapter. Read all the choices carefully because there might be more than one correct answer. Choose all correct answers for each question.

Describing and Using the Features of the Multiuser Environment

1. Which of the following commands or key combinations will move you from one virtual terminal to another?

    A. chvt 4

    B. cnvt 4

    C. SHIFT-F4

    D. ALT-F4

2. What command can you use to see a list of running or suspended tasks?

    A. jobs

    B. tasks

    C. CTRL-Z

    D. jobs -r -s

Using Common Shell Commands and Expressions

3. Which of the following commands would you use to see the last 20 lines of a text file?

    A. tail -n:20 *filename*

    B. tail -l20 *filename*

    C. tail -n20 *filename*

    D. tail *filename* n20

4. Which of the following commands could you use to find all the files in the current directory that start with the letters *pay* and are less than 1MB in size and append the results to a file called *result*?

    A. Find -name 'pay*' -size -1024 -print > result

    B. find -name 'pay*' -size -1024 -print >> result

    C. find -n='pay*' -size+1024 -print -result

    D. find -name '*pay' -size -1024 -print > result

5. Which utility would you use to find a string in a text file?

    A. find

    B. ls

    C. cat

    D. grep

6. Which of the following commands would run a program in the background?

    A. program %

    B. program >bg

    C. bg program

    D. program &

Using Network Commands to Connect to and Manage Remote Systems

7. Why would you use SSH instead of Telnet to connect to a remote system?

    A. SSH works from separate networks. Telnet does not.

    B. SSH is faster than Telnet.

    C. SSH is more secure than Telnet.

    D. SSH is supported by all Linux distributions. Telnet is not.

8. Which ftp command would you use to transfer all the files from the current directory on the local system to remote system?

    A. mput *

    B. mget *

    C. get all

    D. get *

Creating, Extracting, and Editing File and Tape Archives with tar

9. Which of the following commands would you use to see a listing of all the files in a compressed tar archive?

    A. tar tz *tarname*

    B. tar tzv *tarname*

C. testar -z *tarname*

D. tar czv *tarname*

10. Which of the following commands would you use to create a compressed tar archive of all the files in the current directory?

A. tar cf *tarname* *

B. tar all cf *tarname*

C. tar cz *tarname*

D. tar czf *tarname* *

Managing Runlevels with init and shutdown

11. Which of the following runlevels would you set as the default if you wanted your system to boot automatically into a GUI at system startup?

A. 0

B. 3

C. 5

D. 6

12. Which file would you edit to change your default runlevel?

A. /etc/startlevel

B. /boot/inittab

C. /etc/inittab

D. /etc/runlevel

13. Which if the following commands would you use to shutdown and restart a system in 10 minutes?

A. shutdown -r 10

B. shutdown -r -t:10

C. init 0 10

D. shutdown -r 600

Stopping, Starting, and Restarting Services (Daemons) as Needed

14. Which of the following commands would you use to stop the dhcp service on your server?

A. ./dhcp start

B. ./stop dhcp

C. ./dhcp -s

D. ./dhcp stop

Managing Print Spools and Queues

15. Which of the following commands would successfully delete a print job with a number of 793 from the queue for a printer called hplaser?

A. lpr -p hplaser 793

B. lprm -p hplaser -jn 793

C. lpd -p hplaser 793

D. lprm -p hplaser 793

Creating, Editing, and Saving Files with vi

16. Which of the following commands would quit a vi session *without* saving changes to the file?

A. :w!

B. :qw

C. :q!

D. :wq

17. Which of the following commands would take you to line 65 of a file that has been opened in vi?

A. :gtl65

B. :goto65

C. :line 65

D. :65

18. Which command would you use in vi to delete an entire line of text?

A. dd

B. dl

C. ld

D. :dd

Managing and Navigating the Graphical User Interface

19. Which of the following best describes the function of xterm?

A. Terminates an X Window session.

B. xterm is used to terminate specific applications inside of the GUI.

C. Provides a text-based shell from within the GUI.

D. Monitors resource usage from with an X Windows system.

Programming Basic Shell Scripts with Common Shell Commands

20. After writing a shell script, which of the following tasks must be performed?

A. It must be saved as an .exe file.

B. It must be compiled.

C. It must be set as executable.

D. It must be saved as an executable file.

LAB QUESTION

For this lab, create a shell script that will find files on the system that are over a certain size. The user should be able to input the size as a variable. The process for doing this will be very similar that used in the shell script in the chapter, but you will need to use the switches of the find command differently and edit the comments and text to match the purpose of the command. Make sure you comment your file and use the correct syntax.

SELF TEST ANSWERS

Describing and Using the Features of the Multiuser Environment

1. ☑ **A, D.** Both the chvt command and ALT-F*n* combinations will move you between virtual terminal sessions.

☒ **B, C.** Neither this command, which is fictitious, or the SHIFT-F*n* combinations can be used to switch between virtual terminal sessions.

2. ☑ **A.** The jobs command can be used to see a list of running or suspended jobs.

☒ **B.** tasks is not a valid Linux command. **C.** The CTRL-Z combination is used to break into a running job and suspend it. **D.** The CTRL-C combination is used to break into a running job and cancel it.

Using Common Shell Commands and Expressions

3. ☑ **C.** The tail command is used to display the last lines of a text file. The -n switch allows you specify how many lines are to be displayed

☒ **A.** The colon between the **n** switch and the number of lines is not valid and will produce an error. **B.** The correct switch to display a certain number of lines is -**n**, not -l. **D.** the -**n** switch is passed before the filename is supplied, not after.

4. ☑ **B.** This command will produce a list of all files of less than 1,024 bytes and record the path to the files in a file called result. The use of two >> means that the information would be appended.

☒ **A.** Linux commands are case-sensitive. The use of a uppercase *F* in this command would produce an error. **C.** This command uses the **+1024** switch, which looks for files that are more than 1,024 bytes in size. **D.** This command is valid, but the use of a single redirector would mean that the information would overwrite the information in the existing file, not append the information.

5. ☑ **D.** The grep command can be used to search for a string of text in a text file.

☒ **A.** The find command can be used to find a file. **B.** The ls command can be used to find a file. **C.** The cat command is used to display text files.

6. ☑ **D.** To run a command in the background, the ampersand is placed on the command line after the command itself.

☒ **A, B, C.** None of these commands are valid.

Using Network Commands to Connect to and Manage Remote Systems

7. ☑ **C.** SSH offers encryption and other security measures, which Telnet does not, therefore, many administrators prefer to use SSH for remote system access.
☒ **A.** Neither Telnet or SSH is network location–dependant. **B.** SSH is not faster than Telnet. **D.** Both SSH and Telnet are widely supported by most Linux distributions.

8. ☑ **A.** The mput command allows multiple files to be uploaded from a single command. The use of a wildcard (*) indicates that all files in the local directory should be included in the transfer.
☒ **B.** The mget command would download all the files in the working directory of the remote system to the local system. **C.** The get command is a valid ftp command but the **all** switch is not valid with it. **D.** get is intended to download a single file, so the use of a wildcard is erroneous unless there is only a single file in the remote directory.

Creating, Extracting, and Editing File and Tape Archives with tar

9. ☑ **B.** The **t** switch executes a test of the tar file. The **z** switch must be used if the tar file is compressed, and the **v** switch makes the command verbose, meaning that the files will be displayed on screen.
☒ **A.** This is correct command usage, but the omission of the *v* switch means that all the filenames in the archive would not be displayed. **C.** There is no standard utility called testar. **D.** This command includes the **c** switch, which is used to create a tar archive.

10. ☑ **D.** The **c** switch is used to create a new tar file, and the **z** switch makes the newly created tar file compressed. The * wildcard can be used to select all the files in the current directory.
☒ **A.** This command correctly creates the tarfile, but the omission of the -z switch means that it is not be compressed. **B.** The **all** switch is not valid with the tar command. **C.** This command does not specify the files to be included in the tar archive.

Managing Runlevels with init and shutdown

11. ☑ **C.** Setting the default runlevel to 5 will cause the system to boot into a GUI automatically.
☒ **A.** Setting the default runlevel to 0 will cause the system to halt. You must not set 0 as the default runlevel. **B.** runlevel 3 is multiuser mode. This is the most common mode of operation. **D.** Setting a runlevel of 6 causes the system to reboot. You must not set the default runlevel to 6.

12. ☑ C. The default runlevel for a system is defined in the /etc/inittab file.
   ☒ A, B, C. These answers are not valid.

13. ☑ A. This command will successfully shut down and restart the system after 10 minutes.
   ☒ B. This command will halt the system after 10 minutes. It would not trigger a reboot. C. This command is invalid. A time parameter cannot be passed to the init command. D. This command would shut down the system after 600 minutes.

Stopping, Starting, and Restarting Services (Daemons) as Needed

14. ☑ D. This command would correctly stop the DHCP service on a server.
   ☒ A. This command would start the DHCP service, not stop it. B. When starting and stopping a service in this way, the service name comes before the start or stop command. C. The -s switch is not valid in this command. The switch should be start or stop.

Managing Print Spools and Queues

15. ☑ D. This command would successfully delete the job number 793 from the queue for the printer hplaser.
   ☒ A. The lpr command is used to issue print jobs, not to delete them. B. The **jn** switch is not valid for the lprm command. C. the lpd utility is the daemon that manages the printing process on a Linux server, it is not used for deleting print jobs.

Creating, Editing, and Saving Files with vi

16. ☑ C. This command tells vi to quit the current session but to not save the changes. The bang (!) overrides the error message that is given when changes to a file have not been saved before exiting.
   ☒ A. :w! is the command used to write a file that is has special write protection placed on it. B. :qw is not a valid answer. The write command (w) must be issued before the quit command. D. the :wq command is used to save a file and exit.

17. ☑ D. In vi, typing a colon followed by the line number will take you directly to that line number.
   ☒ A, B, C. These are not valid vi commands.

18. ☑ C. The dd command is used to delete an entire line of text
   ☒ A. The dl command will delete a single letter. B. ld is not a valid vi command. D. The use

of a semicolon infers that this command is entered from command mode, whereas the dd command is entered in visual input mode.

Managing and Navigating the Graphical User Interface

19. ☑ **C.** xterm is a program that is run that provides a text-based shell from within the GUI. Most of the most common GUIs offer an easy way to launch on xterm or a variation of xterm. These variations include Konsole for KDE and GNOME Terminal for GNOME.

   ☒ **A.** xterm is not used to terminated an X Window. This can be done effectively using the CTRL-ALT-BACKSPACE key combinations. **B.** xterm is not used to terminate applications. **D.** There are many graphical and command-line tools to monitor resource usage from within Linux, xterm is not one of them.

Programming Basic Shell Scripts with Common Shell Commands

20. ☑ **C.** Because shell scripts are basically text files, they must be set as executable before they can be run. You can set the executable status by using the chmod command.

   ☒ **A.** Linux does not use file extensions such as .exe to signify executable files. **B.** Only source code needs to be compiled. As shell scripts are text files, they do not need to be compiled. **D.** This is not a valid answer. You can't save a file as an executable file.

LAB ANSWER

The shell script you created should look something like this:

```
#! /bin/sh
# This script will search for files that are over a certain size.
echo "What do you want to set the search threshold to (in kbytes)?"
read size
echo Looking for files that are over $size kb in size
find / -size +$size -print > files_over_$size
echo Done!!! A file called files_over_$size has been written
exit 0
```

After creating and saving the shell script, you should use the chmod command to set the execute the permissions. Try running the shell script to see if it runs as expected. If not, check your file for errors and retry.

11

System Maintenance

T here is no easy way to describe the objectives in this domain of the Linux+ certification. In some instances, the information covered is new; for others, it is a case of déjà vu as we revisit topics already covered elsewhere.

Pay special attention to the topics that are repeated, because repetition is an indicator of CompTIA's perceived importance of the topic. From that, you can deduce that the topics being covered again likely will feature prominently in the exam. So, without further ado, let's get to it.

CERTIFICATION OBJECTIVE 11.01

Creating and Managing Local Storage Devices and File Systems

In Chapter 6, we looked at the basics of managing local storage devices, but the utilities that are used during the installation are run automatically, negating the need to actually know how to execute them. After the event, however, you may find it necessary to create partitions, make file systems, and check file systems for errors. There are three utilities that achieve these tasks: **fdisk**, **mkfs**, and **fsck**. We'll take a look at each one separately.

The fdisk Utility

The primary purpose of the **fdisk** utility is to create and manage disk partitions. As such, you should find yourself needing to use it only when you are working with a newly installed device or repartitioning a drive. Outside of such tasks, you should try to steer clear of fdisk, because it is a very powerful tool with only the most rudimentary of menu systems.

Using fdisk is a simple case of issuing the command and nominating which device you want to work on. For example, if you had just installed a new IDE hard disk as the slave on the primary channel, you would use the following command:

```
#fdisk /dev/hdb
```

The initial prompt is simply the following:

```
Command (m for help):
```

So, unless you are familiar with the option you want to use, you'll want to bring up the Command Action menu by pressing M. From there, you can access the various options available. If you find yourself in a place that you don't want to be, pressing Q or CTRL-C will exit you to the command prompt. Remember that for any changes you make to take effect, you have to use the **w** option to write your changes to disk.

e x a m
Watch

*The fdisk **utility is used for creating and managing partitions on the disk. It is not used for checking the file system.***

The mkfs Utility

The make file utility, **mkfs**, is used to create a file system on a device or partition. As with the fsck utility discussed next, mkfs is actually used to call another, file system–specific, utility, such as **mke2fs** for ext2 partitions, or **mkdosfs** for DOS-compatible partitions. Using the mkfs utility is simple insofar as all that you need to do is specify the device and file system that is to be created. For example, if you want to create an ext2 file system on the second partition of a newly installed IDE drive, you use the following command:

```
#mkfs -t ext2 /dev/hdb2
```

Alternatively, the following command creates an MS-DOS-compatible floppy disk:

```
#mkfs -t msdos /dev/fd0
```

In each case, using the file system–specific utility is also valid. If you opt for this method, the -t option is not needed. For example, the file system–specific equivalent of the first of the two commands could be used as follows:

```
#mke2fs /dev/hdb2
```

The process of creating the file system does not take long, and when complete, the file system on the device is ready to use. Note that the basic usage of the mke2fs command uses a set of default parameters that may not be suitable for all situations. Check the man page or documentation for more information.

The fsck Utility

The file system checking utility, fsck, allows you to scan the file system and look for errors. The fsck utility is run during the boot process if the system detects that the file system was not dismounted cleanly. It is also run periodically in any case.

The reliability of Linux and its associated file systems means that the frequency with which fsck needs to be run manually should be low. The fsck command is not actually a file system checker in itself, but is a program that calls another, file system–specific checking utility. The exact utility will depend on the file system being checked, but for the default ext2 file system, it is **e2fsck**.

on the **Job**

The fsck utility will place file fragments found after a file system check in the lost+found directory.

When you issue the fsck command, you can either specify the file system by using the -t option or you can let fsck try to figure it out for itself, which it does by looking at the entry for the device in the /etc/fstab file. If no file system type is specified in the file, the system defaults to the ext2 option.

Here is an example of the fsck command that you use to check the first partition on the second SCSI drive in the system:

```
#fsck /dev/sdb1
```

Alternatively, here is a command that lets you check the file system on a floppy disk with the msdos file system:

```
#fsck -t msdos /dev/fd0
```

One important note about fsck is that it must only be used on unmounted file systems. That means that it may be necessary to unmount the file system in question, run the check, and then remount the file system. If you do try to run fsck on a mounted file system, you'll receive an error message.

Creating and Checking an MS DOS–Compatible Floppy Disk

1. Insert a blank floppy disk in the disk drive.

2. Use the following command to create the msdos file system on the disk:

   ```
   #mkfs -t msdos /dev/fd0
   ```

3. Once the file system creation is complete, copy some files from your system to the floppy disk.

4. Next, use the fsck command as follows to check the file system:

   ```
   #fsck -t msdos /dev/fd0
   ```

5. The result should indicate how many files are on the disk and how many disk clusters are used.

SCENARIO & SOLUTION

Users are reporting problems accessing certain files, and you suspect a problem with the file system.	Use the **fsck** utility or the appropriate file system checking utility.
You need to prepare a newly installed device for use.	Use the **fdisk** utility to create a partition on the device.
You want to make a file system on a device.	Use the **mkfs** utility or the appropriate file system creation utility.

CERTIFICATION OBJECTIVE 11.02

Verifying User and Root cron Jobs and Understanding the Function of cron

Quite often, it is necessary, or merely useful, to run jobs on a regular basis. On a Linux system, this kind of functionality can be used for just about anything you can imagine, from taking backups to reminding you when it's time to go home and so on.

There are two utilities that allow scheduled jobs to run. The first, **at**, only gets a passing mention because it runs jobs once and then removes the job from the queue. That's okay if you want to run something once, but it is more likely that you'll want to schedule jobs to run regularly, which is the function of cron.

cron

cron functionality is provided through the cron daemon, which typically loads on boot. Once it is up and running, cron checks certain files to see if there are any jobs to run. It's possible to schedule cron jobs to run on a minute, hour, day, month, or day of week basis. Because cron simply runs the command or scripts specified, it is very flexible and has a wide variety of applications.

System cron Jobs

Because the system needs to run certain jobs on a regular basis, the system has its own set of cron jobs, which can be edited if need be. System cron jobs are stored in different locations depending on which Linux distribution you are using. Red Hat–based distributions such as Mandrake have directories within the /etc directory called cron.hourly, cron.daily, cron.weekly, and cron.monthly. Within these directories, scripts are placed that run in corresponding frequency with the directory name. Other distributions choose to store the system cron jobs more conventionally, in a file called /var/spool/cron/crontabs/nobody. Neither method has any significant advantages over the other.

User cron Jobs

In addition to system cron jobs, users can create cron jobs for tasks that they want to run on a regular basis. You can control who can add cron jobs by using the cron.allow and cron.deny files. If the cron.allow file exists, users who you want to be able to add cron jobs must be included or else cron will not allow them to create jobs. Equally, if the cron.deny file exists, users who you don't want to add cron jobs must be listed; otherwise, they will be allowed to add cron jobs.

exam
ⓌatchＷatch
The naming of the cron elements can be confusing. The system is called cron, the daemon is called crond, and the command used to create the job file and the file itself is called crontab.

The tool users use to add new jobs for cron is **crontab**. It is a relatively simple command, the most basic usage being the following:

```
$crontab -l
```

This shows the jobs that are in the crontab for the user you are logged in as. The root user can also use the **-u** switch to specify a user ID so that a user's crontab can be viewed. For example, while logged in as root, if you want to view the crontab entries for a user called tom, type the following:

```
#crontab -u tom -l
```

The results might look something like this:

```
# DO NOT EDIT THIS FILE - edit the master and reinstall.
# (/tmp/crontab.859 installed on Wed Sep 12 18:32:36 2001)
# (Cron version -- $Id: crontab.c,v 2.13 1994/01/17 03:20:37 vixie Exp $)
#
#This job gets the sales figures for the previous day.
15 9 * * *    /home/tom/goget
#
#This job sends the sales figures to the sales team
30 7 * * 1,2,3,4,5  /home/tom/issuefig
```

As you can see from the listing, two jobs are listed, each of which is preceded by a comment. The lines that define the jobs have a group of five numbers followed by a command. More about the numbers in a second, but what this is telling us is that two jobs, one called *goget* and another called *issuefig,* are scheduled to run. How frequently the jobs run depends on the numbers, which are one of the most confusing yet simple mechanisms you are ever likely to see.

cron jobs run with the permissions of the corresponding user.

crontab Entries

To understand how a crontab entry is formulated, let's look at the numbering format from the preceding example. As we mentioned, there are five numbers, each of which has a hand in specifying how often the job will be run. The five numbers stand for minute, hour, day, month, and day of week. So, an entry of

15 9 * * *

causes cron to run the specified command every day at 9:15A.M. The numbers

30 7 * * 1,2,3,4,5

cause the system to run the specified command at 7:30 A.M. Monday through Friday. While we are on the subject, the days of the week run from 0 to 6, with Sunday being 0. As you can see, multiple days can be specified by using commas between the desired values. The same approach can be used to specify a job to run every 15 minutes, as follows:

0,15,30,45 * * * *

Table 11-1 contains a few more examples of crontab entries.

TABLE 11-1 Examples of crontab Entries and Their Meanings

crontab Entry	Meaning
0 23 * * 6	Runs the command at 11:00 P.M. on Saturday
30 0,4,8,12,16,20 * * *	Runs the command at 30 minutes past the hour every four hours
0 9 15 * *	Runs the command at 9:00 A.M. on the 15th of each month
0 9 1 3,6,9,12 *	Runs the command at 9:00 A.M. on the first day of March, June, September, and December

Now that we have established how crontab entries are formulated, let's take a look at actually setting them, a process achieved with the **crontab** utility.

cron uses the 24-hour-clock format for entries. For example, 3:15 P.M. would be 15:15.

For an example, we'll create a crontab job that runs the who command every ten minutes. To create a cron job, we'll use the crontab command as follows:

```
$crontab -e
```

When you press ENTER, you are taken into your default text editor. Now, our cron job is entered in the following format:

```
0,10,20,30,40,50 * * * *     who
```

You must be careful not to enter any spaces in the comma-separated list, or they will be interpreted as separators between the values.

When you exit the editor, crontab evaluates the new entry to see if the schedule values are valid. If they aren't valid, it offers to let you reedit. If they are, a message "Installing new crontab" is shown. Now you can see the crontab entry with the following command:

```
$crontab -l
```

All that is left is to sit back and wait for the cron jobs to run, but how will you know whether or not they do run? Any output generated by cron is mailed to the user account of the person who created the job. For this reason, it is a good idea to make sure either that jobs run under cron don't generate too much information or, if they do, that your mailbox is diligently maintained.

Jobs will remain in the crontab indefinitely, which means that you are likely to want to remove the jobs from the file at some point. This can also be achieved with the -e switch, except you just remove the jobs as needed. If you want to remove a crontab completely, you can use the following command:

```
$crontab -r
```

Once again, the root user can specify the **-u** username option and thereby delete a user's crontab file should the need arise.

Adding a Job to crontab

1. Create a user account for Tom by using the following command:

   ```
   #useradd tom
   ```

2. Verify that the user's crontab is empty by using the following command:

   ```
   crontab -u tom -l
   ```

   You should receive a message that says "no crontab for tom."

3. Add a cron job for Tom by using the following command:

   ```
   #crontab -u tom -e
   ```

4. In the editor, enter the following on the first line:

   ```
   0 9 * * * /home/tom/goget
   ```

5. Save the file and exit the editor.

6. To verify that the command has been entered into the crontab file, use the following command:

   ```
   #crontab -u tom -l
   ```

   The crontab file should display the new entry.

7. To delete the crontab for Tom, use the following command:

   ```
   #crontab -u tom -r
   ```

SCENARIO & SOLUTION

You need to prevent a user from adding cron jobs.	Create a /etc/cron.deny file and add the user's name to it.
You need to see what cron jobs a certain user has created.	Use the crontab -u username -l command.
You want to see what system cron jobs are scheduled.	Check the /var/spool/cron/crontabs/nobody file or the cron subdirectories in /etc as appropriate.

CERTIFICATION OBJECTIVE 11.03

Identifying Core Dumps and Removing or Forwarding as Appropriate

As stable as Linux is (and it is), sometimes the system, or the applications or processes running on it, will fail. When it does, a special file called a *core dump* is created and written to the disk. The dump file contains a copy of the data from the memory of the system at the time of the failure. This information can be used for troubleshooting purposes.

Understanding the structure of the core dump files is way beyond the scope of Linux+, but being able to identify core dumps and knowing what to do with them when they are created is included. So we shall focus on that and not worry too much about what causes core dumps or understanding what they contain.

If your system is getting core dumps, it means two things. First, your system is not running that well and might benefit from a little reconfiguration or patching. Second, there is a chance that the core dumps are taking up disk space. In today's world, where hard disk space is cheap and plentiful, you might not be too concerned about a few files taking up space, but you should be. Core dumps can be very large, and unless you are going to do something with them, they can be pretty pointless as well.

Depending on the shell you are using, the limit or ulimit commands can be used to set the maximum size of the core dump. If the size is not set, the core dumps will be the same size as the amount of RAM in the system. Many distributions actually set the limit to 0 by default, which means that core dumps will not be created, a situation that is generally acceptable, because unless you are a developer, they are of little use.

The following is the printout from the ulimit -a command on a Linux Mandrake system. As you can see from the printout, the core dump limit size on this machine is set to 100,000 blocks.

```
#ulimit -a
core file size (blocks)      100000
data seg size (kbytes)       unlimited
file size (blocks)           unlimited
max locked memory (kbytes)   unlimited
max memory size (kbytes)     unlimited
open files                   1024
pipe size (512 bytes)        8
stack size (kbytes)          2040
cpu time (seconds)           unlimited
max user processes           2048
virtual memory (kbytes)      unlimited
```

To set the limit to 0, thereby disabling the core dump feature, you can use the following bash command, though it should be noted that this only sets the new setting for the current session. If you want to set the figure permanently, edit the appropriate shell startup file.

```
#ulimit -c 0
```

Core dumps can be identified by the word "core" in the filename and can be deleted, unless you are going to use them for troubleshooting purposes. The core dump files can normally be found in your home directory or in the root of the file system, although some applications allow you to configure this location if needed.

If you want, you can create a basic script that will search the file system and delete files called core (assuming you don't have any other files called core as well!), but unless you change the minimum from 0, it should not be a problem, because the files will not be created.

The following command can be used to search the file system and track down any core files:

```
#find / -name core -exec rm -f {} \;
```

If you find any core files, the process or application that created the file can be determined by using the following command:

```
#file core
```

If you are experiencing problems with a certain application, you may want to turn on kernel dumping and allow the system to do its thing. What you do next will depend on how much time you have and what you are willing to pay. Many companies that offer Linux consultancy will examine a core dump for you and attempt (normally successfully) to determine what the cause of the problem was, but such services do not come cheaply. Another option is to find someone who will take a look at the dump for you out of interest. Forwarding a dump to the writers of the software may be a valid option, but remember that there are no warranties on free software, and most of the larger vendors will charge you for such services. Also, debugging core dumps on systems other than the one on which it was created presents other challenges that may limit the usefulness of this path. There is a third option, of course, which is that you learn how to read the core dumps for yourself!

CERTIFICATION OBJECTIVE 11.04

Running and Interpreting ifconfig

Although a number of graphical and menu-based utilities are available for configuring the network interfaces on a Linux system, the core configuration utility, **ifconfig**, is what these tools use to manage the configuration of network interfaces on a system.

Viewing Network Information with ifconfig

The most basic usage of **ifconfig** is to simply type the command, which results in all of the network interfaces that are currently "up" to be displayed The result is a listing of the installed network interfaces, basic addressing information, and basic statistical information. If you just want to check the address information for the interfaces enabled on your system, this is the way to go. If you would rather see information for all interfaces, enabled or otherwise, add the **-a** option. The following is the result of the ifconfig -a command:

```
eth0      Link encap:Ethernet  HWaddr 00:60:08:17:63:BF
     inet addr:24.67.185.140  Bcast:24.67.185.255  Mask:255.255.254.0
     UP BROADCAST NOTRAILERS RUNNING  MTU:1500  Metric:1
     RX packets:1051 errors:0 dropped:0 overruns:0 frame:0
         TX packets:409 errors:0 dropped:0 overruns:0 carrier:0
         collisions:0 txqueuelen:100
         Interrupt:16 Base address:0xef00

lo        Link encap:Local Loopback
          inet addr:127.0.0.1  Mask:255.0.0.0
          UP LOOPBACK RUNNING  MTU:3924  Metric:1
          RX packets:0 errors:0 dropped:0 overruns:0 frame:0
          TX packets:0 errors:0 dropped:0 overruns:0 carrier:0
             collisions:0 txqueuelen:0
```

As you can see, two interfaces are listed. The first, eth0, is the information for the first Ethernet network card installed in the system. The second entry, lo, is the software-based loopback adapter that is included in every system configuration by default. This output is typical from a system that has a single network card installed.

The eth0 interface is for the physical network card and includes a variety of information. The top line defines the Link Encapsulation method, which in this case is Ethernet, and also includes address information and the hardware address for the adapter. As you may recall from Chapter 2, this hardware address, or MAC address, uniquely defines this network interface and is used by the network for communication.

The next line details the IP address, broadcast address, and network mask for the interface. This information should be checked if you are experiencing problems with the network connectivity on your system. The next line indicates, among other things, that the interface is up and that the Maximum Transmission Unit (MTU) size is set to 1,500. This is standard for an Ethernet interface. The last field on this line is Metric, which is a number assigned to the interface that is used in routing functions.

The next three lines provide statistical information for the interface. The first, RX, provides information on the packets that have been received, and the TX line gives information on packets that have been transmitted. The third line lets you know how many collisions have been detected by the card and, finally, the transmit queue length. Both of these statistics can be useful when troubleshooting network problems. Each field is identified by a label, followed by a colon, followed by the statistic. The last line of the entry lists what hardware resources are in use by this adapter. The most notable omission from the listing is the host name.

The second entry, lo, is the software-based loopback adapter that is included in every system configuration by default. The loopback adapter allows the system to test itself, and connect to itself as if it were a remote host. The loopback adapter is useful because it allows you to test the network services and connectivity of your system without using another. The loopback adapter is assigned the IP address 127.0.0.1.

Setting Configuration with ifconfig

In addition to viewing information, **ifconfig** can be used to configure network interfaces. To configure a network address for an interface, the syntax is as follows:

```
#ifconfig <interface> <IP address> netmask <netmask> broadcast
<broadcast address>
```

In real terms, this might translate into a command like this:

```
#ifconfig eth0 192.168.100.1 netmask 255.255.255.0
broadcast 192.168.100.255
```

Although convention dictates that the broadcast address must be supplied, ifconfig is able to determine and set a default broadcast address based on the address and subnet mask information if one is not given. Configuring a network interface in this way will automatically bring up the interface with this address information, though there is also an **up** command that allows you to bring up an interface manually if necessary.

A variety of graphical tools are available for configuring the network settings, though, as we have mentioned numerous times previously, knowing the basic utilities that are available on every system is important, because you just never know when you might find that's all you have.

CERTIFICATION OBJECTIVE 11.05

Downloading and Installing Patches and Updates

Patches and updates are a fact of life with any operating system or application, not just Linux. Over time, shortcomings or problems are detected in programs, and patches and updates are released that either repair the functionality that already exists or adds new functionality. Whichever is the case, you must make sure of two things: that you completely read any documentation that is included in the patch, and that you only apply a patch that is needed. In other words, patches should only be applied to fix a specific problem or to add new functionality.

on the Job

The application of patches for no reason is known as **blind patching, and is** *a big no-no in the system administration world. As the old saying goes, "If it's not broken, don't fix it," and the same can be said of patches. No matter how you learn of the availability of a patch, be sure that you understand the purpose of the patch completely before applying it.*

Operating System Patches

Operating system patches are released when it has been decided that a new feature should be included or when a shortcoming in the existing kernel is found. Normally, quite a large number of patches exist for a given Linux kernel version; for example, the 2.2 kernel had 19 patch levels.

Patches can be obtained from a variety of sources, but a good bet is to check your distribution's Web site, which normally provides detailed information on package dependencies and version conflicts that may arise from installing the patch.

on the Job

As with configuration files, it is worth making a backup copy of the kernel before patching it. You can achieve this with the cp *command.*

The patches come in a variety of packages and formats, depending on where the patch is obtained. Because the files can be quite large, **tar** and/or the compression utilities **gzip** and **bzip** are commonly used to compress the files for download. After the patch has been downloaded, it can be installed using the patch command, which applies the changes in the patch file to the original version. The patch command has a number of options, one of the most useful being the **-b** option, which creates a backup copy of the original file; this is always a good idea should you need to revert to the original version.

If you are applying multiple patches, they must be applied in order, from the version you have already to the version you want to reach. In other words, if you are using version 2.2.5 and you want to go to version 2.2.8, you must install 2.2.6, 2.2.7, and then 2.2.8 in sequence. You can find out the current patch level of your system by using the uname -a command. As you may recall from our discussion in Chapter 5 on Linux kernel version numbering, the last of the three digits refers to the patch level.

Application Updates

Application updates or patches are nearly always available from the same place that you downloaded the original program from. If you are looking for an update for a program that was supplied as part of a distribution, a quick search of the Web using the application name should take you to where you need to go in short order. In fact, most distribution sites offer patches and updates for applications, which is another reason why you should make the distribution's Web site your first stop when looking for updates.

on the
job

Some Linux distribution suppliers and consultancies will collect patches and updates together and supply them to you on a CD. This is a good way to go if you are concerned about keeping up to date with what patches are available.

CERTIFICATION OBJECTIVE 11.06

Identifying, Executing, and Killing Processes

Everything that runs on a Linux system is assigned an ID, known as a process ID (PID). This ID number stays with the process for the duration of its life and is used by the system to track each process. Generally, the PID is not that relevant to a system administrator, though if you find yourself having problems with a certain process, you may need to ascertain the PID in order to kill the process. It should be noted, though, that processes don't always get the same PID (with a few exceptions). So, each time you want to kill the process, you must ascertain the PID again.

The ps Command

The Process Search, or ps, command can be used to see what processes are running on your system, who is running them, how long they have been running, and whether the process is still running or has died, by looking at the STAT column. The following is a printout from the ps aux command:

```
USER       PID %CPU %MEM   VSZ   RSS TTY  STAT START  TIME COMMAND
root         1  0.0  0.4  1304   128 ?    S     Sep10  0:06 init [3]
root         2  0.0  0.0     0     0 ?    SW    Sep10  0:00 [kflushd]
root         3  0.0  0.0     0     0 ?    SW    Sep10  0:00 [kupdate]
root         4  0.0  0.0     0     0 ?    SW    Sep10  0:00 [kpiod]
root         5  0.0  0.0     0     0 ?    SW    Sep10  0:00 [kswapd]
root         6  0.0  0.0     0     0 ?    SW<   Sep10  0:00 [mdrecoveryd]
root       267  0.0  0.5  1352   176 ?    S     Sep10  0:00 syslogd -m 0
root       277  0.0  0.5  1596   184 ?    S     Sep10  0:00 klogd
rpc        292  0.0  0.3  1436   112 ?    S     Sep10  0:00 portmap
root       308  0.0  0.0     0     0 ?    SW    Sep10  0:00 [lockd]
root       309  0.0  0.0     0     0 ?    SW    Sep10  0:00 [rpciod]
rpcuser    319  0.0  0.0  1484     0 ?    SW    Sep10  0:00 [rpc.statd]
root       334  0.0  1.3  1276   428 ?    S     Sep10  0:00 /usr/sbin/apmd -poot
root       354  0.0  1.4  5616   432 ?    S     Sep10  0:00 ypbind
root       356  0.0  1.4  5616   432 ?    S     Sep10  0:00 ypbind
root       358  0.0  1.4  5616   432 ?    S     Sep10  0:00 ypbind
nobody     434  0.0  0.0  7580    24 ?    S     Sep10  0:00 [identd]
nobody     438  0.0  0.0  7580    24 ?    S     Sep10  0:00 [identd]
nobody     439  0.0  0.0  7580    24 ?    S     Sep10  0:00 [identd]
nobody     440  0.0  0.0  7580    24 ?    S     Sep10  0:00 [identd]
nobody     441  0.0  0.0  7580    24 ?    S     Sep10  0:00 [identd]
daemon     453  0.0  0.1  1324    56 ?    S     Sep10  0:00 /usr/sbin/atd
root       479  0.0  0.0  1392     0 ?    SW    Sep10  0:00 [cardmgr]
root       494  0.0  1.7  2176   528 ?    S     Sep10  0:00 xinetd -reuse-pi
root       509  0.0  0.2  2428    84 ?    S     Sep10  0:02 /usr/sbin/sshd
lp         533  0.0  0.0  2336     0 ?    SW    Sep10  0:00 [lpd]
lp         537  0.0  2.4  2336   756 ?    S     Sep10  0:00 lpd (Server)des
root       583  0.0  1.0  3132   328 ?    S     Sep10  0:00 sendmail: accept
root       599  0.0  0.4  1316   144 ?    S     Sep10  0:00 gpm -t ps/2
xfs        784  0.0  3.0  4472   948 ?    S     Sep10  0:01 xfs -droppriv -
root       816  0.0  0.6  1268   208 ?    S     Sep10  0:00 rhnsd --interval
root       834  0.0  0.0  1264     0 tty2 SW    Sep10  0:00 [mingetty]
root       835  0.0  0.0  1264     0 tty3 SW    Sep10  0:00 [mingetty]
root       836  0.0  0.0  1264     0 tty4 SW    Sep10  0:00 [mingetty]
root       837  0.0  0.0  1264     0 tty5 SW    Sep10  0:00 [mingetty]
```

```
root     838  0.0  0.0  1264     0 tty6 SW    Sep10  0:00 [mingetty]
root    1441  0.0  3.5  2184  1080 tty1 S     09:27  0:00 login -- root
root    1442  0.0  3.5  2196  1096 tty1 S     09:27  0:00 -bash
lp      1691  0.0  2.7  2340   832 ?    S     14:10  0:00 lpd (Worker)
root    1717  0.0  2.4  2520   748 tty1 R     14:42  0:00 ps aux
```

Some of the common options for running the ps command are listed in Table 11-2.

on the
()ob

The ps command provides similar information to that supplied by the top command, but ps only provides a snapshot, whereas top updates the listing every few seconds.

If you need to, you can use the grep command to pull information on a certain process or even a specific user. For more information on the ps command and the information supplied by it, consult the appropriate man page.

The kill Command

The kill command can be used to send a signal to a process that causes the process to shut down. There are two signals of particular importance: 9, the kill process signal (SIGKILL), and 15, which is the terminate signal (SIGTERM). If you don't specify a signal level, the kill command uses the terminate process (15) signal.

The only required switch for the kill command is the PID, which, as mentioned earlier, can be obtained by using the ps command. Once you have figured out the PID for the process you want to kill, you can use the kill command as follows:

```
#kill 537
```

If a process is being particularly stubborn, you can also specify the signal number you want to send, which will be 9 if you are having problems killing a process.

TABLE 11-2   Common Switches for the **ps** Command

Option	Result
-l	Shows a long format
-a	Show all processes
-u	Shows usernames associated with the processes
-x	Shows processes that do not have a terminal session associated

The command is as follows.

```
#kill -9 537
```

Another useful kill signal to know is 1, which is known as the SIGHUP. Issuing this signal to a process causes the process (in most cases) to reread its configuration files. This command can be issued by specifying the signal number 1 as before, or by using the letters HUP as follows:

```
#kill -1 537
```

The root account can kill any process that's running on the system. Users can only kill processes that they own. The kill command can also be used to see a complete list of the available kill signals. Simply use the -l option as follows:

```
#kill -l
```

The killall Command

The killall command sounds like it is very similar to the kill command, which it is, but it works slightly differently. The killall command can be used to kill all occurrences of a command. For example, if you have a script called *doback* that has stopped processing, you that can issue the following command:

```
#killall doback
```

The command can also be used with signal numbers. For more information, consult the man page.

SCENARIO & SOLUTION	
You want to determine the state of running processes.	Use the ps command and check the STAT column.
You need to kill a process that is not responding.	Use the kill command with the appropriate PID.
You want to kill all occurrences of a process.	Use the killall command.

Differentiating Core Services from Noncritical Services

As we have already discussed, the ps command can be used to determine the PID of a process, which in turn can be used to kill the process if needed. However, before you start killing off processes left, right, and center, it's important to understand which processes do what, and what you can and cannot kill safely.

In the preceding **ps** listing, notice that some of the processes have square brackets around them, which indicates that they are kernel processes and cannot be killed. In addition, the init process cannot be killed, even though the square brackets don't appear around the name itself.

PPIDs

In addition to having a PID, each process also has a parent PID (PPID). The PPID refers to the process that is controlling this process (hence, the term *parent*). The parent of all processes is init, so if there is not other process parent, init (1) will always be listed as the parent process. You can get a listing of the PPIDs by using the **ps -el** command. Here are a few lines from that printout:

F	S	UID	PID	PPID	C	PRI	NI	ADDR	SZ	WCHAN	TTY	TIME	CMD
100	S	0	1	0	0	60	0	-	266	do_sel	?	00:00:06	init
040	S	0	2	1	0	60	0	-	0	bdflus	?	00:00:04	kflushd
040	S	0	3	1	0	60	0	-	0	kupdat	?	00:00:02	kupdate
040	S	0	4	1	0	60	0	-	0	kswapd	?	00:00:00	kswapd
040	S	0	5	1	0	40	-20	-	0	md_thr	?	00:00:00	mdrecover
040	S	0	254	1	0	60	0	-	262	nanosl	?	00:00:00	dhcpcd
140	S	0	295	1	0	60	0	-	357	do_sel	?	00:00:01	syslogd
140	S	0	305	1	0	60	0	-	361	do_sys	?	00:00:00	klogd
040	S	0	318	1	0	67	0	-	320	nanosl	?	00:00:00	crond
140	S	0	362	1	0	60	0	-	272	do_sel	?	00:00:00	gpm
040	S	100	377	1	0	60	0	-	893	do_sel	?	00:00:00	xfs
100	S	0	389	1	0	60	0	-	497	wait4	tty1	00:00:00	login
100	S	0	390	1	0	60	0	-	258	read_c	tty2	00:00:00	mingetty
100	S	0	391	1	0	60	0	-	258	read_c	tty3	00:00:00	mingetty
100	S	0	392	1	0	60	0	-	258	read_c	tty4	00:00:00	mingetty

```
100 S     0    393      1  0  60   0  -   258 read_c tty5 00:00:00 mingetty
100 S     0    394      1  0  60   0  -   258 read_c tty6 00:00:00 mingetty
100 S     0    402    389  0  75   0  -   563 wait4  tty1 00:00:00 bash
100 R     0   5720    402  0  79   0  -   625 -      tty1 00:00:00 ps
```

As you can see, many of the processes at the top of the listing have init as the parent process. Others, such as the bash process, have another process defined as the parent—in this case, 389, the login process. Subsequently, the PPID of 389 is the **init** process, 1.

CERTIFICATION OBJECTIVE II.08

Monitoring System Log Files

The system logs, which are normally located in the /var/log directory, are a useful way of keeping an eye on your system and what is happening with it. There are no set guidelines regarding the frequency with which log files should be checked, so it often depends on company policy or how badly you want to keep your job!

The location of log files, and what is written to them, is defined by the /etc/syslog.conf file. You can edit the syslog.conf file if you want to increase the level of logging or want to define what processes and daemons write logs. There is more information about the purpose of specific log files in Chapter 12.

In the most basic scenario, using the cat command and piping the information into the **less** command will allow you to manually look though the file for unusual activity or inconsistencies. Here is an example of the cat command used in this way to view the /var/log/auth.log file, which records, among other things, logons and user account creation information on certain distributions:

```
#cat /var/log/auth.log | less
```

Alternatively, you can open the text file in a text editor such as **vi**, or pull information from a text file by using the grep command. For more information on using vi and grep, refer to Chapter 10.

What Is "Unusual Activity"?

Unusual activity can be termed as anything that you don't expect to see or anything that seems out of place. Obviously, anything related to security, such as multiple failed logins in the /var/log/auth.log file should be of immediate concern, but other errors should also draw your attention.

In most cases, further investigation of an entry will result in nonissues. It might be that Sadie from accounts really did forget her password six times, and the attempts by an external system to access the FTP server really were genuine mistakes. Over time, you will become adept at identifying which log file entries warrant further investigation and which do not.

on the *Job* *Most ISPs have a department or person who deals with abuse, which is what someone trying to gain access to your systems would be classified as. If you are experiencing problems, contact your ISP and ask them what assistance is available for tracking down who is causing the problems.*

CERTIFICATION OBJECTIVE 11.09

Documenting Work Performed on a System

Back in Chapter 8, we discussed the importance of system documentation and its role in system maintenance and recovery. Because many of the tasks related to server maintenance require that documentation be updated, it is worthy of a separate mention here as well.

SCENARIO & SOLUTION

You need to check log files for unusual activity.	Use the **cat logfile I less** command or a text editor to view the file.
You need to search for a specific string.	Use the **grep** command to extract lines that match a given criteria.
By checking the log files, you determine that an unauthorized entity is trying to access your system.	Attempt to contact the entity or ask your ISP for help in tracking them down and contacting them.

Updating documentation when work is performed on the system is absolutely vital if it is to be of any use. If a configuration change is made and the documentation is not updated, the role of documentation in a troubleshooting scenario may be very limited. Troubleshooting best practices dictate that the documentation be consulted first before attempting any fixes. If the documentation is out of date, two things can happen. First, an annoying result is that the documentation has to be troubleshot before any real steps toward troubleshooting the problem can be taken, which can be a very time-consuming process indeed. An even worse scenario is that the documentation leads the technician, maybe you, maybe not, to start attempting fixes based on the information within it. This might mean that the problem is exacerbated rather than cured. In the best-case scenario, it is a waste of time. So, when performing work on the system, you must make sure that the appropriate documentation is updated. In particular, be sure to include the following information:

- **What was performed**   If the system documentation contains a change log, as it should, update the log with information of exactly what work has been performed.

- **When it was performed**   Note the exact date and time when changes were made. This makes it easier, if the need arises, to track back through log files and find the origin of a problem.

- **Record your name and contact info**   If there are many people who might administer the server, which is often the case in large organizations, be sure to note that it was you who made the changes. It gives another technician the information they need to check in with you should a problem arise.

- **Update backup and hard copies of configuration files**   If the changes you made involved editing or amending configuration files, ensure that new electronic copies and hard copies of the files are made and comment any changes within the file.

Remember, it is essential that documentation is kept up to date by anyone who performs maintenance on the server. It could be you relying on someone else's documentation in a crunch, so consider the changes you make carefully, but make sure you note them.

CERTIFICATION OBJECTIVE 11.10

Performing and Verifying Backups and Restores

Backups are, quite simply, insurance against data loss. Given that, they deserve as much, if not more, attention than any other aspect of system administration. The amount of time taken to rebuild a Linux system pales in significance when compared to the amount of time it takes to reconstruct data. In some cases, it is even impossible to do. Backups make sure that, if the need arises, you can restore your data.

You will find yourself reaching for the backup tape in various situations. Here are some of the main ones:

- **Accidental data loss**   If file permissions are set correctly, the frequency with which data is deleted by mistake will be minimized. Even so, it will happen, and backups present a means of recovering a recent copy of the files so that they can be copied back to the server. In reality, loss of data in this way is far more frequent than any of the other threats discussed here. For this reason, you should choose a backup method that makes it just as easy to restore a file as to back it up.

- **Hardware failure**   There are no prizes for guessing which hardware component is most susceptible to failure. Yes, it's hard disk drives. In fact, a hard disk is twice as likely to fail as the next most susceptible device, which is the power supply. Disks fail, and when they do, they take your data with them. Backups enable you to protect against data loss from disk failure.

- **Theft**   In many cases, the data on your system is worth more than the hardware, but either way, computer systems make an attractive proposition for thieves. Most insurance policies will cover the loss of hardware, but in many cases, will not cover the cost of reconstructing data.

- **Disaster**   Okay, so disaster may sound a little dramatic, but fire, flood, earthquakes, and so on can affect your business, no matter where in the world you are. Having a copy of data securely stored offsite makes it possible to re-create your systems at another location should your original site become unavailable.

Linux, like practically every other NOS, comes with utilities that allow you to back up files on the system. Also like every other NOS, commercially available backup products are available if you prefer not to use the tools that are included. Whether you choose to go with the built-in utilities or purchase another package is a matter of preference, but backups are not the place to cut corners. If you are not completely comfortable with using a command-line utility such as **dump**, discussed in a moment, look to products with a GUI that can make the backup/restore process easier.

Backup hardware must also be considered. There are two main criteria for backup hardware nowadays, namely speed and capacity. Not so long ago, tape drives had capacities that could accommodate all but the largest storage implementations. Now, the drastic fall in the price of hard disks and the ever-expanding needs for data storage mean that you have to check into the storage capacity of drives carefully.

on the **Job**

The mt command can be used to work with tapes.

Generally speaking, the only large-capacity backup choice worth considering are SCSI tape drives. Other means and methods are available, but generally, only SCSI tape drives satisfy the throughput, reliability, compatibility, capacity, and cost criteria for modern systems with large amounts of data. For limited-volume backups, or those occasions when you just need to back up a subset of data, other methods like Zip drives, CD-R, and do forth may actually be more suitable than a high-capacity tape drive, but for system backups, the tape is still king.

exam **Watch**

CD-R is actually well suited to long-term storage of data. A CD-R can hold around 650MB of data, making it ideal for archiving tasks or for holding large files such as those used by computer-aided design (CAD), graphics, and presentation software.

Making a decision to use tapes for backing up is just the start, however. Various formats are available that have different characteristics, such as speed, capacity, and cost. For lower-capacity needs, the Sony-created DDS format still offers a reasonable cost/capacity ratio. For implementations that need higher capacities and speeds, consider some of the 8MM formats from Sony or Mammoth, or the DLT series from Quantum. For those with the need and dollars, the Super DLT or the Ultrium format are the way to go.

on the job

When specifying a tape backup solution, take into consideration the cost of the media. Tapes can be expensive, particularly when you may need a relatively large number for an extended backup cycle.

Capacity is a big factor when choosing a tape drive. The convenience of being able to back up an entire system to a single tape cannot be overstated, nor can the convenience of restoring an entire system from one. If at all possible, choose a backup format that will allow you to fit an entire backup of the system on a single tape.

Just before we finish our discussion of tape drives, we need to cover one more thing: the device naming conventions used for SCSI tape drives.

The first SCSI tape drive in a system is called st0, the second st1, and so on. Simple enough. The only problem with these devices is that they are rewinding tape devices; in other words, when an archive has been written to the tape, the tape rewinds itself. That's all well and good if you only want to store a single archive on a tape, but the likelihood is that, at some point, you will want to place more than one archive on a tape, which is where the nonrewinding SCSI tape devices come in.

Named **/dev/nst***x* (where *x* is the number), these special devices allow more than one archive to be placed on a tape by not rewinding it at the end of the archive process. If you are using a GUI backup utility, you will most likely get a check box to dictate

FROM THE CLASSROOM

Backups and RAID

On occasion, we hear of an environment that has foregone the traditional tape backup for a fault-tolerant RAID implementation. This is a very dangerous strategy indeed. RAID does provide tolerance for the failure of a hard disk, but it doesn't provide against any other data threats. No matter what RAID configuration you are using, the accidental data loss threat still exists. Once data is deleted from the RAID array, it is gone. RAID does not protect against this kind of loss. Theft of the system and loss due to fire, flood, or natural disaster also are not catered for by RAID. The only way to be sure that your data can be recovered is to make a copy of it on removable media and to store that media in a location other than your main site. Any other approach is asking for trouble.

—*Mike Harwood, Linux+ Certified*

whether or not you want a rewind at the end of the archive, but for command-line utilities, understanding the difference and purpose of the **nst** devices is important.

What to Back Up

In the past, the relatively slow speeds of backup devices has meant that people have looked for ways of backing up data other than complete backups because they take up too much time. Nowadays, backup devices accommodate capacities and speeds that mean that in many cases, it is possible to use full backups.

Determining what files need to be backed up is not a difficult task. Simply ask yourself what changes on a regular basis. Once a system is set up and configured, you might choose to take a full backup of the system and then subsequently just back up files that have changed since the full backup. Such a backup is known as a *differential* backup. Alternatively, a more popular approach is to take an *incremental* backup, which backs up all files that have changed or been created since the last full or incremental backup.

This approach is good, because it means that only a small amount of data needs to be backed up each time, making the process much faster than a full backup. The downside is that if you need to do a restore, you'll need the tape containing the full backup, followed by all the tapes from the incremental backups, in order. For this reason, you should intersperse your cycle with regular full backups; otherwise, you face the challenge of restoring a large number of tapes with incremental backups. Table 11-3 summaries the three backup strategies described.

While these different types of backups are standard across operating systems, the mechanisms by which they are implemented differ between platforms and utilities. For example, the dump utility, which we will discuss later, offers "levels" of backup that can be manipulated to produce a certain type of backup. Others, such as tar,

TABLE 11-3   Commonly Used Backup Strategies

Backup Option	Files Backed Up
Full	All files on the system
Differential	All files that have changed since the last full backup
Incremental	All files that have changed since the last full or incremental backup

rely on the modification or creation time of the file or directory to determine whether it should be included in a partial backup.

How Often to Back Up

The answer to this question is relatively simple. How often does your data change? A system running, for example, software for checking in and out books at a library is likely to have data changing at a rapid rate. On the other hand, a system that is acting as a firewall will have relatively little data that changes, apart from log files. Also, the consequences of losing the library database are likely to be more far reaching, because the data is difficult to reconstruct. The data lost from a server acting as a firewall is likely to be easier to reconstruct and less critical.

on the Job

In addition to performing file backups, it is also recommended that you periodically back up the file structure and file permissions of your system. This backup need not be anything fancy, and piping the output from an ls -laR command into a text file is sufficient.

Using criteria such as this, its possible to determine the required frequency of backup. Referring to our example systems again, the library server will need to be backed up daily, if not more often than that. The firewall server could be backed up once a month, or even only when a configuration change is made. If this were the case, you might elect to take a weekly backup of just the log files, because they are the only files that would have changed.

This approach works for all systems. Look at the frequency with which the data changes and ask yourself how important the data is. If you perform your evaluation properly, the backup frequency should be easy to determine.

Backup Cycles

One last general backup concept that deserves attention is that of backup cycles, or in other words, determining how often the tape that you are using needs to be rotated. Rotation of tapes is important because it allows data to be recovered from days or even weeks previous. It also means it's possible to have one backup tape close by for restores while another, still recent backup can be stored offsite for disaster recovery purposes.

Two tape rotation schemes are commonly used: the simple yet effective Grandfather, Father, Son rotation, and the complex yet just as effective Tower of Hanoi scheme, which is based on the popular game. In-depth knowledge of these rotations schemes is not needed for Linux+, but if you want to find out more information on each of them, visit http://www.sansite.com/backup_basics.htm.

Utilities Used to Perform Backups

Various utilities are available for backing up the system, and which one you choose will depend on your needs and on what you feel comfortable using. All of the tools described here are reliable enough to be considered as viable, but some are easier to use than others, and some offer features that others don't. We'll start our discussion with the granddaddy of all the backup utilities, **tar**.

tar

Nowadays, **tar** is more synonymous with downloadable files than backing up, but as the name *tape archive utility* implies, it was, and still is, the choice of many people for performing backups. In Chapter 10, we discussed **tar** as it pertains to creating archive file, and we also discussed how **tar** can be used to write directly to a device. In this section, we will take another look at the tar command and how you can use it to perform backups.

exam
ⓦatch
The tar *utility is commonly used to perform backups and subsequent restores. Be sure you understand the purpose and usage of the tar command.*

Using tar   As you may recall from earlier discussions, tar is a command-line utility with only a very basic set of required options. For example, the following command copies all the files from the /data directory to the first nonrewinding SCSI tape drive and compresses the archive:

```
#tar czf /dev/nst0 /data
```

Multiple specifications can be added to the command simply by separating each designator with a space as follows:

```
#tar czf /dev/nst0 /data/documents /data/ssheets
/data/database/clients /data/database/contacts
```

Restoring with **tar** is not that much more difficult than backing up with it. Rather than use the **c** option to create a **tar** file, you use the **x** option to extract from the archive. Here is an example:

```
#tar xzvf /dev/st0
```

In this example, the data is extracted from the archive on the first SCSI tape drive. As you might recall from our earlier discussions of tar, the **z** option must be used if the archive being written or read from is compressed. Not doing so will generate an error.

While **tar** may have fallen out of favor with many system administrators, it is still widely used and is, perhaps not surprisingly, very good at what it does.

dump

The **dump** utility is also used for making system backups. **dump** is designed to be used as a utility to back up the entire file system. One of the features of **dump** is the *dump level* designator that allows you to customize backups. It should be noted that **dump** is not included with all distributions and is an optional install with others.

on the !job *Unlike tar, dump **does not compress files. This is not too much of a problem because most tape backup devices offer hardware compression of about 2:1**.*

There are 9 dump levels available, with 0 being a full backup. After that, each level backs up files that have been created or modified since the last dump level. For example, if you performed a full dump (level 0) on Friday and a level 1 dump on Monday, only files that had changed since the full dump would be included. On Tuesday, you could use dump level 2, which would only back up files since the 1, and so on. This is essentially an incremental backup. If you were to do a level 0 dump on the Friday and then a 1 Monday through Thursday, you would have a differential backup.

Using Dump   The **dump** utility is simple to use. The following example does a backup of the entire partition from the first IDE hard disk to the first nonrewinding SCSI tape device.

```
#dump -0 -uf  /dev/nrst0 /dev/hda1
```

In this example, the 0 defines the dump level, the **u** indicates that the /etc/dumpdates file, used by **dump** to store information on what files have been backed up, should be updated, and the **f** option specifies the device or filename to dump to. Alternatively, you can specify a file to be created by the dump and a specific directory as follows:

```
#dump -0 -uf /datacopy/newdump /database
```

This command does a level 0 dump of the /database directory to a file called *newdump* in the /datacopy directory. The flexibility of using dump in this way makes it a versatile tool.

Using restore   The partner to the **dump** utility is **restore**, which is used to browse dump archives and allow you to choose the files you want to restore. In its simplest usage, the restore command can be used with just the **f** option, which specifies the device name from which to restore, such as in this example:

```
#restore -rf /dev/st0
```

This causes a complete restore to be performed—handy if you want to restore an entire file system.

If you prefer, you can add the **i** option, which allows you to enter interactive mode. Interactive mode lets you navigate the archive just as if it were a mounted file system and select which files you want to restore. This is a good way to go if you are unsure of exactly which files you want to get back or if you want to specify lots of individual files. The **restore** command with the interactive option looks like this:

```
#restore -ivf /dev/st0
```

Notice that we have also added the **v** option, which makes the utility use verbose logging. This causes the names of the files being restored to be displayed on the screen. One last example. In the following command, we use the **-C** option, which can be used to check that the dump matches the files on the disk, equivalent to a verify.

```
#restore -Cf /dev/st0
```

dump and restore are interesting utilities, because they are more flexible than tar, yet not quite as simple to use as GUI-based products. If you like using the command line and can get the hang of the dump command usage, there is no reason why dump can't be used as your main backup utility. Combine dump with cron and a little shell scripting, and you can have a maintenance- and hassle-free backup system.

EXERCISE 11-3

Using Dump and Restore

1. Insert a blank ext2 floppy disk and mount it using the following command:

   ```
   #mount -t ext2 /dev/fd0 /mnt/floppy*
   ```

2. Use the following command to back up the directory to the floppy drive:

   ```
   #dump 0 -f /dev/fd0 /etc/rc.d
   ```

3. Once the dump is complete, use the following restore command to verify the dump:

   ```
   #restore -Cvf /dev/fd0
   ```

   *This command may need additional or different parameters, depending on your configuration.

Other Backup Packages

As mentioned at the beginning of this section, various backup packages are available for Linux in addition to the tools already mentioned. Some of these products cost thousands of dollars, while others cost less than a $100, and others are free. All of the products offer the same basic backup and restore options, normally through a choice of command-line or graphical utilities. What does differ between the higher-end packages and their less expensive counterparts are features such as disaster recovery functions that allow an entire system to be recovered quickly and easily. That's not to say that the lower-cost products don't offer such features; in fact, nowadays it's hard to find the differences at all sometimes, other than the simple fact that they tend to have a more basic set of tools than the more expensive applications.

If you do elect to go the route of purchasing a backup software package, you should still take the time to understand other utilities such as **tar** and **dump**, because you never know when you might find yourself without your chosen utility.

Testing Your Backups

There is an old saying in the system administration world that goes something like this: "What is the only type of good backup? One that can be restored." These are wise words indeed. Just after a hard disk crash is not the time to discover that the backups you were diligently making contain nothing but a series of log files. Test restores are a vital part of the backup process, and the only real way to tell whether the backups are working correctly. There are no hard and fast guidelines for test restores, but they should probably be performed biweekly; more frequently when the backups are first implemented or if changes are made to the backup process.

In between test restores, you should also check the log files for the backup to see if there have been any errors. Another prudent step is to verify the backup, an option that many backup programs include.

CERTIFICATION OBJECTIVE 11.11

Assessing, Performing, and Verifying Security Best Practices

Nowadays, everyone appears to be concerned about security, yet you would be surprised at just how lax some environments are when it comes to protecting their systems and, more importantly, the data on it. No one in an organization is more responsible for the security of a system than the system administrator, and a good portion of your time should be allotted to the setup and maintenance of security-related tasks and procedures.

exam

ⓦatch

The two CompTIA objectives, Assess Security Risks and Perform and verify security best practices, have a great deal of overlap. As a result, we have chosen to combine them into the same book objective.

Security of systems and data can be broken down into two sections: logical security, which deals with the security of the data while it is on the system, and physical security, which deals with the equipment on which the data resides, be that a server or a backup tape. We'll start by looking at logical security.

Logical Security

Logical security is a complex subject indeed. Part of the reason for this is that computer systems are complex in themselves. The other part is that computer systems often contain data to which people would like to get access. The combination of the two makes for some very interesting challenges.

Rather than cover specific topics that are not part of Linux+ anyway, we'll just look at some of the general considerations for the logical security of your system:

- **Make sure that users have strong passwords** We may be in the 21st century, but the good old username and password combination is still the de facto method of gaining access to the system. Retina scanners and the like are around, but they are still limited to implementations that have the money to use them. For the rest of us, passwords are the order of the day. Passwords should be made strong, as per the guidelines provided in Chapter 7. They should also be kept confidential and not be written on a sticky note tacked to the front of a user's terminal. The example may seem like old hat, but it really does happen. Users should also be educated to notice inconsistencies when entering passwords and know what procedure to follow when something odd does occur. Users should also be educated not to give password information over the phone, even though, from a support perspective, this can be a real pain.

- **Change the root account password** The root account password should be changed at regular intervals or immediately if you think it has been compromised.

- **Make sure password policies are in place** Users should be forced to change their passwords regularly. Password policies can be viewed and set with the chage command. For more information on the chage command, refer to Chapter 9.

- **Use passwords for the BIOS and applications**   Many systems have a BIOS that can be password protected, as do many software applications. Where appropriate, these optional passwords provide an extra layer of security that you should use.

- **Keep file permissions tight**   What the users can't see they won't try to delete! More often than not, data loss is not a malicious act but rather a case of finger trouble. Make sure that the permissions for a user are only enough to do what they need to do and no more. The time taken to set up permissions correctly will pay dividends in the long run.

- **Manage unused accounts**   When an individual leaves the organization, their user account should be removed from the system as soon as is practical. For user accounts that aren't going to be used for some time, such as a user who is on maternity leave, the account could be disabled rather than deleted. The procedure for both of these actions was described in Chapter 9. You should also periodically check the /etc/passwd file to make sure that there are no unauthorized user accounts defined.

- **Manage services appropriately**   Ensure that services that are not necessary are disabled, and that those that are enabled are configured to be as secure as possible. Each and every service that is provided by a system is a potential security hole.

- **Secure sensitive data**   If the system holds sensitive data, special care must be taken to ensure that the permissions for the file system are correct so that people cannot access the sensitive data by accident or intent. If the data is sufficiently sensitive, consider placing it on a completely separate server.

- **Check your system**   Or have your system checked. Various software packages are available to test the security of your system, along with any number of people who are willing to test them for you. Periodic testing of the system can highlight deficiencies before they become a problem. This is particularly relevant if you are offering services to clients on the Internet.

- **Keep information up to date**   Information on security issues is released on a daily basis. Keep an eye and ear out for information that might be relevant to your system and act on information you receive. That said, always be sure of your source before making a change. It has been known for unscrupulous individuals to advise another administrator to make a certain change so that access can be gained to the system. Where possible, verify information is from a trusted source (or two) before acting on it.

■ **Check log files**   Linux has many log files that offer insight into the goings-on of a system. Check the log files regularly and act on anything suspicious.

For more information on Linux security, refer to one of the many excellent books dedicated to the topic.

Physical Security

Some might say that physical security is easier to manage than logical security because you are dealing with the tangible. Even if this is true, physical security deserves no less initial attention than logical security, even if on an ongoing basis it is not as time consuming.

Physical security is about protecting the physical elements of your server, either against accidental damage, such as a spilt cup of coffee, or malicious damage, such as someone actually stealing your system. Here are some guidelines that you should consider:

■ **Ensure that servers are kept in a secure location**   It is very common for servers to be located in a secure room or, at the very least, a locked cupboard. If you are not doing this, consider it. If you are, make sure that access to the area is controlled and limited to only those people who need access.

■ **Control access to system documentation**   Although system documentation should not include really sensitive information such as passwords, there is still enough information contained in it that you would not want it to be seen by people who have no reason to see it. Keep the system documentation in a safe place and, if necessary, create some kind of access control system to regulate who can get at it.

exam
ⓦatch

Most security measures are based on common sense. If you get an exam question and you are unsure of the answer (which is unlikely if you have read the information presented here!), fall back on common sense and take an educated guess. You will most likely be right!

■ **Keep backup tapes secure** A commonly overlooked aspect of data security is that of backup tapes. A backup that contains a full backup of your system contains a copy of every file that is on it. If, as you should do, these tapes are stored offsite, the possibility that someone might think about stealing a tape must be considered. Tapes taken offsite need to be transported and stored securely. Information about the transport and storage of tapes should be on a need-to-know basis, and if possible, tapes should be password-protected and encrypted. This rule should actually be applied to all removable media, not just backup tapes.

on the
Ö o b *No matter how well your server is physically protected, resist the temptation to leave the server logged in with the root account.*

One last note on the subject of security generally is this: security, along with other protective measures such as backups, is designed to protect your investment in the equipment and the data that resides on it. Not taking the necessary precautions can cause an interruption in the operation of your business, not to mention your career.

CERTIFICATION OBJECTIVE 11.12

Setting Daemons and Processing Permissions

When a daemon or process is run, it is run with the permissions of the person who runs it. That means that if the process or daemon attempts, as part of its run, to access a file or process to which the user doesn't have permission, the process or daemon will fail. In most cases, this is okay, because chances are the person shouldn't be running the file in the first place if they don't have the right permissions. On occasion, however, a daemon or process may need access that is not available to the user who runs it. That's where SUIDs and SGIDs come in.

SUID and SGID

If the Set UID (SUID) attribute is set on a file and the file is executable, the process runs with the permissions of the owner of the file, no matter who runs it. That means that a daemon or process can run and access system resources, or other processes that may be needed, without assigning those rights to the person running it. The same can be said for SGID, except that the file gets the rights for the group instead.

To set a file to have the SUID and GUID permissions, you can use the following command:

```
#chmod ug+s filename
```

To remove the permissions from a file, you use the command but just use a minus sign instead of a plus sign. It is also possible to set a SGID permission on a directory, which causes all files created in the directory to have their group set to the directories group.

Having said all this, you need to be aware of the fact that having files with the SUID and SGID set present a serious security issue. Only set the SUID and SGID if you are sure that you need to.

To find files on your system that have the permissions set, use the following command:

```
#find / -perm +ug+s | less
```

This will cause the file system to be searched from the root and the results to be displayed in the **less** utility.

CERTIFICATION SUMMARY

As mentioned at the beginning of this chapter, the Maintenance domain of the Linux+ Exam Objectives is truly one of diverse topics, and covers a range of the tasks that you will find yourself performing in the day-to-day maintenance of a Linux system. Some of the topics covered, such as using fdisk, you will perform rarely. Others, like backing up, will be performed on a daily basis.

As with the other topics covered in this book, the information presented in this chapter is just the basic information for each topic. Spend time learning more about each of the utilities mentioned when you get a chance, and consult the man pages for commands before using them. This is particularly true of utilities such as fdisk, which can cause massive problems if not used correctly and carefully.

TWO-MINUTE DRILL

Creating and Managing Local Storage Devices and File Systems

❏ The fdisk utility can be used to create and manage storage devices.

❏ The mkfs utility is used to call file system–specific utilities that create file systems.

❏ The fsck utility can run automatically when the system is booted or can be run manually for unmounted file systems.

Verifying User and Root cron Jobs and Understanding the Function of cron

❏ cron allows jobs to be scheduled to run at regular intervals.

❏ System cron jobs are stored in subdirectories of the /etc directory.

❏ Users can add cron jobs of their own using the crontab utility.

Identifying Core Dumps and Removing or Forwarding as Appropriate

❏ Core dumps are created when a process or application fails.

❏ Core dump files are named "core" and can be up to the size of the memory in the system.

❏ Core dump files can be deleted or forwarded for troubleshooting purposes.

Running and Interpreting ifconfig

❏ The ifconfig utility enables you to view and set configuration information on network adapters.

❏ The ifconfig utility provides a range of information, including statistics about the network.

Downloading and Installing Patches and Updates

❏ Patches and updates are released to fix problems in a kernel or application or add new functionality.

❑ Patches and updates are commonly provided in compressed format.

❑ Patches or updates should be applied only after you have determined that the changes are necessary for your system. Read accompanying documentation carefully.

Identifying, Executing, and Killing Processes

❑ The ps command can be used to identify processes on the system that have stopped.

❑ The kill command can be used to send a signal to those processes to terminate.

❑ The killall command can be used to kill all occurrences of a process.

Differentiating Core Services from Noncritical Services

❑ Some services are kernel services and cannot be killed.

❑ Each process has a parent, the PID of which is referred to as the parent process ID (PPID).

❑ The parent of all processes is **init**, which is always assigned the PID of 1.

Monitoring System Log Files

❑ Log files should be monitored and checked on a regular basis to detect problems with the system processes and to detect security issues.

❑ Various tools, including cat and grep, can be used to view and extract information from log files.

Documenting Work Performed on a System

❑ Whenever work is performed on the system, documentation should be updated to reflect the changes.

❑ Inadequate or incorrect documentation updates make troubleshooting the system difficult or even impossible.

Performing and Verifying Backups and Restores

❑ Backups protect against data loss from a variety of potential threats.

❑ Linux supports a range of devices that can be used for backups.

❑ A number of utilities are available for backing up Linux.

Performing and Verifying Security Best Practices

❑ Security is a primary concern for any system administrator.

❑ Security typically falls into two categories: logical, which pertains to the security of the data, and physical, which refers to the security of the systems that hold the data.

❑ Security is necessary to protect the investment in data and equipment and to ensure continuity of service.

Assessing Security Risks

❑ File permissions must be configured to be as secure as possible.

❑ Unused user accounts should be disabled or deleted as appropriate.

❑ Access to systems should be closely controlled and systems should be kept secure.

Setting Daemons and Process Permissions

❑ Executable files can have a SUID and SGID set on them that allow the file to be executed with the permission of the file's owner or group rights.

❑ Executable files that require access to other processes or devices may require the SUID or SGID permission to be set.

❑ Files with the SUID and SGID permission represent a security risk, and the permissions should not be assigned unless absolutely necessary.

SELF TEST

The following questions will help determine your level of understanding of the material presented in this chapter. Some of the questions may have more than one correct answer, so be sure to review all answers carefully before choosing all that apply.

Creating and Managing Local Storage Devices and File Systems

1. Which of the following utilities would you use to create a file system?

   A. mkfs

   B. fdisk

   C. cfs

   D. fsck

2. Which two of the following commands could you use to create an ext2 floppy disk?

   A. mke2fs /dev/fd0

   B. mkfs -t ext2 /dev/fd0

   C. mkfs -f ext2 /dev/fd0

   D. mke2fs -t ext2 /dev/fd0

Verifying User and Root cron Jobs and Understanding the Function of cron

3. Which of the following commands would you use to add a job to a user's crontab while logged in as root?

   A. crontab -u tom -l

   B. crontab -u tom -a

   C. crontab -u tom -e

   D. crontab tom -e

Identifying Core Dumps and Removing or Forwarding As Appropriate

4. Which of the following commands would you use to determine what application or process created a core dump?

   A. file

   B. coreid

C. find

D. showcore

5. What are two reasons why the presence of core dumps would concern you?

   A. They can be large and take up lots of disk space.

   B. They indicate that the version of the kernel you are using is a development release.

   C. They indicate that a process is failing.

   D. They indicate that there is a problem in the file system.

Running and Interpreting ifconfig

6. When using the **ifconfig** command to bring up a network interface, which of the following pieces of information would you NOT provide?

   A. IP address

   B. Subnet mask

   C. Hostname

   D. Broadcast address

Downloading and Installing Patches and Updates

7. From reading the latest news section on the Web site for your Linux distribution, you determine that a patch is available for the system. If and when would you install it?

   A. After it has been available for a week or two and tested by other people.

   B. As soon as you can schedule down time for the system.

   C. If your system is running fine, you would not install it.

   D. If the patch cures a specific problem or corrects a certain deficiency on your system.

8. What utility is used to apply Linux kernel patches?

   A. updatep

   B. makeupd

   C. patch

   D. kpupdate

Identifying, Executing, and Killing Processes

9. Which two of the following commands cause a process with a number of 632 to reread its configuration files?

    A. kill -15 632

    B. kill -9 632

    C. kill -1 632

    D. kill -HUP 632

10. What three pieces of information are provided by the **ps** command?

    A. The process ID

    B. The owner of the process

    C. The status of the process

    D. The IP address of the terminal owning the process

11. Which of the following commands would you use to kill a process with a PID of 517?

    A. kill 517

    B. kill pid-517

    C. kill -p 517

    D. kill -s 517

Differentiating Core Services from Noncritical Services

12. What is the significance of square brackets around a process when looking at a listing produced by the ps command?

    A. The process has died.

    B. The task is a kernel task and cannot be killed.

    C. The task is sleeping.

    D. The task is being run from another virtual terminal.

Monitoring System Log Files

13. Which of the following commands would you use to view the mail.log file?

    A. grep mail.log

    B. cat mail.log | less

C.   cat mail.log | grep

D.   view mail.log

Documenting Work Performed on a System

14. Which three of the following pieces of information are included in a documentation update?

A.   Hard copies of updated configuration files

B.   Contact information for the person who completed the update

C.   The time and date the update took place

D.   The amount of time the documentation update took

Performing and Verifying Backups and Restores

15. Which of the following devices would you use to write more than one backup set to the first SCSI tape in the system?

A.   /dev/st1

B.   /dev/sta

C.   /dev/nst0

D.   /dev/st0

16. What does a dump level of 0 cause to happen?

A.   All files on the system that have been changed since the last higher-level backup are backed up.

B.   All files on the system that have changed since the last level 0 backup are backed up.

C.   All the files on the file system are backed up.

D.   All files on the file system that have a dump level value of 0 are backed up.

17. Which of the following options do you use with the restore utility to select individual files for restore?

A.   -r

B.   -v

C.   -i

D.   -C

Assessing Security Risks and Performing and Verifying Security Best Practices

18. Which of the following would you *not* consider a physical security consideration?

    A. Secure transport of backup tapes

    B. Controlling access to the room in which the system is located

    C. Correct setting of file permissions

    D. Controlling access to system documentation

Setting Daemons and Processing Permissions

19. Which of the following commands would you use to set the SUID attribute on a file called commd?

    A. chmod u+s commd

    B. chmod g+s commd

    C. chmod commd g+s

    D. chown g+s commd

20. What is the purpose of the SUID permission?

    A. It allows a file to be executed with the supervisor permission.

    B. It allows a file to be executed with the permissions of the owner.

    C. It allows a file to be executed with the permissions of a group.

    D. It allows a file to be executed with the permissions provided on the command line

LAB QUESTION

In this exercise, you will design a new backup solution for a server system, including specifying hardware and downloading and evaluating backup software.

    The server in question has a total of 30GB of hard disk space and holds a large database that is approximately 15GB in size. Various changes occur to the database file each day. Relatively little other data is on the server, apart from the operating system and some read-only documents that define procedures for working with the database.

        ■ What tape format/backup hardware would you recommend?

- What backup software would you recommend?
- What frequency and type of backups would you recommend?

Use the Internet to find information on each issue, and make recommendations based on the information you find. The cost of the solution is a consideration, so try to recommend the most cost-effective solution available.

SELF TEST ANSWERS

Creating and Managing Local Storage Devices and File Systems

1. ☑ **A.** The mkfs utility can be used to create a new file system on a device.
   ☒ **B.** The fdisk utility is used to partition devices and make them ready for use. **C.** This is not a valid Linux command. **D.** The fsck utility is used to check file systems for errors.

2. ☑ **A, B.** Both of these commands will create an ext2 file system on a floppy disk.
   ☒ **C.** The option that denotes the file system type is **-t**, not **-f**. **D.** The mke2fs command is only used to create ext2 file systems. Therefore, there is no need for the file system to be specified.

Verifying User and Root cron Jobs and Understanding the Function of cron

3. ☑ **C.** This command would allow you to add a cron job for the user Tom while logged in as the root user.
   ☒ **A.** This command would list the cron jobs set for the user Tom. **B.** The -a switch is not valid with cron. **D.** When logged in as root, it is possible to edit the cron jobs for a user, but the **-u** switch must be used and the name supplied.

Identifying Core Dumps and Removing or Forwarding As Appropriate

4. ☑ **A.** The file command can be used to determine what process created a core dump file.
   ☒ **B.** This is not a valid Linux command. **C.** The find command can be used to locate core dump files. **D.** This is not a valid Linux command.

5. ☑ **A, C.** Core dumps are created when a process on the system fails. The files can be quite large, because, unless they are restricted, they will be approximately the size of the memory installed in a system. If core dumps are created often, it will be necessary to investigate the cause.
   ☒ **B.** Kernels that are in development have an odd minor revision number; for example, 2.3.9. Core dumps are created by all Linux versions, irrespective of their being a development release. **D.** Core dumps can be created for a number of reasons. The file system may be an issue but is far less likely than numerous other causes. Certainly, the presence of core dumps is not an indication that there is a problem with the file system.

Running and Interpreting ifconfig

6. ☑ **C.** When using the ifconfig command to bring up a network interface, the hostname parameter is not valid.

  ☒ **A, B,D.** All of these are valid parammeters when using ifconfig.

Downloading and Installing Patches and Updates

7. ☑ **C.** A patch should be installed only after it has been established that it cures a specific problem on your system or corrects a certain deficiency from which you might suffer. Otherwise, patches should not be installed.

  ☒ **D.** Companies and organizations generally only release patches after they have been fully tested, or they make you aware of the fact in the accompanying documentation. Therefore, it should not be necessary to wait for others to try it. **B.** Down time may need to be scheduled, but only after the criteria described in answer D has been established. **C.** The documentation will inform you of what the update addresses. It may be that the deficiency is a security hole; therefore, you must not assume that the patch is not needed just because the system is operating correctly.

8. ☑ **C.** The **patch** command is used to apply Linux kernel patches. Patches must be downloaded and decompressed before they can be applied.

  ☒ **A, B, D.** These are not valid Linux commands.

Identifying, Executing, and Killing Processes

9. ☑ **C, D.** The HUP signal will, in most cases, cause the process to reread its configuration files. The HUP signal can be specified by using the letters HUP or passed using the **1** signal.

  ☒ **A.** This command causes the SIGTERM signal to be issued. The default signal level used by the kill command is 15. **B.** The SIGKILL signal (-9) is used to forcibly destroy a particular process.

10. ☑ **A, B, C.** All of these pieces of information are supplied by the ps command.

  ☒ **D.** The IP address of the terminal owning the process is not supplied by the ps command.

11. ☑ **A.** The only required option for the kill command is the process ID number, or PID.

  ☒ **B.** The PID can be passed on its own. The **pid** switch is not valid. **C.** The -p option for the kill command causes the kill command to display the PID of the named process. **D.** The -s option is used to specify the signal number that is sent to the process. If no signal number is supplied, the default is used.

Differentiating Core Services from Noncritical Services

12. ☑ **B**. Square brackets around a process name in the **ps** command output indicate that it's a kernel task and cannot be killed.
    ☒ **A, C**. The status of a process is provided by the STAT column in the output from the ps -aux command. **D**. The owning terminal for a process is given in the TTY column of the output from the ps -aux command.

Monitoring System Log Files

13. ☑ **B**. The cat command can be used to view files. By piping the output from the **cat** command into the less command, the file can be viewed more easily.
    ☒ **A**. This command would not do anything. **C**. The grep command pulls specified lines of text from a file and displays them. The text to be searched for must be supplied with the grep command, so this usage of the command is incomplete. **D**. The view command is not a valid Linux command.

Documenting Work Performed on a System

14. ☑ **A, B, C**. All of these pieces of information should be included in a documentation update.
    ☒ **D**. This information is irrelevant and does not need to be included in the documentation.

Performing and Verifying Backups and Restores

15. ☑ **C**. The nonrewinding tape driver allows more than one archive to be written to a tape. The designation method is the same as for the standard SCSI tape devices, insofar as the numbering system starts at 0 for the first device.
    ☒ **A**. This designation would be correct for the second nonrewinding SCSI device. **B**. IDE devices use an alphabetical designation, whereas SCSI uses numeric. **D**. This designation would be correct for the first rewinding SCSI tape device.

16. ☑ **C**. A dump level of 0 is used to create a full system backup.
    ☒ **A**. The dump utility uses levels for determining what files should be backed up. Level 0 indicates that all files on the system should be backed up. **B**. dump backs up all files that have changed or been created since the last dump of a lower level. As 0 is the lowest level, all files are backed up. **D**. dump values are not assigned to files.

17. ☑ **C.** The **-i** option takes you into interactive mode when using restore. In this mode, you can select individual files to be restored.

    ☒ **A.** The **-r** option performs a full file system restore. **B.** The **-v** option switches the restore utility into verbose mode, causing filenames to be displayed during the restore. **D.** The **-C** option can be used to verify the contents of a dump.

Assessing Security Risks and Performing and Verifying Security Best Practices

18. ☑ **C.** Correctly setting file permissions would be considered a logical security consideration.

    ☒ **A, B, C.** These would all be considered physical security considerations.

Setting Daemons and Processing Permissions

19. ☑ **A.** The **chmod** command is used to set file permissions. This usage would correctly set the SUID permission for the file commd.

    ☒ **B.** This command is correct for setting the SGID, not the SUID. **C.** The options must be passed before the filename. **D.** The **chown** command is used to change the ownership of a file, not the file permissions.

20. ☑ **B.** The SUID permission allows the files to be executed with the permissions of the file's owner.

    ☒ **A.** Linux has no such permission as supervisor. **C.** The SGID permission must be set for a file to be executed with the permissions of the owning group. **D.** This answer is fictitious.

LAB ANSWER

Because the information on the server is relatively static, after the initial backup is taken, it would only be necessary to back up the database file. However, because the data in the database changes daily, the backups would need to be taken daily as well.

It is good practice to have a backup device that can accommodate the entire disk space, whether or not there is data on it. Therefore, a backup format with at least 30GB capacity is required. Of the current popular formats, this would mean that DDS-4, DLT formats, and 8MM tapes would all be options.

As for the backup software to be used, you could elect to go with the standard utilities such as tar or dump, or you could opt for one of the free-to-use applications such as Amanda (http://ww.amanda.org). Alternatively, you could choose to purchase a backup program.

Given that the database exists within a single file, even the most basic utility would be suitable.

12

Troubleshooting

Troubleshooting is an inescapable part of working with computers and will often comprise a large portion of your daily tasks. Troubleshooting encompasses many facets and requires a diverse range of skills, including knowledge of both hardware and software configurations. You will find yourself troubleshooting in three distinct areas:

- **Workstation** Includes everything related to the workstation computers, from the keyboard to the wall jack.
- **Server** Includes all server-related settings and functioning, which may involve diagnosing and troubleshooting server applications.
- **Network** Includes all network-related equipment and configurations.

Each of these areas requires different approaches, strategies, and knowledge. When you start the troubleshooting process, one of your first steps is to determine which one of these areas will require your attention.

We chose to include hardware troubleshooting much earlier in the book in Chapter 4, because it seemed to fit better as a preinstallation topic rather than a post-installation topic.

This chapter focuses on all three areas of troubleshooting, touching on all the CompTIA objectives along the way. Remember, because troubleshooting plays such an important part in the role of the system administrator, you can expect it to be well represented in the Linux+ exam.

CERTIFICATION OBJECTIVE 12.01

Identifying and Locating the Problem

Troubleshooting is a whole lot easier if you know what it is you are troubleshooting. Before attempting any corrective action, you must first determine whether the problem is a hardware- or software-related issue. Being able to distinguish between the two is a skill that develops over time and increases as you work with computers. Certain errors are a giveaway, such as a system that will not boot or errors given during the boot process. Others, such as memory-related errors, have a nasty way of disguising themselves as software errors or even another hardware error. Although this makes troubleshooting a gray area, you will be required to work through the fog to be able to proficiently manage and troubleshoot Linux systems.

Hardware

Hardware troubleshooting was covered in detail in Chapter 4, but to review, problems with hardware are most likely to be evident on a new system or on a system after new hardware is added. Good administrators are rarely surprised by hardware problems, because they diligently monitor logs and run status utilities on the various hardware components in an effort to preemptively identify hardware errors. But let's be honest: not all of us are that proactive.

Hardware problems, including with memory, hard disks, or CPU, will often show themselves during boot, but not always. For example, a hard drive with bad sectors won't necessarily be detected during the boot process, and the same can be said about incompatible or malfunctioning memory modules. In both instances, you are more likely to notice them during operation, and when they do surface, they may (misleadingly) appear as software errors.

In attempting to diagnose hardware errors, you may need to use the various utilities within Linux to isolate the cause. Resource and status troubleshooting utilities are covered later in this chapter.

Software Errors

Unfortunately, software errors are not that uncommon, and you will be required to troubleshoot them as an administrator. For the most part, software errors seldom come out of nowhere. More likely, you will encounter a software error after the installation of a new application, during the installation or upgrade of Linux itself, or when changes are made to software configurations. Under such circumstances, the problem is easy to locate—that is, of course, if you are aware of the installation of a new application or changes made to the configuration of the system. With this in mind, when you are confronted with a troubleshooting situation, it is a good idea to ascertain whether any changes have been made to the system recently, including the installation of any new software packages. Your first step in this respect should be to check the system documentation, which will include all the changes that have been made. There is more information on documentation in Chapters 8 and 11. Outside of the documentation, the log files created by the system will also play a role.

User Configuration Errors

Undocumented changes to a computer system are the bane of network administrators, and no one is "better" at making these changes than users. It is just a fact that computer users will install programs and change system settings from time to time, forget about it, and then call you to troubleshoot the system. Considering the large number of settings that can be changed, identifying where and what was changed can be very difficult. Over time, however, you will find that you become more efficient at getting to the bottom of these problems, because they tend to be isolated to a few areas, such as printer configuration, networks settings, and various application-specific settings. Not to mention the fact that your questioning and interpretation techniques will improve.

The simple solution to identifying user configuration errors is to question the user for changes made to the system, including any software installations, upgrades, or changes to the configuration. If they deny knowledge of any of these, rephrase the question and gently ask again. Your next recourse is to identify and review system logs for any installation activity. Finally, review all the common configuration hotspots to ensure nothing has changed. Fortunately, many of the settings that can cause user problems are only accessible to the root account and not easily changed.

CERTIFICATION OBJECTIVE 12.02

Describing Troubleshooting Best Practices

When a computer problem arises, computer users tend to get into crisis mode very quickly, and you may find yourself with a roomful of disgruntled users anxiously waiting for you to spin a little Linux troubleshooting magic. The temptation for many administrators in such a situation is to just start fixing things with no rhyme or reason. This can often cause more problems than it fixes. Instead, regardless of the apparent urgency and impending pink slip, a more methodical and polished troubleshooting strategy is needed.

on the **!** job

Sometimes, you may not even be able to get into your Linux system to begin troubleshooting. If this is the case, you can try to boot into single-user mode, which will not start most of the daemons and therefore hopefully get Linux started. Single-user mode can be accessed by typing single *at the LILO prompt.*

Troubleshooting the Scientific Way

A scientific and methodical approach to troubleshooting allows you to determine and eliminate the problem as quickly as possible. It's kind of like hearing a noise in your car's engine; you could immediately start replacing car parts until one fixes the problem, or you could try to isolate the problem first to replace the correct part. That is what the scientific approach is all about.

Within the IT world, there is no agreement on the exact steps a scientific troubleshooting approach should take, but there are some common steps most everyone seems to agree on. With that disclaimer, let's look at some steps you can take, or perhaps should take, when you are trying to get to the bottom of a problem.

Getting the Information

Whatever the problem is you are trying to fix, the first part of the process has to be information gathering. It is important that, before heading off to fix any problem, you take the time to find out as much information as you can about the issue. This information can be gathered from computer users, system log files, other administrators, or error messages generated by the system. Regardless of where you get your information from, you need to address the following questions.

- **Whom does the problem affect?** When troubleshooting a Linux system on a network, you will need to know if it is isolated to a person, a group of people, an entire section of the network, or the entire network. Determining who the issue affects is usually as simple as showing up to work, because you are sure to be greeted by the people who are having difficulty with their systems.

- **What computers are affected?** It may be that the problem is isolated to a single computer, whether a server or workstation, or the problem may affect numerous computers. Knowing what computers are affected can significantly help isolate the problem.

■ **What was the computer doing at the time of failure?**   You will need to know if the problem was occurring during the boot process, while using a specific application, or during any other usage, which can help you to narrow down the problem. Identifying what the computer was doing at the time of failure goes a long way toward reducing the time it takes to isolate the problem and determining if the problem is hardware or software related.

■ **How often does the problem happen?**   You may be trying to troubleshoot a problem that is occurring for the first time or one that occurs frequently. Determining the frequency of the problem is often overlooked in the heat of the crisis, but it can be very helpful in isolating the exact cause, or at least eliminating a few reasons.

■ **What has been done in the past to fix the problem?**   If you are lucky enough, you may be able to determine whether attempts have been made in the past to fix this or a similar problem. Unfortunately, the documentation of past fixes isn't always what it should be and it is often difficult to get the straight scoop from the computer users. If you are able to identify past attempts at fixing the problem, it can save you from going down the same road again.

Making an Informed Guess

After you have all the information gathered, you are ready to take an informed guess at what the problem is. This is actually where most people start the troubleshooting process, but it really does work better when you have the information you need before making the guess. It kind of takes the word *informed* out of the equation if you do not. The information you have gathered allows you to eliminate many potential causes of the problem while simultaneously focusing on the more likely solutions.

Testing Your Hypothesis

Here is where the rubber hits the road. You have all the information you could gather and your best guess in hand. Now, you need to see whether you are right. Of course, this may involve doing a little preemptive work before attempting your fix, such as backups or acquiring the necessary resources. Whether or not your hypothesis was correct, you need to document what you did to try to fix the problem. Include in the documentation the steps you took and any changes to the system that were made. More often than not, you may find yourself retracing your steps to get back to where you were. Troubleshooting is not meant to make the problem worse.

Verifying the Test Results

After you have seemingly successfully remedied the problem, take the time to verify that everything works. Sometimes, the changes you make while troubleshooting may affect other system components or applications. It is worth the effort to try to work with the corrected system in a production scenario, meaning all programs and system tools are tested and verified to be working. It may well be that you do not have the time or means to test immediately, but come back and test thoroughly when you have the chance.

Documenting Procedure

Documentation is as important as any of the other troubleshooting steps. If a problem happens once, it may happen again; the difference is that the next time the problem happens, you can simply refer to your documentation and apply the fix. It is an all-too-rare occurrence when this happens, because documentation procedures often rank very low on the priority list.

You may need to run through these steps more than once to get to the root of the problem. Remember not to skip any of the steps in the troubleshooting process, it might make the process take longer than it needs to be.

FROM THE CLASSROOM

Escalation Procedures

In the pressure cooker that is troubleshooting, it is often the first impulse to agree to fix everything and anything. Sometimes, however, it's just not your problem and the issue should be passed to the appropriate person. In some organizations, escalation procedures for system problems are well documented. In others, you are left to rely on common sense. In short, if you are not comfortable with a problem or procedure, get help. There are many instances on systems—Linux and otherwise—where pursuing the wrong troubleshooting path will make problems go from bad to worse very quickly. Be honest with yourself and know where your limits are.

—*Drew Bird, Linux+ Certified*

CERTIFICATION OBJECTIVE 12.03

Editing Configuration Files Based on the Symptoms of a Problem

As you may have guessed from reading previous chapters, Linux is full of text-based configuration files. From time to time, you will need to get dirty and go through these files as part of your troubleshooting procedures. Some of the more common Linux configuration files are shown in Table 12-1, along with their purposes.

The utilities used to work with these configuration files include **vi** for editing, **grep** for extracting information from them, and **cat** for displaying the files themselves. In fact, when trying to track down a problem in a configuration file, **cat** may be more appropriate because it allows you to display the file without editing it, thereby preventing accidental changes. For example, using **cat** to view the /etc/passwd file and piping the information into the **less** utility lets you read through the file looking for the information you need. An example of this looks like the following:

```
#cat /etc/passwd | less
```

CERTIFICATION OBJECTIVE 12.04

Starting and Stopping Processes Based on the Symptoms of a Problem

In some cases, even after checking configuration files and log files, verifying connectivity, and eliminating user error, you may still find that a service is unavailable, in which case it may be necessary to stop and restart the process. In Chapter 11, we covered the process of identifying and killing processes with the ps and kill commands. In addition, many of the scripts used to start processes have a status option that can be used to determine whether the process is running.

TABLE 12-1   Common Linux Configuration Files and Their Purposes

Filename	Purpose	Potential Error(s)
/etc/lilo.conf	Supplies configuration information for LILO	Boot-related problems; booting directly into an operating system without an option to choose.
/etc/fstab	Defines the file system mounted during boot	If a file system is not mounted at boot, as it is expected to, but can be mounted manually, check the corresponding entry in the fstab file.
/etc/inetd.conf	Defines which network services are available on the server	If a user is unable to connect to a service and the service should be available, ensure that the service is enabled in the inetd.conf.
/etc/host.allow/etc/host.deny	Used to manage access to the system by remote hosts and users	If a user cannot connect to a service, make sure he has correct access rights configured in these files.
/etc/inittab	Controls runlevels	If the system does not boot as expected, check the default runlevel.
/etc/passwd & /etc/shadow	User account information	If a user cannot log on, make sure the user account has not been deleted and the account is still enabled.
/etc/resolv.conf	DNS server information	If you can ping a remote IP address but not the corresponding hostname, check that the DNS configuration is correct.
/etc/X11/XF86Config	X Window configuration	If you experience problems accessing the X Window System, check the configuration or reconfigure using a tool such as Xconfigurator.
/etc/printcap	Printer configurations	If you are experiencing problems with printing or lpd will not load, check the configuration in the /etc/printcap file.

Table 12-2 identifies some common processes, how to start and stop them, and under which conditions this may be necessary. Always remember that starting and stopping a process affects every person that is accessing that service. For this reason, you should start and stop a service only after you have established that the problem does not lie elsewhere.

TABLE 12-2   Common Services, Shutdown Procedures, and Signs of Failure

Process	Script and Options	Signs of Failure
inetd	./inetd start|stop|restart	Unable to connect to any network services.
web server	./httpd start|stop|restart	Web server not functioning correctly.
dns	./named start|stop|restart	Name resolution has failed.
dhcp	./dhcpd start|stop|restart	Systems cannot provide IP addresses to clients.
samba	./smb start|stop|restart	Windows clients cannot access services.
lpd	./lpd start|stop|restart	Unable to print.
nfs	./nfs start|stop|restart	Users cannot connect to NFS shares.

Other services may also need to be stopped and restarted as part of the troubleshooting process.

Using Tools to Determine System Status

To be effective in troubleshooting a computer problem, whether hardware or software, you need to know the tools that are available for you to use. Like many other Linux utilities, when it comes to tools for viewing system resources and statuses, some are available for the GUI while others are strictly command-line tools. If you find yourself working on a Linux server, be prepared to use the command-line utilities, because X Window System may not be installed.

As you might expect, the tool you choose for your troubleshooting largely depends on what resource you are troubleshooting. Table 12-3 shows some of the common utilities.

exam
ⓦatch

You must be able to identify the system resource tools and their functions.

| TABLE 12-3 | Commonly Used Tools for Viewing System Status and Resources |

Tool/Utility	Description
fsck	Used to check and, optionally, repair Linux file systems. fsck automatically detects the file system to be checked and loads the appropriate utility.
e2fsck	Used to examine the ext2 file system for errors, which it will fix along the way. If you are troubleshooting and getting errors when opening files, this command is used to determine whether the file system is at fault.
setserial	Used to give you information on your serial ports, including the device drivers used, I/O address, and IRQ usage.
statserial	Used to show the current status of your serial ports. This command is very useful when troubleshooting a serial port or a modem. You must have root user access to use the **statserial** command.
top	Command-line utility used to monitor CPU, physical, and swap memory usage, and the total number of processes in use. **top** is a dynamic utility and is continually refreshed.
vmstat	Provides summary information about the entire system, including I/O, CPU, and memory statistics. If you suspect a problem with any of these statistics, this utility may be your best friend.
/proc directory	Use of the /proc directory was covered in Chapters 3 and 4. Useful commands for troubleshooting and viewing resources with /proc include /proc/meminfo, /proc/cpuinfo, /proc/dma, and /proc/pci.
ps	Displays a list of currently loaded processes, who is using them, and what resources they are using.

CERTIFICATION OBJECTIVE 12.06

Using Boot Disks in the Recovery Process

Sometimes your system will stop working, and you will need to use Linux rescue disks to get back into your system, at least try and get back in your system. A rescue boot disk can be made during the Linux installation and should be kept current, even after the installation. The process of creating a boot varies between distributions, and it may be necessary to review the distribution's Web site for the exact procedures. The

Linux boot disk is essentially a mini-Linux system on floppy that is fully capable of starting your system. To be used as a repair disk, it has to be able to provide many of the functions and tools that a fully operational Linux system can. Reference to a "boot recovery disk" can be confusing, because it often refers to more than a single disk:

- **Boot disk**   Contains a kernel version that is loaded from the floppy and starts the system. The boot disk is often used when the file system or LILO is corrupt and the system will not boot. Every Linux administrator should have access to a boot disk.

- **Root disk**   Once the kernel has been loaded, the root disk can be used to run the file system independently. The root disk is also known as the rescue disk and can be made with the rescue image file, *rescue.img*. A rescue disk can be used when fixing a damaged Linux system and, as an added bonus, contains a copy of important system files that can be restored if necessary. To be useful, this disk has to be upgraded on a regular basis.

- **Boot/root disk**   It is possible to have the root and boot disk on the same floppy. As you might expect, this can only be done if all of your information fits on a single disk. As your system develops, it is likely you will be forced to use separate disks.

When you read or hear about a boot disk, generally the reference is to both a root and boot disk, but they are separate entities. Both disks should be periodically updated and kept in a secure location.

CERTIFICATION OBJECTIVE 12.07

Determining the Cause of Errors from System Log Files

A key part of Linux troubleshooting is accessing the correct logs to identify and analyze error messages. There are log files in Linux that contain records of almost everything that happens in your Linux system. If you know what you are looking for, you can see whether someone has attempted to access your system, hardware has been loaded properly, or resource conflicts exist.

When it comes to log files, you will be accessing two basic types: software logs, which are generally written by specific applications such as Apache, and system logs, which provide documentation on system processes and at bootup.

Configuring and Reviewing System Logs

Log file configuration is kept in the /etc/syslog.conf file. Configuring this file is not always necessary, because the default settings are generally good enough. Within the syslog.conf file, each entry within the file has both *facility* and *priority* assigned to it. The facility tells from where the message originated, and the priority lets you know how important the message is. By reviewing the syslog.conf file, you can determine where the system is sending the log files.

You will find that, most often, the log files are sent to the /var/log directory, but some or all may not be. It is also possible to redirect log files to a different host or system. This is a good idea if you want to centralize a network's log files. For your own interest, you can explore the syslog.conf file and modify these settings. The configuration of the syslog.conf file falls outside of the Linux+ objectives, but as an administrator, you will need to become familiar with the format and purpose of the file.

Now that you know where log files are configured and where they are kept, you can use the logs when troubleshooting your system. As an example, review a sample section from the syslog file. Are you able to find the error in the log?

```
Sep4 02:52:21 server rc.sysinit: Finding module dependencies succeeded
Sep4 02:52:21 server : Loading module: scsi_hostadapter
Sep4 02:52:21 server rc.sysinit: Checking filesystems succeeded
Sep4 02:52:22 server rc.sysinit: Mounting local filesystems succeeded
Sep4 02:52:22 server rc.sysinit: Checking loopback filesystems succeeded
Sep4 02:52:22 server rc.sysinit: Mounting loopback filesystems:succeeded
Sep4 02:52:22 server rc.sysinit: Turning on user and group quotas for
filesystems:  succeeded
Sep4 02:52:23 server rc.sysinit: Enabling swap space:  succeeded
Sep4 02:52:24 server mandrake_everytime: Building Window Manager Sessions¬
succeeded
Sep4 02:52:25 server init: Entering runlevel: 5
Sep4 02:52:25 server network: Setting network parameters:  succeeded
Sep4 02:52:26 server network: Bringing up interface lo:  succeeded
Sep4 02:52:26 server ifup: Determining IP information for eth0 via dhcpcd
Sep4 02:53:26 server dhcpcd[252]:timed out waiting for DHCP server response
Sep4 02:53:26 server ifup:  failed.
```

```
Sep4 02:53:26 server network: Bringing up interface eth0:  failed
Sep4 02:53:28 server loadkeys:Loading /usr/lib/kbd/keymaps/i386/qwerty/us..
Sep4 02:53:28 server keytable: Loading keymap: us succeeded
Sep4 02:53:28 server loadkeys: Loading /usr/lib/kbd/keymaps/include/com..
Sep4 02:53:28 server keytable: Loading compose keys: compose.. succeeded
Sep4 02:53:28 server keytable:  succeeded
```

By reviewing the log, you can determine that the system was unable to get an IP address from a DHCP server. If you were troubleshooting a network connectivity error, this information could well be the cause of the problem. As another example, consider this printout from the auth.log file:

```
Sep 4 04:44:23 server PAM_unix[13043]: authentication failure;¬
LOGIN(uid=0) -> mary for system-auth service

Sep 4 04:44:23 server login[13043]: FAILED LOGIN 1 FROM (null) FOR mary,
Authentication failure

Sep 4 04:44:27 server login[13043]: FAILED LOGIN 2 FROM (null) FOR mary,
Authentication failure

Sep 4 04:44:30 server login[13043]: FAILED LOGIN 3 FROM (null) FOR mary,
Authentication failure

Sep 4 04:44:37 server PAM_unix[13043]: (system-auth) session opened¬
for user root by LOGIN(uid=0)

Sep 4 04:44:37 server  -- root[13043]: ROOT LOGIN ON tty1

Sep 4 04:47:05 server PAM_unix[13043]: (system-auth) session closed
for user root

Sep 4 04:47:05 server PAM_unix[13043]: 2 more authentication failures;¬
LOGIN(uid=0) -> mary for login service

Sep 4 04:47:11 server PAM_unix[13218]: check pass; user unknown

Sep 4 04:47:11 server PAM_unix[13218]: authentication failure;
LOGIN(uid=0) -> keith for system-auth service

Sep 4 04:47:11 server login[13218]: FAILED LOGIN 1 FROM (null) FOR keith,¬
Authentication failure

Sep 4 04:47:16 server PAM_unix[13218]: check pass; user unknown
```

```
Sep 4 04:47:16 server PAM_unix[13218]: authentication failure;
LOGIN(uid=0) -> kieth for system-auth service

Sep 4 04:47:16 server login[13218]: FAILED LOGIN 2 FROM (null) FOR kieth,¬
Authentication failure

Sep 4 04:47:20 server PAM_unix[13218]: (system-auth) session opened¬
for user root by LOGIN(uid=0)

Sep 4 04:47:20 server  -- root[13218]: ROOT LOGIN ON tty1
```

In this example, two users have had problems trying to log in to the system. The first, Mary, gets her password wrong three times and then gives up, at which point you, as administrator, would have likely gotten a call. At almost the same time, a user called Keith attempts to log in to the system but also fails because the user ID is unknown. On the second attempt, he even manages to misspell the username. While these are mock messages created for the purposes of demonstration, they are quite representative of what might happen in the real world, a place where fact truly is stranger than fiction.

Now that you have looked at examples of how log files can be used to determine problems, Table 12-4 contains a list of the files you may look in to determine problems. Note that the filenames can vary between distributions.

Other log files in your Linux system can be monitored for troubleshooting purposes, but the manner in which you access and read them is essentially the same. Feel free to browse through these logs to see what is happening on your system.

TABLE 12-4   Log Files That Can Be Used Referenced in the Troubleshooting Process

Log File	Function
/var/auth.log	Provides authentication information as well as user and group creation information
/var/boot.log	Provides information on what happens on the system during the boot process
/var/security.log	Provides results from a system security check
/var/cron.log	Provides information on scheduled tasks
/var/log/mail	Provides information on system e-mail
/var/log/daemons/	Hold files that contain messages created by daemons

CERTIFICATION OBJECTIVE 12.08

Solving File System Problems

As stated at the beginning of this chapter, often the easiest solution to a problem is the right one, and when it comes to problems associated with file systems, this may mean that the device in question simply has not been mounted. As you may recall from Chapter 10, for a device to be accessed, it has to be mounted into the file system. Generally speaking, devices like hard disks are mounted automatically at boot through an entry in the /etc/fstab file. Others, such as floppy drives and CD-ROMs, often are not automatically mounted by default and so must be mounted manually.

Again, as you may recall from Chapter 10, two commands, mount and unmount, facilitate the mounting and unmounting of devices. Given that hard disks are normally mounted at boot, we'll focus on floppy drives and CD drives.

A list of the currently mounted devices can be obtained by using the mount command. The following is an example of output from a **mount** command from a system with both the floppy and CD-ROM mounted. The output from your specific system may vary slightly.

```
/dev/hda1 on / type ext2 (rw)
none on /proc type proc (rw)
none on /dev/pts type devpts (rw,mode=0620)
/dev/fd0 on /mnt/floppy type ext2 (rw)
/dev/hdc on /mnt/cdrom type iso9660 (ro)
```

One of the most common mistakes when mounting devices is to change the mount point. In other words, on one day the CD-ROM is accessible through the /mnt/cdrom directory, and the next day it is mounted to another directory. Some distributions make the mounting decision easier by creating directories obviously meant for mounting a certain type of device, whereas others do not. Keeping the mount point consistent and meaningful will make administration easier.

SCENARIO & SOLUTION

You want to review a series of failed logon attempts.	Access the auth.log file to review failed logon attempts.
You need to generate a list of currently mounted devices.	Use the **mount** command.
You need to review information on scheduled tasks.	Review the cron.log file.

CERTIFICATION OBJECTIVE 12.09

Resolving Problems Based on User Feedback

You may have the world's most expensive and well-implemented notification system, but the first indicator that something is going wrong on your Linux system is likely to be a call from a user. There are many problems you can expect to answer and troubleshoot when it comes to user-reported problems—too many to list here. The first thing to determine when troubleshooting user-reported problems is that there is actually a problem in the first place. Users may attribute practically anything as a problem with "the system," even a power outage! After establishing that a problem exists, the next step is to deduce whether the problem lies with the server setup, the workstation, or is a case of user error. Once this is determined, you can begin the troubleshooting process. In the following sections, we look at some of the more common user-reported errors you are likely to encounter, and some general troubleshooting strategies to take, both from the server and the workstation.

Unable to Logon

Probably one of the most common of all user-reported problems is the inability to logon to the system. For the most part, troubleshooting these problems is not too difficult and can often be pinned down to the user entering the wrong username or password. That is not to suggest that an invalid logon can be assumed to be one of these, but it is the first place to look. As with all troubleshooting, the trick is to start with the obvious and easy solutions and work from there.

FROM THE CLASSROOM

User Maintenance

Over the years, much has been made, comic and otherwise, of the relationship between system administrators and users. It must be remembered that the only reason system administrators are needed is that there are users using the services of the system. As such, it is very important to remember that maintenance of the administrator/user relationship is perhaps one of the most important facets of the administrator's role. Ultimately, the goal of both parties is the same, which happens to be the continual provision of service. What the administrator can offer is an understanding that users need the system to be as available as possible and for problems to be fixed in a timely manner. This normally means that users will treat administrators with respect and understand that servers and computer systems are complex and so not easy to manage and administer. On the flip side, administrators must treat users with respect and be courteous and timely in attending to problems.

—*Drew Bird, Linux+ Certified*

exam
Watch

Linux passwords are case-sensitive, so the first thing to check when troubleshooting Linux logon problems is to ensure that CAPS LOCK is off.

From the workstation:

- Visually inspect that the network cables are correctly attached.
- Try logging in with a different account to see if the problem is with the account itself.
- Verify that the network settings have not been changed.
- Confirm that the network card is recognized and working in the workstation computer.

From the Linux server:

- Verify that no changes have been made to the server that might explain the logon failure.
- Verify that the user's account is enabled on the server.
- Verify that there are no restrictions on the user's account.
- Ensure that the server is on the network and can ping other systems on the network.
- Ensure that the server is on the network and can ping workstations on the network.

Cannot Access Files/User Rights

When a user on a network complains that they cannot access certain files, you will need to know whether they have ever had access to those files in the first place. Many times, users try to access files they were never given permissions for. If this is the case, it is an easy fix insofar as you just need to add the permissions to the appropriate files (assuming the users are supposed to have access to those files). Sometimes, however, users cannot access files that they have always been able to. This is where things get a bit more involved. In this case, you can bet that someone has changed a setting somewhere, and it is your job to find out where and why. When troubleshooting file access problems, consider some of the following points. Again, it is likely the most obvious solution will fix the problem.

From the workstation:

- If trying to access files from the network, ensure that the workstation is logged on to the network. This may seem obvious, but it is worth a look. In some cases, the user has become disconnected without knowing it.
- If the user cannot access local files, search the hard disk to see if the file has been moved to a new location.
- Confirm that the user has entered the current path to the location of networked files. This is particularly relevant if the user is accessing more than one server and the file system structures are similar.
- Check that the file system has not been corrupted, by using the fsck command. Remember that the file system should be dismounted for this procedure, so the process may affect more than one user.

■ Check for any virus-related activity. Examples of virus activity may include corrupt files, missing files, or increased error messages.

From the server:

■ Confirm that the permissions for the file have not been changed.

■ Confirm that the files are still accessible through another user account or from a different computer and have not become corrupt.

■ Confirm that the share through which the file is being accessed is still available.

■ Confirm that you still have network access to the workstation trying to access the files.

■ If the directory is accessible but the file within is not, use the **find** command to ensure that the file has not been moved.

Unable to Print

Printing is one of the fundamental services provided by the network, and when printing isn't working, you can expect a call very quickly. The first thing to determine when troubleshooting network printing is to determine whether the problem is isolated to the local computer or is a network printing issue affecting many users. Once you have identified where the problem lies, you are ready to troubleshoot it. Unfortunately, many areas need to be checked when there is a problem with printing. The following lists provide some common areas to get you started.

To check from the workstation:

■ Confirm that the computer is logged on to the network.

■ Verify that the default printer environment variable has not been changed.

■ Confirm the user has not changed their own printer settings.

■ Check that the user is specifying the correct printer.

To check from the server:

■ Check the error log for the printer daemon (lpd).

■ Check that the printer daemon is running.

- Check that the print queue is functioning, by using the lpc status all command.

- If using a network printer, ping the printer to ensure it is on the network.

- If it is a local printer, confirm that the cabling is working.

- Confirm that the /var/spool directory has sufficient space.

- Verify that there are no changes to the /etc/printcap file.

on the **Job** *If you suspect that the lpd daemon is not running, use the lpc status all command; if lpd is not running, you will get an error message.*

E-Mail Not Working

Few failed network services seem to generate as much excitement as the inability to send and receive e-mail. If the e-mail is set up correctly, it should be stable, and problems should be infrequent. As with everything else computer related, however, problems do occur and thus you need to be ready to troubleshoot them. Here are some tips on things to check.

From the workstation:

- Verify that the workstation is connected to the network.

- Confirm that e-mail settings on the system have not been changed.

- Verify that the e-mail username and password are correctly entered.

From the server:

- Check the mail logs for any errors.

- Verify that the daemons associated with mail (SMTP, POP, and IMAP) are functioning correctly. These may have to be stopped and restarted to jumpstart the daemon.

- Check e-mail settings for user accounts.

- Verify the network connectivity of the server.

CERTIFICATION OBJECTIVE 12.10

Recognizing Common Linux Errors

Hang around Linux long enough, and you are sure to encounter some common problems that arise from time to time. Of course, some problems seem to come out of nowhere, but more likely, you will see the same errors creeping up time and again. This section explores some of the more common errors you may encounter and how to deal with them.

Package Dependencies

In an ideal world, you just install a new application and are ready to go. This is not always the case. All software you install on your Linux system has a dependency on other software. Without the dependency software in place, your new application may not run.

You often can tell what dependencies are needed for the new software by reviewing the installation documentation. Within these often-ignored text files are references to which other software is needed for a successful installation. In addition to the installation documentation, some of the Linux distributions list the information on package dependencies along with the application download. If you do install an application and it doesn't work, ensure that you have reviewed and installed all of the required dependencies for the software.

EXERCISE 12-1

Identifying Package Dependencies

1. Log on to the Internet and go to the Red Hat Web site (www.redhat.com).

2. Click Download in the upper-right corner of the screen. You will be taken to the Red Hat application download page (www.redhat.com/apps/download).

3. Scroll down the page to the Find Latest RPMs heading and enter **filerunner** in the By Keyword search box.

4. The Search Results page will be displayed with entries for the FileRunner application. Click one of the links for FileRunner.

5. On the FileRunner download page, you have some information bars, including Package Information, Dependencies, Change Log, and File List. Select Dependencies to see a list of the software that the application needs in order to run.

Library Errors

Linux uses something called *shared libraries*, which are comprised of different functions that programs use so that each individual program does not need to include them. By using these shared libraries, it is possible to keep program and application sizes smaller.

The idea of shared libraries is not unique to Linux and Linux applications; it is used by other operating systems and application software as well. Therefore, all of these pieces of software are subject to the same point of failure, that being outdated or damaged library files.

It is likely that, at some point, you will be attempting to install an application and will be unable to because of outdated or corrupt library files. When you encounter this situation, you have to update the library files on your system. To do this, you will need to go to the Web site for the distribution of Linux you are using and find the updated library files. The library files are usually kept in the /lib, /usr/lib, or /usr/local/lib directory, though if you don't find them there, you may need to do a search for lib directories in other locations.

on the **job**

By using the ldd command, you are able to get a list of the shared libraries required by a program. The command usage is ldd program_name.

Version Conflicts

As part of the troubleshooting process, you may need to identify which library version is installed. The version number associated with the library is contained in the library's name. If you want to determine the library version in use, you need to use the following command:

```
#cd /lib
```

Search through the directory looking for the library file in use by typing the following command:

```
#ls libc.so*
```

The output from the command will display the library version, such as libc.so.6. By cross-referencing this information with the documentation that comes with the application itself, you can determine whether there will be a library version conflict. Other library files located in the /lib directory can be cross-referenced in the same manner.

X Window System Errors

From time to time, you may find yourself troubleshooting a problem with the X server, and most often, X-related problems can be traced to incorrect values in your configuration file. You can use a variety of commands to reconfigure your X system, including the xvidtune and XF86Setup utilities. Details of the utilities you can use to reconfigure the X Window System were covered in Chapter 10.

on the **Job**

If X Window freezes while you are using it, you can kill the X Window session by using the CTRL-ALT-BACKSPACE key combination.

CERTIFICATION OBJECTIVE 12.11

Boot and Login Errors

You will find that most Linux installations go without a hitch; install the software and you will be up and running within an hour, with no sign of any boot errors. If that were always the case, there would be no need to mention boot errors in a troubleshooting chapter.

Numerous issues can cause boot-related problems, both hardware- and software-related. Hardware-related boot problems were covered in Chapter 4, so here we will focus on some of the common software problems that can arise. Table 12-5 summarizes boot-related errors.

TABLE 12-5	Boot-Related Errors and Possible Solutions

Error	Solution
You receive a message: Drive not bootable—insert system disk	This error could indicate that there is a fault with the MBR. Use a rescue disk to fix the system or, if using MS-DOS, use the **fdisk /mbr** command. The error message may also be generated by a nonbootable floppy in the drive.
You receive a "Login incorrect" message.	This error is most likely a result of a mistyped username or password. Confirm that both have been typed correctly. If you are still unable to log in, the account may be corrupt or unavailable.
You receive a message "Shell init permissions denied"	This may indicate that the password file has become corrupt or is erased. The fix for this may be to boot Linux into single-user mode and restore the password file from a backup.
Your system boots into the wrong operating system.	If you have installed Linux on a system that is using a dual-boot configuration, you may find it boots straight into one of the operating systems without the option to choose. To repair this, you will have to modify the boot loader you are using. It may also be that you will need to reinstall the boot loader.

Troubleshooting LILO

LILO is a very flexible boot loader that enables you to load not only Linux but a variety of other operating systems as well. As with everything else, however, sometimes LILO does not function as it should, at which point the troubleshooting process begins. Fortunately, when something goes wrong with the boot loading process, LILO does its best to reveal where the problem lies by using the letters L-I-L-O , with each letter identifying the stage of the boot process. Table 12-6 summarizes the results of LILO failures.

on the job

To update LILO and its map, while logged in as root, type /sbin/lilo.

CERTIFICATION OBJECTIVE 12.12

Identifying Backup and Restore Errors

Having to restore critical system or data files only to have the restore process fail is an event that has to be experienced to really get a feel for it. Having said that, you

| **TABLE 12-6** | LILO Stages, Failures, and Possible Causes |

LILO Stage	Summary
Blank, no letters	LILO did not load at all. This sometimes will happen if LILO was not installed on the active partition or if LILO is corrupt.
L	Only the first stage of LILO loaded correctly and then halted. If this happens, it could be an indication of a bad hard disk or that the hard disk parameters are not set as expected. In our experience, though, a simple reboot, perhaps more than one, fixes the problem. If not, try reinstalling Linux.
LI	Both the first stage and the second stage of LILO loaded correctly, but the second stage could not run or execute. Usually, this problem occurs when there are unexpected disk parameters; more specifically, if the entire boot partition does not appear in the first 1,024 cylinders of the disk. Unfortunately, this error usually means a reinstall of Linux.
LIL/LIL?/LIL-	The second stage of the boot process loaded properly but either could not locate files it needs to proceed or could not read the hard disk. This error is rare, as the boot process that hangs it is more likely to give you the LI error and halt there. If you receive any of these errors, you may need to reinstall LILO or scan your disk for errors.
LILO	All stages for the boot process loaded and executed correctly.

really do not want to experience it. Performing backups and testing them by doing a restore are a few of the most important tasks of the system administrator, and with that responsibility comes the need to troubleshoot backup and restore errors.

Unfortunately, you may not know that a backup has failed until it is too late; "too late" is when you are trying to recover data from a backup. Many backup errors are logged in a file that will report that the backup was unsuccessful. Whenever doing backups on your system, it is necessary to always review the backup or system logs to ensure that it was successful. Just reviewing log files is often not enough. In addition, you will need to periodically test-restore your backups to ensure they work. Doing so verifies that your backup procedures, cartridges, and tape device are functioning. When working with backups, consider the following:

- Ensure the tape is large enough to contain all the data you are trying to back up.
- Ensure that the tape is rewound, formatted, and ready.

- Tape cartridges have a limited lifespan and can fail, so new tapes should be added to your tape rotation, and old ones should be replaced.

- Tape devices should be periodically cleaned to ensure proper functioning. Consult the manufacturer's documentation for more information on the exact procedures.

- To confirm that all backup equipment is functioning adequately, perform periodic restores on the system.

You should also check the backup log files each time a backup is performed. You should also, if supported by the utility you are using, verify the backup was performed correctly. Finally, as mentioned in Chapter 11, you may need to test-restore a backup to ensure that it is functioning correctly.

CERTIFICATION OBJECTIVE 12.13

Server Application Failure

In a networked environment, the server maintains several applications that provide the services the network needs in order to function. When these applications go down, the users accessing the respective services are often unable to function. Because of this, these applications have to be brought back up as soon as possible. When troubleshooting server applications, you will need to know which application has failed. Table 12-7 lists some of the common server applications and the signs that they have failed.

Once you have identified the service that has failed, you can then begin the process of troubleshooting the process. Often, this may involve starting and restarting the service or using the ps command to provide a list of processes being used on the system. As always, once you have identified where the problem lies, you can then troubleshoot it.

TABLE 12-7	Server Application Failure Signs and Symptoms

Application	Failure Indication
Squid	Client machines are unable to access the Internet.
Apache	Web server service is unavailable.
DHCP	Client machines are not automatically assigned IP addresses and cannot log on to the network.
BIND	The system is unable to resolve host names to IP address.
Telnet	A user is unable to establish a telnet session.
FTP	The system is unable to transfer files using the FTP protocol.
POP3	Users are unable to receive e-mail.

SCENARIO & SOLUTION

While working on the server, you notice that client systems are not being assigned IP addresses.	The DHCP server is not functioning. It may need to be stopped and restarted.
During the bootup process, only the letters LI are displayed and the system halts.	It is likely that there is a disk parameter error. Linux will need to be reinstalled.
Clients on your network are unable to receive e-mail.	POP3 allows users to receive e-mail, and if e-mail is unavailable, the POP3 service may be down.

CERTIFICATION OBJECTIVE 12.14

Identifying and Using Troubleshooting Commands

You will find yourself using a variety of commands in the troubleshooting process, some more than others. Each of these commands is intended to be used for a specific purpose, and knowing what each is intended for is required both to administer Linux systems and to pass the Linux+ exam. Table 12-8 identifies some of the commonly used Linux troubleshooting commands.

TABLE 12-8   Common Troubleshooting Commands

Command	Summary
locate	Provides you with a secure way to search for files locally. Using **locate** is faster than using the **find** command, because it looks through a single database file instead of the entire file system.
find	Used to locate files or directories in the system. Enables you to specify where the search is to begin, often with the / directory. You can use the **info** command to identify the options for the **find** command.
whereis	Used to find files, and shows where the files' binary, source, and man pages reside.
grep	Used to search for patterns or strings within a file. Provides an online display of the matching criteria.
?	A wildcard used for a single character. For example, searching for a four-character filename with the first letter *a* and the last letter *d*, you can use the command **ls a ?? d**.
*	The wildcard used to represent a group of characters. For example, searching for a four-character filename with the first letter *a* and the last letter *d*, you can use the command **ls a * d**.
</>	Redirection symbols. The > symbol places the output of a command into a new file. The < symbol allows file input to be integrated with other files.
|	Causes the output from one command to be used as the input for another.
>>/<<	The >> redirection symbol appends the output of a command to an existing file rather than replacing it, whereas the << redirection symbol uses the specified text as input.
cat	Often used to concatenate files together to be viewed as one file and to view other files.
head/tail	Used to quickly view the contents of a file, such as a log file. The **head** command allows you to view quickly a specified number of lines at the beginning of the file, whereas the **tail** command lets you view the specified number of lines at the end of the file.
wc	Used to show a summary of a text file, including the line, word, and byte count of the file.

on the
 J o b   *Many of these commands are not actual troubleshooting commands; however, they can be used as part of the troubleshooting procedure.*

EXERCISE 12-2

Using Redirection Symbols

1. To output the results from an **ls** command into a file called test1, use **ls > test1**.

2. To view the contents of the newly created file, use **cat test1**.

3. Now that you have made a new file and viewed it, you will input additional information into the file using the >> symbols, as follows: **dmesg >> test1**.

4. View the now-appended file using the **cat** command: **cat test1**.

5. The file should now contain not only the input from the **ls** command but also the hardware output from the **dmesg** command.

CERTIFICATION OBJECTIVE 12.15

Using Linux Troubleshooting Resources

Contrary to popular belief, no one person is a Linux information island. Linux is a dynamic, diverse, and complex OS, and working with it requires that you access the appropriate resources. When it comes to troubleshooting, these resources become that much more important. For your own administrative interest and to fulfill the CompTIA objectives, you need to familiarize yourself with the various troubleshooting and information resources available.

Web Pages

Linux is a well-documented OS and the Internet hosts many well-designed Web pages that offer a wide range of support. Finding Linux-related Web pages is not difficult—just type **Linux** in any search engine. The trick is finding quality Linux-related troubleshooting and support sights. In addition to standard Web pages, the Internet hosts numerous USENET newsgroups, discussion boards, and mailing lists that are invaluable for Linux troubleshooting and administrative tasks.

For more information on finding and using Linux resources, refer to Appendix C.

man Pages

The **man** utility is an old standby for Linux users. The man documentation provides a synopsis of commands and their usage. The syntax for using **man** is straightforward. Simply type **man** followed by the command you need information on. For example:

```
#man grep
```

The output from this command will provide you with a brief description of the **grep** command and the options available for **grep**. Even the **man** utility has a number of options that you can use with it. To view the options available for man you can use the following command:

```
#man man
```

How obvious is that?

info Pages

The **info** command is similar to the **man** command and is used to display online documentation. The **info** command allows you obtain detailed information about certain Linux commands. The **info** command is more versatile than the older **man** command and allows you to scroll through menus to gather the information you are looking for. The only way to really understand what the info pages are all about is to experience them. From a Linux command line, type the following command to access the info tutorial:

```
#info info
```

Howto Pages

Want to know how to format a floppy for DOS-based systems? Need to know how to manually mount a floppy drive? When you need to know how to perform a specific task under Linux, you need Linux howto pages.

The Internet houses numerous Web sites that hold howto pages, some of which are covered in Appendix C. These howto pages can easily become a Linux administrator's best friend; however, the information given in a manufacturer's documentation should take precedence over that given in the howto pages. To get an idea of howto pages and how they are used, refer to the following Web sites.

- www.linuxdoc.org
- www.tucows.com
- www.linux.org
- www.linuxhowto.com

As you might expect, this list barely scratches the surface of the available Web sites. By typing **linux howto** in any search engine, you are sure to find numerous other sites.

on the Job

Many of today's Linux distributions include howto documents in their installation packages. This provides an easy way to access them.

LUGs

LUGs, or Linux User Groups, represent for the new Linux user a wealth of support resources. Many of the Linux LUGs go beyond just providing technical information to provide all information Linux-related, including education, support, and just a place to hang out and socialize with other Linux users. To see whether a LUG exists near you, check out the following Web site: www.linux.org/users/index.html.

CERTIFICATION OBJECTIVE 12.16

Using Network Utilities to Identify Network Connectivity Problems

Linux is a network operating system and, as such, you can expect to be troubleshooting a range of network-related problems along the way. Troubleshooting a network requires that you have a knowledge of troubleshooting steps performed from the workstation, as well as those performed from the server, including some basic-observation troubleshooting techniques.

From the workstation:

- Confirm that the network cable is securely plugged into both the network card and the socket.

- Confirm that the cable is not crimped, cut, or near devices that can cause crosstalk or EMI. Recall from Chapter 2 that crosstalk is caused by signals on one cable interfering with signals on another, and EMI is caused by electrical interference from power cables or electrical equipment.

- Verify that the network card link light on the back of the card is on. The existence of a link light (normally a green LED) on the network interface indicates that connectivity between the card and the switch or hub is okay.

- Check the network connectivity of the system by using a tool such as **ping**.

From the server:

- Verify that the server network cable is securely attached to the card and hub or wall socket.

- Verify that the network cards link light is lit.

- Check the network connectivity of the system by using a tool such as **ping**.

Linux provides a variety of tools you can use in the network troubleshooting process. These tools will become your best friend when working in a networked environment. The following section explores some of the common Linux network troubleshooting tools.

The ping Command

Of all the TCP\IP utilities, **ping** is perhaps the most widely used. The **ping** command is most often used to test the connectivity between networked devices. A good example is pinging a computer on the network to see if it is connected. Using **ping** is the easiest way to test if a potential problem lies with the network or with some other area.

The **ping** utility is not complicated and does not require many options to work. Perhaps the most common option is the -**c** option that allows you to specify the number of pings you want to send. Using ping without this option sends continuous packet requests. You can view the rest of the options for the ping command by using the man and info commands.

"Troubleshooting a network connection with ping is a simple process, First, try and ping the local loopback adapter on your system by pinging the address 127.0.0.1. If successful, try pinging your own IP address, then the IP address of another system on the same network as you are. If all of this works, you can verify connectivity to a remote system by pinging the IP address of the default gateway, and lastly the IP address of a system on another network."

ifconfig

The ifconfig command is the Linux network administrator's right arm. If you can't efficiently use it, your job is going to be a lot more difficult. The ifconfig command is used to view and configure the system's network interface devices. There are many options that are used with the ifconfig command. For more information on the ifconfig command, refer to Chapter 11.

route

The route command is used to manipulate or show the routing tables. These route tables are used to dictate how the packets traverse the network. If the routing tables are incorrectly set, data packets will have no idea where they are supposed to go, and the network may not function. The route command is used to add and remove these IP routes. An alternative to using the route command is to use the netstat -r command.

traceroute

Often while troubleshooting network connections, it is necessary to track the path your data packets are taking to get to a destination. This can help you to determine whether and where any of these data packets are being dropped before they reach their destination. Just for practice, we can traceroute to a Web site to see the path it took. To do this, type the following command:

```
#traceroute comptia.org
```

By using this command, you can see a list of the different hosts your data packet travels through to get to www.comptia.org. If you are unable to get all the way to the destination, you will be able to determine where the packet was dropped.

This example shows a traceroute command using the Internet, but you are more likely to be using the command on an internal network, in which case your can identify where exactly, if at all, packets are being dropped.

netstat

The netstat command is a one-stop network information command. Using the netstat command, you can see the current network connections, network interface statistics, and routing tables. Table 12-9 shows some of the common options that can be used with the netstat command.

For more information on the **netstat** options, you can use the man or info command to view further information.

exam
Ⓦatch

Viewing network-related statistics is an important part of administration, and the netstat utility is often used for this process. Such utilities and their options are fair game for the Linux+ exam.

TABLE 12-9   Commonly Used Options for the netstat Command

Option	Description
-r	Displays kernel routing information
-n	Shows numerical addresses
-s	Shows summary statistics for protocols
-I	Displays statistics on network interfaces
-v	Verbose information
-N	Used to resolve hardware names
-e	Used to display additional information
-M	Displays masqueraded connections

CERTIFICATION SUMMARY

Troubleshooting plays a significant part in the overall responsibilities of system administrators and even those maintaining their own private systems. Troubleshooting computer systems will often require that you have at least a basic knowledge of hardware-, software-, and network-related configurations. The ability to distinguish between each of these troubleshooting areas will allow you to isolate the cause of a problem more effectively.

Successful troubleshooting is not a random process; rather, it requires a methodical approach, which includes many steps, such as interviewing users or reading log files to gather information, making an informed guess, testing your hypothesis, verifying test results, and documenting the procedure. Excluding any one of these steps in the process can increase the time it takes to isolate and correct the problem.

When troubleshooting a problem, it is often better to start with the most obvious and simple solution and work from there. For example, in the case of a failed logon attempt, verify that the username and password are correct before verifying network settings. Troubleshooting is a process that may take just a few minutes or many hours. Over time, you will become more adept at determining problems and better able to differentiate between hardware and software problems.

TWO-MINUTE DRILL

Identifying and Locating the Problem

❑ Troubleshooting should be a methodical process.

❑ Before attempting to fix a problem, ensure that the correct problem is being addressed.

Describing Troubleshooting Best Practices

❑ A strong troubleshooting strategy follows a methodical or structured approach.

❑ When forming a hypothesis about a problem, start with the easiest solution and work from there.

Editing Configuration Files Based on the Symptoms of a Problem

❑ Linux uses a range of configuration files for system services.

❑ Many problems can be traced to incorrect entries in files.

Starting and Stopping Processes Based on Symptoms of a Problem

❑ Various mechanisms can be used to determine whether a process is not running as expected.

❑ If it is determined that the process is not running correctly, the process should be restarted or the configuration reloaded.

Using Tools to Determine System Status

❑ Part of the troubleshooting process requires using utilities to view system resources and statuses to see if they are functioning normally.

Using Boot Disks in the Recovery Process

❑ Linux boot disks hold a fully functional Linux kernel that is able to boot the system and can be used to repair boot-related problems.

❑ Root disks are repair disks and hold backups of the key system files that can be used to repair the system in the event of failure

Determining the Cause of Errors from System Log Files

❑ System logs files are kept in the /var/log directory.

❑ Log files can be read and inspected for errors using the **cat** and **grep** commands.

Solving File System Problems

❑ For a file system to be accessible to the system, it has to be mounted.

❑ Mounting and unmounting file systems for the system to use is done with the **mount** and **umount** commands.

Resolving Problems Based on User Feedback

❑ Several common problems reported by users include the inability to log on, print, or access files.

❑ When troubleshooting user feedback errors, start with the most likely solution first and work from there.

Recognizing Common Linux Errors

❑ Over time, you will become more adept at recognizing errors, because many of them reoccur from time to time.

❑ Some common Linux hotspots include package dependency errors, library errors, and version conflicts.

Boot and Login Errors

❑ When troubleshooting a boot error, start with the simplest solution and work from there.

❑ Both hardware and software errors can cause a boot problem, so part of the process is determining which of these is at fault.

Identifying Backup and Restore Errors

❑ After a backup has been performed, you should verify that it has been done correctly.

❑ Critical restore errors can be minimized by periodically performing test restores on the system.

Server Application Failure

❑ Linux servers provide a range of functions to network users; the first indication of a failed application may be when clients can no longer access a service.

❑ The **ps** command can be used to view processes running and can help to isolate application failure. The application-associated daemon may need to be restarted for the service to come back online.

Identifying and Using Troubleshooting Commands

❑ Effective troubleshooting requires the use of specific commands. These commands are used to locate missing files, extract information from configuration files, and manage the overall system.

❑ Common commands used while troubleshooting a Linux system include **grep**, **find**, **locate**, and **cat**.

Using Linux Troubleshooting Resources

❑ Part of effective system administration will involve using Linux support resources.

❑ Common support resources include howto pages, info pages, man pages, LUGs, and various Web sites dedicated to Linux.

Using Network Utilities to Identify Network Connectivity Problems

❑ Part of administering Linux systems will be to identify various network-related problems.

❑ Common tools used to troubleshoot network problems include **route**, **traceroute**, **ifconfig**, **ping**, and **netstat**.

SELF TEST

The following questions will help you measure your understanding of the material presented in this chapter. Read all of the choices carefully because there might be more than one correct answer. Choose all correct answers for each question.

Identifying and Locating the Problem

1. You have been called to troubleshoot a problem with a workstation computer that will not log on to the network. Following troubleshooting best practices, what is your first step?

   A. Check that there are no changes to the network setup.

   B. Verify network connectivity.

   C. Question the workstation user for information on the error.

   D. Log on to the system using the Administrator account.

2. When troubleshooting a logon failure for a single user, which of the following troubleshooting measures is **not** a valid step to take?

   A. Visually inspect network cabling.

   B. Try logging on using a different account.

   C. Confirm that the username and password were correctly typed in.

   D. Restart the server.

Describing Troubleshooting Best Practices

3. A user complains that they cannot access a file on the server. Observing troubleshooting best practices, what is your likely first step in isolating the problem?

   A. Visually inspect that the network cable is attached.

   B. Confirm that the path to the file is still active.

   C. Ascertain whether the user ever had access to the file.

   D. Verify that permissions for the file are correctly set.

Editing Configuration Files Based on the Symptoms of a Problem

4. A user calls and reports that they are unable to print. Upon further investigation, you notice that the lpd will not load. Which of the following configuration files would you review to help locate the source of the problem?

A.   /etc/printcap

B.   /var/printcap

C.   /etc/print.conf

D.   /var/print.conf

Starting and Stopping Processes Based on the Symptoms of a Problem

5.   A user in the administration office calls you to report that they are unable to print. You ask others in the office and determine that only that user is experiencing printing problems. Which of the following represents the best next step in the troubleshooting process?

A.   Ping the printer from the server to confirm network connectivity.

B.   Log off the workstation as the current user and log back on as root user to reinitialize the printer.

C.   Confirm that the user is logged on to the network.

D.   Verify that lpd is running by stopping and restarting the service.

Using Tools to Determine System Status

6.   You need to get information about the serial ports in your computer, including I/O addresses and IRQ usage. Which of the following commands are you likely to use?

A.   Setserial

B.   setserial

C.   Serialset

D.   serialset

Using Boot Disks in the Recovery Process

7.   You have been called in to troubleshoot a Linux system that does not boot. You suspect that the LILO has become corrupt. Which of the following is you next likely troubleshooting step?

A.   Edit the /etc/lilo.conf file.

B.   Reload LILO.

C.   Reboot the system using a boot disk.

D.   Review system logs to isolate the cause.

Determining the Cause of Errors from System Log Files

8. Where would you find the log file configuration file?

  A. /var/syslog.conf

  B. /etc/syslog.conf

  C. /var/logsys.conf

  D. /etc/logsys.conf

Solving File System Problems

9. After booting into your Linux system, you are unable to view the floppy drive. Which command would you use to make the floppy drive available to the system?

  A. fsck

  B. format

  C. mount

  D. /dev/floppy

Resolving Problems Based on User Feedback

10. A user calls and complains that they have been unable to print to a networked printer. They have sent several jobs to the printer but nothing comes out. Based on this feedback, which of the following Linux commands could you use to isolate the problem?

  A. lpr status

  B. lpc status all

  C. lpq status

  D. lprm status all

Recognizing Common Linux Errors

11. You want to troubleshoot a suspected corrupted password file. Where is the password directory kept on the Linux system?

  A. /etc/password

  B. /var/password

  C. /etc/passwd

  D. /var/passwd

Boot and Login Errors

12. After installing your Linux system, your system halts on bootup and displays only the LI letters. What is the likely cause of this error?

    A. The file system is corrupt.

    B. Linux was not installed correctly.

    C. LILO was not completely installed.

    D. The boot partition is too large.

13. When booting your dual-boot system, it goes directly into one of the OSs. Which of the following would explain this issue?

    A. Your boot loader is not functioning.

    B. You are booting into single-user mode.

    C. The password directory is corrupt.

    D. The login username or password likely is incorrect.

Identifying Backup and Restore Errors

14. One of the servers you have been managing has failed, and you are tasked with rebuilding the server, including restoring all data from a recent backup. During the restore process, the tape backup fails. The same happens on subsequent restores tries. What could have been done to prevent the problem?

    A. Confirm the tape drive's compatibility with Linux.

    B. Perform periodic restores from tape device.

    C. Check SCSI termination.

    D. Check SCSI IDs.

Server Application Failure Server

15. After being notified that name resolution in your server has failed, which of the following daemons are not functioning?

    A. inetd

    B. httpd

    C. named

    D. samba

16. After being unable to troubleshoot a printing problem from a user's workstation, you look to the server. What daemon would you verify to be running on the server to troubleshoot the print problem?

    A. lpd

    B. /etc/lpr

    C. /var/lpd

    D. lpq

Identifying and Using Troubleshooting Commands

17. Which of the following commands is used to completely kill an X Window session?

    A. CTRL-ALT-BACKSPACE

    B. CTRL-ALT-ENTER

    C. ALT-ESC

    D. ALT-BACKSPACE

Using Linux Troubleshooting Resources

18. You are unsuccessfully trying to use the grep command and would like more information on it using the manual pages. Which of the following is the correct usage to find out more information?

    A. grep man

    B. man grep

    C. man | grep

    D. /etc/man/grep

Using Network Utilities to Identify Network Connectivity Problems

19. Which Linux command is used to view and configure the network interfaces in your Linux system?

    A. ipconfig

    B. route

    C. ifconfig

    D. netset.conf

20. Which of the following commands is used to test the connectivity between two networked devices?

    A. inetconfig

    B. ping

    C. netstat

    D. ifconfig

LAB EXERCISE

You are called to troubleshoot a problem in which printing is not available to any of the users on the network. The information you have been given is as follows:

- Maintenance has recently been done on the server

- Other network services are available

- The printer was working earlier in the day and then stopped

With this information, where would you start troubleshooting and what guess might you make as to the cause of the problem?

SELF TEST ANSWERS

Identifying and Locating the Problem

1. ☑ C. Good troubleshooting practices dictate that you should ascertain as much information as possible before starting work on the problem.
   ☒ A ,B, D. These are all valid troubleshooting steps, but you should ask for the user's input first.

2. ☑ D. If the problem is confined to a single user, restarting the server likely won't help the problem.
   ☒ A, B, C. When troubleshooting an logon failure for a single user, these are all valid these are all valid troubleshooting steps. Perhaps the first one of these three is to confirm that the username and password were typed in correctly.

Describing Troubleshooting Best Practices

3. ☑ C. When troubleshooting a file access problem, the first step should be to determine whether the user has ever had access to the file. In some cases, they have not, which explains why they cannot see it.
   ☒ A, B, D. These are all valid troubleshooting steps, but would not be performed before first ascertaining whether the user should be able to use the file.

Editing Configuration Files Based on the Symptoms of a Problem

4. ☑ A. The /etc/printcap is a configuration file that holds the configuration files for the printer. If you are experiencing problems with printing or the lpd, it is worth verifying the settings in the configuration to ensure they are correct.
   ☒ B is incorrect, as /var/printcap is not a valid Linux directory. /etc/print.conf and /var/print.conf are not valid Linux files; therefore C and D are incorrect.

Starting and Stopping Processes Based on the Symptoms of a Problem

5. ☑ C. If only a single user is experiencing the problem, chances are that the problem is related to that user ID. A common problem is that the user is either not logged on or has become disconnected from the network.
   ☒ A. Because only a single user is experiencing the problem, network connectivity is unlikely to be an issue. B. This action will not cause the printer to reset. D. Because only a single user is

experiencing problem, restarting the lpd daemon likely won't help and will disrupt printing for other network users.

Using Tools to Determine System Status

6. ☑ **B.** The setserial command provides information on I/O addresses and IRQ usage.

☒ **A,** The setserial command has a small *s*, not a capitalized *S*, and Linux commands are case sensitive, therefore Setserial would be incorrect. **C, D.** The command is setserial, not Serialset, or serialset, these are not valid Linux commands.

Using Boot Disks in the Recovery Process

7. ☑ **C.** Part of the tools available to Linux administrators include a current copy of a boot disk. The boot disk is used when the system refuses to start. Once the system is started with the boot disk, further troubleshooting can take place.

☒ **A** is incorrect, it may be that the lilo.conf file will need to be edited, but this cannot be done unless the system is first booted. The first step would then be to get the Linux system started with the boot disk. As with A, before reloading LILO, you first need to access your system with the boot disk. It is likely that LILO would not need to be reloaded. Therefore answer **B** is incorrect. **D** is incorrect, as you would not be able to review system logs until after the system was able to boot. This may be a valid troubleshooting step, but the machine has to be up and running first.

Determining the Cause of Errors from System Log Files

8. ☑ **B.** The /etc/syslog.conf file contains information about what should be logged and where. The file is used by the syslog daemon.

☒ **A.** The filename is correct but the location is not. The logsys.conf file is not a valid Linux log file, therefore **C** and **D** are incorrect.

Solving File System Problems

9. ☑ **C.** Each device on a Linux system has to be mounted before it is usable by the Linux system. In this case, the mount command will need to be used to mount the floppy device.

☒ **A.** fsck is used to check and correct file system problems. **B. format** is not a valid Linux command. **D.** /dev/floppy is not a command, but rather is a directory.

Resolving Problems Based on User Feedback

10. ☑ B. Because print jobs seem to be frozen in the print queue, it will need to be looked at. The **lpc status all** command will provide status information for all the print queues on the system.
☒ A. The **lpr** command is used to send print jobs to the printer. This command actually attempt to send a file called status to the default printer. C. The **lpq** command is used to query a print queue. D. The **lprm** command is used to remove print jobs from the print queue.

Recognizing Common Linux Errors

11. ☑ C. The password directory is kept in the /etc/passwd directory.
☒ A, B, D. All of the options do not hold the password directory.

Boot and Login Errors

12. ☑ D. Older versions of LILO require that the entire boot partition be within the first 1,024 cylinders of the disk. If it is not, the LILO only gets as far as LI on bootup.
☒ A. The LI message appears before any file systems are mounted. B, C. There is insufficient information to draw these conclusions, because LILO does not get as far as these in the boot process.

13. ☑ A. The most likely explanation when a dual-boot system does not give you an option to choose between operating systems is that the boot loader is not functioning properly or is not configured properly.
☒ B. Single-user mode is used for troubleshooting and will not cause boot-related problems. C. A corrupt password directory will not cause the described boot problem. D. An incorrect username and password would not cause the system to not boot properly.

Identifying Backup and Restore Errors

14. ☑ B. Part of the responsibility of system administrator is to periodically restore backups to ensure that they are functioning properly. No other method is better at testing the success of a backup than an actual restore.
☒ A is incorrect as the tape drive should be tested for compatibility of Linux before it is even installed. Therefore Linux compatibility should not be an issue. Poor SCSI termination and incorrect ID assignment would not cause the problem. At most it would prevent the device from functioning, therefore C and D are incorrect.

Server Application Failure

15. ☑ **C.** The named daemon is responsible for DNS functioning that handles name resolution. If the system is not performing name resolution, then the named daemon may need to be stopped and restarted.

    ☒ **A.** The inetd daemon is responsible for network services. **B.** The httpd daemon is responsible for Web services. **D.** Samba allows Windows systems to use the resources of Linux systems.

16. ☑ **A.** If you suspect that the server is at the bottom of your printer problems, the lpdprinter daemon may not be running. If it is not, you will need to start it, and even if it is running, it may need to be stopped and restarted.

    ☒ **B.** /etc/lpr is not a valid Linux command. **C.** /var/lpd is not a valid Linux command or directory. **D.** **lpq** is used to verify the status of a print queue.

Identifying and Using Troubleshooting Commands

17.   ☑ When an X Window session freezes completely, you can use the CTRL-ALT-BACKSPACE command to kill the X Window session.

    ☒ **B, C, D.** None of these commands has any effect in an X Window session.

Using Linux Troubleshooting Resources

18. ☑ **B.** When using the man pages, the correct usage is **man** followed by the command. In this case it would be **man grep**.

    ☒ **A,C,D,** only **man** followed by the command is the correct usage when using **man** therefore, answers A,C and D are incorrect.

Using Network Utilities to Identify Network Connectivity Problems

19. ☑ **C.** The ifconfig command can be use to view and set configuration parameters on Linux systems.

    ☒ **A.** The ipconfig command cannot be used on Linux systems. **B.** The route command displays the routing table for the system. **D.** This answer is fictitious.

20. ☑ **B.** ping is one of the most common troubleshooting commands used to verify a connection between networked devices. The ping command is arguably the most used tool in the network administrator's tool box.

    ☒ **A.** inetconfig is not a valid Linux command. **C.** netstat is used to view such network statistics as routing tables and interface-related statistics. **D.** ifconfig is used to configure the system's network interfaces.

LAB ANSWER

The first part of the troubleshooting process is to gather the information needed to help isolate the problem. In this case, we know that printing is not a local workstation problem, because all users on the network are unable to print. From this information, we can conclude that the print problem lies with the network, print server, or server itself.

We also know that maintenance has recently been done on the server and that other network services remain available. Because other network services are available, the network can all but be eliminated as the cause of the problem. Recent maintenance to a system is often a red flag and deserves special consideration. In this case, because server changes recently have been made, you need to take note. Finally, we know that the printer worked earlier in the day, meaning that the printer likely doesn't have something physically wrong with it.

So, where does all of this leave us? Without even yet touching a computer system, we have isolated the most likely cause of the printing problem to the server. From there, we would conduct a few tests on the system, such as to check whether the lpd is running, and before long, your printing would be up and running.

Linux+™
COMPUTING TECHNOLOGY INDUSTRY ASSOCIATION

A

Command Summary

Here is a list of the more commonly used commands on a Linux system. This list is not comprehensive. For more information on the usage of each command, consult the appropriate man page or use the --help switch.

adduser   Creates new user accounts.

alias   Creates an alias of a command.

apm   Provides power usage information and management capabilities on APM enabled systems.

bg   Used to run programs in the background.

cat   Displays multiple files and allows them to be joined.

cd (change directory)   Used for moving up and down through the file system.

cfdisk   Utility for partitioning disks.

chage   Sets password aging characteristics and other password related values.

chattr   Changes file attributes on an ext2 filesystem.

checkalias   Displays which aliases are currently in effect.

chgrp   Changes the group ownership of a file or directory.

chmod   Changes access permissions of files or directories.

chown   Changes the user ownership of a file or directory.

chvt   Changes between virtual terminals.

clear   Clears the console screen leaving a single command prompt.

cmp   Compares files and reports on differences.

compress   File compression utility.

cp   Copies files from one location to another.

cpio   Utility for updating tar archives.

crontab   Used to create cron jobs and edit cron tab files.

date   Shows and allows the setting of the system time and date.

dd   Copies a file and in the process can convert between formats.

df   Shows the amount of free space on the disk and other disk usage information.

diff   Compares files and notifies of differences found in the contents of the file.

dir   Lists directory contents and associated information.

dmesg   Lists hardware present in the system that is recognized by the operating system.

du   Displays disk usage information.

dump   Backup utility used with the restore utility.

fdisk   Utility for creating, managing and deleting disk partitions.

fg   Brings a running program from the background to the foreground.

find   Allows the file system to be searched for files and directories that match a given criteria.

finger   Displays information about a specified user that is logged in to a system.

free Shows memory usage statistics for the system.

fsck Utility for diagnosing and fixing problems with the file system.

gpasswd Allows passwords for groups to be changed.

grep Locates and displays information from within text files.

groupadd Allows the creation of new groups.

groupmod Allows information about existing groups to be modified.

groups Shows a list of the current group memberships.

gunzip A file compression utility.

head Displays the first lines of a text file based on a given number.

help Bash command used to obtain help on other commands.

hostname Displays system hostname. Can also be used to set it.

id Displays user and group ID information.

ifconfig Utility for viewing and configuring network settings and related information.

init Command for switching between predefined run levels.

insmod Loads a kernel module.

kill Stops a running process.

less   Allows files to be viewed a page or line at a time and allows movement backward and forward through the file.

ln   Used to create and manipulate file links.

lpc   Line printer control program that allows printer and print queues to be managed.

lpq   Provides information about print queues and the jobs that are in them.

lpr   Command-line utility for printing files from the command line.

lprm   Removes files from a print queue.

ls   Lists files and directories and related information.

lsmod   Lists currently loaded kernel modules.

man   Invokes manual page reader.

mkdir   Creates directories.

mkpasswd   Automatically generates passwords and applies them to users.

mkswap   Creates virtual memory swap files.

more   Allows text files to be viewed a page at a time.

mount   Mounts storage devices into the file system.

mv   Moves files from one location to another.

netstat   Displays statistical information on network connections.

newgrp   Changes a users primary group membership for the duration of the session.

nice   Allows priorities of a program to be modified on execution.

passwd   Allows root to change a users password or a user to change their own password.

ping   Utility used to test connectivity between to network hosts.

ps   Displays current system process usage.

rcp   Allows files to be copied from a local host to a remote host.

restore   Restores files from archives created with the dump command.

rm   Removes files or directories.

rmdir   Removes directories.

rmmod   Unloads kernel modules that are no longer in use.

route   Displays TCP/IP routing information.

scp   Used to copy files securely between hosts.

shutdown   Shuts down a system.

ssh   Opens a secure shell session.

su   Switches between user IDs.

SuperProbe   Utility that allows the detection of video cards and monitors.

tail   Based on criteria, displays the last lines of a text file.

tar   Utility that allows multiple files to be combined into a single file while preserving directory structures.

telinit   Like the *init* command. Used to change run levels.

ulimit   Bash command used to view and set limits for various parameters within the shell.

umask   Sets default file and directory permissions.

umount   Command to dismount an already mounted storage device.

unalias   Removes a previously configured command alias.

unzip   Command to expand a previously compressed file.

useradd   Creates new user accounts.

userdel   Deletes user accounts.

usermod   Allows information on existing user accounts to be modified.

users   Displays a list of currently logged-in users.

who   Displays a list of currently logged-in users.

whoami   Displays information about the user account currently logged in.

yes   Issues recurring Ys to the command line. Used to answer Yes to utilities that require user input.

B

Exercises

Ι n this appendix, we have included some exercises to reinforce some of the skills taught throughout the book.

Exercise B-1

Modifying File Permissions and Ownership

Here we will look at the process of assigning file permissions to a file and changing user and group ownership. For more information on the commands used in this exercise, refer to Chapter 9

1. Log in to the system as root.

2. In root's home directory, create a file by using the following command:

   ```
   #dmesg > testa
   ```

3. View the default permissions that are set on the file by using the following command:

   ```
   #ls -la
   ```

4. Change the permissions on the file so that the owner (root) has read and executed, the group has read and executed, and everyone else has no rights by using the following command:

   ```
   #chmod 750 testa
   ```

5. Use the ls command, as in Step 3, to verify that the permission change has worked.

6. Change the user ownership of the file to another user on your system by using the chown command as follows:

   ```
   #chown username testa
   ```

7. Change the group ownership of the file to another group on your system by using the chgrp command as follows:

   ```
   #chgrp groupname testa
   ```

8. Use the ls command as in Step 3 to view the new file ownership information.

9. Delete the file by using the following command:

```
rm testa
```

Questions

1. How does the file receive these default permission assignments?

2. In Step 4, how else could you have specified the new permission assignments?

3. In Step 9, why were you able to delete the file, even though you were no longer the owner?

Exercise B-2

Mounting and Dismounting a CD-ROM Device

In this exercise, we will examine the process of mounting and dismounting a CD-ROM device. These skills are essential for any Linux system administrator. For more information on mounting and dismounting devices, refer to Chapter 10.

1. Log in to the system as root

2. Insert a CD-ROM into the drive and, from the command line, use the mount command as follows:

```
#mount -t iso9660 -r /dev/cdrom  /mnt/cdrom
```

3. Once the CD-ROM has been mounted, you can access the CD within the drive.

4. To access the drive, you can now switch the drive with the following command:

```
#cd /mnt/cdrom
```

5. If you have successfully mounted the CD-ROM, you can type **ls** to see the contents of the CD. Once you have viewed the contents, use the cd command to change back out of the CD-ROM filesystem.

6. To remove the CD, you will need to unmount the drive. Use the following command to unmount the CD-ROM:

```
#umount /dev/cdrom
```

7. If you receive a "device is busy" message, change directory out of the CD file system. If you don't receive and error and are able to eject the CD, you have successfully dismounted the device.

Questions

1. What is the correct command to mount a floppy drive?

2. If you receive an error when dismounting a CD-ROM, what is a likely cause of the problem?

3. After mounting a CDROM, you are unable to remove the CD from the drive; what is the likely cause?

Exercise B-3

Changing the Default File Permission

When a file is created, it receives the default file permissions of the system. These default permissions can be changed using the umask command. For more information using umask, refer to Chapter 7.

1. Log in to the Linux system using the root account.

2. From the command line or a terminal session, determine the current umask value by typing **#umask.**

3. When typed, the umask command should list the current default file permission setting. To view the setting create a text file using the following command:

```
#dmesg | grep hda > testb
```

The command will create a text file listing the IDE devices in your system called testb.

4. To view the default file permissions of the testb file, type **ls -l** and locate the file.

5. Change the default file permission of your system by typing **umask** and an alternative file mode value. File mode values are listed in Chapter 7. You can use 022, 027, or 077 as an example.

6. Once the umask value is set, create a new text file using the command from Step 3 and compare the permissions between the two.

Questions

1. Which file permissions are granted with a umask of 022?

2. Which umask value would be used to set read and write and permissions for the group but nothing for anyone else?

3. After typing **Umask 022** at the command line, you receive a "command not found" error. What is the likely cause of the problem?

Exercise B-4

Scheduling Jobs Using the *at* Command

In this exercise, we will look at the process of scheduling jobs using the **at** command. Unlike cron, jobs scheduled with **at** are run only once and are then removed from the at queue. For more information on the **at** command, refer to Chapter 11.

1. Log in to the system as a normal user.

2. At the command prompt, type the following command and then press ENTER:

```
#at now + 1 minute
```

You may receive a message that states "this command will be executed using xxxx." Don't be concerned by this.

3. At the at> prompt, type the following command:

```
#ps -aux > atfile1min
```

4. Press CTRL-D to close the **at** prompt.

5. Wait for one minute and then check to see the command has executed and the file created.

6. Schedule two more jobs to run by using the same command as in Step 2, but schedule them to run 15 and 30 minutes from now.

7. View the information in the **at** queue by using the following command:

   ```
   #atq
   ```

8. Remove the second job from the **at** queue by using the following command (where *x* is the job number):

   ```
   #atrm x
   ```

9. Use the atq command again to verify that the job has been removed.

Questions

1. What would you do if you needed to run a job on a regular basis?

2. What command would you use if you needed to run the command at this time tomorrow?

3. How could you restrict users from adding jobs with the **at** command?

Exercise B-5

Backing Up Files Using the tar Command

In this exercise, we will perform a basic backup using the tar command. As you may not have a tape backup device, we will backup to a blank floppy disk. For more information on using tar, refer to Chapter 10.

1. Log in to the system as root.

2. Create a directory in the root home folder called testdir, and copy a group of files from /root into the testdir directory. Make sure that the total size of all the files you copy is less than 1MB, and remember to copy the files, not move them.

3. Insert a blank ext2 floppy disk in the drive and mount it using the following command:

```
#mount -t ext2 -rw /dev/fd0 /mnt/floppy
```

4. Use the following command to create a tar archive on the floppy disk:

```
#tar -czvf /mnt/floppy /backup.tgz /root/testdir
```

The tar will be created and the name of each file displayed as it does so.

5. Once the archive is complete, test the archive that has been created by using the following command:

```
#tar tzvf /mnt/floppy/backup.tgz
```

Questions

5. If you were had a SCSI tape drive in your system, what device would you back up to?

6. If you wanted to extract the tar archive you had created, what command would you use?

7. If you wanted the backup to be taken on a daily basis, what system function would you use?

Exercise B-6

Configuring a Basic Printer Configuration for Testing

In this exercise, we will configure a basic printer configuration for the purposes of testing. You do not need to have a printer connected to complete this exercise, but if you do, you should take it off line to prevent the jobs from being printed. For more information on configuring a printer, refer to Chapter 8.

1. Log in to the system as root.

2. If the file /etc/printcap already exists, make a copy of it. If it doesn't, create a new file by using the following command:

```
#vi /etc/printcap
```

For more information on using vi, refer to Chapter 10.

3. In the file, enter the following lines exactly as they appear:

```
# A printer for testing
        Testprinter
        :sd=/var/spool/lpd/testprinter
        :lp=/dev/lp0:
```

4. Save the file.

5. Using the cd command, change to the /etc/init.d directory.

6. Use the following command to stop the lpd service:

```
./lpd stop
```

7. Use the following command to restart the lpd service:

```
./lpd start
```

8. Change back to your home directory and then use the following command to create a text file called printertest:

```
#dmesg > printertest
```

9. Now to print the file, use the following command:

```
#lpr printertest
```

10. Use the UP ARROW to recall the command from the history and run it three or four times.

11. Use the following command to see a list of print jobs in the queue:

```
#lpq
```

12. Make a note of one of the print job numbers. They are listed in the 'Job' column of the lpq printout.

13. Use the following command to delete a print job, where *x* is the printjob number:

```
#lprm x
```

14. Use the lpq command again to verify that the print job has been deleted. Repeat Step 13 to remove the other jobs from the queue.

Questions

1. What is the syntax and location within the file for adding an alias for the printer?

2. What command would you use to place a hold on all the jobs in the queue?

3. What is the significance of the first printer listed in the /etc/printcap file?

Exercise B-7

Working with Files and Directories

In this exercise, we will work with some of the commands used when managing the Linux file system. For more information on the commands used in this exercise, refer to Chapter 9.

1. Log in to the system as a normal user account.

2. Create a new directory in the users home directory by using the following command:

   ```
   $mkdir testz
   ```

3. Change into the testz directory and create another directory called data.

4. Copy all of the files that start with *m* from the /bin directory to the data directory by using the following command. Substitute the */userhome/dir* field for the name and path of the users home directory (normally /home/username).

   ```
   $cp /bin/m* /userhome/dir/testz/data
   ```

5. Change into the directory data directory by using the cd command. Find out what the largest file that has been copied by using the following command:

   ```
   $ls -la -S | more
   ```

6. Delete the files in the directory that begin with *mo* by using the following command:

   ```
   $rm mo*
   ```

7. Move the rest of the files in the directory to the directory above by using the mv command as follows:

```
$mv * ../
```

8. Change up one level to the testz directory by using the following command:

```
$cd..
```

9. Delete the contents of the testz directory and the data directory in one go by using the following command:

```
$rm * -r
```

10. Change up one level to the users home directory and then use the following command to remove the testz directory:

```
$rmdir testz
```

Questions

1. In Steps 2 and 3, what command could you have used to create both directories at the same time?

2. In Step 6, what switch could have been added to the rm command so that you would not be prompted for input at each file deletion?

3. In Step 9, what is dangerous about this command?

Answer Key

The answers to the question from each exercise are provided here.

Exercise B-1

1. The default rights assignments are set with the umask command.

2. You can specify rights assignments using letters instead of numbers, for example *r,w,x,* and so on.

3. The root user is not subjected to file permissions, and so can delete any file on the system.

Exercise B-2

1. The command to mount a floppy disk drive is

   ```
   #mount /dev/fd0
   ```

2. If you receive an error message, it may be that the files on the device are still in use.

3. Once a CD-ROM is mounted, the device is locked until it is dismounted. This means that to change the disk in the drive, it is necessary to dismount and remount the device.

Exercise B-3

1. A file permission of 022 would be result in no rights for the owner and write permissions for all other users. This is an unusual combination.

2. This configuration would require a umask value of 070

3. In Linux, filenames are case sensitive and so the use of a capital *U* would make the system return a "command not found" error.

Exercise B-4

1. Instead of using the **at** command, you would use cron if you wanted to run jobs on a regular basis.

2. The command to run a job at this time tomorrow would be

   ```
   #at now next day.
   ```

3. You can restrict users from adding jobs with the **at** command by adding entries to the /etc/at.allow and at.deny files.

Exercise B-5

1. If you are backing up to a SCSI tape device, simply substitute /dev/fd0 with /dev/st0.

2. The -t switch, when used with the tar command, allows the archive to be tested and the contents listed.

3. You could use the cron system to schedule the backup jobs to occur on a daily recurring basis.

Exercise B-6

1. To add an alias for a printer entry, you use the pipe separator to the first line of the entry and then list the aliases.

2. The lpc command can be used to perform a range of tasks with the print queue, including placing a hold on all jobs in the queue.

3. The first printer listed in the printcap file is the default printer. When a file is printed or a printing related command executed without a printer being specified, the default printer is used unless it is overridden by the PRINTER variable.

Exercise B-7

1. The -p switch allows you to create multiple directories in a single command.

2. The -f switch when used with the rm command overrides requests for user input.

3. By not asking for any confirmation of file or directory deletion, it's possible to delete an entire directory structure. If the command is executed from the root of the file system, the entire file system would be deleted.

C

Resources

The sheer number of Linux-related resources available is staggering. In this appendix, we have selected a few of these resources that you might find useful as you study for your Linux+ exam. This list is by no means exhaustive, and there are many other useful sources of information that you are likely to encounter.

Linux Distribution Web Sites

These are links to the home pages for some of the more popular Linux distributions.

www.redhat.com   Red Hat.

www.debian.org   Debian.

www.caldera.com   Caldera.

www.suse.com   SuSE.

www.linux-mandrake.com   Mandrake.

www.turbolinux.com   Turbo Linux.

www.slackware.com   Slackware.

For even more distributions (more than any one person could realistically want), visit the Linux Weekly News site and click on the Distributions link at www.linuxweeklynews.com.

Linux-Related Web Sites

www.linux.com   Volunteer-based Web site offering Linux-related articles, weekly features, tutorials, and opinion pieces.

www.tucows.com   The Tucows Linux site provides upgrades, software downloads, patches, and just about anything else you'll need to get the inside scoop on Linux.

www.linux-laptop.net　　This site is devoted to running Linux on laptops. It includes documents and configuration files for a variety of laptops and handheld devices.

www.xfree86.org　　Home of the Xfree86 organization, it includes downloads of the latest software and information on hardware compatibility. The site also includes links to mailing lists, support information, and details on upcoming XFree86 releases.

www.kernel.org　　The place to get the latest version of the Linux Kernel, it includes a set of the Linux documentation project at the following location: www.kernel.org/ldp.

www2.linuxjournal.com　　The online site of the paper-based magazine *Linux Journal*, it includes discussion forums, links and support sources, articles, and even a Linux career center.

www.linux-mag.com　　The online site of the paper-based *Linux Magazine*, it includes a newbies section, product reviews, configuration information, a Guru Guidance section, and feature articles.

www.linuxhq.com　　The Linux headquarters site offers links and some kernel downloads.

www.linuxdoc.org　　If you are looking for a Linux How-to, you are likely to find it here. The site offers more than just how-tos, journals, links, FAQs, and manuals; it is likely you will find what you are looking for on this site. There is a complete list of mirror sites that may be easier to access than the main site.

www.linuxnewbie.org　　As the name suggests, the site is targeted at those in the process of learning Linux basic, although they do seem to overshoot the beginner at times.

Other Sites You Might Want to Check Out

www.lwn.net   Linux Weekly News.

www.linuxtoday.com   Linux Today.

www.UnixReview.com   Unix Review.

www.samag.com   Sys Admin's Web site.

www.onlamp.com   O'Reilly's Linux, Apache, and other technologies' site.

www.freshmeat.net   Free software downloads.

www.gnu.org   The GNU Web site.

We could, quite literally, fill the entire book with links to Linux resources on the Internet. These are some of the best, but there are many others. Spend some time looking around for yourself.

Linux Newsgroups

There are literally dozens of Linux newsgroups ranging from the useful to the bizarre. Here is a list of some of those that fall into the former category. To access them, you'll need newsreader software and the news server information from your ISP. Alternatively, you can access one of the many free Web-based news services such as Deja.com. Here is the list:

General Linux Administration Issues

comp.os.linux and comp.os.linux.admin.

Hardware-Related Issues Such as Installation and Configuration

comp.os.linux.hardware.

General Linux Issues

comp.os.linux.misc, comp.os.linux.networking, comp.os.linux.security, and comp.os.linux.setup.

Discussions on the X Window System

comp.os.linux.x, comp.os.linux.questions, and comp.windows.x.

Discussion on X-Based Applications Issues

comp.windows.x.apps.

In addition to these newsgroups, there are numerous distribution and application specific groups that provide more focused information. Search a newsgroup listing by distribution name to find those that apply to you.

Linux+-Related Information

www.comptia.org CompTIA's Web site provides detailed information on the Linux+ test objectives. When looking for Linux+ information, the CompTIA Web site may be the first place to look.

www.cramsession.com Provides discussion groups and other Linux+ related information.

www.examcram.com Provides some Linux+ news and other related articles.

COMPUTING TECHNOLOGY INDUSTRY ASSOCIATION

D

Glossary

/ Used to refer to the top level of the file system.

/dev directory Directory on a Linux server that contains device drivers.

/proc directory Virtual filesystem that contains routines that provide information about the system.

Absolute path Your current location in the file system, described in full from the top level. For example, /usr/sbin.

Alias In Linux, the creation of a substitute command that performs the same action as an existing command.

Alien A utility that allows common package formats to be converted from one type to another.

Alpha A 64-bit processor based platform offering high levels of performance. Numerous Linux distributions are available for the Alpha platform.

Anti-virus Software that protects a computer from infection by viruses.

Apache A popular Web server application available for Linux, Unix, Windows, and a number of other platforms.

Append The process of data being added to a file, rather than the file being overwritten.

ASCII American Standard Code for Information Interchange. Standard set of codes and corresponding characters used by PCs. Referred to as the ASCII character set.

ATAPI An Interface standard used for the connection of CD-ROM devices on an IDE bus.

Auto-completion   A common capability of shells that allows the automatic completion of a directory path from the first few characters of the name.

Authentication   The process of verifying the identity of someone trying to access the system. The most common authentication system in used is passwords.

awk   Programming utility that is available on multiple platforms. Named after the three people who created it: Alfred Aho, Peter Weinberger, and Brian Kernighan.

Back door   A method of accessing a program or system through a means other than the normal. Generally represents an unwanted or unknown aspect system or application security.

Background   A feature of multiuser operating systems that allows processes to run without any user interface freeing up the command line (foreground) for other uses.

Backup   Process of making duplicate copies of data for the purposes of data recovery.

Bandwidth   The amount of data that can be accommodated by a channel.

BBS   Bulletin Board System. Systems that accommodate remote connections and allow information and files to be stored and then subsequently downloaded.

BIOS   Basic Input Output System. Type of chip that stores instructions used by the computer at boot time.

Boot   The process of starting a computer system up, including the loading of the operating system. A Warm boot is one that does not involve cycling of the power; a cold boot is one that does.

Broadcast   A type of data transmission that is sent to all computers on the network.

BSD   Berkeley Software Distribution. Versions of Unix and Linux developed at The University of California, Berkeley.

Bug   A problem with a computer program.

C   A programming language commonly used to develop applications on Linux and Unix.

Cache   Area of physical memory or disk that is used to store frequently accessed data.

CGI   Common Gateway Interface. Mechanism for transferring data between a Web server and an external program.

CHAP   Challenge Handshake Authentication Protocol. Authentication system in which the server provides a key to the client so that authentication information can be transferred encrypted.

Checksum   Mathematical calculation performed on a file or data set for the purposes of error checking.

CHS   Short for Cylinders, Heads, and Sectors. Used in discussions of hard disk drives.

CIFS   Common Internet File System. File-sharing mechanism that uses SMB over TCP/IP to enable file sharing between systems without the need for additional client software.

CLI   Command-line interface. Generic term used to refer to any system, such as a shell, that allows input from the command line.

CLU   Command-line utility. Any program that is executed from within a command line interface.

Clustering   The process of grouping servers together to provide increased processing power and, in certain circumstances, fault tolerance.

CMOS Complementary Metal Oxide Semiconductor. Type of ROM chip used to store BIOS settings.

COAS Caldera Open Administration System. Caldera-created utility for performing administration and configuration tasks.

Compiling The process of converting source code into machine language.

Concatenate To combine the contents of multiple files into a single one.

Copyleft Copyright system that prevents modification of the license agreement should changes be made to the original software. GPL is often referred to as Copyleft.

Core dump System information written to a file in the event of a critical error. The core dump can be analyzed to determine the cause of the error.

Cracker An individual who attempts to subvert security measures on a system.

Cracking The process of subverting the security measures of a system for the purposes of gaining access, normally unauthorized.

cron Utility that allows the scheduling of tasks.

Cryptography The study of encoding data in such a way that it can only be read by the intended recipients.

Daemon Software components that provide some service to clients or to other daemons.

DEB The Debian package format used to distribute applications.

Debug To eliminate errors from a program or script.

Denial of service   A type of network attack in which the host system is overwhelmed by the number of requests it receives.

Device driver   Software component that interfaces the operating system with a hardware device.

DHCP   Dynamic Host Configuration Protocol. Service that automatically assigns IP addresses to hosts for a predetermined amount of time.

Directory Services   Mechanism by which information on objects, such as users, is stored in a central repository and made accessible by various means.

Disk Druid   Disk Partitioning tool created by Red Hat.

Distribution   Term given to a collection of software, including the Linux Kernel, that is made available for purchase or free download.

DNS   Domain Name Service servers translate hostnames to IP addresses.

Dot file   A file whose name starts with a period. Used to "hide" files that are important to the operation of the system.

Downtime   The amount of time a system is unavailable.

Driver   Software that allows the operating system to communicate with hardware devices.

Dual booting   Term given to a system that has more than one operating system installed and is capable of booting into each one.

Dumb terminal   System that provides access to a multiuser system such as Linux but that provides little or no processing power of its own.

emacs   A popular text editing package.

Encryption   The process of scrambling data so that it can't be read without the correct key.

Environment variable   A setting that affects how the shell appears, operates, or reacts.

Fail-over   The ability for servers or devices to be able to switch over to another in the event of a failure. Most often associated with servers in a cluster configuration.

FAQ   Frequently asked questions. Document that contains answers to questions that are often asked about a product, application, or system.

Fault tolerance   The ability for a device, group of devices, or system to accommodate the failure of a device and continue to run.

FIPS   Disk partitioning utility that allows partitions to be created, deleted, and resized.

Firewall   Device, or group of devices, that protects one network from another.

FreeBSD   An free version of Unix based on the BSD release, which runs on PC hardware.

Freeware   Software that is supplied free of charge.

fsck   Utility that checks and corrects errors in the Linux filesystem.

FTP   File Transfer Protocol. Allows files to be transferred between two hosts.

Full-duplex   Network communication mechanism in which data travels in both directions at the same time. Full-duplex connections require that devices at both ends of the link support it.

Gateway   System, software, or device that provides translation from one entity to another.

GID   Group ID. A unique number assigned to each group that exists on the system.

GIMP   GNU Image Manipulation Program. Software that allows graphic files to be edited and managed. Also enables screenshots to be taken within a X Window session.

Gnome   GNU Network Object Model Environment. Popular desktop environment for Linux.

GNU   GNU's Not Unix. Phrase used to refer to open source software.

GPL   GNU Public License. Document that details the licensing restrictions, or lack thereof, of software created under the umbrella of the GNU project. The GPL licensing scheme is often adopted for other software that is not developed by the GNU project. GPL is often referred to as Copyleft.

Hacker   A computer programmer who seeks an understanding of how software operates for the purposes of making it better. Not to be confused with a cracker.

Half-duplex   Network communication mechanism in which data can travel on the cable in one direction or the other at a time.

Home directory   Directory on the system designed to store files and directories that will only be used by the individual.

Host   A system on the network.

HOWTO   Document that explains how to use certain function or to configure a certain service. Condensed versions, called Mini HOWTOs, are also available for popular topics.

HTML   Hyper Text Markup Language. Tagged text system that enables pages to be constructed with embedded graphics and other features. Used to create Web pages.

Hub   Ethernet networking device that allows multiple devices to be connected creating a physical star configuration.

IMAP   Internet Message Application Protocol. Mechanism for retrieving e-mails from a central server. Similar to POP3 but offers more functionality and security.

inetd   Daemon that acts as a router for incoming network requests. As requests come in, inetd determines the application for which they are destined and forwards the information to that application.

INFO   Command that allows documentation about system utilities and commands to be easily viewed.

init   Command used to switch between run levels on a Linux system.

Intranet   A Web site, or groups of sites, designed to be used internally within an organization.

Intrusion detection   Mechanisms or procedures that detects and notifies of attempts to gain unauthorized entry to the system.

ipchains   Firewall functionality provided in Linux kernel.

iptables   Firewall functionality provided in Linux Kernel versions after 2.2.

IPX/SPX   Internetwork Packet Exchange/Sequenced Packet Exchange. Network communications protocol created by Novell for use on NetWare based networks. IPX/SPX is a fully routable protocol that provides minimal amount of address configuration.

IRC   Internet Relay Chat. Mechanism that allows real-time communication with other IRC users.

ISDN   Integrated Services Digital Network. Networking method that uses data channels and control channels. Used for remote access and, in some cases, wide area networking.

Java   Object-oriented programming language developed by Sun Microsystems.

KDE   The K Desktop Environment. A popular desktop environment included with a number of distributions.

Kernel   The core of the operating system. Provides basic system functionality and hooks that allow services, drivers, and applications to communicate with it.

Kernel mode   Space in which the kernel and the core system functions operate.

korn   A type of shell.

LAN   Local Area Network. A network in which all components are in a single physical location.

LDAP   Lightweight Directory Access Protocol. A mechanism for extracting information from, and inputting data to an LDAP compliant directory.

LILO   Linux Loader. A boot loader system commonly used on Linux systems.

Linuxconf   Menu-based system configuration utility created by Red Hat.

login   The process of gaining access to a system by providing a valid username and password combination

logout   The process of closing a session on the server.

Loopback   Software-based driver that allows network configuration to be tested, even if no actual network connection is present.

lpd   The line printer daemon program, which provides printing functionality on a Linux server.

MAC address   Unique ID that is hard-coded into each network card or interface.

Mailing list   E-mail address that acts as a routing point to other e-mail addresses. Mail sent to the address is automatically sent to all of the addresses on the list. Mailing lists are a popular way for people to communicate about specific topics.

Master boot record (MBR)   Section of a hard disk that contains information on the partitioning system and subsequently is able to locate an operating system if the device holds one.

MDI   Medium Dependant Interface. Port found on Ethernet networking devices in which the wiring is not crossed. Also called an uplink port.

MDI-X   Medium Dependant Interface – Crossed. Port found on Ethernet networking equipment that allows devices to be connected to it. The crossing of certain wires make the transmit line on the sending device become the receive line of the receiving device.

Mounting   The process of making a device available to the system.

Multicast   Network communication that is sent to a group of devices that all share a common multicast address.

NAT   Network Address Translation. The process by which network addresses from an internal system are translated into addresses acceptable on an external network.

Net mask   Also called network mask and subnet mask. Number used to determine what portion of an address refers to the network and which to the node.

Network   Any group of devices that are connected for the purposes of sharing data or resources.

Newsgroup   A message board to which people can post messages about a certain topic. There are thousands of newsgroups covering almost every topic imaginable.

NFS   Network File System. Allows the sharing of files and directories on a network. Most commonly associated with Unix and Linux systems.

NIC   Network interface card. Adapter installed into a system to enable it to connect to the network. Also known as a network card, LAN card, and network adapter.

NNTP   Network Transfer Protocol. Mechanism that is used to connect to newsgroups.

NTP   Network Time Protocol. Part of the TCP/IP protocol suite that allows time information to be communicated between systems.

Open source   Term given to software that makes its source code available to developers.

Package manager   Software that allows preconfigured applications to be installed, removed, or managed on a system.

Packet   Name given to a unit of data that travels across the network.

Packet filter   Process that evaluates the type and content of each packet that is passed through a set of rules. Based on the packet type and contents, it is either forwarded or blocked.

Packet sniffer   Device or software that allows data to be copied from the network and analyzed.

partition   Area of disk assigned to a certain operating system or file system.

Password   An authentication token that must be supplied before access to a system or application is granted.

Path   The list of directories between the current location and the destination file or directory.

PCL   Printer Control Language. Print job formatting language created by Hewlett Packard for use with their popular LaserJet series of printers. Many other printer manufacturers offer PCL compatibility.

Perl   Practical Extraction and Report Language. Programming language. Programming language commonly used to create CGI scripts and so popular for use in Web server applications.

Permission   Field that defines which entities (users and groups) can access a file and directory and also defines what level of access they have.

PID   Process ID. Unique number that is assigned to each process running on the system.

PING   Utility that allows connectivity between two devices to be tested over the network.

Pipe   Mechanism by which the output from one command can be used as the input for another.

POP3   Post Office Protocol 3. Protocol for retrieving e-mail from a central host, which holds the mail items until they are requested.

Port   In TCP/IP, an entry point to the protocol stack. Some ports are preassigned so that the system knows what kind of communication is coming in. Others are able to be assigned dynamically for use by programs after they have established connection.

Postscript   Printer control language that uses special codes to define what is to be printed and at what location on the page.

PPID   Parent Process ID. Each process is assigned a parent process, the ID of which is referred to as the PPID. The init process is the parent ID of all processes.

PPP   Point to Point Protocol. A protocol used for dial-up access over serial connections.

PPTP   Point to Point Tunneling Protocol. A protocol that encapsulates other protocols so that they can be sent and received on an TCP/IP based network.

Print filter   File that defines formatting rules of files that are to be sent to the printer. Analogous to a printer driver on other platforms.

Processor   Casual term for Central Processing Unit (CPU). The key component in a computer system that provides the basis of all processing.

Proxy server   Sever that acts as an intermediary between clients and other hosts.

RAID   Redundant Array of Inexpensive Disks. Disk configuration that uses two or more drives to provide increased performance and/or fault tolerance.

rcp   Remote Copy. Allows files to be copied from one host to another from the command line.

Redirection   The process of outputting the results of a command to another program or file.

Resolution   Defines how many vertical and horizontal lines are displayed on the screen. Resolutions are given in the horizontal and then the vertical—for example, 1024×768.

RFC   Request for comments. Documents, which anyone can contribute to, that define technology standards such as the TCP/IP protocol.

root account   The administrative account on a Linux system. The root account has privileges to perform any action on the system and is not subject to file permission restrictions.

RPM   Red Hat Package Manager.

Run level   Configuration state that causes the system to offer a certain set of services or to react in a certain way. For example, run level 6 causes the system to reboot.

Samba   Service that makes it possible for Windows clients to use a Linux system as a file and print server. It also enables a Linux server to participate in Windows browsing.

Script   An executable file that contains shell commands that are processed in sequence. Can include variables and conditional statements to customize behavior.

Segment   A physical section of the network.

Sendmail   Service that provides e-mail services on a Linux server.

Session   The period of time between a user logging in and logging out of the system.

Shadow password   An encrypted password associated with a user account that is stored in the /etc/shadow file rather than the traditional /etc/passwd file for security reasons.

Shareware   Software that is free for a certain time period, or for a certain application. Any use outside of the free terms requires payment to the software author.

Shell   Environment that provides usability through a command-line interface and numerous utilities.

Single user mode   An operation mode that boots the system with a minimal set of drivers and no networking capabilities. Used for administration purposes.

SMB Server Message Block. File sharing protocol used on Microsoft-based networks.

SMP Symmetrical multi processing. The scheme used to distribute tasks between processors in a multiprocessor system.

SMTP Simple Message Transfer Protocol. A mechanism for the sending and receiving of e-mail.

SNMP Simple Network Management Protocol. A network management mechanism that allows information on system events to be communicated from clients, known as agents, to a central system known as a manager.

Spam Any unsolicited commercial e-mail.

SPM Slackware Package Manager. Packaging system used by Slackware-based distributions.

Spooling The process of a print file being written to disk so that the client does not have to wait for the job to print before continuing other tasks.

SQL Structured Query Language. System for adding, searching, and removing data from a compliant database system.

SSH Secure Shell. Secure method of connecting to and performing tasks on a remote system.

Star Office Suite of free productivity applications for the Linux platform from Sun Microsystems.

Subnet Logical division of a network based on address.

SuperProbe Utility that allows video card and monitor information to be detected.

Superuser   Another name for the root user on a Linux or Unix system.

Switch   Device used on Ethernet networks that switches data between ports based on the MAC address.

Symbolic link   A special file entry that is used as a pointer to the actual file that resides in another location.

Sysadmin   Popular term for a system administrator.

tar   Tape Archive Utility. Linux utility that allows multiple files to be combined into a single archive, referred to as a tarball.

Tarball   A file that has been created with the tar utility.

Telnet   Utility that allows tasks to be performed on a remote system.

UID   A unique ID that is assigned to each user on the system.

Unicast   Network communication between two systems. Unicast is the standard method of communication on a network.

Unmounting   The process of removing a device from the system, thereby making it unavailable.

Uptime   Common term used to refer to the length of time a system has been available.

Usenet   Users' Network. A distributed bulletin board system that provides forums targeted at specific topics.

User mode   The system space in which a user operates and performs tasks.

vi   Popular text editor.

Virtual memory   An area of disk space that is used by the system in the same way as physical memory. Referred to as swap space on Linux systems.

Virtual terminal   Another invocation of the shell that can be called up by pressing a key combination or issuing a command. The new virtual terminal session does not use any information from the original session and operates independently.

Virus   Software component written to corrupt or delete files or disrupt services provided by a system.

VPN   Virtual Private Network. Dedicated path between two hosts that uses a public network, such as the Internet, as a communication mechanism.

WAIS   Wide Area Information Server. Indexed database of documents accessible via the Internet.

WAN   Wide Area Network. A network that spans more than one physical location.

Web server   System that acts as a host for files written in a markup language and makes those pages available to clients upon request.

Wildcard   Character used in commands that acts as a substitute for a single character or a group of characters.

Window Manager   Software that organizes and customizes the appearance of the GUI on an X-11 desktop system.

Worm   A program, normally a virus, which travels from system to system reproducing itself, sometimes changing its form as it does so.

Xconfigurator   Red Hat–based tool that provides menu based configuration of the X Window System.

XF86Setup   X Window configuration utility provided by the XFree86 project. XF86Setup operates with a minimal GUI using the base level of X server.

XML   Extensible Markup Language. Meta-language for the creation of Web pages and other documents.

YaST   Yet another System Tool. GUI utility for configuration and administration of a Linux system. YaST was created by SuSE.

Zipfile   A file, or collection of files, that has been compressed using a utility such as gzip.

Zipping   The process of creating a file using a compression utility such as gzip.

Zone   An area of the DNS namespace.

E

About the CD

This CD-ROM contains the CertTrainer software. CertTrainer comes complete with ExamSim, Skill Assessment tests, and the e-book(electronic version of the book). CertTrainer is easy to install on any Windows 98/NT/2000 computer and must be installed to access these features. You may, however, browse the e-book directly from the CD without installation.

Installing CertTrainer

If your computer CD-ROM drive is configured to autorun, the CD-ROM will automatically start up upon inserting the disk. From the opening screen you may either browse the e-book or install CertTrainer by pressing the Install Now button. This will begin the installation process and create a program group named CertTrainer. To run CertTrainer use Start | Programs | CertTrainer.

System Requirements

CertTrainer requires Windows 98 or higher and Internet Explorer 4.0 or above and 600 MB of hard disk space for full installation. A version of CertTrainer for Linux is also found on the CD, with the files being optimized for Netscape Navigator. The Linux version must be run directly from the CD and is not installable.

CertTrainer

CertTrainer provides a complete review of each exam objective, organized by chapter. You should read each objective summary and make certain that you understand it before proceeding to the SkillAssessor. If you still need more practice on the concepts of any objective, use the In Depth button to link to the corresponding section from the Study Guide.

Once you have completed the review(s) and feel comfortable with the material, launch the SkillAssessor quiz to test your grasp of each objective. Once you complete the quiz, you will be presented with your score for that chapter.

ExamSim

As its name implies, ExamSim provides you with a simulation of the actual exam. The number of questions, the type of questions, and the time allowed are intended to be an accurate representation of the exam environment.

When you launch ExamSim, a digital clock display will appear in the upper-left corner of your screen. The clock will continue to count down to zero unless you choose to end the exam before the time expires.

Saving Scores as Cookies

Your ExamSim score is stored as a browser cookie. If you've configured your browser to accept cookies, your score will be stored in a file named History. If your browser is not configured to accept cookies, you cannot permanently save your scores. If you delete this History cookie, the scores will be deleted permanently.

E-Book

The entire contents of the Study Guide are provided in HTML form. Although the files are optimized for Internet Explorer, they can also be viewed with other browsers, including Netscape.

Help

A help file is provided through a help button on the main CertTrainer screen in the lower-right corner.

Upgrading

A button is provided on the main ExamSim screen for upgrades. This button will take you to www.syngress.com, where you can download any available upgrades.

Linux

A limited version of CertTrainer for Linux is included on the CD. In order to access CertTrainer, browse to the CD-ROM drive and open the folder named Linux. Setup.html will open the HTML version of CertTrainer. These files are optimized for Netscape Navigator. The Linux version includes CertTrainer and e-Book.

INDEX

D

H

I

M

R

INTERNATIONAL CONTACT INFORMATION

AUSTRALIA
McGraw-Hill Book Company Australia Pty. Ltd.
TEL +61-2-9417-9899
FAX +61-2-9417-5687
http://www.mcgraw-hill.com.au
books-it_sydney@mcgraw-hill.com

CANADA
McGraw-Hill Ryerson Ltd.
TEL +905-430-5000
FAX +905-430-5020
http://www.mcgrawhill.ca

**GREECE, MIDDLE EAST,
NORTHERN AFRICA**
McGraw-Hill Hellas
TEL +30-1-656-0990-3-4
FAX +30-1-654-5525

MEXICO (Also serving Latin America)
McGraw-Hill Interamericana Editores S.A. de C.V.
TEL +525-117-1583
FAX +525-117-1589
http://www.mcgraw-hill.com.mx
fernando_castellanos@mcgraw-hill.com

SINGAPORE (Serving Asia)
McGraw-Hill Book Company
TEL +65-863-1580
FAX +65-862-3354
http://www.mcgraw-hill.com.sg
mghasia@mcgraw-hill.com

SOUTH AFRICA
McGraw-Hill South Africa
TEL +27-11-622-7512
FAX +27-11-622-9045
robyn_swanepoel@mcgraw-hill.com

**UNITED KINGDOM & EUROPE
(Excluding Southern Europe)**
McGraw-Hill Education Europe
TEL +44-1-628-502500
FAX +44-1-628-770224
http://www.mcgraw-hill.co.uk
computing_neurope@mcgraw-hill.com

ALL OTHER INQUIRIES Contact:
Osborne/McGraw-Hill
TEL +1-510-549-6600
FAX +1-510-883-7600
http://www.osborne.com
omg_international@mcgraw-hill.com

Custom Corporate Network Training

Train on Cutting Edge Technology   We can bring the best in skill-based training to your facility to create a real-world hands-on training experience. Global Knowledge has invested millions of dollars in network hardware and software to train our students on the same equipment they will work with on the job. Our relationships with vendors allow us to incorporate the latest equipment and platforms into your on-site labs.

Maximize Your Training Budget   Global Knowledge provides experienced instructors, comprehensive course materials, and all the networking equipment needed to deliver high quality training. You provide the students; we provide the knowledge.

Avoid Travel Expenses   On-site courses allow you to schedule technical training at your convenience, saving time, expense, and the opportunity cost of travel away from the workplace.

Discuss Confidential Topics   Private on-site training permits the open discussion of sensitive issues such as security, access, and network design. We can work with your existing network's proprietary files while demonstrating the latest technologies.

Customize Course Content   Global Knowledge can tailor your courses to include the technologies and the topics which have the greatest impact on your business. We can complement your internal training efforts or provide a total solution to your training needs.

Corporate Pass   The Corporate Pass Discount Program rewards our best network training customers with preferred pricing on public courses, discounts on multimedia training packages, and an array of career planning services.

Global Knowledge Training Lifecycle   Supporting the Dynamic and Specialized Training Requirements of Information Technology Professionals

- Define Profile
- Assess Skills
- Design Training
- Deliver Training
- Test Knowledge
- Update Profile
- Use New Skills

College Credit Recommendation Program   The American Council on Education's CREDIT program recommends 53 Global Knowledge courses for college credit. Now our network training can help you earn your college degree while you learn the technical skills needed for your job. When you attend an ACE-certified Global Knowledge course and pass the associated exam, you earn college credit recommendations for that course. Global Knowledge can establish a transcript record for you with ACE, which you can use to gain credit at a college or as a written record of your professional training that you can attach to your resume.

Registration Information

COURSE FEE: The fee covers course tuition, refreshments, and all course materials. Any parking expenses that may be incurred are not included. Payment or government training form must be received six business days prior to the course date. We will also accept Visa/MasterCard and American Express. For non-U.S. credit card users, charges will be in U.S. funds and will be converted by your credit card company. Checks drawn on Canadian banks in Canadian funds are acceptable.

COURSE SCHEDULE: Registration is at 8:00 a.m. on the first day. The program begins at 8:30 a.m. and concludes at 4:30 p.m. each day.

CANCELLATION POLICY: Cancellation and full refund will be allowed if written cancellation is received in our office at least six business days prior to the course start date. Registrants who do not attend the course or do not cancel more than six business days in advance are responsible for the full registration fee; you may transfer to a later date provided the course fee has been paid in full. Substitutions may be made at any time. If Global Knowledge must cancel a course for any reason, liability is limited to the registration fee only.

GLOBAL KNOWLEDGE: Global Knowledge programs are developed and presented by industry professionals with "real-world" experience. Designed to help professionals meet today's interconnectivity and interoperability challenges, most of our programs feature hands-on labs that incorporate state-of-the-art communication components and equipment.

ON-SITE TEAM TRAINING: Bring Global Knowledge's powerful training programs to your company. At Global Knowledge, we will custom design courses to meet your specific network requirements. Call 1 (919) 461-8686 for more information.

YOUR GUARANTEE: Global Knowledge believes its courses offer the best possible training in this field. If during the first day you are not satisfied and wish to withdraw from the course, simply notify the instructor, return all course materials, and receive a 100% refund.

In the US:

CALL: 1 (888) 762-4442

FAX: 1 (919) 469-7070

VISIT OUR WEBSITE:

www.globalknowledge.com

MAIL CHECK AND THIS FORM TO:

Global Knowledge

Suite 200

114 Edinburgh South

P.O. Box 1187

Cary, NC 27512

In Canada:

CALL: 1 (800) 465-2226

FAX: 1 (613) 567-3899

VISIT OUR WEBSITE:

www.globalknowledge.com.ca

MAIL CHECK AND THIS FORM TO:

Global Knowledge

Suite 1601

393 University Ave.

Toronto, ON M5G 1E6

REGISTRATION INFORMATION:

Course title ———

Course location ——— Course date ———

Name/title ——— Company ———

Name/title ——— Company ———

Name/title ——— Company ———

Address ——— Telephone ——— Fax ———

City ——— State/Province ——— Zip/Postal Code ———

Credit card ——— Card # ——— Expiration date ———

Signature ———